The Rorschach: A Comprehensive System, in two volumes
by John E. Exner, Jr.
Theory and Practice in Behavior Therapy
by Aubrey J. Yates

Principles of Psychotherapy
by Irving B. Weiner
Psychoactive Drugs and Social Judgment: Theory and Research
edited by Kenneth Hammond and C. R. B. Joyce
Clinical Methods in Psychology
edited by Irving B. Weiner
Human Resources for Troubled Children
by Werner I. Halpern and Stanley Kissel
Hyperactivity
by Dorothea M. Ross and Sheila A. Ross
Heroin Addiction: Theory, Research and Treatment
by Jerome J. Platt and Christina Labate
Children's Rights and the Mental Health Profession
edited by Gerald P. Koocher
The Role of the Father in Child Development
edited by Michael E. Lamb
Handbook of Behavioral Assessment
edited by Anthony R. Ciminero, Karen S. Calhoun, and Henry E. Adams
Counseling and Psychotherapy: A Behavioral Approach
by E. Lakin Phillips
Dimensions of Personality
edited by Harvey London and John E. Exner, Jr.
The Mental Health Industry: A Cultural Phenomenon
by Peter A. Magaro, Robert Gripp, David McDowell, and Ivan W. Miller III
Nonverbal Communication: The State of the Art
by Robert G. Harper, Arthur N. Wiens, and Joseph D. Matarazzo
Alcoholism and Treatment
by David J. Armor, J. Michael Polich, and Harriet B. Stambul
A Biodevelopmental Approach to Clinical Child Psychology: Cognitive Controls and Cognitive Control Theory
by Sebastiano Santostefano
Handbook of Infant Development
edited by Joy D. Osofsky
Understanding the Rape Victim: A Synthesis of Research Findings
by Sedelle Katz and Mary Ann Mazur
Childhood Pathology and Later Adjustment: The Question of Prediction
by Loretta K. Cass and Carolyn B. Thomas
Intelligent Testing with the WISC-R
by Alan S. Kaufman
Adaptation in Schizophrenia: The Theory of Segmental Set
by David Shakow
Psychotherapy: An Eclectic Approach
by Sol L. Garfield
Handbook of Minimal Brain Dysfunctions
edited by Herbert E. Rie and Ellen D. Rie
Handbook of Behavioral Interventions: A Clinical Guide
edited by Alan Goldstein and Edna B. Foa
Art Psychotherapy
by Harriet Wadeson
Handbook of Adolescent Psychology
edited by Joseph Adelson
Psychotherapy Supervision: Theory, Research and Practice
edited by Allen K. Hess

Continued on back

PREVENTION OF PROBLEMS
IN CHILDHOOD

Prevention of Problems In Childhood

PSYCHOLOGICAL RESEARCH AND APPLICATIONS

Edited by

Michael C. Roberts
The University of Alabama

Lizette Peterson
University of Missouri-Columbia

A WILEY-INTERSCIENCE PUBLICATION
JOHN WILEY & SONS
New York • Chichester • Brisbane • Toronto • Singapore

Library of Congress Cataloging in Publication Data:

Main entry under title:

Prevention of problems in childhood.

"A Wiley-Interscience publication.
Includes index.
1. Mental illness—Prevention. 2. Child mental health services. I. Roberts, Michael C. II. Peterson, Lizette.
RJ499.P7135 1984 618.92'8905 84-7279
ISBN 0-471-87444-2

Printed in the United States of America

10 9 8 7 6 5 4 3 2 1

To our families

Our spouses, Karen B. Roberts and Andrew L. Homer, with gratitude for their support and encouragement for our work in prevention, and to our daughters, Erica Roberts, Alicia Roberts, and Kestrel Homer, the latter two born during our work on this book, for providing external validation of our faith in childhood.

Contributors

Judith E. Albino, Ph.D.
Professor of Behavioral Sciences
School of Dentistry
State University of New York at Buffalo

Peggy Crawford, M.S.N.
Nurse Clinician
Rainbow Babies and Children's Hospital
Frances Payne Bolton School of Nursing
Cleveland, Ohio

Dennis Drotar, Ph.D.
Associate Professor
Departments of Psychiatry and Pediatrics
Case Western Reserve University School of Medicine
Cleveland, Ohio

Martha Brownlee-Duffeck, M.S.
Graduate Student
Department of Psychology
University of Missouri-Columbia

Joseph A. Durlak, Ph.D.
Department of Psychology
Associate Professor
Loyola University of Chicago

Louise Lampi Dyhdalo, M.A.
Graduate Student
Department of Psychology
Wayne State University, Detroit

Pauline D. Elkins, M.A.
Graduate Student
Department of Psychology
University of Alabama, Tuscaloosa

Robert D. Felner, Ph.D.
Associate Professor and Director Clinical/Community Psychology Program
Auburn University, Alabama

Rex L. Forehand, Ph.D.
Professor and Director of Clinical Training
Psychology Department
University of Georgia, Athens

William B. Furey, M.S.
Graduate Student
Psychology Department
University of Georgia, Athens

Mary Ann Ganofsky, M.S.W.
Chief, Pediatric Social Service
Rainbow Babies and Children's Hospital
Cleveland, Ohio

Leonard A. Jason, Ph.D.
Associate Professor
Department of Psychology
De Paul University, Chicago

Phyllis R. Magrab, Ph.D.
Professor of Pediatrics and Director, Child Development Center
Georgetown University
Washington, D.C.

Frank Masterpasqua, Ph.D.
Assistant Professor
Hahnemann University
Assistant Director for Prevention Services
John F. Kennedy Community Mental Health/Retardation Services, Philadelphia

Lizette Peterson, Ph.D.
Associate Professor
Department of Psychology
University of Missouri-Columbia

Beverly A. Powell, M.D.
Assistant Professor
Department of Pediatrics
Georgetown University
Washington, D.C.

Annette U. Rickel, Ph.D.
Associate Professor
Department of Psychology
Wayne State University, Detroit

Michael C. Roberts, Ph.D.
Associate Professor
Department of Psychology
University of Alabama, Tuscaloosa

George P. Royal, M.A.
Graduate Student
Department of Psychology
University of Alabama, Tuscaloosa

Richard L. Smith, Ph.D.
Post-doctoral Student
Department of Psychology
University of Detroit

Anita Miller Sostek, Ph.D.
Associate Professor
Georgetown University
Washington, D.C.

Stephanie B. Stolz, Ph.D
Director
Bureau of Family Health
Kansas State Department of Health and Environment, Topeka

Marshall Swift, Ph.D.
Professor, Hahnemann University
Director, Consultation & Education Services
John F. Kennedy Community Mental Health/Retardation Center, Philadelphia

Eve Holton-Walker
Graduate Student
Department of Psychology
De Paul University, Chicago

Page B. Walley, M.S.
Graduate Student
Psychology Department
University of Georgia, Athens

Series Preface

This series of books is addressed to behavioral scientists interested in the nature of human personality. Its scope should prove pertinent to personality theorists and researchers as well as to clinicians concerned with applying an understanding of personality processes to the amelioration of emotional difficulties in living. To this end, the series provides a scholarly integration of theoretical formulations, empirical data, and practical recommendations.

Six major aspects of studying and learning about human personality can be designated: personality theory, personality structure and dynamics, personality development, personality assessment, personality change, and personality adjustment. In exploring these aspects of personality, the books in the series discuss a number of distinct but related subject areas: the nature and implications of various theories of personality; personality characteristics that account for consistencies and variations in human behavior; the emergence of personality processes in children and adolescents; the use of interviewing and testing procedures to evaluate individual differences in personality; efforts to modify personality styles through psychotherapy, counseling, behavior therapy, and other methods of influence; and patterns of abnormal personality functioning that impair individual competence.

IRVING B. WEINER

University of Denver
Denver, Colorado

Preface

Why a book on prevention of problems in childhood? First, the subject is timely. The current emphasis on extending services to meet expanding needs with dwindling resources calls for a change in strategy from traditional remediative treatments to preventive interventions. Second, experts in many fields are calling for an expanded awareness of prevention. Within the area of health care, it becomes increasingly clear that improvements in health status will come not from improving treatment of disease, but rather from disease prevention through lifestyle changes such as decreased smoking, increased cardiovascular exercise, and improved diet. Similarly, there has been an increased emphasis in mental health on preventing a variety of types of dysfunction, ranging from mild social isolation in preschoolers to drug addiction in adolescents and adults. Finally, a book on prevention in childhood is important now as a positive, optimistic statement about the possibilities of intervening with children. Prevention focuses on competence rather than deficit, on health rather than illness, and on factors which reduce vulnerability instead of those which lead to risk. It implies the ultimate circumvention rather than the treatment of dysfunction.

Why the particular emphasis on childhood? As we note in chapter 1, the emphasis on childhood comes from recognition of several features. First, prevention as a topic area seems uniquely suited to children. Prevention of disorder is most effective if the prevention procedures are applied *before* the onset of the problem. This may necessitate intervention during childhood, since a wide variety of problems ranging from dental phobia to reading problems, from shyness to cigarette smoking, and from obesity to depression, begin prior to adulthood. Thus, prevention in children is the logical extension for much of the work in prevention of physical and mental disorders. Second, childhood must be recognized as a distinct stage of life, requiring special approaches for problems particular to the child at different levels of development. There are special needs and vulnerabilities to be considered in prevention programs with children. Third, the downward extensions of adult-oriented techniques have never sufficed in other areas of mental health intervention, and there is no reason to suspect this approach will work for childhood preventive interventions. Instead, forms of assessment and intervention designed specifically for children are needed. Fourth, prevention work with adults can assume a somewhat steady level of skills and environmental demands, whereas work with children requires a developmental perspective which recognizes the process of continuous change over time in the psychology of the children. Thus, this often requires consideration of special or critical times of change in a child's life. Finally, the developmental perspective also recognizes the "end product" of the childhood development process. Consequently, there is an opportunity to positively influence not only the child but the later adult as well.

How to organize a book on the quickly expanding field of work on prevention in childhood? We found as we discussed current work on prevention that we thought of individuals in the field rather than abstract areas of endeavor. No one organizational scheme seemed suitable for all of the recent research and theory on prevention in childhood. We were both involved in work focusing on specific target responses, such as accident prevention or prevention of anxiety and enhancement of coping in medical settings, and this work cut across settings and developmental levels. Other prevention professionals also took similar approaches. Judith Albino's work on health enhancing habits, such as appropriate dental hygiene, and Dennis Drotar's interventions with chronically ill children were organized similarly toward preventing specific target responses. This must be the way to conceptualize prevention in childhood, we thought.

But we were faced with the question of where to place the important work done by Frank Masterpasqua and Marshall Swift, dealing with community mental health center intervention. That is a setting-based technique, as is some of Leonard Jason's and Joseph Durlak's work on school-based prevention, or Rex Forehand's work on prevention in the home. These interventions cut across developmental levels and specific problem types within settings.

Finally, Phyllis Magrab and Anita Sostek's prevention work during the perinatal period and Annette Rickel's work on prevention with preschoolers is organized by developmental levels or milestones, again cutting across settings and problem types. Robert Felner's emphasis on intervening at specific critical times during childhood is organized in a similar milestone fashion. It could even be argued that some of Durlak's and Jason's work deals with elementary school-aged children rather than with the school setting itself.

We therefore concluded that it was important to allow the current research and theory in the area to dictate the organizational pattern as well as the contributing authors for the book. Consequently, the first group of chapters discusses prevention, utilizing primarily a milestone approach, with prevention focused on selected developmental levels or life stage occurrences in the chapters by Magrab, Sostek, and Powell; Rickel, Dyhdalo, and Smith; Durlak and Jason, and Felner. The second section describes prevention focused on specific target problems with chapters by Roberts, Elkins, and Royal; Albino; Drotar, Crawford, and Ganofsky; and Peterson and Brownlee-Duffeck. The third section describes setting-based prevention attempts through chapters by Jason, Durlak, and Holton-Walker; Forehand, Walley, and Furey; and Masterpasqua and Swift. Finally, Stephanie Stolz keeps these efforts anchored firmly in the pragmatic here and now by describing sources of any impediments to implementation of prevention programs for children.

In completing the book, we believe that the final product fulfills the promise we initially felt was inherent in this kind of approach. Multiple approaches to prevention in childhood are represented here, summarized by some of the leading researchers in the respective areas. They note the problems, pitfalls, strengths, and current status of prevention programs and prevention research. Together, they provide compelling evidence for the future of preventive interventions in childhood.

MICHAEL C. ROBERTS
LIZETTE PETERSON

Tuscaloosa, Alabama
Columbia, Missouri
May 1984

Contents

CHAPTER 1

Prevention Models

Theoretical and Practical Implications

MICHAEL C. ROBERTS AND LIZETTE PETERSON

Interest in the prevention of disorders has been greatly renewed among mental health professionals and others in recent years. This increase is due in part to the recognition that preventing a problem is often easier and more cost-effective than attempting to remediate a problem after it occurs. The concept of prevention in relation to treatment has long been salient (witness Ben Franklin's aphorism, "an ounce of prevention is worth a pound of cure"). In essence, prevention primarily refers to actions taken to avoid the development of a disorder or problem, or secondarily, to identify potential problems early in their development and to take actions to minimize negative effects.

In this chapter, we will first orient the reader to the coverage of this book and the specific applications and approaches to targeting childhood problems detailed by each chapter. Then we will offer a brief introduction to the area of prevention in general by considering the historical background of prevention concepts and activities, and by describing some of the major contributors to the field. We will also describe some of the different orientations to preventive intervention (for example, setting-based, problem-oriented, milestone, population-wide, competency-based, and active versus passive prevention) and relate them to current research. Finally, we will consider some of the controversial areas within the prevention field, including a discussion of the current debate regarding definitional problems, targeting approaches, the knowledge base, evaluation, funding, political/public policy, and professional boundaries. This description of general background and issues will set the stage for detailed coverage by the authors of each chapter.

OVERVIEW TO THIS BOOK

Implications of the Book's Title

We have deliberately chosen the title of the book as *Prevention of Problems in Childhood: Psychological Research and Applications*. The key words or phrases in this title are elaborated throughout the book. A discussion of some of these terms will demonstrate the concepts to be emphasized.

Prevention Orientation

The concept of prevention we have just defined in general, but this concept will be detailed in its complexity in this and following chapters. For many years, remediative treatment of existing problems was the sole method used by professionals, and despite the expenditure of literally billions of dollars only a small proportion of children in need of mental health and physical health services received help (Report of Joint Commission on Mental Health, 1969). Researchers have noted that increasing treatment services is not an adequate answer to the growing problem, as the need for services is expanding more rapidly than the number of service providers. The concept of primary and secondary prevention thus becomes increasingly important for both research and application.

Problems

The choice of the term *problems* was made carefully to convey the broadest meaning. We are discussing not only mental health or psychiatric disorders as often considered, but also more broadly the problems of physical health (or of a medical nature) as well. Thus, while the psychological functioning of children and families receives much attention in this book, further attention is given to psychological applications which directly prevent accidents and illness in children and prevent problems through enhancing positive healthful lifestyles.

Psychological Aspects

The phrase *psychological research and applications* emphasizes both an empirical, research orientation and an applied programming approach to prevention. Research and applications are intertwined since the prevention area has typically employed an innovative and evaluative orientation when applying psychology-based programs to real-world problems. Although the concept of prevention in mental health has been discussed since the 1920s and in public health since before 1855, a renewed emphasis has developed among the helping professionals, particularly psychologists. A variety of specialists within psychology has intensified efforts to design, implement, and evaluate preventive programs for a number of target problems; it is now becoming more common to find programs and articles relating prevention to subdivisions within psychology, such as community, clinical, health, school, and industrial psychologies. Indeed, specialists from an even wider range of professional disciplines contribute behavioral/psychological ideas to prevention. All of these professional interests have profitably applied the prevention notion to various settings and populations. In particular, significant preventive programs have been established which are oriented to various childhood problems. Thus, the *psychological aspects* of this book refer to a behavioral, objective, research-based orientation, not necessarily limited to a single field of professional endeavor. As detailed in this book, the numerous professions contributing important substance include psychology, public health, education, social work, psychiatry, and medicine. We will focus here on psychological research and applications. Prevention is truly a multi-disciplinary and subdisciplinary concept, with each area contributing uniquely important, as well as overlapping, theory, interventions, and techniques.

Emphasis on Childhood

Much of the past prevention literature takes an adult-oriented approach to the topic, reflecting the proclivities of the researchers and authors. A number of fragmented sources exist which incorporate some material on prevention targeted to child-family problems, but childhood is rarely the primary focus. The orientation here to the child years is important for several reasons. First, prevention of disorder is most effective if the prevention procedures are applied *before* any onset of the problem. This may necessitate intervention during childhood, since a wide variety of problems ranging from dental phobia to reading problems, from shyness to cigarette smoking, and from obesity to depression, begin prior to adulthood. Thus, prevention with children is the logical emphasis for much of the work in the area of prevention of physical and mental disorders. Second, childhood must be recognized as a distinct stage of life requiring special approaches for the problems particular to the child at different levels of development. There are special needs and vulnerabilities to be considered in prevention programs with children.

Third, the downward extensions of adult-oriented techniques have never sufficed in other areas of mental health interventions, and there is no reason to suspect this approach will work for preventive interventions for childhood problems. Specialized forms of assessment and intervention are needed. Fourth, prevention work with adults can assume a somewhat steady level of skills and environmental demands, whereas work with children requires a developmental perspective which recognizes the process of continuous change over time in the psychology of the children. This often requires consideration of special or critical times of change in a child's life. Finally, the developmental perspective also recognizes the *end product* of the childhood development process. Consequently, there is an opportunity to positively influence not only the child, but possibly the later adult as well. In sum, our emphasis on prevention in childhood derives from assumptions that a unique set of problems requires a unique set of preventive interventions.

Organization and Chapter Topics

The organization of this book and chapter topics also requires some discussion. The selection of topics and authors was based on a deliberate consideration of the field as it stands and as we think it should be. Our framework includes three parts to reflect different approaches to prevention in children: the milestone approach, the "at risk" or problem-focused approach, and the population-wide approach. Within each approach, chapters discuss different types of problems presenting in childhood which require preventive programming, including scholastic/academic difficulties, psychological/behavioral disorders, accidents and physical health problems. Since presenting problems are inherently related to the setting in which they occur, the chapters will simultaneously focus on the variety of settings for preventive efforts (for example, schools, mental health centers, hospitals, clinics). The chapter divisions will therefore follow this interaction of problem and setting. Furthermore, within each chapter, the age or developmental level of the child targeted for preventive intervention is considered. Finally, the chapters present materials from a number of different professional disciplines and interests concerned with prevention and childhood, including community psychologists and clinical child psychologists. This integration of related but distinct subdisciplines is important since much of the work in this area is so recent and workers in one subdiscipline are often unaware of programs in other subdisciplines.

The chapters provide a framework within which to conceptualize prevention efforts in childhood, review past research by attempting to draw together often disparate sets of literature, and outline innovative and effective prevention programs. The chapters also propose new applications and evaluations. The book explores the work which professionals are doing and can do in the future to prevent problems occurring during childhood; problems of both mental and physical health will be covered. The chapter authors question and to some extent answer the question of what a psychological approach has to offer in preventing mental health and physical problems at this most important point of the development process—during childhood.

Part 1: Milestone Approach.

Part 1 takes the milestone approach in examining prevention at developmental stages and periods. Chapters in this first part consider childhood's problems from a developmental perspective in that prevention is provided to children and families at particular developmental points considered to be important. Consequently, Phyllis Magrab, Anita Sostek, and Beverly Powell (Chapter 2) focus on prevention for the perinatal period (the time before birth including prior to conception, extending through birth, and the early infancy period). Magrab et al. discuss developmentally early preventive interventions for such problems as maternal health, nutrition, and teratogens of alcohol, nicotine, and drugs. They consider several strategies for prevention including health education, family planning, prenatal care, and anticipatory guidance. Thus, Chapter 2 represents programs and research at the critical stages of early development for preventing both immediate and longitudinal problems in children. In Chapter 3, Annette Rickel, Louise Lampi, and Richard L. Smith present psychological prevention programs for preschool-aged children as a milestone in development. These authors describe the variety of preschool programs to prevent school maladaptation as well as social, interpersonal, and behavioral difficulties. These programs include Head Start, problem-solving, relational programs, and the Preschool Mental Health Project. They examine the research base for these early intervention programs, noting the positive aspects as well as the limitations on short- and long-term evaluations. Joseph Durlak and Leonard Jason target the next developmental milestone, school-aged children and adolescents, in Chapter 4. Durlak and Jason describe recent work on preventing social and academic problems, presenting prevention interventions such as affective education programs, coping skills training, cognitive and social skills interventions, and school maladjustment.

Their discussion includes both primary and secondary prevention orientations, noting a generally exemplary record of research and evaluation. In Chapter 5, Robert Felner discusses the recent recognition of certain critical times in children's lives which can have negative and positive consequences for the mental health of the child. He examines, in particular, divorce, illness, and transitions such as geographical relocation and promotions.

Part 2: Problem-Focused Approach.

Part 2 of the book takes a more problem-focused orientation in terms of prevention for children who are at higher risk for difficulties or whose circumstances place them at this higher risk. In Chapter 6, Michael Roberts, Pauline Elkins, and George Royal outline research and applications in preventing childhood accidents and illness. This and Chapter 7 expand the traditional literature in psychological prevention to include physical health prevention and health promotion, considering the contributions of psychological research and applications. Roberts et al. examine childhood accidents in terms of developmental principles, motivational techniques, and methodological procedures. They outline three approaches to prevention for targeting the child's caregiver, the child, and society at large. Judith Albino in Chapter 7 provides an overview to physical disorder prevention through intervening on children's acquisition of health-enhancing habits. Albino further illustrates this health promotion approach by intensively reviewing two important areas of research and application: smoking and dental health. She relates these and other areas of health promotion (for instance, substance abuse, weight control) to children's cognitive and social development. In line with the orientation of Part 2 to reduce risk for problem-focused prevention, Dennis Drotar, Peggy Crawford, and Mary Ann Ganofsky focus on the special needs and circumstances of children who are chronically ill in Chapter 8. They emphasize a family-centered prevention approach to reduce the maladaptive consequences of chronic illness by enhancing the coping strategies of children and families. In Chapter 9, Lizette Peterson and Martha Brownlee-Duffeck review interventions designed to alleviate children's distress associated with medical and dental procedures. They examine both primary and secondary prevention interventions to better prepare children for stressful medical and dental experiences with regard to the research base and practical applications.

Part 3: Population-Wide Approach.

Part 3 of the book takes a population-wide approach to prevention with chapters describing specific settings for intervention with children. In Chapter 10, Leonard Jason, Joseph Durlak, and Eve Holton-Walker view the school as a particularly important setting for prevention. They focus first on prevention of scholastic and academic problems and then on ecological interventions where prevention efforts are attained by manipulating the environment to become more conducive to children's growth and development. Rex Forehand, Page Walley, and William Furey, in Chapter 11, review the available literature on the role of parents and family in preventing childhood problems. They examine preventive interventions for unrealistic parental expectations, inadequate child rearing skills, and parental emotional dysfunction. They find uneven research coverage of these topics and note the need for further research allied with a greater societal commitment to the family. Frank Masterpasqua and Marshall Swift, in Chapter 12, consider prevention programs instituted on a community-wide basis with an orientation to Community Mental Health Center (CMHC) programming. These programs for children at various ecological levels within communities include, for example, mental health promotion, caregiver training in healthy child development, and reinforcement of support systems. They articulate the need for prevention professionals to become applied social scientists as well as political advocates to improve prevention-oriented research and services.

Part 4: Implementation and Dissemination.

Finally, in Part 4, Stephanie Stolz draws conclusions and makes recommendations regarding the implementation and evaluation of prevention programs. She discusses both obstacles and some solutions for these program considerations.

Summary.

The chapters in this book attempt an integration of the field of prevention of childhood problems from a psychological perspective by presenting the state of research knowledge and actual programming. They reflect the contributions of prevention professionals of various theoretical orientations, who often have different emphases for approaches or perceptions of needs. Attempts to maintain an appropriate scholarly objectivity are tempered by a recognition of the critical state of children's needs and what is required to meet them. Alternating states of frustration and optimism will become apparent in the chapters. Nonetheless, the progress that has been made is encouraging and the prospects for future development in preventing childhood problems through psychological research and applications are exciting. Before turning to specific areas of prevention in childhood, it may be helpful to consider the background from which current applications have been drawn and some of the current areas of controversy. Thus, a brief historical overview will be presented first, followed by a consideration of critical points related to prevention.

HISTORICAL PERSPECTIVE

Mental Health Prevention

The foundation for prevention may be traced to numerous conceptual roots in the history of different disciplines. Indeed, public health portrays its prevention roots as being derived from one of the mythological daughters of Aesculapius, Hygeia, who was the prevention and health promotion-oriented daughter, as opposed to medicine's roots with the cure-oriented daughter, Panacea. Prevention in mental health has antecedents within some aspects of the mental hygiene movement originating around 1910 and the resulting changes in ideas about mental illness and health (Bloom, 1977; Joint Information Service, 1980). More recently, community psychologists mark the rise of a community mental health movement significantly oriented to prevention of mental retardation and psychopathology. This movement derived from the Community Mental Health Center Act of 1963 (Price, Bader, & Ketterer, 1980). John F. Kennedy then articulated the mental health orientation to prevention:

> Prevention is far more desirable for all concerned. It is far more economical and it is far more likely to be successful. Prevention will require both selected specific programs directed especially at known causes, and the general strengthening of our fundamental community, social welfare, and educational programs which can do much to eliminate or correct the harsh environmental conditions which often are associated with mental retardation and mental illness. [Kennedy, 1963, p. 2]

Prevention of psychological disorders was thus to have a significant role in the resulting community mental health centers (CMHCs) constructed and funded with federal money (Bloom, 1977). Later, more specific guidelines detailed the original goals for essential services such as consultation and education services. These specific guidelines included under ''indirect services'' the prevention of emotional problems in the CMHC's catchment area through consultation and education (Community Mental Health Center Programs, 1971). Despite President Kennedy's call for prevention to be a fundamental component, CMHCs over the years typically neglected prevention programming, with a few exceptions. Since prevention fell into the consultation and education category, this meant that only 5% of the funds was ultimately expended in the category, which, it should be noted, was not exclusively made up of prevention services (Klein & Goldston, 1977). Fee-for-service models of reimbursement for therapeutic treatment of existing disorders rapidly became the modus operandi of CMHCs; this tendency appears exacerbated today with the decrease in federal support and the need for CMHCs to bring in supporting money from third party payers. Thus, despite considerable fanfare and optimism, and despite the original mandate for prevention in the community mental health movement, prevention services are still not optimally provided.

In recognition of this, the President's Commission on Mental Health appointed by President Jimmy Carter included in its conclusions and recommendations many specifics on prevention of ''mental disability'' and children's mental health needs. In particular, the Commission stated:

> At present our efforts to prevent mental illness or to promote mental health are unstructured, unfocused, and uncoordinated. They command few dollars, limited personnel, and little interest at levels where resources are sufficient to achieve results. If we are to change this state of affairs, as we believe we must, the prevention of mental illness and the promotion of mental health must become a visible part of national policy. [Report to the President, 1978, p. 53]

Some of the Commission's recommendations have now been implemented. However, the change in administration from Carter to Ronald Reagan, with a corresponding alteration in ideological response to social services programming, has precluded implementation of many prevention services proposed in the Mental Health Commission's report and those contained in other health-oriented commissions (Harris, 1981). The recent cuts in budget from the highest federal levels appear to have cut short any progress made toward prevention. However, even without this recent cutback, the reality is that community mental health centers have not significantly included prevention of mental health problems in the routinely programed services.

Despite impediments, prevention in mental health shows a resiliency indicating the continuing strength of the idea. Recently, the National Institute of Mental Health (NIMH) established a Center for Studies of Prevention to encourage, fund, and coordinate research and prevention activities in mental health. (This is in response to the Presidential Commission on Mental Health noted earlier.) Another development has been the emergence of two professional journals which focus on prevention in mental health programming *(The Journal of Primary Prevention,* published by Human Sciences Press and *Prevention in Human Services,* published by The Haworth Press). A number of other well-established journals continue to publish prevention-oriented articles (for example, *Journal of Community Psychology, American Journal of Orthopsychiatry, American Journal of Community Psychology, Community Mental Health Journal).* Several organizations maintain considerable interest in preventive mental health interventions including the National Association of Prevention Professionals, the Divisions of Community Psychology and of Child, Youth and Families in the American Psychological Association, American Orthopsychiatric Association, and the Mental Health Association. Important new books and chapters continue to project the prevention philosophy in mental health (compare Albee, 1982; Price, Ketterer, Bader, & Monahan, 1980; Felner, Jason, Moritsugu, & Farber, 1983). The Vermont Conferences on the Primary Prevention of Psychopathology annually draw active and interested participants on the increasing and diverse range of prevention activities.

Physical Health

We have discussed, thus far, prevention and psychology primarily as related to mental health and psychopathology. The psychological prevention concept, however, shows considerable promise in application to physical health. The recent extensions of health psychology and behavioral health (Matarazzo, 1980, 1982; Matarazzo, Miller, Weiss, Herd, & Weiss, 1984; Millon, Green, & Meagher, 1982) demonstrate the psychological research and applications that can be made to prevent disease and accidents, while promoting healthier lifestyles. As a most recent development in the history of psychological prevention, this expansion into the health area clearly illustrates both the prevention concept and its psychological applications. Scientific journals *(Health Psychology, Journal of Pediatric Psychology),* books (Millon et al., 1982), chapters specifically relating to childhood (Roberts, Maddux, & Wright, 1984; Roberts, Maddux, Wurtele, & Wright, 1982), and articles in this area are rapidly appearing. Professional organizations and interest groups are meeting within psychology and related fields (for example, Division of Health Psychology of the American Psychological Association, Society of Behavioral Medicine, Society of Pediatric Psychology) and federal agencies are increasing funding. These all have major orientations to preventive research and programming in the area of physical health. In many ways, these developments parallel more recent ones in mental health programming. One critical difference appears to be the greater emphasis on prevention in behavioral health than has been evident in mental health.

The Surgeon General's Report on Health Promotion and Disease Prevention, entitled *Healthy People,* clearly states, "improvement in the health status of our citizens will not be made predominantly through treatment of disease, but rather through its prevention" (Califano, 1979, p. 9). A corollary report, by the Select Panel for the Promotion of Child Health, *Better Health for Our Children: A National Strategy,* asserted that: "Many forms of disease prevention and health promotion are demonstrably effective, especially for children and pregnant women, but are still neither widely available nor widely used when they are available" (Harris, 1981, p. 25). The report also points out the psychological contribution to the physical health field:

> It is almost self-evident that behavior is one of the principal determinants of health status. This is especially true of children, both because so many behavioral patterns established in childhood affect long-term health outcomes in adulthood, and because so many of the immediate dangers to children are those related to risk behaviors or situations that admit of behavioral but not medical solutions . . . much of child illness has a psychosocial or behavioral component. [Harris, 1981, p. 46]

This recent historical development in psychological prevention through behavioral health will become apparent in Chapters 6 and 7 by Roberts et al. and Albino, respectively.

Summary

We have noted some of the major historical developments in psychological prevention for problems in mental health *and* physical health. It should be evident that, while progress has been uneven, there is considerable potential and some continual movement toward the utilization of the prevention concepts, albeit often slow movement. Much of the future development depends on the demonstrated utility of prevention in these two general areas of application. Rather than attempting within this chapter to document the utility of prevention across its many applications, we leave it to the following chapters to provide considerable detail of the usefulness of prevention concepts as applied specifically to children and their problems.

MAJOR CONTRIBUTORS TO PREVENTION CONCEPTS

Any list of significant figures in almost any field is inevitably fraught with omissions. This would be patently true here if we attempted to present all of the notable theorists and researchers and relate them to prevention concepts. We have thus elected to present only an illustrative selection of some of the notable contributors to this rapidly expanding area. The selection is based on apparent consensus among professionals for those contributing to prevention in general. More specific names and ideas will become evident in each of the chapters on particular areas of research and application with relevance to childhood problems. Indeed, the selection of authors for the chapters hinged on their contributions to the field in general.

Gerald Caplan

Gerald Caplan, as a psychiatrist heading Harvard's Laboratory of Community Psychiatry (now at Hadassah-Hebrew University, Jerusalem), has been credited with adapting public health concepts to mental disorders and, in doing so, provided an important conceptual model for later prevention work. In particular, his model of prevention intervention included primary prevention, secondary prevention, and tertiary prevention. He defined these as:

> programs for reducing (1) the incidence of mental disorders of all types in a community (''primary prevention''), (2) the duration of a significant number of those disorders which do occur (''secondary prevention''), and (3) the impairment which may result from those disorders (''tertiary prevention''). [Caplan, 1964, p. 16]

In this model, primary prevention includes those efforts that attempt to reduce the number of new problems arising *before* they occur. This can be accomplished by changing the environment so that negative conditions do not produce pathology, or by strengthening an individual's resources to avoid pathology. Examples of primary prevention for psychological problems include early mother-infant contact to foster attachment, social skills training in early adolescence, premedical procedure preparation to reduce anxiety, and preventive intervention prior to parental divorce. Examples of primary prevention for physical problems include immunization against disease, the use of seat belts, dental brushing and flossing, appropriate nutrition, and avoidance of smoking and drug use.

Secondary prevention may be more accurately described as an early treatment orientation, since intervention is made soon after a problem occurs to ameliorate the effects of the disease or disorder early in their development. Early detection of problems or identification of groups at high risk for a problem are important to the success of secondary prevention efforts. Examples of secondary prevention in the mental health area include screening all elementary school children for early identification of school maladjustment so special skills training can be applied. For physical disorders, secondary prevention includes screening tests for cervical cancer and phenylketonuria, early management of childhood obesity, and intervention for neglect and abuse.

Tertiary prevention is, in reality, rehabilitation of existing problems with an aim to limit the severity of outcome and to change the course of the disorder's sequelae. Zax and Cowen (1976, p. 482) emphasize that ''tertiary prevention is prevention in name only'' and not actually a preventive component, although further problems may be forestalled by intervention. In mental health, tertiary prevention would involve all psychological treatments of psychopathology. In physical health, this concept includes restoring physical functioning in any number of ways. We should note that when the term prevention is typically used, it relates to primary and secondary, but not tertiary, prevention. This conveys the unique quality of the prevention concept as being before-the-fact rather than after.

Caplan's (1964) articulation of this prevention model for psychiatry had important impact on the then current work and much subsequent research and services. Empirical evidence for Caplan's idealized goal for mental health—primary prevention—was lacking at the time, but started slowly growing. Caplan (1961) rhetorically asked: "In the absence of such studies, how valid is it to discuss the prevention of mental disorders in children, and how useful is it to plan and implement programs in this area?" (p. 6). He then answered his own question by pointing to the public health area where effective preventive interventions often predated an understanding of etiology and sound scientific research. He further made a call for research, but noted:

> Paradoxically, it would appear that only after social inertia has been overcome by the development of preventive programs on an admittedly inadequate scientific basis will the scientific research be developed that can act as the eventual foundation for stable and valid operations. [Caplan, 1961, p. 7]

Thus, one particular contribution of Caplan was as a catalyst for prevention programming at the same time data were being gathered.

Caplan (1964) modified some other notions basic to prevention in public health to mental health. First, he argued that primary prevention should be a community- or population-directed concept rather than individual-oriented as typified by traditional psychiatry and psychology. The goal of prevention programs is the reduction of problems in the total population which can translate to a number of individuals, but this latter aspect is not the direct concern. Factors at the community level that increase the rate of pathology should be examined and changed or programs should focus upon increasing the ability of children to cope with these factors. "Clearly defined populations at special risk" (p. 8) are within such a community/population orientation. Not all prevention professionals necessarily agree with a sole *community* orientation. Caplan (1964) also presented the "crisis model" of psychopathology wherein "repeated periods of individual and social disequilibrium of human development" disrupt normal developmental processes. These "at risk" or life crisis periods are opportunities for preventive intervention which both avoid pathology and facilitate subsequent psychological growth. For example, this concept becomes clearly applied in the work outlined in Chapter 5 by Felner on prevention interventions at particular periods of vulnerability for stress. Through the several concepts noted here as well as several other contributions, Caplan serves as a recognized leader in influencing prevention programming and research.

Emory Cowen

Emory Cowen has been an active contributor to the prevention area through various activities in program development, evaluation projects, the community psychology movement, and training of other prevention professionals. As elaborated in Chapter

3 by Rickel et al., Cowen and his colleagues developed an exemplary prevention program for the early detection and intervention for school maladjustment (Primary Mental Health Project: PMHP) which continues in operation to date. The PMHP has served as a model intervention program through its emphasis on both service and research (Cowen, Spinell, Wright, & Weissberg, 1983; Cowen, Trost, Izzo, Lorion, Dorr, & Isaacson, 1975; Weissberg, Cowen, Lotyczewski, & Gesten, 1983). The PMHP has been emulated by other programs across the country. In a similar way, Cowen has attempted to clarify the confused state of the prevention field by articulating not just abstract definitions of prevention, but also by arguing for more specific operationalizations and more concrete identification of prevention variables (Cowen, 1977, 1980). In particular, Cowen (1982) defines primary prevention more narrowly than many other writers in order to facilitate the future generation of true primary prevention research:

> "primary prevention" must meet three structural requirements:
> (1) It must be group or mass-, rather than individually-oriented (even though some of its activities may involve individual contacts).
> (2) It must have a before-the-fact quality, i.e., be targeted to groups not yet experiencing significant maladjustment (even though they may, because of their life situations or recent experiences, be at risk for such outcomes).
> (3) It must be intentional, i.e., rest on a solid, knowledge-base suggesting that the program holds potential either for improving psychological health or preventing maladjustment. [Cowen, 1982, p. 132]

Moreover, he adds that "to *be* primary prevention requires one further (often overlooked) critical element, *data* showing positive program effects" (p. 132). Cowen claims this definition is necessary because the term primary prevention is misused too frequently through application to programs that do not utilize true prevention, but simply are labeled as prevention by the programmer. The definitional confusion impedes bona fide prevention research and programs. Many more references will be made to Cowen in later pages because of his eminent position in psychological research and applications.

George W. Albee

George Albee's contributions to primary prevention have encompassed theoretical and conceptual contributions to the field as well as an outspoken political advocacy of the merits of primary prevention. As professor of psychology at the University of Vermont, Albee organized the first National Conference on Primary Prevention in 1975. Subsequent years have established this annual conference, now entitled "The Vermont Conference on the Primary Prevention of Psychopathology," as the source of some of the most influential papers on primary prevention (for example, Albee & Joffe, 1977; Joffe & Albee, 1981). In 1978, President Carter established a new President's Commission on Mental Health and Albee served as chair of the Task Panel on Prevention (1978). The recommendations of this panel included augmenting efforts within primary prevention on a nationwide basis, with specific emphasis on primary prevention with children.

Albee demonstrates a balance between concern over the conceptualization and evaluation of primary prevention and concern over the social implementation of preventive efforts. While noting the role which public health approaches have played in conceptualizing the prevention of mental illness (Kessler & Albee, 1975), Albee argues that conceptualizations of disturbed functioning which are based upon physical indices, such as genetic or neurological structure, will never contribute to real primary prevention. The belief that disturbance stems from socially learned behaviors which can be altered by social intervention is central to his conceptualization of prevention (Albee, 1982a). He proposes the following method of describing the incidence of mental disorders as a first step to organizing prevention efforts:

$$\text{Incidence} = \frac{\text{organic factors} + \text{stress}}{\text{coping skills} + \text{self-esteem} + \text{support groups}}$$

He notes that preventive efforts to reduce the incidence of emotional disturbance can intervene at any of the levels described in the equation. Organic factors can be attacked, for example, by preventing brain damage due to lead poisoning or automobile accidents. Stress reduction is one of the primary goals of prevention and Albee suggests that social stresses such as poverty and racism are among the most important targets for attack. Similarly, building coping skills or self-esteem and increasing community support are commonly viewed end-products for successful preventive intervention.

Albee describes primary prevention as the "fourth mental health revolution" (Albee, 1982b) and he approaches the question of prevention as militantly as any revolutionist. He notes that for a revolution to succeed, there must be six critical steps. First, there must be widespread injustice; Albee notes that of the 32 million persons with serious mental and emotional problems, only seven million are seen annually by the mental health system. Children are particularly underserved, constituting widespread injustice. Second, there must be an overt challenge to authority; for example, suggesting that the medical model for emotional disturbance in children is no longer useful or accurate constitutes such a challenge. Third, a revolution requires a widely understood political position; Albee (1982b) suggests "no mass disorder afflicting human kind has ever been eliminated through one-to-one intervention but only as a result of successful prevention" (p. 9) as such a position. Fourth, a core of leaders are required; Albee suggests joining forces with others interested in mental health to produce those leaders. Fifth, the field needs to be prepared for strong resistance; the current retrenchments of mental health funding may be one index of such resistance. Albee discusses other forms of resistance at length elsewhere (Albee, 1982a). Finally, unstable power structures bring about revolutions and the current dissatisfaction within the field of mental health may signal such instability. Albee and his colleagues have provided many of the basic texts reviewing the literature on primary prevention (for example, Albee & Joffe,

1977; Joffe & Albee, 1981; Kessler & Albee, 1975) and he continues to be a vital source of innovation and support within the area of primary prevention.

Bernard Bloom

Bernard Bloom, a psychologist at the University of Colorado, has over the years repeatedly described the changing state of prevention and provided conceptual frameworks for prevention ideas. As others have also done, Bloom (1977) relates prevention of mental health problems to the public health model and more specifically to epidemiology. This relationship to public health relies on the concepts of host, environment, and agent. The *host* refers to the individual or population vulnerable to a disease or problem. The *agent* is the source or process that leads to the problem development. The *environment* includes those aspects surrounding the individual or population that relate to physical or psychological stress. Prevention interventions can be made to each of these influence categories. Further public health applications noted by Bloom derive from epidemiology and the study of prevalence of a disease or disorder (that is, the number of cases identified at a particular time). Prevalence involves two concepts: (1) incidence—the number of *new* cases identified in a specific period, and (2) duration—the amount of time from first diagnosis to some terminating end point (recovery, cure, or death). Bloom (1977) notes that primary prevention attempts to reduce incidence, while secondary and tertiary prevention try to reduce duration; all efforts attempt to reduce prevalence. As Bloom did initially, other writers extend the relationship between psychology and public health in more detail (compare Runyan, DeVellis, McEvoy-DeVellis, & Hochbaum, 1982; Singer & Krantz, 1982).

Bloom (1977, 1979) sees important changes in the orientation of the mental health profession. He notes that presently in the field more energy is given to considering the precipitating and perpetuating factors in mental illness than is spent in considering predisposing factors contributing to mental illness. Thus, professionals now attend to those factors or agents that hold potential for producing psychopathology or maladaptive behavior (such as stressful life events or situations). Finally, we note Bloom's (1971) seven principles for developing programs in community mental health. These serve as important points for the prevention professional to recognize before attempting community-oriented programming and include: "If you want to know about a community's mental health needs, ask them . . . Let the community establish its own priorities . . .", and "You should work toward the equitable distribution of power in the community" (Bloom, 1971, pp. 10–12).

Joseph Matarazzo

In addition to other professional contributions, Joseph Matarazzo deserves mention for articulating the challenge to psychology and related disciplines of maintaining health and preventing illness and dysfunction (Matarazzo, 1980, 1982). This developing area of behavioral health (and of health psychology) moves beyond the traditional mental health concepts of primary prevention for psychiatric disability, mental illness, or psychological problems. A behavioral health orientation suggests psychological intervention upon physical health through application of psychological research and principles. In this view, it is interesting that mental health professionals' adaptation of public health concepts (for example, primary and secondary prevention) has come full circle to being reapplied by psychologists to physical health aspects much in the same way as they were originally developed. Matarazzo (1982) describes the "role of the individual's behavior and lifestyle in health and dysfunction" (p. 12) and the behavior and lifestyle are within the domain of psychological/behavioral professionals and of prevention interventions, in particular. Matarazzo and others relate the behavioral health conceptualization to prevention of children's physical health problems (Matarazzo et al., 1984; Roberts et al., 1984; Roberts et al., 1982). For one example, the developmental perspective reveals the greatest susceptibility to becoming a habitual smoker occurs around age 12. The prevention interventions on this critical health risk should be centered at or before this age (Matarazzo, 1982). In this way, Matarazzo and the behavioral health model clearly relate the prevention of physical problems to intervention in childhood. Two chapters in this volume (Albino, Chapter 7; Roberts et al., Chapter 6) detail this theme further in relating psychological research and applications to the prevention of accidents and illness as well as the promotion of healthful lifestyles for children.

Other Contributors to Prevention

In addition to the contributors to the prevention literature noted above, there are several other contributors whose theorizing, writing, and research applications are of importance. Of particular relevance are those professionals whose work bears much direct relationship to prevention in childhood. (Of course, many of the individuals noted earlier were also working in this child-oriented field.) These additional professionals and their ideas will be briefly noted here.

Helen Reinherz, for example, recommends a very practical model of intervention in this area: (1) community mental health centers must commit themselves to long-term primary prevention for children's problems, (2) prevention programs are necessary for children at all developmental levels, (3) the child and his or her family should be considered as a unit, (4) enhancement of mental health should be tied to the enhancement of all functions including physical functioning, and (5) current resources are not sufficient for primary prevention due, in part, to reliance on third party payments for mental health center activities which must change (Reinherz, 1980).

Charles Adam (1981) emphasizes the differences in prevention and treatment by arguing that prevention is: (1) proactive—preventionists engage in intervention before distress occurs, not in reaction to distress as in treatment, (2) generic—prevention is organized toward the broad goal of "wellness" and competency rather than to specific problem remediation, (3) developmental—prevention focuses on the development of personal skills and strengths throughout the lifespan, (4) experiential—prevention works best when the recipients perceive the prevention intervention as directly relevant to their own life experiences and needs, and they feel close personal involvement, (5) systemic—since developmental and experiential facets must be a part of prevention programs from the start, preventionists must have a theoretical framework to work within; general systems theory, dealing with systems such as communities, schools, and churches exemplifies such an approach, and (6) collaborative—prevention relies on a collaborative or ecological perspective in which the prevention system interlocks and exchanges resources with other systems.

Coming from the psychiatric profession, William Bolman categorizes prevention programs as: (1) child-centered, (2) family-centered, or (3) society-centered (Bolman, 1967; Bolman & Westman, 1967). Each of these has implications for mental health services directed to children. Child-centered programs would involve prevention measures targeted at individual children, for example, prenatal and perinatal problems, children with handicaps, and problems arising from hazardous or traumatic events in development during childhood (such as illness, grief, divorce of parents). Family-centered programs would include interventions directed at different constellations of family units—intact, broken/disorganized, or disadvantaged families. Society-centered programs are oriented toward making changes on an entire community-wide basis including community development, social action, and education programs, among others. Bolman (1967) outlined preventive psychiatric interventions for children using a categorization of 15 population groups as well as describing the goals of intervention, the type and approach (for instance, primary/secondary, milestone, high-risk, community-wide), and the resources available for intervention. Among the 15 potential targets of prevention he listed were: (1) prenatal infants (for example, prevent maternal disease, genetic counseling), (2) newborn (reduce casualty due to deprivation), (3) infants and preschool children (for instance, early detection of developmental problems), (4) children with special problems (blindness, deafness, mental retardation), (5) children exposed to stressful events (such as hospitalization, parent loss), (6) children with chronic illness (for example, diabetes), (7) children with parental deprivation, (8) children exposed to family disorganization, and (9) children failing in school. Each of these can be further analyzed for what types of professional intervention need to be made by medical personnel, mental health professionals, the judicial system, educational system, or governmental agencies. Bolman and Bolian (1979) similarly outline "biomedical" intervention programs potentially viable for problems such as high-risk pregnancies, children with special needs, and families with stressful circumstances. They further list prevention programs for teenagers including pregnancies, school problems, and delinquency. The value of Bolman's various outlines comes from the organization of prevention programming into a framework for conceptualizing interventions as well as for determining research and application priorities.

We do not intend to overlook valuable contributions of many other individuals. The following chapters and their reference lists document the large number of authors, researchers, programmers, and programs particularly important in the child-oriented prevention area. This section has highlighted only some of the contributors and their ideas.

DIFFERENT ORIENTATIONS FOR PREVENTION INTERVENTIONS

There are perhaps as many ways of viewing preventive interventions as there are prevention programs, but there are some commonalities between approaches which link prevention programs within broad categories or orientations toward prevention. Most of the orientations overlap somewhat; rather than being mutually exclusive, these categories often have several features in common. The factor which determines how a program might be categorized should be the predominant focus of that program. Some programs are organized primarily toward reaching all members of a given population and their primary thrust is toward *population-wide* or *community* intervention. Other programs restrict themselves to only certain individuals at a given age or developmental level, characterizing *milestone* or *developmental* intervention. Still other programs are organized around a particular problem or a particular setting rather than a specific population, demonstrating a *problem-oriented* intervention or a *setting-based* intervention. Prevention may also be viewed as an increase in *competency*, or decisions may be made concerning whether *active or passive* forms of prevention are the most cost-effective and feasible. Each of these overlapping, broad categories of prevention programs is briefly discussed below and two or three programs characteristic of the approach are described, providing a limited overview to the possible orientations of preventive interactions.

Population-wide or Community Intervention

A program which is directed toward all individuals within a given geographical area demonstrates a population-wide intervention. Many population-wide interventions have utilized the media to reach large numbers of individuals within a given district or series of neighborhoods. Media interventions have typically had a mixed level of success. Peterson (1980), for example, demonstrated that national public service announcements concerning the importance of obtaining immunizations had little impact on immunization activity in a Midwest population, whereas media announcements of a local rubella epidemic were followed by large increases in the number of individuals obtaining immunizations. Similarly, Maccoby, Farquhar, Wood, and Alexander (1977) reported on the effects of a community-based media campaign on risk factors for cardiovascular disease. Television, radio, newspaper advertisements and stories, as well as billboards and bus cards were used to impact dietary behavior, smoking, and other risk related behavior. These investigators also noted mixed results, with large decreases in dietary cholesterol and saturated fat, but very small changes in smoking reduction. In discussing their program, Maccoby and Alexander (1980) suggested that to be successful, a media campaign must do more than simply persuade, it must achieve five stages: (1) agenda setting or bringing the matter to the public attention, (2) informing the layman about the problem,

(3) training members of the population to modify their risk related behaviors, (4) giving motivation to change and reinforcement for changes, and (5) shifting to self-control from externally based control. They concluded that

> certain kinds of behavior associated with risk reduction can be learned through exposure to mass media . . . while others require a different constellation of media events which contain a considerable amount of skills training (for example, cigarette smoking cessation). [p. 367]

There is some evidence that certain preparations for select health behaviors may be impacted by population-wide mass media programming. However, it is undoubtedly the case that the number of attempts at such contact overreaches the data suggesting their effectiveness. Children's Saturday morning viewing, for example, is now replete with media based announcements regarding diet, dental habits, and so forth. Several messages have been produced to limit the impact of televised advertisements on children, with little evidence demonstrating any positive effects (Peterson, Note 1).

Milestone or Developmental Approach

While population-wide approaches typically are oriented toward all viewers within a community, they often have special emphasis for a particular portion of that community. Thus, television advertisements may be potentially viewed by all members of a population, they are targeted more to specific viewing audiences. For example, admonitions to children to brush their teeth accompany the "Smurfs" cartoon hour on Saturday morning, while suggestions to teenagers to avoid smoking are presenting during "American Bandstand." This illustrates the overlap between a strictly population-wide and a milestone approach. The milestone approach has as its main thrust an orientation toward intervening at different developmental levels, when the individual might be thought to be particularly at risk for certain problems. This approach is so clearly a child-oriented approach that several later chapters in this book are organized around interventions specifically for infancy, preschool, and school-aged children. Attending prenatal medical care classes, sensitively introducing the preschool child to the first out-of-home experiences, requiring immunizations of school-aged children as a requisite for entering school, providing information on contraceptives to junior high school students, and requiring a driver's test before awarding the first driver's license are all forms of milestone prevention attempts.

In one milestone program designed to prepare children for entering school, Frangia and Reisinger (1979) combined assessment and treatment for the child and for the parent. The Early Intervention Program (EIP) gave parents training in behavior management and in methods of instructing the child in self-help skills. In addition, parents were taught methods of decreasing interfering behaviors such as tantrums and noncooperative responding. Part of the parents' training included methods of assessment of the effectiveness of their own treatment by graphing both the child's and the parents' behavior. One novel aspect of the program was that the training was not conducted by professionals but rather by previously trained parents at the repayment rate of five hours of service for every hour of treatment, thus making the treatment not only timely but cost-effective. The children's later benefits in appropriate classroom behavior demonstrate the utility of this milestone approach.

The onset of adolescence with a concomitant increase in social anxieties, heterosexual stresses, and a lack of a sense of identity has also been noted as a critical milestone event. Botvin (1982) argues that the changes adolescents experience in the way they reason, make decisions, and define themselves leave them vulnerable toward a variety of health risking behaviors such as alcohol and drug use, and cigarette smoking. He advocates a psychosocial approach to smoking prevention in which emphasis is placed upon the acquisition of life skills. Specifically, the orientation is toward improved general personal competence (for example, self-image, decision making, coping with anxiety, basic social skills, assertiveness). Botvin noted that the program can be implemented by outside health professionals, older peer leaders, and regular classroom teachers and that it has typically reduced new cigarette smoking by at least 50%.

Milestone approaches have a great potential for influencing behaviors which occur at predictable junctures throughout development. However, because these approaches attempt to intervene upon each child who passes the developmental milestone, they may not be suitable for prevention of relatively infrequent problems or for disorders which may occur at several developmental levels. Such problems may be better prevented using a problem-oriented intervention.

Problem-Oriented Intervention

As noted above, some problems are of sufficiently low baserate that a population-wide approach would not seem warranted and they may occur at differing points throughout the development cycle. Prevention attempts for such problems must be oriented toward the problem itself, whenever and wherever it appears. This does not mean that individuals at differing developmental levels will be treated in exactly the same fashion, only that developmental level per se will not function as the primary cue for intervention.

One example of a problem which has long troubled prevention professionals is that of child abuse. The majority of "screening instruments" to identify families at risk for child abuse have not proven effective (Newberger & Daniel, 1979) and some say traditional, individual-oriented prevention programs in this area are "doomed to failure" (Zigler, 1979). Garbarino (1980) noted that there are a variety of levels of problem-oriented intervention which must take place for child abuse, including promoting family-centered childbirth, early community support for the family caretaker which taps into "natural helping networks," principles of effective child rearing such as avoiding physical punishment and increasing the use of reinforcement articulated in the media, and early identification of child neglect and maltreatment. Other researchers have offered problem-cued intervention such as a family outreach program which used trained volunteers to serve as family consultants to those families showing early signs of neglect and abuse (Rosenstein, 1978) or have combined the role of educators and families in the early identification and treatment of child abuse and neglect (McCaffrey & Tewey, 1978). Much additional research is needed in the area of child abuse and, because of its relatively low baserates and occurrence throughout the developmental cycle, such research is likely to utilize a problem-oriented focus.

Similarly, problems in children which occur secondary to parental death or divorce are usually best dealt with in terms of a problem-oriented intervention focusing on prevention of heightened anxiety and aggression, depression, anger, and loneliness (Wallerstein & Kelly, 1974, 1976). Programs aimed at preventing such problems including the Children of Divorce project (Wallerstein & Kelly, 1977), and social support groups for children of divorce (Guerney & Jordon, 1979) provide positive anecdotal data concerning the utility of these programs, but few interventions have empirically documented the prevention of distress due to parental separation and divorce. This is another problem-oriented area which demands additional evaluation.

Although often serious, relatively low baserate behaviors are among the most difficult targets for clear demonstration of prevention, there have been a variety of successful programs which have had such a problem-oriented focus. Interventions to prevent academic skill deficits provide one excellent example. Most programs oriented toward prevention of academic problems have utilized either a school-based approach (such setting-based interventions are described in more detail in the next section) or a milestone approach, as in the Early Intervention Program discussed earlier. However, some programs clearly demonstrate a problem-oriented approach, cutting across settings and traditional developmental levels. In one such project described by Rodick and Henggeler (1980), students with academic deficits received one of three interventions: a home-based, parental administered program (Rev. Jesse Jackson's "PUSH for Excellence"), a standard school based remedial reading course, or an intervention which utilized undergraduate tutors implementing the SMART (Staats Motivation Activating Reading Technique) program. Immediately after termination of the program, students receiving the SMART program demonstrated greater increases in achievement motivation and academic skills than students in either of the other groups. However, by the six month followup both students in the home-based PUSH program and the tutor-oriented SMART program showed maintained gains in academic ability and achievement motivation.

Problem-oriented approaches will continue to be valuable in conceptualizing preventive endeavors, particularly in breaking free of some of the restrictions found implicit in other orientations. However, because problem-oriented approaches begin with neither the population nor setting defined, structuring such programs demands creative thinking and consideration of exploitable locations for prevention.

Setting-Based Intervention

Setting-based interventions typically focus upon an "exploitable" or "captive" population, brought together for purposes other than those of the prevention program and receiving the preventive treatment by virtue of being in the location. Child-based prevention of necessity occurs in locations in which children are typically found: preschool and elementary schools, churches, doctors' and dentists' offices, and hospitals. The strength of most setting-based prevention endeavors is their relevance to the location in which they are based. While occasionally the setting has nothing to do with the preventive attempt (such as performing immunizations at local churches and supermarkets as noted in Peterson, 1980), more often it is directly relevant to the setting.

For example, Shure and Spivack (1979) have employed preventive procedures in preschool settings for students who were thought to be impulsive (often disruptive, aggressive, and uncooperative) or withdrawn (passive, confused, and noninteracting). These children have received intensive, interpersonal cognitive problem-solving training over two years of preschool and thus may enter kindergarten with the requisite behaviors for both social and academic success. Since many people regard this as the principal aim of preschool education, such programming appears appropriate.

Another type of location which has received much attention recently as an important source of preventive intervention is medical settings. Peterson and Ridley-Johnson (1980) reported on a survey of pediatric hospitals in this country which demonstrated that 74% of these institutions employed formal setting-based prevention programs. During the last decade, programs based in hospital settings and oriented toward prevention of anxiety and pain due to medical and surgical procedures have demonstrated the effectiveness of providing information on the sensations to be experienced (Johnson, 1975), filmed modeling (Melamed & Siegel, 1975), and coping techniques such as relaxation and cognitive distraction (Peterson & Shigetomi, 1981). Such setting-based programs are likely to become more prevalent and better evaluated in the coming years, as more consumers begin to view prevention as one of the legitimate and necessary functions of settings which serve children. Ultimately, the goal of prevention programs in locations like preschools and pediatric wards may be not only to prevent harm from the experience but to instill self-confidence and build coping skills, so the child emerges from the setting better able to meet the next challenge of life than when the setting was first encountered.

Prevention as Competency

This orientation, as implied above, suggests that prevention should do more than accomplish the short-term avoidance of problems. This orientation suggests that preventive programming should add to the child's growing collection of skills, that the child should experience increments in abilities which may cut across settings and developmental levels. Kessler and Albee (1975), in the introduction to their chapter entitled "Primary Prevention," may have stated this point of view best:

> Our reading for a year leads us to the conclusion that practically every effort aimed at improved child rearing, increased communication, building inner control and self-

> esteem, reducing stress and pollution, etc.—in short, everything aimed at improving the human condition, at making life more fulfilling and meaningful—may be considered to be part of primary prevention of mental or emotional disturbance. [p. 557]

Kornberg and Caplan (1980) also describe the promotion of competence as a primary source of prevention, both of specific disorders such as academic deficits as well as general problems such as learned helplessness and hopelessness in low income mothers. Similarly, Reinherz (1980) noted that "all definitions of primary prevention clearly include the concept of defending against the emergence of mental health problems by building strength and coping capacity . . . and enhancing competency" (p. 6). This view of prevention pervades many of the previously discussed structures for prevention. Investigators utilizing population-wide prevention discuss training individuals in the requisite skills to reduce risk behavior; milestone approaches attempt to train parenting skills or social skills for adolescents; problem-oriented programs focus upon substituting child rearing skills for abusive parental responding or training academic competence to overcome deficits in reading; and setting-based programs attempt to train problem-solving to replace impulsive behavior, or coping skills to replace anxious responding in medical settings. An increased emphasis on increasing competence rather than focusing on deficit behavior is likely to continue to characterize prevention programs with children (Kirschenbaum, 1983).

Active versus Passive Prevention

This orientation toward prevention more than any other focuses upon the pragmatic or cost benefit considerations of any prevention program. Prevention was first discussed in the context of a health enhancement rather than disease model (Caplan, 1964) and in that context it has been clearly demonstrated that passive as opposed to active preventive intervention occurs at lower cost, with more individuals contacted with more regularity. Fluoride in the drinking water prevents cavities as effectively as topical application, but requires no active intervention to remember and correctly apply the substance. Child proof containers have greatly cut down on the number of child poisonings in this country and yet require little active intervention on the part of caregivers. The controversy between seat belts and airbags in automobiles may be a good example of the contrast between active and passive intervention. Seat belts require active participation each time individuals are transported by automobiles. Injuries to children, which could be prevented by appropriate use of seat belts or safety restraints, continues to be a leading cause of childhood death in this country. Programs to increase the use of safety restraints for children show mixed success at best. Air bags in cars, by comparison, would require no active intervention to be effective, but would become available in case of an accident, effectively preventing injury and death.

In addition to passive intervention methods which may protect children's health, there may be similar methods which may influence children's emotional well-being.

Increases in neighborhood support networks and in the presence of appropriate child care facilities may decrease parental stress (Garbarino, 1980) and thus result in an emotionally healthier child. Routine psychological preparation prior to medical procedures may require little active intervention by the parent or child, but can result in far less distress experienced by the child patient (Peterson & Ridley-Johnson, 1980). The use of affective education, including communication and group process skills, perspective taking, values clarification, self-control, decision making and problem-solving as a routine part of school curriculum, could result in increased emotional competence in young children (Cooper, Munger, & Ravlin, 1980). These are only a few illustrations of approaches which might require less active participation of parents and children to realize prevention goals.

Bloom (1980) noted that the issue of active versus passive prevention has received insufficient research attention. He noted three levels of prevention on a continuum ranging from (1) the most recipient passive (for example, fluoride in water), (2) informing the public of risks and providing screening, but requiring intervention on the part of the recipient as a second approach (for instance, blood pressure screening for hypertension treatment), and (3) placing the entire burden of prevention upon the recipient as the most active approach (seat belt use, brushing teeth). Bloom argued that there is a moral dilemma whenever the proposed program demands "involuntary participation as the price for optimal results" (p. 21). He suggests the cautious use of both active and passive strategies, with sensitivity to issues of both effectiveness and political concerns. The utility and acceptability of passive approaches for prevention should continue to be seriously examined within child prevention programs.

Summary

This section has outlined some of the different orientations or approaches for prevention. Examples and research demonstrate these approaches, which are elaborated in each following chapter. As noted, some of the approaches overlap, some are mutually exclusive, and not all have application with all potential childhood problems.

CRITICAL CONSIDERATIONS FOR PREVENTION

We have, thus far, outlined key concepts and approaches, historical developments, and major contributions related to psychological research and application in prevention. The rest of the book is devoted to a more detailed examination of prevention issues for particular problems, populations, and settings. We assert that such focused discussions will be more fruitful in reaching conclusions about prevention of problems in childhood, rather than making simplistic and general conclusions. There are, however, some considerations requiring critical attention that will be discussed in this section because of universal relevance to prevention research and application. This section will raise the problems of: definitions, targeting approaches, prevention's knowledge base, evaluation, funding, political and public policy, and professional boundaries.

Definitional Problems

We have previously mentioned some problems with definitions of prevention. Cowen (1982), in particular, has criticized the "overly elasticized use of the term primary prevention" (p. 131). Kessler and Albee (1975) document the vast array of programs claiming a position under the rubric of primary prevention; Cowen (1982), among others, would assert that most of these programs do not belong in that category. Cowen (1982) and Broskowski and Baker (1974) agree that the abstract definitions of primary prevention are generally "consensually validated."

However, more concrete operationalization within the abstract definition becomes more difficult when "virtually anything done to improve man's lot can be called primary health prevention" (Zax & Cowen, 1976, p. 479). Various models have been advanced for conceptualizing the various operationalizations (compare Caplan, 1961: primary, secondary, and tertiary prevention; Cowen, 1982: criteria of group-oriented, before-the-fact quality, and intentionality; Munoz, 1976: four approaches of developmental, functional areas, specific disorders, and specific populations; and many other conceptual models). These models certainly have their valued place in the field and there are many more conceptualizations, some having less value. We suggest that there has been much more theorizing and over-conceptualizing beyond these viewpoints than would be anticipated from the facts derived from research and programming in prevention. We wonder, is there a point where such over-organizing and frameworking becomes less useful and self-defeating? While clarity of conceptualization is important, overconcern with semantical precision or theoretical superstructuring can render down the concept at issue—essentially, what interventions can be developed and validated that can prevent problems from occurring? Although some segments of this book necessarily focus on conceptual and theoretical issues, much more is devoted to research and application.

Targeting Approaches

A second issue assumes the validity of the prevention concept, but emerges from debate concerning which is the most appropriate approach for preventive intervention: a global, social action program aimed at eradicating poverty, discrimination, injustice, and other stress-producing social conditions (Albee, 1982a; 1982b; Brickman, 1970) or a more specific targeting of programs to the more discrete components of problems (Cowen, 1977; Poser, 1970). This argument over prevention at the "macro or micro" level may impede necessary communication even among professionals who agree prevention is a worthy goal. Furthermore, as articulation to the public and to policy makers concerning prevention goals becomes garbled and confused, resistance to prevention concepts can be generated. The many different levels and approaches to prevention currently seen in both mental health and physical health areas seem appropriate to us. Of course, this division resolves to the now rather traditional dichotomy in primary prevention models of "people-centered" and "system-centered approaches." There is a need and, indeed, room for all approaches in the prevention camp. Joffe (1982), arguing against limiting definitional standards, makes the point more poetically by imploring us "to let a thousand flowers bloom" (p. 55).

A related issue is debate of whether it is more profitable to intervene on general categories of either problems or populations, or to target specific problem groups within the populations at higher risk for problems. For the former position, Bolman and Bolian (1979) argue that no evidence exists for identifying and intervening with high-risk children and that "programs are better accepted when they are generalized, not when they are directed toward a specific group or category" (p. 229). Thus, they suggest that, for example, parent education should be provided for all mothers, not just high-risk ones, such as those in poverty. On the other hand, Goldston (1977a, 1977b) argues that a more cost-effective approach is to implement prevention services only for those groups of individuals or populations that appear to be at higher risk for developing problems, and therefore, in greatest need of preventive services. This at risk approach also encompasses a newer model of identifying situations that place people at higher risk for difficulties. Certainly, in times of limited resources, the specific targeting of groups or situations may be most cost-effective.

Knowledge Base

Professionals in science-related fields typically hold the axiom that an area of research and application is only as good as the quality of information on which it is based. In the prevention field, a number of professionals hold a second axiom that, in the words of Cowen (1982), "we're awfully short on good primary prevention research" (p. 134). In contrast, many would assert that the knowledge base for prevention is better than it was and is developing steadily (Albee, 1982a). Others would argue that progress can be made even with a dearth of adequate knowledge. Since there does appear to be a robust knowledge base (albeit not without gaps) for physical health, the discussion here will focus on primary prevention of mental health problems, where there is some debate and controversy. Before turning to what makes up the knowledge base for prevention of mental health problems, there are several indices of the knowledge base and its development which can be described.

One milestone of prevention development as a source of empirical data in psychology came in 1973 when "prevention" became an index term for *Psychological Abstracts*. This milestone could be meaningless, of course, if the index identifies articles inaccurately or the studies so noted fail to meet some criteria as appropriately prevention. A second problem arises when the term indexes relatively few items, thus indicating a lack of production in the topical area. For example, Bloom (1981) analyzed the knowledge base for prevention as reflected in different information retrieval systems including *Psychological Abstracts, Social Science Citation Index,* and *Exceptional Child Education Index.* He found between two and four prevention articles for every thousand articles listed in the various indices. Computer-based systems (such as MEDLINE and ERIC) produced similarly low ratios of items on prevention. He further concluded that the information retrieval systems inadequately indexed material on prevention since a personal search of the prevention topic produced many more relevant articles than did either conventional systems or computer-based systems. An additional conclusion appears warranted: relative to the awesome totality of articles in psychology and related fields (particularly, therapeutically oriented fields), the number of articles on prevention is extremely low, perhaps indicating a relative inadequacy of the knowledge base. Cowen (1973) obtained a similarly dismal finding in his search of articles in the *Community Mental Health Journal,* which yielded only about 3% of articles dealing with prevention relative to other clinical intervention articles.

Several recent developments may assist in better identifying the prevention knowledge base. As noted before, two new journals focus primarily on prevention: *The Journal of Primary Prevention* and *Prevention in Human Services.* Additionally, the *Journal of Primary Prevention* publishes abstracts and other information available from the newly established Primary Prevention Program Clearinghouse (Psychology Department, Dewey Hall, University of Vermont, Burlington, VT 05405). These and other developments should help develop the field by providing forums for exchange of information, program descriptions, and research. Thus, identification of the knowledge base may be less of a problem in the future. However, the fact that adequately designed and evaluated prevention programs are infrequent poses significantly more problems for the knowledge base than mere identification of what does exist in the literature. As an aside, we should note our personal observation that much more quality work does exist than typically receives credit. This occurs either because of an individual author's ignorance of the work or that individual's iconoclasm. Going back to Cowen's (1982) statement above, many writers assert that what literature does exist is of poor quality and is not "true prevention" or prevention under a rigorous definition. Zax and Cowen (1976) charge that "we are still without hard empirical data to justify prevention" (p. 509). On the other hand, Albee (1982a) states emphatically, "a large and growing literature demonstrates the effectiveness of prevention programs in eliminating or reducing the incidence of later disturbance" (p. 1044).

This division over whether there is as yet an adequate knowledge base may be less dramatic than is apparent. First, there appears to be both public and private faces to prevention. When "selling" the concepts publicly, there is a need to assert the more positive aspects. When talking "within house," quasi-privately to fellow prevention professionals, perhaps through specialty journals, the position de rigueur is to urge greater efforts at generating a prevention research base of evaluation. Second, both statements can be true simultaneously. As even Cowen (1982) admits, "although primary prevention's current generative base cannot be described as robust, it is sufficient to justify development of diverse primary prevention programs" (p. 136). It will be demonstrated in each of the following chapters, reflecting the field at large, that whereas this knowledge base is becoming adequate, in many instances research justification is still developing. Additionally, it appears that specific, targeted prevention interventions are able to show considerably more beneficial effects than more global interventions. For example, it is relatively easier to demonstrate preventive effects of hospital preparation for psychological problems of anxiety and behavior disorders than it is to show prevention of schizophrenia, in part due to more clearly delineated independent variables, dependent measures, and conceptualizations of etiology. The state of the knowledge base is ever changing and, it is hoped, improving. This volume presents numerous aspects of this base, while pointing out where more evaluation is needed.

Evaluation

Critical examination of the outcome of prevention programming remains at the core of the knowledge base noted above. Dusenbury-Kelly (1982) succinctly presents the reasons for more adequate evaluation of prevention programs:

> If our dream is to see prevention become a major component of our mental health system, it is imperative that research demonstrate to the cynics that community programs of prevention can achieve their goals effectively. Adequate research design enables us to make a measured, reliable, valid assessment of what a program was and what it accomplished. Adequate evaluation gives credibility to claims that prevention programs are effective. Credibility is essential in influencing skeptics who control funding; research and program money is too scarce to throw away on programs whose effectiveness has not or cannot be proved. [pp. 228–229]

Almost every conceptual review paper, every chapter, and every book dealing with prevention underscores this need for research and evaluation. Indeed, the original Community Mental Health Center Act of 1963 (amended in 1965) chartered research and evaluation activities as a fundamental facet of CMHCs.

This discussion is again slanted to mental health evaluation. The requirements for demonstration and evaluation of prevention programs are no less important for the physical health area, but the state of sophistication and orientation to evaluation in physical health may be better relative to mental health. There are several important issues regarding evaluation in prevention since there are several levels at which evaluation can take place. First, Edgerton (1971) and others (Heller, Price, & Sher, 1980) note the distinction between research and evaluation. The purpose of research is to generate new knowledge without concern for its immediate application. Evaluation, in contrast, considers the degree to which an intervention (technique or program) accomplishes its objectives. Of course, this distinction becomes blurred when considering "applied research" as opposed to "basic research." Second, this distinction often leads some prevention professionals to lament over the problems of applied or evaluation research and, consequently, to propose "softer" standards to judge evaluation research. Contrasted with this position, other professionals contend that no less rigor should be required of evaluation research in the field or naturalistic setting than is required for laboratory research (Cowen, 1982; Dusenbury-Kelly, 1982). Perhaps the nature of the scientific rigor required may change with the setting and with adaptation to the peculiarities of circumstance, but a constant demand for quality is required. Thus, while some precision may be sacrificed in experimental control, for example, other considerations become important such as actual utility and meeting real-life needs (Hermalin, 1981).

Some professionals suggest that rigor should not be a singular goal to the detriment of useful and meaningful research (Sarason, 1981). Nonetheless, there is a clear need for both basic and applied research (evaluation) to advance the field (Heller et al., 1980). A third issue concerns *what* is being evaluated. There are several interrelated questions regarding what target variables evaluators should select. For example, evaluative consideration of both the implementation process and the program outcome can be considered important since each interacts with the other (Snowden, Munoz, & Kelly, 1979). Both of these are discussed for different settings and problems in several of the chapters to follow. Peterson and Brownlee-Duffeck (Chapter 9) note difficulties in attempting to summarize outcome studies, some of which focus upon research and careful empirical measurement, and others upon implementation, where outcome is discussed in anecdotal and general ways. Masterpasqua and Swift (Chapter 12) report the problems of setting up community-wide prevention programs and note that intervention, not evaluation of the intervention outcome, is the focus of most community centers. MacMahon, Pugh, and Hutchison (1961) articulate this question differently by distinguishing between evaluation of accomplishment (that is, does the program have beneficial impact?) and evaluation of technique (how is the program being implemented?)

Despite the need for information on programs and implementation, we caution that there appears to be an overabundance of narrative/descriptive "evaluations" of the implementation process compared to more data-based evaluation. While many such reports can be valuable, Dusenbury-Kelly (1982) discussed 67 programs nominated for a prevention award from the Mental Health Association and noted that most of the programs' reports lacked clarity and did not include adequate evaluation. In contrast, Cowen et al. (1975) describe in detail the extensive research base for the Primary Mental Health Project as well as elaborating the difficulties of setting up and maintaining the program, the selection of personnel, the interactions with various agencies, and the funding arrangements, among other implementation aspects. Their reports are not limited to clearly documented phenomena; they also note the informal nature of some "indirect consequences" of their program in terms of teacher, principal, and parent reactions, for example. Similarly, Rolf, Bevins, Hasazi, Crowther, and Johnson (1982) describe the problems of the Vermont Vulnerable Child Development Project in terms of gaps between prevention theory and practice while also noting the research base of the project (Crowther, Bond, & Rolf, 1981; Rolf, Fischer, & Hasazi, in press).

A fourth consideration of evaluation targets is the question of which effects should be monitored: short-term or long-range effects (Heller et al., 1980). Many prevention evaluations tend to measure short-term effects of the interventions—those found immediately upon completion of a program. In many instances, these are relatively easier to obtain. However, the typical lack of measurement over time precludes examination of any long lasting benefit that may be of more importance. Another potential problem is that many prevention programs do not or cannot show such short-term effects due to the very nature of the problem requiring the intervention. For example, successful prevention of coronary disease or periodontal problems cannot be shown until later adulthood; and prevention of children's school maladjustment may not be truly documented until the child graduates without having had problems. Of course, researchers can identify short-term steps on the continuum over the long-term where early and intermediate points might show results. Rickel et al. (Chapter 3) depict this process in their discussion of the Head Start program wherein the immediate gains were then followed over a period of years. We assert, however, that in many cases the short-term effects of an intervention (however defined by the programmer) may be at least as important as the long-term effects. That is, immediate positive effects of an intervention can be of particular utility. For example, a program to prepare children for the hospital may only have beneficial effects for that particular hospitalization and may not generalize to other situations or future hospitalizations. However, the target of immediate reduction of pain and anxiety is achieved. Rolf et al. (1982) present the ultimate goals of their Vermont Project as including the prediction and influencing of adult outcome from childhood factors. Yet, they also note the short term goals which were easier to obtain and document. These types of specific and relatively short-term effects should not be denigrated by some professionals' demands for massive, long-term, high impact prevention interventions (compare Rutter, 1982). In summary on evaluation of short-term versus long-term effects, consideration of both appears requisite.

Finally, the issue of *what* is evaluated also comes from the need to measure the actual effects of the prevention program rather than only the intentions of the programmer (Cowen, 1982). Many well-intentioned programs either have a minimal effect or have unexpected effects (sometimes opposite the original intentions). Attention to the total ecology of the prevention situation is required.

Requirements for Evaluation.

Several writers have suggested conceptual requirements for prevention evaluation. These frameworks or guidelines are useful for specifying how to evaluate evaluations of prevention programs. Some of these guidelines will be briefly noted here and are described further in the references cited. Hermalin (1981) synthesized the requirements of prevention evaluation as including demonstration of utility, specification and individualization to target groups, sound measurement, follow-up evaluations of long-term effects, controls on extraneous variables, and alliances between researchers and service programmers. Similarly, Heller et al. (1980) ask the following questions for program evaluation:

> What specific end state is to be prevented?
> What specific programmatic objectives could be expected to contribute to the reduced incidence of the end state in question?

Was the intervention successfully implemented?
What changes occurred as a result of the intervention?
Were changes in targeted groups different from changes in comparison groups; or were changes in targeted groups different from changes in these same groups during initial baseline periods of nonintervention?
Were there any changes in significant others or nearby "systems"?
What were the financial and social costs associated with the intervention? [p. 307]

Edgerton (1971), Morell (1981), Bloom (1968), and Flanagan (1971) advance similar frameworks and question requirements for evaluation in the prevention field.

Programming versus Research.

One final issue that repeatedly arises regarding evaluation requirements of prevention is posed by Hollister (1981) in his editorial title: "Program Development versus Research: Which First?" This issue remains controversial due in part to more recent problems of funding and difficult decisions about allocation of scarce resources. A more fundamental aspect of this issue comes from a perceived schism between research-oriented professionals and "on-line, prevention service providers." The former group demands evaluation, the latter group argues that the costs and difficulties of conducting evaluation can impede innovation and implementation. (See a discussion of this issue in Hollister, 1981, by Bernard Bloom, Ruth Knee, and Eli Bower, with later responses by Blackman, 1982, and Hollister, 1982a.) Other writers attend more fully to this dilemma than we can here (Snowden et al., 1979). We raise the issue not only to note its presence, but also to presage its importance in questioning priorities within different settings and problems as discussed in many of the following chapters. The evaluation component of the prevention field comprises many aspects. Problems and solutions (or the lack thereof) for evaluation are discussed by chapter authors specific to their topical areas. Additionally, Stolz (Chapter 13) discusses implementation and evaluation issues in more detail.

Funding of Prevention

We have already noted the relatively low rate of financial support for prevention research and programs. Albee (1982a) asserts that within the budget of the National Institute of Mental Health, no more than 2% of mental health money is spent on prevention. Commensurate with this, CMHCs now allocate less energy to "consultation and education" and more to clinical services (even less than that originally mandated, which at no time approached the energy spent on treatment; see Perlmutter, 1974; Snow & Newton, 1976). A newer orientation of "fee for service" appears to permeate many CMHCs for survival wherein third party reimbursements are sought for treatment, not prevention activities (D'Augelli, 1982). Indeed, Baxter (1977) poses the essential question by asking "Who pays when nobody's sick?" in a chapter title. Different solutions to this funding question have been proposed including governmental sources, charitable organizations, and private industry (Baxter, 1977; Cromwell, 1978; Griswold, 1980; Gullotta, 1981).

Critics of prevention argue that the funding problems are well-placed since there is an inadequate supply of money available and what funds are available should be given to mental health treatment and clinical services as a higher priority than prevention (Henderson, 1975; Lamb & Zusman, 1979). One particular issue in the debate for prevention funding revolves around cost-effectiveness, with proponents arguing that prevention represents the best cost-benefit ratios available (Harper & Balch, 1975) and opponents arguing that benefits are unproven to justify the cost (Lamb & Zusman, 1979). It may be difficult to resolve this issue on a general level, but evidence is accumulating that support for prevention is justified for specific disorders and certain types of prevention intervention. This evidence is amply documented in this book. However, this conclusion does not mean that all programs have been proven effective and a blanket endorsement of prevention can be made at this time. With unanimity, the chapter authors here point to areas requiring further development before an unequivocal stand can be taken. But, certainly the conclusion is warranted that funding for proven programs is still inadequate, even without considering support for innovative programs or those still needing research evaluation.

We should also note here that funding for prevention in physical health parallels the low priority in mental health.

Some writers argue that funding for prevention will continue at low levels until a "constituency" of social forces can be brought to bear demanding prevention services. This issue will be discussed in the next section.

Political/Public Policy

Broskowski and Baker (1974) see the largest barrier to prevention as the lack of demand by a "well identified and powerful constituency" (p. 717). That is, no group is lobbying effectively for prevention. This lobbying involves not only trying to affect the legislative process of appropriations or the third party payments mechanism, but also lobbying for the attention and interest of the population at large to demand prevention programming activities. Broskowski and Baker (1974) suggest "it is difficult to organize a constituency that defines its needs as the maintenance of a positive state of affairs" (p. 716). Hastings (1982) makes a similar point by noting that the concept of prevention cuts across categories and services and is not a casualty area, but is one which "implies wholeness, developing individuals to their fullest potential, and stopping some event from happening" (p. 52). There may be some movement toward a coalescing of interests which may ultimately build a constituency for prevention in mental health and physical health areas (Gelfand & Hartmann, 1977; Matarrazo, 1982). To build on this movement, Hollister (1982b) urges professional attention toward the development of community support and citizen advocacy. This has been a fundamental element of many community interventions over the years (Bloom, 1971; Snowden et al., 1979), but may be even more important now.

Recent administrative and philosophical changes at the federal level have produced some changes in support of prevention as it relates to social services. It is still a political axiom, however, that loud, well-articulated and organized power entities will get a response from the political system, where factually-based, prevention advocates may be given minimal attention without any political clout. Hastings (1982) suggests that

> if prevention is to survive, those who currently believe and participate in the prevention field must be willing to measure program effectiveness and build public awareness of these programs where measurable gains can take place. Through many avenues, prevention advocates can build a constituency which can promote better local, state, and federal prevention policy. This constituency can become the basis for a new politics in prevention . . . a politics which can provide incentives for systematic development and funding of prevention programs within both public and private sectors. [p. 53]

If prevention is "right," and if impact on public policy is necessary, then constituency building takes on a higher priority for prevention professionals in both mental and physical health fields.

Professional Boundaries

We have suggested that no one professional discipline or subdiscipline owns the prevention concept. Numerous professions and professionals assist in various prevention program developments and evaluations. "Turf" issues and disciplinary isolation have often impeded progress. Thus, we find it all too common that literature reviews or position papers ignore related and excellent work which is outside a writer's personal specialty. We also acknowledge, correspondingly, that we may be guilty of this as well in the writing of this chapter and in our editing of the following chapters, since the habit of reading and discussing within relatively closed circles is hard to break. For example, Broskowski and Baker (1974) found that perceptions of competitiveness or interference by different professions impeded program development. They cite Sanford's (1970) treatise that different explanations of alcoholism, each specific to the various specialty disciplines, have impeded alcoholism prevention programming. Such professional chauvinism can likely be found for unfortunately innumerable topics. To the extent possible, the chapter authors in this volume attempted to look beyond community psychology, clinical psychology, or even psychology at large, in order to draw on valuable resources wherever they may be found relative to the prevention of childhood problems. Although this is a psychologically-oriented book by the title, we acknowledge the statement of Cowen (1977) that mental health professionals "are not architects, engineers, nutrition specialists, recreation specialists, politicians, or urban planners; nor can we assume a near-infinity of such roles" (pp. 4–5). We do assert that psychologists and related professions have something positive to contribute to many diverse prevention roles. Our position is that all professions can well afford to break down barriers with others.

One particular professional boundary has been alluded to already, namely the division between practitioners and researchers in prevention (Broskowski & Baker,

1974). While many prevention professionals transcend this dichotomy, this schism all too frequently divides the "preventive house." Many of the following chapters attend to such boundaries of orientation (for example, Peterson & Brownlee-Duffeck, Chapter 9; Masterpasqua & Swift, Chapter 12). As becomes apparent in some of the outstanding examples of prevention programming, there is no reason that program development and implementation cannot inherently involve research and vice versa.

A second boundary worth brief rementioning is one often erected between the professional and "outsiders" or lay-persons. To be successful, liaison is necessary between preventionists and consumers, opinion leaders and legislators, for example. The recommended constituency building and community involvement are primary components of future prevention programming in general.

Finally, Albee (1982a; 1982b) notes that mental health professionals often resist prevention programs because of prior financial and training investment in clinical services (diagnosis, treatment, and rehabilitation). Gullotta (1981) takes this a step further by suggesting that "professional human beings (social workers, psychologists, nurses, doctors, and members of other helping professions) profit off of the illness and misery of their clients" (p. 18). Gullotta recommends using this issue to improve prevention funding by appealing to profit motives. However, together with Albee's statement and those of others, it becomes apparent that the past and present emphasis in mental health has been on treatment services rather than prevention activities. Perlmutter (1974) predicts that prevention will need to separate from treatment-oriented agencies in order to maintain a viable identity and existence. Despite some differences in orientation and priorities, we see no professional reason for a hostile coexistence of prevention and treatment. A "chip-on-the-shoulder" attitude serves nobody. And, within Caplan's model of primary, secondary, and tertiary prevention, prevention per se and treatment are compatible. A reordering of some priorities may, of course, be necessary, but professional antagonisms need not prevail as a boundary.

Summary

In this section, we have discussed several critical considerations currently being debated within the area of prevention. The discussion of each issue has been admittedly brief and fairly general, but serves to introduce the different investigators and their points of view for further reference. Particular relevance to the childhood period as the focus of this book was only infrequently raised. Our intention has been to note the issues related to prevention as a general concept; it remains for each chapter to present the specifics for particular topics in childhood prevention.

REFERENCES

Adam, C. T. A descriptive definition of primary prevention. *Journal of Primary Prevention*, 1981, *2*, 67–79.

Albee, G. W. Preventing psychopathology and promoting human potential. *American Psychologist,* 1982, *37*(9), 1043–1050. (a)

Albee, G. W. A brief historical perspective on the primary prevention of childhood mental disorders. In M. Frank (Ed.), *Primary prevention for children and families.* New York: Haworth, 1982. (b)

Albee, G. W., & Joffe, J. M. (Eds.), *The primary prevention of psychopathology: The issues.* Hanover, NH: University Press of New England, 1977.

Baxter, F. Z. Funding—who pays when nobody's sick. In D. C. Klein & S. E. Goldstein (Eds.), *Primary prevention: An idea whose time has come* (DHEW ADM Publication No. 77-447). Washington, D. C.: Government Printing Office, 1977.

Blackman, S. Creative controversy. *Journal of Primary Prevention,* 1982, *3,* 55–56.

Bloom, B. L. The evaluation of primary prevention programs. In L. M. Roberts, N. S. Greenfield, & M. H. Miller (Eds.), *Comprehensive mental health: The challenge of evaluation.* Madison: University of Wisconsin Press, 1968.

Bloom, B. L. Strategies for the prevention of mental disorders. In Division 27, American Psychological Association, Task Force on Community Mental Health (ed.), *Issues in community psychology and preventive mental health.* New York: Behavioral Publications, 1971.

Bloom, B. L. *Community mental health: A general introduction.* Belmont, CA: Wadsworth, 1977.

Bloom, B. L. Prevention of mental disorders: Recent advances in theory and practice. *Community Mental Health Journal,* 1979, *15,* 179–191.

Bloom, M. A working definition of primary prevention related to social concerns. *Journal of Prevention,* 1980, *1,* 15–23.

Bloom, M. Analysis of the knowledge base of primary prevention. *Journal of Primary Prevention,* 1981, *2,* 6–13.

Bolman, W. M. An outline of preventive psychiatric programs for children. *Archives of General Psychiatry,* 1967, *17,* 5–8.

Bolman, W. M., & Bolian, G. C. Crisis intervention as primary or secondary intervention. In I. N. Berlin & L. A. Stone (Eds.), *Basic handbook of child psychiatry. Volume 4: Prevention and current issues.* New York: Basic Books, 1979.

Bolman, W. M., & Westman, J. C. Prevention of mental disorders: An overview of current programs. *American Journal of Psychiatry,* 1967, *123,* 1058–1068.

Botvin, G. J. Broadening the focus of smoking prevention strategies. In T. Coates, A. Peterson, & C. Perry (Eds.), *Promoting adolescent health: A dialog on research and practice.* New York: Academic Press, 1982.

Brickman, H. R. Mental health and social change: An ecological perspective. *American Journal of Psychiatry,* 1970, *127,* 413–419.

Broskowski, A., & Baker, F. Professional, organizational, and social barriers to primary prevention. *American Journal of Orthopsychiatry,* 1974, *44,* 707–719.

Califano, J. A., Jr. *Healthy people: The Surgeon's General's report on health promotion and disease prevention.* Washington, D.C.: U.S. Government Printing Office, 1979.

Caplan, G. (Ed.), *Prevention of mental disorders in children.* New York: Basic Books, 1961.

Caplan, G. *Principles of preventive psychiatry.* New York: Basic Books, 1964.

Community mental health center programs operating handbook, (DHEW) Washington, D.C.: Government Printing Office, 1971.

Cooper, S., Munger, R., & Ravlin, M. M. Mental health prevention through affective education in schools. *Journal of Prevention,* 1980, *1,* 24–34.

Cowen, E. L. Social and community interventions. *Annual Review of Psychology,* 1973, *24,* 423–472.

Cowen, E. L. Baby-steps toward primary preventions. *American Journal of Community Psychology,* 1977, *5,* 1–22.

Cowen, E. L. The wooing of primary prevention. *American Journal of Community Psychology,* 1980, *8,* 258–284.

Cowen, E. L. Primary prevention research: Barriers, needs and opportunities. *Journal of Primary Prevention,* 1982, *2*(3), 131–137.

Cowen, E. L., Spinell, A., Wright, S., & Weissberg, R. P. Continuing dissemination of a school-based mental health program. *Professional Psychology: Research and Practice,* 1983, *14,* 118–127.

Cowen, E. L., Trost, M. A., Izzo, L. D., Lorion, L. D., Dorr, D., & Isaacson, R. V. *New ways in school mental health: Early detection and prevention of school maladaptation.* New York: Human Sciences Press, 1975.

Cromwell, E. Estimating costs of community services. *Social Work,* 1978, *13,* 159–161.

Crowther, J., Bond, L., & Rolf, J. The incidence prevalence and severity of internalizing and externalizing behavior problems among preschool children in day care. *Journal of Abnormal Child Psychology,* 1981, *9,* 23–42.

D'Augelli, A. R. A funny thing happened on the way to the community: Consultation and education in community mental health centers, or how I learned to stop worrying about prevention and love third-party payment. *Journal of Primary Prevention,* 1982, *2,* 235–239.

Dusenbury-Kelly, L. Between the dream and the reality: A look at programs nominated for the Lela Rowland Prevention Award of the National Mental Health Association. *Journal of Primary Prevention,* 1982, *2,* 217–234.

Edgerton, J. W. Evaluation in community mental health. In Division 27, American Psychological Association, Task Force on Community Mental Health (Ed.), *Issues in community psychology and preventive mental health.* New York: Behavioral Publications, 1971.

Felner, R. D., Jason, L., Moritsugu, J., & Farber, S. S. (Eds.), Preventive psychology: Theory, research and practice in community interventions. New York: Pergamon Press, 1983.

Flanagan, J. C. Evaluation and validation of research data in primary prevention. *American Journal of Orthopsychiatry,* 1971, *41,* 117–123.

Frangia, E. W., & Reisinger, J. J. Parent implementation of a preschool intervention system. *Journal of Clinical Child Psychology,* 1979, *8,* 64–68.

Garbarino, J. Preventing child maltreatment. In R. H. Price, R. F. Ketterer, B. C. Bader, & J. Monahan (Eds.), *Prevention in mental health: Research, policy, and practice.* Beverly Hills: Sage, 1980.

Gelfand, D. M., & Hartmann, D. P. The prevention of childhood behavior disorders. In B. B. Lahey & A. E. Kazdin (Eds.), *Advances in clinical child psychology* (Vol. 1). New York: Plenum Press, 1977.

Goldston, S. E. Defining primary prevention. In G. W. Albee & J. M. Joffe (Eds.), *Primary prevention of psychopathology: The issues* (Vol. 1). Hanover, NH: University Press of New England, 1977. (a)

Goldston, S. E. Primary prevention: A view from the federal level. In G. W. Albee & J. M. Joffe (Eds.), *Primary prevention of psychopathology: The issues (Vol. 1). Hanover, NH: University Press of New England, 1977. (b)*

Griswold, P. M. A family practice model for clinical psychology. *Professional Psychology,* 1980, *11,* 628–636.

Guerney, L., & Jordon, L. Children of divorce: A community support group. *Journal of Divorce,* 1979, *2,* 283–294.

Gullotta, T. P. An unorthodox proposal for funding primary prevention. *Journal of Primary Prevention,* 1981, *2,* 14–24.

Harper, R., & Balch, P. Some economic arguments in favor of primary prevention. *Professional Psychology,* 1975, *6,* 17–25.

Hastings, M. M. The politics of prevention. *Journal of Primary Prevention,* 1982, *3,* 52–53.

Harris, P. *Better health for our children: A national strategy. The Report of the Select Panel for the Promotion of Child Health.* Washington, D.C.: U.S. Government Printing Office, 1981.

Heller, K., Price, R. H., & Sher, K. J. Research and evaluation in primary prevention: Issues and guidelines. In R. H. Price, R. F. Ketterer, B. C. Bader, & J. Monahan (Eds.), *Prevention in mental health: Research, policy, and practice.* Beverly Hills, CA: Sage, 1980.

Henderson, J. Object relations and new social psychiatry: The illusion of primary prevention. *Bulletin of the Menninger Clinic,* 1975, *39,* 233–245.

Hermalin, J. Introduction: Evaluation and prevention in human services. *Prevention in Human Services,* 1981, *1,* 3–5.

Hollister, W. Program development vs. research: Which first? *Journal of Primary Prevention,* 1981, *2,* 56–58.

Hollister, W. G. Fiscal myopia or constituency building. *Journal of Primary Prevention,* 1982, *3,* 3–5. (a)

Hollister, W. G. Hollister replies. *Journal of Primary Prevention, 1982, 3,* 56–57. (b)

Joffe, J. M. Let a thousand flowers bloom? *Journal of Primary Prevention,* 1982, *3,* 53–55.

Joffe, J. M., & Albee, G. W. (Eds.), *Prevention through political action and social change.* Hanover, NH: University Press of New England, 1981.

Johnson, J. E. Stress reduction through sensation information. In I. G. Sarason & C. C. Spielberger (Eds.), *Stress and anxiety* (Vol. 2). Washington, D.C.: Hemisphere, 1975.

Joint Information Service of the American Psychiatric Association. *Preventing mental illness: Efforts and attitudes.* Washington, D.C.: American Psychiatric Association, 1980.

Kennedy, J. F. *Message from the President of the United States relative to mental illness and mental retardation.* (88th Congress, First Session, U. S. House of Representatives Document No. 58). Washington, D.C.: U.S. Government Printing Office, 1963.

Kessler, M., & Albee, G. W. Primary prevention. *Annual Review of Psychology,* 1975, *26,* 557–591.

Kirschenbaum, D. S. Toward more behavioral early intervention programs: A rationale. *Professional Psychology: Research and Practice,* 1983, *14,* 159–169.

Klein, D. C., & Goldston, S. E. (Eds.), *Primary prevention: An idea whose time has come.* (DHEW ADM Publication No. 77--447). Washington, D.C.: Government Printing Office, 1977.

Kornberg, M. S., & Caplan, G. Risk factors and preventive intervention in child psychopathology: A review. *Journal of Prevention,* 1980, *1,* 71–133.

Lamb, H. R., & Zusman, J. Primary prevention in perspective. *American Journal of Psychiatry,* 1979, *136,* 12–17.

McCaffrey, M., & Tewey, S. Preparing educators to participate in the community response to child abuse and neglect. *Exceptional Children,* 1978, *45,* 114–122.

Maccoby, N., & Alexander, J. Use of medicine in lifestyle programs. In P. O. Davidson & S. M. Davidson (Eds.), *Behavioral medicine: Changing health lifestyles.* New York: Brunner/Mazel, 1980.

Maccoby, N., Farquhar, J. W., Wood, P. D., & Alexander, J. Reducing the risk of cardiovascular disease: Effects of a community-based campaign on knowledge and behavior. *Journal of Community Health,* 1977, *3,* 100–114.

MacMahon, B., Pugh, T. F., & Hutchison, G. B. Principles in the evaluation of community mental health programs. *American Journal of Public Health,* 1961, *51,* 963–968.

Matarazzo, J. D. Behavioral health and behavioral medicine: Frontiers for a new health psychology. *American Psychologist,* 1980, *35,* 807–817.

Matarazzo, J. D. Behavioral health's challenge to academic, scientific, and professional psychology. *American Psychologist,* 1982, *37,* 1–14.

Matarazzo, J. D., Miller, N. E., Weiss, S. M., Herd, J. A., & Weiss, S. M. (Eds.), *Behavioral health: A handbook of health enhancement and disease prevention.* New York: Wiley, 1984.

Melamed, B. G., & Siegel, L. J. Reduction of anxiety in children facing hospitalization and surgery by use of filmed modeling. *Journal of Consulting and Clinical Psychology,* 1975, *43,* 511–521.

Millon, T., Green, C. J., & Meagher, R. B. (Eds.), *Handbook of clinical health psychology.* New York: Plenum Press, 1982.

Morell, J. A. Evaluation in prevention: Implications from a general model. *Prevention in Human Services,* 1981, *1,* 7–40.

Munoz, R. F. The primary prevention of psychological problems. *Community Mental Health Review,* 1976, *1*(6), 1–15.

Newberger, E., & Daniel, J. Knowledge and epidemiology of child abuse: A critical review of concepts. In R. Bairne & E. Newberger (Eds.), *Critical perspectives on child abuse.* Lexington, MA: D. C. Heath, 1979.

Perlmutter, F. D. Prevention and treatment: A strategy for survival. *Community Mental Health Journal,* 1974, *10,* 276–281.

Peterson, L. *Prevention and community compliance to immunization schedules.* Columbia, Missouri: University of Missouri-Columbia, 1980. (Eric Document Reproduction No. ED 191559).

Peterson, L., & Ridley-Johnson, R. Pediatric hospital response to survey on prehospital preparation for children. *Journal of Pediatric Psychology,* 1980, *5,* 1–7.

Peterson, L., & Shigetomi, C. The use of coping techniques to minimize anxiety in hospitalized children. *Behavior Therapy,* 1981, *12,* 1–14.

Poser, E. G. Toward a theory of "behavioral prophylaxis." *Journal of Behavior Therapy and Experimental Psychiatry,* 1970, *1,* 39–43.

Price, R. H., Bader, B. C., & Ketterer, R. F. Prevention in community mental health: The state of the art. In R. H. Price, R. F. Ketterer, B. C. Bader, & J. Monahan (Eds.),

Prevention in mental health: Research, policy, and practice. Beverly Hills, CA: Sage Hills, 1980.

Price, R. H., Ketterer, R. F., Bader, B. C., & Monahan, J. (Eds.), *Prevention in mental health: Research, policy, and practice.* Beverly Hills, CA: Sage, 1980.

Reinherz, H. Primary prevention of emotional disorders of children: Mirage or reality. *Journal of Prevention,* 1980, *1,* 4–14.

Report of Joint Commission. *The mental health of children: Challenge for the 1970's.* New York: Harper & Row, 1969.

Report to the President from The President's Commission on Mental Health (Vol. 1). Washington, D.C.: U.S. Government Printing Office, 1978.

Roberts, M. C., Maddux, J. E., & Wright, L. The developmental perspective in pediatric behavioral health. In J. D. Matarazzo, N. E. Miller, S. M. Weiss, J. A. Herd, & S. M. Weiss (Eds.), *Behavioral health: A handbook of health enhancement and disease prevention.* New York: Wiley, 1984.

Roberts, M. C., Maddux, J. E., Wurtele, S. K., & Wright, L. Pediatric psychology: Health care psychology for children. In T. Millon, C. J. Green, & R. B. Meagher (Eds.), *Handbook of Clinical Health Psychology.* New York: Plenum Press, 1982.

Rodick, J. D., & Henggeler, S. W. The short-term and long-term amelioration of academic and motivational deficiencies among low-achieving inner-city adolescents. *Child Development,* 1980, *51,* 1126–1132.

Rolf, J. E., Bevins, S., Hasazi, J. E., Crowther, J., & Johnson, J. Prospective research with vulnerable children and the risky art of preventive intervention. In H. A. Moss, R. Hess, & C. Swift (Eds.), *Early intervention programs for infants.* New York: Haworth Press, 1982.

Rolf, J., Fischer, M., & Hasazi, J. Assessing preventive interventions for multiple-risk preschoolers: A test case. In M. Goldstein (Ed.), *The prevention of schizophrenia.* Rockville, MD: NIMH, in press.

Rosenstein, P. J. Family outreach: A program for the prevention of child neglect and abuse. *Child Welfare,* 1978, *57,* 519–525.

Runyan, C. W., DeVellis, R. F., McEvoy-DeVellis, B., & Hochbaum, G. M. Health psychology and the public health perspective: In search of the pump handle. *Health Psychology,* 1982, *1,* 169–180.

Rutter, M. Prevention of children's psychosocial disorders: Myth and substance. *Pediatrics,* 1982, *70,* 883–894.

Sanford, N. Community actions and alcoholism. In D. Adelson & B. L. Kalis (Eds.), *Community psychology and mental health: Perspectives and challenges.* Scranton, PA: Chandler, 1970.

Sarason, S. B. *Psychology misdirected.* New York: Free Press, 1981.

Shure, M. B., & Spivack, G. Interpersonal problem-solving and primary prevention: Programming for preschool and kindergarten children. *Journal of Clinical Child Psychology,* 1979, *8,* 89–94.

Singer, J. E., & Krantz, D. S. Perspectives on the interface between psychology and public health. *American Psychologist,* 1982, *37,* 944–960.

Snow, D. L., & Newton, P. M. Task, social structure, and social process in the community mental health center movement. *American Psychologist,* 1976, *31,* 582–594.

Snowden, L. R., Munoz, R. F., & Kelly, J. G. The process of implementing community-based research. In R. F. Munoz, L. R. Snowden, J. G. Kelley & Associates (Eds.), *Social and psychological research in community settings.* San Francisco: Jossey-Bass, 1979.

Task Panel on Prevention, President's Commission on Mental Health. *Report on primary prevention.* Washington, D.C.: U.S. Government Printing Office, 1978.

Wallerstein, J. S., & Kelly, J. B. The effects of parental divorce: The adolescent experience. In E. J. Anthony & C. Kaupernek (Eds.), *The child in his family: Children at psychiatric risk* (Vol. 3). New York: Wiley, 1974.

Wallerstein, J. S., & Kelly, J. B. The effects of parental divorce: Experiences of the child in later latency. *American Journal of Orthopsychiatry,* 1976, *46,* 256–269.

Wallerstein, J. S., & Kelly, J. B. Divorce counseling: A community service for families in the midst of divorce. *American Journal of Orthpsychiatry,* 1977, *47,* 4–22.

Weissberg, R. P., Cowen, E. L., Lotyczewski, B. S., & Gesten, E. L. The Primary Mental Health Project: Seven consecutive years of program outcome research. *Journal of Consulting and Clinical Psychology,* 1983, *51,* 100–107.

Zax, M., & Cowen, E. L. *Abnormal psychology: Changing conceptions* (2nd ed.). New York: Holt, Rinehart, & Winston, 1976.

Zigler, E. Controlling child abuse in America: An effort doomed to failure? In R. Bourne & E. Newberger (Eds.), *Critical perspectives on child abuse.* Lexington, MA: D. C. Heath, 1979.

REFERENCE NOTE

1. Peterson, L. *Training consumerism in children's judgments of televised advertisements.* Manuscript submitted for publication, University of Missouri-Columbia, 1983.

PART ONE

Milestone Approach

Prevention at Selected Developmental Stages and Times

CHAPTER 2

Prevention in the Perinatal Period

PHYLLIS R. MAGRAB, ANITA MILLER SOSTEK, AND BEVERLY A. POWELL

In the consideration of both health prevention and health promotion, the perinatal period plays an important role in the developmental outcome of the infant. The Select Panel for the Promotion of Child Health (1981a) pointed out that some of the most potent influences on child health include the social environment, the physical environment, nutrition, and health-related behaviors. These factors wield their effects well before the child is born. This chapter will examine the prenatal, neonatal, and postnatal factors related to developmental outcome in infants as well as suggested prevention strategies.

During the prenatal period, maternal practices including nutrition, smoking, substance abuse, maternal health, and maternal age must be considered. Related prevention strategies, such as health education, family planning services, screening for health problems and genetic disorders, antenatal diagnosis and genetic services, prenatal care, anticipatory guidance and environmental safety, and regionalization of perinatal services are discussed.

The latter portion of this chapter describes possible complications of labor and delivery with particular emphasis on prematurity and intensive care nursery hospitalization. Parents with infants whose medical status requires prolonged hospitalization have special emotional and often practical needs. Family adjustment to both the normal and the at-risk infant is also discussed. Finally, the chapter describes assessment and intervention strategies aimed at infant cognitive, motor, and affective development.

PRENATAL INFLUENCES ON DEVELOPMENTAL OUTCOMES OF THE INFANT

The psychological and physical growth of the infant and child is to some extent determined by the physical health and social-emotional status of the pregnant mother. To prevent negative sequelae and to promote healthy outcomes for the child, there are a number of important prenatal influences such as nutrition, environmental factors, infection, maternal age and genetics that must be considered. The first part of this section will delineate these factors and the second part will address strategies to reduce environmental risks, to improve the health status of the mother, and to provide needed prenatal services.

Maternal Nutritional Practices

Nutritional practices of the mother throughout her lifetime have a major impact on the status of the fetus and whether a healthy baby results. The relationship between maternal nutrition and pregnancy outcome has been well established (Lechtig, Delgado, Martorell, Richardson, Yarbrough, & Klein, 1978; U.S. National Institutes of Health, 1971; Winick, 1974). The mother must be well enough nourished to support her own nutritional needs as well as those of the baby. In the last decade there has been increased attention to sufficient maternal intake and greater weight gain to provide optimum nutritional potential for the fetus. Maternal weight and height and weight gain during pregnancy have a direct relationship to infant birthweight (Lechtig et al., 1978; Naeye, 1979; Naeye, Blanc, & Paul, 1973).

The fetal malnutrition that can occur when the mother is significantly undernourished is practically synonymous with small-for-gestational age (SGA) infants. Those infants who are small in height and weight and especially head circumference for their gestational age are at high risk for mortality, morbidity, congenital anomalies, continued growth retardation during childhood, and neurodevelopmental disorders (Lubchenco, 1976; Westwood, Kramer, Munz, Lovett, & Watters, 1983; Winick, 1974). It is not surprising that there is an increased incidence of SGA in lower socioeconomic groups where poverty influences the mother's ability to obtain sufficient quantities of quality food.

The critical importance of prenatal nutrition was recognized by the Select Panel for the Promotion of Child Health (1981a). They identified the period of pregnancy as a major point of impact on the health of infants. Research has demonstrated that food supplementation programs, nutritional counseling and prenatal diet are associated with increased birthweight and lower perinatal mortality (Habicht, Yarbrough, Lechtig, & Klein, 1972; Higgins, 1973; Lechtig et al., 1978). Specifically it was recommended that the Supplemental Food Program for Women, Infants, and Children (WIC) be enlarged to serve all who are eligible by income and nutritional risk.

The WIC program currently provides supplemental, nutritious food to low income pregnant and lactating women, infants, and children who are at nutritional risk. It is administered by the U.S. Department of Agriculture. Local agencies implementing the program must see that health services are available to WIC participants. Yet, despite the thrust of this program, many women who are nutritionally in need cannot participate because of inadequate funding or federal, state or local policies. Others may not utilize the program because of motivational or educational factors, and thus a number of women complete pregnancies without benefit of prenatal nutritional counseling, diet or food supplement programs.

Teratogens and Pregnancy Outcomes

During pregnancy, there are a number of substances that may cause harm to the growing fetus. The use of teratogens such as alcohol, cigarettes and drugs may result in behavioral and physical abnormalities in the infant (Davies, Gray, Ellwood, & Abernathy, 1976; Fielding & Yankauer, 1978; Terris & Gold, 1969). Alcohol abuse has been associated with a cluster of infant outcomes now known as fetal alcohol syndrome (Jones & Smith, 1973; Ouelette, Rosett, & Rosman, 1977). The affected infants show pre- and postnatal growth deficiencies in height, weight, and head circumference, hypertonicity, dysmorphic features, as well as abnormalities in the liver, heart and muscular-skeletal system. In addition, there may be delayed motor and language development and cognitive impairments which can lead to poor academic achievement (Erb & Andresen, 1978; Streissguth, 1976). Because the level of alcohol consumption required to produce undesirable outcomes in infants is not known, alcohol consumption during pregnancy is discouraged (Karn & Penrose, 1951; Select Panel for the Promotion of Child Health, 1981a).

Cigarette smoking by the pregnant mother has been implicated in a variety of ways in the health outcome of the infant. A retarded rate of fetal growth, an increased risk of spontaneous abortion, and a doubled risk of having a low birthweight infant have been documented (U.S. Department of Health, Education, and Welfare, 1979a, 1979b; Meyer, 1977). It has been further found that children born to smoking mothers may not catch up and achieve the same growth rate or achievement levels of children of mothers who did not smoke during pregnancy (Department of Health, Education and Welfare, 1980). Health education efforts targeted at pregnant mothers to quit smoking could significantly affect infant health (American College of Obstetricians and Gynecologists, 1979).

When the mother is addicted to drugs such as heroin, there are often pronounced effects on the fetus and long-term implications for development. Maternal heroin addiction causes trauma during pregnancy and often produces low birthweight infants who suffer from withdrawal symptoms such as convulsions, hypertonicity and tremors (Finnegan, 1976; Green, Alston, & Rich, 1975; Kennell, Slyter, & Klaus, 1970). During school age, latent developmental deficits may begin to appear (Sardeman, Madsen, & Friis-Hansen, 1976). Research on the effect of other drugs such as the array of hallucinogens continues to suggest that they influence fetal development, but the evidence is less conclusive.

The exposure of either parent during childhood and young adult years to environmental toxins such as chemical substances or excess radiation poses an additional threat to the developing infant because of unique susceptibilities early in the life cycle (Select Panel for the Promotion of Child Health, 1981a). Over 20 agents are known to be associated with human birth defects (McAlister, 1979). Some common examples include the recent reports of birth defects in infants whose fathers were exposed to Agent Orange and the higher incidence of birth defects in infants or mothers who have frequent contact with certain anesthetic agents (Corbett, Cornell, Endres, & Lieding, 1974; Wilson, 1977a). The importance of genetic counseling for these problems is well recognized.

In 1979, the Surgeon General reported over 34,000 chemicals in the work environment that have toxic effects (McAlister, 1979). Furthermore, exposure to pesticides and chemical waste also poses a threat to the pregnant mother and to the father (Select Panel for the Promotion of Child Health, 1981a). To reduce the environmental threat to the developing fetus requires extensive public health efforts and improved legislative controls.

A unique group at particular risk for teratogenic effects on their offspring are the survivors of childhood cancer such as leukemia or Hodgkin's disease. These patients typically have been exposed to both high dose chemotherapy, which is potentially teratogenic, and to radiation. In current treatment of teenagers and young adults with these problems, every effort is made to protect their reproductive organs from unnecessary injury. However, there may be increased incidence of chromosome breakage and a higher risk of birth defects among the offspring of survivors of childhood cancer (Jaffe, 1976; Nicholson, 1968).

The use of medication during pregnancy is a serious concern. While the Federal Food and Drug Administration (FDA) attempts to regulate prescription drugs, nonprescription drugs such as aspirin, sleeping pills, antihistamines, and numerous others may pose a significant risk to the pregnant woman and are not under FDA monitoring. Typically obstetricians discourage the use of such drugs during pregnancy (Select Panel for the Promotion of Child Health, 1981a).

Sometimes chronic health problems in the mother such as epilepsy require the use of medication during pregnancy in order to assure an optimal outcome to the infant. In cases such as hypothyroidism or seizure disorder, the appropriate dosage and level of medication are important as well as the selection of a medication with lower teratogenicity to the infant. One anticonvulsant medication known to produce multiple birth defects in infants is Dilatin, sometimes resulting in the Fetal Hydantoin Syndrome. For this reason, it is often recommended that an adult woman with epilepsy consult her physician prior to conceiving in order to determine whether a medication less toxic for the infant can be safely adopted before the pregnancy is begun (Hanson & Smith, 1975; Wilson, 1977b).

Maternal Health

There are a number of aspects of maternal health that can influence the outcome of pregnancy. Infections such as rubella, cytomegaloviruses, toxoplasmosis, herpes virus, syphilis, and varicella are commonly known to relate to developmental deficits (Cooper, 1977; Hanshaw, Sheiner, Moxley, Gaev, & Abel, 1975; Sever, 1977) as do maternal medical conditions such as diabetes mellitus (Grathe, 1977).

Improved medical care for women with chronic medical conditions such as juvenile diabetes and sickle cell anemia have resulted in their ability to carry pregnancies to term. However, a team of medical experts is frequently required to collaborate closely around the prenatal management of these mothers. Phenylketonuria (PKU) and cystic fibrosis are two other serious chronic disorders which can significantly affect the developing infant in utero and complicate prenatal care significantly. In some of these conditions, delivery of the baby prior to 40 weeks gestation may be indicated and care of the mother in a tertiary care center or perinatal care center is mandatory for optimal outcome. Infants of this very high-risk pregnancy population have a much higher than average incidence of congenital anomalies, inborn errors of metabolism, or perinatal complications requiring intensive care in the neonatal period (Zaleski & Casey, 1979).

PKU is a disorder which previously led invariably to mental retardation. Effective screening of newborns for this disorder and appropriate dietary management during childhood have allowed affected individuals to enter adulthood with normal intelligence. Many states now have mandatory screening to identify at-risk children.

Because women with PKU now live to the age of reproduction, they must be adequately counseled regarding the potential risks to their infant during infancy. If they choose to conceive, they require very complex medical management for their health and safety as well as optimal outcome for the infant. Likewise, a woman with any chronic endocrine or metabolic disorder such as diabetes, hypothyroidism, or hypertension should have her problem under optimal medical control and share any plans for pregnancy with physicians involved in her care.

Maternal Age

The age of the mother during pregnancy may also be a significant factor in developmental outcome. Mothers at both ends of the reproductive continuum represent a threat to the infant. Adolescent mothers are at increased risk for perinatal mortality and premature delivery of low birthweight infants. Neurological abnormalities are significantly higher in infants of teenage mothers (Bremberg, 1977; Cooper, 1977; Fielding, 1978; Klein, 1974). The fact that teenage mothers frequently come from lower socioeconomic groups augments their risk status. Numerous programs such as comprehensive clinics, parenting training programs and home visitor programs have emerged over the last decade to impact on teenage pregnancy; they have had varying degrees of success (Olds, 1981; Purvis, 1982; Wallace, Weeks, & Medina, 1982).

At the other end of the reproductive continuum, there is also a greater probability of developmental delay and intellectual deficit in infants born to mothers 40 years of age and over. In some cases, the older mothers are at high risk due to earlier obstetrical difficulties. Also, the incidence of some chromosomal abnormalities increases with age. During the prenatal period, genetic factors play an important role in determining developmental outcome. A number of genetic conditions are accompanied by mental retardation such as phenylketonuria, galactosemia, maple syrup urine disease, and Tay-Sachs disease (Nora & Fraser, 1974). In terms of prevention for chromosomal and genetic disorders, our ability to identify the relevant causative factors in cases such as maternal and paternal age in Down's Syndrome has implications for prevention of chromosomal disorders (Abrams & Bennett, 1979).

It is currently recommended that women over the age of 35 be counseled regarding the advisability of amniocentesis to detect an infant with significant chromosomal abnormality such as one of the trisomies. Families at risk for some of the inborn errors of metabolism and rare neurodegenerative diseases can be identified through a careful examination of the family pedigree. Some racial and ethnic groups such as the Ashkenazi Jews are at particular risk for certain types of developmental deficits or genetic syndromes and information is being disseminated through religious and cultural organizations concerning these risk factors. In a disorder such as Tay-Sachs disease, adults of childbearing age can undergo blood tests to determine their carrier status. If one or both members of a couple is determined to be a carrier for genetic disease, further medical examination as well as extensive genetic counseling services may be obtained through either the public or private sector.

In addition to known carriers for chromosomal or endocrine metabolic disorders, the following risk factors would also warrant referral for genetic counseling services:

1. history of three or more miscarriages or a stillbirth
2. history of any child with significant medical or developmental problems in either the immediate or extended family
3. exposure to probable mutagens

PREVENTION STRATEGIES IN THE PRENATAL PERIOD

There are multiple approaches to prevention of developmental disorders in the prenatal period. The value of these is of great significance in terms of financial cost to society and more importantly, the human cost to the child and the family. The strategies discussed below, which have been employed to prevent developmental disability during the prenatal period, include the provision of:

1. health education
2. family planning services
3. screening for health problems and genetic disorders
4. antenatal diagnosis and genetic services
5. prenatal care and other health maintenance programs
6. anticipatory guidance and environmental safety
7. regionalization of perinatal services

Health Education and Family Planning Service

Public education is a powerful vehicle to influence health practices that affect the infant's developmental outcome. Mullen (1981) delineates several principles that relate to effective planning of health education programs: early participation of both consumers and providers in designing the program, establishing an appropriate level of intensity and duration of the program, and integrating the program into larger program systems. To improve pregnancy outcome, she gives an example of how to develop an educational strategy to meet this goal. Table 2.1 illustrates how the settings of the clinic, the community, the school, and the media/market can be used to develop such a health education program.

Dissemination of knowledge about such problems as the effects of smoking, alcohol, and drugs on the developing fetus is important, particularly for shaping attitudes in the childbearing years and younger. Techniques such as media and advertising campaigns as well as the specific labelling of product containers on their suitability for use by pregnant women have been successful in communicating information. Pamphlets regarding appropriate nutritional practices and habits such as sleep, exercise, and avoidance of alcohol and tobacco during pregnancy are readily available in health clinics and doctors' offices as well as through the lay press and in shopping areas (Food and Drug Adminstration, 1981).

Inclusion of these topics in a health education curriculum for junior and senior high school students has occurred significantly over the past 10 to 15 years. There is a wide array of programs being implemented in schools, with varying reports of success (McAlister, Perry, Killen, Slinkard, & Maccoby, 1980; Miller & Smith, 1975; North Carolina Division of Health, Safety and Physical Education, 1974;

Table 2.1. Examples of Educational Strategies to Improve the Health of Mothers, Children, and Youth

	Settings			
Goal/Behaviors	Clinical	Community	School	Media/Market
Improve pregnancy outcomes				
Entry into prenatal care; reduction of smoking, alcohol and drug use, including over-the-counter drugs, exposure to x-rays, and occupational hazards	Specific counseling for infertility patients and other women planning a pregnancy, for women with positive pregnancy tests planning to continue the pregnancy (that is, in family planning clinics), or during regular prenatal care	Inclusion in childbirth education classes, education through other organizations that reach young women to increase general awareness	Inclusion in curricula	Warning labels on products harmful to pregnant women; general awareness campaign through multimedia
Family planning (especially adolescents)	Outreach to high-risk groups; anticipatory counseling by primary care provider	Education for parents to discuss sexuality and family planning with children; counseling and discussion groups through youth-serving organizations, including those for boys	Inclusion in curricula, including support for abstinence	Radio to reach teenagers

Parcel, 1976; Perry, Killen, Tetch, Slinkard, & Danaher, 1980; School Health Education Study, 1967).

Classes to prepare expectant couples for labor and delivery have become very popular and have expanded to include information regarding a healthful pregnancy and optimal outcome for mother, infant, and the developing family unit. These childbirth education classes are frequently offered by hospitals or independent organizations to expectant parents (for example, International Childbirth Education Association). Education in parenting skills is also widely recognized as a valuable component and is being provided as a service to individuals of all ages through adult education and community mental health programs as well as in high schools and college curricula. Hospitals, community centers, or civic organizations may hold parenting classes or groups with a structured curriculum (for example, Rothenberg, Hitchcock, Harrison, & Graham, 1981) or informal discussion groups covering a wide range of child care skills including feeding, health, stimulation, and developmental concerns (Wandersman, 1982). In addition to providing expert guidance, many of the parenting groups offer support for new parents dealing with the new responsibilities and emotional demands. Although benefits accrue for many parents, parent-infant or perinatal support programs have particular importance for the primary prevention of child abuse (Gray, 1982). High-risk parents can be identified and then provided perinatal services. Gray (1982) describes programs of this type funded by the National Center on Child Abuse and Neglect. For example, the Perinatal Positive Parenting Program at Michigan State University provides support and education for mothers in the hospital and through follow-up home visits, newsletters, a telephone call-in service, and a parent support group. The Rural Family Support Project in Indiana enlists community support for providing pregnancy related services to parents in rural counties (Kelly, 1982). The Vanderbilt University School of Medicine program attempts to increase postpartum contact (rooming-in) between parents and child (for example, O'Connor, Vietz, Sherrod, Sandler, & Altemeier, 1980; O'Connor, Vietz, Sherrod, Sandler, Gerrity, & Altemeier, 1982). Other prevention programs offer guidance to low income families (for example, Parent-Child Developmental Center, New Orleans, Gross & Gross, 1978) and to teenage mothers (Infant Stimulation/Mother Training Classes in Cincinnati, Badger, 1977; Badger & Burns, 1980; Badger, Burns, & Rhoads, 1976). Although critical evaluation is needed for many preventive programs, evidence is accumulating for their effectiveness. (Masterpasqua & Swift, in Chapter 12 of this volume, also describe several prenatal and early intervention programs emanating from mental health centers and neighborhood health centers.)

Closely aligned to these efforts is the availability of family planning services that allow young couples to choose optimal times for conceiving their infant and to improve the outcome of pregnancy, particularly for the at-risk population. Family planning services include provision of information, counseling and outreach to the schools and the community, media advertisements, clinical contraceptive services, distribution of nonprescription contraceptive methods, counseling and provision of condoms to males, information on sexual transmission of disease, and voluntary sterilization for both males and females.

One example of a prevention program for unwanted pregnancies and venereal disease is "Developing Responsible Relationships" in Opelika, Alabama (Kelly, 1982). This education program targets grades 7–12 with information on emotional development, sexuality, and birth control.

One way to insure better developmental outcome for infants and to reduce childhood problems is to be sure that children born are wanted. Studies have shown that planning and spacing children is related to infant health, resulting in fewer low birthweight infants, lower infant mortality, and fewer stillbirths (Select Panel for the Promotion of Child Health, 1981a). The Select Panel for the Promotion of Child Health asserted that family planning programs, both public and private, have made much progress in reducing the number of unintended pregnancies. But programs for family planning are fraught with controversial issues such as contraception for teenagers without parental approval, funding constraints, and insurance coverage problems. Additionally, the programs are vulnerable to changing administrations and shifting public policy.

Antenatal Diagnosis and Genetic Services

The whole arena of antenatal diagnosis and genetic services is one that continues to expand in response to the enormous need. Genetic disorders are present in over 5% of live births; each mother has a 3% chance of having a child with a genetic disorder (U.S. Department of Health, Education, and Welfare, 1979a, 1979b). Families who are at risk for producing children with chromosomal or other developmental disorders require access to genetic counseling services to identify their specific risk factors and case statistics. Genetic counseling services should be available to couples prior to conception and during pregnancy in order to identify the need for specific antenatal intervention.

New secondary screening techniques of ultrasound, fetoscopy and amniocentesis are routinely available. Measurement of fetal growth in utero can be done through a combination of physical examination and a noninvasive procedure known as the sonogram (ultrasound). Ultrasound produces a shadow picture which reveals details about the fetus and the placenta and can record fetal heart rate. Through this technique, the physician can monitor not only the growth of the infant in utero and the position and size of the placenta, but can actually assess potential birth defects in the infant.

When sonography is not adequately detailed, further visual inspection of the infant can be accomplished through fetoscopy. This invasive procedure involves insertion of a small fiberoptic endoscope through the mother's abdomen into the uterus. Malformations associated with certain genetic disorders can be seen through this procedure.

A process known as amniocentesis can be performed under careful sonography to assure the safety of the fetus when it is necessary to obtain amniotic fluid for testing. For detection of some congenital abnormalities the fluid is then subjected to biochemical analysis and karyotyping. The karyotype is a photographic representation of the fetus' chromosomes. The application of amniocentesis has recently been expanded and it is currently recommended for pregnant women over 35. Conditions such as spina bifida, sickle cell disease, metabolic disorders, and chromosomal abnormalities such as the trisomies can be identified. Amniocentesis is also used later in pregnancy to determine lung maturity when an early delivery may be imminent.

Genetic counseling is an important component of genetic services. It is a communication process whereby a family is helped to understand (1) the medical facts including the diagnosis and treatment of any given genetic disorder, (2) the ways heredity contributes to the occurrence of the disorders (statistical probabilities) and the risk factors involved, such as mortality, developmental deficits, and reoccurrence, (3) the alternatives for dealing with the risks (abortion, adoption, acceptance), (4) selecting a course of action that is consistent with the family's goals and beliefs, and (5) making the best possible adjustment to the occurrence of a genetic disorder.

Technology is just now expanding to provide some medical or surgical treatments to the fetus. As an example, prenatal transfusions have been utilized to decrease the severity of hematologic disorders such as Rh incompatibility. Microsurgical techniques have been developed to relieve obstructions in the genito urinary tract, to prevent severe kidney damage, and to relieve pressure in the brain in cases of congenital hydrocephalus. The provision of perinatal care by teams of obstetrical and neonatal physicians has greatly enhanced our capability for early identification and treatment in utero of problems that would present a risk to the infant.

Prenatal Care

Provision of comprehensive prenatal care, the continuous surveillance and management of the pregnant woman, is an invaluable tool for early identification of pregnancies which are not progressing in the expected fashion, so that early intervention for complications can be instituted. The American College of Obstetricians and Gynecologists recommends a routine schedule of prenatal care to include visits every fourth week until the twenty-eighth week of gestation, every two weeks thereafter until 36 weeks and then every week until delivery. Regular contact with a care provider such as a nurse/midwife or obstetrician provides an opportunity, in addition to monitoring the growth and development of the fetus in utero, for regular health education. Table 2.2 outlines the components of prenatal care services described by the Select Panel for the Promotion of Child Health (1981a).

As a part of prenatal care, there are many health screening devices which complement the usual routine. One of these is periodic blood and urine studies to monitor the mother's kidney function, blood pressure, risk for developing gestational diabetes, and her status with regard to prenatal and genital infections. Titers for rubella and herpes and vaginal cultures, if necessary, can be performed at varying stages of pregnancy to determine whether the mother and infant are at risk, to note any developing signs or symptoms of infection, and to allow decisions regarding appropriate interpartum management. For example, if an active genital herpes in-

Table 2.2. Prenatal Care Services

Intervention for physical/mental conditions existing before pregnancy	Identification, treatment, management
Continuing health and mental assessment of pregnant woman and fetus	Prevention, early detection, and management of potentially threatening conditions: Screening for hypertension, diabetes, Rh isoimmunization, anemia, abnormal fetal development, unusual emotional stress
History	General, medical, social and occupational, family and genetic background, health, previous and current pregnancy
General physical examination	Height, weight, blood pressure, fetal development
Laboratory tests (as needed)	Rh determination, irregular antibody screening, Papanicolau smear, G.C. culture, hemoglobin, hematocrit, urinalysis for sugar and protein, rubella tests, blood group determination
Intervention for fetal genetic disorders (neuraltube defects, chromosomal abnormalities)	Screening, diagnosis (amniocentesis) and counseling with abortion services available
Identification of actual or potential high risk pregnancy	Arrangement for appropriate care includes services for labor and delivery
Nutritional assessment and services	Provision of vitamins, iron and other supplements as needed; Referral to WIC
Continuing education to the pregnant woman to promote health of the fetus	Education on enviromental hazards, teratogens, sexually transmittable diseases
Education to pregnant woman and her husband or other support person on labor and delivery	Childbirth education classes
Anticipatory guidance	Information to prepare the mother and father to meet the physical, psychological, and health needs of their newborn
Intermediate levels of care for special problems, but ones that do not require hospitalization	Management of pregnant woman with diabetes, questionable preeclampsia, or threatened premature labor. Use of home visits, hospital day care, or nurse-supervised residential care
Antenatal pediatric visit	Preparation for health care of the newborn

fection is identified in the latter weeks of the third trimester, a Cesarean section decision would be made to prevent exposing the infant to the virus during passage through the birth canal. Also, part of the routine admission procedure to labor and delivery suites is the screening of the mother for syphilis and other sexually transmitted diseases that may have been acquired in the latter weeks of pregnancy. If a positive test is obtained, the mother and infant are evaluated further so that appropriate medical treatment can be instituted.

Should a positive finding for prenatal or perinatal infection such as cytomegalovirus be identified, then important public health measures would be taken to prevent the exposure of other pregnant mothers. For example, if the infant is going to be in the nursery or a daycare setting, pregnant caretakers should be screened for their immune status to the viral agent and they should not have contact with direct secretions of any infant actively excreting the virus.

Once a problem has been identified during the pre- or perinatal period, early intervention and further screening for developmental disabilities is available at many health centers. Examples of this would be the administration of blood tests for metabolic disorders such as PKU and hypothyroidism, and the provision of infant stimulation to high-risk newborns even in the intensive care nursery setting. Early diagnosis and intervention measures for infants are discussed later in detail.

Prenatal care has been positively related to improved pregnancy outcome; the pregnant woman who has not had prenatal care is three times as likely to have a low birthweight infant and a four times higher infant death rate (American College of Obstetricians and Gynecologists, 1980; U.S. Department of Health, Education, and Welfare, 1979). The federal program of Maternity and Infant Care Projects which provide prenatal services as a high priority have consistently been associated with declines in infant mortality and low birthweights (Select Panel for the Promotion of Child Health, 1981a). Unfortunately, there have been no studies to determine the precise components of prenatal care associated with these differences.

The Select Panel for the Promotion of Child Health in 1981 reported that one-quarter of all pregnant women receive either belated or no prenatal care. The reasons for this include: (1) An inadequate reimbursement system: prenatal care is frequently not covered by third party reimbursement programs and Medicaid does not cover first pregnancies. Even where it does cover prenatal care, reimbursement is low. (2) Maldistribution of services: rural areas lack trained personnel to provide adequate prenatal services. (3) Lack of services coordination and inadequate coordination among publicly supported programs involved in aspects of prenatal care as well as between public and private providers. (4) Lack of sufficient outreach resulting in insufficient assistance to many high-risk women who lack the necessary motivation or health awareness to obtain prenatal care.

Anticipatory Guidance and Environmental Safety

Both the obstetrician and the pediatrician can provide anticipatory guidance to parents before the birth. The promotion of optimal parent-infant bonding in order to minimize the incidence of abuse and neglect during early childhood and the assurance of an adequate environment for the infant are all a part of anticipatory guidance. Anticipatory guidance during the prenatal period consists of discussing with the woman and her spouse or partner the plans for place of delivery; type of delivery (natural or assisted childbirth) and feelings about anesthesia; infant nutritional needs and feeding practices such as breast feeding; parenting skills, with specific attention to detecting potentially abusive or negligent parents; planning for continuous pediatric care including an antenatal visit; emotional and social changes related to the birth of the baby; and considering the special needs of the mother during the postpartum period.

There is a growing trend toward contact between the pediatrician or family practitioner and the couple in the prenatal period. The antenatal visit enables the pediatrician to interview the family, determine their preparedness for parenting, and begin the process of education around safety measures such as poison control and the use of a car seat for transporting the infant home from the hospital. Evidence shows that the prenatal period is the best time to make recommendations that will be acted on by the parents (see Roberts, Elkins, & Royal, Chapter 6 of this volume). The prenatal interview also gives the health professional an opportunity to screen the family history and perform additional testing, if indicated, for factors indicating risk of developmental disabilities. If necessary, the pediatrician can then refer the couple for appropriate services such as genetic counseling. Finally, for the high-risk population such as the pregnant adolescent or low-income parent, a careful assessment by a home visitor may be necessary during the latter stage of the pregnancy to assure a safe environment for the infant and to promote education concerning the normal needs of a newborn.

The Optimal Growth Project in Florida (Kelly, 1982) provides prenatal and postnatal home visits by paraprofessionals offering mental health and physical health instruction. This prevention program is aimed at pregnant adolescents and low-income (migrant) parents, and has, in a preliminary evaluation, resulted in decreased child abuse, more positive interactions, and higher developmental indices (Kelly, 1982).

Regionalization of Services

Regionalization implies the ordering of health services within a geographic area to promote efficiency, avoid duplication, achieve greater quality and equity of services, and meet consumer needs. In 1976 a major impetus toward improving pregnancy outcome was identified through the recommendation of perinatal regionalization services (Committee on Perinatal Health, 1976). Level I, II, and III service units were described as well as their interrelationships. These three levels provide progressively expanded services to the pregnant woman. It is the Level III center that has full services for all types of fetal and neonatal illnesses and abnormalities and is prepared to manage any complication in pregnancy or the newborn. This type of organized health delivery system would provide optimum prenatal services for all women. Table 2.3 summarizes the guidelines for referral from a Level II to a Level III unit.

The Select Panel for the Promotion of Child Health (1981a) recommended further development of the regional perinatal care network to assure all high-risk pregnant women and newborns access to regionalized care systems. As part of this effort, the panel encouraged the trend toward regionalized genetic services, including pooling laboratory diagnostic facilities and the availability of consultation.

BIRTH

Clearly, events around labor and delivery have broad implications for the infant's short- and long-term condition. Although most deliveries yield normal newborns, difficult labor and other birth complications can reduce the amount of oxygen re-

Table 2.3. Guidelines for Referral from a Level II Unit to a Level III Unit

Maternal-Fetal Abnormalities

1. Severe preeclampsia and eclampsia
2. Severe isoimmune disease
3. Intrauterine growth retardation
4. Unexplained previous perinatal death
5. Labor at less than 34 weeks' gestation
6. Anticipated severe neonatal infection
7. Anticipated need for major neonatal surgery
8. Major conditions which may significantly alter the usual management of pregnancy or the newborn
   a. Diabetes mellitus, requiring insulin
   b. Severe toxemias of pregnancy; eclampsia
   c. Serious cardio-respiratory disease
   d. Serious renal disease
   e. Malignancy
   f. Severe, unresponding infection
   g. Severe hemoglobinopathy
   h. Drug addiction

Newborn Abnormalities

1. Gestation of less than 34 weeks, birthweight of less than 2,000 grams
2. Respiratory distress other than mild, transient tachypnea
3. Sepsis
4. Seizures
5. Persistent hypoglycemia
6. Congenital abnormalities requiring surgery

ceived by the brain and cause direct damage to the central nervous system (CNS). Anoxia (lack of oxygen) can result from lowered fetal heart rate, prenatal or birth asphyxia or ingestion of fluid into the lungs. Damage to the CNS can also occur when there is direct trauma to the head during delivery. Immediate distress caused by such complications may be reflected by low Apgar ratings (Apgar, 1953). The Apgar sums ratings to 0, 1 or 2 for each of five physical dimensions (heart rate, respiration, muscle tone, skin color and reflex responses) at one and five minutes after birth. Apgar scores of 7 or better at five minutes are considered normal. Markedly depressed Apgar scores (between 0 and 3) at five minutes reflect that the infant may have sustained serious damage. If resuscitation is required, the more rapidly it can be performed the better the expected outcome.

Some of the delivery complications that might compromise the newborn can be managed surgically by performing a cesarean delivery under general or regional (epidural) anesthesia. Primary cesarean births are prevalent when the fetus is in a breech (foot first) rather than a vertex position, the fetal head is large in relation to the mother's pelvic bone structure, contractions are ineffective, the fetus is in distress, or the placenta or cord are abnormal. Under these circumstances, cesarean deliveries can serve to reduce birth trauma and prevent anoxia and subsequent brain damage (Babson, Benson, Pernoll, & Benda, 1975). Malformed fetuses with anomalies such as hydrocephalus, which would be exacerbated by passage through the birth canal, can also benefit from a cesarean delivery.

Cesareans are also frequently performed on subsequent births to women who had already delivered surgically. The routine performance of "repeat cesarean" has recently been challenged as a major contributor to our presently high rates of 15–30% cesareans (National Institute of Child Health and Human Development, 1981). Developmental follow-up has revealed no differences between infants born vaginally or by cesarean at eight months, although the vaginally born infants had a slight developmental advantage earlier in infancy (Field & Widmayer, 1980).

Increasingly, researchers and other health professionals have been focusing on the possible influence of obstetric agents, such as medications used for labor and delivery or behavior. Although obstetrical anesthestics and analgesics reduce sensory responsivity in the newborn (Stechler, 1964; Tronick, Wise, Als, Adamson, Scanlon, & Brazelton, 1976), there is little convincing evidence of long-term effects. Considering the newborn's remarkable capacity to recover from even fairly serious problems, it is unlikely that monitored obstetrical medication would cause permanent deficits. Subtle effects are suggested by a recent report of anesthesia-related differences in development and mother-infant interaction at one month of age (Murray, Dolby, Nation, & Thomas, 1981).

Most parents and many physicians today prefer to minimize the use of medication for delivery for both pharmacologic and psychological reasons. If the immediate postpartum period represents a sensitive time for the development of attachment (Klaus & Kennell, 1982), it would be beneficial for the mother to be optimally alert and for the infant to be as responsive as possible.

It is generally felt that problems and events during the perinatal period are responsible for a significant proportion of developmental and neurological handicaps seen in children. To minimize these handicaps, it is essential to identify as accurately and early as possible which infants are at risk. These infants usually come from approximately 30% of pregnancies broadly defined as high risk because of maternal disease affecting the fetus, problems during labor and delivery, or complications of a previous pregnancy as discussed earlier. The vast majority of infants resulting from these pregnancies do well in the neonatal period as a result of careful prenatal monitoring and preventive care of the mother and infant during pregnancy, labor and delivery. In spite of this, however, a small group of high-risk infants will be subjected to one or more life threatening conditions. If the infant survives, he or she may remain at risk for later physical and psychological handicaps (Field, Sostek, Goldberg, & Shuman, 1979; Friedman & Sigman, 1981).

Prematurity

Birthweight and gestational age are the most important factors influencing mortality and neurodevelopmental morbidity (Avery, 1981; Babson et al., 1975). The incidence of prematurity (gestational age less than 37 weeks) is approximately 10% among white populations and 20% among black populations with increasing risk at lower socioeconomic levels. Survival and outcome of infants less than 37 weeks vary with gestational age. In the last decade, mortality ranged from approximately 2% in infants of 36 weeks to as high as 8% in those born at 31 weeks (Babson et al., 1975). More recently, survival rates have become even more favorable.

When one looks at preterm infants, it is clear that outcome is quite variable, with overall survival now approaching 70% in most intensive care nurseries. Infants of less than 32 weeks gestation comprise the most vulnerable group. Although they represent less than 2% of live births, they account for nearly half of the neonatal deaths (Chase & Byrnes, 1970). Even in this premature group, increasing gestational age carries an increased survival rate. Factors adversely affecting outcome include respiratory distress, asphyxia, intraventricular hemorrhage, sepsis, hyperbilirubinemia, metabolic problems, anemia, and nutritional inadequacies (Avery, 1981).

Most of these complications have direct implications for development of the central nervous system. Respiratory distress, asphyxia and anemia affect oxygenation, and intraventricular hemorrhage can cause damage to particular portions of the brain. The deleterious effects of IVH multiply if the hemorrhage leads to hydrocephalus.

It is self-evident that appropriate medical management of these kinds of complications is critical. The recent trend toward regionalization of health services has improved the quality of health care to mothers and newborns (Babson et al., 1975). Ideally the high-risk infant will be delivered in a tertiary level hospital with a special care nursery. This can be accomplished by referring care of the higher-risk mother to such a center early in the pregnancy or by transporting her physically when she goes into labor. When the high-risk baby is born at a community hospital without a special care nursery, the best alternative is prompt transport of the infant to a hospital that has respiratory support equipment and other specialized equipment appropriate for newborn infants. Additionally, pediatric subspecialty support must be available from such disciplines as surgery, cardiology, endocrinology, pulmonary therapy, radiology, neurology and child development. Medical intervention would then not only be available to the infant, but could also be delivered rapidly.

In addition to providing appropriate medical care, the intensive care nursery staff may attempt to structure sensory stimulation for the preterm infant. Tactile and vestibular stimulation such as rocking, stroking, and extra handling have been shown to enhance the organization of behavioral state and social responsiveness (Shaefer, Hatcher, & Barglow, 1980). Physical recovery may also be affected by supplementary stimulation (Kramer & Pierpont, 1976; Solkoff, Weintraub, Yaffe, & Blase, 1968). Patterning of the stimulation rather than simple addition of sensory experiences is critical to the effectiveness of any nursery enrichment program (Korner, 1980).

Supporting Parents During the Hospitalization

To aid in prevention of parenting problems, it is essential that the physician and other health professionals be sensitive to the emotional needs of parents during hospitalization of the high-risk infant (see Drotar, Crawford, and Ganofsky, Chapter 8 of this volume). Drotar, Baskievicz, Irwin, Kennell, and Klaus (1975) describe the states of adaptation to an infant with early problems. Shock or disbelief is the first apparent reaction, followed by immobility, feelings of sadness, and often anger. There is a sadness over the loss of the anticipated perfect child and there may be anger on the part of each parent at himself or herself and at each other. The anger may actually be a reaction to guilt. During this time many factors make it difficult for the parents to become attached to their infant, including the fear that the child may die.

While the parents are working through these first three stages, there are a number of things that hospital staff can do to facilitate the parents' task. First, it is important for the staff members to recognize that the parents' feelings are normal. Parents should not be judged to be unfeeling or inadequate because they temporarily find it difficult to accept and love their infant. Second, as soon as possible, the parents should be encouraged to see and touch their infant (Klaus & Kennell, 1982). What the parents imagine about their child is likely to be worse than the reality. Although what is wrong with the infant should be explained and the parents' grief should be acknowledged, what is normal, healthy, and appealing should be emphasized in order to reassure the parents that their infant is one they can grow to love. If the infant does die, the parents' attachment does not make mourning more difficult; in fact, it may even facilitate grieving (Kennell et al., 1970).

During this time it is important that the parents be allowed to express their feelings. Nursing, medical, and other personnel should spend time with the parents, helping them to explore their emotional reactions (Korner, 1980; Minde et al., 1981). Encouraging the parents to share their sadness, guilt, and fears will help them become more aware of their own feelings. Other sources of positive social support such as friends or relatives should be explored (Cynic, Greenberg, Ragozin, Robinson, & Basham, 1983). Parents with similar experiences in the past may provide invaluable emotional and informational support.

Once these processes begin, the parents will soon be able to move into the final stages of equilibrium and then reorganization. During this time, the parents begin to cope with their infant's problems and their role in his or her care. Parents benefit greatly from being assured that their presence is important for the infant as well as for themselves (Barnett, Leiderman, Grobstein, & Klaus, 1970; Quinn, Sostek, & Davitt, 1978). Even though much of their grieving is past, a new crisis in the premature infant may cause fear and sadness to reappear. When a child is permanently handicapped, sadness may never be gone completely, but will resurface periodically or remain subdued but chronic (Olshonsky, 1962).

In planning for discharge, the parents should feel comfortable in their ability to care for their infant. They should be given the opportunity to ask questions and voice whatever fears or anxieties they may have about their child's health. As much as possible, they should be given realistic expectations and clear instructions on how to identify and handle possible problems.

There is a fine line between providing accurate information and unduly increasing anxiety. It is important to inform parents that most available measures of early infant development display limited predictability due to the variety of factors contributing to measurement outcome. Unless strong evidence points to the contrary, reassurance that, as far as can be determined, the baby's future looks optimistic is helpful for them and for their relationship with the infant.

Family Adjustment to a High-Risk Infant

In families where the adaptation does not seem to be proceeding well, professional help (from psychiatric, social work, or other mental health fields) should be offered and encouraged. There is a higher incidence of marital dissolution in families with a retarded or chronically ill child and caregiving disorders are more prevalent when parents and newborn infants have been separated for prolonged periods (Fanaroff, Kennell, & Klaus, 1972; Leifer, Leiderman, Barnett, & Williams, 1972).

Behaviorally, preterm infants have been described as more difficult in temperament than full term babies of similar background (DiVitto & Goldberg, 1979; Field, Hallock, Dempsey, & Shuman, 1978). They are less rewarding initially because it takes them longer to develop sustained periods of alertness, to regulate their sleep-waking patterns, and to respond socially. Mothers of preterm infants tend to engage in more caregiving behaviors and less play, smile less frequently, and maintain less ventral body contact (Goldberg, Brachfeld, & DiVitto, 1980; Leifer et al., 1972). During the hospital period, the prematures' mothers must exert effort to feed their infants and months later, at home, they are often less emotionally and verbally responsive (Bakeman & Brown, 1980). More important than these relatively subtle differences, there is extensive evidence that low birthweight infants are more likely to be battered, abused, and neglected (Elmer & Gregg, 1967; Klein & Stern, 1971).

These interactional differences probably have a variety of causes. The premature or ill infant is likely to be unresponsive to parental stimulation, especially during the early part of hospitalization. Because of the process of the mourning for the full-term normal newborn they anticipated and anxiety about the child's future, parents may be unwilling to invest themselves emotionally in the infant.

Parents of high-risk infants may also be frustrated by the difficulty of visiting their infant. In the past, many intensive care nurseries restricted visiting and direct handling of the infants. Even under the most liberal conditions, parents and high-risk newborns experience far more separation than parents and full-term normal newborns. It may also be logistically difficult for some families such as those with older children to visit the nursery often. Parents of high-risk babies should be assured of the value of their visits both for themselves and their infants (Brazelton, 1981). The benefits of maximizing parent-infant contact during hospitalization have been widely documented in both high-risk and normal populations (Klaus & Kennell, 1982; Sostek, Scanlon, & Abramson, 1982; Trause, 1981).

Another source of parental anxiety lies in the uncertainty that the parents of preterm infants have in knowing what development pattern to expect from their infants. The tendency of preterm infants to show transient abnormalities and uneven spurts of progress makes the situation more stressful. The popular literature on childbearing provides little help because the information on prematurity is very limited. Only recently have supportive and informative books specifically addressing parents or preterm infants been published (Brazelton, 1981; Nance, 1982).

Problems of Attachment in the Normal Infant

For parents of the vast majority of normal infants, there are challenges in the first weeks after birth that may form the basis of future interactions. Most fundamentally, the parents intensify whatever attachment to the infant they had prenatally. Attachment can be defined as a unique, long-term positive relationship between two people (Klaus & Kennell, 1982). Behaviors that reflect attachment include kissing, fondling, cuddling and prolonged gaze; each is affectionate and serves to maintain contact between individuals.

Attachment typically proceeds during the postpartum hospitalization and may be facilitated by the supportive attitudes and policies of the hospital staff. Present-day policies for normal postnatal care generally provide extensive opportunities for mother-infant contact. Mothers are no longer encouraged to remain inactive after childbirth and to be with their newborns only for feedings. Most hospitals allow mothers to spend as many daytime hours with their babies as they wish and to assume responsibility for the basic care of their babies at a time when the nursing staff is available to answer questions. The mothers have opportunities to become acquainted with their babies physically, learn how the baby reacts to hunger, fatigue and satiation, and experience his or her periods of alertness and responsivity. Pacing interactions around the infant's active and quiet times can establish the basis for reciprocity later in infancy. The importance of such synchrony and rhythmic patterning has been emphasized by Stern, Jaffe, Beebe, and Bennett (1975).

Opportunities for mother-infant contact are particularly beneficial for those women having first babies or who have not had previous caregiving experience (Greenberg, Rosenberg, & Lind, 1973). Sostek et al. (1982) found increased maternal confidence and decreased anxiety shortly after birth when first mothers had extensive contact with their normal, full-term babies during the days immediately following delivery.

The benefits of early contact apply to fathers as well. The majority of hospitals today do not consider fathers to be visitors and allow them to spend as many hours as they desire with the mother and baby. Given ample opportunity to interact with their infants, fathers have behaved toward their newborns very much like mothers (Parke & O'Leary, 1976). Previous opinions about the uniqueness of the attachment between mothers and infants may have been the result of limited interaction opportunities for fathers.

Interactional difficulties in the newborn period or later in infancy might be indicated by lack of interest, consistent negative affect, poor responsiveness in the mother, father or newborn, or insensitivity of the parents to the infant's cues (Ainsworth, Blehar, Waters, & Wall, 1978). Counseling about the needs and capabilities of the newborn as well as caregiving and interaction demonstrations may be helpful in the postpartum period. It is often helpful to provide an opportunity to observe the Brazelton Neonatal Assessment Scale (Brazelton, 1973) which demonstrates the sensory, social, motoric and state regulation capabilities of the infant. Various techniques for comforting and alerting the infant are also employed. Widmayer and Field (1980) have established the efficacy of parents' observing of the Neonatal Assessment Scale as an intervention.

Optimally, long-term continuity of this type of care should be available if necessary from the infant's pediatrician. When problematic interaction patterns are encountered, intervention can be approached on many levels. If the underlying cause is family stress, assistance from social workers may be helpful in order to arrange services, develop support networks, improve practical circumstances or change family interaction patterns. When the infant has a difficult temperament, the parents can be instructed directly on infant bonding techniques and counseled in both the development of the infant's states of arousal and methods of coping. Finally, if the difficulty seems rooted in the mother's or father's personality or expectations about parenthood, therapy or counseling may be advisable. In all cases, availability of a broad support network to provide sympathy, information and respite care is invaluable (Korner, 1980). Field (1978, 1982) also describes infant-adult "interaction coaching" as a prevention intervention to modify interaction disturbances.

Developmental Screening for Normal Infants

It has been frequently pointed out that although infants born with medical problems have a greater risk of developmental difficulties, the majority of infants with developmental disabilities come from the medically normal newborn population (Scott & Masi, 1979). Efforts aimed at prevention of developmental problems should include regular screening of all infants. Practically, the most efficient way of screening is during well-baby visits for primary pediatric care. Within five to 10 minutes, the pediatrician or pediatric nurse practitioner can administer age-appropriate developmental tasks such as the Denver Developmental Screening Test (Frankenburg, VanDoorninck, Liddell, & Dick, 1976). Infants who seem to be markedly delayed on a consistent basis should then be referred to a multidisciplinary diagnostic center where the extent of the problem can be diagnosed.

Developmental Follow-Up for Infants At-Risk

In order to reduce the incidence and degree of developmental disability, it is also necessary to have periodic and prospective screening of the groups at greatest risk. Essentially, these services are part of the continuum of perinatal care. A sample of neonatal criteria typically used for such follow-up is outlined in Table 2.4 (Sostek, Quinn, & Davitt, 1979). Although infants with such complications are at increased risk of developmental difficulties, outcome is quite variable. Knowing only the perinatal history, it is impossible to make accurate specific predictions for individual infants. For groups of infants, perinatal complications have been found to predict poor IQ and language skill at four years of age (Bee, Barnard, Eyres, Gray, Hammond, Spietz, Snyder, & Clark, 1982). In part, limited prediction reflects the

Table 2.4. Criteria for Inclusion for Developmental Follow-Up Program

Birthweight less than 1,800 grams
Gestational age less than 34 weeks
Respiratory distress requiring oxygen for longer than 48 hours or assisted ventilation.
Major congenital malformation
Asphyxia requiring resuscitation longer than five minutes or with complications
Sepsis
Meningitis
Intraventricular hemorrhage and/or hydrocephalus
Necrotizing entercolitis
Congenital infection
Chromosomal abnormality or dysmorphic syndrome
Birthweight less than 2,250 grams (5 pounds) at term
Any significant persistent neurological abnormality noted in the nursery (seizures, spasticity)
Hyperbilirubinemia exceeding albumin-binding capacity or requiring exchange transfusion

Note: Any of the above criteria qualify infant for follow-up.

extensive influence of socioeconomic and environmental factors (Ramey & Brownlee, 1981). The ability to predict outcome improves if performance and medical events in the first months of life are considered in addition to newborn data (Littman, 1979).

Periodic developmental evaluations of infants at risk as well as those with identifiable handicaps may be available from single health care agencies such as Crippled Children's Services, University Affiliated Facilities, or Rehabilitation Centers, or from private diagnosticians in several disciplines (Maternal and Child Health, 1980). The evaluations serve several purposes. First, they enhance the accuracy of prediction about individual infant's developmental prognosis which is of value for families, school systems and health care specialists (Parmelee, Kopp, & Sigman, 1976). Next, they aid in matching infants to intervention programs and in designing specific activities for each infant. Additionally, they offer the families a regular opportunity to air developmental concerns with a group of professionals particularly experienced in development of infants at risk. The staff can provide the parents with developmental expectations and can address the parents' feelings of anxiety or depression. They can also counsel against overprotection, a frequent reaction to neonatal complications that can impede development if it leads to restriction of activities (Lewis, 1979). Preventive measures can therefore be directed either at developmental problems or parent-infant interaction difficulties. For psychosocial support, the parents may be directed to Parents of Preemies groups or assisted in contacting parents with similar experiences. In general, parental adjustment seems to be easier when adequate social support is available (Cynic et al., 1983).

The optimal model for prospective developmental follow-up is interdisciplinary (Lipsitt, 1981). At a minimum, a high-risk infant should be evaluated by a psychologist for mental functioning, a pediatrician or neurologist for neurological status, and an occupational or physical therapist for motor functioning (Tjossem, 1976). Professionals from several additional disciplines should be readily available for possible consultation. These include nursing, speech and language, nutrition, and social work. Ideally, infants at risk would be followed into the school years to evaluate learning and attention skills as well as overall level of development. Periodic multidisciplinary follow-up allows the various specialists to make recommendations for promoting optimal development and parent-infant attachment (Kass, Sigman, Bromwich, & Parmelee, 1976). When there are no severe disabilities the parents should be counseled regularly on developmental expectations relative to the infant's skill level rather than chronological age. Home stimulation suggestions should encompass the mental, motor and language areas (Bricker & Bricker, 1976). If consistent and marked developmental lags or neurologic abnormalities are detected, the follow-up staff may recommend remedial stimulation.

Prevention of Developmental Disabilities in High-Risk Infants

Several guidelines have been proposed for early assessment and intervention programs (Maternal and Child Health, 1980). The staff should remain sensitive to the infant's general health and nutritional condition, parent-infant interaction patterns, and the parents' perception of the infant's developmental progress. For continuity of care, periodic reports should be provided to the infant's primary health provider. When repeated medical or surgical procedures are necessary, losses and gains of developmental skills should be monitored before and after treatment. Medical progress should be paralleled by developmental recovery. At these times, close coordination between developmental and medical/surgical personnel working with any particular infant is critical.

Intervention directed toward improving cognitive, motor and language skills may take the form of specific therapies or more general stimulation. Specific therapies can be directed at any one or a combination of the following: speech and language development, cognitive/fine motor skills, gross motor progress, or neurodevelopmental functioning. Typically, stimulation in these areas is carried out by therapists from one or more of the following disciplines: speech and language, developmental psychology, infant education, physical or occupational therapy, or pediatricians. The therapy should be received at regular intervals, either in the home or at a developmental center. In either setting, parents should be taught follow-through activities to conduct with the infant at home (Bricker & Bricker, 1976).

Overall infant stimulation combines these forms of therapy in order to provide the more compromised infant with stimulation in every area of development. General stimulation is also recommended for most infants with identified developmental difficulties, such as mental retardation, cerebral palsy, and congenital malformations with functional implications. Infant stimulation programs tend to be offered in developmental centers and can serve several valuable functions. First, the therapy can directly facilitate acquisition of skills; second, the parents can learn tasks appropriate for the infant's developmental level and can incorporate such activities into their routines at home; and third, the parents may benefit from regular contact with professionals familiar with infants who have developmental difficulties and, perhaps more importantly, other parents in similar situations (Nielson, Collins, Meisel, Lowry, Engh, & Johnson, 1975). As stated by Bromwich and Parmelee (1979):

> Intervention which helps parents enjoy their baby and which strengthens sensitivity, responsiveness and skills creates a parent-child system in which the parent experiences success and the infant progresses to his maximum potential. [p. 390]

Naturally, the role of the parents must be respected in planning an intervention program (Bromwich & Parmelee, 1979). It is important to assess parent-infant interaction patterns, parent attitudes and environmental resources of the family (Kass et al., 1976). When problems of attachment are detected, parent education or provision of social services may be effective. Goals for parents of any infant, and particularly one in an infant stimulation program, include understanding of the child's awareness of his or her skills and developmental progress, effectiveness in handling the infant and managing problem behaviors, and development of mutually satisfying patterns of interaction (Denhoff & Hyman, 1976). Positive interaction behaviors in the parent can typically be facilitated by increasing sensitivity to the infant's signals, improving the parent's sense of competence, and providing psychosocial support especially to families of infants with special needs (Kass et al., 1976). Finally, it is also crucial to recognize that developmental disabilities or delays during the first year of life are often transient (Sigman & Parmelee, 1979). The decision to recommend therapy must be weighed against the impact of labelling the child as one who needs therapy and the resultant anxiety it may cause the parents.

SUMMARY

During the perinatal period a number of factors contribute to optimum developmental outcome for the infant. In addressing prevention issues, it is important to examine prenatal influences as well as birth events that will affect the infant. Prevention strategies must address such areas as maternal practices, maternal health, labor and delivery events, and family adjustment to the birth of a high-risk infant. This chapter has summarized a variety of prevention approaches during the perinatal period including health education, family planning services, screening, antenatal diagnosis, prenatal care, and regionalization of services.

Events around labor and delivery can influence the infant's long-term condition. Some complications can be prevented by performing cesarean deliveries and avoiding excess medication at the time of birth. One of the most important factors for development is the maturity of the newborn. Preterm infants have variable outcomes and, although most develop normally, they are at increased risk for delay and disabilities. Measures to prevent prematurity, to manage the preterm infant optimally, and to provide appropriate stimulation can reduce the incidence of developmental problems. Parents of preterm or ill neonates may refuse support in their acceptance of the infant and attachment to him or her. Even parents of full-term infants can benefit from early contact and a broad network of support.

Periodic developmental screening should be provided to all infants and those at particular risk should have regular, prospective evaluations of mental, motor and neurologic functioning. Disabilities can be reduced by directed intervention in the form of specific therapies or general stimulation. Professionals planning intervention programs must remain sensitive to the role of the parents.

The prevention approaches outlined in this chapter are in use in programs around the country. It would be impossible to document all that have developed. All too often, however, these programs are instituted without an appropriate conceptualization and most frequently without adequate evaluation of effects (Gray, 1982; Kelly, 1982; Wandersman, 1982). In order to provide more comprehensive and effective prevention services to benefit children and families, programs should focus more efforts on their development and evaluation components. The knowledge about useful prevention services is growing; attention must also turn to implementation and evaluation.

REFERENCES

Abrams, K. I., & Bennett, J. W. Parental age and Trisomy-21. *Down's Syndrome,* 1979, *2,* 6–7.

Ainsworth, M. D. S., Blehar, M. C., Waters, E., & Wall, S. *Patterns of attachment: A psychological study of the strange situation.* Hillsdale, NJ: Laurence Erlbaum Associates, 1978.

American College of Obstetricians and Gynecologists. Cigarette smoking in pregnancy. *ACOG Technical Bulletin,* Sep. 1979, *53.*

Apgar, V. A proposal for a new method of evaluation of the newborn infant. *Current Researches in Anesthesia and Analgesia,* 1953, *32,* 260–268.

Avery, G. B. *Neonatology,* 2nd Edition. Philadelphia: Lippincott, 1981.

Babson, S. G., Benson, R. C., Pernoll, M. L., & Benda, G. I. *Management of high-risk pregnancy and intensive care of the neonate.* St. Louis: C. V. Mosby, 1975.

Badger, E. The infant stimulation/mother training project. In B. Caldwell & D. Stedman (Eds.), *Infant education: A guide to helping handicapped children in the first three years.* New York: Walker, 1977.

Badger, E., & Burns, D. Impact of a parent education program on the personal development of teenage mothers. *Journal of Pediatric Psychology,* 1980, *5,* 415–422.

Badger, E., Burns, D., & Rhoads, B. Education for adolescent mothers in a hospital setting. *American Journal of Public Health,* 1976, *66,* 469–472.

Bakeman, R., & Brown, J. V. Early interaction: Consequences for social and mental development at three years. *Child Development,* 1980, *51,* 437–447.

Barnett, C. R., Leiderman, P. H., Grobstein, R., & Klaus, M. H. Neonatal separation: The maternal side of interactional deprivation. *Pediatrics,* 1970, *45,* 197–205.

Bee, H. L., Barnard, K. E., Eyres, S. J., Gray, C. A., Hammond, M. A., Spietz, A. L., Snyder, C., & Clark, B. Prediction of IQ and language skills from perinatal status, child performance, family characteristics, and mother-infant interaction. *Child Development,* 1982, *52,* 1134–1156.

Brazelton, T. B. *Neonatal behavioral assessment scale,* London: Heinemann, 1973.

Brazelton, T. B. *On becoming a family: The growth of attachment.* New York: Delacorte, 1981.

Bremburg, S. Pregnancy in Swedish teenagers. Perinatal problems and social situation. *Scandinavian Journal of Social Medicine,* 1977, *5* (1) 15.

Bricker, W. A., & Bricker, D. D. The infant, toddler and preschool research and intervention project. In T. Tjossem (Ed.), *Intervention and strategies for high risk infants and young children.* Baltimore: University Park Press, 1976.

Bromwich, R., & Parmelee, A. An intervention program for pre-term infants. In T. Field, A. Sostek, S. Goldberg, & H. H. Shuman (Eds.), *Infants born at risk: Behavior and development.* New York: Spectrum Publications, 1979.

Chase, H. C., & Byrnes, M. E. Trends in prematurity: United States, 1950–1967. *American Journal of Public Health,* 1970, *60,* 1967–1983.

Committee on Perinatal Health. *Toward improving the outcome of pregnancy. Recommendations for the regional development of maternal and perinatal health services.* New York: The National Foundation-March of Dimes, 1976.

Cooper, T. Present HEW policies in primary prevention. *Preventive Medicine,* 1977, *6* (2), 198.

Corbett, T. H., Cornell, R. G., Endres, J. L., & Lieding, K. Birth defects among children of nurse-anesthetists. *Anesthesiology,* 1974, 41, 341–344.

Cynic, K. A., Greenberg, M. T., Ragozin, A. S., Robinson, N. M., & Basham, R. B. Effects of stress and social support on mothers and premature and full-term infants. *Child Development,* 1983, *54,* 209–217.

Davies, D. P., Gray, O. P., Ellwood, P. C., & Abernathy, M. Cigarette smoking in pregnancy: Associations with maternal weight and fetal growth. *Lancet,* 1976, *1* (7956), 385–387.

Denhoff, E., & Hyman, D. Programs for developmental management. In T. Tjossem (Ed.), *Intervention strategies for high risk infants and young children.* Baltimore: University Park Press, 1976, 381–401.

DiVitto, B., & Goldberg, S. The development of parent-infant interaction in full-term and premature infants over the first four months of life. In T. Field, A. Sostek, S. Goldberg, & H. H. Shuman (Eds.). *Infants born at risk: Behavior and development.* New York: Spectrum Publications, 1979.

Drotar, D., Baskievicz, A., Irwin, N., Kennell, J., & Klaus, M. The adaptation of parents to the birth of an infant with a congenital malformation: A hypothetical model. *Pediatrics,* 1975, *56,* 710–721.

Elmer, E., & Gregg, G. S. Developmental characteristics of abused children. *Pediatrics,* 1967, *40,* 596–602.

Erb, L., & Andresen, B. The fetal alcohol syndrome: A review of the impact of chronic maternal alcoholism on the developing fetus. *Clinical Pediatrics,* 1978, *17,* 644–649.

Farnaroff, A. A., Kennell, J. H., & Klaus, M. H. Follow-up of low birth weight infants—the predictive value of maternal visiting patterns. *Pediatrics,* 1972, *49,* 287–290.

Field, T. The three Rs of infant-adult interactions: Rhythms, repertoires, and responsivity. *Journal of Pediatric Psychology,* 1978, *3,* 131–136.

Field, T. Interaction coaching for high-risk infants and their parents. *Prevention in Human Services,* 1982, *1* (4), 5–24.

Field, T., Hallock, N., Dempsey, J., & Shuman, H. H. Mother's assessment of term infants with respiratory distress syndrome: Reliability and predictive validity. *Child Psychiatry and Human Development,* 1978, *9,* 75–85.

Field, T. M., Sostek, A. M., Goldberg, S., & Shuman, H. H. (Eds.) *Infants born at risk: Behavior and development.* Jamaica, New York: Spectrum Books, 1979.

Field, T., & Widmayer, S. M. Developmental follow-up of infants delivered by cesarean section and general anesthesia. *Infant Behavior and Development,* 1980, *3,* 253–264.

Field, T., Widmayer, S., Greenberg, R., & Stroller, S. Effects of parent training on teenage mothers and their infants. *Pediatrics,* 1982, *69,* 703–707.

Fielding, J. E. Adolescent pregnancy revisited. *New England Journal of Medicine,* 1978, 299 (16), 893.

Fielding, J., & Yankauer, A. The pregnant smoker. *American Journal of Public Health,* 1978, *68,* 835.

Finnegan, L. Clinical effects of pharmacologic agents on pregnancy, the fetus and the neonate. *Annals of the New York Academy of Sciences,* 1976, *281,* 74–89.

Food and Drug Administration. Surgeon General's advisory on alcohol and pregnancy. *FDA Drug Bulletin,* July, 1981, *11* (2), 9.

Frankenburg, W. K., Van Doorninck, W. J., Liddell, T. N., & Dick, N. P. The Denver Prescreening Developmental Questionnaire (PDQ). *Pediatrics,* 1976, *57,* 744–753.

Friedman, S., & Sigman, M. *Preterm birth and psychological development.* New York: Academic Press, 1981.

Goldberg, S., Brachfeld, S., & DiVitto, B. Feeding, fussing and play: Parent-infant interaction in the first years as a function of prematurity and perinatal medical problems. In T. Field, S. Goldberg, D. Stern, & A. Sostek (Eds.), *High-risk infants and children.* New York: Academic Press, 1980.

Gray, E. B. Perinatal support programs: A strategy for the primary prevention of child abuse. *Journal of Primary Prevention,* 1982, *2,* 138–152.

Green, M., Alston, F. K., & Rich, H. Prenatal exposure to narcotics: What is the risk of long-term damage to the central nervous system. *Pediatrics Annals,* 1975, *4,* 418–423.

Greenberg, M., Rosenberg, I., & Lind, J. First mothers rooming-in with their newborns: Its impact on the mother. *American Journal of Orthopsychiatry,* 1973, *43,* 783–788.

Gross, B., & Gross, R. Model programs in six cities to teach mothers and children the fundamentals of family life. *Parents',* July, 1978, *53,* 72–75.

Habicht, J.P., Yarbrough, C., Lechtig, A., & Klein, R. E. *Relation of maternal supplemental feeding during pregnancy to birthweight and other socio-biological factors.* Paper presented at the Symposium on Intrauterine Malnutrition, New York, November, 1972.

Hanshaw, J., Sheiner, A., Moxley, A., Gaev, L., & Abel, V. CNS sequelae of congenital cytomegalovirus infection. In S. Krugman & A. Gershon (Eds.), *Progress in clinical and biological research* (Vol. 3). New York: Alan R. Liss, 1975.

Hanson, J., & Smith, D. The fetal hydantoin syndrome. *Journal of Pediatrics,* 1975, *87,* 285–290.

Higgins, A. C. *Montreal diet dispensary study in nutritional supplementation and the outcome of pregnancy.* In Proceedings of a Workshop, National Academy of Sciences, Washington, D.C., 1973, 93–104.

Jaffe, N. Late side effects of treatment. In N. Jaffe (Ed.) *Symposium on Pediatric Oncology.* Philadelphia: Saunders, 1976.

Jones, K. L., & Smith, D. W. Recognition of the fetal alcohol syndrome in early infancy. *Lancet,* 1973, *2 (7836), 999–1001.*

Kandall, S. R., Albin, S., Lowinson, J., Berle, B., Eidelman, A. L., & Gartner, L. M. Differential effects of maternal heroin and methadone use on birthweight. *Pediatrics,* 1976, *58,* 681–685.

Karn, H. N., & Penrose, L. S. Birth weight and gestation time in relation to maternal age, parity and infant survival. *Annals of Eugenics,* 1951, *16,* 147.

Kass, E. R., Sigman, M., Bromwich, R. F., & Parmelee, A. H. Educational intervention with high risk infants and young children. In T. Tjossem (Ed.), *Intervention strategies for high risk infants and young children.* Baltimore: University Park Press, 1976.

Kelly, L. D. Between the dream and the reality: A look at the programs nominated for the Lela Rowland Prevention Award of the National Mental Health Association. *Journal of Primary Prevention,* 1982, *2,* 217–234.

Kennell, J. H., Slyter, H., & Klaus, M. H. The mourning response of parents to the death of a newborn infant. *New England Journal of Medicine,* 1970, *283,* 344–349.

Klaus, M. H., & Kennell, J. K. *Maternal-infant bonding.* St. Louis: C. V. Mosby Company, 1982.

Klein, L. Early teenage pregnancy, contraception and repeat pregnancy. *American Journal of Obstetrics and Gynecology,* 1974, *120,* 249.

Klein, M., & Stern, L. Low birth weight and the battered child syndrome. *American Journal of Disabled Children,* 1971, *122,* 15–18.

Korner, A. F. Infancy, what we know and what we need to know as a basis for intervention. In Office of Maternal and Child Health (Ed.), *Guidelines for early intervention programs.* Salt Lake City, Utah: College of Nursing, University of Utah, 1980.

Kramer, L. I., & Pierpont, M. E. Rocking waterbeds and auditory stimuli to enhance growth of preterm infants. *The Journal of Pediatrics,* 1976, *88,* 297–299.

Lechtig, A., Delgado, H., Martorell, R., Richardson, D., Yarbrough, C., & Klein, R. E. Effect of maternal nutrition on infant mortality. In W. H. Mosley (Ed.), *Nutrition and human reproduction,* New York: Plenum Press, 1978, 147–174.

Leifer, A. D., Leiderman, P. H., Barnett, C. R., & Williams, J. A. Effects of mother-infant separation on maternal attachment behavior. *Child Development,* 1972, *43,* 1203–1218.

Lewis, M. Psychology. In P. J. Valetutti & F. Christoplos (Eds.), *Preventing physical and mental disabilities: Multidisciplinary approaches.* Baltimore: University Park Press, 1979.

Lipsitt, L. P. The importance of collaborative and continuous research efforts in the study of perinatal risk and developmental follow-up. In V. L. Smeriglio (Ed.), *Newborns and parents: Parent-infant contact and newborn sensory stimulation.* Hillsdale, NJ: Lawrence Erlbaum Associates, 1981.

Littman, B. The relationship of medical events to infant development. In T. M. Field, A. M. Sostek, S. Goldberg, & H. Shuman (Eds.), *Infants born at risk: Behavior and development.* New York: Spectrum, 1979.

Lubchenco, L. Interauterine growth and neonatal morbidity and mortality. In L. Lubchenco (Ed.), *The high risk infant*. Philadelphia: Saunders, 1976.

Maternal and Child Health (Office of). *Guidelines for early intervention programs*. Salt Lake City, Utah: College of Nursing, University of Utah, 1980.

McAlister, A. L. Tobacco, alcohol, and drug abuse: Onset and prevention. In *Healthy people: The Surgeon General's report on health promotion and disease prevention* (Vol. 2). U.S. Department of Health, Education, and Welfare, Public Health Service. Washington, D.C.: U.S. Government Printing Office, 1979.

McAlister, A., Perry, C., Killen, J., Slinkard, L. A., & Maccoby, N. Pilot study of smoking, alcohol, and drug abuse prevention. *American Journal of Public Health*, 1980, *70*, 719–721.

Meyer, M. B. Effects of maternal smoking and altitude on birth weight and gestation. In D. M. Reed & F. J. Stanley (Eds.), *The epidemiology of prematurity*. Baltimore-Munich: Urban & Schwarzenberg, 1977, 81–104.

Miller, J., & Smith, D. *Web of life*. Washington, D.C.: Department of Health, Education and Welfare, 1975.

Minde, K., Marton, P., Manning, D., & Hines, B. Some determinants of mother-infant interaction in the premature nursery. *Journal of the American Academy of Child Psychiatry*, 1980, 19, 1–21.

Mullen, P. D. Behavioral aspects of maternal and child health: Natural influences and educational intervention. In Select Panel for the Promotion of Child Health. *Better health for our children: A national strategy*, Vol. 4, 1981, 127–188.

Murray, A. D., Dolby, R. M., Nation, R. L., & Thomas, D. B. Effects of epidural anesthesia on newborns and their mothers. *Child Development*, 1981, *52*, 71–82.

Naeye, R. L. Weight gain and the outcome of pregnancy. *American Journal of Obstetrics and Gynecology*, 1979, *135*, 3–9.

Naeye, R. L., Blanc, W., & Paul, C. Effect of maternal nutrition on the human fetus. *Pediatrics*, 1973, *52*, 494–503.

Nance, S. *Premature babies: A handbook for parents*. New York: Arbor House, 1982.

National Institute of Child Health and Human Development. *Consensus development conference on cesarean childbirth: Report of the task force on cesarean childbirth*. Washington, D.C.: Public Health Service, 1981.

Nicholson, H. Cytotoxic drugs in pregnancy. *Journal of Obstetrics and Gynaecology of the British Commonwealth*, 1968, *75*, 307–312.

Nielson, G., Collins, S., Meisel, J., Lowry, M., Engh, H., & Johnson, D. An intervention program for atypical infants. In B.Z. Friedlander, G. M. Sterritt, & G. E. Kirk (Eds.) *Exceptional infant. Volume 3: Assessment and intervention*. New York: Brunner/Mazel, 1975.

Nora, J. J., & Fraser, F. C. *Medical genetics: Principles and practices*. Philadelphia: Lea & Febiger, 1974.

North Carolina Division of Health, Safety and Physical Education, Department of Public Instruction. *Life skills for health: Focus on mental health*, 1974.

O'Connor, S., Vietze, P. M., Sherrod, K. B., Sandler, H. M., & Altemeier, W. A. Reduced incidence of parenting inadequacy following rooming-in. *Pediatrics*, 1980, *66*, 176–182.

O'Connor, S., Vietze, P., Sherrod, K., Sandler, H. M., Gerrity, S., & Altemeier, W. A.

Mother-infant interaction and child development after rooming-in: Comparison of high-risk and low-risk mothers. *Prevention in Human Services,* 1982, *1* (4), 25–43.

Olds, D. L. The prenatal/early infancy project. An ecological approach to prevention of developmental disabilities. In J. Belsky (Ed.), *In the beginning: Readings on infancy.* New York: Columbia University Press, 1981.

Olshonsky, S. Chronic sorrow: A response to having a mentally defective child. *Social Casework,* 1962, *43,* 190–193.

Ouellete, E. M., Rosett, H. L., & Rosman, N. P. Adverse effects on offspring of maternal alcohol abuse during pregnancy. *New England Journal of Medicine,* 1977, *297,* 528–530.

Parcel, G. S. Skills approach to health education: A framework for integrating cognitive and affective learning. *Journal of School Health,* 1976, *46* (7), 403–406.

Parke, R. D., & O'Leary, S. Father-mother-infant interaction in the newborn period: Some findings, some observations, and some unresolved issues. In M. K. Riegel & J. Meacham (Eds.), *The developing individual in a changing world. Volume 2: Social and environmental issues.* The Hague: Mouton, 1976.

Parmelee, A. H., Kopp, C. B., & Sigman, M. Selection of developmental assessment techniques for infants at risk. *Merrill-Palmer Quarterly,* 1976, *22,* 177–199.

Perry, C., Killen, J., Tetch, M., Slinkard, L.A., & Danaher, B. G. Modifying smoking behavior of teenagers: A school base intervention. *American Journal of Public Health,* 1980, *70,* 722–725.

Purvis, G. A. Teenage pregnancy: A contemporary crisis. *Pediatric Basics,* 1982, *32,* 1–3.

Quinn, P. O., Sostek, A. M., & Davitt, M. K. The high risk infant and his family. In P. Magrab (Ed.), *Psychological management of pediatric problems, Volume 1: Early life conditions and chronic diseases.* Baltimore: University Park Press, 1978.

Ramey, C., & Brownlee, J. Improving the identification of high-risk infants. *American Journal of Mental Deficiency, 1981, 85,* 504–511.

Rothenberg, B. A., Hitchcock, S., Harrison, M. L., & Graham, M. *Parentmaking: A practical handbook for teaching parent classes about babies and toddlers.* Menlo Park, CA: Banster Press, 1981.

Sardeman, H., Madsen, K. S. & Friis-Hansen, B. Follow-up of children of drug-addicted mothers. *Archives of Disease in Childhood,* 1976, *51,* 131–134.

Schaefer, M., Hatcher, R., & Barglow, P. Prematurity and infant stimulation: A review of research. *Child Psychiatry and Human Development,* 1980, *10* (4), 199–212.

School Health Education Study. *Health education: A conceptual approach.* Washington, D.C.: School Health Education Study, 1967.

Scott, K. G., & Masi, W. The outcome from and utility of registers of risk. In T. M. Field, A. M. Sostek, S. Goldberg, & H. H. Shuman, (Eds.), *Infants born at risk: Behavior and development.* New York: Spectrum Publications, 1979.

Select Panel for the Promotion of Child Health. *Better health for our children: A national strategy. Volume 1: Major findings and recommendations.* Washington, D.C.: U.S. Government Printing Office, 1981a.

Select Panel for the Promotion of Child Health. *Better health for our children: A national strategy. Volume 4: Background papers.* Washington, D.C.: U.S. Government Printing Office, 1981b.

Sever, J. L. Intrauterine infections. In A. Goldstein (Ed.) *Advances in perinatal medicine.* New York: Stratton Intercontinental Medical Book Corporation, 1977, 107–112.

Sigman, M., & Parmelee, A. Longitudinal evaluation of the pre-term infant. In T. Field, A. Sostek, S. Goldberg, & H. H. Shuman (Eds.), *Infants born at risk: Behavior and development.* New York: Spectrum Publications, 1979.

Solkoff, N., Weintraub, D., Yaffe, S., & Blase, B. Effects of handling on the subsequent development of premature infants. *Developmental Psychology,* 1969, *1,* 765–769.

Sostek, A., Quinn, P., & Davitt, M. Behavior, development and neurologic status of premature and full-term infants with varying medical complications. In T. Field, A. Sostek, S. Goldberg, & H. H. Shuman (Eds.), *Infants born at risk: Behavior and development.* New York: Spectrum Publications, 1979.

Sostek, A. M., Scanlon, J. W., & Abramson, D. C. Postpartum contact and maternal confidence and anxiety: A confirmation of short-term effects. *Infant Behavior and Development,* 1982, *5,* 323–329.

Stechler, G. Newborn attention as affected by medication during labor. *Science,* 1964, *144,* 315–317.

Stern, D. N., Jaffe, J., Beebe, B., & Bennett, S. L. Vocalizing in unison and in alternation: Two modes of communication within the mother-infant dyad. *Annals of the New York Academy of Science,* 1975, *283,* 89–100.

Streissguth, A. P. Psychologic handicaps in children with fetal alcohol syndrome. *Annals of the New York Academy of Science,* 1976, 273, 140–145.

Terris, M., & Gold, E. M. Epidemiologic study of prematurity in relation to smoking, health volume, employment and physique. *American Journal of Obstetrics and Gynecology,* 1969, *103,* 358–370.

Tjossem. T. (Ed.). *Intervention strategies for high risk infants and young children.* Baltimore: University Park Press, 1976.

Trause, M. A. Extra postpartum contact: An assessment of the intervention and its effects. In V. L. Smeriglio (Ed.), *Newborns and parents: Parent-infant contact and newborn sensory stimulation.* Hillsdale, NJ: Lawrence Erlbaum Associates, 1981.

Tronick, E., Wise, S., Als, H., Adamson, L., Scanlon, J., & Brazelton, T. B. Regional obstetric anesthesia and newborn behavior: Effect over the first ten days of life. *Pediatrics,* 1976, *58,* 94–100.

U.S. Department of Health, Education and Welfare, Public Health Service. *Healthy people: The Surgeon General's report on health promotion and disease prevention.* Washington, D.C.: U.S. Government Printing Office, 1979. (a)

U.S. Department of Health, Education, and Welfare, Public Health Service, Office of the Assistant Secretary for Health, Office on Smoking and Health. *Smoking and Health: A report of the Surgeon General.* Washington, D.C.: U.S. Government Printing Office, 1979. (b)

U.S. Department of Health, Education and Welfare, Office of the Assistant Secretary for Health, Public Health Service Office on Smoking and Health. *The health consequences of smoking for women: A report to the Surgeon General,* January 14, 1980.

U.S. National Institutes of Health. *Collaborative perinatal study of the National Institute of Neurologic Diseases and Stroke: The women and their pregnancies.* U.S. Department of Health, Education, and Welfare, National Institutes of Health, Bethesda, Maryland, 1971.

Wallace, H., Weeks, S., & Medina, A. Services to pregnant teenagers in large cities of the U.S. 1970–80. *JAMA,* Nov. 12, 1982, *248* (18), 2270–2273.

Wandersman, L. P. An analysis of the effectiveness of parent-infant support groups. *Journal of Primary Prevention,* 1982, *3,* 99–115.

Westwood, M., Kramer, M. S., Munz, D., Lovett, J. M., & Watters, G. V. Growth and development of full-term nonasphyxiated, small-for-gestational-age newborns: Follow-up through adolescence. *Pediatrics,* 1983, *71* (3), 376–382.

Widmayer, S. M., & Field, T. M. Effects of Brazelton demonstration on early interactions of preterm infants and their teenage mother. *Infant Behavior and Development,* 1980, *3,* 79–89.

Wilson, J. G. Embryotoxicity of drugs in man. In J. G. Wilson & F. C. Fraser (Eds.), *Handbook of Teratology.* New York: Plenum Press, 1977, 309–356. (a)

Wilson, J. G. Environmental chemicals. In J. G. Wilson & F. C. Fraser (Eds.), *Handbook of Teratology.* New York: Plenum Press, 1977, 357–385. (b)

Winick, M. *Nutrition and fetal development.* New York: Wiley, 1974.

Zaleski, L.A., & Casey, R. E. Maternal PKU: Dietary treatment during pregnancy. *Canadian Medical Association Journal,* 1979, *121,* 1591FF.

CHAPTER 3

Prevention with Preschoolers

ANNETTE U. RICKEL, LOUISE LAMPI DYHDALO, AND RICHARD L. SMITH

Aside from the family, the school is perhaps the most powerful socializing agent which affects virtually all people during the course of their formative years. Yet, for many children, the classroom experience can be a very stressful one. Glidewell and Swallow (1969) found that three out of every 10 American elementary-age children suffer moderate to severe difficulties with adjustment to school. While families are often inaccessible and impractical to deal with individually, the school is an ideal medium for intervention; however, its traditional system of mental health service delivery has been inadequate (Cowen, Trost, Izzo, Lorion, Dorr, & Isaacson, 1975).

For the past several years, the authors have been involved in developing and evaluating a preventive mental health program for preschool-age children and their parents in the Detroit Public Schools. The Preschool Mental Health Project, which will be a major focus of this chapter, is a secondary preventive effort, designed to provide early screening, diagnosis, and remediation to high-risk children evidencing difficulties such as learning, acting out, or withdrawal problems. In conjunction with the secondary preventive intervention program, which deals with preschool children who are already experiencing problems, a primary preventive parent training program was also developed and aimed at enhancing parent-child interaction skills. This primary prevention program was by definition educational in nature and had as its goal the creation of psychologically healthy environments that enhance adaptation.

Teachers vary tremendously in their definitions and modes of dealing with school maladaptation (Cowen et al., 1975). Because teachers are education oriented, their identification of a problem child depends largely upon their personal tolerance threshold for disruptive behavior and patience with learning difficulties. Teachers often overlook behavioral problems when academic performance is satisfactory or when the behavior involved does not disrupt the classroom routine, as in the case of a shy, withdrawn child. Further, a child who needs the guidance of a mental health professional may not be referred for such help by a teacher who perceives this as an admission that he or she cannot handle the problem. Once the teacher has singled out a child as an adjustment problem, it is up to that teacher to decide how severe the maladaptation is and what recourse is appropriate in the particular case. Whether the difficulty is considered (1) one which the child will eventually "grow out of," (2) one requiring a consultation with parents, or (3) one that requires the attention of a mental health professional, is a decision made by teachers on the basis of their idiosyncratic definitions of maladaptation and their perceptions of the urgency and severity of the measures necessary to alleviate the problem.

The more drastic means of dealing with maladaptation in the traditional school system often lead to further unfortunate consequences, for example, labeling the child as a misfit, isolating the child, or further undermining his or her educational and interpersonal capabilities. Other children with less obvious difficulties often remain unidentified. Many of these children, crippled by their inefficient functioning, manage to coast from grade to grade but never realize their full potential. Zax, Cowen, Rappaport, Beach, and Laird (1968) have shown there is a strong tendency for unaddressed school maladaptation problems to later develop into more serious psychological/educational difficulties. To cap this rather grave situation, most public school systems have very limited personnel and resources to devote to mental health services. The demand almost invariably outdistances the supply of professionals affordable by the schools to remedy the problems at hand.

Ideally, a prevention program would allow the reengineering of classroom environments to promote mental health initially, rather than treat subsequent behavioral and educational failings as the traditional system has attempted to do unsuccessfully. However, in the absence of the skills and resources to implement such a total revamping of the system, what is needed and feasible at this time is an efficient and parsimonious means of screening, diagnosis, and remediation of early school maladaptation.

EARLY INTERVENTION PROGRAMS WITH PRESCHOOLERS

Historically, the notion that preschool education could serve as an impetus to the cognitive and emotional growth of children arose from the social, economic, and political changes of the early 1960s as well as advances in the area of developmental psychology. Focus on the physical/psychological welfare of the nation's indigent, and the emerging recognition that the preschool years are critical in children's cognitive development, resulted in a new concept of the function early education should serve. The research of Piaget (1950), Bruner (1961), and others demonstrated that the child is an active learner, a participant in the learning process. A major shift in the orientation of preschool education led to a change in emphasis from the mere provision of good day care and opportunities for children to interact with their peers in a supportive environment to the actual structuring of learning experiences and the provision of appropriate stimulation to promote cognitive growth. It was hoped that the building of a child's cognitive structure might even be accelerated by matching appropriate activities with the child's cognitive level. From this, the notion was conceived that preschool could serve as an intervention for those children who lagged behind their peers in cognitive development. A wide variety of experimental early childhood programs emerged, reflecting diverse theoretical approaches. But most, again in accordance with the zeitgeist of the 1960s, were aimed at enabling disadvantaged children to achieve cognitive parity with their middle class peers. The introduction of Project Head Start, one of the most influential social experiments in our history, began a new and exciting era in American preschool education.

The inception of Head Start in 1965 started the controversy over whether or not early intervention programs for the disadvantaged are effective in producing gains in children's intellectual development that persist with time (Zigler, 1978). The assumption underlying the creation of Head Start, a multifaceted preschool education program, was that if high-risk, disadvantaged children were provided with the opportunity to acquire learning readiness skills during the preschool years, then their subsequent adaptation to and success in the formal educational system would be facilitated. It was believed that this intervention would ultimately result in increased educational and occupational opportunities for these disadvantaged children, thereby disrupting the poverty cycle (Weinberg, 1979). This, of course, assumed that the positive effects of the intervention would endure with time.

Early evaluations of Head Start's intervention effectiveness were unfavorable. Although many studies comparing children who experienced the program and control children who had not received a Head Start intervention indicated that participating children did exhibit significant gains on cognitive and personality measures, the Head Start program was still considered a failure because these gains were not maintained after the first two or three years of elementary school (Zigler, 1976). This "wash-out" phenomenon was interpreted by many researchers to mean that a one-year Head Start program does not produce lasting, positive changes in behavior.

Evaluative reports by Wolff and Stein (1966) and the Westinghouse Learning Corporation (1969) are well-known examples of negative findings which led to these early conclusions regarding the effectiveness of the Head Start program. However, as Weinberg (1979) points out, the evaluation of Head Start and other preschool intervention programs was approached in a naive fashion. These programs were not initially designed as longitudinal studies, nor were they designed for later between-program comparisons. Lacking adequate evaluation technology, researchers encountered many difficulties in measuring the impact of an intervention. Difficulties arose because program models were conceptually diverse even within a single project, such as Head Start, and methodological errors characterized many evaluations of the earlier preschool intervention programs.

A good example is the Westinghouse Learning Corporation (1969) Head Start evaluation. As noted earlier, this study is a well-known, early, negative finding and is often cited as evidence that preschool intervention is futile (Cicerelli, 1969). Actually, this finding was not totally negative since children were found to benefit from the full-year Head Start programs. Nevertheless, the eight-week summer Head Start programs were found to have a negative effect on the achievement of Head

Start subjects. The Westinghouse study was controversial from the start and was called "sloppy" by Robert Finch, then Secretary of Health, Education and Welfare. Campbell and Erlebacher (1970) and Smith and Bissell (1970) have discussed the biases in sampling and the defects in the design and analysis of this study.

Barnow (Note 1) reanalyzed the Westinghouse data using an analysis of covariance and concluded that the summer programs were effective for certain groups of subjects. Barnow found that both the summer and full-year programs were effective for white children from mother-headed families, but were ineffective for white children from families with two parents. For black children, participation in Head Start produced a five-point gain in IQ when tested in the first grade. However, follow-up testing in second and third grade indicated that no gains were retained for this greater length of time. The study revealed no differences in effects between participation in full-year or summer programs for either black or white children. Rindskopf (Note 6) further reanalyzed these summer Head Start data, allowing for unreliability in a measure of SES. Significant positive effects for reliability estimates as low as 0.3 were discovered. Magidson (1977) also reexamined the Westinghouse summer data using a path analysis procedure. Magidson corrected for SES bias in the comparison groups and his results showed a positive impact from the summer program.

In view of this new evidence, it is clear that the Westinghouse report must be considered a positive finding. However, with the advantage of hindsight, we can assert that the controversy surrounding the evaluation of Head Start programs (and other early intervention efforts) and the need to reanalyze data might have been avoided had the appropriate evaluation strategies been generated when goals were being established in the initial development of such programs. Even with our expanded evaluation technology, difficulties still arise in the assessment of preschool mental health programs. Nevertheless, evaluation is essential. The unequivocal demonstration of long-term humane and fiscal benefits will encourage the establishment of early intervention programs as a routine procedure.

One such preschool program model, developed on the basis of constant evaluation, is that of Jason and his associates. He has described the six-year evolution of their educational intervention program for economically disadvantaged preschoolers (Jason, DeAmicis, & Carter, 1978). Over this period of the program's development, decisions regarding the effectiveness of various aspects of the intervention and the inclusion of new components were made based upon the results of ongoing evaluation research. The program aims to facilitate the social, behavioral, and academic skills of center city preschoolers who have been identified through routine pediatric examination to exhibit marked evidence of social and behavioral difficulties, although they are physiologically and neurologically healthy.

The program format which eventually emerged combined the effective elements of relational and behavioral approaches, both of which had been evaluated previously by Jason (1977). This included home and health center sessions with the children as well as parents. The health center provided an enriched environment equipped with educational toys, books, and games. Helping agents developed a warm relationship with the children and rewarded prosocial behavior. At both home and center sessions, the helping agents also taught a hierarchical curriculum of lessons that emphasized language skills. This behavioral series of 61 lessons was arranged along a continuum of simple to more complex tasks, which the children master in sequence (Jason, 1977). Parent involvement was obtained by having parents observe and then participate in the teaching activities with their children during home sessions. They also attended weekly parent group meetings where the program and its goals, child rearing issues, and personal concerns were discussed. The intervention continued for three months, with three child sessions weekly.

Jason's various intervention efforts have resulted in significant gains in a broad range of areas, including academic skills (Jason, 1977), increased interest in the environment, more sociable behavior (Jason, Clarfield, & Cowen, 1973), and improved motor skills (Jason, Gesten, & Yock, 1976). The program has also been shown to improve maternal child rearing attitudes (Jason et al., 1973). Sustained gains in academic skills at the three month follow-up were attributed by Jason (1977) to the extensive involvement of parents in the program. Through the home sessions and parent group meetings, Jason believes that parents were provided with the skills and desire to continue teaching program elements after termination of the formal project, thereby reducing "erosion" effects.

Another program model by Risley and his co-workers emphasizes language skills and the constant monitoring of children's behavior to determine effects of the intervention. Risley (1972), like Jason, also believes that the positive impact of early intervention is more likely to be maintained if conditions following termination promote the continued use and elaboration of program lessons. Risley achieves this goal by teaching young children specific skills (such as following directions), attitudes (the desire to please the teacher and avoid trouble-makers), and concepts (being on time), which schools maintain. Risley refers to this approach as *survival training,* a means of ensuring academic success.

Risley has noted a number of survival training techniques and their rates of effectiveness (Risley, Reynolds, & Hart, 1970). These are behavioral procedures for remediating various aspects of language deficits found in disadvantaged preschool children. Risley's focus is based upon the high correlation between language skills and public school success. For example, Risley describes how the child's rate of talking can be increased by making the social and material reinforcements of the preschool environment contingent upon spontaneous speech and oral responses to questions. Teachers are able to increase the child's talking time (observed during free play periods) from 10% to 75% by interacting with the child only when he or she speaks and by dispensing materials to the child when he or she requests them and is able to answer several questions about their use. Techniques for other verbal behaviors such as talking at appropriate times, social skills, and various imitation skills were also developed and the children were observed to evaluate the impact of these techniques on their behavior.

Programs emphasizing social skills training often assume that the competencies they promote will generalize to extra-intervention situations and thus be maintained.

For example, Spivack and Shure (1974) designed a classroom environment for young children which promotes interpersonal problem-solving behavior. Their program specifies activities which help children develop a cognitive problem-solving style for real-life situations and to generate their own ways of solving the typical interpersonal conflicts that arise daily. Children learn to cope more effectively and manifest this improvement in increased overt behavioral adjustment. In order to achieve this level of overt functioning, the language and cognitive skills needed to solve social problems are promoted, and children are taught how to use these skills in solving real-life interpersonal difficulties. All children participate together in these regular classroom activities regardless of their adjustment status. Thus, for maladjusting preschoolers, the program activities serve a remediational purpose, with the additional benefit of affording opportunities to interact with adjusted peer models who may be more skilled in interpersonal problem-solving. For children without significant difficulties, the program functions as a primary preventive effort, using classroom exercises to further build and reinforce adjusted behavior, thereby reducing the probability of later-developing problems.

Initial evaluative data collected by the Spivack and Shure group indicated that as a result of their program intervention, preschool children increased their ability to generate alternative solutions and consequences to deal with interpersonal conflicts. These improved cognitive skills were reflected in teachers' ratings of increased behavioral adjustment (Spivack, Platt, & Shure, 1976). However, other researchers employing similar strategies have had less consistent success in training social problem-solving skills (Gesten & Weissberg, Note 2).

Social problem-solving training does not produce skills which consistently transfer to classroom performance (Krasnor & Rubin, Note 3). For example, social skills training implemented by Berler, Gross, and Drabman (1982) improved the responses of socially deficient, learning disabled children to role-play situations. However, these increased skills did not generalize to the classroom setting nor did they have impact upon ratings of peer acceptance. Finally, Rickel, Eshelman, and Loigman (1983) point out in their follow-up study of interpersonal problem-solving training that relatively few investigators have examined the endurance of successfully entrained problem-solving abilities (Houtz & Feldhusen, 1976; Pitkanen, 1974; Stone, Hinds, & Schmidt, 1975). Follow-up investigations which have been implemented suggest that initially positive results are not sustained for even four months (McClure, Chinsky, & Larcen, 1978; Rickel et al., 1983). Thus, it seems that on many counts, social skills training produces results which are rather equivocal.

Other program models focus on the remediation of more specific problem behaviors, such as impulsivity (Kendall & Wilcox, 1980). On the basis of research with young aggressive boys, Camp (1977) and Camp, Zimet, Van Doorninck, and Dahlem (1977) suggest that these children often fail to use verbal mediational activity in the appropriate situations. When covert mediational activity is utilized, it often fails to achieve functional control over behavior. Camp et al. (1977) believe that an ineffective linguistic control system may be responsible for the learning and behavioral difficulties experienced by aggressive boys. However, they conclude that training in the use of self-guiding verbalizations may help to increase self-control and decrease aggression in these children.

Zahavi and Asher (1978) examined the effect of direct verbal instruction in an attempt to modify children's aggressive behavior. Children in a day-care center who were observed to be most prone to fighting, using physical and verbal abuse, and engaging in uncooperative behavior, were individually instructed by their teacher. Through conversations with the child, teachers conveyed three basic concepts: (1) aggressive acts harm others and make them unhappy, (2) aggression is ineffective as an interpersonal strategy, and (3) prosocial alternatives in conflict situations yield more positive outcomes. As a result of this instruction, a decrement in the children's aggressive behavior was observed as well as an increase in the incidence of positive behaviors. Low levels of aggression were maintained over a two-week posttraining period.

Robin, Schneider, and Dolnick (1976) evaluated a procedure for helping children control their aggressive impulses called the "Turtle Technique." Children attending a school for the emotionally disturbed who were identified as being highly aggressive on the basis of teacher reports received instruction from their teachers in the four components of this technique. As a reaction to aggressive impulses, the children were taught: (1) the "turtle response," keeping arms close to the body, closing eyes and lowering the head, picturing oneself as a turtle withdrawing into the shell, (2) muscle relaxation to dissipate emotional tension aroused by the negative situation, (3) social problem-solving to generate prosocial alternative strategies for coping with negative situations that prompt the turtle response, and (4) peer support of appropriate use of the technique. The children were taught to emit the turtle response whenever they anticipated an aggressive encounter with a peer, when they felt frustrated or angry with themselves and were tempted to throw a temper tantrum, or when the teacher or a classmate called out "turtle." The investigators found that this procedure produced significant reductions in teacher ratings of aggressive behavior among these emotionally disturbed children.

Lasting Gains from Early Intervention

Project Head Start has inspired alternative models of early intervention, psychoeducational remediation, and preschool education (White, Day, Freeman, Hantman, & Messenger, 1973), and has paved the way for federal funding of innovative intervention programs. Recently, a great deal of new evaluative evidence has emerged. In fact, there are now over 100 major studies of longitudinal experiments and Head Start evaluations (Brown, 1978). A number of longitudinal studies of early intervention began in the 1960s, and the preschool children who were involved in these programs are now in their later years of childhood and adolescence. They are old enough to give reliable IQ and achievement scores and have spent enough time in school to allow an overall inspection of their academic performance. This opportunity to obtain valuable data has been recognized and acted upon.

In an attempt to surmount methodological problems associated with statistical significance and small numbers of subjects, the Developmental Continuity Consortium has analyzed 14 major longitudinal studies of early intervention begun in the 1960s by pooling results and using a common set of measures to collect additional rounds of follow-up data. The goal of the consortium, involving 12 principal investigators, was to provide better information on the actual effects of preschools on low income children who are predominantly black, and who ranged from nine to 18 years of age at the time of follow-up. Consortium results (Lazar, Hubbell, Murray, Rosche, & Royce, 1977) not only indicated long term gains on cognitive measures, but also revealed evidence for increased emotional adjustment. Significant attitudinal differences were found, such as program children's more positive self-ratings of their school work compared to the same ratings of control children. In addition, early intervention was found effective in reducing the number of children placed in special education classes and the number of children retained in grades, making it possible for them to maintain their position in the classroom with non-disadvantaged peers. Finally, several consortium investigators have found evidence for late developing gains, or "sleeper effects," which appear to be permanent (Palmer, 1978; Seitz, Apfel, & Efron, 1978). These positive effects were not apparent in the scores of the same children during the first few years after preschool intervention (Palmer & Anderson, 1979).

The consortium's most recent follow-up studies provide evidence that gains following the Head Start or other preschool experience may last well into the high school years (Darlington, Royce, Snipper, Murray, & Lazar, 1980). Long-lasting effects of early education were also found in relation to the child's ability to meet basic school requirements, increased intelligence and achievement test scores, children's attitudes and values (for example, achievement orientation), and improved maternal attitudes toward school performance (Lazar & Darlington, 1982). In reference to the consortium findings, Muenchow and Shays' (1980) definitive report to the president of the United States declared that educational benefits enduring as long as 13 years after the child's preschool intervention experience have now been documented.

The diversity of intervention programs implemented in the last 20 to 30 years have met with varying degrees of success. However, important lessons have been learned. First, as has been seen, evaluation planning should be an essential issue in the initial development of intervention programs. Recognizing the continuity of development, the evaluation methodology must be preplanned so that the longitudinal impact of early childhood intervention can be carefully studied. The advantage of evaluation planning and longitudinal assessment is that it allows the differentiation of effective and noneffective programs, thus furthering the cause of establishing secondary prevention efforts in the schools. Second, as Weinberg (1979) points out, IQ's should not continue to be used as the major dependent variable in outcome evaluations of early intervention. This is an abuse of intelligence tests and neglects the impact of early intervention on children's development in the social-emotional realm. The notion of "competence," which intervention should bring about, must include a healthy interaction with the social environment as well as academic success. The importance of treating the total child is paramount, giving attention to both cognitive and affective facets of the child's development to promote the greatest change. Programs that focus only on learning deficits may be disregarding important, underlying social-emotional needs that may actually be generating the learning difficulties. On the other hand, for children from disadvantaged, unstimulating home environments, the cognitive remediation is equally important.

Enhancing Parenting Skills

While secondary preventive intervention efforts with preschool children have been proposed to foster social and academic success, preschool intervention can achieve optimal success when parents are involved in the educational process (Bronfenbrenner, 1975; Valentine & Stark, 1978; Zigler, 1978). Primary preventive parent training programs have been developed in conjunction with child intervention efforts, which are aimed at reducing dysfunctional parenting behavior and creating psychologically healthy environments that will build mental health and competence in children. The importance of the parenting role in influencing the optimal development of children is based on the contention that the child's earliest and most influential experiences take place in the context of parent-child relationships.

Working with parents to modify children's behavior by helping them to modify their own represents a relatively new approach for dealing with the problems of children and their parents. It provides greater access to the natural environment of children, which more often than not is composed primarily of family. The parents can, therefore, become not merely recipients of therapy but also active behavior cotherapists (Berkowitz & Graziano, 1972). Traditionally, experts have attempted to directly influence the child and change his or her behavior. However, according to Glogower and Sloop (1976), behavior change may be brought about more effectively by controlling the child's environment through the manipulation of behavioral contingencies. Parents, who are the primary socializing agents of the child (Baumrind, 1971), are in a better position to bring about change than are professionals who see the child for only a few hours each week (see Forehand, Walley, & Furney, Chapter 11 of this volume).

Mash, Lazere, Terdal, and Garner (1973) conducted a study using a group of mothers to modify their children's deviant behaviors. Their focus was on the modification of maladaptive mother-child interactions. They found that the altered response repertoires of the mothers resulted in behavior change on the part of their children. They pointed out that their results supported the usefulness of working with the child-care agents as vehicles for modifying children's behavior. Other studies have demonstrated positive results using parents as change agents and have indicated that they are very effective in eliciting positive changes in children who exhibited a wide range of behavior problems (Johnson & Katz, 1973; McPherson & Samuels, 1971; O'Dell, 1974; Reisinger, Frangia, & Ora, 1976; Tavormina, 1974). These problems included antisocial and immature behavior, speech dysfunction, school phobias, encopresis and enuresis, seizures, self-injurious behavior, and oppositional behavior. The authors, however, pointed out that the success of therapeutic intervention by parents depends on the ability of a backup therapist to produce reliable changes in the behavior of parents toward their children.

Some work with parents has focused not only on the remediation of problems but also on a preventive mental health approach (Reisinger & Lavigne, 1980). The Early Intervention Program (EIP) for Preschoolers and Parents emphasizes parent training and skill development through the application of behavioral-social learning principles. The EIP is organized into service modules that focus on specific needs of the child or the parent, such as the individual tutoring module and the child management module (Reisinger & Lavigne, 1980). This strategy teaches parents more effective ways to deal with child rearing and child management issues and consequently stands in contrast to the more traditional child or parent therapy-oriented approaches (Tavormina, 1974).

Methods for Modifying Inappropriate Child Rearing Attitudes and Behaviors

There have been essentially two methods employed in working with parents, one a more traditional reflective approach and the other a behavior modification approach. The reflective approach emphasizes parental awareness, understanding, and acceptance of the child's feelings. This model uses cognitively mediated variables as a means of altering parent-child interactions. The behavioral approach attempts to eliminate cognitive variables and emphasizes actual behavior. Training is directed toward teaching parents to manipulate their responses to the child in order to affect the child's subsequent behavior (Tavormina, 1974).

The reflective approach is best exemplified by Hereford (1963), Auvenshine (1974), and Swenson (1970), who were able to produce significant changes in the attitudes of parents through use of parent discussion groups. Stearn (1971) and Hanley (1974) demonstrated that the use of Parent Effectiveness Training (PET), a reflective method, yielded substantial changes in attitudes. They found that parents became more accepting of their children and their behavior, and developed more democratic attitudes toward their families.

The behavioral approach has also been shown to be effective in changing inappropriate attitudes and behaviors. Zeilberger, Sampen, and Sloane (1968) showed that parents could control undesirable behaviors in their children through the use of differential reinforcement contingencies. O'Leary, Turkewitz, and Taffel (1973) also involved parents in the treatment of their children and produced important therapeutic changes. Their focus was on consulting with parents concerning how they could change their children's behavior through systematic shaping of inappropriate behavior, timing of punishment, modeling appropriate behavior, and the establishment of incentive systems. Patterson (1974, 1980) and his associates (Taplin & Reid, 1977), in one of the most extensive parent-mediated child treatment programs for aggressive boys, obtained significant reduction in targeted deviant behavior by parents through the use of behavior modification procedures.

Variations of the reflective and behavioral approaches have met with both success and failure. Johnson (1970) conducted an interesting study in which she compared mother versus child groups and traditional versus behavior modification procedures in the treatment of disobedient children. She found the behavior groups for both mother and child showed slight increases in general adjustment from post- to follow-up testing, while the reflective group showed a slight decrease during the same periods. Tavormina (1975) evaluated the relative effectiveness of a behavioral and reflective group counseling procedure. He found that both types of counseling had beneficial effects relative to the untreated controls, but that the behavioral method resulted in significantly greater improvement. He concluded that the behavioral technique was the treatment of choice for counseling parents because it provided them with an understandable, consistent, and effective way to deal with the specific problems they were facing in raising their children.

Thus, with this review of intervention efforts for young children and their parents, the importance of a well planned, integrative approach to the identification and remediation of mental health problems becomes apparent. We will now present our model of early intervention.

THE PRESCHOOL MENTAL HEALTH PROJECT

The 1975–76 academic year marked the inception of the Wayne State University Preschool Mental Health Project conducted in the Detroit Public Schools (Rickel, 1977; Rickel & Smith, 1979). The program was designed to prevent maladjustment in children and to promote positive cognitive and emotional growth through early screening, diagnosis and remediation. The program builds, in part, on the pioneering work of Emory Cowen in the public school system in Rochester, New York (Cowen et al., 1975). Cowen's Primary Mental Health Project focuses on young (primary grade) children and emphasizes the use of systematic screening for early detection of behavioral and learning problems (see also Durlak & Jason, Chapter 4 of this volume).

A key aspect of Cowen's program is that it modifies the role of the school mental health professional to increase their impact. The school mental health professional, in conjunction with the classroom teacher, is involved in screening, diagnosis, and the development of intervention strategies for children experiencing school adjustment problems. Nonprofessional child aides (housewives) are trained to implement the interventions under the school mental health professionals' supervision. This approach enables a multiplicative expansion of the efforts of the professional.

The Wayne State University/Detroit Public School Preschool Project uses a similar approach to expand the delivery of preventive mental health services. However, the Preschool Project departs from the model provided by the Cowen program to make innovations in three areas: (1) the age at which screening and intervention is made, (2) the manner in which the multiplication of the mental health professionals' impact is achieved, and (3) the research design. For illustrative purposes, we will describe a single year's activity of the Project as well as a two year follow-up designed to determine the lasting effects of the program.

Intervention at Early Age

It is a basic philosophy of the Preschool Project that interventions which take place early in the child's development are more likely to be successful. In younger children, maladaptive patterns are less firmly established and when identified may be more amenable to positive and long lasting change. For these reasons, the Project focuses on preschool age children.

The Mental Health Professional's Role

In the Preschool Project, the mental health professional's efforts are concentrated on diagnosis, training, and supervision. Using diagnostic tests, children with behavioral or learning difficulties are first identified with the help of teachers. Then specific prescriptive interventions are developed and tailored to each child's identified problem(s). In the context of the classroom setting, the interventions are implemented through the use of Wayne State University senior level psychology students. These students are trained and are under the supervision of professionals. The Project also addresses itself to the fact that the child's home is likely to be a contributing factor if not a primary source of the problems identified by the program. Parent training and discussion sessions are held to foster more effective parenting techniques.

Emphasis on Research Design

A key aspect of the Project is the use of a carefully planned, well-controlled research design. Important features of the design are the use of a control group and of blind assessments. Since a control group was used, interventions designed to correct the observed problems of adjustment were not extended to all members of the preschool population identified as experiencing problems. While it is recognized that withholding treatment may disadvantage children in need of help, it was the judgment of the Project staff that any short-term social costs involved in withholding treatment are more than offset by the ability of a control group design to clearly establish the effect of the treatment employed. Furthermore, the use of a blind assessment procedure insured that the treatment effects were not an artifact of the assessor's knowledge of the treatment the child received.

The Preschool Mental Health Project involved two major facets. The first of these took place within the classroom context and consisted of a program of prescribed interventions for high-risk children. The other main facet of the program was a parent training program designed to improve the child's home environment by improving the parent's child rearing techniques. Each of these facets is explained in greater detail in the following two sections.

The Child Program

The child program consisted of the following four phases: (1) initial observation of children's classroom behavior, (2) identification of high-risk children and the assignment to treatment conditions, (3) training of student aides and the implementation of prescriptive interventions, and (4) program evaluation.

The Period of Initial Observation.

The first five weeks of the school year were established as a period in which the children were to become acclimated to the preschool setting, and the teachers familiarize themselves with each child. In this period the children were engaged in traditional preschool activities. The teachers interacted with all children individually and observed each child's interactions with other children. In this phase of the program, there were 240 preschool children. All children were enrolled in Title I Preschool Programs in three schools in Region 7 of the Detroit Public School system.

Diagnosis and Treatment Assignment.

Following the period of initial observation, screening and diagnosis were performed to identify those children who were experiencing difficulty adjusting to the preschool setting. Three instruments were employed in this assessment: the Caldwell Preschool Inventory, the AML, and the Classroom Adjustment Rating Scale (CARS).

The Caldwell Preschool Inventory is an individually administered assessment procedure for use with children aged three to six years, and yields a total score and subtest scores for Personal-Social Responsiveness, Associative Vocabulary, Concept Activation-Numerical, and Concept Activation-Sensory (Caldwell, 1970). The AML is a quick screening device for detecting school adaptation problems consisting of three subscores: Aggressive, Acting-Out Behavior (A Scale), Moody-Internalized Behavior (M Scale) and Learning Disabilities (L Scale) and a total score (Cowen et al., 1975). The Classroom Adjustment Rating Scale (CARS) is also an instrument for measuring school adaptation problems which yields three subscale scores: Aggression (A scale), Shy-Anxious (S scale) and Learning Problems (L scale) and a total score (Clarfield, 1974).

The Caldwell Preschool Inventory, the AML, and the CARS were completed by each child's teacher after the teacher was thoroughly instructed in the use of these instruments.

A developmental history was also obtained on each child. This information was supplied by the child's parent(s) and consisted of the child's physical characteristics, such as sex, age, birthweight, speech or hearing abnormalities, and the child's social history characteristics, such as the parents' living arrangements, their education, occupation, and the number of siblings in the home.

On the basis of the assessments gathered, 64 children were identified as being high risk. Specifically, children were considered high risk if they were in the highest third of the maladjustment range on either the Caldwell, the AML or both, or if they had physical problems (for example, speech abnormalities), which were deemed severe enough to interfere with the child's adjustment to school. Once identified, these 64 high risk children were randomly assigned to either a prescriptive remediation program or a placebo control group. The random assignment was done irrespective of the school in which the child was enrolled or their problem type; as such, there were experimental and control children in each of the classrooms. The experimental group consisted of 13 aggressive and 19 shy-withdrawn children, while the control group was composed of 10 aggressive and 22 shy-withdrawn children. All 64 children had learning problems of some type. In addition, the teachers were unaware of the group assignment of each child, as well as the subsequent nature of the experimental and control group experiences.

Training and Intervention.

Twelve Wayne State University senior level psychology students functioned as intervention aides in the classroom program, receiving academic credit for their participation. The students were required to have an overall grade point average of 3.0 (B) or better and were screened for participation on the basis of an interview with one of the project staff. All aides received general training which consisted of didactic presentations, reading assignments on normative preschool behavior, and discussion of appropriate techniques for handling various child management situations.

Half of the aides were selected by means of random assignment to work with experimental children, the remaining half were assigned to work with control children. Each of these groups then received additional training unique to their group. In the context of this training, no indication was given to either group regarding the experimental or control nature of their training.

Those aides assigned to the experimental children received supplemental training in prescriptive intervention techniques. This training familiarized the aides with the behavioral symptoms of the following specific problem types: the shy-withdrawn child, the hostile or aggressive child, and the child experiencing learning difficulties.

A thorough understanding of the prescriptive techniques is best achieved by reading the program training manual (Rickel, 1979). However, the intervention techniques had general features which are briefly described below. Prescriptive techniques for dealing with the shy-withdrawn child and the aggressive child were developed and discussed separately. However, in the case of these two problem types, the intervention techniques had the following common features:

1. When dealing with feelings of shyness and insecurity on the part of the shy-withdrawn child or feelings of hostility on the part of the aggressive child, the aides were taught to encourage the child to recognize these feelings as something all people feel at different times and in different situations.

2. Techniques to encourage children to think and talk about different ways of dealing with problem situations were presented. For example, in dealing with an aggressive child who often fights to achieve his or her objectives, the aide was taught how to engage the child in a discussion and to challenge the child to think of and talk about other ways of dealing with frustrating situations.

3. Instruction was given to aides in developing dramatic play in order to encourage children to practice and improve social skills. For example, with the shy child, the aide would be instructed in how to structure situations for dramatic play. A typical pattern for involving the shy child in dramatic play would be for the aide to elicit the child's help in planning the room and furniture arrangement. As the ar-

rangement was being made, additional participants would be introduced gradually, and scenes to be played could be suggested. As this activity became self-perpetuating, the aide would gradually move out of the situation and function only as an observer.

4. The aides were instructed in the importance of using reward or praise for successively more appropriate approximations of desired behavior. Aides were encouraged to carefully observe the children to which they were assigned and to systematically reward positive changes in behavior. The aides were further instructed in the importance of gradually making the rewards contingent on higher levels of performance.

The aides were also instructed in prescriptive interventions designed to assist the child experiencing learning difficulties. These prescriptive interventions consisted of a variety of activities and exercises in the following areas: motor development (basic body movement, directionality, fine motor activities), perceptual development (auditory discrimination, shape recognition), conceptual development (classification, relational concepts), oral language expression (naming and defining, sentence building). These activities were described in detail and arranged for the aide in a series of increasing difficulty to encourage gradual improvement.

Aides who were assigned to work with control children received supplemental training based on a control training manual. The manual and the training consisted of instructions for conducting a variety of traditional preschool activities, for example, playing with blocks, coloring, and singing songs.

The intervention phase of the program was begun in the third month of the school year (November). The project staff developed a program of prescriptions and activities for each experimental and control child. These programs were written in a standard form, reviewed with each aide, and referenced specific activities in the training manual. For the experimental children, the prescriptive interventions were tailored to the child's diagnosed problem. In the case of the control children, the activities referenced a collection of traditional nursery school tasks.

As the program progressed, the project staff made on-site visits once a month to observe each child and the child's aide. Separate meetings for experimental and control aides were conducted by the staff every four weeks. In these meetings, the progress of each child was reviewed and the prescriptive program was updated as needed by the project staff.

The intervention phase of the program lasted eight months (November–June). In this period, each child was scheduled to be seen four times a week by the aide for 15–20 minutes each session. Due to illness and weather, this was not always achieved. However, each child was worked with at least twice a week for approximately 20 minutes each session.

Evaluation of the Classroom Program

The effect of the program was evaluated twice. The first evaluation took place at the completion of the program. A second evaluation, designed to assess the lasting quality of the program's impact, was done two years after program completion.

The first evaluation showed a definite advantage for treatment children relative to control children. Comparisons were made of the children's scores on the Caldwell, AML and CARS. As previously indicated, teachers who administered these instruments were blind to the treatment status of the children (Rickel, Smith, & Sharp, 1979). A factorial Multivariate Analysis of Variance (MANOVA) and follow-up univariates were performed on postprogram scores. The two factors used in these analyses were treatment (treatment versus control) and problem type (shy versus acting-out/aggressive). The analysis of the Caldwell, AML, and CARS total scores revealed the treatment effect to be highly significant favoring the experimental children.

Secondary univariate analyses on the 10 subscale scores of the instruments revealed significantly better scores for treatment children on five of the 10 subscales. The subscales which revealed clear differences between treatment and control children were the Personal-Social Responsiveness (P Scale) and Sensory Concept (S Scale) of the Caldwell, the Aggressive, Acting-Out Behavior (A Scale) and the Moody-Internalized Behavior (M Scale) of the AML, and the Shy-Anxious Behavior (S Scale) of the CARS.

The analysis also revealed the expected differences between problem types (shy children versus aggressive children) on instruments measuring these behaviors. Interestingly, the interaction between treatment and problem type failed to reach significance, suggesting the program of prescriptive interventions was equally effective for both problem types.

In general, postprogram analyses suggest that the Preschool Mental Health Project was effective in addressing the problems of high-risk children, facilitating a much more satisfactory adjustment to the classroom environment than was observed in the control group children. In order to determine whether these effects were temporary or of a more lasting quality, these same children were reevaluated two years after the completion of the program.

The two-year follow-up was done with 70 children who were then in the first grade. Of those, 42 were originally diagnosed as high risk and were involved in the intervention program either as experimental children or as control children. A group of 28 subjects, initially identified as low-risk children, were also included in this study to serve as a normal standard of comparison for the high-risk groups. The two-year follow-up analysis compared data from three time periods, pre, post, and follow-up, using the Caldwell and AML Scales as criterion measures.

A series of contrasts were performed using MANOVA to compare the groups on the Caldwell and AML scores at the three time periods (Rickel & Lampi, 1981). The group means which were analyzed are shown in Table 3.1. In general, the results of these analyses revealed significantly more maladjustment for high-risk controls than for the low-risk, normal controls at each time period. Conversely, contrasts between the high-risk treatment groups and the normal controls generally revealed nonsignificant differences at posttreatment and follow up. Also, as shown in Table 3.1, the shy treatment children experienced greater benefits from the intervention at follow-up than did the aggressive treatment children.

The results of this follow-up establish the extended effectiveness of the Preschool Mental Health Project's program of prescriptive interventions. Two years after the

Table 3.1. Mean and Standard Deviation of Caldwell and AML

Total Pre, Post and Follow-up Scores by Group and Risk

Group		Caldwell			AML		
		Pre	Post	Follow-up	Pre	Post	Follow-up
High-risk shy control	*M*	21.87	38.00	49.13	29.29	35.57	25.71
(n = 12)	SD	9.22	5.98	6.30	4.79	7.85	3.25
High-risk aggressive control	*M*	15.83	39.67	48.33	27.00	32.33	27.33
(n = 9)	SD	8.50	3.62	2.42	11.80	7.63	6.31
Low-risk ''normal'' control	*M*	35.14	53.50	57.64	22.93	18.36	17.71
(n = 28)	SD	7.30	11.84	4.28	9.94	7.30	5.72
High-risk shy experimental	*M*	14.50	46.43	53.50	25.21	23.07	21.57
(n = 11)	SD	10.59	7.49	5.53	13.01	9.11	9.55
High-risk aggressive experimental	*M*	25.14	50.00	55.71	26.53	25.67	22.40
(n = 10)	SD	8.13	6.53	4.86	8.29	5.62	5.37

intervention program, the high-risk treatment children more closely approximated the low-risk normal controls than did the high-risk control group children.

Taken in concert, the postprogram evaluation and two-year follow-up establish the effectiveness of the Preschool Project's program of prescriptive interventions. At the conclusion of the program, children initially diagnosed as high risk who received the project's treatment intervention program were rated as signficantly more adjusted by teachers blind to the child's treatment status than comparable high-risk children who received no treatment. In addition, children who received intervention treatment as preschoolers continued to be rated as better adjusted than high-risk control children two years after the completion of the program. Furthermore, treated children compared favorably with children originally diagnosed as low risk or normal.

The Parent Training Program

Another major objective of the Preschool Mental Health Project was to extend the influence of the project into the home by means of a parent training program. This extension was as much a research endeavor as it was a program of service delivery. As such, the goals of the Parent Training Program were twofold. First, the program sought to develop additional insight into the relationship between the parenting styles to which the child is exposed and the child's social skills; and second, the program was an effort to gain a greater understanding of how to conduct an effective training program in parenting techniques.

In order to develop greater understanding of the relationship between parenting style and the child's classroom behavior, an initial assessment of parenting styles was made in the context of the parenting program. This measure of parenting technique was then related to an assessment of the child's social skills as measured in the classroom. The assessment of parenting technique employed a modified version of the Block Child Rearing Practices Report (CRPR) developed by Rickel and Biasatti (1982). The original Block Child Rearing Practices Report consisted of 91 statements of self-reported child rearing practices administered in a Q-sort format (Block, 1965). The modified version of the Block CRPR consists of 40 of the original 91 items which are presented in the form of a questionnaire utilizing a six-point Likert Scale. In its modified form the Block CRPR yields scores on two subscales, Nurturance and Restrictiveness. These two subscales have an alpha coefficient of .82 for the restrictiveness scale and .82 for the nurturance scale (Rickel & Biasatti, 1982). These measures of self-reported parenting style were examined for a relationship to the social problem-solving strategies of 72 preschoolers in the Detroit Public School Preschool Programs. The measure of the child's social problem-solving strategies was obtained from a modified version of the Preschool Interpersonal Problem Solving Test (PIPS) (Spivack & Shure, 1974). When related to the measures of maternal parenting style, restrictiveness was found to be positively associated with the use of evasion and negatively associated with the use of personal appeal and negotiation strategies. In addition, maternal nurturance was negatively related to the child's use of reliance on authority as a problem solution strategy. In general, children whose mothers reported using more nurturant and less restrictive parenting techniques were more likely to confront interpersonal problem-solving situations independently and to use verbal strategies such as personal appeal and negotiation (Jones, Rickel, & Smith, 1980).

The existence of a link between the mother's self-report of parenting styles used in the home and the social problem-solving strategies used by the child suggests that a complete program to correct maladaptive behaviors of children should focus on the parents and the home environment as well as on the child's classroom behaviors. Toward this end, a parent training program was developed and piloted with parents of Detroit Public School Preschool children during the same year that the classroom interventions were conducted.

The training program consisted of five consecutive weekly sessions and a follow-up session of approximately two and one-half hours each, held at the local school during regular school hours. At each session, topics were introduced by the group leaders, including how to handle a child's expression of anger, children's fights, and appropriate discipline techniques. Parents were generally instructed in what is typical and atypical behavior for a preschool child. Techniques for dealing with inappropriate child behaviors were explained. Handout sheets outlining the most important points discussed in each session were also distributed to each parent for future reference. Parents were given a notebook for keeping the handouts and additional notes they might have taken in the sessions or at home.

For the majority of each session, the parents practiced the concepts which were presented through the use of role playing and games. Since for most parents these were new experiences, every effort was made to help them feel comfortable in discussing their thoughts and feelings.

Each session ended with a behavioral homework assignment. The assignment encouraged the parent to use some aspects of the new techniques at home. In addition, parents were encouraged to discuss these concepts with their spouse or others with whom they lived. At the beginning of each session, parents were asked to share the experiences they had had in using the techniques at home. The content of each of these sessions is briefly described below (Berman & Rickel, 1979).

Session 1: Positive Assertions.

The session explained the differences between assertive, nonassertive, and aggressive behavior (Alberti & Emmons, 1970). In the context of the session, the importance of commenting positively on a child's behavior for the purpose of increasing the child's feelings of self-esteem and increasing desired behaviors was emphasized.

Session 2: Listening.

This session stressed the importance of listening to children. Parents were encouraged to develop the habit of talking and listening to the child simply to share an experience and to gain insight regarding the child's perspective.

Session 3: Making Requests and Expressing Anger.

This session discussed the use of positive direct techniques for making requests, such as positioning one's self in front of the child, establishing eye contact and speaking in a calm, firm voice. The session also presented methods for openly and honestly expressing anger to a child, such as discussing how the child's actions have made the parent feel and why.

Session 4: Conflict Resolution.

A multistep method for conflict resolution was presented. It involved sitting down and talking about the problem, allowing each individual to state their desires; second, each family member was instructed to state what he or she thought the other's desires were; and finally, possible solutions were discussed and agreements attempted.

Session 5: Discipline.

This session discussed discipline as a method of teaching cooperative and contributive behaviors. The importance of stating the choices a child faces in the context of discipline was emphasized. The statement of alternatives allows for a discussion of the thinking the child engages in concerning alternatives. Also, the importance of allowing children to experience the consequence of actions was emphasized.

Follow-up Session.

In order to evaluate how successful the parents had been in using the techniques they had learned, a follow-up session was conducted five weeks after training. Techniques the parents had forgotten or were having difficulty incorporating into their behavior at home were reviewed.

In general, the sessions were received very favorably by the parents, who indicated that they felt better about themselves as parents. Parents also reported feeling more confident about their ability to handle specific problem situations.

The effectiveness of the training program was evaluated with a control group format involving both center city and suburban parents. (In addition to the center city parents being trained as a part of the Preschool Mental Health Project, training was also conducted with suburban parents.) The placebo control group programs consisted of the same number and length of sessions as those in the treatment programs, but were nondirective discussions of the participants' parenting experience.

Prior to the program, center city parents as a whole were more restrictive (that is, they expected conformity to demands) than suburban parents as measured on the modified Block CRPR. There was no preprogram difference between center city parents and suburban parents on the nurturance dimension. From pre- to postprogram, experimentally trained parents decreased significantly on self-reports of restrictiveness. Further, a significantly greater change was noted for center city experimental parents trained in conjunction with the Preschool Project than for the suburban parents given the experimental training (Rickel, Dudley, & Berman, 1980).

The main limitation of the results obtained is that the criterion measure is a self-report of parenting behavior. As such, the parent training program continues to be evaluated. Currently, direct observations of parent-child interactions are being obtained pre- and posttraining using videotape procedures to more effectively assess behavioral change (Rickel & Dudley, 1983). It will be of interest to determine in future research whether or not the training program is having a positive effect on the behavior of children. To address this issue, research of a longitudinal nature is planned, which focuses on the effect of the parent training approaches on the social-emotional adjustment of children whose parents have received the training (Rickel, Williams, & Loigman, Note 5).

Overview of Preschool Mental Health Project Findings

The Preschool Project provides for the screening and identification of early behavioral and learning difficulties as children enter preschool, and prescribes individualized remediational strategies implemented by trained undergraduate child aides to deal with lags in conceptual and social-emotional development. The intervention team, which includes project staff psychologists, graduate students, preschool teachers, and college student aides, works together to promote the child's total development. In addition, parent training extends the influence of the program into the child's home environment. By providing preschool intervention, the program strives to prevent more profound deficiencies in children which may evolve from these early indications of maladjustment.

Immediate and long-term assessments of the Preschool Program's impact were conducted. At the conclusion of the intervention year, experimental treatment children demonstrated a distinct advantage over program control children (Rickel et al., 1979). Both shy and aggressive, acting-out children with learning difficulties benefited equally at the immediate close of the program in areas of cognitive as well as social-emotional adjustment. The children receiving prescriptive interventions were clearly aided in their increased overall adjustment to the classroom environment.

Follow-up evaluation of the same children two years later testifies to the endurance of the program's positive impact (Rickel & Lampi, 1981). Both aggressive and shy treatment children demonstrated a performance superior to that of their high-risk control counterparts. The shy treatment children experienced relatively greater benefits from the intervention at follow-up than did the aggressive treatment children. Cowen, Gesten, and Wilson (1979) also report that the Primary Mental Health Project has been more effective with shy-anxious children than with those who are aggressive, acting-out or learning disabled. In his review of work with high-risk children, Garmezy (1974) reports results that are generally similar. It should be noted that the finding of differential effects for children with various behavioral difficulties is in itself supportive of the intervention programs such as the Preschool Project or Cowen's program, which treat maladjustment as a possible source of educational shortcomings. The Preschool Project staff is currently developing supplemental prescriptive activities so that future intervention efforts will more effectively deal with children identified as aggressive, acting-out, or learning disabled. The differential gains observed, however, should not overshadow the fact that the performance of both treatment groups exceeded that of the high-risk control children.

Comparison of the treatment groups to low-risk control subjects also yielded favorable results at follow-up testing. The performance of the experimental treatment children was, for the most part, not significantly different from that of the low-risk control children who had not experienced behavioral or learning difficulties. This suggests that in terms of both cognitive and social-emotional development, the shy and aggressive treatment children are better able to compete with their adjusted peers, and are now less likely to require placement in special education classes or to be retained in a grade.

It may be argued that the effect of maturation is as strong as the treatment effect, and that the positive gains exhibited by the experimental treatment groups reflect the passage of time rather than the impact of the intervention program. The longitudinal findings of the Preschool Mental Health Project indicate that all groups improved to some degree over time, perhaps reflecting maturation. However, the positive gains of the experimental treatment groups placed them much closer to the performance of the low-risk control group, while the high-risk control children remained at a lower level of competence. Thus, the Preschool Program's intervention has a positive impact that goes beyond the benefits of maturation.

As noted earlier, several investigators have found evidence of "sleeper effects" several years after participation in preschool intervention projects (Palmer, 1978; Seitz et al., 1978). Immediate gains shown at the conclusion of a program sometimes fade out and late-developing gains appear when the children reach later elementary grades. Therefore, children involved in the Preschool Project should be retested, since the positive gains found after a two-year period may be even more impressive and more extensive as they progress in their academic careers.

The Parent Training Program was also evaluated. This component of the Preschool Project was shown to effectively reduce maternal restrictiveness, a dimension previously associated with less desirable parenting strategies (Rickel et al., 1980). The Parent Training Program was particularly successful with center city parents (as opposed to suburban parents) receiving this instruction.

Directions for Future Research

Though program development has come a long way since the founding of Head Start, there is still much to be done. Brown (1978) points out that there are yet other aspects of early intervention which should be considered. He raises questions such as: (1) Does intervention have some part in facilitating the parent-child relationship through critical periods? (2) Is the mother's life situation expanded by a preventive program? (3) Does intervention help to spare children from special placement, abuse, or neglect? While the results of the longitudinal studies discussed earlier are very encouraging, these questions give us some idea of the amount of work yet to be attempted.

Additionally, investigators in early intervention need improved research tools. Measures are needed that go beyond an assessment of school adjustment or achievement level. A most interesting aspect of such research would be to discover whether early intervention increases the child's competence in adapting to other facets of his or her world outside the classroom and, if so, which type of program is most beneficial in this respect. Further, what type of project would enable the child to cope with stresses in his or her family and social life? Even if a program was designed specifically with these ends in mind, we currently have few appropriate measures of intervention effectiveness in increasing coping or adaptive behavior outside of the classroom (Brown, 1978).

In view of the long-standing debate over the long-term effectiveness of early intervention, particularly with regard to studies such as the Westinghouse Report (1969) and the various reanalyses of that data (Barnow, Note 1; Rindskopf, 1976; Magidson, 1977), it is clear that we need more efficient experimental designs and methods of statistical analysis. The Preschool Project illustrates Weinberg's (1979) essential point that programs which are designed as longitudinal studies, with appropriate evaluation strategies being generated during initial development, can result in well-controlled, accurate measures of long-term intervention effectiveness. This preplanning avoids the necessity for reanalysis of data which may or may not result in a more accurate assessment of treatment impact, given that the program was not designed to facilitate a tightly controlled measure of intervention effectiveness in the first place.

Finally, early intervention should be established in the schools as a routine procedure. Our rapidly increasing knowledge of child development could be incorporated into working programs catering to each child's needs. If more teacher and administrative involvement is encouraged, these individuals begin to view early intervention as an asset rather than an intrusion on class time. Preschool and primary grade teachers could easily administer relatively brief screening devices (such as the Caldwell and AML tests) to their new students every fall and, with the help of mental health professionals and aides, see that problem children regain their foothold among class peers. This extra effort would short-circuit later, potentially more serious and disruptive difficulties, making the tasks of both teachers and administrators much easier in the long run.

Primary Prevention as an Ultimate Goal

Once preschool intervention is established in the schools as a regular procedure, further enhancement of program effectiveness should involve working toward the ultimate goal of primary prevention of school maladjustment. The first step toward this goal might be a consideration of the ways in which classrooms can be initially restructured to promote mental health. The Preschool Project could be expanded to include a revamping of regular classroom activities, based upon research findings indicating the types of environments which promote mental health and academic competence. Research has shown, for example, that predictable environments promote the development of an internal locus of control in children and adolescents. Nowicki and Barnes (Note 4) and Moore and Brassel (1971) utilized behavior modification techniques with a strong emphasis on success and reward to create a highly predictable environment which led children to significantly move in the direction of an internal locus of control. Creating a classroom environment which promotes internal locus of control is desirable since studies have shown that children who test as highly internally controlled both achieve better in school (especially boys) and have higher morale with regard to school (Flanders, Morrison, & Brode, 1968).

A second step toward the goal of primary prevention might be to extend the comprehensiveness of the Preschool Project outside the classroom. This might include a monitoring and analysis of parent-child interactions involving parents of both low-risk and maladjusting preschoolers. Since some children enter preschool with social-emotional and learning difficulties (Rickel & Smith, 1979), it is likely that the quality of parental behavior prior to their child's school entrance is one important factor contributing to classroom maladjustment. Research has repeatedly demonstrated the relationship between child-rearing practices and academic performance as well as interpersonal skills and other behaviors relevant to classroom functioning. Even a cursory review of the literature clearly indicates that parental child-rearing practices have an influence on all aspects of maladjustment, including academic underachievement (Gronlund & Knowles, 1969), shy-anxious/dependent behavior (McCandless, 1970), and aggressive, acting-out behavior (Fontana, 1964). The effectiveness of the Preschool Project's parent education program has already been discussed. However, other parent-mediated child treatment programs have also been effective in reducing undesirable parent behaviors which often result in child difficulties. For example, Patterson (1974) and his associates have developed an extensive program for aggressive boys which leads to a significant reduction in observed targeted deviant behavior through the use of parental behavior modification procedures.

In an effort to achieve primary prevention, parent education programs should include parents of both maladjusting and low-risk children. All parents could be given guidance in child management techniques, encouraged to evaluate their own stimulus value in the home, and to recognize the kinds of models they present to their children. This aspect of an intervention program might involve school-based meetings to discuss the effects of various child-rearing practices as well as utilize naturalistic observations of parent-child interactions in the home setting. Such an approach will make individual parents aware of the particular behaviors they encourage which may lead to undesirable results in their children's school performance. This would serve a remedial purpose for children already exhibiting adjustment difficulties in preschool as well as a preventive technique for those who may develop problems later if parental behaviors are not altered.

Weinberg's (1979) point that programs must be designed with long-term evaluation in mind, cannot be overemphasized. If programs such as the Preschool Project are expanded in the direction of primary prevention, we must be able to show, with confidence, that these revisions produce lasting, positive changes in children's behavior. Children are our investment in the future, and through effective early intervention we can make sure that every child acquires the skills necessary to meet that future with the highest possible level of competence.

REFERENCES

Alberti, R. E., & Emmons, M. L. *Your perfect right.* San Luis Obispo, CA: Impact, 1970.

Auvenshine, W. R. The parent discussion group: An additional dimension to the role of the school counselor. *Dissertation Abstracts International,* 1974, *34,* 3859A.

Baumrind, D. Current patterns of parental authority. *Developmental Psychology Monograph,* 1971, *4,* 1–103.

Berkowitz, B., & Graziano, A. Training parents as behavior therapists: A review. *Behavior Research and Therapy,* 1972, *10,* 297–317.

Berler, E. S., Gross, A. M., & Drabman, R. S. Social skills training with children: Proceed with caution. *Journal of Applied Behavior Analysis,* 1982, *15,* 41–53.

Berman, S. F., & Rickel, A. U. Assertive training for low income black parents. *Clinical Social Work Journal,* 1979, *7,* 123–132.

Block, J. H. *The childrearing practices report.* Berkeley: University of California, Institute of Human Development, 1965.

Bronfenbrenner, U. Is early intervention effective? In M. Guttentag & E. L. Struening (Eds.), *Handbook of Evaluation Research* (Vol. 2). Beverly Hills, CA: Sage Publications, 1975.

Brown, B. Long-term gains from early intervention. In B. Brown (Ed.), *Found: Long-term gains from early intervention.* Boulder, CO: Westview Press, 1978.

Bruner, J. *The process of education.* Cambridge, MA: Harvard University Press, 1961.

Caldwell, B. *The preschool inventory* (Revised Edition). Princeton, N.J.: Educational Testing Service, 1970.

Camp, B. W. Verbal mediation in young aggressive boys. *Journal of Abnormal Psychology,* 1977, *86,* 145–153.

Camp, B. W., Zimet, S. G., Van Doorninck, W. J., & Dahlem, L. Verbal abilities in young aggressive boys. *Journal of Educational Psychology,* 1977, *69,* 129–135.

Campbell, D. T., & Erlebacher, A. How regression artifacts in quasi-experimental evaluations can mistakenly make compensatory education look harmful. In J. Hellmuth (Ed.), *The disadvantaged child. Volume 3: Compensatory education: A national debate.* New York: Brunner/Mazel, 1970, 185–210.

Cicirelli, V. G. *The impact of Head Start: An evaluation of the effects of Head Start on children's cognitive and affective development (Vols. 1 and 2).* A report presented to the Office of Economic Opportunity pursuant to contract B89-4536, June, 1969. Ohio University, Westinghouse Learning Corporation, 1969.

Clarfield, S. P. The development of a teacher referral form for identifying early school maladaptation. *American Journal of Community Psychology,* 1974, *2,* 199–210.

Cowen, E. L., Gesten, E. L., & Wilson, A. The primary mental health project (PMHP): Evaluation of current program effectiveness. *American Journal of Community Psychology,* 1979, *7,* 293–303.

Cowen, E. L., Trost, M. A., Izzo, L. D., Lorion, R. P., Dorr, D., & Isaacson, R. V. *New ways in school mental health: Early detection and prevention of school maladaptation.* New York: Human Sciences Press, 1975.

Darlington, R. B., Royce, J. M., Snipper, A. S., Murray, H. W., & Lazar, I. Preschool programs and later school competence of children from low-income families. *Science,* April 11, 1980, *208* (4440), 202–204.

Flanders, N. A., Morrison, B. M., & Brode, E. L. Changes in pupil attitudes during the school year. *Journal of Educational Psychology,* 1968, *59,* 334–338.

Fontana, V. J. *The maltreated child.* Springfield, IL: C. C. Thomas, 1964.

Garmezy, N. The study of competence in children at risk for severe psychopathology. In E. J. Anthony & C. Koupernik (Eds.), *The child in his family: Children at psychiatric risk.* New York: Wiley, 1974.

Glidewell, J. C., & Swallow, C. S. *The prevalence of maladjustment in elementary schools: A report prepared for the Joint Commission on the Mental Health of Children.* Chicago: University of Chicago Press, 1969.

Glogower, F., & Sloop, E. W. Two strategies of group training of parents as effective behavioral modifiers. *Behavior Therapy,* 1976, *7,* 177–184.

Gronlund, E., & Knowles, L. Child-parent identification and academic under-achievement. *Journal of Consulting and Clinical Psychology,* 1969, *33,* 495–496.

Hanley, D. Changes in parent attitudes related to a parent effectiveness training and a family enrichment program. *Dissertation Abstracts International,* 1974, *34,* 7044-A.

Hereford, C. F. *Changing parental attitudes through group discussion.* Austin: University of Texas Press, 1963.

Houtz, J., & Feldhusen, J. The modification of fourth-graders problem-solving abilities. *Journal of Psychology,* 1976, *93,* 229–237.

Jason, L. A. A behavioral approach in enhancing disadvantaged children's academic abilities. *American Journal of Community Psychology,* 1977, *5,* 413–421.

Jason, L., Clarfield, S., & Cowen, E. L. Preventive intervention with young disadvantaged children. *American Journal of Community Psychology,* 1973, 1, 50–61.

Jason, L. A., DeAmicis, L., & Carter, B. Preventive intervention programs for disadvantaged children. *Community Mental Health Journal,* 1978, *14,* 272–278.

Jason, L. A., Gesten, E., & Yock, T. Relational and behavioral interventions with economically disadvantaged toddlers. *American Journal of Orthopsychiatry,* 1976, *46,* 270–278.

Johnson, C. A., & Katz, R. C. Using parents as change agents for their children: A review. *Journal of Child Psychology and Psychiatry,* 1973, *14,* 181–200.

Johnson, S. A. *A comparison of mother versus child groups and traditional versus behavior modification procedures in the "treatment" of disobedient children.* Urbana: University of Illinois Press, 1970.

Jones, D. C., Rickel, A. U., & Smith, R. L. Maternal child rearing practices and social problem-solving strategies among preschoolers. *Developmental Psychology,* 1980, *16,* 241–242.

Kendall, P. C., & Wilcox, L. E. Cognitive-behavioral treatment for impulsivity: Concrete versus conceptual training in non-self-controlled problem children. *Journal of Consulting and Clinical Psychology,* 1980, *48,* 80–91.

Lazar, I., & Darlington, R. Lasting effects of early education: A report from the Consortium for Longitudinal Studies. *Monographs of the Society for Research in Child Development,* Serial No. 195, 1982, Vol. 47, Nos. 2–3.

Lazar, I., Hubbell, V., Murray, H., Rosche, M., & Royce, J. *The persistence of preschool effects: A long-term follow-up of fourteen infant and preschool experiments.* (Summary report of the Consortium on Developmental Continuity, Education Commission of the States, Grant 18-76-07843). Washington, D.C.: U.S. Department of Health, Education, and Welfare, 1977.

Magidson, J. *Toward a causal model approach for adjusting for pre-existing differences in the non-equivalent control group situation: A general alternative to ANCOVA.* New York: Abt Associates, 1977.

Mash, E., Lazere, R., Terdal, L., & Garner, A. Modification of mother-child interaction: A modeling approach for groups. *Child Study Journal,* 1973, *3,* 131–143.

McCandless, B. R. *Adolescents: Behavior and development.* Hinsdale, IL: Dryden, 1970.

McClure, L. F., Chinsky, J. M., & Larcen, S. W. Enhancing social problem-solving performance in an elementary school setting. *Journal of Educational Psychology,* 1978, *4,* 504–513.

McPherson, S., & Samuels, C. Teaching behavioral methods to parents. *Social Casework,* 1971, (March), 148–153.

Moore, T. C., & Brassell, W. R., Jr. *The success environment: An approach to community educational improvement.* Atlanta Public Schools, End of Budget Period Report for grant from U. S. Public Law 89-10, Title III, Director: Marion Thompson, 1971.

Muenchow, S., & Shays, S. *Head Start in the 1980's: Review and recommendations.* A report requested by the President of the United States, Administration for Children, Youth, and Families (DHHS), Washington, D.C., Project Head Start. St. Paul, Minn., Bush Foundation, September, 1980.

O'Dell, S. Training parents in behavior modification: A review. *Psychological Bulletin,* 1974, *81,* 418–433.

O'Leary, K. D., Turkewitz, H., & Toffel, S. Parent and therapist evaluation of behavior therapy in a child psychological clinic. *Journal of Consulting and Clinical Psychology,* 1973, *41,* 279–283.

Palmer, F. H. The effects of early childhood intervention. In B. Brown (Ed.), *Found: Long-term gains from early intervention.* Boulder, CO: Westview Press, 1978.

Palmer, F. H., & Anderson, L. W. Long-term gains from early intervention: Findings from longitudinal studies. In E. Zigler & J. Valentine (Eds.), *Project Head Start: A legacy of the War on Poverty.* New York: The Free Press, 1979.

Patterson, G. R. Retraining of aggressive boys by their parents: Review of recent literature and follow-up evaluation. *Canadian Psychiatric Association Journal,* 1974, *19,* 142–158.

Patterson, G. R. Mothers: The unacknowledged victims. *Monographs of the Society for Research in Child Development,* 1980, *45,* 1–64.

Piaget, J. *The psychology of intelligence.* Trans. M. Percy & D. E. Berlyne. London: Routledge and Kegan Paul, 1950.

Pitkanen, L. The effect of simulation exercises on the control of aggressive behavior in children. *Scandinavian Journal of Psychology,* 1974, *15,* 169–177.

Reisinger, J. J., Frangia, G., & Ora, J. Parents as change agents for their children: A review. *Journal of Community Psychology,* 1976, *4,* 103–123.

Reisinger, J. J., & Lavigne, J. V. An early intervention model for pediatric settings. *Professional Psychology,* 1980, *11,* 582–590.

Rickel, A. U. Screening and remediation of preschool children from low income families. *Perceptual and Motor Skills,* 1977, *45,* 757–758.

Rickel, A. U. *Preschool mental health project: Training manual.* State of Michigan, Department of Mental Health, 1979.

Rickel, A. U., & Biasatti, L. R. Modification of the Block Child Rearing Practices Report. *Journal of Clinical Psychology,* 1982, *38,* 129–134.

Rickel, A. U., & Dudley, G. A parent training program in a preschool mental health project. In R. Rosenbaum (Ed.), *Varieties of short term therapy groups: A handbook for mental health professionals.* New York: McGraw-Hill, 1983.

Rickel, A. U., Dudley, G., & Berman, S. An evaluation of parent training. *Evaluation Review,* 1980, *4,* 389–403.

Rickel, A. U., Eshelman, A. K., & Loigman, G. A. Social problem solving training: A follow-up study of cognitive and behavioral effects. *Journal of Abnormal Child Psychology,* 1983, *11,* 15–28.

Rickel, A. U., & Lampi, L. A. A two-year follow-up study of a preventive mental health program for preschoolers. *Journal of Abnormal Child Psychology,* 1981, *9,* 455–464.

Rickel, A. U., & Smith, R. L. Maladapting preschool children: Identification, diagnosis, and remediation. *American Journal of Community Psychology,* 1979, *7,* 197–208.

Rickel, A. U., Smith, R. L., & Sharp, K. C. Description and evaluation of a preventive mental health program for preschoolers. *Journal of Abnormal Child Psychology,* 1979, *7,* 101–112.

Risley, T. Spontaneous language and the preschool environment. In J. C. Stanley (Ed.), *Preschool programs for the disadvantaged: Five experimental approaches to early childhood education.* Baltimore, MD: Johns Hopkins University Press, 1972.

Risley, T., Reynolds, N., & Hart, B. The disadvantaged: Behavior modification with disadvantaged preschool children. In R. H. Bradfield (Ed.), *Behavior modification: The human effort.* San Rafael, CA: Dimensions Publishing Co., 1970.

Robin, A., Schneider, M., & Dolnick, M. The turtle technique: An extended case study of self-control in the classroom. *Psychology in the Schools,* 1976, *13,* 449–453.

Seitz, V., Apfel, N. H., & Efron, C. Long-term effects of early intervention: The New Haven Project. In B. Brown (Ed.), *Found: Long-term gains from early intervention.* Boulder, CO: Westview Press, 1978.

Smith, M. S., & Bissell, J. S. Report analysis: The impact of Head Start. *Harvard Educational Review,* 1970, *40,* 51–104.

Spivack, G., & Shure, M. B. *Social adjustment in young children.* San Francisco: Jossey-Bass, 1974.

Spivack, G., Platt, J., & Shure, M. B. *The problem-solving approach to adjustment: A guide to research and intervention.* San Francisco: Jossey-Bass, 1976.

Stearn, M. B. The relationship of parent effectiveness training to parent attitudes, parent behavior and child self-esteem. *Dissertation Abstracts International,* 1971, *32,* 1885-1886B.

Stone, G., Hinds, W., & Schmidt, G. Teaching mental health behaviors to elementary school children. *Professional Psychology,* 1975, *6,* 34–40.

Swensen, S. S. Changing expressed parental attitudes toward childrearing practices and its effects on school adaptation and level of adjustment perceived by parents. *Dissertation Abstracts International,* 1970, *31,* 2118-2119A.

Taplin, R. S., & Reid, J. B. Changes in parent consequences as a function of family intervention. *Journal of Consulting and Clinical Psychology,* 1977, *45,* 973–981.

Tavormina, J. B. Basic models of parent counseling: A critical review. *Psychological Bulletin,* 1974, *81,* 827–835.

Tavormina, J. B. Relative effectiveness of behavioral and reflective group counseling with parents of mentally retarded children. *Journal of Consulting and Clinical Psychology,* 1975, *43,* 22–31.

Valentine, J., & Stark, E. The social context of parent involvement in Head Start. In E. Zigler & J. Valentine (Eds.), *Project Head Start: A legacy of the War on Poverty.* New York: The Free Press, 1979.

Weinberg, R. A. Early childhood education and intervention: Establishing an American tradition. *American Psychologist,* 1979, *34,* 912–916.

Westinghouse Learning Corporation, Ohio University. *The impact of Head Start: An evaluation of the effects of Head Start on children's cognitive and affective development.* Washington, D.C.: U. S. Office of Economic Opportunity, 1969.

White, S. H., Day, M. C., Freeman, P. K., Hantman, S. A., & Messenger, K. P. *Federal programs for young children: Review and recommendations* (Vols. 1–4), Washington, D.C.: U. S. Department of Health, Education and Welfare, 1973.

Wolff, M., & Stein, A. *Factors influencing the recruitment of children into the Head Start Program, summer 1965: A case study of six centers in New York City (Study II),* New York: Yeshiva University, 1966.

Zahavi, S., & Asher, S. R. The effect of verbal instructions on preschool children's aggressive behavior. *Journal of School Psychology,* 1978, *16,* 147–153.

Zax, M., Cowen, E. L., Rappaport, J., Beach, D. R., & Laird, J. D. Follow-up study of children identified early as emotionally disturbed. *Journal of Consulting and Clinical Psychology,* 1968, *32,* 369–374.

Zeilberger, J., Sampen, S., & Sloane, H. N. Modification of a child's problem behaviors in the home with the mother as therapist. *Journal of Applied Behavior Analysis,* 1968, *1,* 47–53.

Zigler, E. F. Head Start: Not a program but an evolving concept. In J. D. Andrews (Ed.), *Early childhood education: It's an art? It's a science?* Washington, D.C.: National Association for the Education of Young Children, 1976.

Zigler, E. F. America's Head Start Program: An agenda for its second decade. *Young Children,* 1978, *33,* 4–11.

REFERENCE NOTES

1. Barnow, B. S. *The effects of Head Start and socio-economic status on cognitive development of disadvantaged children.* Doctoral dissertation, University of Wisconsin, 1973.
2. Gesten, E. L., & Weissberg, R. *Social problem-solving training and prevention: Some good news and some bad news.* Paper presented at the meeting of the American Psychological Association, New York, September, 1979.
3. Krasnor, L. R., & Rubin, K. H. *Preschooler's verbal and behavioral solutions to social problems.* Paper presented at the annual meeting of the Canadian Psychological Association, Ottawa, June, 1978.
4. Nowicki, S., Jr., & Barnes, J. *Effects of a structured camp experience on locus of control orientation.* Paper presented at the Southeastern Psychological Association meeting, New Orleans, May, 1971.
5. Rickel, A. U., Williams, D. L., & Loigman, G. L. *Personal and situational predictors of child rearing: Implications for intervention.* Paper presented to the American Psychological Association Convention, Washington, D.C., 1982.
6. Rindskopf, D. *A comparison of various regression-correction methods for evaluating non-experimental research.* Doctoral dissertation, Iowa State University, 1976.

CHAPTER 4

Preventive Programs for School-Aged Children and Adolescents

JOSEPH A. DURLAK AND LEONARD A. JASON

The ambitious goal of this book is to attain comprehensive coverage with a minimum of content overlap. Therefore, the first order of business in this chapter is to describe its contents and indicate how this material interfaces with the rest of this volume.

This chapter discusses individually-oriented, competency-building preventive programs for school-aged children and adolescents. Competency-building programs are those that attempt to intervene directly with youths, either individually or in groups, to teach them important behaviors or skills that will directly enhance their current functioning and thus prevent future problems. It is assumed that enhanced functioning resulting from skill acquisition will ultimately be preventive for any number of reasons. For example, individuals will be better able to deal with stress, be more adept in social situations, have greater self-confidence, or be interpersonally more flexible or adaptable.

However, not all competency building programs for school-aged children and adolescents are discussed here. For example, preventive programs that directly promote academic competencies or indirectly influence school age children and adolescents through environmental manipulations are discussed by Jason, Durlak, and Holton-Walker in Chapter 10; programs involving parents by Forehand, Walley, and Furey in Chapter 11; and those attempting to prevent alcohol and drug abuse are covered by Albino in Chapter 7. Four major sections follow the introductory comments in this chapter. In the first section, primary prevention programs for elementary school-aged children are discussed; in the second, primary prevention programs for junior high and high school-aged students are reviewed. In the third section, secondary prevention programs directed at school maladjustment, social isolation, and hyperactivity are described. The final section contains some general comments concerning the evaluation of preventive programs for school-aged children and adolescents. Rather than a comprehensive review, representative programs in each area are discussed. The major intent of this chapter is to describe the most promising strategies and to further encourage research and practice.

PRIMARY PREVENTION FOR SCHOOL-AGED CHILDREN

Affective Education

The most popular of all primary prevention programs has been school-based programs that fall under the general rubric of affective education. Affective education includes such programs as the Human Development Program ("Magic Circle"), Teacher Effectiveness Training, Developing Understanding of Self and Others (DUSO), Ojemann's Causal Approach, Interpersonal Problem Solving Training, Schools Without Failure, and various program modifications (Baskin & Hess, 1980; Elardo & Elardo, 1976; Medway & Smith, 1978). In general, affective education refers to teaching children certain intrapersonal and interpersonal skills considered to be important in promoting psychological growth and social development. The focus is to help children understand personal and peer attitudes, feelings and values, and then to use this increased knowledge to guide their behavior in social situations. In effect, affective education attempts to influence children's emotional and social-cognitive development, which will then hopefully improve their overt, behavioral adjustment.

Affective education has become popular for both conceptual and practical reasons. Conceptually, these programs coincide with the growing educational philosophy that children's social and affective development is as important as their academic growth (that is, educate the total person). Practically, the use of these programs has been greatly facilitated by the development of commercially available curriculum packages that include a carefully sequenced teacher's lesson plan and all the necessary audiovisual aides, workbooks and exercise materials. Thousands of pupils in school districts throughout the country have been exposed to affective education in one fashion or another.

Table 4.1 presents an overview of representative affective education programs. Baskin and Hess (1980) note that program goals generally fall into three areas: intrapersonal, social-cognitive, and behavioral. Intrapersonal goals usually relate to improving self-esteem, developing more positive attitudes toward school, and learning and accepting more responsibility for one's actions. Social-cognitive goals typically involve improved cognitive problem-solving and perspective-taking skills. Finally, these programs attempt to modify children's adjustment overtly as reflected by possible changes in communication skills, peer relations, and discipline and management problems. Invariably, the affective education programs listed in Table 4.1 have multiple goals that fall into all three of these areas.

Current affective education programs vary widely in complexity and procedural application. Most programs are implemented by teachers who are sometimes assisted by undergraduate students or community volunteers; school counselors have conducted programs in some cases. Lesson plans have been developed for most programs so that the program is presented systematically and sequentially for use in structured small or large group sessions. However, some programs are unstructured and depend on the judicious application of program techniques. For example, Teacher Effectiveness Training attempts to teach children how to communicate

Table 4.1. Characteristics and Outcomes of Representative Affective Education Programs

			Outcome Research[a]	
Program	Visual Target Population	Mode of Presentation	Type of Outcome Measure	Ratio of Studies Obtaining Positive Results on Each Measure
Ojemann's (1958) Causal Approach	Grade 1–6	Daily, 10–30 min. group sessions	(a) Self-concept (b) Self-responsibility (c) Anxiety (d) Social causation (e) Attitudes to school	(a) 2 of 2 (b) 2 of 2 (c) 2 of 2 (d) 2 of 2 (e) 2 of 2
Human Development Program (Bessell & Palomares, 1970)	Preschool—Grade 6	Daily, 10–30 min. group sessions	(a) Self-esteem (b) Peer relationships (c) Attitudes to school (d) Academic achievement	(a) 4 of 7 (b) 1 of 1 (c) 2 of 2 (d) 2 of 2
DUSO (Dinkmeyer, 1970)	Kindergarten—Grade 4	Daily, 20–30 min. group sessions	(a) Self-esteem (b) Social awareness (c) General adjustment (d) Academic performance	(a) 3 of 8 (b) 1 of 1 (c) 1 of 1 (d) 1 of 1
School without Failure (Glasser, 1969)	Grades 4–12	Classroom-wide meetings formed as needed	(a) Self-esteem (b) Attitudes to school (c) Discipline problems (d) Academic achievements	(a) 0 of 1 (b) 1 of 1 (c) 1 of 1 (d) 0 of 1
Teacher Effectiveness Training (Gordon, 1974)	Any grade	No structured curriculum	(a) Discipline problems	(a) 3 of 4
Interpersonal Problem-Solving Training (Spivack & Shure, 1974, and others)	Preschool—Grade 6	Daily, 20–30 min. group sessions	(a) Problem solving skills (b) General adjustment (c) Peer relationships (d) Self-esteem (e) Locus of control	(a) 10 of 11 (b) 5 of 7 (c) 0 of 4 (d) 0 of 3 (e) 2 of 2

[a]These outcome data are drawn from the studies reviewed by Baskin & Hess (1980), Durlak (1983b), Elardo & Elardo, (1976), and Medway & Smith (1978).

clearly about personal feelings and how to resolve interpersonal conflicts in mutually satisfying ways. Teachers must therefore be attuned to conflicts as they arise during the school day and assist children in discussing feelings and possible problem solutions in a satisfactory way as the situation arises. In order to give the reader a feeling for affective education programs, details on two representative programs are presented here.

Attempts to train children in interpersonal problem-solving skills are one example of affective education. Spivack, Shure, and their colleagues (Spivack & Shure, 1974; Spivack, Platt, & Shure, 1978) have theorized that children's ability to solve interpersonal problems is an important determinant of their school adjustment. They maintain that certain cognitive skills determine problem-solving ability and that these cognitively based problem-solving skills are applicable to many situations. Spivack and Shure have broken the problem-solving process into cognitive components which are the primary targets of training. The major hypothesis is that a central core of cognitive problem-solving processes mediates adjustment; improving these processes should lead directly to improved interpersonal functioning.

Spivack and Shure have developed methods to assess these various problem-solving skills and have also prepared a structured curriculum to teach preschool and primary grade children these skills using a series of small group activities ranging from stories and visual aids to puppet play and discussion. Training for preschool and young primary grade children proceeds in three phases. Children are first taught basic language and cognitive concepts such as same-different, and-or, and if-then, and how to distinguish among emotions such as mad, happy, or frustrated. Then children are taught how to generate alternative solutions to problems, how to anticipate the consequences of different behaviors, and how to pair alternate and consequential thinking skills together and apply them to real-life and simulated interpersonal problems. Usually one or two leaders work with groups of five to eight children. The strategy of training children in cognitive problem-solving skills has become a popular school-based primary prevention intervention (Durlak, 1983a).

DUSO represents another type of affective education program and is appropriate for children ages five to ten (Dinkmeyer, 1970). DUSO helps children learn to identify feelings, understand how feelings, goals, and behaviors are related, and finally how to communicate clearly and effectively about these socio-emotional elements. For example, among the stories in the DUSO curriculum, a girl feigns sickness at home in order to avoid a stressful situation at school; a boy teases and aggresses against his peers because he feels rejected by them; and another child is torn between giving up or continuing to try to reach a difficult goal. The DUSO curriculum is structured so that teachers can pause frequently to elicit children's opinions and observations. For example, clues are presented suggesting the "real" feelings of story characters. Children are prompted to consider both verbal and nonverbal behavior in understanding the thoughts and feelings behind story characters' actions. Children are also helped to predict successfully what will happen next in stories and why. As problems arise, children are asked to change aspects of the situation to achieve satisfying solutions for all involved parties. As with most affective education programs, DUSO is flexible enough so that real-life situations and problems presented by children can be incorporated into group activities and discussions.

The DUSO curriculum focuses upon eight major developmental tasks or themes, such as understanding feelings, understanding goals and purposive behavior, and understanding choices and consequences. The program employs an appealing array of educational materials consisting of storybooks, records and cassettes, posters and puppets. Each instructional unit is devoted to one of the major themes and involves a complementary sequence of activities, such as a central story, a problem situation frequently encountered by children, role-playing exercises, puppet play, and discussion. Supplementary activities are also possible. The complete DUSO curriculum is implemented in daily 20-minute sessions for a full school year.

Programs such as DUSO are attractive and interesting to children. Most children remain attentive and involved during program activities. The major concern is whether affective education consistently achieves significant positive changes in children's adjustment. The following section reviews outcome studies evaluating affective education programs.

Evaluation of Affective Education Programs

Outcome studies of affective education programs have been discussed by several reviewers (Baskin & Hess, 1980; Durlak, 1983b; Elardo & Elardo, 1976; Medway & Smith, 1978). The results of this outcome research are summarized in the last two columns of Table 4.1.

At first glance, evaluations of affective education seem very encouraging; the majority of studies have attained some positive results. Nevertheless, conclusions regarding the effectiveness of affective education must be made cautiously for several reasons. For example, the experimental design of many studies has been weak. Children often have not been assigned randomly to experimental conditions; assessment devices with questionable reliability and validity have been used; and controls for nonspecific treatment effects were lacking. Few studies have employed objective outcome measures to assess changes in overt behavioral adjustment, focusing instead on potentially biased child self-reports and teacher ratings. Moreover, few follow-up data have been collected so the preventive effects of intervention cannot be determined.

Another important limitation is that the basic theoretical or conceptual rationale of affective education programs has not been convincingly established. For example, most affective education programs hypothesize that certain variables, such as understanding of self and others, affective communication skills, social-cognition, or cognitive problem-solving skills, mediate adjustment and that improvement along these dimensions is responsible for the positive results obtained in outcome studies. However, there are insufficient research data to support such hypotheses. Research on interpersonal problem-solving serves as an illustration.

Spivack and Shure have consistently obtained positive effects on children's adjustment as a result of problem-solving training (Shure & Spivack, 1978, 1979, 1982; Spivack & Shure, 1974). Their findings suggest that children who improve in cognitive problem-solving skills show a corresponding change in classroom adjustment. However, other investigators implementing problem-solving training programs modeled after the Spivack and Shure approach have either failed to obtain positive changes on various adjustment measures (Allen, Chinsky, Larcen, Lochman, & Selinger, 1976; McClure, Chinsky, & Larcen, 1978), or have noted that children's improvement, if obtained, fails to correlate with gains in problem-solving ability (Weissberg, Gesten, Rapkin, Cowen, Davidson, de Apodaca, & McKim, 1981; Weissberg, Gesten, Carnike, Toro, Rapkin, Davidson, & Cowen, 1981). Moreover, additional studies have failed to find significant relationships between children's problem-solving skills and other indices of adjustment, including naturalistic observations of classroom and play behavior, teaching ratings and sociometric status (Gillespie, Durlak, & Sherman, 1982; Press, Alvarez, Cotler, & Jason, in press; Rickel & Burgio, 1982; Butler, Note 1). Therefore some programs may misdirect efforts at variables not directly relevant to mental health. Accordingly, the important elements of affective education programs need reexamination and clarification.

In summary, the current status of affective education is perplexing. On the one hand, there is enthusiasm for the introduction of affective education into many schools and this intervention approach is intuitively appealing. On the other hand, research data have yet to clearly establish the preventive value of various affective education programs. No clear resolution of this predicament is possible without further information from carefully controlled studies.

Nevertheless, it should be pointed out that insufficient program implementations may have contributed to the limited impact of many current programs. For example, as noted earlier, there are carefully prepared lesson plans for many programs that suggest a sequential and structured approach to program implementation. In practice, however, many teachers pick and choose among different instructional units based on their personal preferences and the entire program is not always conducted. As a result, affective education has not always been put to an adequate test in previous program evaluations. Some programs have been conducted for much shorter periods than recommended and there are some data suggesting that lengthier programs are more likely to be effective (Medway & Smith, 1978; Weissberg et al., 1981). Moreover, as pointed out by Medway and Smith (1978), implementing an affective education program requires an understanding of child development, skill in group dynamics, and an ability to facilitate the expressions of feelings. Such skills cannot be learned solely from a teacher's manual or lesson plan. Therefore, it is important to train and supervise teachers effectively.

A recent study evaluated 32 teachers' implementation of an affective education program (Thompson-Rountree & Musun-Baskett, 1981). Two groups consisting of teachers with high and low skills were identified. Although no outcome differences in terms of the teachers' skill levels were found among children at the primary grade level (grades 1-3), in the intermediate grades (4-6), children of teachers in the high skill group demonstrated significantly more positive changes in adjustment than children of teachers in the low skill group. Similarly, another study reported that children of teachers trained in implementing an affective education program showed greater gains in measures of problem-solving ability and social cognition than children of teachers who implemented the program without training (Ojemann, Levitt, Lyle, & Whiteside, 1955).

In summary, it is not known how many teachers have conducted affective education programs in their classrooms without the skill training or consultation required for effective program implementation.

Notwithstanding the above problems, the primary prevention value of affective education cannot be underestimated. Barrios and Shigetomi (1980) have noted that a successful prevention program must have several characteristics: (1) be available to large populations, (2) have an efficient method of service delivery (not require extensive monetary or personnel costs), (3) be politically and personally acceptable (not induce strong resistance to its implementation), and (4) be effective in producing significant, desirable outcomes and few undesirable side effects. Except for the latter requirement, affective education fulfills these characteristics.

As a school-based intervention, affective education has the greatest potential to reach the most children of all primary prevention efforts. Moreover, these programs do not require mental health professionals as direct service agents. Teachers, aides, and community volunteers have effectively implemented programs. Professionals can more effectively serve as trainers and consultants for those conducting different programs. Most importantly, the goals and principles of affective education are congruent with current educational values and practices; affective education has been sanctioned by teachers, principals, and administrators throughout the country as a valid educational enterprise. As an intervention strategy then, affective education has successfully resolved the complex political and administrative issues related to gaining program entry, support and maintenance in the school, an important social institution. Few community programs, let alone those with a preventive thrust, can make this claim. Therefore, the challenge that remains for investigators is to identify what growth-enhancing factors exist in affective education programs in order to develop new programs or modify existing ones as needed.

PRIMARY PREVENTION FOR SCHOOL-AGED ADOLESCENTS

Intervention for High-Risk Populations

Up to now, preventive programming for elementary aged school children has been emphasized. In this section, however, four research efforts directed at junior high and high school aged adolescents are discussed. Moreover, these investigations involve high risk youth. The notion of risk is relative, having different connotations depending upon the situation. In general, however, primary prevention programs for high-risk groups concentrate on those members of a population who, in comparison to their peers, are most likely to exhibit subsequent adjustment problems.

In the studies noted, investigators have been careful in identifying a target group, specifying the notion of risk, delineating the problem or problems to be prevented, and using multi-outcome measures to evaluate intervention effects. Furthermore, most of these studies have conducted follow-up assessment of program effects and are therefore good examples of primary prevention programs for high-risk adolescents.

Schinke and his colleagues have been interested in the prevention of unwanted teenage pregnancy, currently occurring at epidemic proportions throughout the country (Schinke, Blythe, & Gilchrist, 1981; Schinke, Gilchrist, & Blythe, 1980; Schinke, Blythe, Gilchrist, & Burt, 1981; Schinke, Gilchrist, & Small, 1979). Approximately 1.3 million teenagers become pregnant each year (Tietze, 1978). Not only is unwanted pregnancy a significant social problem in its own right, but early unwanted pregnancy can also seriously impede and complicate a youth's vocational, social, and personal development (Schinke et al., 1979). Contemporary research data indicate that adolescents are often unable to deal effectively with their developing sexuality. For example, many adolescents are ignorant of basic information concerning sexuality and contraception. Moreover, adolescents are often unaware of the physical and affective changes occurring within themselves and their peers that result from sexual maturation. Finally, adolescents may have difficulty in expressing their feelings and asserting themselves effectively in sexual situations. The above factors coalesce to place many adolescents at risk in terms of unwanted pregnancy.

The Schinke group has developed a multicomponent program directed at reducing these risk factors. Instruction, role-playing and discussion are used first to insure that adolescents perceive and comprehend basic sexual information accurately. The next stage of intervention helps adolescents integrate sexual information into their value systems and lifestyles. Social learning principles are used to train adolescents in effective decision making, interpersonal problem-solving, communication skills, and assertiveness. Training takes place in small groups and helps adolescents refuse unreasonable demands, make appropriate requests of others, and communicate their feelings positively and specifically.

Several research studies indicate this training approach to pregnancy prevention is promising. Compared to untrained controls, trained adolescents usually acquire more accurate sexual information, show increased self-confidence, become better problem solvers, and behave more effectively in problematic interpersonal situations; follow-up data also suggest that trained adolescents use more successful methods of contraception (Schinke, Blythe, & Burt, 1981; Schinke et al., 1981; Schinke et al., 1980). Whereas research by the Schinke group concentrates on the specific prevention of unwanted pregnancy, the following three research efforts attempt to prevent a variety of intrapersonal and social adjustment problems.

Research reported by Poser and Hartman (1979) and Hartman (1979) represents a two-stage process in developing a primary prevention intervention for high risk adolescents. In this case, adolescents were considered at risk for future psychological problems because of their current inability to cope effectively with environmental and intrapersonal stress. First, the authors took pains to develop an experimental method to distinguish low from high risk adolescents (Poser & Hartman, 1979). Essentially, this method involves a two dimensional approach that evaluates individual coping mechanisms in combination with environmental pressures. Data suggest that combinations of measures assessing assertiveness, self-esteem, anxiety, peer status, and both reinforcing and stressful life events yielded consistent risk classifications. Once a method of evaluating youths was developed, an intervention designed to modify their risk potential was implemented and evaluated (Hartman, 1979).

Following an initial assessment, low and high risk high school students were randomly assigned to either an eight-week preventive program or a nontreatment control condition. A teacher was trained to conduct the program, which attempted to correct the skills deficits that presumably placed the students at risk. The program incorporated a variety of behaviorally-focused techniques for this purpose, including cognitive restructuring, rational emotive and behavioral self-control training, stress management, and social skills training.

Outcome data collected two and 12 weeks after the program ended were positive. Whereas controls tended to display few changes over time, most outcome measures reflected significant improvement in high risk students; moreover, these results were typically maintained three months later. Data also indicated that low-risk students benefited from the intervention but not to the same degree as high risk youths. Poser and Hartman (1979) admit that their classification procedures still require more study and confirmation. Nevertheless, the attempt by these researchers to operationalize and empirically validate risk indices for adolescents is exemplary and could be profitably emulated by others.

A third study represents still another innovative approach to improving the functioning of high-risk adolescents (Sarason & Sarason, 1981). In this case, adolescents attending a multi-ethnic urban high school were targeted. Several indices suggested students at this school were at risk for subsequent academic and social problems. For example, as a group the student body was characterized by low academic achievement and high dropout and delinquency rates. This study is noteworthy because systematic information was collected prior to intervention to pinpoint students' problems. Interviews were conducted with a cross-section of students, school staff, school dropouts and local citizens. Interview data suggested that students were frequently impulsive, were ineffective problem solvers, lacked social skills in interactions with peers and adults, and were not socially adept during job interviews with potential employers.

Sarason and Sarason (1981) developed a 13-week intervention specifically directed at these students' typical cognitive and social skills deficits. Treatment was offered during the regular high school health course, and modeling and role-playing predominated among the procedures used to improve students' interpersonal functioning.

The results were positive. Compared to control students who were not involved in the special health course, experimental students improved their interpersonal problem-solving skills and also performed more effectively during actual job interviews conducted four months later. At one-year follow-up, school records indicated that program participants were absent and tardy less frequently and were less often referred for behavioral problems.

Another research group focusing on high risk students began their intervention when the students were in seventh grade (Bry, 1982; Bry & George, 1980; Bien & Bry, 1980). Inspection of school records and contacts with school staff identified a group of 40 students considered at risk for subsequent school failure and social maladaptation. Identified students had at least two of the following characteristics: (1) low academic motivation, (2) family problems, or (3) a record of serious or frequent school disciplinary referrals. Students were randomly assigned to treatment or control conditions. The basic approach to treatment consisted of daily and weekly monitoring of students' school behavior and systematic feedback to students designed to help them increase their positive behavior and resolve their difficulties. Social and token reinforcement was emphasized. A multicomponent intervention was established that included twice weekly meetings between students and the research staff, biweekly teacher consultations, and periodic contact and consultation with parents which was designed to increase involvement in their children's behavior.

Program effects were assessed immediately following treatment and at 12 months, 18 months, and five-year follow-up points. Immediately following treatment, the treated children improved significantly over the untreated control group in terms of school grades, attendance, and disruptive classroom behavior (Bry & George, 1980). No effects were found on measures of tardiness and school disciplinary actions.

School data collected at the one-year follow-up indicated significant treatment effects on a composite measure of school problems, including disciplinary action, tardiness, absenteeism, and grade promotions. Interview data collected from students at the 18-month follow-up indicated significant positive effects on employment history, self-reported drug abuse and criminal behavior. Finally, inspection of court records five years after treatment indicated that treated students were less frequently involved in the juvenile criminal justice system.

Finally, Cradock, Cotler, and Jason (1978) were interested in the prevention of public speaking anxiety in high school freshman girls. Test and performance anxiety, of which public speaking is one variant, is a large-scale problem affecting as much as 20% of the school population at one time or another (Eysenck & Rachman, 1965). Students who did not take an available elective speech course were screened using a self-report measure found useful in prior research (Personal Report of Confidence as a Speaker), and individuals considered vulnerable to public speaking anxiety, but who were not yet demonstrating clinically elevated levels of distress, were targeted for intervention. Cradock et al. (1978) found that a brief, six-hour cognitive restructuring treatment resulted in significant increases in public speaking confidence compared to that of individuals in an untreated control group.

Other Programs

Space limitations do not permit a discussion of all primary prevention programs, but a few other interventions can be briefly cited. Glidewell and his colleagues in St. Louis were among the first to demonstrate the potential of preventive programming for school-age children (Glidewell, Gildea, & Kaufman, 1973). The St. Louis Project attempted to prevent the emergence of academic and social difficulties in young elementary school children. A primary feature of the St. Louis Project was a discussion group program for parents, conducted by specially selected and trained community volunteers. The discussion groups were designed to promote positive mental health attitudes and child-rearing skills in parents of elementary school-aged children. Results suggested this program was successful. Other school oriented programs have reported positive changes in children's anxiety, impulse control and behavior problems (Miller & Kassinove, 1978; Rogeness, Stokes, Bednar, & Gorman, 1977). Finally, there have been several investigations that have increased specific abilities in children and adolescents, such as communication skills (Haynes & Avery, 1979; Vogelsong, 1978) and sharing and cooperative behaviors (Barton & Osborne, 1978; Sagotsky, Wood-Schneider, & Konop, 1981). Each of these investigations has relevance to preventive programming by illustrating change techniques that can be successfully applied toward the promotion of potentially important developmental competencies.

SECONDARY PREVENTION FOR SCHOOL-AGED CHILDREN

The distinction between primary and secondary prevention is important. Secondary prevention is prompt intervention for early-detected dysfunction that is uncovered through a systematic population-wide case finding or screening approach. In contrast to primary prevention, which involves essentially nondysfunctional populations, secondary prevention programs are directed at individuals who are already maladapting to mild or moderate degrees. Such programs are preventive in the sense that early-identified problems could worsen over time in the absence of any intervention. Secondary prevention programs are best discussed in terms of the target problems that change agents attempt to prevent. The following sections discuss efforts directed at the prevention of school maladjustment, social isolation, and hyperactivity.

School Maladjustment

The most well known school-based secondary prevention program is the Primary Mental Health Project (PMHP) in Rochester, New York (Cowen, Trost, Dorr, Lorion, Izzo, & Isaacson, 1975). PMHP is a large scale, school-based effort for early detection and prevention of school maladjustment. PMHP has been in operation for more than 25 years and is impressive in its conceptualization, delivery, and evaluation of school-based preventive mental health services; over 150 published articles have described the program's procedures and outcomes. There are four primary components to PMHP: (1) a focus on young children, (2) systematic mass screening efforts to detect school maladaptation, (3) use of paraprofessionals to work with target children, and (4) changing roles for mental health professionals emphasizing program development, consultation, and evaluation in lieu of direct therapeutic activity (see also Rickel, Dyhdalo, & Smith, in Chapter 3 of this volume).

Beginning in 1972, PMHP staff members have actively pursued a systematic national and regional strategy to encourage other school districts to develop conceptually similar programs. PMHP's dissemination effort has been very successful. A survey conducted in 1977 indicated there were 35 additional school districts that had been or were operating secondary prevention programs influenced by the PMHP program model (Cowen, Davidson, & Gesten, 1980). These programs incorporated at least three of the four primary components of PMHP, including the use of paraprofessionals. During the 1976–1977 school year, approximately 3,250 children from more than 200 schools received help through PMHP-related programs. A 1981 follow-up survey indicated a continued growth in the application of the PMHP model, with programs being implemented in 109 different school districts throughout the country. Altogether, approximately 7,500 children from 330 schools had been served (Cowen, Spinell, Wright, & Weissberg, Note 2).

Table 4.2 presents summary information on representative programs that have been influenced by PMHP and have published the results of various program evaluations. Also included in Table 4.2 are several programs that have apparently developed independently of PMHP but which share similar conceptual features (Butler, Meizitis, Friedman, & Cole, 1980; Maher & Barbrack, 1982).

Because of space limitations, it is not possible to discuss all the programs listed in Table 4.2. The Social Skills Program will be presented to provide more concrete details on how school-based secondary prevention programs operate. This program has been introduced into three separate school districts (in Heidelberg, West Germany; Augusta, Georgia; and Carbondale, Illinois); in each case some programmatic features have varied, but the core program has remained the same. The Social Skills Program is basically oriented at identifying those children who are alternatively referred to in the literature as externalizers (acting-out children) or internalizers (shy withdrawn children). Although the largest group of selected children falls into the former category, most children have a combination of problems including learning difficulties. All children in first through third grades at each program school are first screened using the AML, a brief teacher rating scale (which will be described in more detail later). The AML data are then supplemented by a lengthier teacher checklist, interviews with teachers, and observations of classroom behavior.

Children receiving the highest AML ratings (reflecting school maladaptation) are targeted for treatment. Personnel available to serve as group leaders are recruited in each community, including teachers and school counselors (Durlak, 1977) and undergraduate and graduate psychology students have been used (Durlak & Mannarino, Note 3). Group leaders work in pairs and see the children for one hour a week outside the classroom but during the school day. Groups consist of from five to eight children, usually drawn from the same grade but from as many different classrooms as possible. Both relationship and behavioral treatment techniques have been used; since outcome data suggest some advantages for the latter techniques (Durlak, 1980; Durlak & Mannarino, Note 3), these are described here.

Using all available screening and assessment data, group leaders consult with the supervising professional to develop individualized treatment goals for each child. Basically, the major treatment strategy have been to reinforce positive social behavior which is incompatible with typical dysfunctional school behavior. Both social and token reinforcement have been used. Acting-out children are rewarded for such behaviors as waiting their turn, listening to others, or following directions; shy-withdrawn children are rewarded for joining in discussions, talking to or working with others.

Group leaders direct each weekly meeting using a range of activities designed to give children the opportunity to practice different social skills related to self-control, cooperation and sharing. Depending on their initial experience and skill levels, group leaders receive four to eight hours of preprogram training in group skills and behavioral reinforcement techniques as well as weekly group supervision. In addition, the supervisor directly observes several of the group meetings at school, provides immediate feedback to group leaders, and suggests changes in group leaders' behavior. During the program, group leaders also maintain contact with teachers and share information regarding children's progress in the groups and in the classroom. Further details on program practices and issues involved in implementing and evaluating school-based programs are available elsewhere (Durlak, 1977; Mannarino & Durlak, 1980).

The Social Skills Program appears to be cost-effective. On the one hand, outcome evaluations indicate that treated children improve significantly over the control group in their school adjustment and maintain their gains during follow-up periods (Durlak, 1977, 1980; Durlak & Mannarino, Note 3). Moreover, the majority of children respond favorably to intervention. A recent evaluation suggested that 83% of participating children displayed a clinically significant improvement in their school adjustment as a result of program participation (Durlak & Gillespie, Note 4). On the other hand, program "costs" have been relatively minimal with brief, group-oriented treatments (a maximum of 20 treatment sessions during the school year) contributing to the program's economy. A social worker or clinical psychologist has assisted the program director in each program implementation, and the programs have required an average expenditure of 10 hours per week to administer. Not counting professional staff time, financial expenses have been minimal and have been covered jointly by the host schools, local community groups or through a small university research grant. The cost-efficiency of programs such as the Social Skills Program makes them particularly attractive as preventive interventions.

In general, research on the secondary prevention of school maladjustment has focused primarily on two issues: the early identification of school maladjustment and the impact of interventions provided to target children.

Identifying School Maladjustment

Identifying maladapting school children is a sensitive undertaking. On the one hand, secondary prevention programs run the risk of labeling or stereotyping children because some are selected for treatment whereas others are not. On the other hand, it is fundamentally important to detect adjustment problems as quickly as possible. It is assumed that the more quickly children's current difficulties are identified and are attended to, the greater the likelihood of precluding more serious problems from developing.

For wide-scale applications, procedures to identify maladapting children must

Table. 4.2. Characteristics and Outcomes of Representative School-based Secondary Prevention Programs

Program[a]	Experimental Group: *N* and Grade Level	Major Method of Intervention	Primary Change Agents	Major Findings: Significant Changes in E Group Compared to Controls
Allen, Chinsky, Larcen, Lochman, & Selinger (1976)	20, grades 1–6	Individual behavioral treatment	Undergraduates	Increase in peer social interactions
Butler, Miezitis, Friedman, & Cole (1980)	28, grades 5 and 6	Group roleplaying & cognitive restructuring	Unidentified	Reduction in depressive symptoms and increase in internal locus of control
Cowen, Gesten, & Wilson (1979)	215, primary grades 1–3	Individual, relationship treatment	Housewives	Reduction in maladjustment
Durlak (1977)	56, grades 1–3	Group behavioral treatment	School counselors, teachers and undergraduates	Reduction in maladjustment
Durlak (1980)	93, grades 1–3	Group behavioral or relationship treatment	Graduate and undergraduate students	Behavioral treatment more effective than relational in reducing maladjustment
Kirschenbaum (1979)	273, grades 1–6	Structured group sessions and/or teacher consultation	Community volunteers and teachers	Reduction in maladjustment
Maher & Barbrack (1982)	24, 9th graders	Behavioral group counseling	School counselors and high school students	Increase in school attendance and grades, reduction in disciplinary referrals

Mannarino, Durlak, Christy, & Magnussen (1982)	32, grades 1–3	Group problem solving training	Undergraduates	Reduction in maladjustment and increase in sociometric status
Rickel, Smith, & Sharp (1979)	32, preschoolers	Eclectic individual treatment based on nature of child's problems	Undergraduates	Reduction in maladjustment and improvement in academic achievement
Sandler, Duricko, & Grande (1975)	19, kindergarten—grade 3	Individual and group relationship treatment	Community volunteers, parents, and teachers	Reduction in maladjustment
Tefft & Kloba (1981)	22, kindergarten—grade 4	Individual, relationship treatment	High school students	Reduction in maladjustment for acting-out children

[a]Programs sought to reduce early signs of general school maladaptation with the exception of the interventions by Allen et al. (1976) and Butler et al. (1980), which sought to specifically reduce social isolation and depressive symptomatology respectively.

not only be reliable and valid, but also efficient and economical. That is, procedures that require extensive professional personnel or that make time-consuming and intrusive demands on teachers are unlikely to gain widespread use. One measure that appears to fulfill the above criteria rather effectively, and which has received the most research attention in secondary prevention school-based programs, is the AML.

The AML is an 11-item, three-factor, quick screening teacher rating scale designed to detect early school maladjustment (Cowen, Dorr, Clarfield, Kreling, McWilliams, Pokracki, Pratt, Terrell, & Wilson, 1973). Ratings provide information on children's acting-out and shy-withdrawn classroom behaviors and their learning difficulties. The AML provides important information quickly and efficiently; a teacher can rate a child in only a minute or two. Despite its brevity, the AML has acceptable psychometric properties in terms of internal consistency, test-retest reliability and a stable factor structure (Cowen et al., 1973). AML scores also correlate significantly with information obtained on lengthier, more complicated assessment procedures which are designed to detect school maladaptation, such as naturalistic observations of children's classroom behavior (Cowen et al., 1973; Dorr, Stephens, Pozner, & Klodt, 1980; Durlak, Stein, & Mannarino, 1980). Distributions of AML scores for different school populations have been presented (Carberry & Handal, 1980; Cowen et al., 1973), providing investigators with normative guidelines concerning the range of scores to be expected in different school-age populations. Furthermore, data suggest that the AML is a relatively effective screening instrument. Kirschenbaum, Marsh, and DeVoge (1977) asked for teacher referrals to their secondary prevention program and then also screened all elementary school children using the AML. Comparing both AML ratings and teacher referrals with clinical judgments of the children's adjustment status, Kirschenbaum et al. found that the AML effectively identified more than twice as many maladapting children.

Carberry and Handal (1980) compared AML ratings with professionals' independent evaluations of children's school adjustment; 86% of the children with high AML ratings were confirmed by professionals as having problems (true positives) while 13% with high AML scores were not considered by professionals as maladaptive (false positives). Finally, Gillespie and Durlak (Note 5) compared the classroom behavior of 57 children targeted for intervention (based on their high AML ratings) with the behavior of 114 of their peers selected randomly. Based upon peer data, criteria were established to determine the range of normal behavior in each classroom; 53 of the 57 target children displayed behavior considered beyond normal limits, suggesting a 93% accuracy rate for the AML in identifying true positives.

Notwithstanding the above data, there are reservations regarding the AML's use. The long-term predictability of AML ratings is unknown as is the number of false negatives obtained in AML screening (that is, what percent of children with low AML ratings are actually demonstrating dysfunctional school behavior). Moreover, the AML can only provide an initial estimate of school maladaptation; more information using other assessment procedures must be gathered in order to identify a child's specific difficulties and to plan effective remediation. Nevertheless, the AML appears to provide an economical, yet discriminating, initial assessment of a school child's adjustment status.

Evaluating Program Effectiveness

Current outcome data offer clear and consistent support for the value of secondary prevention school-based programs. Results of current programs are impressive, not because of the findings from any single program, but because of the consistency of positive effects independent investigators obtain while working in diverse community settings. In other words, investigators have obtained impressive convergent evidence concerning the value of a generic school-based secondary prevention program model. Evaluations conducted in 15 different school districts have indicated that prompt attention to early-detected dysfunction is effective in improving young children's school functioning. Positive outcome data have been obtained using a variety of measures including teacher ratings (Cowen, Gesten, & Wilson, 1979; Kirschenbaum, 1979; Sandler et al., 1975), independent observations of classroom behavior (Durlak & Mannarino, Note 3; Durlak & Gillespie, Note 4), sociometric data (Mannarino, Durlak, Christy, & Magnussen, 1982) and standard psychological tests (Rickel et al., 1979). Moreover, follow-up data collected in five settings have indicated that program effects are not transitory; the enhanced adjustment demonstrated by participating children immediately following treatment has, by and large, been maintained for anywhere from a few weeks to several years (Durlak, 1977, 1980; Lorion, Caldwell, & Cowen, 1976; Tefft & Kloba, 1981; Rickel & Dyhdalo, Note 6). Overall, there is probably more evidence for the effectiveness of school-based secondary prevention programs than for any other type of preventive approach.

Nevertheless, there are several issues yet to be resolved. For example, the long-term preventive implications of current programs are unknown; program children may still experience adjustment difficulties later in their school careers. Some programs have obtained differential effects as a function of the nature and seriousness of children's school maladaptation. In general, children with acting-out or more severe problems respond less favorably to interventions, particularly relationship-oriented treatment. As a result, there is the need to specify which children are best served by current programs and to understand the reasons for these results.

Finally, it is important to assess the value of different programs' practices. For example, as Table 4.2 indicates, despite conceptual similarity, there have been many variations in the ways current programs have been implemented. Some programs emphasize behavioral treatment; others emphasize relationship-oriented techniques; and some combine therapeutic strategies. Both individual and group interventions have been provided to target children, and parents and teachers have been involved in some programs. The primary therapeutic agents in different programs have included teachers, housewives, high school and college students, community volunteers, and school counselors and nurses. However, the differential effectiveness of various program practices is still unknown. Although Kirschenbaum (1983) has recently argued that behavioral techniques are the treatment of choice in preventive programs, this conclusion may be premature given the paucity of direct comparative studies.

Social Isolation

This section discusses programs directed at improving the social skills and peer interactions of socially withdrawn or isolated children. Socially isolated children are often selected for intervention because such children typically do not have good peer relationships. The quality of childhood peer relationships has been linked to a variety of later difficulties, such as delinquency, poor school and social adjustment, and various mental disorders (see Conger & Keane, 1981; Wanlass & Prinz, 1982). However, from a preventive standpoint the relationship between childhood peer relationships and later adjustment is correlational in nature and one cannot assume that improving peer relations will automatically prevent subsequent problems.

Conger and Keane (1981) and Wanlass and Prinz (1982) have reviewed and evaluated interventions for socially withdrawn children. Therefore, this section merely discusses a few representative programs. In each case, treatment seeks to improve the social skills and peer relations of identified children, but the studies differ in terms of initial assessment of social withdrawal, the target measures chosen for treatment, the specific intervention techniques used, and general evaluation procedures.

Oden and Asher (1977) screened twelve classrooms using a peer sociometric measure to identify socially isolated children in the third and fourth grades. Their experimental intervention involved instructing children in social skills related to making friends, having them practice these skills in play interactions with peers, and then reviewing with each child the use of the coached skills and their possible application in future peer situations. The social skills on which children were trained or coached included such behaviors as paying attention, listening, taking turns, and providing social reinforcement. Behavioral observation data did not reflect positive intervention effects, but sociometric data did indicate significant improvement in coached versus control children. Moreover, coached children continued to show improvement in sociometric standing one year later.

Ladd (1981) identified children with poor peer relations on the basis of sociometric screening and behavioral observations of peer interactions. Selected children were trained in three basic skills: asking questions, making leading responses (offering suggestions or directions), and offering social support. In addition, trained children were taught how to use self-rehearsal and self-evaluation when practicing and applying the target skills. Analysis of observed behavioral outcome data indicated that trained children improved significantly in question asking and leading responses immediately following treatment and at four weeks, whereas untreated controls and attention-placebo control children did not change. Analysis of sociometric data also significantly favored trained children at posttreatment and at follow-up. Children in the above two studies were treated by experimenters outside the classroom; in the following two reports the intervention was implemented in a classroom setting.

Walker, Greenwood, Hops, and Todd (1981) identified 18 socially withdrawn elementary school children on the basis of counselor referrals, behavioral observations of peer interactions, and teacher-completed behavior checklist data. Selected children were treated by a specially trained teacher and teacher's aide in an experimental classroom setting. During four months of treatment, token reinforcement techniques were used to reinforce children for initiating, responding to, or maintaining social interactions. A series of three experiments involving reversal and DRO procedures (differential reinforcement of other behavior) clearly indicated that the intervention was successful in producing large increases in children's positive social behavior.

Finally, teachers bringing withdrawn children to the attention of investigators were trained in modifying these children's social behaviors (Weinrott, Corson, & Wilchesky, 1979). Behavioral observations and standardized checklist data confirmed that there were deficiencies in referred children's social behavior. Teachers were trained to use modeling procedures, social reinforcement, and individual and group contingencies in their regular classrooms. These procedures resulted in a significant increase in target children's social behavior compared to the untreated control group. Moreover, the five-week follow-up indicated that the level of appropriate social behavior demonstrated by target children was similar to that displayed by a normal peer group not considered to be deficient in social behavior.

In summary, secondary prevention programs designed to modify the behavior of socially withdrawn children have met with promising results. Current outcome data should encourage future research and practice in the area and help to establish more standardized assessment and intervention procedures for children whose inhibited interpersonal style impedes their psychological development.

Hyperactivity: Lack of Effective Self-Control

The topic of hyperactivity deserves attention here because some estimates indicate that hyperactivity (attention deficit disorder) is the single largest diagnostic problem of maladjusted children and may be implicated in up to 50% of all referrals to child guidance clinics (Gelfand, Jenson, & Drew, 1982). If so, then the effective prevention of hyperactivity could have a sizable impact on childhood and adolescence maladjustment. However, several complications exist. First, as is the case with most diagnostic categories, there is still disagreement regarding the etiology, defining characteristics, developmental progression, and prognosis of hyperactivity. Second, attempts to review preventively-oriented efforts for hyperactive children are difficult due to investigators' failure to employ common referral and assessment techniques and to use the same terminology in identifying target groups. Whereas one investigator may use techniques A and B to identify "impulsive" children, another investigator may use techniques C and D to select "hyperactive" children and still another may use technique E to study "non-self-controlled" children. Under such circumstances, it is difficult to tell if different investigators are dealing with the same clinical phenomenon.

Since a complete discussion of hyperactivity is beyond the scope of this chapter, this discussion centers upon programs designed to change self-control, a target variable germane to hyperactivity. Hyperactive children are frequently described as impulsive, overactive, emotionally labile, and unable to attend to and concentrate upon relevant tasks. In general, hyperactive children cannot adequately control their cognitive, affective, and behavioral responses. Interventions to improve children's self-control have implications not only for the prevention of hyperactivity, but also for several other adjustment problems in which children and adolescents have difficulty regulating their own behavior, such as juvenile delinquency, aggression, alcohol and drug abuse, and various behavior management problems.

The concept of self-control is complex, and theoreticians disagree regarding its exact components. The processes that are most commonly identified include self-instruction, self-determined performance standards, self-assessment, and self-reinforcement. Current programs differ in terms of which of these dimensions are targeted for intervention.

A cognitive-behavioral emphasis (stressing the importance of integrating thought processes with behavior) has recently assumed prominence in the field of self-control. Evidence is accumulating that many groups of dysfunctional children (labeled as hyperactive, aggressive, impulsive, learning disabled, or acting-out) do not use language effectively to guide their own behavior. Hence, many cognitive-behavioral programs teach children how to "talk to themselves," "think aloud," or "stop, look, and listen" before, during, and after their performance on different tasks. The major goal is to train children to bring their own behavior under more effective cognitive control. There are several excellent analyses of cognitive-behavioral strategies and self-control programs for children (Kendall, 1981; O'Leary & Dubey, 1979; Rosenbaum & Drabman, 1979). The studies presented here illustrate different procedural applications of self-control training.

In the investigation by Kendall and Zupan (1981), children whose lack of self-control was creating social and academic problems in the classroom were referred by teachers. Self-instructional training and reinforcement contingencies were emphasized in the 12-session training program that was developed. Children were taught how to verbally define a problem, develop a strategy to solve the problem, and then evaluate their behavioral performance and reinforce themselves accordingly. The trainer first modeled effective self-instructional procedures and then reinforced the child for correct imitation of these behaviors. A response-cost procedure was utilized in which children were penalized if they made errors during the self-instructional practice sessions by losing tokens that could otherwise be used to gain material reinforcers. Compared to attention-placebo controls, children trained individually or in groups improved significantly in self-control, according to teachers' ratings of classroom behavior. Furthermore, the self-control of children in both training conditions was within normal limits when compared to nonproblem peers, who were also rated by teachers. This latter finding was consistent one year later in the individually trained children only. However, the group-trained children did not differ at follow-up from their normal peer group when specific ratings of hyperactivity were examined (Kendall, 1982). Such findings indicate that the context of self-control training, in this case individual or group, may produce differential treatment effects.

Another study used self-instructional training to help aggressive children regulate their behavior more effectively (Camp, Blom, Hebert, & van Doorninck, 1977). Similar to the Kendall and Zupan (1981) study, children were instructed to think aloud during their task performance. Children practiced self-instructional techniques that focused on identifying a problem exactly, specifying a possible solution, and then evaluating their resultant performance. Instructions, modeling, and social reinforcement were used during training as the children worked on both academically related tasks and interpersonal problem situations. Trained children improved their performance on a battery of cognitive and academic tests resulting in their final performance differing significantly from untrained controls, but not from a tested normal peer group. Trained children also improved their interpersonal problem-solving ability and classroom behavior.

In another study, Glynn and his associates applied self-control training procedures to academic behaviors. In one investigation, a teacher-administered token reinforcement system effectively increased rates of on-task behavior to acceptable levels in a class of second graders (Glynn, Thomas, & Shee, 1973). Glynn et al. were then interested in whether appropriate levels of on-task behavior could be maintained and teacher responsibility for monitoring and controlling the reinforcement system diminished when children were taught self-control procedures. The results were positive. Children were able to learn how to self-assess their rates of on-task behavior, to self-record their behavior, to self-determine if their behavior merited reinforcement, and finally, to self-administer the necessary reinforcement. In addition, rates of on-task behavior were more stable in the classroom under the self-control condition than under the teacher-administered condition. Ballard and Glynn (1975) also demonstrated that self-management techniques could be used successfully to improve the writing skills of third graders. Children were able to improve the quantity and quality of their work output during English composition exercises as they learned to monitor, evaluate and reinforce themselves for different elements of their writing styles. Data also reflected improvement in children's on-task behavior during the self-control phase of the study, and ratings from independent judges confirmed that the children's writing had improved in quality.

The preventive value of self-control training procedures has not yet been adequately evaluated. Furthermore, there are many practical and experimental issues that have to be resolved before self-control training can be most efficiently applied to different target groups and problems. Nevertheless, self-control training has enormous potential value to the field of prevention. Programs that assist children in controlling their hyperactive and aggressive behavior and improve their academic performance and on-task behavior can be applied to a wide array of populations and settings. Interested readers would do well to pursue the references cited in this section that evaluate the advantages and limitations of current self-control interventions for children and adolescents.

FUTURE DIRECTIONS

Previous sections of this chapter have included evaluations or critiques of specific programs. This final section discusses some general issues that apply to most preventive programs for school-aged children and adolescents. In terms of program evaluation, four important issues deserve additional attention: (1) identifying those critical competencies that mediate adjustment, (2) demonstrating the long-term impact of interventions, (3) assessing how specific components of a program contribute to outcome, and (4) effectively matching interventions to the needs of target populations.

Competencies That Mediate Adjustment

As noted earlier, competency building preventive programs attempt to promote social competency in target groups. The ultimate success of this approach is, of course, dependent upon correctly identifying the skills or competencies critical to adaptive functioning and which mediate adjustment in school aged children and adolescents. Which skills are these? For the most part, the studies reviewed in this chapter have elected to modify children's and adolescents' social skills on one dimension or another. Social skills may be defined as "the ability to interact with others in a given social context in specific ways that are societally acceptable or valued and at the same time personally beneficial, mutually beneficial, or beneficial primarily to others" (Combs & Slaby, 1977, p. 163). For example, investigators have chosen the following social skills for intervention: interpersonal problem-solving skills (Spivack & Shure, 1974), self-control processes (Kendall & Zupan, 1981), the ability to reinforce others (Oden & Asher, 1977), assertiveness (Schinke et al., 1979), communication skills (Ladd, 1981), and listening to and helping others (Durlak, 1977). Do such social skills mediate adjustment for school-aged children and adolescents? Unfortunately, current data do not allow us to reach definite conclusions.

The literature on social skills has increased dramatically in recent years, and writers suggest that social skills may contribute a major amount of the variance in social competence (Combs & Slaby, 1977; Foster & Ritchey, 1979). However, recent reviews have emphasized the four major conceptual and methodological problems in social skills research (Combs & Slaby, 1977; Foster & Ritchey, 1979; Green & Forehand, 1980; Van Hanselt, Hersen, Whitehill, & Bellack, 1979). First, many investigators have offered limited validation for those behaviors used to assess social skills. Often social skills targeted for intervention are chosen on a face-valid basis to suit the preferences or convenience of investigators. As a result, there may be very limited empirical justification for training children and adolescents in those behaviors that lie at the core of the intervention. Second, little attention has been paid to the situational or cultural context of social behaviors: the same behavior can be viewed as "assertive" under some circumstances but "aggressive" under others. Investigators have not always recognized that social skills must be studied in relation to the environment in which such behaviors occur. In fact, as an isolated variable, the concept of social skill has little meaning. Third, teachers, parents, and peers undoubtedly influence the development and expression of social skills, but the nature and extent of these influences remain largely unknown. Fourth, normative data are also lacking for competent behavior at different age levels so that the developmental evolution and progression of social skills are unclear.

In addition to the above problems, from a preventive perspective the two most serious limitations in the current social skills literature involve the causal influence and predictive validity of social skills. Many studies indicate that maladapting and adapting children or adolescents differ in one or more social skills. However, such investigations implicate the role of social skills in adjustment in a correlational, not causal, way. Because a group of maladapting children differs from their well adjusting peers on certain social skills does not imply that these social skills account for the differential adjustment status of these two groups. Changing maladjusting children's social skills may or may not change their adjustment status.

Finally, life history research has suggested a relationship between certain indices of children's early adjustment and their later functioning (Cass & Thomas, 1979). For example, children with good peer relations tend to have few adjustment problems during adolescence and young adulthood, with the converse being true for those with poor peer relations. However, these findings are only correlational in nature. In the absence of clear empirical documentation, we cannot assume that improving children's peer relations will necessarily prevent the appearance of later problems. Accordingly, Green and Forehand (1980, p. 152) have concluded that "at this time there is little reliable valid research evidence from longitudinal or retrospective studies relating childhood social skills difficulties with later adult psychopathology." In summary, prevention-oriented interventions that improve children's and adolescents' social skills have had some positive results, but whether these programs target those skills that are most critical to adjustment for these populations has yet to be convincingly demonstrated.

Long-Term Impact

To be completely successful, preventive programs must first demonstrate that some important negative outcome has been prevented, and then that the effects of intervention are relatively long lasting. Whereas some programs have achieved the former goal, only a few have begun to approach the latter criterion. Therefore, there is a need for more follow-up studies. In particular, competency building programs should include some measures of maladjustment among their outcome measures. By definition, competency building programs attempt to promote mental health, but it is important to know how success at mental health promotion reduces the subsequent appearance of new problems. For example, Poser and Hartman (1979) have observed that the functional relationship between positive behaviors that were increased or enhanced and negative behaviors or problems that were subsequently reduced must be shown before the claim of prevention can be accepted. Otherwise, it is difficult to tell exactly what has been prevented.

Relating Program Features to Outcome

Most of the programs discussed in this chapter have been complex multicomponent interventions (for example, affective education and school-based secondary prevention programs) whose exact mechanisms are unknown. In other words, we do not know what the specific factors are that account for positive results in different programs. Therefore, an important task in future research is to isolate the active ingredients of different interventions. Investigations employing a dismantling treatment strategy can be effective in this regard. A dismantling strategy is the process whereby a complex treatment is broken down into its primary components, each of which is assumed to play a possible role in producing behavior change. Comparisons are then made among groups receiving different components. Group A may receive all three of the primary components of a particular treatment; Group B may receive only two of the three components, and Group C receives only one.

Over time, investigations employing this strategy can successively converge upon the most potent therapeutic factors of an intervention; at the same time, ineffective elements can be identified and eliminated from future program implementations.

Matching Interventions to Individual Needs

As the field of preventive psychology matures, global questions regarding program effectiveness must give way to more sophisticated and refined forms of psychological inquiry. Instead of asking "Does a program work?" it becomes important to determine which preventive interventions in which settings are most effective with different target groups. The situation is analogous to that of psychotherapy, where global assessment of treatment outcome is seen as far less helpful than determination of the specific conditions under which different treatments for different types of problems and clients are most beneficial (Kiesler, 1971). The need for differentiating program impact implies multidimensional assessment of both treatments and program participants. The dismantling treatment strategy discussed earlier, which isolates active treatment ingredients, must be combined with multidimensional assessment of program participants.

For example, the mastery of different life tasks usually requires a combination of behavioral, social, and cognitive abilities. Program participants' status along these dimensions should be assessed prior to program implementation and then related to outcome. It is likely that children within any age group will respond differentially to the same intervention as a function of their specific strengths and limitations. Other factors that would interact to affect program outcome include the environmental settings in which programs are implemented and the type of competency or problem. Even these factors could be expanded upon (that is, take into account participants' sex and racial status and their social and cultural background and milieu). Nevertheless, the point is clear. Attempts to develop the most economical and effective programs will be largely dependent upon exact specification of how preventive interventions should vary to account for children's and adolescents' developmental status, particularly their behavioral deficits and strengths. Some target groups might require an intensive skill building effort, while others may only need a small part of a proposed program.

Peering into the Future

In closing, it might be useful to consider the functions schools might assume in the future and the potential that exists for preventive programs. As is pointed out by Jason, Durlak, and Holton-Walker in Chapter 10, sophisticated technological systems such as computers might increasingly assume teaching functions, particularly in the development of basic academic skills (Banet, 1978). Also, larger chunks of instruction could conceivably occur at home or in neighborhood locations as well as in schools (Gleason, 1981). The exciting consequence of such developments is that the high percentage of school time devoted to instruction in basic academic areas would be greatly reduced, freeing schools to develop other curricula. Prevention-oriented professionals might have influence in developing the alternative curricula. Communication workshops, friendship building seminars, and other programs designed to promote adaptive behavior, coping responses, and creativity may eventually occupy a larger component of classtime. In addition, field work experience and training, with an emphasis on helping and caring for others (such as visiting isolated elderly community residents), could also be a part of a more humanistic, growth-enhancing educational experience. Prevention-oriented professionals can work cooperatively with educators in introducing empirically tested curricula which foster competencies in academic, social, affective, and health areas.

REFERENCES

Allen, G. J., Chinksy, J. M., Larcen, S. W., Lochman, J. E., & Selinger, H. V. *Community psychology and the schools: A behaviorally oriented multilevel preventive approach.* Hillsdale, N.J.: Lawrence Erlbaum Associates, 1976.

Ballard, K. D., & Glynn, T. Behavioral self-management in story writing with elementary school children. *Journal of Applied Behavior Analysis,* 1975, *8,* 387–398.

Banet, B. Computers and early education. *Creative computing,* 1978, *4,* 90–95.

Barrios, B. A., & Shigetomi, C. C. Coping skills training: Potential for prevention of fears and anxieties. *Behavior Therapy,* 1980, *11,* 431–439.

Barton, E. J., & Osborne, J. G. The development of classroom sharing by a teacher using positive practice. *Behavior Modification,* 1978, *2,* 231–250.

Baskin, E. J., & Hess, R. D. Does affective education work? A review of seven programs. *Journal of School Psychology,* 1980, *18,* 40–50.

Bessell, H., & Palomares, U. *Methods in human development: Theory manual and curriculum activity guide.* San Diego: Human Development Training Institute, 1970.

Bien, N. Z., & Bry, B. H. An experimentally designed comparison of four intensities of school-based prevention programs for adolescents with adjustment problems. *Journal of Community Psychology,* 1980, *8,* 110–116.

Bry, B. Reducing the incidence of adolescent problems through preventive intervention: One- and five-year follow-up. *American Journal of Community Psychology,* 1982, *10,* 265–276.

Bry, B. H., & George, F. E. The preventive effects of early intervention on the attendance and grades of urban adolescents. *Professional Psychology,* 1980, *11,* 252–260.

Butler, L., Miezitis, S., Friedman, R., & Cole, E. The effect of two school-based intervention programs on depressive symptoms in preadolescents. *American Educational Research Journal,* 1980, *17,* 111–119.

Camp, B. W., Blom, G. E., Hebert, F., & van Doorninck, W. J. "Think aloud": A program for developing self-control in young aggressive boys. *Journal of Abnormal Child Psychology,* 1977, *5,* 157–169.

Carberry, A. T., & Handal, P. J. The use of the AML scale with a Headstart population: Normative and validation studies. *American Journal of Community Psychology,* 1980, *8,* 353–363.

Cass, L. K., & Thomas, C. B. *Childhood pathology and later adjustment: The question of prediction.* New York: Wiley, 1979.

Combs, M. L., & Slaby, D. A. Social-skills training with children. In B. B. Lahey & A. E. Kazdin (Eds.), *Advances in clinical child psychology* (Vol. 1). New York: Plenum, 1977.

Conger, J. C., & Keane, S. P. Social skills intervention in the treatment of isolated or withdrawn children. *Psychological Bulletin,* 1981, *90,* 478–495.

Cowen, E. L., Davidson, E. R., & Gesten, E. L. Program dissemination and the modification of delivery practices in school mental health. *Professional Psychology,* 1980, *11,* 36–47.

Cowen, E. L., Dorr, D., Clarfield, S. P., Kreling, B., McWillaims, S. A., Pokracki, F., Pratt, D. M., Terrell, D. L., & Wilson, A. B. The AML: A quick screening device for early identification of school maladaptation. *American Journal of Community Psychology,* 1973, *1,* 12–35.

Cowen, E. L., Gesten, E. L., & Wilson, A. B. The Primary Mental Health Project (PMHP): Evaluation of current program effectiveness. *American Journal of Community Psychology,* 1979, *7,* 293–303.

Cowen, E. L., Trost, M. A., Dorr, D. A., Lorion, R. P., Izzo, L. D., & Isaacson, R. V. *New ways in school mental health: Early detection and prevention of school maladaptation.* New York: Human Sciences Press, 1975.

Cradock, C., Cotler, S., & Jason, L. A. Primary prevention: Immunization of children for speech anxiety. *Cognitive Therapy and Research,* 1978, *2,* 389–396.

Dinkmeyer, D. *Developing understanding of self and others.* Circle Pines, MN: American Guidance Service, 1970.

Dorr, D., Stephens, J., Pozner, R., & Klodt, W. Use of the AML scale to identify adjustment problems in fourth, fifth, and sixth grade children. *American Journal of Community Psychology,* 1980, *8,* 341–352.

Durlak, J. A. Description and evaluation of a behaviorally oriented school-based preventive mental health program. *Journal of Consulting and Clinical Psychology,* 1977, *45,* 27–33.

Durlak, J. A. Comparative effectiveness of behavioral and relationship group treatment in the secondary prevention of school maladjustment. *American Journal of Community Psychology,* 1980, *8,* 327–339.

Durlak, J. A. Providing mental health services to elementary school children. In C. E. Walker & M. C. Roberts (Eds.), *Handbook of clinical child psychology.* New York: Wiley-Interscience, 1983. (a)

Durlak, J. A. Social problem-solving as a primary prevention strategy. In R. D. Felner, L. A. Jason, J. Mortisugu, & S. S. Farber (Eds.), *Preventive psychology: Theory, research and practice.* New York: Pergamon, 1983. (b)

Durlak, J. A., Stein, M. A., & Mannarino, A. P. Behavioral validity of a brief teacher rating scale (the AML) in identifying high risk acting-out school children. *American Journal of Community Psychology,* 1980, *8,* 101–115.

Elardo, P. T., & Elardo, R. A critical analysis of social development programs in elementary education. *Journal of School Psychology,* 1976, *14,* 118–130.

Eysenck, H. J., & Rachman, S. *The causes and cures of neurosis.* San Diego: Knapp, 1965.

Foster, S. L., & Ritchey, W. L. Issues in the assessment of social competence in children. *Journal of Applied Behavior Analysis,* 1979, *12,* 635–638.

Gelfand, D. M., Jenson, W. R., & Drew, C. J. *Understanding child behavior disorders.* New York: Holt, Rinehart & Winston, 1982.

Gillespie, J. F., Durlak, J. A., & Sherman, D. Relationship between kindergarten children's interpersonal problem-solving skills and other indices of school adjustment: A cautionary note. *American Journal of Community Psychology,* 1982, *10,* 149–153.

Glasser, W. *Schools without failure.* New York: Harper and Row, 1969.

Gleason, G. T. Microcomputers in education: The state of the art. *Educational Technology,* 1981, *21,* 7–18.

Glidewell, J. C., Gildea, M. C. L., & Kaufman, M. K. The preventive and therapeutic effects of two school mental health programs. *American Journal of Community Psychology,* 1973, *1,* 295–329.

Glynn, E. L., Thomas, J. D., & Shee, S. M. Behavioral self-control of on-task behavior in an elementary classroom. *Journal of Applied Behavior Analysis,* 1973, *6,* 105–113.

Gordon, T. *P.E.T. in action.* New York: Wyden Books, 1976.

Green, K. D., & Forehand, R. Assessment of children's social skills: A review of methods. *Journal of Behavioral Assessment,* 1980, *2,* 143–159.

Hartman, L. M. The preventive reduction of psychological risk in asymptomatic adolescents. *American Journal of Orthopsychiatry,* 1979, *49,* 121–135.

Haynes, L. A., & Avery, A. W. Training adolescents in self-disclosure and empathy skills. *Journal of Counseling Psychology,* 1979, *26,* 526–530.

Kendall, P. C. Cognitive-behavioral interventions with children. In B. B. Lahey & A. E. Kazdin (Eds.), *Advances in clinical child psychology* (Vol. 4). New York: Plenum, 1981.

Kendall, P. C. Individual versus group cognitive-behavioral self-control training: 1-year follow-up. *Behavior Therapy,* 1982, *13,* 241–247.

Kendall, P. C., & Zupan, B. A. Individual versus group application of cognitive-behavioral self-control procedures with children. *Behavior Therapy,* 1981, *12,* 344–359.

Kiesler, D. J. Experimental designs in psychotherapy research. In A. E. Bergin & S. L. Garfield (Eds.), *Handbook of psychotherapy and behavior change.* New York: Wiley, 1971.

Kirschenbaum, D. S. Social competence intervention and evaluation in the inner city: Cincinnati's Social Skills Development Program. *Journal of Consulting and Clinical Psychology,* 1979, *47,* 778–780.

Kirschenbaum, D. S. Toward more behavioral early intervention programs: A rationale. *Professional Psychology,* 1983, *14,* 159–169.

Kirschenbaum, D. S., Marsh, M. E., & DeVoge, J. B. The effectiveness of a mass screening procedure in an early intervention program. *Psychology in the Schools,* 1977, *14,* 400–406.

Ladd, G. W. Effectiveness of a school learning method for enhancing children's social interaction and peer acceptance. *Child Development,* 1981, *52,* 171–178.

Lorion, R. P., Caldwell, R. A., & Cowen, E. L. Effects of a school mental health project: A one-year follow-up. *Journal of School Psychology,* 1976, *14,* 56–63.

Maher, C.A., & Barbrack, C.R. Preventing high school maladjustment: Effectiveness of professional and cross-age behavioral group counseling. *Behavior Therapy,* 1982, *13,* 259–270.

Mannarino, A. P., & Durlak, J. A. Implementation and evaluation of service programs in community settings. *Professional Psychology,* 1980, *11,* 220–227.

Mannarino, A. P., Durlak, J. A., Christy, M., & Magnussen, M. G. Evaluation of social competence training in the schools. *Journal of School Psychology,* 1982, *20,* 11–19.

McClure, L. F., Chinsky, J. M., & Larcen, S. W. Enhancing social problem-solving performance in an elementary school setting. *Journal of Educational Psychology,* 1978, *70,* 504–513.

Medway, F. J., & Smith, R. C. Jr. An examination of contemporary elementary school affective education programs. *Psychology in the Schools,* 1978, *15,* 260–269.

Miller, N., & Kassinove, H. Effects of lecture, rehearsal, written homework, and IQ on the efficacy of a rational emotive school mental health program. *Journal of Community Psychology,* 1978, *6,* 366–373.

Oden, S., & Asher, S. R. Coaching children in social skills for friendship making. *Child Development,* 1977, *48,* 495–506.

Ojemann, R. H. The human relations program at the State University of Iowa. *Personnel and Guidance Journal,* 1958, *37,* 199–206.

Ojemann, R. H., Levitt, E. E., Lyle, W. H., & Whiteside, M. F. The effects of a "causal" teacher-training program and certain curricular changes on grade school children. *Journal of Experimental Education,* 1955, *24,* 95–114.

O'Leary, S. G., & Dubey, D. R. Application of self-control procedures by children: A review. *Journal of Applied Behavior Analysis,* 1979, *12,* 449–465.

Poser, E. G., & Hartman, L. M. Issues in behavioral prevention: Empirical findings. *Advances in Behavior Research and Therapy,* 1979, *2,* 1–25.

Press, S., Alvarez, J., Cotler, S., & Jason, L. A. Developing a problem-solving program in an elementary school setting. *Education,* in press.

Rickel, A. U., & Burgio, J. C. Assessing social competencies in lower income preschool children. *American Journal of Community Psychology*, 1982, *10*, 635–645.

Rickel, A. U., Smith, R. L., & Sharp, K. C. Description and evaluation of a preventive mental health program for preschoolers. *Journal of Abnormal Child Psychology*, 1979, *7*, 101–112.

Rogeness, G. A., Stokes, J. P., Bednar, R. A., & Gorman, B. L. School intervention program to increase behaviors and attitudes that promote learning. *Journal of Community Psychology*, 1977, *5*, 246–256.

Rosenbaum, M. S., & Drabman, R. S. Self-control training in the classroom: A review and critique. *Journal of Applied Behavior Analysis*, 1978, *12*, 467–485.

Sandler, I. N., Duricko, A., & Grande, L. Effectiveness of an early secondary prevention program in an inner-city elementary school. *American Journal of Community Psychology*, 1975, *3*, 23–32.

Sagotsky, G., Wood-Schneider, M., & Konop, M. Learning to cooperate: Effects of modeling and direct instruction. *Child Development*, 1981, *52*, 1037–1042.

Sarason, I. G., & Sarason, B. R. Teaching cognitive and social skills to high school students. *Journal of Consulting and Clinical Psychology*, 1981, *49*, 908–918.

Schinke, S. P., Blythe, B. J., & Gilchrist, L. D. Cognitive-behavioral prevention of adolescent pregnancy. *Journal of Counseling Psychology*, 1981, *28*, 451–454.

Schinke, S. P., Blythe, B. J., Gilchrist, L. D., & Burt, G. A. Primary prevention of adolescent pregnancy. *Social Work with Groups*, 1981, *4*, 121–135.

Schinke, S. P., Gilchrist, L. D., & Blythe, B. J. Role of communication in the prevention of teenage pregnancy. *Health and Social Work*, 1980, *5*, 54–59.

Schinke, S. P., Gilchrist, L. D., & Small, R. W. Preventing unwanted adolescent pregnancy: A cognitive-behavioral approach. *American Journal of Orthopsychiatry*, 1979, *49*, 81–88.

Shure, M. B., & Spivack, G. *Problem-solving techniques in child rearing*. San Francisco: Jossey-Bass, 1978.

Shure, M. B., & Spivack, G. Interpersonal cognitive problem-solving and primary prevention: Programming for preschool and kindergarten children. *Journal of Clinical Child Psychology*, 1979, *8*, 89–94.

Shure, M. B., & Spivack, G. Interpersonal problem-solving in young children: A cognitive approach to prevention. *American Journal of Community Psychology*, 1982, *10*, 341–356.

Spivack, G., Platt, J. J., & Shure, M. B. *The problem-solving approach to adjustment*. San Francisco: Jossey-Bass, 1976.

Spivack, G., & Shure, M. B. *Social adjustment of young children: A cognitive approach to solving real-life problems*. San Francisco: Jossey–Bass, 1974.

Tefft, B. M., & Kloba, J. A. Underachieving high school students as mental health aides with maladapting primary-grade children. *American Journal of Community Psychology*, 1981, *9*, 303–319.

Thomson-Rountree, P., & Musun-Baskett, L. A further examination of Project Aware: The relationship between teaching behaviors and changes in student behavior. *Journal of Social Psychology*, 1981, *19*, 260–266.

Tietze, C. Teenage pregnancies: Looking ahead to 1984. *Family Planning Perspectives*, 1978, *10*, 205–207.

Van Hasselt, V. B., Hersen, M., Whitehill, M. B., & Bellack, A. S. Social skill assessment and training for children: An evaluative review. *Behavior Research and Therapy,* 1979, *17,* 413–437.

Vogelsong, E. L. Relationship enhancement training for children. *Elementary School Guidance and Counseling,* 1978, *12,* 272–279.

Walker, H. M., Greenwood, C. R., Hops, H., & Todd, N. M. Differential effects of reinforcing topographical components of social interaction. *Behavior Modification,* 1979, *3,* 291–321.

Wanlass, R. L., & Prinz, R. J. Methodological issues in conceptualizing and treating childhood social isolation. *Psychological Bulletin,* 1982, *92,* 39–55.

Weinrott, M. R., Corson, J. A., & Wilchesky, M. Teacher-mediated treatment of social withdrawal. *Behavior Therapy,* 1979, *10,* 281–294.

Weissberg, R. P., Gesten, E. L., Carnike, C. L., Toro, P. A., Rapkin, B. D., Davidson, E., & Cowen, E. L. Social problem-solving skills training: A competence-building intervention with 2nd–4th grade children. *American Journal of Community Psychology,* 1981, *9,* 411–423.

Weissberg, R. P., Gesten, E. L., Rapkin, B. D., Cowen, E. L., Davidson, E., de Apodaca, R. F., & McKim, B. J. The evaluation of a social problem-solving training program for suburban and inner-city third grade children. *Journal of Consulting and Clinical Psychology,* 1981, *49,* 251–261.

REFERENCE NOTES

1. Butler, L. J. *The relationship between interpersonal problem-solving skills and peer relations and behavior.* Paper presented at the meeting of the Canadian Psychological Association, June, 1978.
2. Cowen, E. L., Spinell, A., Wright, S., & Weissberg, R. P. *Continuing dissemination of a school-based mental health program.* Manuscript submitted for publication, 1982.
3. Durlak, J. A., & Mannarino, A. P. *Behavioral versus relationship treatment in the secondary prevention of school maladjustment.* Manuscript submitted for publication, 1982.
4. Durlak, J. A., & Gillespie, J. F. *Assessing the applied significance of treatment effects in a school-based preventive mental health program.* Paper presented at the meeting of the Midwestern Psychological Association, Minneapolis, May 1982.
5. Gillespie, J. F., & Durlak, J. A. *Screening children at risk for school maladjustment.* Paper presented at the meeting of the Midwestern Psychological Association, Minneapolis, May 1982.
6. Rickel, A. U., & Dyhdalo, L. L. *Secondary preventive interventions with preschool children: A follow-up study.* Paper presented at the Midwestern Psychological Association, Detroit, May, 1981.

CHAPTER 5

Vulnerability in Childhood

A Preventive Framework for Understanding Children's Efforts to Cope with Life Stress and Transitions

ROBERT D. FELNER

Prevention has increasingly been accorded a position of central importance in mental health. As a heuristic, it has helped to spur the exploration of factors relating to optimal growth and development and identify hazards to such development. As a model for intervention, taking a preventive stance in dealing with emotional dysfunction has received increasing support while dissatisfaction with more traditional approaches has grown (Felner, Jason, Moritsugu, & Farber, 1983). Unfortunately, while the idea of preventive intervention has been embraced, the lack of a well-established generative knowledge base to guide such efforts has impeded the effective development of such efforts (Price, 1983). With increased recognition of this knowledge gap has come intensified efforts to alleviate it. Felner, Jason, Moritsugu, and Farber (1983) have identified a number of lines of inquiry, developed to serve as focal points for prevention research, which form solid foundations for preventive interventions. Investigations of social networks and support systems, social environments, and the component skills of social competence are all well into their second and third "generations" and offer much to the prevention specialist. Assuredly, each of these somewhat distinct lines of investigation has unique contributions to make toward furthering the effective development of preventive interventions. On a broader level, they share a common focus as well. They each contribute to the resolution of the quintessential prevention concern; that is, the elaboration of those conditions and circumstances which influence the degree of vulnerability of an individual or population to the development of disorder.

Organizing frameworks for prevention research and programs which derive most directly from this concern with differential vulnerability are those which view the times at which individuals experience significant life events as being critical points in their development. This chapter evaluates the current status of work in the area of life events and transitions as it relates to children (including toddlers through adolescents)—groups for whom preventive efforts may be particularly appropriate (Cowen, 1980; Felner, Jason, Moritsugu, & Farber, 1983). The first section elaborates on the theoretical models of life events and life change, particularly as they define the relevance of such occurrences for preventive efforts with children. Next, against this backdrop, representative empirical literature on the association between life events and transitions and the adaptation of children is presented and current preventive efforts are discussed. Of particular concern will be the further refinement of theoretical models of life events and changes which facilitate understanding of such experiences in ways that are compatible with prevention's goals. Attention is paid to both the effects of life change events and to factors which mediate the relative vulnerability of these children following such events. Of primary concern is the development of a more coherent model for understanding and reducing vulnerability while also allowing for developmental enhancement. Finally, current conceptual models of life events are evaluated for their utility for guiding further research and the design of preventive interventions.

MODELS OF LIFE EVENTS AND LIFE CHANGE

For prevention, particularly with children, there are aspects of the experience of life events and change which make these events critical to future development; hence, they are very appealing as organizing foci for intervention efforts. A number of arguments have been advanced to substantiate this position. Generally, three perspectives on life events have been most influential in focusing and shaping prevention's concerns with life events. These three views emphasize, respectively, (1) the crises which may accompany the experience of significant events, (2) the stress and pathogenic outcomes which may result, and (3) the changes that life events may precipitate in the lives of individuals.

Crisis Theory

The first model is based heavily in crisis theory (Caplan, 1964). Essentially, crisis theory views the normal state of the organism to be one of homeostatic balance. Crises are seen as events which create demands on individuals which cannot be met through their normal and available coping resources (Murphy, 1961). This ''overload'' throws the organismic system into a state of flux which opens the system to rapid change. Caplan (1964) has emphasized this ''temporal'' quality of crisis. That is, crises may have a telescoping effect on development, with significant changes in adaptation and coping styles occurring in a relatively short time period which may have important long-term consequences. In this same vein, Lindemann (1956) and others (Caplan, 1961; Felner, Stolberg, & Cowen, 1975; Morley, Note 1; Stein, 1970) note that crises may be either adaptively or maladaptively resolved with either outcome having important consequences for the resolution of future crises as well as for more general adaptive functioning. Individuals who effectively cope with crises are thought to further build and strengthen their adaptive resources, while ineffective coping efforts may predispose the individual to enduring maladjustment.

Stress and Life Events

A second perspective on life events which is drawn upon to guide preventive efforts views such events as significant sources of social and environmental stress. A key set of assumptions underlying this position is that changes in the lives of individuals associated with such events engender heightened levels of psychosocial stress. This stress, in turn, is seen to be an important etiological factor in physical and psychological disorder and distress (Dohrenwend, 1979; Dohrenwend, 1978; Sandler, 1979). Studies of the association between stressful life events and disorder have been characterized by two primary approaches. The first of these is concerned not with particular discrete life events but rather with the cumulative stress and consequent dysfunction resulting from the experience of a number of life events within a relatively short period of time (generally one to two years). The second approach is concerned with particular, single life events which, in themselves, may confront the individual with adaptive challenges of such magnitude that they may be significant sources of stress.

Many of the recent studies of the association between cumulative stress life events and disorder stem from the work of Holmes and Rahe (1967). A primary goal of this work, and one which has been relatively unquestioned as a central aspect of subsequent studies, was to identify antecedents or precipitants of disease onset (Holmes, 1979). Moreover, Holmes and Rahe's work has served to establish a methodological paradigm which has, with some modification, been employed in subsequent studies. Typically, work of this type has been characterized by efforts to develop scales on which "stress," "readjustment," or "change unit" weightings are assigned to life events. The amount of stress a child or adult is said to be experiencing is computed by summing the weightings assigned to those events as they occurred within a specified time period. For adults, events included on such scales range from death of a spouse to minor traffic violations, while for children scale items may range from parent death or divorce to residential relocation and arguments with parents (Coddington, 1972a; Holmes & Rahe, 1967).

The development of these instruments for both children and adults has been carefully reviewed elsewhere and general methodological problems in the use of such scales to clarify the association between cumulative life events and dysfunction have been extensively discussed (Dohrenwend & Pearlin, 1981; Felner, Farber, & Primavera, 1983; Johnson, 1982; Sandler, 1979). Later in this chapter representative work in this area will, however, be considered as it relates specifically to helping or hindering effforts to better understand the essential qualities of life events that are important for preventive efforts aimed at enhancing or maintaining children's adjustment.

A number of authors have offered models for understanding the adaptive consequences of discrete stressful life events in ways that may be relevant for prevention

(Bloom, 1979, Dohrenwend, 1978; Felner, Farber, & Primavera, 1980). Much of this work builds on a model offered by Dohrenwend (1978), which includes several key elements. Life events which are of particular concern for prevention are those which are frequently associated with heightened levels of psychosocial stress and consequent psychopathology. The immediate stress reaction following the event is the central focus of the adaptive process examined in this model. The model recognizes that not all events are equally stressful and dysfunction-producing for those who experience them, and hypothesizes personal, psychological and environmental variables present during and immediately following the event as mediators of these differential outcomes. Personal and psychological mediators include the individual's age, sex, emotional and cognitive maturity, success in coping with similar prior experiences, coping abilities and their social competencies (Dohrenwend, 1978; Felner et al., 1980; Felner, Farber, & Primavera, 1983; Turk, 1979). Situational mediators encompass such elements of the individuals' meaningful environment as their social supports and social networks, economic resources, and the presence of other environmental stressors.

Limitations of Life Crisis and Life Stress Models for Primary Prevention

Felner and his colleagues (Felner, Farber, & Primavera, 1983) have examined the adequacy of the preceding stressful life events frameworks for explicating the links between critical life events and adjustment, particularly those used for primary prevention development. They argue that although this work may be important for prevention on both heuristic and practical grounds, the conceptualization and methodology may also have had unintended adverse consequences on the development of frameworks better suited to guide primary prevention programs for individuals experiencing critical events. On the positive side, Felner, Farber, and Primavera (1983) note that prior work has contributed to our ability to identify individuals who are at risk for the development of disorder before such difficulties are observed. In this way such information may aid in the shaping of "before the fact" programs, a central focus of primary prevention. Toward this end, for example, such work may provide mental health professionals who were trained in more reactive rather than proactive service delivery models with acceptable and clear indicators of the need for preventive programs (Felner & Aber, 1983).

A second key contribution of research on life events is its elaboration of the important role of psychological and situational mediators in exacerbating or reducing the potential adverse consequences of stress associated with such events. The identification of salient mediators is important for further refinement of procedures to predict and assess the level of risk of individuals or populations. Further, knowledge of such mediators may facilitate the design of prevention programs by enabling professionals to address deficits in individuals and their environments which affect their relative vulnerability (Felner, Farber, & Primavera, 1983).

These contributions notwithstanding, prior work on life crises and stressful life events is, in other ways, problematic for prevention. With few exceptions, studies of stressful life events have been primarily concerned with the potential pathogenic consequences of such events (Bloom, 1979; Dohrenwend, 1978; Holmes, 1979; Johnson, 1982; Sandler, 1979). As a result of this emphasis, the focus of such work has been primarily on negative events. Increasingly overlooked by those working from a life stress perspective have been both the adaptive significance of positive events as well as the potential of life events and changes to facilitate the development of adaptive strengths and coping skills. This state of affairs is one which does not adequately reflect primary prevention's concerns with enhancement and mastery (Felner, Jason, Moritsugu, & Farber, 1983). The implications of this issue for the targeting and design of prevention efforts are considerable. If our concern is primarily with psychopathology, then the death of a parent, being expelled from school, or a serious injury or illness may be more salient events than more predictable, and supposedly positive, events (such as school promotion or graduation). However, if prevention's focus is broadened to include the full range of potential adaptive outcomes, then positive events may be of equal salience. Although studies of life events have not found consistent associations between positive events and adaptive outcome, there is no doubt that the way in which an individual or family masters the adaptive challenges posed by such positive events as marriage, birth of a child, or receiving a desired promotion, can have important implications for their well-being, life satisfaction, and happiness (Felner, Farber, & Primavera, 1983). If primary prevention is concerned with the enhancement of functioning and the reduction of vulnerability, it seems clear that preventive efforts focused on life events need to develop a perspective which better attends to the potential for positive growth that may be associated with life events. This concern was a key element underlying the initial focus of attention on life crises, and it needs to be resurrected from the secondary status to which it has been relegated in more recent work on life events.

A related issue is the almost synonymous use of the terms *stress* and *life change* that has characterized prior work. A fundamental assumption of this position is that life events lead to stress because the organism is relatively intolerant of change (Pearlin, Menaghan, Lieberman, & Mullen, 1981). The work of Holmes and Rahe (1967) reflects this assumption clearly in its use of *life change units* to define the degree of stress an individual experiences. Indeed, Uhlenhuth (1979) argues that the greatest contribution of the work of Holmes and Rahe is its operationalization of stress in everyday life as the demand for social readjustment that is placed on the person by events.

It is perhaps ironic that the initial goal of Holmes and Rahe was quantification of life change (Holmes, 1979), as the research which has derived from their work has been increasingly concerned with stress at the expense of changes which may accompany life events. This may, in part, be accounted for by the aforementioned emphasis on dysfunction. Given such an emphasis, the stressful, pathogenic properties of life events became an overriding concern. Additional factors which have shifted the focus from change to stress have been: (1) the emphasis of stressful life events models on the event per se, and (2) the structure of life events inventories themselves. For example, in Dohrenwend's (1978) framework the focus is on the event as subjectively defined by the individual and the immediate context in which it occurs. Ignored by this framework is the period which follows the event, the changes the individual confronts during this period, and the process by which the adaptive outcome is shaped. Similarly, life events inventories as constructed tend to suggest that all of the events included are similar in some overriding fashion. Felner, Farber, and Primavera (1983) argue that, if our concern is primarily with the stressfulness of such experiences, this assumption may be justified. However, they note that the inventories may be less successful in elaborating the adaptive challenges the events pose for individuals. Illustratively, a statement by Holmes (1979) nicely demonstrates the way in which life event inventories which seek to quantify, on a similar metric, "events" which have highly disparate long-term consequences for the individual. Based on life change unit weights assigned by raters to items on the Social Readjustment Rating Scale, Holmes concludes "that essentially, worldwide, death of a spouse requires twice as much change and adjustment as marriage and 10 times as much as a traffic ticket" (Holmes, 1979, p. 47).

Certainly while in some rare instances receiving 10 traffic tickets may require as much long-term change in an individual's life as would the death of his or her spouse, were this the general case it would be a sad commentary on marital relationships. Approaching this statement from a primary concern with phenomenological, immediate stress, it becomes somewhat less absurd and perhaps more defensable. Whatever the case, this illustration should help to illuminate how the life event scales and models discussed to this point may not adequately deal with process of adaptation engendered by at least some of the critical experiences on which they focus.

A Life Transitions Perspective

A model for viewing life events which may more adequately reflect the full range of prevention's goals, as well as facilitate the development of a better understanding of the adaptive process required by at least some of these events, has been suggested by Felner, Farber and Primavera (1980, 1983). They note that among the events considered by life stress researchers some are limited both temporally and in the repercussions they engender in people's lives. Hence, they are "true" events. Other events, however, are generally markers or precipitants of major changes in an individual's life, which may lead to further stress and changes and require additional adaptive effort. It is argued that, for the latter events, a preventive focus would be better served by a framework which considers the entire transitional period of the individual adapting to the changes he or she is experiencing, rather than viewing occurrences such as divorce and death of a parent as unitary events.

Another element of this expanded Life Transitions model (Felner, Farber, & Primavera, 1980, 1983) relates to turning from a primary focus on stress and its pathogenic consequences to the nature of the changes which characterize such transitions and the process of adapting to them. Felner, Farber, and Primavera (1983) state: "the stress involved in adapting to these changes is but one element of a larger process which includes mastery of the range of adaptive task engendered by the life transition" (p. 207). This shift in focus offers several advantages for prevention.

First, it legitimizes an equal emphasis on positive life changes. It may be hypothesized that such occurrences, although of potential critical importance for adaptive functioning, may have any negative adaptive impact (associated with failure to adequately master them) ''masked'' or obscured by the closer temporal association of subsequent negative events with such outcomes. What needs to be recognized more clearly is that these latter negative events themselves may result from a failure to adequately master and adapt to the initial positive life changes. Thus, for example, there may seem to be a heightened incidence of dysfunction associated with divorce. From a preventive standpoint, however, this association may be somewhat misleading for determining where and when intervention should occur as well as for understanding the importance of adjustment to marriage. Although the divorce may be stressful for the individuals involved, both the dysfunction associated with it and the divorce itself may be the result of the individuals' failure to adequately master the adaptive challenges of such positive events as the planned birth of a child or even the marriage itself. It should also be noted that from a perspective which focuses on the mastering of life change, it becomes readily apparent that congruent with early crises theory, the divorce and the changes associated with it may provide an opportunity to reverse maladaptive patterns of interacting and lead to the eventual reduction of what may have been chronically high levels of stress in the lives of parents and children which were present prior to the divorce. As will be seen in the following section, recent data are increasingly demonstrating that such a sequence of events is typical. Thus, it is important to remember that, at least from an adaptive/developmental enhancement perspective, some negative events may actually be positive life changes.

A concern with positive as well as negative events may be useful for the prevention of dysfunction, which results from failure to master the adaptive challenges presented by positive events. Such concern may also lead to facilitation of successful adaptation to such events and thus serve to enhance the quality of life for individuals, aid in the development of competencies, and decrease vulnerability to dysfunction in the face of other stressors. For example, recent literature on quality of life and social support (Campbell, Converse, & Rogers, 1976; Gottlieb, 1981) clearly shows that individuals whose marriages are stable and mutually satisfying are generally happier and more satisfied with their lives, as well as better able to deal with stress than those who have less satisfactory relationships.

If there is a shift in focus to include adaptive change, rather than merely the reduction or containment of stress, then preventive psychologists are confronted with the need to: (1) define the nature of the changes which must be dealt with, particularly those which are common to most life transitions and, hence, may be defining features of them, and (2) elaborate those factors which influence adaptation and mastery of these changes. Against the backdrop of these frameworks for life events, the following sections address these concerns as they relate to children and adolescents. Specifically, drawing on representative empirical literature on the salience of life events and transitions for the adaptation of children, the adequacy of our current knowledge base to guide prevention programs for children experiencing such events is elaborated. Following this discussion, the utility of frameworks for understanding life events will be considered and suggestions offered for further refinement of an integrated framework to guide future work.

CUMULATIVE LIFE EVENTS AND LIFE CHANGE IN CHILDHOOD AND ADOLESCENCE

Johnson (1982) points out that much of the existing life stress research has been carried out with adult populations. As a consequence more is known about the relation of life events to adult physical and emotional problems than about similar associations for children or adolescents. A similar state of affairs exists pertaining to our understanding of the coping process and moderator variables. This is not to say, however, that a knowledge base to guide the understanding of life stress and change in children and adolescents is not rapidly developing.

Children's Life Events Scales

The relationship between cumulative life changes or stresses and adaptation in children has recently received increased attention (Johnson, 1982). Pioneer work in this area was carried out by Coddington (1972a), who developed separate Social Readjustment Rating Questionnaires for children and adolescents in different age groups (preschool, 6–11, 12–16, and 16 and above). Drawing from the literature on child development, a number of events that were judged to be frequently experienced by children and adolescents in each age group were identified. Events were initially rated by pediatricians, teachers, and mental health workers for the degree of readjustment each event would require of a child in a particular age group. In keeping with similar adult work (compare Holmes & Rahe, 1967), raters were asked to compare each event against a standard "anchoring" one, in this case birth of a brother or sister, as the standard arbitrary value of 500 life change units. After comparison ratings were completed, mean weighting values were obtained for each event. By simply summing the weighted life change units associated with those events experienced by the child over a specific time period, the amount of social-psychological readjustment required of the child was determined. Life events included on Coddington's scales encompassed such events as outstanding personal accomplishment, death of a parent, serious illness requiring hospitalization, suspension from school, and not mastering an extracurricular activity. In a follow-up, Coddington (1972b) administered the scales to a sample of more than 3,500 children whose ages ranged across the target groups. This work provided normative data for various age groups while allowing the observation of developmental shifts in life changes experienced by children. Of particular interest are the findings that overall there was a strong positive relation between age and the amount of life change experienced.

Following up on this work, Monaghan, Robinson, and Dodge (1979) sought to develop a British Life Events Inventory for Children and attempted to further refine scoring procedures and items included on such scales. Focusing only on children ages 6–11, they followed procedures similar to those employed by Coddington (1972a). Two items from the original scale were excluded: becoming involved with drugs or alcohol and having a visible congenital deformity. In the former case, the authors justified its removal by arguing that it is quite rare for this age group. As to the latter, they argued that it cannot be strictly classified as an event. Further, three items thought by the authors to be indicative of significant change in the lives of children were added: moving to a new house and increase or decrease in the number of arguments with brothers and sisters. High levels of agreement on ratings were found between the three groups of raters (pediatricians, mental health workers, and teachers) as well as with the scores reported by Coddington's American raters (Monaghan et al., 1979).

Cumulative Life Events and Accidents or Illness

Studies with these life event scales and similar ones have found significant associations between the experience of life events in the recent past (generally the previous two years is the period of focus) and a wide array of psychological and physical disorders in children. In one study Padilla, Rohsenow, and Bergman (1976) found that seventh grade boys with high life change scores experienced more accidents over a five month period than those with low life change scores. Similarly, Heisel, Ream, Raiz, Rappaport, and Coddington (1973) found that children who were displaying a range of physical health problems had significantly high life stress scores compared to the normal children on Coddington's (1972a) scale. In an early study, Meyer and Haggerty (1962) found that, for children where there were documented streptococcal infections or clinically identifiable upper respiratory problems, there was a marked increase in the number of stressful events they had experienced in the preceding two weeks. The severity and duration of respiratory illnesses displayed by preschool children have also been found to positively relate to the life stress levels experienced (Boyce, Jensen, Cassell, Collier, Smith, & Raimey, 1973). At the level of more serious illness, Jacob and Charles (1980) found that children with cancer had in the year prior to onset experienced significantly more life change than control subjects. Additional work on the association between life stress and physical health problems in childhood has demonstrated links to the course and onset of chronic illness (Bradley, 1979; Bedell, Giordani, Amour, Tavormina, & Boll, 1977; Grant, Kyle, Teichman, & Mendels, 1974), as well as to more general health states (Hotaling, Atwell, & Linsky, 1978).

Limitations of Cumulative Life Events Scales for Children and Adolescents and Moderators of Outcome

Despite the general consistent findings linking life events and physical disease in childhood, there is some disagreement about the degree of strength of this relationship. Johnson (1982), after reviewing many of the above studies, as well as others, argued that there seems to be reasonable ground for suggesting that such a relationship exists. Rutter (1981) argues, however, that findings to date provide only modest and equivocal support for this view. A closer look at the strength of the association between cumulative life stress and psychological adjustment in childhood might resolve these differences of agreement. Although the results of prior work are generally consistent, they are still modest at best (for example, Barrera, 1981; Douglas, 1973; Gersten, Langner, Eisenberg, & Simcha-Fagan, 1977; Heisel et al., 1973; Hotaling et al., 1978; Sandler & Block, 1979; Siegel, Note 1). Indeed, across both child and adult samples the absolute magnitude of correlations between life stress and dysfunction generally falls in the .30 range (Dohrenwend, 1979; Rabkin & Streuning, 1976).

Several limitations of life change scales in general, and for children in particular, have recently been identified which may help us understand these findings. Johnson (1982) has pointed to several factors which he feels may help clarify the relationship between cumulative life change and physical or emotional difficulties in children. He argues that a principal difficulty with prior work is its failure to adequately attend to differences in the adaptive significance of positive and negative life events. While much prior work views both types of life change as stressful to the individual, Johnson (1982) argues that it is perhaps more appropriate to conceptualize life stress in terms of undesirable events and changes, rather than in terms which view both desirable and undesirable changes as of equal importance.

The use of mean stress weightings for items, derived from other raters rather than the children themselves, is also seen as problematic. For example, the stressfulness of events may vary as a function of the experiencing child's cognitive appraisal (Rutter, 1981). Hence, the use of ratings provided by others on the stressfulness of an event may be misleading. Further, not only may the ratings of the event's stressfulness be unrepresentative of the child's experiences, but the events included on the scales may be similarly unrepresentative. It is argued that we should obtain information from the child as to the events they actually experience as stressful, rather than depending solely on prior literature or clinical experience for the identification of potential stressors (Johnson, 1982).

With these concerns in mind, Johnson and McCutcheon (1980) developed the Life Events Checklist for use with older children and adolescents. The scale includes a list of 46 events plus four blank spaces for reporting events not listed but which have been experienced by the child. Items were selected after: (1) an examination of previous literature, and (2) open-ended surveys with 44 black and white adolescents were carried out. This scale calls for several responses. First, respondents are asked to indicate whether or not an event has occurred in the previous year. In contrast to prior scales where such an indication would result in the assignment of a predetermined stress/change score, on this instrument the respondents are further asked to indicate whether they view the event as desirable or undesirable and, to also indicate on a four point scale the degree of impact they feel the event had on their life. Hence, for each respondent, separate positive and negative life change scores may be derived in addition to a total life change score.

The potential utility of this scale for predicting maladjustment resulting from life change has been demonstrated in several studies. Gad and Johnson (1980) found, with an adolescent population, that negative life change scores were significantly associated with a range of indices of physical, personal and school adjustment problems. By contrast, positive change scores were only found to relate to fewer visits to physicians' offices and less so to the level of personal problems reported. With a second adolescent sample, Johnson and McCutcheon (1980) examined the differential association of positive and negative life changes to dysfunction. Although significant correlations between undesirable event scores and depression, anxiety, emotional maladjustment, and external locus of control were found, desirable event scores were only found to be related to greater internal locus of control scores.

Sandler and his colleagues have also attempted to elaborate conditions which may moderate the effects of life events on children. In one study, Sandler and Ramsey (1980) sought to identify the qualitative properties of life events that related to children's adjustment problems. A sample of 12 clinical child psychologists was employed to rate 32 life events on how stressful they might be for a child, as well as the similarity of the events to each other. Usable ratings were obtained from nine judges, and factor analysis of the similarity ratings yielded seven interpretable factors. Qualitative groupings of life events so identified included: loss, entrance, family troubles, sibling problems, primary environment change, physical harm, and positive events (Sandler & Ramsey, 1978). Analyses were then carried out to determine the relationships between the experience of events on each of these dimensions and child adjustment problems as assessed by parents and teachers. A group of 99 kindergarten through third grade children, identified by teachers as displaying emotional maladjustment, and a matched control group of 44 nonmaladapting children comprised the full sample. From this sample, parent ratings of child adjustment problems and life events were available for 71 of the maladapting children and 33 of the control children. Scores on two of the life change dimensions, family troubles and entrance events, discriminated between the control and maladaptive groups. Further, both of these dimensions, as well as primary environment change, significantly correlated with ratings of aggression while family troubles alone significantly related to inhibition problems.

Using the same sample, Sandler and Block (1979) obtained scores for total life changes experienced using Coddington's weightings as well as a sum of the total number of changes, and separate desirable and undesirable life change scores. Further, using the latter two dimensions, an undesirable/desirable difference life change score was obtained. On four of the five stress measures, the life stress scores were higher for the maladaptive children than for the controls. Only positive changes failed to successfully discriminate between these two groups. An examination of the demographic characteristics of the groups revealed that more children's families in the maladaptive group than the control group received welfare. Hence, further analyses were carried out to examine the moderating effect of this variable. When analyses were carried out for welfare and nonwelfare populations separately, the results indicated stress contributed significantly to the adjustment problems in the nonwelfare group but not the welfare group. For the nonwelfare group the same four stress scores discriminated the maladaptive and control group children and significantly correlated with parent ratings of children's adjustment problems on the Louisville Child Behavior Checklist. Sandler (1979) hypothesized that these differences may be explained by postulating that as the parents in the nonwelfare samples were primarily in unskilled and relatively unstable jobs, and that the economic struggle they confronted prevented them from providing the support their children might need to adapt to stress.

Several recent studies have attempted to identify potential moderators of adaptive outcomes other than the desirability or qualitative aspects of the events themselves. One variable of particular concern has been social support. Sandler (1980), using data again drawn from the Sandler and Ramsey (1978) study, examined the effects of three types of social support (that is, one versus two parents, having an older sibling, or ethnic congruence with the community) on the association between life stress and parents' ratings of child behavior problems. The presence of higher levels of both parent and sibling support were both found to relate to lower levels of maladjustment, although ethnic congruence was not. By contrast, Gad and Johnson (1980) found little evidence that social support played a significant moderating role between life stress and adjustment for adolescents. They reported that adolescents from lower income families, regardless of race, experienced heightened levels of stress and maladjustment. However, they found no evidence that social support played a significant moderating role between these two variables.

Cauce, Felner, and Primavera (1982) have noted that a key difference between the work of Sandler (1980) and Gad and Johnson (1980) is that in the former case, social support was broken down into separate components; however, in the latter study, adolescents' subjective ratings of the amount of support they received from different sources were summed and the obtained overall ratings of support level used to examine any moderating effect. They argue that such a global approach to assessing social support may obscure important differences in the relationship of different types or sources of support to adjustment. To explore this question, Cauce et al. (1982) sought to identify clearly distinguishable and meaningful dimensions of social support for adolescents. Once this was done, they then examined the degree to which these dimensions were differentially perceived as useful or were related to indices of personal and academic adjustment as a function of the age, sex, and ethnic background of the adolescent. Ten sources of social support potentially available to adolescents were identified based on previous literature. In keeping with prior work demonstrating the central importance of perceived support as a critical predictor of adaptive outcome in studies with adults (Heller & Swindle, 1983), 250 adolescents from high stress backgrounds were asked to rate how helpful they perceived each of the 10 sources of social support to be on a three point scale. Principal components factor analysis of the 10 items of the Social Support Rating Scale (Cauce et al., 1982) yielded three separate psychologically-meaningful factors with eigenvalues greater than one and which accounted for approximately 95% of the total variance. The three social support factors were labeled family support (parents), formal support (teachers) and informal support (friends) based on the characteristics of the items with the highest loadings appearing on each factor.

Overall the results supported the authors' contention that measures of social support which utilize global ratings may obscure important differences in the nature and differential adaptive influence of various sources of social support. The perceived helpfulness of the three support dimensions as well as total support were found to vary by sex, grade, and ethnic background. More important was the study's demonstration of the differential relationship between the adolescents' levels of social support on these dimensions and their adjustment in different spheres. Of particular interest is the finding that in some cases social support was negatively related to certain measures of adjustment; a consideration generally overlooked in prior work. Although higher levels of peer self-concept were positively related to informal, formal and total support scores, family support was not significantly related to this variable. By contrast family support was the only support dimension that was found to be positively related to scholastic self-concept. A key finding was that adolescents with higher levels of informal support (that is, from friends) showed significantly poorer academic adjustment as reflected by grades and absences.

In a subsequent work, Felner, Aber, Primavera, and Cauce (in press) examined the role of several aspects of the social environment, in addition to social support, as moderators of the vulnerability of adolescents to the maladaptive impact of life stress. Specifically, the study examined the degree to which high risk adolescents' experience of the social environment of the school and their families' levels of functioning and organization, in addition to the extent of social support they perceived as available were related to differential vulnerability. Measures assessing the adolescents' perceptions of the high school social environment and of their families, as well the social support they perceived as available to them, were administered to 250 adolescents who were at high risk for the development of maladaptation due to experiencing multiple life stressors. In addition, measures of school adjustment (such as grades and absences) and self-concept were obtained. Regression analysis revealed different dimensions of the adolescent's social environment to be differentially salient as moderators of adaptation as a function of the specific area of adjustment assessed. The authors argue that, in the future development of models for understanding the moderating effects of personal and situational variables, it is important to not simply question which factors relate to differential vulnerability to heightened levels of stress, but also to carefully specify what area of functioning is of concern.

This general pattern of findings notwithstanding, Felner and his colleagues note that two aspects of the environment were found to be significantly associated with more favorable outcomes across domains of adjustment (Felner, Aber, Primavera, & Cauce, in press). These components of the environment were the levels of cohesion adolescents perceived as present in their family systems, as well as the level of teacher support they perceived as present in the school environment. These variables will be returned to when the issue of adaptation to single life events is considered. For the moment, however, they will only be considered within the overall pattern of findings relating to moderators of cumulative life stress in children and adolescents.

CUMULATIVE LIFE EVENTS AND PREVENTION

Before going on to an examination of single life changes as critical influences on the child's development, let us briefly consider how current models and data from the work on multiple life events may enhance or detract from efforts to design effective prevention programs for children. Several features of this work appear to be of particular value for such efforts. First, it is clear from these findings that a marked increase in the experience of life events, particularly negative ones, may be important markers of increased risk for the development of physical or emotional disorder. Second, recent research seems to underscore the need to consider potential moderating variables which may bear on the child's ability to adaptively cope with the stresses resulting from life change.

Although the foregoing are important contributions, both heuristically and practically, to preventive efforts with children, that is not to say that the work on cumulative life stress events and changes has been as helpful in these ways as it might. Consistent with the arguments of Felner, Farber, and Primavera (1983) regarding the need for a life transitions model rather than a stressful events one, it may be seen that some aspects of this work, particularly its conceptualization and goals, may have actually had limiting or adverse effects on the development of theoretical frameworks for viewing life events that are more compatible with the goals of primary prevention. Two aspects of prior work may be particularly problematic in this way. These are: (1) the emphasis on the stressful properties of life events and their potential for pathological outcomes, and (2) the use of methodologies which may by their implicit assumptions obscure qualitative differences among items that are included on scales as events (Felner, Farber, & Primavera, 1983).

As is illustrated by the assertions of Johnson (1982), most of the criticisms of the work of Coddington (1972a) and of other early life events scales have not focused on ways of increasing our understanding of life change per se. Rather, the key element for workers in this area has been the further development of the ability of such scales to predict negative adaptive outcomes. One cannot, in fairness, criticize this emphasis in any absolute sense. Indeed, given the epidemiological, public health tradition in which much of the work on cumulative life events is rooted, an emphasis on prediction of pathology is to some extent appropriate. However, if our broader concern is with primary prevention and its full range of goals (that is, positive enhancement of adaptation as well as prevention of dysfunction) then this emphasis becomes less acceptable as it allows for too little emphasis on the potential positive adaptive consequences of major life events.

As should be clear from the pathology focus of prior work on cumulative life change, failure to pay sufficient attention to the paradigmatic regularities of the epidemiological model underlying it may also constrain the degree to which a preventive stance in psychology may be as clean a break with the traditional medical model as prevention advocates claim it is (Rappaport, 1977). Not enough attention has been paid to the fact that the public health model, from which much of our thinking about prevention and life events has been borrowed, is fundamentally still a medical model that is more concerned with disease reduction than enhancement of functioning in individuals (Felner, Farber, & Primavera, 1983).

If, in keeping with primary prevention's goals, we shift our focus to give equal weight to enhancement and positive outcomes, as well as to avoidance of pathology, then several other features of prior work on cumulative life stress become of concern. A primary argument underlying the greater emphasis on undesirable as opposed to desirable life events has been the stronger immediate association of the former with negative adaptive consequences. Given the shift in focus, this difference is no longer as salient. Instead, what may now be more clearly seen is that the ways in which individuals adapt to positive events may have important implications for their overall level of adaptation, although perhaps not in ways which are immediately detectable on indices of pathology.

Another corollary of such a shift in emphasis is the need to reexamine the properties of life events with which we are most concerned. If our concern lies with pathological outcomes, then the stressful properties of life events are of primary concern. However, if we are interested in both the positive and negative adaptive implications of life events then we need to question whether or not other characteristics of such occurrences might be of equal or greater importance. Of particular concern may be the need to question the virtually synonymous use of the terms *life change* and *life stress* that has been argued for by some (Holmes, 1979; Holmes & Rahe, 1967; Uhlenhuth. 1979). Instead, given our broadened framework, the adaptive tasks and types of changes which life events precipitate for the individual can be seen to have importance in their own right. Further, the degree of stress associated with life events becomes but one factor with which people must cope when attempting to master such changes.

A second aspect of the work on cumulative stress from life events which limits its compatibility with the full range of prevention's goals derives from an assumption suggested by the current format of life events inventories. That is, there seems to be an implicit assumption that the items are sufficiently similar in some overriding manner to justify their mutual inclusion on the scale. When the focus is kept on the stressfulness of such experiences this assumption may be justified. However, from a preventive perspective this position is less defensible. A key concern here is the inability of the inventories as constructed to capture or illuminate qualitative differences in adaptive challenges for individuals. The previously cited quote by Holmes (1979) concerning traffic tickets and the death of a spouse illustrates the greatly misleading position which may result from the use of procedures which seek to somehow quantify, on a similar metric, life change or stress resulting from qualitatively different occurrences.

INDIVIDUAL LIFE EVENTS AND CHANGES

Studies of cumulative life events and single life events, while not entirely overlapping in their assumptions and goals, converge at a number of important points for prevention. Hence, before we further consider "goodness of fit" between work on cumulative life events and prevention it may be helpful to consider the status of current work on the role of single life events or changes in children's development. Efforts to address the potential impact of specific life events on children and adolescents have generally taken one or the other of two major approaches or have followed a middle path. The first approach has sought to establish specific adaptive consequences associated with particular life events, while the second has sought to clarify variables related to differential outcomes of the same event for different children.

Conceptually, attempts to document specific adaptive outcomes frequently associated with particular life events stem from several sources. The crisis model of Caplan (1964), which emphasizes the potential long-term adaptive impact of relatively short-term events or experiences, served to focus attention on this question. Building on this crisis model, recent authors (Bloom, 1979; Dohrenwend, 1978) have emphasized that a key first step toward organizing preventive efforts is the identification of specific stressful life events, which are associated with undesirable consequences in a significant proportion of the population. Of particular concern to both of these approaches is the use of life events as markers of increased risk and hence as useful indicators of the need for intervention efforts before actual dysfunction is present (Felner & Aber, 1983).

Specific Life Events and Their Import

For children and adolescents, a number of potentially critical events or life changes have been identified which may be associated with heightened risk for enduring maladaptation. Among these are hospitalization or serious illness, the birth of a sibling, the death or serious illness of a sibling, loss of a parent through death or divorce, adoption, geographic relocation, and predictable or unpredictable school transitions. As far as hospitalization is concerned, studies suggest children may exhibit signs of distress for some months after they return home with significant potential for this disturbance becoming a fixed pattern (Felner, Norton, Cowen, & Farber, 1981; Jessner, Blom, & Waldfogel, 1952; Peterson & Ridley-Johnson, 1983; Rutter, 1981). Children's reactions to hospitalization are described further by Peterson and Brownlee-Duffeck in Chapter 9 of this volume. Similarly, serious illness in a child has been found to be associated with heightened levels of disruptive behavior, anxiety and depression and school adjustment problems; moreover, overall rates of psychiatric disorders have been found to be significantly higher for chronically ill and handicapped children than for physically healthy children (Pless & Roghmann. 1971; Pless, Roghmann, & Haggerty, 1972; Rutter, 1981, Drotar, 1977, 1981; Johnson, 1982; Wright, 1979). An often overlooked risk group are the siblings of seriously ill children or those who have died due to illness or accident. Siblings of seriously or terminally ill children have been found to evidence a wide array of adjustment problems including school difficulties, greater anxiety and depression and heightened levels of disruptive behaviors (Binger, Ablin, Feurstein, Kuchner, Zoger, & Mikkelsen, 1969; Breslau, 1982; Breslau, Weitzman, & Messenger, 1981; Burton, 1975; Lavigne & Ryan, 1979; Tew & Laurence, 1973). Similarly, siblings of children who died due to terminal illness have been found to have a number of difficulties in coping. Although some of the symptoms may have actually become manifest during the course of the sibling's terminal illness, more severe disturbances became evident following the death of the sibling. Disorders associated with sibling death include enuresis, depression, impaired school adjustment and performance, severe anxiety and abdominal pain (Binger, 1973; Binger et al., 1969). These issues are discussed further by Drotar, Crawford, and Ganofsky in Chapter 8 of this volume.

Children's reactions to the birth of a sibling have also received attention. Moore (1975) found that 15% of the children examined developed difficulties following the birth of a sibling, generally manifested through increased acting-out behaviors or difficulties in the mother-child relationship. Dunn, Kendrick, and MacNamee (1981) found that in a group of 40 children age two and three there were increases in tearfulness, sleep disturbance, and toileting problems following the birth of a sibling. As to long-term effects of the birth of a sibling, Rutter (1981) suggests that oldest children may have a slightly increased risk of emotional disturbance in later childhood. He notes, however, that the evidence is not conclusive at this point and may be open to interpretations other than that they are sequelae of the event itself. Instead, for example, they may be due to shifts in family organization following the birth of the younger sibling.

The potential effects of parental loss due to death or divorce have also received extensive study. Hetherington (1972) reported that adolescent girls experiencing either parental divorce or death displayed significantly more difficulties in their interactions with males than did girls from intact families. A series of clinical studies by Wallerstein and Kelly (1974, 1975, 1976, 1977) have shown parental divorce to be associated with a range of behavior problems in children from preschool age through adolescence. Other studies have demonstrated links between parent death or divorce and such health problems as juvenile diabetes, childhood cancer, or respiratory problems (Jacobs & Charles, 1980; Johnson, 1982; Leaverton, White, McCormick, Smith, & Sheikholislam, 1980; Stein & Charles, 1971). In some studies, parent death has also been shown to relate to later psychiatric problems, particularly depression (Barry, Barry, & Lindemann, 1965; Birtchnell, 1969; Sugar, 1970; Rutter, 1966). Other studies, however, have failed to obtain similar findings concerning the enduring effects of parent death (Blaine & Carmen, 1968; Gregory, 1966; Munro, 1966).

The question of whether different types of parental separation or loss lead to different outcomes has also been raised. Glueck and Glueck (1950) found that a significantly higher proportion of delinquent boys came from homes broken by parent death than by divorce. Felner and his colleagues studied school adjustment problems associated with parental divorce in both referred and normal populations of primary graders (Felner, Stolberg, & Cowen, 1975; Felner, Ginter, Boike, & Cowen, 1981). Children with histories of parent death tended to manifest heightened shyness, hostility, and withdrawal, whereas those from divorced or separated families were more likely to show aggressive antisocial problems.

Adoption may be considered as a special form of parent loss and family reconstitution. Moderators of its potential impact certainly may have much in common with both parent divorce or death. Two sets of findings deserve attention here. When evaluated against the general population of children, evidence suggests adopted children have more adjustment problems than nonadopted children (Bohman, 1972; Cunningham, Cadoret, Loftus, & Edwards, 1975; Eisen, 1979; Schechter, Carlson, Simmons, & Work, 1968). But when compared with foster children, a group whose backgrounds may be more similar to adoptees than to nonadoptive children, adoptees display fewer intellectual and emotional difficulties (Bohman & Sigvardsson, 1978; Eisen, 1979; Tizard, 1977).

School transitions and geographic relocation may also be significant events which pose adaptive problems for children. The incidence of such events alone makes them intriguing targets for prevention activities. At one point or another in their educational careers almost all children experience predictable, normative school changes (such as promotion to high school). Moreover, with increasing frequency, children are experiencing such less predictable extrasystemic transfers as those due to residential mobility. As a result of increased mobility in the United States, 20 to 30% of the children enrolled in public schools are new transfers each year (Holland, Kaplan, & Davis, 1974). Both cumulative and single school transfers have been found to be related to poorer academic achievement (Felner, Primavera, & Cauce, 1981; Levine, Wesolowski, & Corbett, 1966; Schaller, 1975), increased classroom behavior problems (Keeme, 1971), and heightened anxiety, particularly over gaining peer acceptance and meeting school expectations (Levine, 1966; Rakieten, 1961). Other investigators, however, have failed to find an association between poor school adjustment and either cumulative school transfers (Collins & Coulter, 1974; Cramer & Dorsey, 1979; Goebel, 1978) or any single school change precipitated by residential mobility (Felner, Primavera, & Cauce, 1981). By contrast, the normative transition into high school has been clearly demonstrated to be a time of increased vulnerability to school maladjustment. In a recent study, Felner, Primavera, and Cauce (1981) examined changes in the academic adjustment of students during and following the transition to high school. Significant decreases in academic performance and increases in absenteeism were found to be associated with this life change. Moreover, further exploration of the relative vulnerability of students during this transition found that students who are typically seen as being at heightened risk for school failure, that is, minorities and those with histories of higher levels of mobility (U.S. Department of Health, Education & Welfare, 1975), were particularly vulnerable during this transition.

Limitations of Discrete Life Event Impact Studies

These and other studies, which seek to identify specific adaptive consequences that different life events may have for children, have played an important role in focusing prevention's attention on such events. Moreover, such work may at times help us to better understand the different adaptive challenges which confront children who experience them. However, generally inconsistent findings as well as the range of problems associated with each event make it clear that the search for a constellation of general effects for each event may not be the most productive approach for understanding the adaptive processes required, nor for addressing the shape that preventive efforts should take. No life event or change is equally stressful, nor does it have the same adaptive consequences for all children and adolescents who experience it (Felner et al., 1975). Congruent with the models for understanding single life events and changes of Dohrenwend (1978) and Felner, Farber, and Primavera (1983), the literature on cumulative life events made clear the need to consider personal coping styles and attributes, as well as situational variables which may influence the child's appraisal of the stressfulness of the event and the level of threat they experience. Hence, if we are to understand children's differential vulnerability to isolated life events, it seems that rather than ask what specific effect an event may have, we should determine what personal and situational factors may be associated with differing levels of adaptive success within and across events.

It should also be further noted that efforts to elaborate specific consequences associated with particular life events or changes have generally focused on potential adverse outcomes. Several studies with children have indicated that changes in competencies and strengths of adjustment may also accompany such negative events as parental death or divorce (Felner, Ginter, Boike, & Cowen, 1981; Finkel, 1975). Therefore, it seems important, based both on the data and the previously discussed need for preventive specialists to consider the full range of adaptive outcomes of life changes and events, to consider the elements of life events which may lead to positive as well as negative developmental outcomes.

Finally, the question of what effects a specific event may have on a child or adolescent reflects an implicit assumption that the experience which is of adaptive significance is the event per se, rather than any more prolonged adaptive process which it may precipitate. As noted earlier, recent work has suggested that the specific life event framework for considering the impact of life changes may be too narrow in its focus (Felner, Farber, & Primavera, 1983). Rather than simply focusing on the impact of the event, what needs to be further untangled is the relative contribution of other changes and stressors which may accompany the event.

A LIFE TRANSITIONS MODEL FOR UNDERSTANDING THE PROCESS OF COPING WITH LIFE CHANGE

Recent empirical literature is generally supportive of a position which views the process of coping or adaptation (engendered by life change in childhood or adolescence) as one extended over a period of time which confronts the child with a complex set of personal and environmental changes and tasks (Felner, Farber, & Primavera, 1980; Johnson, 1982; Rutter, 1981). A detailed consideration of all the moderator variables and environmental challenges associated with each of the major life changes a child may experience is well beyond the scope of this chapter. Drawing on representative studies of children's responses to life changes, an attempt will be made to identify personal and situational factors which, across life events, may be associated with differing levels of risk and coping efficacy. Of particular concern will be the way in which this literature may aid in the refinement of a framework for understanding life transitions that will facilitate the organization of a knowledge base for preventive efforts targeted at childen experiencing such shifts in their lives (Felner, Farber, & Primavera, 1980, 1983).

Child Factors

Among the basic characteristics children bring to the adaptation process, which may influence adjustment to life events and changes, are age and sex. The need to consider the child's age at the time of the life change as a potential moderator of outcome has been well documented. Studies of children who have experienced parental divorce (Farber, Primavera, & Felner, in press; Felner, Farber, & Primavera, 1983; Wallerstein & Kelly, 1975, 1976), bereavement (Bradley, 1979; Rutter, 1966, 1981), birth of a sibling (Breslau, 1982; Dunn et al., 1981; Koocher & O'Malley, 1981; Moore, 1975), had a sibling who is chronically or terminally ill or has died, as well as other events (such as school transfer) have demonstrated that the child's age at the time of the event may be an important mediator of both the form of the child's adaptive efforts and its potential outcome. Sex differences may also be associated with differing levels of response or adaptive outcome following these and other major life changes (Dunn et al., 1981; Farber et al., 1983; Felner, Farber, & Primavera, 1980; Hetherington, Cox, & Cox, 1978; Rutter, 1981). Other fixed characteristics which have received some attention as potential mediators of adaptation to stress and change are temperament factors (Dunn et al., 1981) and ethnic background (Felner, Farber, & Primavera, 1980; Felner, Primavera, & Cauce, 1981; Neito, 1972; Rutter, 1981). However, although there are some suggestive data, there is very little direct evidence on the contribution of either of these latter factors, particularly temperament, to children's adaptation to life events or changes (Rutter, 1981).

Knowledge of the child's age and sex as they relate to outcomes following specific events or changes may be helpful in targeting programs to populations and problems. More importantly, however, for understanding children's efforts to cope with life changes is the association these variables may have with other potential moderator variables which are more program addressable, that is, able to be modified by intervention efforts. A child's age, sex, temperament, or ethnic background are variables which, with the possible exception of temperament, cannot be modified through intervention efforts. Their significance for determining the degree of success of the child's coping efforts may, however, be less a function of properties of these specific variables than their association with variables which can be modified and therefore determine the shape of preventive efforts. For example, the children's age or sex may relate to parallel differences in social or cognitive development, which in turn, may affect the children's perception and understanding of the changes taking place in their life as well as the type of coping style they employ (Felner, Farber, & Primavera, 1980). Such a position is consistent with that of Lazarus and Launier (1978), who underscore the importance of an individual's cognitive appraisal of an event as an important determinant of coping outcome. Children at differing ages and associated levels of cognitive development, or with different socialization experiences (such as those which may be associated with sex differences), may appraise the meaning and significance of an event quite differently. Girls, for example, have been shown to appraise and cope with failure experiences quite differently than boys, giving up more quickly and attributing their failure to cope to their own lack of ability (Dweck & Bush, 1976; Dweck, Davidson, Nelson, & Enna, 1978). By contrast, boys may expend greater effort and, if they still fail, may attribute it to not trying hard enough, thus maintaining the feeling that they could cope adequately if they really chose to do so (Rutter, 1981).

Recently, several studies have focused more directly on attempting to elaborate the dimensions and adaptive implications of children's coping styles. Siegel (Note 2) studied 70 children between the ages of eight and 14 hospitalized for minor surgery. Children who were more successful at coping (that is, lower in anxiety and discomfort from physical procedures, more cooperative) were more active in seeking information about the hospital and the procedures they were to undergo than were those less successful in coping. Similarly, Burstein and Meichenbaum (1979) reported that children who were less defensive prior to hospitalization for minor elective surgery, and who actively played with stress associated toys, were less anxious and distressed following surgery. While these studies are suggestive of the role of children's coping styles in adapting to life events, the general paucity of literature on this topic, particularly as it relates to children's efforts to adapt to life changes other than hospitalization, make generalized conclusions impossible.

Those concerned with the development of preventive efforts need to further elaborate the nature of children's coping styles and clarify the differences in children's perceptions and appraisals of life changes that are associated with differential vulnerability before we can take steps to modify such appraisals to reduce stress and enhance coping through preventive efforts. Preliminary work in this area has demonstrated the potential efficacy of such an approach (Peterson & Ridley-Johnson, 1983; Peterson & Shigetomi, 1981).

The availability or responsiveness of environmental factors which potentially enhance the child's ability to cope with life changes also may differ as a function of the child's characteristics. Illustratively, Rutter (1981) argues that the greater vulnerability of boys to some stressors may be a function of parents being less supportive of boys in their coping efforts and being more likely to respond negatively to signs of distress from the child. Similarly, he notes that patterns of parent-child interaction may also vary as a function of the child's temperament. Again, there is a need for further clarification of ways in which the child's characteristics may interact with environmental coping resources or exacerbate other potential sources of stress which may aid prevention specialists. This is particularly true in the design of programs which modify environmental circumstances to increase resources and reduce threat. There is programmatic evidence which supports the viability of efforts of this type (for example, Felner, Ginter, & Primavera, 1981). In summary then, both fixed characteristics of children (age, sex, and temperament), and ones more amenable to programmatic modification (cognitive appraisal of the event, coping styles, and competencies), may act both directly, as well as interact with environmental factors to influence the adaptive processes required by life change. Rather than merely seeking to examine how specific characteristics of the child relate to outcomes following specific events, a second, and perhaps more fruitful, avenue for the prevention professional appears to be the systematic elaboration of how specific characteristics of the child may interact with environmental circumstances and changes that are common across transitions to increase or decrease vulnerability.

ENVIRONMENTAL COPING RESOURCES AND ADAPTIVE TASKS

Although attention has been focused only recently on environmental mediators of children's adaptation to life change, some factors which seem to be consistently important mediators of outcomes have emerged. Before discussing representative literature, though, in keeping with the prior discussion of life event frameworks, a distinction needs to be made between two views of how situational factors may mediate outcomes. In stress or pathology focused approaches to life events (Dohrenwend, 1978), environmental factors such as social support or family organization are viewed as factors which mediate the level of stress experienced by individuals who, with the exception of their role in appraising the event, are relatively passive. Environmental resources and stressors either are or are not present at some preexisting level and the individual is ''acted upon'' by them (Felner, Farber, & Primavera, 1983). However, if we shift our focus to one that is more consistent with the range of prevention's goals, (that is, to an individual's or system's efforts to adapt to change rather than merely cope with stress and avoid its pathogenic effects), then some shifts in the way environmental mediators of adaptation are viewed are necessitated. It has been suggested that a life transitions perspective (Felner, Farber, & Primavera, 1983), with its emphasis on change rather than stress, involves the elaboration of the types of changes which confront the individual during transition. These changes are then viewed as tasks which may engender active efforts on the part of the person to master them, with the final level of stress associated with the tasks and changes resulting from transactions between the individual and his or her environment (Felner, Farber, & Primavera, 1983; Lazarus & Launier, 1978). Moreover, it recognizes that a transition is not a time-limited event with which one copes, but a process which may extend over some time and require prolonged adaptive efforts (Felner, Farber, & Primavera, 1983).

Such a transactional, adaptive perspective has direct consequences for the way in which potential environmental mediators are viewed. The child's characteristics, competencies, and coping efforts assume a far more central role in determining the adaptive outcome achieved when viewed from this model. They may act both directly on such outcomes, as well as indirectly through their influence on the acquisition and shape of the environmental coping resources which may enhance coping efforts. To some extent then, the quality of environmental mediators available as coping resources, as well as the presence of additional stressors, *may be as reflective* of the adequacy or success of the child's coping skills and efforts as they are mediators of such adaptation.

A framework which views certain life events as precipitants or markers of transitional processes, rather than as more time-limited events, also makes it critical to identify common characteristics and tasks of transitions which have adaptive significance. Life changes in childhood, such as birth of a sibling, school transfer, parental divorce, or developing a chronic illness, may appear to be quite different. However, in the types of adaptive tasks or changes they engender, they may be quite similar (Felner, Farber, & Primavera, 1983). For children, as for adults, a number of possible common environmental changes and tasks which may play important roles in shaping adaptive efforts may be identifiable from the existing literature.

For children and adolescents both the level of family organization and interaction prior to the transition, as well as shifts in these circumstances which are precipitated by the life transition, may be the most salient mediators of adaptation. This issue has been perhaps best elaborated in studies of children's adaptation to parental divorce. One key set of circumstances relates to the pre- and post-divorce parental relationship. Parental conflict surrounding the divorce appears to have a pronounced effect on the coping efforts of children. Recent reviews of research in this area have concluded that parental separation or divorce does not necessarily have an enduring negative impact on the child, but the parental conflict which precedes or follows it may (Emery, 1982; Felner, Farber, & Primavera, 1980; Rutter, 1981). Studies of children who have experienced parental divorce have found that many of the problems they had were at least initially identifiable before the divorce (Lambert, Essen, & Head, 1977). Moreover, other studies have found that children from intact homes in which there was marital discord, unhappiness, high conflict levels, were more likely to have problems than children from lower conflict families where a divorce had already occurred (Nye, 1957; Raschke & Raschke, Note 3; Zill, Note 4). Hence, the "emotional divorce" of parents may be far more of a hazard to children's development, particularly if not accompanied by actual separation, than legal divorce.

Additional support for the view that interparental conflict and not divorce per se may be the cause of increased behavioral problems often associated with divorce is provided by Felner and his colleagues. The school adjustment patterns of primary grade children who had experienced either parental divorce or death were compared in a series of studies. In two independent samples of children referred to a school-based early identification and prevention program, those children who had experienced parental divorce displayed significantly more acting-out problems than those from homes where a parent had died (Felner et al., 1975). These findings were replicated with a nonreferred group of primary grade students (Felner, Ginter, Boike, & Cowen, 1981). Moreover, the second study focused on measures of adaptive strengths and competencies as well. Again, children who had experienced parental divorce fared more poorly than those who had experienced parental death with the same pattern of behavior reported. Moreover, the former group were noted by teachers as having significantly fewer competencies overall, as well as in the specific areas of frustration tolerance and peer sociability, than those in either the latter group or children from generally intact households. These authors argue, as have others (Birtchnell, 1969; Tuckman & Regan, 1967), that the poorer adaptive outcomes and heightened levels of acting-out behavior associated with divorce rather than parent death, are at least in part a function of differences in the family climate leading up to them. That is, divorce usually follows a chronic, conflict-laden, dissatisfying interactive pattern between the parents, whereas parent death generally does not.

For other life transitions in childhood the potentially deleterious effects of interparental difficulties on coping efforts have also been suggested. Adaptation by children to chronic illness, birth or death of a sibling, hospitalization, a parent going to jail, or geographic relocation may all be influenced to some extent by the levels of conflict and cohesion in the home (Felner, Farber, & Primavera, 1983; Johnson, 1982; Nannis, Susman, Strope, Woodruff, Hersh, Levine, & Pizzo, 1982; Rutter, 1981; Wolff, 1969). However, the specific implications of such circumstances for adaptation to these life changes have been elaborated less than they have for parental divorce.

Another set of factors relating to family organization which may have significant implications for children's efforts to cope with life changes are the pretransition nature and quality of parent-child relationships, as well as changes which may take place in them as a consequence of the life event. Hetherington et al. (1978) found that, following divorce, changes may occur in both the quality and quantity of parent-child interactions, which may relate to the level of problems the child displays. Moreover, of particular note is their finding that the efficacy of parent management behavior may continue to change for a period of up to two years following the divorce before reaching stable equilibrium. This once again underscores the notion that rather than dealing with an event, what children are really coping with is a more prolonged reorganization of their environment.

Felner, Farber, Ginter, Boike, and Cowen (1980) report results which further substantiate this position. They found that children with histories of parental separation or divorce experienced significantly lower levels of educational stimulation from parents and greater parental rejection and economic stress than those from homes disrupted by parent death. It has also been reported that parents' levels of communication with their children, affection, and degrees of protectiveness may be lower in divorced than in intact homes (Hetherington et al., 1978). Again, however, these findings may be less a function of the divorce per se than the process which surrounds it. The difference in post-event organization between homes broken by divorce or parent death may actually reflect differences in family functioning prior to the actual event. While divorce is, as noted above, often preceded by chronically conflictual family interaction patterns, as a result of which significant disruption in parent–child interaction may have occurred, parental death may have no such systematic relationship to prior family functioning. For example, in high conflict households there may be less sharing of parenting duties and the parent who is responsible for such duties may be already overtaxed by the high level stress and relatively low level of support existing in the relationship (Felner, Farber, Ginter, Boike, & Cowen, 1980). Rather than leading to poorer levels of parent-child interaction, the reorganization following the divorce or a subsquent remarriage may actually provide an opportunity to change long-standing problematic interactions patterns in a relatively short time. This may be a key issue for prevention specialists to understand due to its implications for enhancement of functioning.

A study by Boike, Ginter, Cowen, Felner, and Francis (1978) lends further support to the argument that existing or new difficulties in parent-child interactions following divorce, rather than the divorce itself, may account for some of the behavior difficulties shown by children. Focusing on patterns of family interaction similar to those examined in the study by Felner, Farber, Ginter, Boike, and Cowen (1980), they report that children from both intact and divorce homes (where there were lower levels of educational stimulation) had higher levels of acting-out problems. By contrast, those experiencing more pressure to succeed displayed higher levels of anxious behavior. Given the previously noted associations between parental death or divorce and such behaviors, as well as between these events and the patterns of parent-child interaction being discussed, it is clear that at least part of the association between the parent divorce or death and the subsequent behavior problem patterns found may be related to systematic changes in family organization that are precipitated by or associated with the event.

Similar results have been reported for other major life changes. Hospitalization of a child may result in heightened levels of parental anxiety which, in turn, may play as large role in any distress the child experiences as does the hospital procedure they undergo (Rutter, 1981). Further, as for divorce, preexisting and unchanged difficulties in the parent-child relationship may influence coping efforts. Persistent disturbance in the child's adaptive function following hospitalization is more likely to occur when the child comes from a family in which parent-child relationships were already poor (Quinton & Rutter, 1976; Rutter, 1981).

For seriously or terminally ill hospitalized children, as well as for their healthy siblings, parental care and attention in addition to help in understanding changes in the parents' behavior may also have adaptive implications (Koocher & O'Malley, 1981). For the healthy siblings of seriously ill children this may be particularly difficult. Once their sibling is home from the hospital children often assume life can go on as before the illness. Often, this is not the case, and continued parental focus on the patient may cause jealousy and resentment in their siblings (Binger, 1973; Kagen-Goodheart, 1977; Koocher & O'Malley, 1981).

Following the birth of a sibling, the parent-child relationship may again be a salient mediator of adequate outcome. Rutter (1981) states, "In the case of birth of a sibling, the stress to the elder child seems to largely lie in the effects this has on the pattern of family interaction" (p. 332). Empirical findings support this contention. Dunn et al. (1981) argue, based on their findings, that the relationship between a mother and her two to three year old is often difficult and the changes which accompany the birth of a sibling at this age may exacerbate these difficulties. Dunn and Kendrick (1980a,b) report findings which support this position. They found that following the birth of a second child, mothers show more negative verbal interactions, confrontations, and prohibitions with the first child and engage in less playful interactions with them.

Two other key environmental variables which may mediate the child's adaptation to a transition are the level of social support available and the degree of complexity or organization of the environment itself. Much of the literature on the influence of social support on children's adaptation to life change has already been discussed. Additionally, it should be clear that the disruption in parent-child interaction or interparental relationships associated with life changes may lead to reduced levels of support being available to the child (Farber, Primavera, & Felner, in press). In a positive vein, however, preexisting, good relationships with a parent may buffer the effect of life changes if these relationships are not disrupted. Several authors found that following a divorce in which the relationship of the child and a parent could be classified as very good, the typical detrimental effects associated with divorce were avoided (Emery, 1982).

The degree of complexity of the social environment which children confront both during and following the life change may also play a critical role in their success at mastery. Felner, Primavera, and Cauce (1981) examined the relationship between cumulative school transfers, single unpredictable school transfers precipitated by residential changes, and the transition to high school to academic adjustment. High rates of school mobility were found to relate to poor academic performance, particularly for high-risk minority students. Of more significance for the present work, however, was the finding that while no single school transition due to residential mobility had a significant impact on the student's post-transfer adjustment, the normative "desirable" transition to high school did. This latter change was associated with significantly lowered academic performance and increased absences. The authors argue that, in contrast to the relatively stable environment confronted by students transferring at other times, those making the change into high school are confronted by an entire social system in flux. All students in their grade are simultaneously confronted by a new physical environment and a larger, generally unfamiliar set of peers and school personnel. Children's mastery of transitional tasks, such as gaining an understanding of the school's expectations and regularities or reconstructing and reorganizing his or her formal and informal support system, may be made more difficult by the increased complexity of the social setting (Felner, Primavera, & Cauce, 1981). Just as the degree of complexity of children's larger social environment may increase the difficulty of the adaptive tasks they confront and influence their adaptation to life change, so too may the organization of their family system shift and increase the complexity of their environment. For example, recent work has shown that the maintenance or reestablishment of stable, predictable patterns of family functioning and household routine may significantly enhance a child's adaptation to parental divorce (Hetherington et al., 1978; Wallerstein, 1977). Similarly, association between the maintenance of family or environmental stability and positive coping outcomes have also been reported for seriously ill children (Koocher & O'Malley, 1981; Nannis et al., 1982).

The utility for primary prevention programs of focusing on both social support or reducing the degree of difficulty of the adaptive tasks confronted by the child following life changes has been demonstrated in a recent study by Felner, Ginter, and Primavera (1982). They report on a primary prevention program for children making the transition to high school which sought to enhance the coping efforts of children by reducing the degree of complexity in the school/social environment as well as increasing the level of social support available. The program involved two aspects. First, the social system the student was entering was partially reorganized to reduce flux and facilitate the student's restructuring of stable peer support systems. This was, in part, accomplished by increasing the degree of overlap and consistency in the group of students in each of the child's classes. An additional goal here was to increase the child's perception of the school as a stable, well-organized, understandable, and cohesive place. A second component involved assigning guidance functions to homeroom teachers. This was done to increase the amount of instrumental and affective social support available to students and reduce the difficulty with which students could gain access to information concerning school expectations, rules and regulations.

Overall, the results of the project indicate the major goals were achieved. By the end of ninth grade the children who participated in the program showed significantly better attendance records and academic achievement, as well as more stable self-concepts, than children going through the transition who did not participate in the programs. Further, project participants reported perceiving the school environment as having greater clarity of expectations and organizational structure and higher levels of teacher support than did nonproject students.

SUMMARY AND CONCLUDING COMMENTS

The preceding discussion of potential mediators of children's adaptations to life changes is not intended to be exhaustive. Other factors such as preexisting levels of or shifts in parental adjustment and well-being or economic resources may also play important roles in influencing adaptation to the transition. The discussion is intended to be illustrative of a perspective on life changes which may lead to more effective preventive efforts being developed for children. The studies reviewed indicate that the immediate stress associated with the critical life event may play a far lesser role in making such events significant hazards to development than do changes and stressors in the child's social environments associated with the event. Indeed, any continuing stress the child experiences may be less a function of the event per se than the subsequent shifts in conditions in the child's environment. In this vein, Felner, Farber, and Primavera (1983) have argued that a perspective which differentiates between proximal and distal stressors may fit well with a life transitions approach (DeLongis, Coyne, Dakof, Folkman, & Lazarus, 1982). Major life events are seen as distal stressors, while the residual, day-to-day stressors engendered or exacerbated by them are proximal stressors. Life events are considered as distal because they do not directly describe the conditions and adaptive demands which result from them. By contrast, proximal stressors are seen as those person-environment transactions that are part of the child's daily life and pose adaptive challenges directly (for example, adapting to a new family routine or pattern of parental attention). A life transition perspective with its emphasis on change and the ongoing process of adaptation which surrounds the marker event easily accommodates such a view. Clearly, most of the major potential mediators of adaptive outcomes may be viewed as potential proximal stressors of adaptive tasks. While the marker event may produce some acute and lasting distress, it is the specific changes in circumstances and associated adaptive tasks that precede or follow the event and the children's ability to master these changes and tasks that may be of central importance in actually determining their ultimate adjustment.

The general goals of this chapter have been to examine current views of the developmental importance of critical life events in childhood and, drawing on empirical literature, to further refine an explanatory model that may contribute to the development of preventive efforts. Prior frameworks placed an overemphasis on pathology and stressful occurrences at the expense of understanding life changes more generally, and the specific circumstances and resultant adaptive challenges with which the child must cope when experiencing major life changes. This shift in focus was seen to bring the adaptive implications of positively valenced life events into sharper focus than models which are more pathology focused. These shifts are critical ones for balancing the investment of preventive psychologists in the complementary spheres of developmental enhancement and pathology avoidance (Felner, Farber, & Primavera, 1983). If the focus is change and adaptation to it, rather than merely the avoidance of the adverse consequences of stress, then it is important that some preventive efforts are targeted toward producing positive outcomes and enhancement of the ability of children to be resilient in the face of other potentially dysfunction predisposing circumstances.

It has also been argued here that we need to shift our focus to efforts to adapt to change, rather than merely reduce stress. By doing so our view of the tasks involved is that they are to be mastered, that is, to be acted on by the child with others (for example, parents and teachers) though active problem solving. This is by contrast to a life stress view where mediators of stress act on a relatively passive child. As a function of this shift in the view of the adaptive process, the child's coping skills and problem-solving abilities assume a far more central role in determining the outcome. Now, not only may these factors directly influence adaptive effects as in Dohrenwend's (1978) model, they may also act indirectly through their influence on environmental factors. For example, in stress focused approaches to life events, situational mediators such as social support are viewed as factors which influence or buffer the child's experience of stress by their presence or absence. If, however, it is recognized that children may be actively engaged in adapting to change, then it should also be evident that they may actively employ their coping skills or problem-solving abilities to gain or reshape environmental resources that they may draw upon for their adaptive efforts. Thus, from this perspective, among those tasks which children confront during transitions may be the active reorganization and modification of such environmental mediators of stress as their social networks and supports, the routines that characterize their daily lives, their interactions with parents, and their psychosocial roles. Further research is necessary to fully delineate the nature and range of such tasks (Felner, Farber, & Primavera, 1983).

Finally, it should be clear that the preceding framework is one which lends itself to research strategies which attempt to elaborate factors related to the differential vulnerability of children at risk due to the experience of life events. Felner, Aber, Primavera, and Cauce (in press) have argued that our ability to further refine and develop a knowledge base to guide preventive efforts for children at risk due to the experience of life events or changes depends on two key elements. First, we need a well articulated framework for viewing children's efforts to cope with such events. It is hoped that the preceding discussion has moved us further toward this goal. Of equal importance, however, is the need to identify factors which contribute to successful adaptive outcomes. Toward this end they argue that prevention may do well to borrow from a paradigm developed by psychopathology researchers, that is, examine factors which differentiate between children experiencing life changes who show high levels of vulnerability compared to those who are relatively ''invulnerable'' (Garmezy, 1975, 1976). The relative paucity of research that relates to these children in the prevention area has been underscored by several authors (Cowen, 1980; Felner et al., in press), as has been the need for additional clarification of the conditions associated with positive psychological outcomes in such high risk children. The life transitions framework for understanding life events as presented in this chapter enables us to shift our focus from a preoccupation with pathology to a search for factors associated with competence and positive adaptation. Such a strategy would be one particularly well suited to expanding our understanding of children's efforts to cope with life changes.

ACKNOWLEDGMENT

The author wishes to thank Karen Wolfe for her critical comments on the earlier drafts of this manuscript as well as for her encouragement and assistance throughout the preparation of this chapter.

REFERENCES

de Araujo, G., Van Arsdel, P. P., Holmes, T. H., & Dudley, D. L. Life change, coping ability and chronic intrinsic asthma. *Journal of Psychosomatic Research*, 1973, *17*, 356–363.

Barrera, M. Social support's role in the adjustment of pregnant adolescents: Assessment issues and findings. In B. H. Gottlieb (Ed.), *Social networks and social support in community mental health*. Beverly Hills: Sage Publications, 1981.

Barry, H., Jr. Barry, H. III, & Lindemann. E. Dependency in adult patients following early maternal bereavement. *Journal of Nervous and Mental Disease*, 1965, *40*, 196–206.

Bedell, J. R., Giordani, B., Amour, J. L., Tavormina, J., & Boll, T. Life stress and the psychological and medical adjustment of chronically ill children. *Journal of Psychosomatic Research*, 1977, *21*, 237–242.

Binger, C. M. Childhood leukemia—Emotional impact on siblings. In E. J. Anthony & C.

Koupernick (Eds.), *The child in his family: The impact of disease and death*. New York: Wiley-Interscience, 1973.

Binger, C. M., Ablin, A. R., Feuerstein, R. C., Kuchner, J. H., Zoger, S. & Mikkelsen, C. Childhood leukemia: Emotional impact on patient and family. *New England Journal of Medicine*, 1969, *280*, 414–418.

Birtchnell, J. The possible consequences of early parent death. *British Journal of Medical Psychiatry*, 1969, *42*, 1–12.

Blaine, G. B., & Carmen, C. R. Causal factors in suicide attempts by male and female college students. *American Journal of Psychiatry*, 1968, *125*, 146–149.

Bloom, B. L. Prevention of mental disorders: Recent advances in theory and practice. *Community Mental Health Journal*, 1979, *15*, 179–191.

Bohman, M. A study of adopted children, their back-ground, environment and adjustment. *Acta Paediatrica Scandinavia*, 1972, *61*, 90–97.

Bohman, M., & Sigvardsson, S. An 18-year prospective, longitudinal study of adopted boys. In E. J. Anthony, C. Koupernick, & C. Chiland (Eds.), *The child in his family: Vulnerable children*. (Vol. 4). New York: Wiley, 1978.

Boike, M. F., Cowen, E. L., DeStefano, M., Felner, R. D., & Gesten, E. L. A comparison of rural, suburban, and urban teachers' perceptions of class environment, problems and mental health services: Implications for secondary prevention. *Journal of Preventive Psychiatry*, 1982, *1*, 337–348.

Boike, M. F., Ginter, E. L., Cowen, E. L., Felner, R. D., & Francis, R. The relationship between family background problems and the competencies of young normal children. *Psychology in the Schools*, 1978, *15*, 283–290.

Boyce, T. W., Jensen, E. W., Cassell, J. C., Collier, A. M., Smith, A. H., & Raimey, C. T. Influence of life events and family routines on childhood respiratory tract illness. *Pediatrics*, 1973, *60*, 609–615.

Bradley, C. Life events and the control of diabetes mellitus. *Journal of Psychosomatic Research*, 1979, *23*, 159–162.

Bramwell, S. T., Masuda, M., Wagner, N. N., & Holmes, T. H. Psychosocial factors in athletic injuries. *Journal of Human Stress*, 1975, *1*, 6–22.

Breslau, N. Siblings of disabled children: Birth order and age-spacing effects. *Journal of Abnormal Child Psychology*, 1982, *10*, 85–96.

Breslau, N., Weitzman, M., & Messenger, K. Psychological functioning of siblings of disabled children. *Pediatrics*, 1981, *67*, 344–353.

Burstein, S., & Meichenbaum, D. The work of worrying in children undergoing surgery. *Journal of Abnormal Child Psychology*, 1979, *7*, 121–132.

Burton, L. *The family life of sick children: A study of families coping with chronic childhood diseases*. London: Routledge and Kegan Paul, 1975.

Campbell, A., Converse, P. E., & Rodgers, W. L. *The quality of American life: Perceptions, evaluations and satisfactions*. New York: Russell Sage Foundation, 1976.

Caplan, G. (Ed.). *Prevention of mental disorder in children*. New York: Basic Books, 1961.

Caplan, G. *Principles of preventive psychiatry*. New York: Basic Books, 1964.

Caplan, G. *Prevention of mental disorders in children*. New York: Basic Books, 1964.

Cauce, A. M., Felner, R. D., & Primavera, J. Social support systems in high risk adolescents: Structural components and adaptive impact. *American Journal of Community Psychology*, 1982, *10*, 417–428.

Coddington, R. D. The significance of life events as etiological factors in the diseases of children: I. A survey of professional workers. *Journal of Psychosomatic Research*, 1972, *16*, 7–18. (a)

Coddington, R. D. The significance of life events as etiological factors in the diseases of children: II. A study of a normal population. *Journal of Psychosomatic Research*, 1972, *16*, 205–213. (b)

Collins, J. M., & Coulter, F. Effects of geographical movement on the social and academic development of children of army personnel. *Australian and New Zealand Journal of Sociology*, 1974, *10*, 222–223.

Cowen, E. L. The wooing of primary prevention. *American Journal of Community Psychology*. 1980, *8*, 258–284.

Cramer, W., & Dorsey, S. Are movers losers? *The Elementary School Journal*, 1979, *70*, 387–390.

Cunningham, L., Cadoret, R. J., Loftus, R., & Edwards, J. R. Studies of adoptees from psychiatrically disturbed biological parents: Psychiatric conditions in childhood and adolescence. *British Journal of Psychiatry*, 1975, *126*, 534–549.

DeLongis, A., Coyne, J. C., Dakof, G., Folkman, S., & Lazarus, R. S. Relationships of hassles, uplifts, and major life events to health status. *Health Psychology*, 1982, *1*, 119–136.

Dohrenwend, B. P. Stressful life events and psychopathology: Some issues of theory and method. In J. E. Barrett (Ed.), *Stress and mental disorder*. New York: Raven Press, 1979.

Dohrenwend, B. P., & Pearlin, L. I. *Report of the panel of life events from the committee for research on stress in health and disease*. Institute of Medicine, National Academy of Sciences, Washington, D.C., 150–169, 1981.

Dohrenwend, B. S. Life events as stressors: A methodological inquiry. *Journal of Health and Social Behavior*, 1973, *14*, 167–175.

Dohrenwend, B. S. Social stress and community psychology. *American Journal of Community Psychology*, 1978, *6*, 1–14.

Douglas, J. W. B. Early disturbing events and later enuresis. In I. Kolvin, R. MacKeith, & S. R. Meadow (Eds.), *Bladder control and enuresis*. London: SIMP/Heinemann, 1973.

Drotar, D. Clinical practice in the pediatric hospital. *Professional Psychology*, 1977, *8*, 72–80.

Drotar, D. Psychological perspectives in chronic childhood illness. *Journal of Pediatric Psychology*, 1981, *6*, 211–228.

Dunn, J., & Kendrick, C. Study temperament and parent-child interaction: Comparison of interview and direct observation. *Developmental Medicine and Child Neurology*, 1980, *4*, 484–496.(a)

Dunn, J., & Kendrick, C. The arrival of a sibling: Change in patterns of interaction between mother and first born. *Journal of Child Psychology and Psychiatry*, 1980, *21*, 119–132.(b)

Dunn, J., Kendrick, C., & MacNamee, R. The reaction of first-born children to the birth of a sibling: Mothers' reports. *Journal of Child Psychology and Psychiatry*, 1981, *22*, 1–18.

Dweck, C. S., & Bush, E. S. Sex differences in learned helplessness: I. Differential debilitation with peer and adult evaluators. *Developmental Psychology*, 1976, *12*, 147–156.

Dweck, C. S., Davidson, W., Nelson, S., & Enna, B. Sex differences in learned helplessness. II. The contingencies of evaluative feedback in the classroom and III. An experimental analysis. *Developmental Psychology*, 1978, *14*, 268–276.

Eisen, P. Children under stress. *Australian and New Zealand Journal of Psychiatry*, 1979, *13*, 193–207.

Emery, R. E. Interparental conflict and the children of discord and divorce. *Psychological Bulletin*, 1982, *92*, 310–330.

Farber, S. S., Primavera, J., & Felner, R. D. Parental separation/divorce and adolescents: Examination of factors mediating adaptation. *American Journal of Community Psychology*, in press.

Felner, R. D., & Aber, M. S. Primary prevention for children: A framework for the assessment of need. *Prevention in Human Services*, 1983, *2*, 109–121.

Felner, R. D., Aber, M. S., Primavera, J., & Cauce, A. M. Adaptation and vulnerability in high risk adolescents: An examination of environmental mediators. *American Journal of Community Psychology*, in press.

Felner, R. D., Farber, S. S., Ginter, M. A., Boike, M. F., & Cowen, E. L. Family stress and organization following parental divorce or death. *Journal of Divorce*, 1980, *4*(2), 67–76.

Felner, R. D., Farber, S. S., & Primavera, J. Transitions and stressful life events: A model for primary prevention. In R. H. Price, R. F. Ketterer, B. C. Bader, & J. Monahan (Eds.), *Prevention in mental health: Research, policy, and practice*. Beverly Hills, CA: Sage Publications, 1980.

Felner, R. D., Farber, S. S., & Primavera, J. Transitions and stressful life events: A model for primary prevention. In R. D. Felner, L. A. Jason, J. N. Moritsugu, & S. S. Farber (Eds.), *Preventive psychology: Theory, research, and practice*. New York: Pergamon Press, 1983.

Felner, R. D., Ginter, M. A., Boike, M. F., & Cowen, E. L. Parental death or divorce and the school adjustment of young children. *American Journal of Community Psychology*, 1981, *9*, 181–191.

Felner, R. D., Ginter, M. A., & Primavera, J. Primary prevention during school transitions: Social support and environmental structure. *American Journal of Community Psychology*, 1982, *10*, (3), 227–290.

Felner, R. D., Jason, L. A., Moritsugu, J., & Farber, S. S. Preventive psychology: Evolution and current status. In R. D. Felner, L. A. Jason, J. N. Moritsugu, & S. S. Farber (Eds.), *Preventive psychology: Theory, research and practice*. New York: Pergamon Press, 1983.

Felner, R. D., Norton, P. L., Cowen, E. L., & Farber, S. S. A prevention program for children experiencing life crisis. *Professional Psychology*, 1981, *12*, 446–452.

Felner, R. D., Primavera, J., & Cauce, A. M. The impact of school transitions: A focus for preventive efforts. *American Journal of Community Psychology*, 1981, *9*, 449–459.

Felner, R. D., Stolberg, A., & Cowen, E. L. Crisis events and school mental health referral patterns of young children. *Journal of Consulting and Clinical Psychology*, 1975, *43*, 305–310.

Finkel, N. J. Stress, trauma and trauma resolution. *American Journal of Community Psychology*, 1975, *3*, 173–178.

Gad, M. T., & Johnson, J. H. Correlates of adolescent life stress as related to race, SES, and levels of perceived social support. *Journal of Clinical Child Psychology*, 1980, *9*, 13–16.

Garmezy, N. The experimental study of children vulnerable to psychopathology. In A. Davis (Ed.), *Child personality and psychopathology: Current topics* (Vol. 2). New York: Wiley-Interscience, 1975.

Garmezy, N. *Vulnerable and invulnerable children: Theory, research, and intervention.* Washington, D.C.: American Psychological Association, 1976.

Gersten, J. C., Langner, T. S., Eisenberg, J. G., & Simcha-Fagan, O. An evaluation of the etiologic role of stressful life events in psychological disorder. *Journal of Health and Social Behavior*, 1977, *18*, 228–244.

Glueck, S., & Glueck, E. *Unravelling juvenile delinquency.* Boston: Harvard University Press, 1950.

Goebel, B. L. Mobility and education. *American Secondary Education*, 1978, *8*, 11–16.

Gottlieb, B. H. Social networks and social support in community mental health. In B. H. Gottlieb (Ed.), *Social networks and social support.* Beverly Hills: Sage Publications, 1981.

Grant, I., Kyle, G. C., Teichman, S., & Mendels, J. Recent life events and diabetes in adults. *Psychosomatic Medicine*, 1974, *36*, 121–128.

Gregory, I. Retrospective data concerning childhood loss of a parent. I: Category of parental loss by decade of birth, diagnosis and MMPI. *Archives of General Psychiatry*, 1966, *15*, 362–367.

Harris, P. W. The relationship of life change to academic performance among selected college freshmen at varying levels of college readiness. Unpublished doctoral dissertation. East Texas State University, 1972.

Heisel, J. S., Ream, S., Raitz, R., Rappaport, M., & Coddington, R. D. The significance of life events as contributing factors in the diseases of children. *Behavioral Pediatrics*, 1973, *83*, 119–123.

Heller, K., & Swindle, R. W. Social networks, social support and coping with stress. In R. D. Felner, L. A. Jason, J. Moritsugu, & S. S. Farber (Eds.), *Preventive psychology: Theory, research and practice.* New York: Pergamon Press, 1983.

Hetherington, E. M. Effects of father absence on personality development in adolescent daughters. *Developmental Psychology*, 1972, *8*, 313–326.

Hetherington, E. M., Cox, M., & Cox, R. The aftermath of divorce. In J.H. Stevens, Jr. & M. Mathews (Eds.), *Mother/child father/child relationships.* Washington, D.C.: National Association for the Education of Young Children, 1978.

Holland, J. V., Kaplan, D. M., & Davis, S. D. Interschool transfers: A mental health challenge. *Journal of School Health*, 1974, *44*, 74–79.

Holmes, R. H., & Rahe, R. H. The social readjustment rating scale. *Journal of Psychosomatic Research*, 1967, *11*, 213–218.

Holmes, T. H. Development and application of a quantitative measure of life change magnitude. In J. E. Barrett (Ed.), *Stress and mental disorder.* New York: Raven Press, 1979.

Hotaling, G. T., Atwell, S. G., & Linsky, A. S. Adolescent life changes and illness: A comparison of three models. *Journal of Youth and Adolescence*, 1978, *7*, 393–403.

Hough, R. L., Fairbank, D. T., & Garcia, A. M. Problems in the ratio measurement of life stress. *Journal of Health and Social Behavior*, 1976, *17*, 70–82.

Hudgens, R. W. Personal catastrophe and depression: A consideration of the subject with respect to medically ill adolescents, and a requiem for retrospective life-event studies. In B.S. Dohrenwend & B.P. Dohrenwend (Eds.), *Stressful life events: Their nature and effects.* New York: Wiley, 1974.

Jacobs, T. J., & Charles, E. Life events and the occurrence of cancer in children *Psychosomatic Medicine*, 1980, *42*, 11–24.

Jessner, L., Blom, G. E., & Waldfogel, S. Emotional implications of tonsilectomy and adenoidectomy in children. In R. S. Eisslen (Ed.), *The psychoanalytic study of the child*. New York: International Universities Press, 1952.

Johnson, J. H. Life events as stressors in childhood and adolescence. In B. B. Lahey & A. E. Kazdin (Eds.), *Advances in clinical child psychology* (Vol. 5). New York: Plenum Press, 1982.

Johnson, J. H., & McCutcheon, S. M. Assessing life stress in older children and adolescents: Preliminary findings with the life events checklist. In I. G. Sarason & C. D. Spielberger (Eds.), *Stress and anxiety* (Vol 7). Washington, D.C.: Hemisphere, 1980.

Johnson, J. H., & Sarason, I. G. Life stress, depression and anxiety: Internal-external control as a moderator variable. *Journal of Psychosomatic Research*, 1978, *22*, 205–208.

Johnson, J. H., & Sarason, I. G. Moderator variables in life stress research. In I. G. Sarason & C. D. Spielberger (Eds.), *Stress and anxiety* (Vol. 6). Washington, D.C.: Hemisphere, 1979.

Kagen-Goodheart, L. Re-entry: Living with childhood cancer. *American Journal of Orthopsychiatry*, 1977, *47*, 651–658.

Kemme, M. L. Factors relevant to the mobile child's management of entry into a new school. *Dissertation Abstracts International*, 1971, *32*, 1849.

Koocher, G. P., & O'Malley, J. E. *The Damocles syndrome: Psychosocial consequences of surviving childhood cancer*. New York: McGraw-Hill, 1981.

Lambert, L. Essen, J., & Head, J. Variations in behavior ratings of children who have been in care. *Journal of Child Psychology and Psychiatry and Allied Health Professions*, 1977, *18*, 335–346.

Lavigne, J. V., & Ryan, M. Psychologic adjustment of siblings of children with chronic illness. *Pediatrics*, 1979, *63*, 616–626.

Lazarus, R. S., & Launier, R. Stress-released transactions between person and environment. In L. A. Pervin & M. Lewis (Eds.), *Perspectives in interactional psychology*. New York: Plenum Press, 1978.

Leaverton, D. R., White, C. A., McCormick, C. R., Smith, P., & Skeikholislam, B. Parental loss antecedent to childhood diabetes mellitus. *Journal of the American Academy of Child Psychiatry*, 1980, *19*, 678–689.

Levine, M. Residential change and school adjustment. *Community Mental Health Journal*, 1966, *2*, 61–69.

Levine, M., Wesolowski, J. C., & Corbett, F. J. Pupil turnover and academic performance in an inner city elementary school. *Psychology in the Schools*, 1966, *3*, 153–156.

Lindemann, E. The meaning of crises in individual and family living. *Teachers' College Record*, 1956, *57*, 310–315.

Markush, R. E., & Favero, R. V. Epidemiological assessment of stressful life events, depressed mood, and psychophysiological symptoms—A preliminary report. In B. S. Dohrenwend & B.P. Dohrenwend (Eds), *Stressful life events: Their nature and effects*. New York: Wiley, 1974.

Masuda, M., & Holmes, T. H. Life events: Perceptions and frequencies. *Psychosomatic Medicine*, 1978, *40*, 236–261.

Meyer, R. J., & Haggerty, R. J. Streptococcal infections in families. *Pediatrics*, 1962, *29*, 539–549.

Monaghan, J. H., Robinson, J. O., & Dodge, J. A. The children's life events inventory. *Journal of Psychosomatic Research*, 1979, *23*, 63–68.

Moore, T. Stress in normal childhood. In L. Levi (Ed.), *Society: Stress and disease. Volume 2: Childhood and adolescence*. London: Oxford University Press, 1975.

Munro, A. Parental deprivation in depressive patients. *British Journal of Psychiatry*, 1966, *112*, 443–457.

Murphy, L. B. Preventive implications of development in the preschool years. In G. Caplan (Ed.), *Prevention of mental disorder in children*. New York: Basic Books, 1961.

Myers, J.K., Lindenthal, J. J., & Pepper, M. P. Social class, life events, and psychiatric symptoms: A longitudinal study. In B. S. Dohrenwend & B. P. Dohrenwend (Eds.), *Stressful life events: Their nature and effects*. New York: Wiley, 1974.

Nannis, E. D., Susman, E. J., Strope, B. E., Woodruff, P. J., Hersh, S. P., Levine, A. S., & Pizzo, P. A. Conception of cancer: The perspectives of child and adolescent patients and their families. *Journal of Pediatric Psychology*, 1982, *7*, 75–84.

Nieto, J. The Puerto Rican child. In I. R. Stuart & L. E. Abt (Eds.), *Children of separation and divorce*. New York: Grossman, 1979.

Nuckolls, K. B., Cassel, J., & Kaplan, B. H. Psychosocial assets, life crisis and the prognosis of pregnancy. *American Journal of Epidemiology*, 1972, *95*, 431–441.

Nye, F. I. Child adjustment in broken and in unhappy, unbroken homes. *Marriage and Family Living*, 1957, *19*, 356–361.

Padilla, E. R., Rohsenow, D. J., & Bergman, A. B. Predicting accident frequency in children. *Pediatrics*, 1976, *58*, 223–226.

Paykel, E. S. Life stress and psychiatric disorder: Applications of the clinical approach. In B. S. Dohrenwend & B. P. Dohrenwend (Eds.), *Stressful life events: Their nature and effects*. New York: Wiley, 1974.

Pearlin, L. I., Menaghan, E. G., Lieberman, M. A., & Mullen, J. R. The stress process. *Journal of Health and Social Behavior*, 1981, *22*, 337–356.

Peterson, L., & Ridley-Johnson, R. Prevention of childhood disorders. In C. E. Walker & M. C. Roberts (Eds.), *Handbook of clinical child psychology*. New York: Wiley-Interscience, 1983.

Peterson, L., & Shigetomi, C. The use of coping techniques to minimize anxiety in hospital children. *Behavior Therapy*, 1981, *12*, 1–14.

Pless, I. B., & Roghmann, K. J. Chronic illness and its consequences: Observations based on three epidemiological surveys. *Journal of Pediatrics*, 1971, *79*, 351–359.

Pless, I. B., Roghmann, K. J., & Haggerty, R. J. Chronic illness, family functioning and psychological adjustment: A model for the allocation of preventive mental health services. *International Journal of Epidemiology*, 1972, *1*, 271–277.

Price, R. H. The education of the preventive psychologist. In R.D. Felner, L. A. Jason, J. Moritsugu, & S. S. Farber (Eds.), *Preventive psychology: Theory, research and practice*. New York: Pergamon Press, 1983.

Prugh, D. G., Staub, E. M., Sands, H. H., Kirschbaum, R. M., & Lenihan, E. A. A study of the emotional reactions of children and families to hospitalization and illness. *American Journal of Orthopsychiatry*, 1953, *23*, 70–106.

Quinton, D., & Rutter, M. Early hospital admissions and later disturbance of behavior: An attempted replication of Douglas' finding. *Developmental Medicine and Child Neurology*, 1976, *18*, 447–459.

Rabkin, J. G., & Streuning, E. L. Life events, stress and illness. *Science*, 1976, *194*, 1013–1020.

Rahe, R. H., Mahan, J. L., & Arthur, R. J. Prediction of near-future health changes from subjects: Preceding life changes. *Journal of Psychosomatic Research*, 1970, *14*, 401–406.

Rakieten, H. The reactions of mobile elementary school children to various elementary school induction and orientation procedures. Unpublished doctoral dissertation. Teachers College, Columbia University, 1961.

Rappaport, J. *Community psychology: Values, research and action*. New York: Holt, Rinehart & Winston, 1977.

Rutter, M. *Children of sick parents*. Maudsley Monograph No. 16. New York: Oxford University Press, 1966.

Rutter, M. Stress, coping and development: Some issues and some questions. *Journal of Child Psychology and Psychiatry*, 1981, *22*, 323–356.

Sandler, I. N. Life stress events and community psychology, In I. G. Sarason & C. Speilberger (Eds.), *Stress and anxiety* (Vol. 6). New York: Halstead Press, 1979.

Sandler, I. N. Social support resources, stress and maladjustment of poor children. *American Journal of Community Psychology*, 1980, *8*, 41–52.

Sandler, I. N., & Block, M. Life stress and maladaptation of children. *American Journal of Community Psychology*, 1979, *7*, 425–440.

Sandler, I. N., Duricko, A., & Grande, L. Effectiveness of an early secondary prevention program in an inner-city elementary school. *American Journal of Community Psychology*, 1975, *3*, 23–32.

Sandler, I. N., & Ramsey, T. B. Dimensional analysis of children's stressful life events. *American Journal of Community Psychology*, 1980, *8*, 28–302.

Sarason, I. G., Johnson, J. H., & Siegal, J. M. Assessing the impact of life changes: Development of the life experiences survey. *Journal of Consulting and Clinical Psychology*, 1978, *46*, 932–946.

Schaller, J. The relationship between geographic mobility and school behavior. *Man-Environment Systems*, 1975, *5*, 185–187.

Schechter, M., Carlson, P., Simmons, J., & Work, H. Emotional problems in the adoptee. *Archives of General Psychiatry*, 1968, *10*, 109–118.

Stein, K. A. A challenge to the role of the crisis concept in emergency psychotherapy. *Dissertation Abstracts International*, 1970, *30*, 5045B.

Stein, S. P., & Charles, E. Emotional factors in juvenile diabetes mellitus: A study of early life experiences of adolescent diabetics. *American Journal of Psychiatry*, 1971, *128*, 56–60.

Sugar, M. Divorce and children. *Southern Medical Journal*, 1970, *63*, 1458–1461.

Tew, B. J., & Laurence, K. M. Mothers, brothers, and sisters of patients with spina bifida. *Developmental Medicine and Child Neurology*, 1973, *15* (Suppl. 29), 69–76.

Tizard, B. *Adoption: A second chance*. London: Open Books, 1977.

Turk, D. C. Factors influencing the adaptive process with chronic illness: Implications for intervention. In I. G. Sarason & C. D. Spielberger (Eds.), *Stress and anxiety* (Vol. 6). Washington, D.C.: Hemisphere Publishing, 1979.

Tuckman, S., & Regan, R. A. Intactness of the home and behavioral problems in children. *Journal of Child Psychology and Psychiatry*, 1967, *7*, 225–233.

Uhlenhuth, E. H. Life stress and illness: The search for significance. In J. E. Barrett (Ed.), *Stress and mental disorder*. New York: Raven Press, 1979.

U.S. Department of Health, Education and Welfare. *Dropout prevention*. Washington, D.C.: Educational Resources Information Center, 1975 (ERIC Document Reproduction Service No. ED 105 354).

Wallerstein, J. S. Responses of the preschool child to divorce: Those who cope. In M. F. McMilliam & S. Henas (Eds.), *Child psychiatry: Treatment and research*. New York: Brunner/Mazel, 1977.

Wallerstein, J. S., & Kelly, J. B. The effects of parental divorce: The adolescent experience. In E. J. Anthony & C. Koupernik (Eds.), *The child in his family: Children at psychiatric risk* (Vol. 3). New York: Wiley, 1974.

Wallerstein, J. D., & Kelly, J. B. The effects of parental divorce: The experiences of the preschool child. *Journal of American Academy of Child Psychiatry*, 1975, *14*, 600–616.

Wallerstein, J. S., & Kelly, J. B. The effects of parental divorce: Experiences of the child in later latency. *American Journal of Orthopsychiatry*, 1976, *46*, 256–269.

Wallerstein, J. S., & Kelly, J. B. Divorce counseling: A community service for families in the midst of divorce. *American Journal of Orthopsychiatry*, 1977, *47*, 4–22.

Wolff, S. *Children under stress*. New York: Basic Books, 1969.

Wright, L. A comprehensive program for mental health and behavioral medicine in a large children's hospital. *Professional Psychology*, 1979, *10*, 458–466.

Zautra, A., & Simons, L. S. Some effects of positive life events on individual and community mental health. *American Journal of Community Psychology*. 1979, *7*, 441–452.

REFERENCE NOTES

1. Morley, W. *Treatment of the patient in crisis*. Unpublished manuscript, Los Angeles Psychiatric Service, 1964.
2. Siegel, L. J. *Naturalistic study of coping strategies in children facing medical procedures*. Paper presented at the Southeastern Psychological Association. Atlanta, Ga., 1981.
3. Raschke, H. J., & Raschke, V. J. *Family conflict and children's self concepts: A comparison of intact and single parent families*. Presented at the 72nd Annual Meeting of the American Sociological Association. September, 1977.
4. Zill, N. *Divorce, marital happiness and the mental health of children: Findings from the Foundation for Child Development National Survey of Children*. Prepared for the National Institute of Mental Health Workshop on Divorce and Children, Bethesda, Maryland, 1978.

PART TWO

Reducing Risk

Problem-Focused Prevention

CHAPTER 6

Psychological Applications to the Prevention of Accidents and Illness

MICHAEL C. ROBERTS, PAULINE D. ELKINS, AND GEORGE P. ROYAL

Psychology traditionally has been associated with the study and remediation of mental health problems. Increasingly, however, psychological research and applications are being made in a wider range of areas. As a prime example, protecting and enhancing physical health and safety, particularly of children, has become an important new emphasis for the application of psychological knowledge (Matarazzo, 1982; Roberts, Maddux, & Wright, 1984; Roberts, Maddux, Wurtele, & Wright, 1982). This development derives from the increased awareness of the psychological and behavioral relationships in health promotion and physical disorder prevention. For example, professionals from a number of disciplines including psychology, medicine, and public health assert that further significant improvements in quality of human life (physical status, longevity, and so forth), will be made not by technological advancements, but through individual actions related to behavior and lifestyle. In other words, it is what people *do* that will determine the quality of life. People *doing* is the realm of psychology, the science of behavior. Indeed, examination of just a few statistics bears out the relationship of physical health and behavior. In general, accidents are the leading cause of deaths in childhood (Wright, Schaefer, & Solomons, 1979). Motor vehicle accidents, in particular, produce the largest number of child injuries and deaths—over 4,000 children under 15 years annually die in such accidents (National Safety Council, 1979). These deaths are primarily attributable to the lack of proper child restraints, excessive speed, or alcohol consumption by a driver. These causes are behaviorally based. Similarly, nonintentional poisoning of children produces a considerable number of injuries and deaths—a multitude of children ingest toxic substances each year including drugs, pesticides, and a variety of common household agents. Poison control in the household is a behavior that can prevent such accidents. Whereas communicable diseases previously accounted for the majority of childhood deaths, acquiring immunization against disease is a behavioral act with singular implications for preventing illness. Other preventable accidents and illnesses with significant behavior components include fires and burns, shooting accidents, cuts from sharp objects, playground accidents, and so forth. The list is virtually endless. This is not to say that behavioral aspects are the only causes or that behavioral interventions are the only solution for accident and illness prevention, but behavior is intrinsic to both.

In considering prevention of physical disorders and injury in this chapter, we intend not to just repeat the call for improved safety for children but to show how psychological principles can be utilized in understanding and improving children's safety and reducing disease risk. Thus, we will note the accident or disease potential of various situations and also note the preventive actions necessary. But more importantly, we will discuss how psychological techniques might be applied to implement preventive actions. For example, particular accidents are preventable by relatively simple actions: poisoning risk is reduced by storing toxic agents out of children's reach; vehicle collision injuries are reduced by restraint in a child safety seat; pedestrian injuries are reduced by proper street crossing. Psychology has relatively little to add to these proposed preventive actions which have been repeatedly articulated by other concerned groups (for example, the American Academy of Pediatrics Committee on Accidents and Poison Prevention, Insurance Institute for Highway Safety, and Physicians for Automotive Safety). Psychology can contribute, however, in understanding behavior and encouraging parents to take preventive actions or to teach their children appropriate behavior.

The fact that most accidents are not just random, unavoidable, inexplicable events based on chance has led to a recent preference for the term *inadvertent injuries and injury control* rather than *accidents and prevention* (Haddon & Baker, 1981). In line with this, our use of the term *accidents* here is not an endorsement of the latter terminology, but is used as a term more readily understandable and extant in the literature. We firmly believe the data indicate that most accidents are preventable and are not merely capricious events.

The importance of illness and injury prevention can be measured by several parameters: (1) number of children injured or killed, (2) the financial cost to parents and society over a long term, and (3) the psychological correlates of such problems (Baker, 1980). These three parameters are discussed throughout this chapter and especially in a later section on cost-effectiveness issues. To preview the rest of the chapter, the goal of prevention efforts in this realm is to ameliorate or preclude these three undesirable outcomes of illness and injury.

Overview of Chapter

In this chapter we focus on psychology's contributions to the prevention of accidents and illness in childhood. We first examine actual and potential applications of psychological ideas as applied to individual and demographic correlates of behavior, developmental principles, motivational techniques, and methodological procedures. Next, we discuss three major approaches to prevention of physical disorders: (1) targeting the caregiver, (2) targeting the child, and (3) targeting society at large.

We then turn to the obstacles or problems associated with prevention efforts, including the complexity of the preventive behavior, cost-effectiveness issues, financial support, and availability of services. Throughout the following sections, we refer to existing research and literature. Where limited sound research exists, we note descriptive, anecdotal, or clinical reports, while reaffirming the need for more substantive empirical efforts. Much of the literature upon which this chapter is based comes from disciplines other than psychology, including pediatrics, public health, and nursing. Psychology in many forms is increasingly involved in prevention of accidents and illness; greater contributions can be made.

ACTUAL AND POTENTIAL APPLICATIONS OF PSYCHOLOGY

Psychology as the science of behavior and mental processes has much to offer the topic of prevention. As noted above, what people *do* is the realm of psychology. Both the content of psychological understanding (for example, behavioral laws, developmental principles) and the scientific process by which that content is acquired (such as research methodology and evaluation techniques) are major contributions to prevention programming. Several examples of applications specific to accidents and illness will be noted briefly, including individual and demographic correlates, developmental principles, motivation of behavior change for preventive action, educational and learning principles, and scientific methodology.

Individual and Demographic Correlates

Accident Proneness.

Understanding human behavior as a major aspect of psychology has included the examination of "accident proneness" in children. Researchers have observed that certain individual and demographic characteristics correlate regularly with types and rates of accidents. At the simplest level, the concept asserts that there are some common characteristics in those children who account for accidents more often than other children. Psychological research has pointed to personality and behavioral characteristics that identify children of high accident liability: extraversion, aggression, impulsivity, greater activity, distractibility, inattention to situational cues and to ongoing task requirements (Manheimer & Mellinger, 1967; Matheny, 1980; Matheny, Brown, & Wilson, 1971, 1972). This research is, of course, correlational and only suggestive of causative factors. Additionally, some researchers dispute the accident proneness thesis since it minimizes the contribution to accidents made by hazardous environments, and in essence, "blames the victim" for an accident (Haddon & Baker, 1981; Sass & Crook, 1981). The emphasis on personality characteristics of accident proneness has diminished somewhat as researchers eschew *trait* implications in favor of accident repeaters or accident liable children. The concept is useful, however, as this research contributes to the identification of potential accident interactions (namely, a dangerous situation and an accident prone child) with a goal of preventing such occurrences (Matheny, 1980). This psychological research on child accident proneness can therefore contribute to prevention programming by identifying children at higher risk for particular accidents.

Epidemiology.

As noted later in this chapter, certain demographic characteristics have been studied in relation to accidents and illness from an epidemiological standpoint. For example, age differences emerge in the types of childhood accidents; "poisonings are more common among toddlers, drownings more common among preschoolers, and pedestrian injuries more common among children of school age" (Matheny 1980, p. 344). Other studies indicate boys are more likely than girls to be involved in accidents, and children from lower class families tend to have more accidents (Manheimer, Dewey, Mellinger, & Corsa, 1966; summarized by Matheny, 1980). Epidemiology studies also help identify children particularly at risk and in need of prevention efforts.

A few illustrations demonstrate the nature and utility of epidemiology. Studies of dog bites and attacks reveal several conclusions: (1) spring and summer months witness higher rates of dog bites for older children, whereas younger children have a fairly stable rate throughout the year, (2) boys receive more dog bites than girls, (3) pet dogs without a history of biting predominate the biting reports, (4) attacking dogs outweigh their victims, and (5) infants less than one year old receive more fatal dog attacks than other age groups (Chun, Berkelhamer, & Herold, 1982; Pinckney & Kennedy, 1982). These conclusions point to possible targets for prevention, although no dog attack prevention programs are known to us. Similar epidemiological studies, for example, have been conducted on child car passenger accidents resulting from collisions or falls from vehicles (Baker, 1979; Bell, Ternberg, & Bower, 1980; Williams, 1981), safety restraint use (Pless & Roghmann, 1978), childhood strangulation (Feldman & Simms, 1980), playground accidents and equipment characteristics (Reichelderfer, Overbach, & Greensher, 1979; Sweeney, 1979; Werner, 1982), unsafe sleeping conditions (Smialek, Smialek, & Spitz, 1977), and childhood poisoning (Rogers, 1981). As noted, the contribution of these types of epidemiology studies is in the identification of situations and victim characteristics requiring preventive intervention.

Developmental Principles

A primary tenet of psychology is that *change* in behavior, attitudes, emotions, and intellectual properties is essential to human development. For children, the changes develop rapidly. With such change over the lifespan comes the need to target different preventive services based on the needs and characteristics of a particular age group. The discipline of psychology provides a perspective on the developmental process with applications for prevention. Certainly, it is well understood that establishing early healthful lifestyles and safety-conscious behavior has ramifications for later behavior, health, and quality of life.

Developmental psychology can be applied to determine how preventive actions are decided by individuals and what may influence their decisions. This line of research indicates *when* and *what* particular types of preventive efforts might be most powerful. For example, prevention efforts might be best taken when the parent or child is most receptive or when critical decisions are made. Kanthor (1976) presents evidence which suggests that parents are most likely to acquire infant car safety seats when advised to do so during the prenatal period. Smoking prevention programs might be most effective if targeted to children in the 12–13 year old age group who are entering the critical decision-making stage and are more susceptible to developing smoking habits (Hunter, Webber, & Berenson, 1980; Matarazzo, 1982). Further psychological research might explicate other such particular developmental periods for *when* prevention intervention might be most successful.

A second developmental application comes from the study of *when* prevention services are especially needed in the lifespan, that is, periods of high risk. For example, poison control is critically needed for children ages one to four years since most accidental poisonings occur during this age period (Vaughan & McKay, 1975). The nature of child pedestrian accidents indicates a need for training programs at ages five to nine years (Yeaton & Bailey, 1978; Yeaton, Greene, & Bailey, 1981). Safety with recreational equipment (bicycles, playgrounds, skateboards) needs to be emphasized for children ages 6–11 because the leading causes of accidents for this developmental period include these apparatus (Califano, 1979; Reichelderfer et al., 1979; Sweeney, 1979; Werner, 1982). Immunization schedules should be followed for high-risk preschool age children who are not covered by mandatory inoculation laws for school attendance or who have low rates of compliance (Yokley & Glenwick, in press; Peterson, Note 1).

Pediatrics identifies this type of prevention as anticipatory guidance (Brazelton, 1975; Roberts & Wright, 1982). This concept utilizes the knowledge base in child development and growth to anticipate the type of abilities emerging at different ages and the corresponding accidents for which parents should be alert. For example, the child in his or her first year has accidents of falls, inhalation of foreign objects, and drownings because of normal behavior characteristics of squirming and rolling, placing things in the mouth, and being helpless in the water. In anticipatory guidance, the pediatrician instructs parents in preventive precautions including not leaving the child alone on a table or in a tub of water and keeping small objects and harmful materials out of reach (Vaughan & McKay, 1975, p. 214).

A third application based on an understanding of developmental processes derives from *what* types of programming would be most effective. For example, the research by Evans suggests that antismoking programs for junior high students should be present-oriented, not future-oriented (Evans, Rozelle, Mittelmark, Hansen, Bane, & Havis, 1978). Utilizing a developmental perspective, Gallagher and Moody (1981) suggest that, since adolescents and young adults are greatly concerned with personal appearance, dentist encouragement for oral hygiene might emphasize this aspect. Fear appeal messages to eliminate maternal alcohol intake and prevent fetal alcohol syndrome should include information about alcoholic effects on both mother and fetus during pregnancy (Labs, Note 2). Prevention programs requiring active participation (role-playing, behavioral rehearsal, or guided practice) by children are more effective than instruction alone (see example for dental preventive behaviors in Levy, Lodish, & Pawlack-Floyd, 1982). These examples illustrate how developmental research contributes to determining preventive program designs and components.

This discussion of developmental psychology applications illustrates the utility of developmental principles in determining *when* and *how* to implement prevention programming: (1) when services might be most powerful, (2) when services are critically needed, and (3) what types of services are most effective.

Motivation of Behavior Change for Prevention Action

Several subareas within the broad domain of psychology have developed theoretical frameworks for understanding and influencing human behavior. We will use some of these to illustrate the actual and potential utility of the psychology of behavioral change and motivation to the prevention of accidents and illness: fear appeals, reward and punishment, prompting, and modeling.

Fear Appeals.

Within social psychology, behavior and attitude change have been studied as a result of fear appeals or informational messages which try to evoke emotional arousal or threaten impending harm (Rogers, 1975; 1983). Preventive action, including the elimination or change of particular behaviors, may be taken by an individual to avoid feared aversive consequences. Many health messages contain such fear appeals, for example, television public service commercials which inform parents of the tragic consequences of not using seat belts, of not immunizing children against diseases, of not brushing teeth, of home fires, and so forth. The psychological research base for fear appeals (for example, protection motivation theory) is growing to indicate their efficacy in encouraging preventive behaviors in some situations (Rogers, 1983). However, some workers have noted there may be problems in relying on fear appeals and health hazard warnings. Etzioni (1978) suggests that overwarning the public may lead to some people discounting or ignoring each new hazard warning because they are already overwhelmed with warnings. Christophersen (Note 3) suggests that fear appeals likely lose their effect when the negative health behavior occurs with no aversive consequences. For example, when parents leave their children unrestrained without seat belts, the child is at greater risk for an accidental injury. The probability, however, is relatively low that an accident will occur. Therefore, the parents are not punished for ignoring a fear message by suffering the negative consequences of not restraining their child in cars. In general, this example of fear appeals research and debate about efficacy points to the need for continuing examination of this psychological application to prevention. Nonetheless, this type of research demonstrates one psychological application in motivating behavior and attitude change for preventive and health topics.

Reward and Punishment.

A second application of the knowledge base of psychology to prevention comes from learning theory research. The basic premise is that behavior followed by a reward increases in frequency, while punished behavior is suppressed or decreases in frequency. Application of reward and punishment paradigms may occur with either planned consequences or natural happenings. For example, more effective toothbrushing and flossing to prevent dental caries was increased through planned rewards provided by classroom teachers or parents (Claerhout & Lutzker, 1981; Swain, Allard, & Holborn, 1982). Rewarding children on school buses through contingent music playing for decreases in noise and disruptive behavior resulted in less distraction of the driver's attention (Barmann, Croyle-Barmann, & McLain, 1980), and lowered the potential for accidents. External reinforcement (money, discounts) to parents has increased preventive acts of bringing their children in for dental checkups (Reiss, Piotrowski, & Bailey, 1976) and acquiring child immunizations (Yokley & Glenwick, in press; White, 1976). Providing free or low cost preventive devices, such as car safety seats (Reisinger & Williams, 1978) and cabinet locking devices (Dershewitz, 1979), is a form of external reinforcement, but one which has not proven to effectively alter the use of all apparatus provided. However, free electrical outlet covers have been used with high frequency (Dershewitz, 1979). Other examples of planned reinforcement procedures for prevention will be noted in later sections. Externally imposed punishment effects are demonstrated by state laws requiring child restraints in cars (Williams, 1979). Fines levied against parents in Tennessee, for example, decreased nonuse of proper safety restraints (Williams & Wells, 1981). Promoting prevention behavior through naturally occurring reinforcement and punishment has received less attention, primarily because the experimental controls are difficult to determine. Additionally, many potential rewards and punishments for behavior in the natural setting never occur, or are long range rather than immediate. For example, a child who never wears a seatbelt may never be involved in a vehicle accident. Failure to maintain dental hygiene may result in dental disease and eventual loss of teeth only at later ages. Additionally, many preventive acts are avoidances of aversive consequences which usually means the status quo is maintained. For instance, practicing water safety avoids drowning, but no overt reward, other than continued life, goes to the safe swimmer or boater. Some instances of naturally-occurring reinforcement have been postulated by researchers. Christophersen and Gyulay (1981) present data to support that use of car safety seats for children becomes naturally rewarding to parents because restrained children exhibit more appropriate behavior. Failure to restrain the child results in a naturally occurring punishment because of increased inappropriate behavior in the car (Christophersen, Note 3). Both planned and naturally-occurring consequences as psychological phenomena have the potential to change and maintain preventive behavior.

Prompting.

Another psychological phenomenon derived from learning theory is that of prompting or presenting discriminative stimulus cues to people to engage in preventive behavior. Examples of cues or reminders to take action may be observed in seatbelt buzzers in passenger cars, flashing yellow street lights, and school zone signs. Applied research has found that systematic prompts (for example, telephone calls or mailings) increases the likelihood of keeping dental and pediatric appointments (Nazarian, Mechaber, Charney, & Coulter, 1974; Reiss et al., 1976), prenatal visits for high risk mothers (Duer, Note 4), and immunization (Yokley & Glenwick, in press; Young, Halpin, Johnson, Irvin, & Marks, 1980; Yokley, Glenwick, Hedrick, & Page, Note 5). However, this positive effect of prompting is not always found in immunization rates (Martin, Fleming, Fleming, & Scott, 1969; Peterson, Note 1). Nonetheless, behaviorally-based prompts are another example of psychological applications.

Modeling.

The psychological principle of modeling has been used to change attitude and behavior through vicarious experience—observation of a model exhibiting a particular behavior (Bandura, 1971). In terms of accident and illness prevention, current television public service commercials demonstrate, for example, what to do in house fires, how to correctly brush teeth, what protection to use while swimming or skateboard riding, how to correctly store household toxic substances, and so on. In controlled studies, modeling has been a prime component of techniques for the promotion and demonstration of preventive actions. Modeling, along with other psychological educational procedures, was employed in different training programs to successfully teach children self-protective behaviors to prevent abduction and molestation (Poche, Brouwer, & Swearingen, 1981), emergency actions in home fires (Jones, Kazdin, & Haney, 1981a, 1981b), identification of emergencies and making telephone calls (Jones & Kazdin, 1980; Rosenbaum, Creedon, & Drabman, 1981), how to properly cross streets (Yeaton & Bailey, 1978), and how to brush teeth (Levy et al., 1982; Murray & Epstein, 1981; Swain et al., 1982). In such programs, modeling as a singular component is rarely evaluated. The basis for including modeling as a technique, however, derives from an extensive set of psychological research—both basic and applied.

Educational Principles

Psychology has contributed considerably to the understanding of how people learn. This has particular implications for health education which is the most widely used approach to preventing health problems (for example, nutrition information, dental hygiene). The basic idea is to provide information about health hazards and let the individual (parent, child) determine the proper preventive action. Research from psychology and other disciplines can be used in the development and evaluation of educational programs. More often, however, programs are based on common sense or intuition and fail to utilize relevant psychological or educational principles. Furthermore, these programs are rarely evaluated. When conducted, the findings from empirical studies of health education show equivocal results. Some education efforts demonstrate effects on knowledge acquisition and later behavior; many do not. (A review of health education is available elsewhere [Paulson, 1981], therefore only a few examples of preventive programs will be presented here.) The most extensive effort at preventive health education has been to get parents to acquire and use child safety restraints in cars (Reisinger, Williams, Wells, John, Roberts, & Podgainy, 1981). Pless (1978) reviewed the pediatric literature on physicians' attempts to encourage use of restraints. He concluded that the efficacy of health education appears "limited." He also noted that "both a sophisticated television campaign and $51 million advertising campaign were dismal failures" (Pless, 1978, p. 434, citing study by Robertson, Kelley, O'Neill, Wixom, Eisworth, & Haddon, 1974). This conclusion is also based on controlled studies that had physicians or health educators present information on the safety benefits of child restraints through a variety of modalities (including one-to-one presentations, group discussion, and films). In general, usage of child car seats in these studies was not significantly increased over a control group's baseline average of around 25% (Cliff, Catford, Dillow, & Swann, 1980; Miller & Pless, 1977; Reisinger & Williams, 1978).

Similarly, in a study with follow-ups on compliance, health education instructions to mothers for making their homes safer (with free safety devices of cabinet locks and electrical outlet covers) resulted in only limited change in safety compliance (Dershewitz, 1979; Dershewitz & Williamson, 1977). Levy et al. (1982) reported mixed results for a program that taught school children about dental health, with components included to encourage the children to take responsibility for their own dental care. Dental knowledge increased with the extra training, but other assessments of behavior (role-plays and self-reports) found no change. Project Burn Prevention was a large scale public education program to increase awareness of burn hazards and thus reduce the incidence and severity of burn injuries. This program was successful only in increasing the knowledge of school children. Adults, who were targeted through a media campaign and community meetings, did not benefit. Furthermore, the evaluation found no evidence that the program reduced burn incidence or severity in either population (McLoughlin, Vince, Lee, & Crawford, 1982).

In contrast to these generally negative results from education efforts, some studies have found positive behavior changes. For instance, some child restraint studies showed high rates of child seat usage after instruction, but these used self-report measures of safety compliance (Simons, 1977). Additionally, since these efforts were targeted to parents during the prenatal or newborn period (Allen & Bergman, 1976; Kanthor, 1976; Scherz, 1976), generalization to other at-risk age groups was restricted. Nevertheless, these studies do indicate some positive effect of health education. Other comprehensive programs have also shown increases of preventive behavior. For example, the dental program called "Alabama Smile Keeper" showed beneficial effects on oral hygiene and dental knowledge (Rose, Rogers, Kleinman, Shory, Meehan, & Zumbro, 1979). Specific health instruction increased rubella immunization (Woodhead, Ghose, & Gupta, 1980); defensive driving courses for adults generally improved driver skills (Planek, Shupak, & Fowler, 1974); pedestrian training improved children's street behavior (Yeaton et al., 1981); and training children to identify emergencies and make telephone calls was also successful (Jones & Kazdin, 1980). Two key elements in many of these effective programs appear to be the degree of specificity in the instructional material and the comprehensiveness of procedures.

As a side note, the work of Christophersen (1977) suggests that parental (and probably child) education should focus on positive aspects of preventive behavior which are not necessarily descriptive of health benefits. For example, parents who require children to ride in safety restraints will be rewarded by improved behavior and, "this immediate and continuing reward for the parent's altered behavior is clearly superior to the procedure of merely providing threat about the possible negative consequences for continued failure to use car seats" (Christophersen & Gyulay, 1981, p. 311). General health promotion appears to also be moving away from an emphasis on aversive behavior consequences to emphasizing only the positive benefits of a healthful lifestyle.

All in all, the major problems for health education come back to psychological processes which have been typically neglected in these programs. These include: (1) attention processes—the participant must pay attention to and acquire the message before any action can be taken, and (2) motivational processes—getting people to actually take preventive action.

Scientific Methodology

Psychology, as a science, is comprised of a set of standard procedures for gathering and evaluating information. Of course, this scientific method is not exclusive to psychology. Many important contributions to prevention derive from the scientific methods psychology share with other disciplines. A primary one, the body of knowledge leading toward understanding human behavior, has already been noted and was developed through this basic scientific methodology. The procedures themselves, particularly the evaluation techniques, are applicable to all aspects of prevention of accidents and illness. Economy of presentation precludes a detailed examination of methodological contributions since most underlie prevention research, but few are unique to it. There are a number of basic and advanced texts elaborating the psychological scientific process and procedures (Kerlinger, 1973; Vasta, 1979), but one particularly useful methodology will be addressed here.

In this chapter, we frequently describe and cite several studies from the behavior analysis literature. Characteristics of note for this approach include: (1) identification of critical problems, (2) careful determination of constituent behaviors in the problem, (3) direct intervention using effective behavior change techniques (rewards, modeling), and (4) evaluation of effects through data collection and direct observation. These characteristics of sound research methodology are evident in prevention programs using behavioral analysis, previously cited for children's emergency behavior (Jones & Kazdin, 1980; Rosenbaum et al., 1981), pedestrian skills (Yeaton & Bailey, 1978), self-protection (Poche et al., 1981), dental hygiene (Swain et al., 1982), and behavior on school buses (Barmann et al., 1980; Greene, Bailey, & Barber, 1981). Programs targeting caregivers' behavior have also used behavior analysis. For example, applications have been evaluated for car speeding control (Van Houten, Nau, & Marini, 1980), prompting parents to require immunizations for children (Peterson, Note 1), prompting high-risk women to keep prenatal care appointments (Duer, Note 4), and encouraging parents to use child restraints

(Christophersen, 1977; Christophersen & Gyulay, 1981). Peterson (Note 6) utilized this methodology in successfully developing and evaluating the "Safe at Home" game for latch-key children (those left without parental supervision at home). These children are at special risk for injury or personal trauma. Thus, after analyzing the need for such a prevention program, Peterson examined the areas of parental concern and training relevance to include components on emergencies, encountering strangers, and safe daily habits. Each response to be trained received external validation from either a physician, a nutritionist, or personnel from the fire, police, and civil defense departments. A training program was devised utilizing instructional drilling and incentives. Evaluation of the training included information acquisition measures and behavioral role-playing. The results clearly demonstrated positive gains by the children. This research exemplifies the behavior analytic approach to prevention of physical problems. Several sources exist detailing behavior analysis in general (Gelfand & Hartmann, 1975; Roberts & La Greca, 1981) and, in particular, applications to community education and prevention programs (Fawcett, Fletcher, & Mathews, 1980; Michelson, 1981; Yeaton et al., 1981). Behavior analysis encourages application of psychological procedures and knowledge to real-life problems. This contribution needs to be further developed.

This section demonstrates the variety of psychological applications to the prevention of accidents and illness in childhood. While numerous aspects are described, these are not exhaustive. Although psychology has been typically considered a mental health discipline, this discussion demonstrates the actual and potential utility of psychology in the physical health area. The next section considers the different approaches or models for preventive programming for which psychology has relevance.

APPROACHES TO PREVENTION OF PHYSICAL DISORDERS IN CHILDHOOD

Overview

Although other conceptualizations exist, we have chosen a rather simple categorization for prevention approaches particularly relevant to childhood physical disorders. We consider the three targets of prevention programs: (1) caregivers of the child, (2) the individual child, and (3) the environment and institutions. Our categorization permits an examination of prevention approaches with particular regard to psychological research and applications.

Target Caregivers for Preventive Actions

Numerous caregivers, including parents, teachers, and babysitters, take responsibility for a child's behavior and well-being. Child caregivers are an obvious resource to take accident and illness prevention actions since they have control over various aspects of the child's life. They control not only their own behavior, but also influence the child's behavior and select much of the makeup of the surrounding environment. The following discussion examines the approach of targeting the child's caregiver to take preventive actions. Three categories of caregiver behavior are discussed: (1) the caregiver's own unsafe behavior, (2) the caregiver's behavior on behalf of the child, and (3) the caregiver's behavior to change the child's behavior.

Caregiver's Own Unsafe Behavior.

Obviously, adults exhibit a multitude of unsafe behaviors; prevention professionals are particularly interested in targeting for intervention those which directly affect the safety of the child. In this situation, the adult might take a preventive action which benefits both adult and child. For example, when a parent refrains from drinking alcohol and driving with a child as a passenger or potential pedestrian, he or she is behaving to benefit his or her own health and safety as well as the child's. Similarly, a pregnant woman who does not drink during pregnancy takes a health action for herself and one which prevents fetal alcohol syndrome in her child (Labs, Note 2). The adult who stops smoking decreases his or her own health risk as well as the chance of asthma in his or her children (Gortmaker, Walker, Jacobs, & Ruch-Ross, 1982). Community programs to decrease speeding benefit children who are passengers or pedestrians in addition to decreasing the accident risk for the adult driver. Other programs targeting caregiver behavior which benefits both caregiver and child include encouragement to install fire and smoke detectors in the home or school, to maintain proper gun safety, and to improve home safety in general. There are many prevention efforts which use this approach of targeting the caregiver to take actions which are mutually beneficial to the adult and the child. Television commercials and brochures have been produced for all these problems. However, the efficacy of these materials is unknown and potentially unmeasurable, although controlled experimental studies have demonstrated the positive effects of some of these materials (for example, see Labs, Note 2). But, studies have not considered whether it is actually useful to target the caregiver to take preventive action on his or her own unsafe behavior in order to improve the well-being of a child.

Caregiver's Behaviors on Behalf of the Child.

A second type of caregiver preventive behavior is that which primarily benefits the child without necessarily benefiting the adult. The caregiver makes choices for the child's well-being, which may include making the surrounding environment safer or requiring the child to do healthful things. For environment improvement, programs or brochures can instruct parents in safe toy selection, babysitter training, household safety precautions for falls, suffocation, poisoning, burns, and shocks (Because You Care for Kids, 1980; Child Safety, 1981; Don't Risk Your Child's Life, 1981; Locked Up Poisons Prevent Tragedy, 1981; Sitting Safely, 1976; Young Children and Accidents in the Home, 1976). A study of playground accidents indicated that the equipment is less at fault than the lack of proper supervision by caregivers (Nixon, Pearn, & Wilkey, 1981). Thus, day-care teachers can become protectors of the child's safety through the selection of equipment and supervision of activities (Solomons, Lakin, Snider, & Paredes-Rojas, 1982). Parents also must assume this responsibility. As frequently noted, no controlled studies evaluated the written materials noted above although considerable effort and money are expended on them. Some evidence exists to indicate that certain types of prevention efforts can increase some caregivers' behaviors such as the acquisition and use of car safety restraints (Kanthor, 1976) and the improvement of crib selection (Consumer Product Safety Commission, 1979). On the other hand, some research also shows informational programs directed at caregivers do not have intended effects. For example, programs showing no increase in caregiver preventive behavior include car restraint acquisition at later ages (Miller & Pless, 1977), poison control in the home (Lacouture, Minisci, Gouveia, & Lovejoy, 1978), and general injury prevention (Dershewitz & Williamson, 1977; Schlesinger, Dickson, Westaby, Lowen, Logrillo, & Maiwald, 1966). These examples illustrate the caregiver's actions to structure a safe environment for the child. Other behaviors can be targeted to enhance the child's health through the caregiver's control. For example, parents can be primed to bring their children in for periodic medical and dental health checkups to prevent or catch early physical problems and acquire immunizations, but the success of such priming has been demonstrated in only a few controlled studies. Immunizations for preschoolers were not increased in two studies (Yokley & Glenwick, in press; Peterson, Note 1), while pediatric dental checkups were increased (Levy et al., 1982; Reiss et al., 1976). One study has shown that provision of nutritional meals for the child is another caregiver action successfully amenable to physicians' instructions (Pisacano, Lichter, Ritter, & Siegal, 1978). Further evaluation is obviously needed to resolve the efficacy issue for targeting the caregiver's preventive behavior on behalf of the child, whether it is designed to render the environment safer or to require healthful actions of the child.

Caregiver Behavior to Change Child Behavior.

This section emphasizes the caregiver's active, direct efforts to change the child's behavior more or less permanently rather than simply having the caregiver make preventive decisions for the child. Successful prevention programs of this type would include parents or classroom teachers arranging reward systems for teaching and promoting tooth brushing and dental flossing (Claerhout & Lutzker, 1981; Poche, McCubbrey, & Munn, 1982; Swain et al., 1982), self-protective behavior (Poche et al., 1981), emergency behavior (Jones et al., 1981), and pedestrian behavior (Yeaton & Bailey, 1978). These behavioral instruction programs are provided by caregivers to change the child's behavior. The emphasis here is on targeting the caregiver to take the responsibility for actually changing the child's behavior. Little evidence has accumulated demonstrating success or failure in such attempts. In a singular case, however, Yeaton et al. (1981) report that school crossing guards can be taught to provide pedestrian training to children.

Target the Child for Preventive Actions

As opposed to directing efforts to the caregiver, other preventive programming targets the child to take responsibility for his or her own behavior in preventing accidents or illness. Influencing the child to change behavior results in longer lasting effects and contributes to positive lifestyle changes. This targeting approach might be seen as learning new skills or competence which may then be applicable to potentially hazardous conditions. Successful programs of this nature have been noted previously. Various personnel (parents, teachers, program managers) are effective trainers of children for a variety of identified preventive behaviors. Preschool children have been trained to identify emergency situations (fires, people unconscious or falling), and to make appropriate telephone calls (Jones & Kazdin, 1980; Rosenbaum et al., 1981). Through similar comprehensive training efforts, grade school children were trained to respond correctly to home fire situations (Jones et al., 1981a, 1981b). Preschool children have been taught to resist the different lures of simulated child molesters (Poche et al., 1981) and school children have been taught street crossing skills through an instructional package with follow-up training (Yeaton & Bailey, 1978).

Not all programs directed at children's behavior show such positive effects. For example, health education attempting to improve dental habits is generally found ineffective (Levy et al., 1982; Podshadley & Schweikle, 1970; Podshadley & Shannon, 1970). Driver's education programs have been directed to improving the skills of beginning drivers, with no evidence of positive effects (Goldstein, 1969; Haddon, 1967). Instead, researchers are now suggesting driver's education may increase accident rates for adolescents by allowing them to drive earlier (Robertson, 1980; Robertson & Zador, 1978).

The difficulty in summarizing the approach of targeting the child is further complicated by the lack of careful evaluation for many existing programs (for example, for water and bicycling safety education). These programs have a common component of actively teaching the child appropriate behavior in response to particular situations. Targeting the child to take responsibility for preventive and health behavior is intuitively appealing, with empirical support still developing.

Target Environment and Institutions

A third approach to prevention is through changes made in the environment or institutional makeup. Prevention of this type typically relies upon various governmental laws and regulations, in effect, to prevent accidents or illness. Some require active compliance by individuals (for example, maintain the 55 mile per hour speed limit); others require only passive acceptance by individuals (fluoride in drinking water, for example). The latter have been called passive prevention. In part due to the problem with other prevention programs, many professionals now conclude that passive prevention will prove maximally effective because "such protection is totally independent of the wisdom, caution, skill, and psychological make-up of the individuals who are protected" (Baker, 1980, p. 467). In a similar statement, the Select Panel for the Promotion of Child Health concluded:

> The evidence suggests that many kinds of injuries and health problems can be more economically and more effectively reduced by changing environments than by trying

to change behaviors directly. Often the most effective strategies are those that work automatically, without action on the part of the person being protected. [Harris, 1981, p. 75]

Passive prevention works because it requires little or no action by a caregiver or child. This approach often requires formulation of legal requirements before a preventive action is taken by designers and manufacturers of products used by individuals. In this approach, there is less direct application of psychological principles to actual problems, but it may prove to be the most effective in reducing accidents and illness across all ages. Even a brief examination of regulated prevention reveals that such measures decrease accidents and illness. Regulatory action is not inevitable or always necessary, but has been found generally effective. A prime example is the Poison Prevention Packaging Act of 1970 which requires special child-proof caps on products harmful to children. Fifteen categories of substances are now regulated including prescription and nonprescription drugs, solvents, and petroleum products. The instances of poison ingestions, hospital emergency room visits, and deaths due to accidental ingestions have dropped significantly as a result of the federal act and intervention by the Consumer Product Safety Commission (CPSC) (McIntire, 1977; Walton, 1982). Regulations requiring the manufacture of flame retardant sleepwear have resulted in a decrease in admissions to burn units, a decrease in burn deaths, and an increase in survival rates of sleepwear fire victims (McLoughlin, Clarke, Stahl, & Crawford, 1977). CPSC regulations on the design and construction of infant cribs has led to a reduction of injuries and deaths previously attributed to unsafe or defective cribs (Consumer Product Safety Commission, 1979). Regulations are not always required, as exemplified by the voluntary standards of water heater manufacturers which prevent water scalds by installing automatic thermostats on heating units (Harris, 1981). The proposed use of air bags in passenger cars is another example of passive prevention necessitated by generally low use of seat belts and poor results of promotional programs (Williams, 1979).

Other prevention measures require some limited action by individuals. Baker (1980) points out that one-time action is more effective than prevention requiring repeated actions; for example, smoke detectors that require no further service after installation (for example, battery replacement) are more likely to function. Similarly, one-time installation of window guards has been shown to significantly reduce children's falls from windows in New York City (Spiegel & Lindaman, 1977). A limited series of immunizations in childhood has also prevented a number of previously disabling diseases (Vaughan & McKay, 1975).

Other types of prevention regulation require continuing active effort such as compliance with laws. The 55 mile per hour speed limit, originally mandated to conserve energy, has decreased the number of car accident fatalities and injuries (Califano, 1979). When the speed limit is enforced, or at least approximated, accidents continue to decrease (Baker, 1980). However, the average speed has generally increased and correspondingly, the number of accidents has risen (Committee on Accident and Poison Prevention, 1981; Harris, 1981). Children as passengers and pedestrians are directly affected by speeding accidents.

The United States has yet to pass mandatory seat belt laws for adults, but other countries which have done so have found fairly positive results in compliance and the reduction of fatalities (Harris, 1981; Williams, 1979). Several states in the U.S. have passed legislation requiring children under certain ages to be restrained in car safety seats; Tennessee passed the first such law effective in 1978. Evaluation of this law's effects continues, but there is evidence that the use of restraints modestly increased after the law was passed (Williams & Wells, 1981). Several factors diminish the efficacy of such laws, including legal exemptions if a child is in the rear seat or is held in an adult's arms. Spotty enforcement of the law further compromises its benefits.

Prevention through regulation attempts to influence behavior of the population in general. A particular problem with overreliance on regulations to attain prevention is the issue of personal rights and freedoms (Michelson, 1981). For example, Califano (1979) notes:

> Motorcyclists often contend that helmet laws infringe on personal rights and opponents of mandatory laws argue that since other people usually are not endangered, the individual motorcyclist should be allowed personal responsibility for risk. But the high costs of disabling and fatal injuries, the burdens on families, and the demands on medical care resources are borne by society as a whole. [p. 112]

When laws requiring motorcycle helmets are repealed, the number of fatal head injuries doubles (Califano, 1979). Similar objections to the starter ''interlock'' system requiring seat belt use (based on federal regulation) increased the number of users, but was met with such vehement opposition and circumvention that the standards were repealed within a year (Haddon & Baker, 1981). Regulation by the government is in particular political disfavor at this time; acceptance or rejection by the citizenry of regulated behavior either reflects or produces this disfavor. However, not all passive prevention requires massive intrusion into people's lives. Other passive prevention benefits are realized through environmental improvements, such as improved design and construction in playgrounds, highways, or car interiors (Baker, 1980; Haddon & Baker, 1981; Harris, 1981), sanitation and disease vector control (Harris, 1981; Health Systems Plan, 1981), and air quality standards (''Relax Air-Pollution Standards?,'' 1982).

As noted, psychology is less fundamental in the prevention approach of targeting the environment and institutions. This does not mean that psychologists should not be involved. Individual and group efforts can be directed to the prevention of accidents and illness of children, regardless of a direct link to the discipline. A psychological contribution can come through motivating behavior change in legislators, designers and manufacturers, governmental agencies, and others in position to implement passive or regulatory prevention. An exemplary effort at influencing passage of child passenger safety laws in Kansas came through psychologically derived data, psychological principles of behavior analysis, and involvement of psychologists themselves (Fawcett & Seekins, Note 7). Psychologists and other professionals allied with state legislators in a common goal of influencing public policy designed to reduce the incidence of injury and death in motor vehicle accidents. This effort required: (1) knowledge and application of policy research, (2) behavioral assessment of the low incidence of restraint usage without a law, (3) polling to determine the positive views of the state citizenry (that is, social validity of the issue and intervention), and (4) legislative testimony on behalf of the restraint bill presenting the findings of the research. This case of involvement clearly demonstrates a combination of psychological contributions necessary to prevent childhood accidents and illness.

DISCUSSION

Throughout this chapter, we have attempted to identify numerous applications of psychology to the prevention of accidents and illness in childhood. As noted, despite psychology's traditional realm of mental health, a wealth of actual and potential applications exists in the realm of physical health. While psychologists have been neither the predominant nor an extensively active force, psychological principles are intrinsically involved.

Complexity of the Phenomena

Human behavior is inherently complex. Because prevention and accidents or illness primarily involve behavior, they are also complex even though the concepts appear superficially simple. Hence, simple models for conceptualizing the problem do not assist; simple preventive interventions likely do not work. Baker (1980) notes that prevention program effectiveness depends on three things: "they must work when properly used, that is, they must be efficacious; second, they must be used; and third, they must be used properly" (p. 466). A breakdown in any of these areas renders such measures ineffective. The preceding examples demonstrate that each component is incredibly difficult to guarantee in prevention programming. The second and third factors particularly relate to psychological applications. Involved in these factors are attentional, motivational, and learning principles, all of which are subject to additional factors including social and individual characteristics and developmental issues. Because of this psychological complexity, prevention is not a "quick fix."

A further complication is that health behaviors often do not intercorrelate (Langlie, 1979; Williams & Wechsler, 1972). That is, many people report inconsistent preventive actions exhibiting healthful behavior of one type, but not another (for example, they may stop smoking, but do not wear seat belts). Each behavior results from a multitude of influences, not from a general health orientation. Specific behaviors are typically resistant to general health education efforts. Thus, special preventive programs or interventions are required to promote behavioral change for each specific action. Results from the numerous health education studies support such a conclusion. Given the vast number of preventive behaviors requiring promotion, the prospect of services directed to each one seems overwhelming.

To compound the complexity, every prevention effort affects numerous entities and interested parties. Political, financial, cultural, and religious considerations enter the prevention decision making process. While sometimes important, well-meaning, and relevant, such considerations can also forestall, dilute, contaminate, or sabatoge prevention efforts. For example, the original Tennessee legislative bill requiring infant car restraints was amended during passage to exempt children held in the arms of an older person. This exemption severely compromises the concept and benefits of the act since compliance can be avoided through this loophole in the law. Such on-lap travel is potentially more hazardous than children being unrestrained in a seat because the adult might crush the child if an accident occurs (Williams, 1979; Robertson & Williams, Note 8). Starfield (1979), in regard to the Tennessee exemption, notes that ''everyone has competing needs, and decisions are often not formed by logic'' (p. 969). Similar incidents compromising prevention efforts include religious exemptions to immunization laws; political reelection considerations affecting strict enforcement of speeding and drunk driving laws; political accusations against fluoride water treatment; philosophical objections to regulations governing behavior in general.

Additionally, many preventive actions have side effects which compound the original problem or create new ones. For example, some of the flame retardant chemicals used in children's sleepwear apparently have mutagenic properties (Blum & Ames, 1977), asbestos extensively used for fireproofing schools is now considered a carcinogen (Nicholson, Rohl, Sawyer, Swozowski, & Todaro, 1978), drivers' education mandated to improve adolescent driving skills appear to only lower the age of driving onset, increase the number of miles driven, and increase the potential of accidents (Robertson & Zador, 1978), and the swine flu vaccination program produced higher rates of Guillain-Barre syndrome (Silverstein, 1981). These examples demonstrate the need for careful consideration before implementation of any prevention program. All these considerations lend further complexity to already complex phenomena. This complexity should not dissuade professionals from taking on the task, but should alert them to the difficulties involved.

Cost-Effectiveness Issues

Related to complexity are frequent, but necessary, comparisons of the cost of prevention versus the benefits derived. Studies repeatedly and convincingly demonstrate the cost-benefit advantage of prevention over curative or rehabilitation interventions in physical health (Harris, 1981). This conclusion does not blanketly endorse every prevention service, but does support continued consideration of well-designed and evaluated programs. Thus, determination of cost-benefit requires an essential component of prevention—evaluation. The accountability issue can be raised for every type of prevention programming—does the program do what it intends to do? Answers are sometimes difficult to ascertain because some manifestations of prevention benefit are often long term, but short-term benefits are also valuable and should not be overlooked (Harris, 1981). A few examples here illustrate the cost-effectiveness for prevention of accidents and illness. Measles vaccinations costing $180 million from 1966 to 1974 saved $1.3 billion in services that would have been required for negative side effects of the disease (Witte & Axnick, 1975). The polio immunization program from 1963 to 1978 cost $189 million and saved almost $2 billion (Califano, 1981). In 1980, Muller estimated that an annual net benefit of $61 million in medical care and rehabilitation costs would be expected if all motorcyclists nationwide used helmets. Fluoridation in community water can achieve the benefits of reducing the number of cavities by 60%. Comparisons of the cost of dental care show children in fluoridated areas have one-half the costs of those in nonfluoridated communities (Health Systems Plan, 1981). (For other considerations of cost-effectiveness, refer to Chapter 1 by Roberts & Peterson and Chapter 13 by Stolz in this volume.)

Of course, such cost savings figures do not reflect the savings of lives or the lessening of disability resulting from prevention efforts—the stark figures of decreased fatalities and injuries do. For example, Walton (1982) determined that childhood poisoning deaths declined from a rate of two per 100,000 children to .5 as a result of the Poison Prevention Packaging Act. Many beneficial effects of services are often difficult to document; the nonoccurrence of an event is difficult to observe and epidemiological findings such as those above must be used.

Financial Support

Despite evidence of efficacy, prevention funding remains low in relation to expenditures for rehabilitation services. Financial support for mental health programming in prevention has been minimal and appears to be declining (Fishman & Neigher, 1982). Funding for some physical health related measures (for example, immunization) is somewhat higher, but still less than expenditures for curative interventions. Indeed, Califano (1981) reports that of the almost $50 billion spent by the federal government on health care, only 4%, or under $2 billion, was spent on disease prevention and health promotion. Existing systems for health care (which would encompass prevention of accidents and illness) are not viable for prevention funding (Califano, 1981; Harris, 1981). That is, current health care funding provides little incentive for prevention services since reimbursement to hospitals and physicians, for example, pays more for technology-based procedures and patient hospitalization than for health counseling. Consequently, the Select Panel for the Promotion of Child Health recommends modifying reimbursement practices and policies to include health promotion and disease and accident prevention (Harris, 1981). The Panel recommends changes in public and private third-party payers including private health insurers, Medicaid, and national health financing through grants. Others propose funding prevention and promotion activities through affiliation with various private industries. Gullotta (1981) suggests primary prevention professionals might affiliate with the private sector to improve industries' profits. Other proposals suggest implementing industry workplace health promotion which, in turn, would improve the productivity and morale of workers (Naditch, 1981; Wilbur, 1981). Unless children and families receive coverage through their parents' plans as workers, this critical group is neglected. Such proposals also overlook those people not covered—primarily the poor who are consistently not helped by the health care system, but who also represent the highest risk for many physical disorders.

We note the problem of inadequate funding for prevention services, but cannot provide an answer. The problem demands a major effort to develop funding support from various sources. For the present, many of the programs noted here and others continue to be supported on an ad hoc, underfinanced basis, usually with a psychologist receiving personal support for other activities (for example, as researchers, educators, or community practitioners, see Benedict, Note 9). Psychologists, as part of the health care system and part of the prevention effort, might assist the development of other funding arrangements by applying psychological techniques and knowledge. More influential presentations of needs and remedies might be made to secure additional financing; more economical and effective programs might be developed to better use existing resources.

Availability of Services

Many prevention interventions with documented efficacy are experimental programs limited in time, funding, and affected population. Numerous settings and social institutions offer opportunities for preventive interventions benefiting children: schools, physicians' offices, hospitals, television programming, mental health centers, and so forth. Yet not nearly enough is being provided or is proving effective, as evidenced by statistics reflecting high rates of accidents and injury.

Certain prevention measures and services may require population-wide application. For instance, comprehensive disease prevention necessitates immunization of all children. These types of prevention measures address population-based outcomes as well as individual benefits (for example, general fatality rates decrease through the use of child safety restraints, which translates into one's child, a neighbor's child, and so on, being saved). Other programming is necessary for particular population subgroups who are at greater risk for accidents or disease. Such at-risk programming may be based on overlapping criteria, including: (1) developmental perspectives (for example, infants are more susceptible to death in car accidents; toddlers require added poison control); (2) behavioral and psychological characteristics (for example, accident prone or accident repeating children; Type A behavior); (3) special needs due to living circumstances (low income pregnant women have poor prenatal care and low income children get sick more often); and (4) special risks posed by particular activities (car or motorcycle riding, recreational activities). Targeting prevention services to groups at risk makes maximum use of scarce resources (Harris, 1981). Additionally, special target groups may include the caregiver, the child, or the environment following careful consideration of needs and outcome.

Even given effective techniques, prevention cannot be effective if unavailable. Maximum availability of cost-effective programming is a goal, not nearly a fact at this time. Innovative programming can achieve this through participation by psychologists with expertise in a variety of specialties (Matarazzo, 1982). Effective prevention of accidents and illness requires an enhanced and continuing effort to which psychology as a science and profession has much to offer. Some things are not amenable to prevention; obstacles frequently frustrate implementation. Yet, psychological research and practice, in combination with many other professional disciplines, can accomplish much.

REFERENCES

Allen, D. B., & Bergman, A. B. Social learning approaches to health education utilization of infant auto restraint devices. *Pediatrics,* 1976, *58,* 323–328.

Baker, S. P. Motor vehicle occupant deaths in young children. *Pediatrics,* 1979, *64,* 860–861.

Baker, S. P. Prevention of childhood injuries. *The Medical Journal of Australia.* 1980, *1,* 466–470.

Bandura, A. *Social learning theory.* New York: General Learning Press, 1971.

Barmann, B. C., Croyle-Barmann, C., & McLain, B. The use of contingent-interrupted music in the treatment of disruptive bus-riding behavior. *Journal of Applied Behavior Analysis,* 1980, *13,* 693–698.

Because you care for kids. . . (No. 620-225/3892). Washington, D.C.: U.S. Government Printing Office, 1980.

Bell, M. J., Ternberg, J. L., & Bower, R. J. Low velocity vehicular injuries in children ''run-over'' acidents. *Pediatrics,* 1980, *66,* 628–631.

Blum, A., & Ames, B. N. Flame retardant additives as possible cancer hazards: The main flame retardant in children's pajamas is a mutagen and should not be used. *Science,* 1977, *195,* 17–22.

Brazelton, T. B. Anticipatory guidance. *The Pediatric Clinics of North America,* 1975, *22*(3).

Califano, J. A., Jr. *Healthy people: The Surgeon General's report on health promotion and disease prevention.* Washington, D.C.: U.S. Government Printing Office, 1979.

Califano, J. A., Jr. *Governing America: An insider's report from the White House and the Cabinet.* New York: Simon & Schuster, 1981.

Child Safety. New York: Metropolitan Life Insurance Company, 1981.

Christophersen, E. R. Children's behavior during automobile rides: Do car seats make a difference? *Pediatrics,* 1977, *60,* 69–74.

Christophersen, E. R., & Gyulay, J. Parental compliance with car seat usage: A positive approach with long-term follow-up. *Journal of Pediatric Psychology,* 1981, *6,* 301–312.

Chun, Y., Berkelhamer, J. E., & Herold, T. E. Dog bites in children less than 4 years old. *Pediatrics,* 1982, *69,* 119–120.

Claerhout, S., & Lutzker, J. R. Increasing children's self-initiated compliance to dental regimens. *Behavior Therapy,* 1981, *12,* 165–176.

Cliff, K. S., Catford, S. C., Dillow, I., & Swann, C. M. Promoting the use of seat belts. *British Medical Journal,* 1980, *281,* 1477–1478.

Committee on Accident and Poison Prevention. The 55 miles per hour maximum speed limit. *Pediatrics,* 1981, *67,* 304.

Consumer Product Safety Commission. *Impact of crib safety activities on injuries and deaths associated with cribs*. Washington, D.C.: CPSC, February, 1979.

Dershewitz, R. A. Will mothers use free household safety devices? *American Journal of Diseases of Children,* 1979, *133,* 61–64.

Dershewitz, R. A., & Williamson, J. W. Prevention of childhood household injuries: A controlled clinical trial. *American Journal of Public Health,* 1977, *67,* 1148–1153.

Don't risk your child's life! Rye, NY: Physicians for Automotive Safety, 1982.

Etzioni, A. Caution: Too many health warnings could be counterproductive. *Psychology Today,* 1978, *12,* 20–22.

Evans, R. I., Rozelle, R. M., Mittelmark, M. B., Hansen, W. B., Bane, A. L., & Havis, J. Deterring the onset of smoking in children: Knowledge of immediate physiological effects and coping with peer pressure, media pressure, and parent modeling. *Journal of Applied Social Psychology,* 1978, *8,* 126–135.

Fawcett, S. B., Fletcher, R. K., & Mathews, R. M. Applications of behavior analysis in community education. In D. Glenwick & L. Jason (Eds.), *Behavioral community psychology*. New York: Praeger, 1980.

Feldman, K. W., & Simms, R. J. Strangulation in childhood: Epidemiology and clinical course. *Pediatrics,* 1980, *65,* 1079–1085.

Fishman, D. B., & Neigher, W. D. American psychology in the Eighties: Who will buy? *American Psychologist,* 1982, *37,* 533–546.

Gallagher, E. B., & Moody, P. M. Dentists and the oral health behavior of patients: A sociological perspective. *Journal of Behavioral Medicine,* 1981, *4,* 283–295.

Gelfand, D. M., & Hartmann, D. P. *Child behavior analysis and therapy*. New York: Pergamon, 1975.

Goldstein, L. G. The "case" against driver education. *Journal of Safety Research,* 1969, *1,* 149–164.

Gortmaker, S. L., Walker, D. K., Jacobs, F. H., & Ruch-Ross, H. Parental smoking and the risk of childhood asthma. *American Journal of Public Health,* 1982, *72,* 574–579.

Greene, B. F., Bailey, J. S., & Barber, F. An analysis and reduction of disruptive behavior on school buses. *Journal of Applied Behavior Analysis,* 1981, *14,* 177–192.

Gullotta, T. P. An unorthodox proposal for funding primary prevention. *Journal of Primary Prevention,* 1981, *2,* 14–24.

Haddon, W. An introduction to the traffic safety problem. In W. Smith (Ed.), *Traffic safety: A national problem.* New Haven, CT: Payne & Lane, 1967.

Haddon, W., Jr., & Baker, S. P. Injury control. In D. Clark & B. McMahon (Eds.), *Preventive and community medicine.* Boston: Little, Brown & Company, 1981.

Harris, P. *Better health for our children: A national strategy. The report of the Select Panel for the Promotion of Child Health.* (DHHS(PHS) Publication No. 79-55071). Washington, D.C.: U. S. Government Printing Office, 1981.

Health Systems Plan for 1981–85. West Alabama Health Council, Health Service Area 2, November, 1981, 5th Edition, Tuscaloosa, AL.

Hunter, S. M., Webber, L. S., & Berenson, G. S. Cigarette smoking and tobacco usage behavior in children and adolescents: Bogalusa Heart Study. *Preventive Medicine,* 1980, *9,* 701–712.

Jones, R. T., & Kazdin, A. E. Teaching children how and when to make emergency telephone calls. *Behavior Therapy,* 1980, *11,* 509–521.

Jones, R. T., Kazdin, A. E., & Haney, J. I. Social validation and training of emergency fire safety skills for potential injury prevention and life saving. *Journal of Applied Behavior Analysis,* 1981, *14,* 249–260. (a)

Jones, R. T., Kazdin, A. E., & Haney, J. I. A follow-up to training emergency skills. *Behavior Therapy,* 1981, *12,* 716–722. (b)

Kanthor, H. A. Car safety for infants: Effectiveness of parental counseling. *Pediatrics,* 1976, *58,* 320–328.

Kerlinger, F. N. *Foundations of behavioral research* (2nd ed.). New York: Holt, Rinehart, & Winston, 1973.

Lacouture, P., Minisci, M., Gouveia, W. T., & Lovejoy, F. H. Evaluation of a community-based poison education program. *Clinical Toxicology,* 1978, *13,* 623–629.

Langlie, J. K. Interrelationships among preventive health behaviors: A test of competing hypotheses. *Public Health Reports,* 1979, *94,* 216–225.

Levy, R. L., Lodish, D., & Pawlack-Floyd, C. Teaching children to take more responsibility for their own dental treatment. *Social Work in Health Care,* 1982, *7,* 69–76.

Locked up poisons prevent tragedy. (No. 0-355-692-QL3). Washington, D.C.: U. S. Government Printing Office, 1981.

McIntire, M. S. Safety packaging: A model for successful accident prevention. *Pediatric Annals,* 1977, *6,* 706–708.

McLoughlin, E., Clarke, N., Stahl, K., & Crawford, J. D. One pediatric burn unit experience with sleepwear-related injuries. *Pediatrics,* 1977, *60,* 405–409.

McLoughlin, E., Vince, C. J., Lee, A. M., & Crawford, J. D. Project burn prevention: Outcome and implications. *American Journal of Public Health,* 1982, *72,* 241–247.

Manheimer, D., Dewey, J., Mellinger, G., & Corsa, L. 50,000 child-years of accidental injuries. *Public Health Reports,* 1966, *81,* 519–533.

Manheimer, D., & Mellinger, G. Personality characteristics of the child accident repeater. *Child Development,* 1967, *38,* 491–514.

Martin, D. A., Fleming, S. J., Fleming, T. G., & Scott, D. C. An evaluation of the immunization status of white children in a Kentucky county. *Public Health Reports,* 1969, *84,* 605–610.

Matarazzo, J. D. Behavioral health's challenge to academic, scientific, and professional psychology. *American Psychologist,* 1982, *37,* 1–14.

Matheny, A. P., Jr. Visual-perceptual exploration and accident liability in children. *Journal of Pediatric Psychology,* 1980, *5,* 343–351.

Matheny, A. P., Jr., Brown, A., & Wilson, R. S. Behavioral antecedents of accidental injuries in early childhood: A study of twins. *Journal of Pediatrics,* 1971, *79,* 122–124.

Matheny, A. P., Jr., Brown, A. M., & Wilson, R. S. Assessment of children's behavioral characteristics: A tool in accident prevention. *Clinical Pediatrics,* 1972, *11,* 437–439.

Michelson, L. Behavioral approaches to prevention. In L. Michelson, M. Hersen, & S. M. Turner (Eds.), *Future perspectives in behavior therapy.* New York: Plenum Press, 1981.

Miller, J. R., & Pless, I. B. Child automobile restraints: Evaluation of health education. *Pediatrics,* 1977, *59,* 907–911.

Muller, A. Evaluation of the costs and benefits of motorcycle helmet laws. *American Journal of Public Health,* 1980, *70,* 586–592.

Murray, J. A., & Epstein, L. H. Improving oral hygiene with videotape modeling. *Behavior Modification,* 1981, *5,* 360–371.

Naditch, M. P. The Control Data Corporation Staywell Program. *Behavioral Medicine Update,* 1981, *4,* 9–10.

National Safety Council. *Accident facts.* (1979 Ed.). Chicago: Author, 1979.

Nazarian, L. F., Mechaber, J., Charney, E., & Coulter, M. Effect of a mailed appointment reminder on appointment keeping. *Pediatrics,* 1974, *53,* 349.

Nicholson, W. J., Rohl, A. N., Sawyer, R. N., Swoszowski, E. J., & Todaro, J. D. *Control of sprayed asbestos substances in school buildings: A feasibility study.* Report to the National Institute of Environmental Health Sciences, June 15, 1978. In Oversight Hearings on Asbestos Health Hazards to School Children by the Subcommittee on Elementary, Secondary, and Vocational Education of the Committee on Education and Labor, U. S. House of Representatives, January 8, 1979, pp. 27–117. Washington, D.C.: U.S. Government Printing Office, 1979.

Nixon, J., Pearn, J., & Wilkey, I. Death during play: A study of playground and recreation deaths in children. *British Medical Journal.* 1981, *283,* 410.

Paulson, J. A. Patient education. *The Pediatric Clinics of North America,* 1981, *28.*

Pinckney, L. E., & Kennedy, L. A. Traumatic deaths from dog attacks in the United States. *Pediatrics,* 1982, *69,* 193–196.

Pisacano, J. C., Lichter, H., Ritter, J., & Siegal, A. P. An attempt at prevention of obesity in infancy. *Pediatrics,* 1978, *61,* 360–464.

Planek, T. W., Schupack, S. A., & Fowler, R. C. An evaluation of the National Safety Council's Defensive Driving Course in various states. *Accident Analysis and Prevention,* 1974, *6,* 271–297.

Pless, I. B. Accident prevention and health education: Back to the drawing board? *Pediatrics,* 1978, *62,* 431–435.

Pless, I. B., & Roghmann, K. J. Safety restraints for children in automobiles: Who uses them? *Canadian Journal of Public Health,* 1978, *69,* 289–292.

Poche, C., Brouwer, R., & Swearingen, M. Teaching self-protection to young children. *Journal of Applied Behavior Analysis,* 1981, *14,* 169–176.

Poche, C., McCubbrey, H., & Munn, T. The development of correct toothbrushing technique in preschool children. *Journal of Applied Behavior Analysis,* 1982, *15,* 315–320.

Podshadley, A. G., & Schweikle, E. S. The effectiveness of two educational programs in changing the performance of oral hygiene by elementary school children. *Journal of Public Health Dentistry,* 1970, *30,* 17–20.

Podshadley, A. G., & Shannon, T. H. Oral hygiene performance of elementary school children following dental health education. *Journal of Dentistry for Children,* 1970, *37,* 298–302.

Reichelderfer, T. E., Overbach, A., & Greensher, J. Unsafe playgrounds. *Pediatrics,* 1979, *64,* 962–963.

Reisinger, K. S., & Williams, A. F. Evaluation of programs designed to increase the protection of infants in cars. *Pediatrics,* 1978, *62,* 280–287.

Reisinger, K. S., Williams, A. F., Wells, J. K., John, C. E., Roberts, T. R., & Podgainy, H. J. Effects of pediatricians' counseling on infant restraint use. *Pediatrics,* 1981, *67,* 201–206.

Reiss, M. D., Piotrowski, W. D., & Bailey, J. S. Behavioral community psychology: Encouraging low-income parents to seek dental care for their children. *Journal of Applied Behavior Analysis,* 1976, *9,* 387–397.

Relax air-pollution standards? *U.S. News and World Report,* May 24, 1982.

Roberts, M. C., & La Greca, A. M. Behavioral assessment. In C. E. Walker (Ed.), *Clinical practice of psychology: A practical guide for mental health professionals.* New York: Pergamon Press, 1981.

Roberts, M. C., Maddux, J. E., & Wright, L. The developmental perspective in behavioral health. In J. D. Matarazzo, N. E. Miller, S. M. Weiss, J. A. Herd, & S. M. Weiss (Eds.), *Behavioral health: A handbook of health enhancement and disease prevention.* New York: Wiley, 1984.

Roberts, M. C., Maddux, J. E., Wurtele, S. K., & Wright, L. Pediatric psychology: Health care psychology for children. In T. Millon, C. J. Green, & R. B. Meagher (Eds.), *Handbook of clinical health psychology.* New York: Plenum Press, 1982.

Roberts, M. C., & Wright, L. The role of the pediatric psychologist as consultant to pediatricians. In J. Tuma (Ed.), *Handbook for the practice of pediatric psychology.* New York: Wiley-Interscience, 1982.

Robertson, L. S. Crash involvement of teenaged drivers when driver education is eliminated from high school. *American Journal of Public Health,* 1980, *70,* 599–603.

Robertson, L. S., Kelley, A. B., O'Neill, B., Wixom, C. W., Eisworth, R. S., & Haddon, W., Jr. A controlled study of the effect of television messages on safety belt use. *American Journal of Public Health,* 1974, *64,* 1071–1080.

Robertson, L. S., & Zador, P. L. Driver education and fatal crash involvement of teenaged drivers. *American Journal of Public Health,* 1978, *68,* 959–965.

Rogers, J. Recurrent childhood poisoning as a family problem. *The Journal of Family Practice,* 1981, *13,* 337–340.

Rogers, R. W. A protection motivation theory of fear appeals and attitude change. *Journal of Psychology,* 1975, *91,* 93–114.

Rogers, R. W. Cognitive and physiological processes in fear appeals and attitude change: A revised theory of protection motivation. In J. Cacioppo & R. Petty (Eds.), *Social psychophysiology.* New York: Guilford Press, 1983.

Rose, C., Rogers, E. W., Kleinman, P. R., Shory, N. L., Meehan, J. T., & Zumbro, P. E. An assessment of the Alabama smile keeper school dental health education program. *Journal of the American Dental Association,* 1979, *98,* 51–54.

Rosenbaum, M. S., Creedon, D. L., & Drabman, R. S. Training preschool children to identify emergency situations and make emergency phone calls. *Behavior Therapy,* 1981, *12,* 425–435.

Sass, R., & Crook, G. Accident proneness: Science or non-science? *International Journal of Health Services,* 1981, *11,* 175–189.

Scherz, R. G. Restraint systems for the prevention of injury to children in automobile accidents. *American Journal of Public Health,* 1976, *66,* 451.

Schlesinger, E. R., Dickson, D. G., Westaby, J., Lowen, L., Logrillo, V. M., & Maiwald, A. A. A controlled study of health education in accident prevention. *American Journal of Diseases of Children,* 1966, *111,* 490–496.

Silverstein, A. M. *Pure politics and impure science: The swine flu affair.* Baltimore: The Johns Hopkins University Press, 1981.

Simons, P. S. Failure of pediatricians to provide automobile restraint information to parents. *Pediatrics,* 1977, *60,* 646–648.

Sitting Safely. New York: Metropolitan Life Insurance Company, 1976.

Smialek, J. E., Smialek, P. Z., & Spitz, W. U. Accidental bed deaths in infants due to unsafe sleeping situations. *Clinical Pediatrics,* 1977, *16,* 1031–1036.

Solomons, H. D., Lakin, J. A., Snider, B. C., & Parades-Rojas, R. R. Is day care safe for children? Accident records reviewed. *Children's Health Care,* 1982, *10,* 90–93.

Spiegel, C. N., & Lindaman, F. C. Children can't fly: A program to prevent childhood morbidity and mortality from window falls. *American Journal of Public Health,* 1977, *67,* 1143–1147.

Starfield, B. Love, logic, and other approaches to prevention. *Pediatrics,* 1979, *64,* 968–969.

Swain, J. J., Allard, G. B., & Holborn, S. W. The good toothbrushing game: A school-based dental hygiene program for increasing the toothbrushing effectiveness of children. *Journal of Applied Behavior Analysis,* 1982, *15,* 171–176.

Sweeney, T. B. X-rated playgrounds? *Pediatrics,* 1979, *64,* 961.

Van Houten, R., Nau, P., & Marini, Z. An analysis of public posting in reducing speeding behavior on an urban highway. *Journal of Applied Behavior Analysis,* 1980, *13,* 383–395.

Vasta, R. *Studying children.* San Francisco: W. H. Freeman & Company, 1979.

Vaughan, V. C., & McKay, R. J. *Nelson textbook of pediatrics.* Philadelphia: W. B. Saunders, 1975.

Walton, W. W. An evaluation of the poison prevention packaging act. *Pediatrics,* 1982, *69,* 363–370.

Werner, P. Playground injuries and voluntary product standards for home and public playgrounds. *Pediatrics,* 1982, *69,* 18–20.

White, J. Because we care. *American Education,* 1976, *12*(10), 26–28.

Wilbur, C. S. The Johnson & Johnson Live For Life Program. *Behavioral Medicine Update,* 1981, *4,* 7–8.

Williams, A. F. Restraint use legislation: Its prospects for increasing the protection of children in cars. *Accident Analysis & Prevention,* 1979, *11,* 255–260.

Williams, A. F. Children killed in falls from motor vehicles. *Pediatrics,* 1981, *68,* 576–578.

Williams, A. F., & Wechsler, H. Interrelationship of preventive actions in health and other areas. *Health Services Reports,* 1972, *87,* 969–976.

Williams, A. F., & Wells, J. K. The Tennessee child restraint law in its third year. *American Journal of Public Health,* 1981, *71,* 163–165.

Witte, J. J., & Axnick, N. W. The benefits from ten years of measles immunization in the United States. *Public Health Reports,* 1975, May-June, *90,* 205–207.

Woodhead, J., Ghose, R., & Gupta, S. Health education to improve rubella immunization. *British Medical Journal,* 1980, *281,* 649–650.

Wright, L., Schaefer, A. B., & Solomons, G. *Encyclopedia of pediatric psychology.* Baltimore: University Park Press, 1979.

Yeaton, W. H., & Bailey, J. S. Teaching pedestrian safety skills to young children: An analysis and one-year followup. *Journal of Applied Behavior Analysis,* 1978, *11,* 375–329.

Yeaton, W. H., Greene, B. F., & Bailey, J. S. Behavioral community psychology strategies and tactics for teaching community skills to children and adolescents. In B. B. Lahey & A. E. Kazdin (Eds.), *Advances in clinical child psychology,* (Vol. 4). New York: Plenum Press, 1981.

Yokley, J. M., & Glenwick, D. S. Issues in mounting behavioral programs to increase the immunization of preschool children. *Behavioral Counseling Quarterly,* in press.

Young children and accidents in the home. (DHEW Publication No. (OHD)76-30034). Washington, D.C.: U.S. Government Printing Office, 1976.

Young, S. A., Halpin, T. J., Johnson, D. A., Irvin, J. J., & Marks, J. S. Effectiveness of a mailed reminder on the immunization levels of infants at a high risk of failure to complete immunizations. *American Journal of Public Health,* 1980, *70,* 422–424.

REFERENCE NOTES

1. Peterson, L. *Increasing immunization levels in high risk preschool children.* Paper presented at the meeting of the Midwestern Psychological Association, St. Louis, May 1980.
2. Labs, S. M. *Primary prevention of fetal alcohol syndrome: Effects of target, threat noxiousness, and self-efficacy on the abstinence intentions of prospective mothers.* Unpublished dissertation, University of Alabama, 1982.
3. Christophersen, E. R. Untitled presentation. In L. Wright (Chair) *Applying general principles of behavior to health and accident problems in childhood.* Symposium at the convention of the American Psychological Association, Los Angeles, August 24, 1981.
4. Duer, J. D. *Telephone prompts for high-risk prenatal appointments.* Paper presented at the convention of the Association for Advancement of Behavior Therapy. Toronto, November 1981.
5. Yokley, J. M., Glenwick, D. S., Hedrick, T. E., & Page, N. D. *Increasing the immunization of high risk preschoolers: An evaluation of applied community interventions.* Paper presented at the convention of the Association for Advancement of Behavior Therapy. New York, November 1980.
6. Peterson, L. The "Safe at Home" game: Training comprehensive prevention skills in latch-key children. Unpublished manuscript submitted for publication, University of Missouri-Columbia, 1982.
7. Fawcett, S. B., & Seekins, T. *Behavior analysis and policy research: A case of state legislation regarding child passenger safety.* Unpublished manuscript submitted for publication, University of Kansas, 1982.
8. Robertson, L. S. & Williams, A. F. *Some international comparisons of the effects of motor vehicle seat belt use and child restraint laws.* Paper presented at the Child Passenger Safety Conference, Nashville, May 1978.
9. Benedict, A. *Getting paid for primary prevention.* Paper presented at the convention of the American Psychological Association, Los Angeles, August 1981.

CHAPTER 7

Prevention by Acquiring Health-Enhancing Habits

JUDITH E. ALBINO

The critical role of personal behavior in health and illness is becoming increasingly clear. Twentieth century advances in the control of communicable diseases resulted in a clear shift away from morbidity and mortality patterns associated with high rates of acute and infectious conditions. Today, chronic disease is the number one killer. Cardiovascular disease alone now accounts for more than 50% of deaths in the United States each year. The incidence of these medical conditions is correlated with diet and exercise patterns, smoking, stress, and other lifestyle variables, suggesting that the problem is to a high degree avoidable. The etiologies of other major medical disorders, including cancer and diabetes, have been linked to behavior and environment, as have less severe but far more prevalent health problems such as dental caries.

The situation was described succinctly by Knowles (1977) in his volume on health in America: ''the health of human beings is determined by their behavior, their food, and the nature of their environment. Over 99% of us are born healthy and suffer premature death only as a result of personal misbehavior and environmental conditions'' (p. 79). More simply, much of what ails us today could be prevented.

The urgent concern with which chronic diseases are now viewed by our society is reflected in the directions of biomedical research and in government efforts to encourage the development and evaluation of health programs aimed at primary prevention. The 1979 report of the Surgeon General (Califano, 1979) was an explicit statement of the federal government's intended emphasis on health promotion and disease prevention. Specific recommendations for a healthy lifestyle are now being made, and it is apparent that widespread adoption of these recommendations will require the expertise of psychologists and others knowledgeable about behavior change. As a result, the interdisciplinary field of ''behavioral health'' has become recognized as the subspeciality of behavioral medicine and is focused on health promotion and the primary prevention of medical disorders (Matarazzo, 1980, 1982). In economic as well as humanitarian terms, primary prevention represents the preferred approach to control of chronic disease. To the extent that individuals are able or trained to adopt health-enhancing lifestyles, they will increase their probability of avoiding or delaying the suffering and expense of some of the most prevalent health problems.

Schoenberger (1982) pointed out that in most cases risk factors recognized in adults also apply to children. Furthermore, a "dose-response" interaction seems to exist for risk factors and disease. The assumption here is that low levels of risk over many years are roughly equivalent to higher levels over a shorter term. This relationship is apparent for risks such as smoking, obesity, elevated blood pressure, and blood cholesterol elevation. It appears that the presence of risk factors even at low levels should be considered important in children.

Schoenberger (1982) also suggested other reasons for promoting health-enhancing behaviors in children. He noted that it is generally easier to change short-term habits than to change behaviors that have persisted over many years. Furthermore, at some point damage occurring as the result of long-term practices cannot be reversed. This occurs in the atherosclerotic process after extreme scarring of blood vessel walls and ischemic damage to the heart or other organ tissues, for example.

In spite of such compelling arguments, we cannot simply assume that what is good primary prevention for adults is equally good for children. To begin with, it is not clear in all cases that the behaviors recommended as health-enhancing for adults are also important, or even healthy, for children. This is particularly true in the areas of diet and exercise where children and adults often have different physical needs and capabilities. Children also differ from adults in their ability to understand health issues and to assume responsibility for health behaviors (Roberts, Maddux, & Wright, 1984).

Applying the goals and approaches associated with behavioral health to a childhood population raises other special issues and concerns. In working with adults toward health enhancement and the primary prevention of disease, most models stress the need for participant cooperation and shared responsibility. This implies respect for an individual's right to make decisions about his or her own health. When working with children it means being concerned with the rights of individuals who are especially vulnerable by virtue of cognitive, social, and emotional immaturity. Obviously, this increases the burden on health care providers and researchers to be sensitive to the individual's rights, personal views and concerns.

With children, even more than with adults, the concern for individual needs and preferences overlaps a concern for social and environmental influences. The child's cultural and family ties and the peer network are all aspects of the social context that must be considered. In varying degrees at any given time these different sources of influence shape a child's attitudes and behaviors, and these influences may not always be in harmony with a particular thrust for primary prevention and health enhancement. In the case of such conflict, health care providers must concern themselves not only with promoting physical health, but also with the impact of their efforts on the child's psychological well-being. Failure to acknowledge and respect these social and developmental issues has implications for the results of primary prevention efforts. Lack of attention to cognitive and social factors could result in the rejection of health messages.

Issues of concern in working with children toward health enhancement also include questions related to methodology and assessment. Selection of criteria is always problematic in primary prevention research. While research aimed at evaluating the treatment of a disorder involves the assessment of decreases in symptoms or undesirable conditions, prevention research requires assessment of health status in the absence of symptoms. In many cases, prevention research seeks to evaluate improvement in that which is already acceptable. In working with children, care must be taken to appropriately interpret physiological measures. Average blood pressure readings are expected to be lower for children than for adults, but based on the dose-response hypothesis, even high normal readings for children may need to be treated as risk indicators.

The issues and concerns described here provide a focus for the next three chapter sections. These sections will describe major research and evaluation efforts related to two aspects of health enhancement: smoking avoidance and dental health. Each of these involves some unique demands on the target populations and raises some special problems of research methodology. Thus, the degree to which cognitive and social developmental issues have been addressed will be considered, and methodological issues related to program development and evaluation or research design will be discussed. Conclusions and recommendations regarding program effectiveness and impact will also be offered. By providing an intensive look at just two representative areas of health enhancement, it is hoped that maximum clarity of major conceptual issues can be achieved. Parallels with primary prevention efforts in other areas, such as substance abuse, diet and nutrition, stress management, and exercise do occur, of course, and examples or brief discussions of conceptual issues from these areas will be included.

PREVENTION OF SMOKING IN ADOLESCENTS

The negative effects of smoking on health have been extensively documented. A 1979 report of the Surgeon General (U.S. Public Health Service, 1979a) referred to smoking as the single most important factor contributing to current morbidity and mortality. The risk for both lung cancer and cardiovascular disease is extremely high for smokers. Oral and other cancers, and emphysema and non-neoplastic diseases of the respiratory system also are associated with smoking. Studies of trends in smoking behavior between 1968 and 1974 indicate that while the number of adult smokers decreased as a result of new information about the potential harmful effects, the number of adolescent smokers went up, particularly among females (U.S. Public Health Service, 1976). Although more recent reports (U.S. Public Health Service, 1982) indicate a tapering off of this trend in adolescent smoking, there continues to be cause for concern. Only within the last five to ten years, however, have researchers begun to see the development of carefully conceptualized and *effective* programs to decrease the onset of adolescent smoking.

In a review of smoking education programs from 1960-76, Thompson (1978) reported that most of the earlier antismoking efforts comprised campaigns to publicize the health hazards of smoking. Unfortunately, while such efforts have often increased the level of knowledge about health and smoking, they have had virtually no impact on the rate at which young people initiate smoking. Iammarino, Heit, and Kaplan (1980) studied 1,117 eighth grade students who had participated as elementary school children in the School Health Curriculum Project, which included an antismoking educational program now used in 200 schools. While they found significantly more desirable attitudes toward smoking on the part of participants, there were no differences between participants and controls on actual smoking behavior. Rabinowitz and Zimmerli (1974) also found positive changes in attitudes and knowledge but no improvements in smoking behaviors when they assessed response to a junior high school educational program focused on health hazards. In their critical review of the literature, Evans, Henderson, Hill, and Raines (1979a) concluded that health education efforts to prevent smoking generally have been disappointing when information alone was relied on to bring about behavior changes.

One of the hallmarks of adolescence is an egocentric sense of time (Elkind, 1967, 1978) and an accompanying inability to view oneself as old or in danger of poor health. From a cognitive developmental perspective, therefore, we might speculate that young people would not be strongly influenced by information about the devastating effects of years of smoking. The work of Creswell, Huffman, Stone, and Newman (1969) and Creswell, Stone, Huffman, and Newman (1971) has borne out this supposition, and suggests the need to focus on the immediate effects of smoking. While we should not yet conclude that it is futile to inform adolescents about the long-range health hazards, results such as these underscore the importance of going beyond the standard communication of this information to increase relevance and focus on the actual behaviors we wish to influence.

McAlister, Perry, and Maccoby (1979) have pointed out that traditional approaches to the primary prevention of smoking in adolescence have paid too little attention to the social context within which such behaviors are adopted. They cite sources indicating that most young smokers begin smoking before the ninth grade, and that they do so in response to pressure from a favorite peer. Recognizing the importance of peer values and acceptance to the adolescent struggling to form an identity independent of his or her parents, it is understandable that smoking (a social behavior generally reserved for adults) could symbolize that independence. It may appear somewhat contradictory that smoking in adolescence has been shown to be correlated with parental smoking (Borland & Rudolph, 1975). However, Wake (1979) argues that children model parental behavior with regard to issues perceived as serious or involving risk, while they model peer behavior when the level of perceived risk or concern about an issue is lower. He also points out that the modeled behavior in social learning need not involve conscious imitation, and suggests that both peer and parental modeling can influence the adolescent's decision to smoke. Botvin (1982) has expressed concern about what he perceives to be a narrow definition of peer pressure with reference to initial smoking. He believed that this pressure may often occur in the form of more subtle self-imposed pressure to conform to group norms, rather than direct and coercive pressure to smoke.

Social learning theory has been useful in understanding other aspects of the adoption of smoking by adolescents as well. McAlister et al. (1979) pointed to the strong influence on this age group of the attractive and adventurous young people shown in cigarette ads, as well as the models provided by parents and peers. Cognitive development generally enhances this effect. While younger children tend to be absolute in their thinking and are likely to be moralistic in their negative attitudes toward smoking, adolescents are attaining cognitive processes that allow them to be more relativistic (Schneider & Vanmastrigt, 1974). Since the developmental tasks of this age are largely focused on forming a unique sense of self and independence from parents, adolescents are likely to use their new thinking skills in testing the demands or opposing the expectations of the adult world. They are ready to model the behaviors of powerful adults, and if this action is rebellious it is even more attractive.

The case for ''readiness'' to smoke in adolescents is made even stronger by their perceptions of time, which are unlikely to induce fear of the long-term health consequences of smoking. Botvin (1982) has also suggested that because adolescents frequently do not perceive their smoking as part of a continuing pattern of behavior, they do not feel vulnerable to the health hazards of smoking. Many effective programs, therefore, have focused on the immediate or most salient issues related to adolescent smoking (Evans, Hansen, & Mittelmark, 1977; Fodor & Glass, 1971; McAlister et al., 1979; Perry, Killen, Telch, Slinkard, & Danaher, 1980). These issues have been conceptualized in terms of the toxicity of smoking by-products, the physical effects of smoking on fitness for sports or other activities, and on appearance and breath, rather than on long-term susceptibility to cardiovascular disease and cancer. With respect to social issues, emphasis is best placed on recognizing the pressures from peers or other reference groups, who may provide models for smoking behavior. In most cases, this task has been operationalized in terms of training social skills, as well as providing health information relevant to adolescent decisions concerning how to live today.

Evans, Rozelle, Mittelmark, Hansen, Bane, and Havis (1978) reported one of the first carefully designed studies of an attempt to influence adolescents' responses to social pressures regarding smoking. Having determined that the seventh grade represents a high risk period for beginning smoking, they chose as their study participants 750 seventh grade students in ten Houston, Texas junior high schools. These children were randomly assigned to one of three conditions or to a control group. Data obtained on students who reported smoking even one cigarette within the previous month (31%) were excluded from analyses, since they were classified as smokers. All four groups were present in two schools, and each treatment was also present alone in two other schools. All groups were pretested to assess smoking behavior and each experimental group was posttested at intervals of one, five, and ten weeks. The control group was posttested only after ten weeks. Accuracy of the smoking behavior assessment was insured by use of a spectrometric nicotine-in-saliva analysis. All students were shown a film demonstrating and explaining the spectrometric technique, and all were required to provide saliva samples at each test interval although, in fact, saliva samples were not analyzed.

The treatment group of greatest interest involved use of four videotapes, each featuring peers as narrators and actors. The first tape provided basic information about the dangers of smoking and the immediate advantages of not smoking in terms of health, fitness, and attractiveness, then focused on depictions of peer pressure. A second tape focused on adolescents' modeling of parents' smoking, and a third focused on exposing the persuasive appeals in cigarette advertising. The fourth tape summarized the others. After viewing each tape, students answered content questions and participated in small group discussions focused on ideas for coping with pressures to smoke. Posters based on the videotapes were displayed in the classrooms to serve as reminders. After each posttest, students in this group received feedback about their classmates' smoking behavior. The second and third experimental groups were structured to evaluate the possibility of treatment effects occurring as a result of the feedback alone, or from the influence of testing. Thus, the second group received feedback and assessment only, and the third, assessment only.

Analyses of their data indicated that almost twice as many children (18.3%) in the control group began smoking as did children in the treatment, feedback, and testing groups (10%, 8.6%, and 10.3%, respectively). The number of control group participants who began smoking was unexpectedly low, however. The investigators speculated that, since the videotape describing the saliva analysis focused on the immediate effects of nicotine on the body, this may have served as a relatively powerful treatment for young people with a strong ''present time'' orientation. Another explanation for the performance of the control group was suggested by McAlister et al. (1979) in commenting on this study. They suggested that the measurement techniques used may be viewed fearfully by adolescents, who suspect that smoking might be reported to their parents or to school authorities.

In additional longitudinal studies, Evans and his group are tracking children's smoking behaviors over a three-year period and investigating specific components of the treatment described here. The initial data, however, confirmed the effectiveness of dealing with the social context and behavioral models, and of focusing on immediate, rather than future consequences.

Others working in the area of smoking prevention also have used concepts from social learning theory with considerable success. McAlister et al. (1979) suggested that the program developed by Evans and his colleagues was still too closely tied to adult authority to maximize the modeling of nonsmoking as a reflection of the peer culture. They recommended presentation of such programs by peers, preferably teenagers slightly older than the target group. The concept of psychological ''inoculation'' represents a major component of efforts conducted by the Stanford University Heart Disease Prevention Program in their school-based programs for adolescents (Coates & Perry, 1981; McAlister et al., 1979; McAlister, Perry, Killen, Slinkard, & Maccoby, 1980; Perry et al., 1980). Similar to Evans' work in which students are exposed to the social pressures for smoking, this approach seeks to actually provide training and rehearsal of interpersonal skills for resisting social pressure to smoke.

In the Stanford program, ''attractive'' peer leaders are selected from volunteers at nearby high schools. After training, these peer leaders implement a seven session curriculum for sixth and seventh grade students. Students are encouraged to make a commitment to nonsmoking based on information presented in the first session.

Then they spend the next two sessions learning, discussing, and trying out responses for dealing with advertisements, dares of friends, and other pressures to smoke. Four more sessions spread over the school year function as review, or "boosters" for the original three day inoculation. Initial data from the study showed that at the end of a school year, using assessment techniques similar to those described by Evans et al. (1977, 1978), 9.9% of the control group, but only 5.6% of the treatment group, reported having smoked during the previous week. In another trial (McAlister et al., 1980), 21-month followup data showed an 8.4% annual smoking onset rate for the control group, compared with only 3.2% for the experimental group. Thirty-three month followup data reported by Telch, Killen, McAlister, Perry and Maccoby (1982) showed that the earlier differences between treatment and control subjects were maintained. At this point, only 5.1% of the treatment group were smokers, while 14.8% of the controls were classified as smokers.

Smoking prevention programs evaluated and reported by Botvin and Eng (1980, 1982) and by Botvin, Eng, and Williams (1980) have also used a peer leadership approach. Theirs differs from the Stanford program, however, in the placement of greater emphasis on psychological factors that can render adolescents more vulnerable to social pressure. In this way, they hoped to counter pressures to conform, as well as more explicit pressure to smoke. They reported significantly lower levels of smoking onset for 121 students enrolled in a program designed to increase knowledge about smoking, develop skills for resisting pressure to smoke, and to develop greater autonomy, self-esteem, self-confidence, and an ability to cope with social anxiety. In a subsequent study, Botvin and Eng (1982) tested this program as implemented by peer leaders in the manner recommended by McAlister et al. (1979). Focusing on 426 seventh graders, Botvin and Eng pretested and provided a 12 session program to children in one suburban New York school. Two posttests were conducted at intervals of three months and one year. Control group children in a comparable school received the pre- and posttest measures only. Saliva samples were obtained to enhance the accuracy of self-reported smoking behavior, as recommended by Evans et al. (1977). In addition to assessing smoking behavior, measures of knowledge about smoking, psychosocial factors in smoking, and advertising were obtained, as well as scores on measures of locus of control, self-esteem, social anxiety, and the ability to be influenced. The confidentiality of all assessments was emphasized to the students, however, and 25% of the posttest saliva samples were actually analyzed for thiocyanate levels.

The twelve one-hour sessions used group discussion, modeling, and behavior rehearsal techniques, and were conducted by trained peer leaders who were popular, attractive nonsmokers recruited from a nearby high school. In addition to sessions focused specifically on smoking or behavior related to smoking, there were sessions dealing with general communication and social skills, assertiveness, decision-making, anxiety management, and other life skill topics. Homework assignments required practice of these skills. Student participants also carried out a self-improvement project in which they were involved in setting short- and long-term goals and charting progress related to changing some personal behavior.

As in the Evans et al. (1978) study, Botvin and Eng (1982) eliminated data for pretest smokers prior to analyses. After three months, 19% of the control group and 8% of the experimental group reported having smoked at least once during the previous month, with 8% and 5% reporting smoking in the preceding week. This difference was supported by the results of saliva analyses. In addition, analyses of covariance revealed significant differences in the expected directions between experimental and control subjects on all knowledge measures and on social anxiety and the ability to be influenced. After one year, 24% of the experimental group and 32% of the control group reported having smoked in the preceding month. For the preceding week, these reports were 11% and 25%, respectively. Botvin and Eng suggest that the apparent erosion of treatment effects indicates a need for continued intervention, possibly booster sessions, over a period of years.

The programs and evaluations described here are representative of the most effective work being done in primary prevention of smoking. As a group, these programs are an example of the type of effort most needed in primary prevention; that is, systematic applied research guided by theory and highly cognizant of previous and on-going work. While the results obtained in these efforts do not attain the ideal of no new adolescent smokers, they clearly represent a major step in the right direction. Furthermore, the possibility should not be overlooked that the criteria used in these studies have been altogether too stringent. Many adolescents may smoke once or twice a month over a period of a few years but never develop a habit or smoke at all after their teen years. There is not yet enough information about either the long-term implications of occasional smoking or the determinants of habitual smoking. Smoking the first cigarette is a necessary condition for the development of a smoking habit; it is not a sufficient condition, however. Furthermore, Perry et al. (1980) have demonstrated that the same techniques used for primary prevention of smoking could be used to modify current smoking behaviors. Tenth grade smokers, who participated in social skills training and informational programs focusing on the immediate effects of smoking, reported significantly less smoking at the end of a semester than did control subjects exposed to a traditional program emphasizing long-term health risks. We have seen the failure of drug abuse programs that threatened the youthful experimenter with addiction (Tennant, Weaver, & Lewis, 1973). Now there are indications that smoking programs that are too insistent on total abstinence or that focus only on the severe, long-term effects of smoking could also fail.

A program reported by Hurd, Johnson, Pechacek, Bast, Jacobs, and Luepker (1980) provides some information based on less stringent criteria related to smoking behaviors. While also focusing on the immediate consequences of smoking and also utilizing peers for teaching, this work involved a stronger attempt to personalize the treatment. A total of 1,526 seventh grade students participated over an eight month period. In addition to a control group and a group receiving assessment only, there were two treatment groups participating in five sessions. One of these saw the same videotaped materials on social pressures used by Evans et al. (1978) and participated in small group activities led by college age students. The last group participated in all of these activities and also viewed videotapes of some of their own peers discussing smoking. Next they wrote a statement describing their commitment and reasons for not smoking, were videotaped while presenting their statements orally, and then viewed their presentations.

Saliva thiocyanate measures were described to program participants and saliva samples were obtained at a pretest (except for the control group) and after the second and last sessions. A longer behavioral self-report questionnaire than in previous studies was used, and students were classified as nonsmokers, experimenters, smokers (twice or more a month), and quitters. The number of nonsmokers in all treatments declined over the year and the number of experimenters and smokers increased, although in the intervention involving personalization and commitment techniques these changes reflected lower levels of smoking. The number of smokers who quit was also higher in the treatment groups.

While Hurd et al. were not able to demonstrate the separate effects of the commitment and personalization components of their program, their theoretical rationale is persuasive. Studies in other areas have sometimes shown that making a public commitment can substantially affect future behavior (for example, Levy, Yamashita, & Pow, 1979). This activity also provides information about peer values and behavior and forces students to confront their own inconsistencies if they do choose to smoke. This technique has parallels in the belief congruence model described by Rokeach (1971), which has also been operationalized in the area of dental hygiene (Albino, 1978). Combining these activities with the modeling and inoculation techniques already used successfully has apparently strengthened the prevention technique and suggests that other multi-method approaches should be explored.

Another major program has produced promising findings by combining media, teacher training, and home family activity strategies with modeling and social inoculation techniques (Flay, D'Avernas, Best, Kersell, & Ryan, 1982; Flay, Johnson, & Hansen, 1984; Flay, Hansen, Johnson, Sobol, & Alvarez, Note 1; Flay, Johnson, & Hansen, Notes 2, 3; Sobol, Flay, Johnson, Hansen, Alvarez, Grossman, & Simmons, Note 4). This large scale program involved the use of five heavily promoted five-minute video segments aired on commercial television. These segments were correlated with classroom activities directed by peer leaders who worked with teachers trained in social and behavioral skills. Parents were asked to participate in homework assignments and printed materials were also made available. The week following this program, five additional television segments focusing on smoking cessation were aired and "self-help quitting kits" were made available. Preliminary data obtained one month after the program activities reflected impressive positive changes for children in experimental school conditions compared to those in control conditions. The differences included increased knowledge and only half as many new smokers among children in the schools receiving the program. In addition, in 23% of all viewing homes, a smoker was reported to have quit. Flay (1981) has proposed an integrative model of attitude and behavior change that would guide the use of such multiple program components to enhance a variety of health education efforts. The use of television is viewed as a central concept, since mass media dissemination of information is by nature efficient and effective for this purpose.

Other activities and approaches can be used to strengthen and personalize the behavior change effort.

The programs described here are promising and offer great hope for the elimination of a major health risk. Fisher (1980) has provided a caveat that should temper our expectations, however. In smoking prevention, as in other fields involving psychology and education, he points out that there is no reason to believe desired results will be maintained over long periods of time and in the absence of social and environmental support. While early adolescence may be the single most critical time to intervene, the need for boosters and their appropriate timing are issues that should be explored. It has already been suggested that informational approaches may be useful during the elementary years. These can later provide a symbolic model from which children can draw when they are first confronted with pressure to smoke. Such material could strengthen their commitment and receptivity to social skills training provided to them later as young adolescents. It is possible that the last years of high school and the early college years also represent a critical time requiring still another approach as these young adults begin to develop in other-directedness and to establish a concept of themselves in the adult world.

Botvin (1982) has pointed out a tendency in smoking prevention programs to focus on social skills while ignoring other important social factors. Efforts to reduce the number of positive role models who smoke represents one way of providing essential environmental support for adolescents. Botvin (1982) also has suggested that smoking prevention programs should not be conducted as "single-issue" efforts. Since cigarette smoking tends to occur in adolescents along with other health compromising activities, such as alcohol or drug use, an approach that acknowledges this larger pattern will have a greater likelihood of success. Still another issue that has received relatively little attention is the role of personality variables. Botvin believes that personality factors are influential primarily as moderators of the response to environment and in particular to social pressures related to smoking. He recommends expansion of research aimed at identifying young people who are more highly susceptible to these pressures.

Having considered a number of theoretical and design issues in programs aimed at preventing smoking, it is time to comment on some practical issues and implications of these efforts. By the standards of most school systems, the programs described here would appear carefully designed, but also time-consuming and expensive. Many would perceive such programs as beyond their reach, in terms of both material and human resources. As the health messages related to smoking become more broadly disseminated, there will be increasing pressure to include smoking prevention in school health curricula. As a result, there is a real danger that less expensive, information-oriented programs will be put in place, in spite of the data suggesting they are ineffective and inappropriate for the adolescent population at greatest risk. This could be an example of a case in which a little money and effort thrown at a problem is worse than none at all. The ineffectiveness of "token effects" often serves to discredit all efforts. The next important step for those interested in primary prevention is to package these new approaches for easier and less expensive implementation in the schools or other community settings. It will also be important to develop the data base that will substantiate, and therefore sell, such packages. It is unpopular to place a dollar value on health or life. Nevertheless, the cost of adequate primary prevention can be compared convincingly with the cost of treatment for those whose illnesses and deaths can be attributed to smoking.

INITIATING AND SUSTAINING DENTAL HEALTH BEHAVIORS

While primary prevention with respect to smoking is operationalized as an effort to *avoid* or *inhibit* the initiation of a behavior that places the individual at risk, there are other issues that require the *adoption* of specific health behaviors. Dental hygiene is a good example of this latter form of primary prevention.

Although a recent study suggests that important reductions in the rate of dental caries among school children have been achieved over the past ten years (U.S. Public Health Service, 1981), this dental problem remains the most common disease of childhood. Dental caries is rampant among teenagers and eventually affects 95% of the population. The average number of carious lesions in young adulthood is 14.9, and by this time the costs have been considerable in terms of pain and loss of school time, as well as dollars. Furthermore, thousands of children under the age of three years are diagnosed annually as victims of "nursing bottle syndrome" or extensive caries associated with unrestricted use, particularly during sleep, of bottles containing infant formula or other sweetened liquids.

The second most prevalent oral health problem is periodontal, or gum disease, which reaches its peak after the age of 35 and affects three-quarters of the adult population. Thirty-two percent of the population over 45 have no teeth, usually as a direct result of advanced periodontal disease and the loss of supporting bone structure that frequently accompanies it (U.S. Public Health Service, 1979b). Yet in spite of their prevalence, caries and periodontal disease are largely preventable.

While their etiologies are complex and not fully understood, the occurrence of both caries and periodontal disease is clearly associated with the presence of certain microorganisms. Regular brushing and flossing to remove bacterial plaque is a highly effective procedure for the prevention of periodontal disease, and there are also indications that oral hygiene offers protection against dental caries. In early childhood, and possibly prenatally as well, use of fluoride compounds significantly increases the resistance of tooth enamel to dental caries. Diet can also play a role in the elimination of oral disease by controlling the availability of a suitable substrate for microbial growth (Stamm, 1980). Each of these factors in dental disease is susceptible to influence either by individual behavior, or in the case of water fluoridation, community behavior.

The problem of preventing major dental diseases is ameliorated by a relatively clear relationship between behavior and health—far more clear and direct, for example, than the relationships between hypertension and exercise, or cancer and diet. Contributing to this generally positive situation is the fact that primary prevention of dental diseases is neither expensive nor time-consuming. It is possible to reduce dental disease substantially by spending as little as 10 to 15 minutes daily properly brushing and flossing the teeth.

Achieving sustained adherence to recommended dental preventive behaviors has proved to be quite difficult, however, in both adults and children. Horowitz (1979) has suggested that oral hygiene procedures should not be relied on as a major component of primary prevention programs in dental health, precisely because it is so difficult to achieve sustained efforts of regular and thorough plaque removal. Kegeles (1963) has attributed this difficulty to the relatively low perceived severity of dental problems. Another problem may be the typically insidious progression of dental diseases that obscures the relationship between preventive behaviors and dental health. Still another difficulty is the tendency to overlook home oral hygiene care in early childhood. Knowing the children will lose their deciduous teeth after only a few years, many parents and dentists tend to wait until children have their permanent teeth before emphasizing oral hygiene. In doing so, however, they may miss out on one of the most important times for social learning—the preschool years when children are particularly receptive to parental models. Unfortunately, there has not been enough research to permit adequate assessment of the suggestion that the best time for initiating dental hygiene behaviors is in early childhood.

The research literature does contain a number of well-designed dental health program evaluations which incorporate various instructional and motivational techniques aimed at very young and older children. Among these is the report by Martens, Frazier, Hirt, Meskin, and Proshek (1973) of an effort to increase oral hygiene behavior in second grade children. They achieved sustained reductions in plaque scores with a program incorporating contingent reinforcement along with discovery learning approaches and individual interaction with a dental hygienist.

In the Martens et al. (1973) study, children received tokens which could be used to purchase toys when examinations revealed improved plaque scores. Tokens were worth 10 points, five points, or one point to reflect the children's performance levels. Twenty examinations were scheduled during the school year to simulate a variable interval schedule for reinforcing oral hygiene behaviors. Instruction in oral hygiene skills was provided only in response to students' direct requests, and this instruction was highly personalized. Instructional sessions involved group and individual activities related to dental health and oral hygiene skills. Participation was "contracted" by each child and activities were structured to the individual levels of curiosity and interest. In addition, parents were invited to informational sessions and were asked to encourage their children's oral hygiene efforts. Plaque scores obtained by children in the six experimental group classrooms were compared with those of the six control group classrooms. Six months after completion of the program (a full year after the program began), the plaque scores of experimental group children remained significantly lower than those of control group children. The results are particularly impressive because the post-treatment interval included the summer vacation period when there was no in-school monitoring or brushing. This pattern was unaffected by sex, reading level, or IQ scores, or by involvement of the parents.

These results suggest that positive reinforcement may be highly effective in changing oral hygiene behaviors. This success could be partly attributable to the age and readiness of the child participants, as it may be easier to structure reinforcement for children at this age and easier to avoid competing needs or stimuli. The effects of various instructional and motivational components of the program were particularly difficult to determine. Would positive reinforcement techniques have been as effective if not conducted within a discovery learning context where children received considerable individual attention? While the less impressive results of other studies which focused on such learning activities seem to suggest that positive reinforcement techniques are the critical component, it was not possible to identify the discrete effects of various program aspects.

For all its methodological shortcomings, the study by Martens et al. (1973) represents one of the best attempts to implement and evaluate a dental hygiene program that focuses specifically on changing behaviors, rather than knowledge or attitudes. Historically, most published reports of primary prevention efforts have described information-oriented programs conducted in schools. Frazier (1980) reviewed the content of these programs and concluded that they focus primarily on very basic information about caries and proper brushing and flossing techniques. As a result, such programs change children's knowledge, but only rarely their behavior. Rayner and Cohen (1974) strongly recommended that dental health education move away from information approaches to more innovative techniques for effecting behavior change. Both reviews documented the ineffectiveness of programs based on information and/or skill approaches alone, and the last decade has brought an increase in the efforts aimed at changing behavior. Most of these can be very broadly described either as (1) behavioral or contingency management approaches, or (2) cognitive approaches, including components such as affect arousal or other persuasive techniques and those utilizing social learning framework components.

Contingency Management

Albino, Juliano, and Slakter (1977) and Albino, Tedesco and Lee (1980) reported the use of behavior modification techniques along with other motivational approaches. Adolescents were the target subjects in this program, rather than the early elementary age children of the Martens et al. (1973) study. This research extended over a three-year period and originally involved 1,500 students in public and parochial schools. Classrooms of children were assigned randomly to three groups: (1) a control group receiving a standard dental health lecture and a dental prophylaxis each year, (2) a treatment group receiving the same treatment as the control group as well as topical fluoride treatments and sealants applied to the occlusal surfaces of their teeth, and (3) a group receiving all treatments described for the first two groups, and a variety of instructional, motivational activities. For a subsample of children, these included a parent-monitored program of contingent reinforcement for brushing and flossing.

After 30 months, the third group had significantly lower plaque scores, although this difference declined over the succeeding six months. Within the treatment group, which participated in intensive instructional and motivational activities, some differences could also be identified. Results suggested that the parent-monitored behavior modification program involving weekly administration of tangible reinforcers produced the greatest improvements in plaque scores. These data were confounded, however, by the fact that in the last year of the program, only those students with the poorest plaque control and those identified as class leaders received the behavior modification approaches.

Several studies have used positive reinforcement techniques without instruction or dental procedures to improve brushing in children, including a study by Lattal (1969) conducted in a summer camp. This work provides a more careful analysis of the effectiveness of contingency management alone for increasing toothbrushing. The subjects were eight 10–12 year old boys observed over a 53 day camping session. The criterion measure in this study was frequency of brushing, rather than a plaque score or some other assessment of oral hygiene. Swimming was made contingent on the campers' brushing their teeth. A four-day baseline period was followed by a second eight-day baseline period in which a verbal announcement to "go and brush your teeth" was made each day. Then, swimming was made contingent on brushing for the next 22 days; and finally the contingency was abandoned during a final nine-day extinction period. From baselines reflecting almost no brushing behaviors, this contingency arrangement produced virtually a 100% level of brushing, and no need for verbal prompts after 17 days. During the extinction period, brushing dropped off markedly, although there were some problems in accurately assessing extinction.

Although the lack of controls limited their study, Stacey, Abbott, and Jordan (1972) also employed contingency management techniques during a summer camp experience. The 17 participants, aged five to 17, received individualized instruction in brushing. This was followed by supervision of brushing and four examinations, scheduled at irregular intervals, to assess oral hygiene performance. Those who met their goals were rewarded with toys or passes to play miniature golf. Results of the examinations showed that all children demonstrated at least modest improvements in oral hygiene, although children with poor manual dexterity demonstrated less improvement than those with greater skill levels. The authors point out that modeling and competition may also have prompted improved performance.

Other investigators have examined children's compliance with dental regimens in response to various school- or home-based contingency management procedures. Using multiple baselines across flossing and brushing responses and other design variations, Claerhout and Lutzker (1981) found substantial increases in self-initiated compliance for four children ages seven to nine. The contingency management approaches included point systems, direct cash payments, award of stars, and money-based token systems, all administered by parents who offered no other help, encouragement, or prompting. Swain, Allard, and Holborn (1982) reported improved oral hygiene for 22 first graders and 23 second graders who participated in "The Good Toothbrushing Game." The game required toothbrushing at home. At school, each class was divided into two teams and four children from each team were randomly selected every day at school for hygiene checks. In addition to specific feedback and praise for individuals, winning teams had their names on a winners' poster and received special stickers. Using multiple baselines across each of the groups, they found reductions in plaque that were essentially maintained after nine months.

Lund, Kegeles, and Weisenberg (1977) reported that contingent reward approaches were superior to information on techniques or to a discussion technique used along with the information approach. Their work focused on achieving compliance among seventh graders in a school-based program for application of topical fluoride. Subjects were 335 students in lower income urban areas or higher income suburban areas. Group differences were assessed for volunteering, obtaining parental permission for participation, and participation in each of the three fluoride applications. Although the "prizes," or contingent rewards offered for participation were worth only 25 cents to $1.00 (or $3.00 for participation in all three fluoride applications), 73% of those in the urban schools who received the rewards and 79% in the suburban schools participated fully in the program. These figures compare with only 67% and 56% for those receiving information only, and 48% and 52% for those involved in the peer group discussion sessions.

In a similar study assessing achievement of adolescent participation in a home mouth rinse program, Kegeles, Lund, and Weisenberg (1978) again found the use of small rewards to be more effective than information or discussion approaches alone, both for obtaining participation and for maintaining compliance over a period of time. In still another mouth rinse program, Lund and Kegeles (1982) found that the effect of contingent rewards on compliance could be enhanced by the use of simple action instructions, although reminders alone did not increase compliance. These action instructions, it was thought, prompted mental rehearsal of a clear course of action, in the manner described earlier by Leventhal, Singer and Jones (1965). Surprisingly, however, the significant improvement in compliance gained by action instructions occurred only for urban, lower income children. It was suggested that suburban, higher income children reacted to highly structured instructions that seem to belittle their competence and ability to act independently. The authors have no data to support this explanation, although it would be consistent with Brehm's (Brehm, 1966; Wicklund & Brehm, 1968) work on psychological reactance.

One attempt to use aversive contingencies was recently reported by White (1980). Orthodontic patients who did not brush well or who reported for appointments with loose bands were required to use an unpleasant tasting dentifrice to clean their teeth. While there was no control group, the decrease in percentage of patients appearing with poor hygiene suggested they were willing to change their behaviors in order to avoid this unpleasant experience.

These studies reveal contingent reinforcement techniques are an effective approach to increasing preventive dental behaviors. Based on the work presented, but without considering the variety of ways in which contingency management has been implemented and often enhanced by other factors, these approaches appear to be equally applicable across an age span of at least 12 years. Furthermore, the objective value of the reinforcer need not be great which is an additional, practical advantage. Yet behavioral techniques have not been widely adopted by those working in preventive dentistry.

Kegeles et al. (1978) have suggested that the failure to adopt behavioral approaches can be attributed to the perceived problem of extinction and loss of "intrinsic motivation," and to practical issues related to the financial and personal costs of such programs. These issues reflect empirical questions, but comparative studies of reinforcement schedules have not been conducted in this area, and there are few reports of work related to the streamlining of contingency management techniques. Kegeles et al. (1978) have suggested that self-monitoring and self-reinforcement programs might be used to cut down on the resources required for frequent monitoring and rewards. Weinstein and Getz (1978) have described such an approach for use within a clinical setting. The literature on self-management could also be very useful here (for example, Kanfer & Karoly, 1982; Williams & Long, 1979).

Cognitive Approaches

Cognitive or persuasive approaches have been applied most frequently with adolescents, and some have included the mobilization of peer pressure within a social learning paradigm similar to the smoking prevention programs already described. Unfortunately, this work does not reflect the same level of cohesiveness and mutual cognizance that was found in the work on smoking. Nevertheless, there are interesting and instructive findings available.

"Fear appeals" have been implemented in preventive dentistry by Evans and his colleagues (Evans, Rozelle, Lasater, Dembroski, & Allen, 1968, 1970). They conducted a series of investigations of the effects and interactions of aroused fear and persuasive messages on self-reported dental behaviors and oral hygiene measures reflecting actual behaviors. Subjects were junior high school students who were randomly assigned to receive either fear-arousing messages concerning the effects of neglected oral hygiene (high threat or low threat), or positive messages about the importance of good dental health and its social rewards. All communications were followed by recommendations and instructions for brushing, flossing, and disclosing plaque to check brushing. A fourth group received only these recommendations, and a fifth group received a more elaborate set of instructions. Plaque scores and measures of reported behavior changes were obtained five days and again six weeks after the sessions. Results suggested that reported changes and actual changes in oral hygiene were affected differently by fear arousal and persuasive messages. Reported behavior changes were most responsive to the high fear message and recommendations only, which was generally consistent with Leventhal and Singer's (1966) earlier finding that a high-fear message was more effective in changing subjects' dental hygiene beliefs and acceptance of recommendations. However, the Evans studies revealed greater improvements in plaque scores, representing actual behavior, when elaborated recommendations and positive appeals were used.

For all of Evans' groups, the five-day measures produced positive changes and regression occurred at the six-week testing period. Only the low fear groups regressed to below baseline levels, however. Evans (1978) also reported that later studies showed that simply testing subjects at irregular intervals was as persuasive as messages involving fear arousal. In summarizing the work on fear arousal and persuasive communication in preventive dentistry, Evans concluded that increasing neither the amount of information nor the level of emotion arousal could be expected to bring about behavior changes.

Leventhal (1971), however, noted that the data from fear arousal studies are not consistent across various health issues. He reviewed this research and discussed the work in terms of alternate theories, the "drive-reduction" model and a "parallel response" model. The drive model assumes that responses to the health message involving fear arousal are the result exclusively of the drive to reduce the negative emotion of fear. The alternate hypothesis, however, suggests that there may be competing responses—one intended to reduce fear and the other to cope with, or manage the health issue itself. Thus, not only must the amount of fear be balanced in order to control irrational responses such as denial, but the properties of the message that provide the subject with a means for controlling the health problem danger must also be balanced. Leventhal suggested that it is important for health practitioners to understand the absolute value and the utility of information provided. In particular, it is important to understand whether information is directed at controlling fear or controlling danger, since the two processes may have very different relationships to the stimulus situation.

Leventhal's parallel response model is convincing and seems to explain some of the contradictory results obtained in experimental attempts to motivate preventive dental behaviors. Interestingly, some of the recommendations both he and Evans have made seem to suggest a return to approaches that focus on information and instruction. Their work has made it quite clear, however, that if we are to depend on instruction, the structure, context, timing, and content of preventive messages are important. In ignoring one or more of these aspects of the prevention message, traditional instructional approaches have failed. The consideration given to these factors in the antismoking programs, including presentation by peers to children at the most vulnerable age for onset of smoking and limitation of content to immediate consequences, provides an example that could be used in promoting dental health as well.

Several dental health studies have involved attempts to mobilize peer group influence to support participation in preventive dentistry programs. The studies by Kegeles et al. (1978) and Lund et al. (1977), as already described, revealed both contingent reward techniques and a control approach based on information only to be superior to peer group discussions for enhancing participation in topical fluoride and fluoride rinse programs. Other studies have offered support for the use of approaches focused on peer values.

Albino (1978) reported an attempt to mobilize peer influence using a "belief consistency" technique inspired by Rokeach's (1971) work in which individuals are made aware of inconsistencies within their systems of values and beliefs. The study involved 171 seventh grade students in three schools, who were randomly assigned to four treatments. Three weeks after instruction in brushing and flossing, adolescents in the belief consistency group were seen in individual sessions and asked to rank order a set of 12 personal characteristics. It was emphasized that these characteristics had been selected by a large group of their peers, and participants were reinforced for their top choices with information about the large numbers of children who gave high ratings to the same characteristics. Children were then asked to relate one or more of the characteristics they rated highest to dental health. After discussion of these relationships, they were asked to rate their satisfaction with their brushing and flossing behaviors. This session was followed five weeks later by another instructional session and an additional three weeks later by another belief consistency review session. In this last session, the subjects were also shown color photographs, taken in baseline assessment sessions, of their own mouths with red dye staining the plaque on their teeth. At this point they were forced to confront not only any inconsistencies between their own beliefs and those of their peers, but also the inconsistencies between their own beliefs about oral hygiene and the behaviors reflected in the photographs. This technique appears to directly address the problem of adolescents' frequent inability to see relationships between the ideals they espouse and their day-to-day behaviors, a pattern that Elkind (1967, 1978) has described as "apparent hypocrisy."

In addition to baseline assessments, posttest plaque scores were obtained one week, six weeks, and twelve weeks after the final session. Analyses of these data indicated that significantly greater reductions in plaque scores were achieved by the belief consistency treatment group than by a control group, or a group that received only the instructional sessions. Another experimental group, which participated in the behavior rehearsal session focussing on mental rehearsal and imagining of brushing and flossing, achieved scores equal to those of the belief consistency group after one week, but by six weeks were regressing. The belief consistency group, on the other hand, continued to improve their plaque scores after twelve weeks. The interpretation of results was rendered problematic by the fact that there were many elements combined in one approach. It is impossible to know whether peer modeling, the value clarification process, the photographic feedback, or some other element, was most crucial to the observed dental health changes. Nevertheless, the data reflect a very positive response to approaches focused on cognitive change within a social learning paradigm.

In summary, while approaches utilizing contingency management can be successfully applied to initiate oral health behaviors in almost any age group, there is also evidence that approaches utilizing the social context of health decisions may be effective in improving and sustaining oral hygiene behaviors of adolescents. In fact, some of the more successful contingency management programs have been substantially enhanced by the use of cognitive restructuring and social learning approaches. As already suggested, techniques used within the smoking prevention programs could be applied to strengthen oral hygiene programs. For example, high school students could be trained to present programs involving information, oral hygiene skills, value clarification, and social skills to junior high school students. Levy, Lodish, and Pawlak-Floyd (1982) reported a pilot study concerning training skills for problem solving and decision making. This work used role play simulation and discussion methods in helping 11- and 12-year-old children to begin taking responsibility for their dental health care. While their results were weak, children who participated in this group showed greater knowledge and reported and role-played more desirable behaviors than did those in a control group. There are a number of ways in which this program could be improved, but it represents a useful first step toward integrating preventive dental behaviors with life and social skills training for adolescents.

With respect to prevention of childhood dental problems, there is clearly a need to develop more programs to focus on preschool and the elementary years. While data reported by Korins, Sposato, Leske, and Ripa (1982) suggest that most first grade children cannot brush their teeth well enough to achieve desirable levels of oral hygiene, there are other indications that even very young children can learn the necessary motor skills. Murray and Epstein (1981) reported two experiments designed to evaluate the effectiveness for normal preschool children of a strategy successfully employed by Horner and Keilitz (1975) for the acquisition of toothbrushing skills in mentally retarded children. The approach involved a videotaped program showing 15 behavioral steps in toothbrushing and verbal instruction, observation of skilled performers, practice, and physical prompting. In comparison with those of a matched control group, the oral hygiene scores of five four to six-year-old children improved significantly over a five day period. In the second study, scores of children exposed to the same treatment were compared with those of a group receiving feedback as demonstrated in the Martens et al. (1973) study. While both of these groups improved, results with the video approach were superior and did not decline until the sixth week after exposure. Poche, McCubbrey, and Munn (1982) reported successful skills acquisition by three- and four-year-old children using 16 steps for the actual manipulation of the brush in the mouth. Although they did not use videotaped instruction, simple instructions, modeling, physical guidance, and descriptive praise were used, as in the Horner and Keilitz (1975) approach. Such work shows that with adequate analysis and training of component behaviors, preschool children are capable of essential preventive procedures.

From a social psychological perspective, however, a practical and potentially devastating barrier to children's dental hygiene programs is encountered in the unreliability of parental models. Effective programs for young children often require the participation of parents, whose availability and enthusiasm may not approach that of their young children. This suggests a need for concurrent approaches for children and their parents or guardians. Lee (1978) has described one successful program using traditional instruction in which kindergartners' parents attended a school dental health program. Since parent participants were volunteers, however, we cannot assume they were not already highly motivated.

The fear arousal techniques described in this section might prove more useful within a population of adults approaching the years of greatest vulnerability to periodontal disease and the accompanying threat of losing their teeth. We could not predict, however, the extent to which parents' responses would be supportive of health-enhancement for their children. The contingency reinforcement program described by Reiss, Piotrowski, and Bailey (1976) suggests an approach aimed at the children of program recipients that shows more promise for primary prevention adaptation. They were able to increase the use of restorative dental services for the children of lower income rural residents by providing a $5.00 incentive. This technique was more cost-effective than the use of repeated telephone reminders. While Iwata and Beckfort (1981) used fee reductions to increase oral hygiene behaviors in adults, there have been no reports of programs using such incentives for parents who are able to effect improved oral hygiene in their children. Olson, Levy, Evans, and Olson (1981) reported significant increases in utilization of dental services as a function of individualized feedback and personal contact. While only 12% of the control children whose parents received notices of treatment needs received those services, 53% of the treatment group received the dental services they needed. Approaches like these need to be explored as potentially useful adjuncts to the instruction and persuasion of children in the adoption of effective oral health behaviors.

IMPLICATIONS FOR HEALTH ENHANCEMENT

In this chapter, we have reviewed in some depth the primary prevention research related to two specific issues in childhood—smoking and dental health. These two health concerns differ in a number of ways that influence the selection of approaches to prevention, yet they are also alike in certain important respects. A closer examination of these similar and dissimilar aspects should be instructive for a broader consideration of health enhancement in children.

The primary prevention task, in the case of most work on smoking, is to avoid the onset of smoking to eliminate an important risk factor related to morbidity and premature mortality in adulthood. Although these diseases are most likely to occur after the fifth decade, primary prevention is focused on early adolescence, since this is when individuals usually smoke their first cigarette. In the case of dental health also, early adolescence is frequently targeted for primary prevention efforts. This choice is probably because of the high caries rate which affects adolescence and has made this time of life known as the "caries-prone years." But again, there is no *immediate* perceived relationship between the unhealthy behavior and its negative consequences which may occur over the life span in the form of caries, periodontal disease, and the loss of teeth. Still, the threat of dental disease is more immediate than that of lung cancer. It also is a relatively mild threat as most adolescents have experienced the restoration of one or more teeth. To adequately compare the two health issues, it must be noted that most smoking prevention programs ask young people to completely reject a social behavior that may have great symbolic value in the development of self-concept and assertion of identity. Oral hygiene behaviors, however, are more private and do not ordinarily carry these personal and social values.

In reviewing the behavior change characteristics required in both prevention efforts, it becomes quite clear that task characteristics could interact with cognitive and social developmental characteristics of the targeted population. In the cases reviewed here, the earlier adolescents frequently targeted probably represent the age group least capable of responding to the tasks presented. Adolescents tend to be oriented to present rather than future consequences, and they tend to espouse peer values to the point of rejecting everything associated with the adult world and the authority it implies. So important are these aspects of adolescent culture that we might expect primary prevention efforts to be successful in direct proportion to the extent to which they are *not* associated with adult values or authority and the extent to which they *are* focused on immediate, rather than long range effects.

It has already been suggested that health behaviors are more likely to result in the formation of strong habits that will be maintained throughout life if they are learned earlier, presumably prior to adolescence. This approach would have more validity in some cases than others. Although there has been some question about the effectiveness of their skills, data indicate that very young children can learn the psychomotor skills important for oral hygiene and generally are receptive to attempts to establish dental health routines, particularly when parental support is available. These habits probably can be maintained over time, so long as there is no serious disruption of lifestyle. Early acquisition can also be highly effective in decreasing the total experience with dental caries. In the case of smoking, however, there is no reason to expect that attitudes held strongly in childhood will translate to refusal to smoke in adolescence. There are other aspects of prevention tasks that need to be considered in planning intervention strategies. Smoking represents an addictive behavior and this complicates the issue considerably. As in the case of alcohol and drug use, there is a conceptual problem related to the goal. Should we attempt to prevent initial (that is, *any*) use of an addictive substance or should we be aiming at the prevention of substance abuse? The answer is not simple, and the question tends to evoke political as well as scientific responses. To further confound the question, there are problems of definition. When does substance use become abuse? Some recent research indicates that very moderate consumption of alcohol may actually reduce health risks related to cardiovascular disease. While common sense suggests that this relationship would not hold true in adolescence, this issue places a strong demand on health program planners to understand the physiological, as well as behavioral, aspects of the health issues under consideration.

There are other similarities among the issues of tobacco, alcohol, and drug use. Long-term use of these substances has the potential for devastating effects in terms of lost health, physical suffering, and psychological pain for both the victim and his or her family. Yet these behaviors typically begin in adolescence when they may have strong positive value within the peer culture. As smoking does, alcohol and drug use can symbolize both adult behavior and the rejection of adult rules and authority. In the media, drug and alcohol use continue to be depicted as exciting and sophisticated. Alcohol use now tends to begin in early adolescence; the numbers of young people who drink has grown in recent years, with a higher rate of increase for females than for males (Hamburg, Elliott, & Parron, 1982). This last fact is particularly disturbing in light of the increase in teenage pregnancies and the risk of fetal alcohol syndrome.

McAlister (1979) has identified other common factors in smoking, alcohol, and drug use behaviors. All are more common among the poor and poorly educated, and among the unhappy and dissatisfied. Finally, peer models and standards play an important role. Just as there are social groups (often focused on athletic or social activities) that reject these behaviors, there are other groups defined by their common interest in alcohol or drugs. Although Schaps, Churgin, Palley, Takata, and Cohen (1980) pointed out in their review that many of the most promising alcohol and drug prevention programs have been inadequately evaluated, it appears that some of the most successful strategies to date have been similar to those employed to prevent initial smoking. They have included use of peer communications to enhance skills for coping with pressures toward alcohol and drug abuse (McAlister, 1979; McAlister et al., 1980). Such approaches take into consideration the cognitive developmental levels of the target group and work within their social structure. They tend to focus on the immediate pressures experienced by these young people while also presenting important information relevant to effects on one's health and potential offspring.

The need to fully understand relevant biological mechanisms is particularly cogent in considering the issue of weight control and improvement of nutrition in children. The risks associated with overweight children have appeared relatively clear, since at least one-third of obese adults were overweight themselves as children (Lloyd & Wolff, 1980). More recently, however, Mallick (1983) has challenged this assumption, citing methodological flaws in the research and providing evidence that health problems related to weight control are quite common and that even physician-monitored dieting has negative effects on children's growth and development. This work suggests the need to focus on nutrition, rather than weight per se. Overweight in adult life, of course, is associated with cardiovascular disease, diabetes, and other major medical disorders, and it greatly decreases general fitness and physical ability. Yet the control of obesity and improvement of nutrition in childhood represent a particularly resistant behavior problem.

The task of changing eating behaviors requires attention to some of the same issues that comprise obstacles to changing addictive behaviors. Eating provides its own reinforcement in the form of immediate pleasurable sensation. To exacerbate this situation, eating usually has social value. Candy is used to reinforce desired behavior in small children, and teenagers have their favorite (not necessarily healthy or nutritious) peer culture foods. The former example suggests that parents, and perhaps even school personnel, must be involved in prevention efforts related to weight control. The latter example indicates that peer support and approval should be utilized in programs for adolescents. Coates and Thoreson (1978) reviewed the literature and offered three recommendations for the treatment of obesity in children and adolescents. These are: (1) insure that the environment will promote and support ongoing efforts to control weight, (2) provide highly structured programs, and (3) reward weight loss rather than habit change to maximize opportunities for people to find their own successful approaches.

Among the specific strategies that evaluation efforts have shown to be useful are monetary deposits refunded for weight loss (Coates, Jeffrey, Slinkard, Killen, & Danaher, 1982), and behavior modification and exercise management provided along with nutrition education (Botvin, Cantlon, Carter, & Williams, 1979). Researchers at the Stanford Five City Multifactor Risk Reduction Program have reported encouraging results in a program for adolescents that emphasizes the learning of skills for both short- and long-term weight control (Coates & Perry, 1981). Another program for elementary age children used social learning strategies, including modeled behaviors, behavioral commitments, feedback and incentives, and family involvement (Coates, Jeffrey, & Slinkard, 1981). This program focused on proper nutrition rather than specific weight loss, a concept that is particularly important in terms of the potential problems caused by over-emphasis on weight control. Mallick (1983) has discussed basic issues of adequately providing for the nutritional needs of growth and development. Among adolescents, particularly females, there also is the possibility of contributing indirectly to the onset of anorexia nervosa. This disorder often begins with simple dieting but develops into obsessive weight loss which can result in extensive morbidity and an approximately 15% mortality incidence (Pinkerton, Hughes, & Wenrich, 1982). It is possible that some adolescents are not able, cognitively or psychologically, to realistically evaluate either their own body images or social norms related to weight and appearance.

Other prevention problems have their unique characteristics as well. Increasing regular participation in aerobic physical activity, for example, suggests the need to add a generally acceptable and socially approved activity. In this sense, the problem is more similar to initiating oral health behavior patterns than it is to preventing the onset of smoking. There are, however, some important barriers to acquiring good habits in physical activity and exercise. The absence of positive models at home for young children and peer models for adolescents can be a major deterrent. Furthermore, in school districts where budget cuts have resulted in reduced physical education and athletic programs, children may be faced with fewer opportunities to learn about and participate in physical activities. At the other extreme, in schools where competitive athletics are heavily supported, there may be a tendency to leave out the less athletically talented. Regardless of such institutional variables, however, there is a need to encourage aerobic and life long forms of exercise that young people will be more likely to carry with them into adulthood.

Research on initiating and maintaining exercise patterns in children is relatively sparse, and much of it has been conducted within the context of weight control programs directed at obese children (Mayer, 1975; Moody, Wilmore, Girandola, & Royce, 1972). These programs have shown immediate results in terms of weight or skinfold reductions, but not in terms of exercise maintenance. Dishman's (1982) extensive review of the literature, however, points out that both weight and percentage of body weight in fat are negatively related to, and the best predictors of, adherence to exercise programs. While this may suggest either that exercise is more difficult for heavier individuals or that leaner persons are already more physically active, it appears important to consider weight in planning exercise programs for young people. Other variables may also be considered, including the physical and practical demand characteristics of various activities and individual preferences for types of exercise.

Working with college students, Wysocki, Hall, Iwata, and Riordan (1979) found sustained aerobic fitness 12 months after a program that used contingency contracting and deposits of valued objects. This may indicate that similar approaches could be effectively applied with younger people. Similar to the dental health interventions reviewed here, it is likely that contingency management approaches might be enhanced by the use of cognitive or social learning strategies, including skills training, and mobilization of support and clarification of values through peer discussion. These may be particularly important because exercise is a relatively public, time-consuming behavior and, therefore, may require choices between this and other behaviors.

Stress management is another area of health enhancement for which there is a clear need to target persons at risk and to individually tailor programs. Stress has been implicated as a risk factor in such diverse medical disorders as asthma, influenza, hypertension, depression, alcoholism, and drug abuse. It is relatively clear that individual vulnerability to stress is affected by both genetic and psychosocial factors, and that genetic and environmental mediators may influence biological reactions and clinical responses to stress (Hamburg et al., 1982). Furthermore, recent research suggests that the availability of social support makes individuals less vulnerable to illness and early death (Berkman & Syme, 1979; Syme & Berkman, 1976). It appears that social support may serve a number of purposes, including acting as a buffer and facilitating the development of coping responses. Pilisuk (1982) has suggested that the deterioration of traditional natural ties involving family and stable community groups has created a need for formal social support for health-related activities. Hamburg et al. (1982) suggest the use of such groups in early adolescence, when both internal and external changes may present stressful events with which many young people are not yet ready to cope. Group work with adolescents, such as that described in the smoking prevention programs, provides models for dealing with other stressful issues as well.

Related stress and coping is the presence of the Type A or coronary-prone behavior pattern (Friedman & Rosenman, 1974) in children. While it is not yet clear whether this pattern in children is identical to that in adults, preliminary evidence reflects similarities (Bortner, Rosenman, & Friedman, 1970; Lawler, Allen, Critcher, & Standard, 1981; Matthews, 1977; Matthews & Krantz, 1976) and indicates the potential for early behaviors associated with increased risk of cardiovascular disease (Coates, Perry, Killen, & Slinkard, 1981). While there have been no published reports of programs directed specifically at modifying Type A behavior in children, the nature of the problem and work on behavior modification in adults (Chesney, Eagleston, & Rosenman, 1981; Friedman & Rosenman, 1974) suggests the need for a strong cognitive program. This would focus on recognition of sources of stress and the specific Type A behaviors they elicit, identification and use of alternative behaviors, and possibly relaxation techniques as well.

This discussion admittedly raises more questions than it answers. If primary prevention efforts in childhood are to be effective for avoiding health problems in childhood and later ages, these questions must be addressed in a highly critical manner. In this spirit, Leventhal (1973) challenged three popular notions: (1) that children are more open to positive influence, (2) that they learn new behaviors more efficiently, and (3) that behavioral patterns learned in childhood are more likely to last. He reviews a number of variables that could interfere with these assumptions, including developmental factors and environmental influences. The area of social and cultural influences has been largely ignored in prevention research, yet we know that availability and quality of social support may have important implications for health behavior and response to illness (Schaefer, Coyne, & Lazarus, 1981). Further exploration of these issues represents one of the most critical challenges for primary prevention and health enhancement.

A FINAL COMMENT

I will conclude with some brief general remarks on this new field of behavioral health which is now benefiting from an influx of many enthusiastic psychologists and other behavioral scientists. Previously I have attempted to outline what I believe to be the most important roles for psychologists in this field (Albino, 1983) and will present here some caveats for psychologists in health promotion.

First, there is a temptation for psychologists interested in behavioral health to approach these behavior change issues from a clinical perspective, one that is usually focused on building competence within individuals. While this objective is not inappropriate it also is not necessarily enough. Efforts to inform people on health issues and to help them develop relevant preventive or self-help skills will not succeed if there is no support for these behaviors within the environment. In Chapter 6 of this volume, Roberts, Elkins, and Royal discussed in greater detail some of the possibilities for targeting society, as well as children and their caregivers, with efforts for preventing accidents and illness. Changes are needed within schools, community organizations, health care and social services, and other institutions serving children, as well as in legislation. It is the responsibility of those interested in health-enhancement to find ways of effecting these changes, as well as changes in individuals.

Finally, I believe that psychologists interfering with the lifestyles of healthy people must proceed with unprecedented caution, particularly in working with interventions where effectiveness is unproved. It is tempting to take for granted the effectiveness of recommendations that appear to carry a stamp of medical approval. The field of primary prevention is a relatively new one in medicine too, however, and all the data are *not* in—particularly in terms of childhood health enhancement. It behooves psychologists working in this area to become well educated concerning the physical and medical aspects, as well as the behavioral aspects, of the problems they are exploring. Meaningful contributions to behavioral health will come only out of systematic research and long-term follow up that is fully sensitive to both behavioral and physical health perspectives. The value of contributions produced in this manner will be unlimited.

REFERENCES

Albino, J. E. Evaluation of three approaches to changing dental hygiene behaviors. *Journal of Preventive Dentistry,* 1978, *5,* 4–10.

Albino, J. E. Health psychology and primary prevention: Natural allies. In R. D. Felner, L.

A. Jason, J. Moritsugu, & S. S. Farber (Eds.), *Preventive psychology: Theory, research, and practice in community interventions*. New York: Pergamon, 1983.

Albino, J. E., Juliano, D. B., & Slakter, M. J. Effects of an instructional-motivational program on plaque and gingivitis in adolescents. *Journal of Public Health Dentistry*, 1977, *5*, 4–10.

Albino, J. E., Tedesco, L. A., & Lee, C. Z. Peer leadership and health status: Factors moderating response to a children's dental health program. *Journal of Clinical Preventive Dentistry*, 1980, *2*, 18–20.

Albino, J. E., Tedesco, L. A., & Phipps, G. T. Social and psychological problems of adolescence and their relevance to dental care. *International Dental Journal*, 1982, *32*, 184–193.

Berkman, L. F., & Syme, S. L. Social networks, host resistance, and mortality: A nine-year follow-up study of Alameda County residents. *American Journal of Epidemiology*, 1979, *109*, 186–204.

Borland, B. L., & Rudolph, J. P. Relative effects of low socioeconomic status, parental smoking and poor scholastic performance on smoking among high school students. *Social Science and Medicine*, 1975, *9*, 27–38.

Bortner, R. W., Rosenman, R. H., & Friedman, M. Familial similarity in pattern A behavior. *Journal of Chronic Diseases*, 1970, *23*, 39–43.

Botvin, G. J. Broadening the focus of smoking prevention strategies. In T. Coates, A. Peterson, & C. Perry (Eds.), *Promoting adolescent health: A dialog on research and practice*. New York: Academic Press, 1982.

Botvin, G. J., Cantlon, A., Carter, B. J., & Williams, C. L. Reducing adolescent obesity through a school-health program. *Journal of Pediatrics*, 1979, *95*, 1060–1062.

Botvin, G. J., & Eng, A. A comprehensive school-based smoking prevention program. *The Journal of School Health*, 1980, *50, 209–213.*

Botvin, G. J., & Eng, A. The efficacy of a multi-component approach to the prevention of cigarette smoking. *Preventive Medicine*, 1982, *11*, 199–211.

Botvin, G. J., Eng, A., & Williams, C. L. Preventing the onset of smoking through life skills training. *Preventive Medicine*, 1980, *9*, 135–143.

Brehm, J. W. *A theory of psychological reactance*. New York: Academic Press, 1966.

Califano, J. A., Jr. Objectives for the nation. In Public Health Service (Eds.), *Healthy people: The Surgeon General's report on health promotion and disease prevention*. U. S. Department of Health and Human Services, Public Health Service, Publ. No. (PHS) 79-55071A. Washington, D.C.: U.S. Government Printing Office, 1979.

Chesney, M. A., Eagleston, J. R., & Rosenman, R. H. Type A behavior: Assessment and intervention. In C. K. Prokop & L. A. Bradley (Eds.), *Medical psychology: Contributions to behavioral medicine*. New York: Academic Press, 1981.

Claerhout, S., & Lutzker, J. R. Increasing children's self-initiated compliance to dental regimens. *Behavior Therapy*, 1981, *12*, 165–176.

Coates, T. J., Jeffrey, R. W., & Slinkard, L. A. Heart healthy eating and exercise: Introducing and maintaining changes in health behaviors. *American Journal of Public Health*, 1981, *71*, 15–23.

Coates, T. J., Jeffrey, R. W., Slinkard, L. A., Killen, J. D., & Danaher, B. G. Frequency of contact and contingent reinforcement in weight loss, lipid change, and blood pressure reduction in adolescents. *Behavior Therapy*, 1982, *13*, 175–185.

Coates, T. J., & Perry, C. Multifactor risk reduction with children and adolescents taking care of the heart in behavior group therapy. In D. Upper & S. Ross (Eds.), *Behavior group therapy: An annual review.* Champaign, IL: Research Press, 1981.

Coates, T. J., Perry, C., Killen, J., & Slinkard, L. A. Primary prevention of cardiovascular disease in children and adolescents. In C. K. Prokop & L. A. Bradley (Eds.), *Medical psychology: Contributions to behavioral medicine.* New York: Academic Press, 1981.

Coates, T. J., & Thoreson, C. E. Obesity in children and adolescents. A review. *American Journal of Public Health,* 1978, *68,* 143–151.

Creswell, W. H., Huffman, W. J., Stone, D. B., & Newman, I. M. University of Illinois anti-smoking education study. *Illinois Journal of Education,* 1969, *60,* 27–37.

Creswell, W. H., Stone, D. B., Huffman, W. J., & Newman, I. M. Anti-smoking education study at the University of Illinois. *HSMHA Health Reports,* 1971, *86,* 565–576.

Dishman, R. K. Compliance/adherence in health-related exercise. *Health Psychology,* 1982, *1,* 237–267.

Elkind, D. Egocentrism in adolescence. *Child Development,* 1967, *38,* 1024–1034.

Elkind, D. Understanding the young adolescent. *Adolescence,* 1978, *13,* 127–134.

Evans, R. I. Motivating changes in oral hygiene behavior: Some social psychological perspectives. *Journal of Preventive Dentistry,* 1978, *5,* 14–17.

Evans, R. I., Hansen, W. B., & Mittelmark, M. B. Increasing the validity of self-reports of smoking behavior in children. *Journal of Applied Psychology,* 1977, *62,* 521–523.

Evans, R. I., Henderson, A. H., Hill, P. C., & Raines, B. E. Current psychological, social, and educational programs in control and prevention of smoking: A critical methodological review. In A. M. Gatto & R. Paoletti (Eds.), *Atherosclerosis Reviews* (Vol. 6), New York: Raven Press, 1979.(a)

Evans, R. I., Henderson, A., Hill, P., & Raines, B. E. Smoking in children and adolescents: Psychosocial determinants and prevention strategies. In *Smoking and health: A report of the surgeon general,* U. S. Department of Health, Education, and Welfare, Public Health Service, Publ. No. (PHS) 79-50066. Washington, D.C.: U.S. Government Printing Office, 1979.(b)

Evans, R. I., Rozelle, R. M., Lasater, T. M., Dembroski, T. M., & Allen, B. P. New measure of effects of persuasive communications: A chemical indicator of toothbrushing behavior. *Psychological Reports,* 1968, *23,* 731–736.

Evans, R. I., Rozelle, R. M., Lasater, T. M., Dembroski, T. M., & Allen, B. P. Fear arousal, persuasion, and actual versus implied behavior change: New perspective utilizing a real-life dental hygiene program. *Journal of Personality and Social Psychology,* 1970, *16,* 220–227.

Evans, R. I., Rozelle, R. M., Mittelmark, M. B., Hansen, W. B., Bane, A. L., & Havis, J. Deterring the onset of smoking in children: Knowledge of immediate physiological effects and coping with peer pressure, media pressure, and parent modeling. *Journal of Applied Social Psychology,* 1978, *8,* 126–135.

Fisher, E. B. Progress in reducing adolescent smoking. *American Journal of Public Health,* 1980, *70,* 678–679.

Flay, B. R. On improving the chances of mass media health promotion programs causing meaningful changes in behavior. In M. Meyer (Ed.), *Health education by television and radio.* Munich, Germany: Saur, 1981.

Flay, B. R., D'Avernas, J. R., Best, J. A., Kersell, M. W., & Ryan, K. B. Cigarette smoking: Why young people do it and ways of preventing it. In P. McGrath & P.

Firestone (Eds.), *Pediatric and adolescent behavioral medicine.* New York: Springer-Verlag, 1982.

Flay, B. R., Johnson, C. A., & Hansen, W. B. Evaluation of a mass media enhanced smoking prevention and cessation program. In J. P. Baggaley & J. Sharpe (Eds.), *Experimental research in TV instruction* (Vol. 5). Montreal, Canada: Concordia University, 1984.

Fodor, J. T., & Glass, L. H. Curriculum development and implementation of smoking research: A longitudinal study. *Journal of School Health,* 1971, *44,* 324–330.

Frazier, P. J. School-based instruction for improving oral health: Closing the knowledge gap. *International Dental Journal,* 1980, *30,* 257–268.

Friedman, M., & Rosenman, R. H. *Type A behavior and your heart.* New York: Knopf, 1974.

Hamburg, D. A., Elliott, G. R., & Parron, D. L. *Health and behavior: Frontiers of research in the biobehavioral sciences.* Washington, D.C.: National Academy Press, 1982.

Horner, O. R., & Keilitz, I. Training mentally retarded adolescents to brush their teeth. *Journal of Applied Behavior Analysis,* 1975, *8,* 301–309.

Horowitz, A. M. A comparison of available strategies to affect children's dental health: Primary prevention procedures for use in school-based dental programs. *Journal of Public Health Dentistry,* 1979, *39,* 268–274.

Hurd, P. D., Johnson, C. A., Pechacek, F., Bast, L. P., Jacobs, D. R., & Luepker, R. V. Prevention of cigarette smoking in seventh grade students. *Journal of Behavioral Medicine,* 1980, *3,* 15–28.

Iammarino, N., Heit, P., & Kaplan, R. School health curriculum project: Long-term effects on student cigarette smoking and behavior change. *Health Education,* 1980, *11,* 29–31.

Iwata, B. A., & Beckfort, C. M. Behavioral research in preventive dentistry: Educational and contingency management approaches to the problem of patient compliance. *Journal of Applied Behavior Analysis,* 1981, *14,* 11–20.

Kanfer, F. H., & Karoly, P. *Self-management and behavior change: From theory to practice.* New York: Pergamon Press, 1982.

Kegeles, S. S. Why people seek dental care: A test of a conceptual formulation. *Journal of Health and Human Behavior,* 1963, *4,* 166–173.

Kegeles, S. S., Lund, A. K., & Weisenberg, M. Acceptance by children of a daily home mouthrinse program. *Social Science and Medicine,* 1978, *12,* 199–210.

Knowles, J. H. *Doing better and feeling worse: Health in the United States.* New York: Norton, 1977.

Korins, J. I., Sposato, A., Leske, G. S., & Ripa, L. W. Toothbrushing efficiency of first-grade children. *The Journal of Pedodontics,* 1982, *6,* 148–158.

Lattal, K. A. Contingency management of toothbrushing behavior in a summer camp for children. *Journal of Applied Behavior Analysis,* 1969, *2,* 195–198.

Lawler, K. A., Allen, M. F., Critcher, E. C., & Standard, B. A. The relationship of physiological responses to the coronary-prone behavior pattern in children. *Journal of Behavioral Medicine,* 1981, *4,* 203–216.

Lee, A. J. Parental attendance at a school dental program: Its impact upon the dental behavior of the children. *The Journal of School Health,* 1978, *48,* 423–427.

Leventhal, H. Fear appeals and persuasion: The differentiation of a motivational construct. *American Journal of Public Health,* 1971, *61,* 1208–1224.

Leventhal, H. Changing attitudes and habits to reduce risk factors in chronic disease. *The American Journal of Cardiology,* 1973, *31,* 571–580.

Leventhal, H., & Singer, R. P. Affect arousal and positioning of recommendations in persuasive communications. *Journal of Personality and Social Psychology,* 1966, *4,* 137–146.

Leventhal, H., Singer, R., & Jones, S. Effects of fear and instructions on how to cope with danger. *Journal of Personality and Social Psychology,* 1965, *2,* 20–29.

Levy, R. L., Lodish, D., & Pawlak-Floyd, C. Teaching children to take more responsibility for their own dental treatment. *Social Work in Health Care,* 1982, *7,* 69–76.

Levy, R. L., Yamashita, D., & Pow, G. The relationship of an overt commitment to the frequency and speed of compliance with symptom reporting. *Medical Care,* 1979, *17,* 281–284.

Lloyd, J. K., & Wolff, O. H. Overnutrition and obesity. In F. Falkner (Ed.), *Prevention in childhood of health problems in adult life.* Geneva World Health Organization, 1980.

Lund, A. K., & Kegeles, S. S. Increasing adolescents' acceptance of long-term personal health behavior. *Health Psychology,* 1982, *1,* 27–43.

Lund, A. K., Kegeles, S. S., & Weisenberg, M. Motivational techniques for increasing acceptance of preventive health measures. *Medical Care,* 1977, *15,* 678–692.

Mallick, M. J. Health hazards of obesity and weight control in children: A review of the literature. *American Journal of Public Health,* 1983, *73,* 78–82.

Martens, L. W., Frazier, P. J., Hirt, K. J., Meskin, L. H., & Proshek, J. Developing brushing performance in second graders through behavior modification. *Health Services Reports,* 1973, *88,* 818–823.

Matarazzo, J. D. Behavioral health and behavioral medicine: Frontiers for a new health psychology. *American Psychologist,* 1980, *35,* 807–817.

Matarazzo, J. D. Behavioral health's challenge to academic, scientific, and professional psychology. *American Psychologist,* 1982, *37,* 1–14.

Matthews, K. Caregiver-child interactions and the Type A coronary-prone behavior pattern. *Child Development,* 1977, *48,* 1752–1756.

Matthews, K. A., & Krantz, D. S. Resemblances of twins and their parents in pattern A behavior. *Psychosomatic Medicine,* 1976, *28,* 140–144.

Mayer, J. Obesity during childhood. In M. Winik (Ed.), *Childhood obesity.* New York: Wiley, 1975.

McAlister, A. L. Tobacco, alcohol, and drug abuse: Onset and prevention. In U. S. Public Health Service (Ed.), *Healthy people: Background papers.* Department of Health and Human Services, Public Health Service. Publ. No. (PHS) 79-55071A. Washington, D. C.: U. S. Government Printing Office, 1979.

McAlister, A. L., Perry, C., & Maccoby, N. Adolescent smoking: Onset and prevention. *Pediatrics,* 1979, *63,* 650–658.

McAlister, A., Perry, C., Killen, J., Slinkard, L. A., & Maccoby, N. Pilot study of smoking, alcohol, and drug abuse prevention. *American Journal of Public Health,* 1980, *70,* 719–721.

Moody, D. L., Wilmore, J. H., Girandola, R. N., & Royce, J. P. The effects of a jogging program on the body composition of normal and obese high school girls. *Medicine and Behavior in Sports,* 1972, *2,* 210–213.

Murray, J. A., & Epstein, L. H. Improving oral hygiene with videotape modeling. *Behavior Modification,* 1981, *5,* 360–371.

Olson, D. G., Levy, R. L., Evans, C. A., & Olson, S. K. Enhancement of high risk children's utilization of dental services. *American Journal of Public Health,* 1981, *71,* 631–634.

Perry, C., Killen, J., Telch, M., Slinkard, L. A., & Danaher, B. G. Modifying smoking behavior of teenagers: A school-based intervention. *American Journal of Public Health,* 1980, *70,* 722–725.

Pilisuk, M. Delivery of social support: The social inoculation. *American Journal of Orthopsychiatry,* 1982, *52,* 1, 20–31.

Pinkerton, S. S., Hughes, H., & Wenrich, W. W. *Behavioral medicine: Clinical applications.* New York: Wiley, 1982.

Poche, C., McCubbrey, H., & Munn, T. The development of correct toothbrushing technique in preschool children. *Journal of Applied Behavior Analysis,* 1982, *15,* 315–320.

Rabinowitz, H. S., & Zimmerli, W. H. Effects of a health education program on junior high students' knowledge, attitudes, and behavior concerning tobacco use. *Journal of School Health,* 1974, *44,* 324–330.

Rayner, J. F., & Cohen, L. K. A position on school dental health education. *Journal of Preventive Dentistry,* 1974, *1,* 11–23.

Reiss, M. L., Piotrowski, W. D., & Bailey, J. S. Behavioral community psychology: Encouraging low-income parents to seek dental care for their children. *Journal of Applied Behavior Analysis,* 1976, *9,* 387–397.

Roberts, M. C., Maddux, J. E., & Wright, L. Developmental perspectives in behavioral health. In J. D. Matarazzo, N. E. Miller, S. M. Weiss, J. A. Herd, & S. M. Weiss (Eds.), *Behavioral health: A handbook of health enhancement and disease prevention.* New York: Wiley, 1984.

Rokeach, M. Long-range experimental modification of values, attitudes, and behaviors. *American Psyhologist,* 1971, *26,* 453–459.

Schaefer, C., Coyne, J. C., & Lazarus, R. S. The health-related functions of social support. *Journal of Behavioral Medicine,* 1981, *4,* 381–406.

Schaps, E., Churgin, S., Palley, C. S., Takata, B., & Cohen, A. Y. Primary prevention research: A preliminary review of program outcome studies. *The International Journal of the Addictions,* 1980, *15,* 657–676.

Schneider, F. W., & Vanmastrigt, L. A. Adolescent-preadolescent differences in beliefs and attitudes about cigarette smoking. *The Journal of Psychology,* 1974, *87,* 71–81.

Schoenberger, J. A. Why cardiovascular health education in the schools: From a medical perspective. *Health Education,* 1982, *35,* 15–16.

Stacey, D. C., Abbott, D. M., & Jordan, R. D. Improvement in oral hygiene as a function of applied principles of behavior modification. *Journal of Public Health Dentistry,* 1972, *32,* 234–238.

Stamm, J. W. Cause of oral diseases and general approaches to their prevention. *Family and Community Health,* 1980, *3,* 13–21.

Swain, J. J., Allard, G. B., & Holborn, S. W. The Good Toothbrushing Game: A school-based dental hygiene program for increasing the toothbrushing effectiveness of children. *Journal of Applied Behavior Analysis,* 1982, *15,* 171–176.

Syme, S. L., & Berkman, L. F. Social class, susceptibility and sickness. *American Journal of Epidemiology,* 1976, *104,* 1–8.

Telch, M. J., Killen, J. D., McAlister, A. L., Perry, C. L., & Maccoby, N. Long-term follow-up of a pilot project on smoking prevention with adolescents. *Journal of Behavioral Medicine,* 1982, *5,* 1–8.

Tennant, F. S., Weaver, S. C., & Lewis, C. E. Outcomes of drug education. *Pediatrics,* 1973, *52,* 246–251.

Thompson, E. L. Smoking education programs, 1960-1976. *American Journal of Public Health,* 1978, *68,* 250–257.

U. S. Public Health Service. *Teenage smoking. National patterns of cigarette smoking ages 12 through 18, in 1972 and 1974,* Department of Health, Education, and Welfare, Public Health Service, National Institutes of Health. Publ. No. (NIH) 76-931. Washington, D.C.: U. S. Government Printing Office, 1976.

U. S. Public Health Service. *Smoking and health: A report of the Surgeon General,* Department of Health, Education and Welfare, Public Health Service. Publ. No. (PHS) 79-50066. Washington, D.C.: U. S. Government Printing Office, 1979.(a)

U. S. Public Health Service. *Basic data on dental examination findings of persons 1-74 years, United States, 1971-74,* Department of Health, Education, and Welfare, Public Health Service, National Center for Health Statistics. Publ. No. (PHS) 79-1662. Washington, D.C.: U. S. Government Printing Office, 1979.(b)

U. S. Public Health Service. *The prevalence of dental caries in United States children, 1979-80,* Department of Health and Human Services, Public Health Service, National Institutes of Health. Publ. No. (PHS) 82-2245. Washington, D.C.: U. S. Government Printing Office, 1981.

U. S. Public Health Service. *The health consequences of smoking: Cancer. A report of the Surgeon General,* Department of Health and Human Services, Public Health Service, Office on Smoking and Health. Washington, D.C.: U.S. Government Printing Office, 1982.

Wake, F. R. Preventing the onset of smoking. In UICC (Eds.), *Papers presented at the Fourth World Congress on Smoking and Health, Stockholm, Sweden, 20 June, 1979.* Geneva: UICC, 1979.

Weinstein, P., & Getz, T. *Changing human behavior: Strategies for preventive dentistry.* St. Louis: C. V. Mosby, 1978.

White, L. W. Behavioristic technique or oral hygiene—an update. *American Journal of Orthodontics,* 1980, *77,* 568–570.

Wicklund, R. A., & Brehm, J. W. Attitude change as a function of felt competence and threat to attitudinal freedom. *Journal of Experimental Social Psychology,* 1968, *4,* 64–75.

Williams, R. L., & Long, J. D. *Toward a self-managed life style.* Boston: Houghton Mifflin, 1979.

Wysocki, T., Hall, G., Iwata, B., & Riordan, M. Behavioral management of exercise: Contracting for aerobic points. *Journal of Applied Behavior Analysis,* 1979, *12,* 55–64.

REFERENCE NOTES

1. Flay, B. R., Hansen, W. B., Johnson, C. A., Sobol, D., & Alvarez, L. *The USC/KABC-TV smoking prevention/cessation programs: A general description.* Unpublished manuscript, 1982. (Available from Health Behavior Research Institute, University of Southern California, 1985 Zonal Avenue, Los Angeles, CA 90033.)

2. Flay, B. R., Johnson, C. A., & Hansen, W. B. *Theoretical basis of USC smoking and drug abuse prevention programs.* Unpublished manuscript, 1982. (Available from Health Behavior Research Institute, University of Southern California, 1985 Zonal Avenue, Los Angeles, CA 90033.)
3. Flay, B. R., Johnson, C. A., & Hansen, W. B. *The USC/KABC-TV smoking prevention/cessation program: Preliminary short-term results.* Unpublished manuscript, 1982. (Available from Health Behavior Research Institute, University of Southern California, 1985 Zonal Avenue, Los Angeles, CA 90033.)
4. Sobol, D., Flay, B. R., Johnson, C. A., Hansen, W. B., Alvarez, L., Grossman, L., & Simmons, R. *The effectiveness of teacher training in implementing an innovative smoking prevention curriculum.* Paper presented at the meeting of the American School Health Association, Phoenix, Arizona, October, 1982.

CHAPTER 8

Prevention with Chronically Ill Children

DENNIS DROTAR, PEGGY CRAWFORD, AND MARY ANN GANOFSKY

The stresses of chronic physical illness affect the lives of many children and assume special importance as a focus of preventive intervention. Prevention of severe behavior problems associated with childhood chronic illness emphasizes reduction of the maladaptive consequences of illness-related stress by enhancement of effective coping strategies. Goals of preventive intervention include: (1) mastery of anxieties related to illness and their physical management, (2) reasonable understanding of and adherence to medical regimens, (3) integration of illness into family life including the reconciliation of family needs with those of ill children, and (4) adaptation to hospital, school, and peers. Optimal preventive work takes place in long-term relationships between professional caregivers and families and is characterized by continuity, mutual participation, advocacy, and the attainment of competencies in illness-related and life situations. In this chapter, the principles of family-centered preventive intervention with chronically ill children in schools, with chronically ill peers, with reconstituted families, and with the life-threatening sequelae of psychosomatic illness are illustrated through case vignettes taken from clinical practice.

The implementation of prevention within complex, disease-focused medical cultures requires special consideration of institutional obstacles, the emotional impact on the professional caregiver, and training in prevention. Priorities for prevention research include systematic documentation of health professional-family transactions, long-term outcome studies of survivors of childhood chronic illness, and treatment outcome studies. Comprehensive care programs which combine clinical intervention and research are seen as critical to understanding ways of reducing the maladaptive consequences of chronic illness-related stress.

Chronic physical illness affects the lives of a great many children and their families (Pless & Douglas, 1975; Pless & Roghmann, 1971) and assumes special importance as a focus of preventive mental health intervention for several reasons. Each and every family whose child is affected with a chronic illness experiences some form of compelling psychological stress which compromises their quality of life. In addition, although the majority of chronically ill children and their families cope well enough to maintain adequate psychological adjustment, a significant number (Mattsson, 1972) develop psychological disturbances serious enough to warrant the attention of mental health professionals. Prevention of the psychological sequelae of childhood chronic illness is a multifaceted enterprise which includes: (1) reduction of the maladaptive consequences of illness-related stress by enhancement of effective coping strategies, (2) early recognition of psychological difficulties associated with chronic illness and intervention designed to reduce the severity of these disturbances, and (3) containment of already existing psychological problems to prevent serious disruption of disease management. Health care settings provide a unique context for these preventive efforts. Chronically ill children and their families are followed continuously by physicians and other health care professionals in ways that allow earlier recognition of psychological disturbance and hence, greater potential access to preventive intervention than is possible in traditional mental health services. Moreover, the increasing numbers of mental health and health care professionals working with chronically ill children and their families in medical settings provide important resources for prevention.

However, the challenging issues raised by the prevention of psychological problems in childhood chronic illness requires special consideration, especially since most descriptions of psychosocial intervention in this area concern treatment of already present, severe disturbances rather than prevention. In addition, the language and intervention strategies characteristic of prior descriptions of intervention are pathology-centered and not especially useful conceptualizations of prevention (Iscoe, 1981). This chapter reflects the progression in the authors' ideas from pathology-focused intervention models to an emphasis on enhancement of chronically ill children's adjustment potential through ongoing family-centered, advocacy-based intervention. This chapter is organized in the following topics: (1) identification of major stresses associated with chronic illness, (2) the principles and illustrations of preventive interventions with chronic illness populations, (3) various problems in implementing prevention, and (4) implications for health promotion and future research in childhood chronic illness.

THE STRESSES OF CHRONIC PHYSICAL DISEASE

Prevention with chronically ill children begins with a thorough understanding of the general and unique stresses posed by chronic illnesses. Illness-related stresses intersect with other social and psychological factors to affect coping, and ultimately lead to psychological resilience or disturbance. For this reason, clinicians and researchers concerned with prevention must become familiar with major illness-related stressors, characteristic modes of child and familial coping, and patterns of psychopathology frequently associated with chronic illness. The major classes of stresses associated with a chronic physical illness include physical symptoms, treatment regimens and procedures, physical impairment and deterioration, and threat to life. As a guide for subsequent discussions of preventive stress management, the nature of these stresses and their potential import for prevention are elaborated here.

Physical Symptoms

Depending on their disease, chronically ill children endure various physical symptoms, including pain, shortness of breath, lethargy, and so forth. These symptoms cannot be completely prevented, becoming a part of their day-to-day existence which must be accepted to enhance normal living. Individual chronic illnesses vary considerably with respect to the affected organ system, the nature and degree of physical symptoms and pain, and the way in which life functioning is disrupted by disease-related symptoms (Mattsson, 1972; Steinhauer, Muskin, & Rae-Grant, 1974). For example, most children with chronic conditions such as mild asthma or heart disease do not experience severe physical symptoms nor need to cope with demanding treatments on a daily basis. As a consequence, they may have lifestyles very much like physically healthy children except for their need to cope with activities such as visits to physicians and periodic medical regimens. On the other hand, children with conditions such as cystic fibrosis face daily reminders of their disease in their arduous physical treatments (McCollum & Gibson, 1970). Physical symptoms and their consequences assume considerable importance in preventive work, both as a focus of psychological distress and as a fixed reality with which the chronically ill child must cope. For this reason, supportive prevention interventions often have the goal of enhancing adaptive coping with physical symptoms, so that the child's life functioning and subjective sense of well-being are not unduly disrupted by symptom-related stress.

Every chronic illness includes a unique constellation of symptoms which may also represent a source of anxiety. For example, epileptic seizures appear to have specific psychological meaning in terms of loss of control (Heisler & Friedman, 1981; Whitt, Dykstra, & Taylor, 1979), while symptoms such as tiredness may affect one's general outlook and sense of efficacy. A chronic illness also can change physical appearance in ways that are potentially stigmatizing, restrict mobility, or result in physical isolation, with significant implications for social development (Steinhauer et al., 1974). Finally, the symptoms of a chronic illness also differ dramatically in responsiveness to family environments. For example, chronic psychosomatic illnesses such as asthma (Purcell, Brady, Chai, Muser, Mock, Gordon, & Means, 1969; Purcell, Muser, Miklich, & Dietiker, 1969) or juvenile diabetes (Minuchin, Rosman, & Baker, 1978) can be highly responsive to environmental stressors, particularly those engendered by family dysfunction. In such instances, preventive interventions may be profitably directed toward reduction of the maladaptive consequences of family dysfunction on physical symptoms or compliance with disease-related regimens.

Treatment Regimens, Hospital and Physical Procedures

The diagnosis of a chronically ill or malformed child ordinarily triggers a major family crisis characterized by feelings of shock, sadness, and anger (Drotar, Baskiewicz, Irvin, Kennell, & Klaus, 1975; McCollum & Gibson, 1970). For the formerly healthy child, diagnosis presents a multifaceted crisis which requires the child to adapt to loss of normal functioning, tolerate and comply with new medical procedures, and struggle with feelings about the meaning of the disease and its treatment (Geist, 1979). For this reason, the point of diagnosis is recognized as a potential focal point for preventive intervention directed toward crisis management, information sharing, and emotional expression (Drotar et al., 1975; Power & Dell Orto, 1980). Following diagnosis, chronically ill children are called upon to cope with treatment regimens which run the gamut from the relatively benign regimen of the asymptomatic asthmatic child and the daily insulin injections needed by the juvenile diabetic, to the complex, energy draining physical treatments required by cystic fibrosis and dialysis for end-stage renal failure.

An inherent goal of any preventive comprehensive care program is enhancement of the child and family compliance with treatment regimens. In certain conditions, the degree of adherence to medical regimens can have a profound effect on subsequent psychological development and physical well-being. For example, adherence to the diet prescribed for phenylketonuria, a rare metabolic disorder, can prevent severe mental retardation. Similarly, assiduous compliance with medication regimens can make a critical difference in acceptance versus rejection of a kidney and, hence, in the subsequent quality of life (Korsch, Negrete, Gardner, Weinstock, Mercer, Grushkin, & Fine, 1973).

The way in which physical demands of treatment regimens affect the balance of interpersonal relationships within the family also provides a target for preventive interventions. For example, chronically ill children and their parents must cooperate in demanding physical treatments that can stimulate dependency or conflict and can affect adjustment. In some families, poor adherence to medical regimens is a sign of severe family dysfunction that may require intervention. Treatment regimens also impose special burdens on parents to negotiate their roles, responsibilities, time, energy and finances, and to reconcile career versus family demands (Turk, 1967; Vance, Fazan, Satterwhite, & Pless, 1980).

In accord with the disease course and the dictates of medical management, a chronic illness may involve periodic or regular visits to physicians and hospitalizations which entail such stresses as separating from parents and familiar routines, becoming dependent, and losing control of one's autonomy (Hofmann, Becker, & Gabriel, 1976; Vernon, Foley, Sipowicz, & Schulman, 1965). Hospital-based diagnostic and treatment procedures can include injections, surgery, and immobilization which involve actual or imagined assaults to bodily integrity, autonomy, and sexuality and in turn threaten body image and self concept (Bergmann, 1965; Eissler, Freud, Kris, & Solnit, 1977; Freud, 1952; Geist, 1979). Physical treatments such as medication can also have serious side effects which disturb physical appearance and well-being (Korsch, Fine, Grushkin, & Negrete, 1971). Certain adjustment reactions, especially those that engendered by reactions to painful procedures or to medical regimens that change physical appearance, are not completely preventable. However, preventive programs for hospitalized children can address these inevitable stresses by reducing anxiety and providing opportunities for the patient to express his or her feelings (Ack, 1978; Adams, 1976; Plank, 1971).

Disruption of Adjustment in Life Contexts as a Consequence of Illness

Hospitalizations inevitably remove the child from the familiar settings of school and home, require adjustment to an unfamiliar hospital social and physical environment, and create yet another transition back to home (Kagan-Goodheart, 1977). For this reason, transitions from hospital to home settings provide opportune points for preventive interventions, designed to aid the chronically ill child's mastery of change. It is also not uncommon for the emotional problems of chronically ill children to develop disturbances in academic, social, or vocational functioning which necessitate interventions in such contexts. One of the more common adjustment problems associated with a chronic illness is school avoidance (Drotar, 1978a; Lansky, Lowman, Vats, & Gyulay, 1975), which may be accompanied by functional somatic symptoms.

For example, Kate, a 12 year old with cystic fibrosis, developed chronic tiredness and vague pains which were not explainable by organic factors. Kate had not attended school for over a year and gradually lost interest in peers and outside activities. Feeling that her peers did not accept her because of her illness, she had given up trying to tell them about it. At home, her parents had gradually given up efforts to involve her in activities. Kate's problems benefited from both individual and family discussions, which clarified her isolation and the parents' feeling of grief.

Physical Impairment and Deterioration

Illness-related impairments can limit the child's physical activity, capacity to function at work or school, and independence. Although many chronic illnesses afford a very reasonable quality of life for extended periods, conditions such as spina bifida, which involve multiple organ systems and entail severe physical immobility, impose a social isolation that cannot be easily overcome (Dorner, 1973; Holroyd & Guthrie, 1979). Moreover, the advanced stages of progressive illnesses such as cystic fibrosis or cancer entail painful losses of physical capacities and cherished activities, as well as troubling adjustments in life goals. Significant changes in physical status require extraordinary coping strategies and can be a focus for the type of preventive intervention which maximizes the potential for life functioning at any level of disease severity. Some children with relatively severe diseases make astonishing progress toward life goals in the midst of extraordinary physical obstacles (Drotar, 1978a), while others with relatively mild physical diseases can become functionally debilitated far beyond the level of their actual physical impairment (Bergman & Stamm, 1967).

Life-Threatening Illness

Life-threatening illnesses pose unique psychological problems which transcend those of nonlife-threatening diseases (Kagen-Goodheart, 1977; Koocher & O'Malley, 1981; Spinetta & Maloney, 1975). For example, the prospect of raising a child with a potentially fatal illness generates extraordinary fears and child rearing dilemmas for parents (Friedman, Chodoff, Mason, & Hamburg, 1963; McCollum & Gibson, 1970; Natterson & Knudson, 1960). These parents must manage their anxieties in order to encourage a reasonable level of life functioning for their children, yet not become unduly preoccupied with the prospect of death (Koocher & O'Malley, 1981). Since the entire family is affected by the death of a chronically ill child, supportive preventive intervention may enhance family coping during and subsequent to this stressful life experience (Drotar, 1977; Spinetta, Swarner, & Sheposh, 1981).

The Setting of Physical Treatment

Families of chronically ill children must not only adapt to the demands of an individual illness and its treatments, but also negotiate transactions with caregivers in unfamiliar hospital environments. The medical care of chronically ill children occurs in many settings including ambulatory environments, inpatient hospitals, and special treatment settings such as dialysis or intensive care units, each with distinctive subcultures (Drotar, 1976). Most chronically ill children are treated in highly specialized medical training centers (Kanthor, Pless, Satterwhite, & Myers, 1974) where structural and organizational problems (Mechanic, 1974; Tefft & Simeonsson, 1979) impede communication among professionals as well as between physician and family members. The time pressures, emphasis on action, and absence of privacy can severely constrain caregivers' transactions with children and families (Drotar, Benjamin, Chwast, Litt, & Vajner, 1981). Transactions with chronically ill children and their families frustrate physicians (Artiss & Levine, 1973; Ford, Liske, & Ort, 1963), partially because this work requires special communication skills which are not usually a part of the pediatrician's repertoire (Haggerty, Roghmann, & Pless, 1975). Social-emotional issues appear to be neglected in communicating with parents about well-child care (Korsch & Morris, 1968) and evaded in the care of adolescents with some chronic conditions (Raimbault, Cachin, Limal, Elincheff, & Rappaport, 1975). Finally, physical treatments for chronic life-threatening conditions, such as cancer and renal failure, dramatically affect the quality of life and raise profound ethical questions and uncertainties for caregivers and families alike (Fox, 1975; Fox & Swazey, 1978; Illich, 1976; Katz & Capron, 1975), further affecting communication between physicians and family members. Given such constraints, the interpersonal context of physical treatment can itself be a stressor and a salient target for preventive intervention.

ADJUSTMENT PROBLEMS OF CHRONICALLY ILL CHILDREN

Considering the nature of illness-related stresses, it is surprising that chronically ill children and their families do not develop severe problems more frequently than they do (Drotar, Doershuk, Boat, Matthews, & Boyer, 1981; Pless & Pinkerton, 1975; Tavormina, Kastner, Slater, & Watt, 1976). In contrast to early case reports, which emphasized the adjustment problems associated with chronic illness, recent controlled research indicates that: (1) the personality and adjustment strengths of chronically ill children outweigh their deficits, (2) for the most part, chronically ill children resemble their physically healthy peers with respect to mental health, (3) chronic illness is best construed as a life stressor which contributes to additional mental health risk, but is not a primary cause of adjustment problems (Drotar, 1981; Pless & Pinkerton, 1975).

Chronically ill children demonstrate the same emotional problems as physically healthy children, such as anxiety reactions (Drotar, 1975a, 1978a; Drotar, Ganofsky, & Makker, 1979; Mattsson, 1972), depression and suicidal behavior (Drotar, 1978a; Sterns, 1959; Weinberg, 1970), overly dependent behavior (Lansky & Gendel, 1975; Mattsson, 1972), and learning and behavioral problems (Drotar, 1978a; Spencer, 1968). Chronically ill children also experience stress-related adjustment reactions and problems with compliance, which are more strictly disease-related. Through experience, seasoned clinicians learn to distinguish between understandable stress reactions and more severe, potentially intractable problems, which often relate to maladaptive premorbid adjustment. For example, although a certain degree of depression and upset is inevitable in illness-related crises, prolonged retreat from the demands of school, peers, or family generally signals a more severe disturbance (Drotar, 1978a).

PRINCIPLES OF PREVENTIVE INTERVENTION

Our long-term experiences as professional caregivers in comprehensive care centers for chronic illness populations (Drotar, 1975a; Drotar, Crawford, & Bush, 1984; Drotar & Ganofsky, 1976; Ganofsky, Drotar, & Makker, 1983) indicate that a useful conceptual framework for prevention focuses on enhancement of potential rather than psychological deficits. Unfortunately, such perspectives are not only difficult to acquire in traditional, pathology-oriented clinical training (Drotar, 1981; Mohr, Note 1), but also difficult to implement in disease-focused medical cultures. In practice, physicians tend to refer the most seriously disturbed chronically ill children and families to mental health professionals. Thus, it was no accident that our initial clinical exposure to chronic illness involved physicians' requests to intervene with severe emotional disturbances, compliance difficulties, and family problems (Drotar, 1975a; Drotar & Ganofsky, 1976). Our cumulative clinical experiences have taught us the wisdom of abandoning the language of deficit for that of coping. We have also reframed our treatment goals to include competency enhancements (Hobbs, 1975; Mattsson, 1972) including: (1) mastery of potentially disruptive anxiety related to the disease and its physical management, (2) a reasonable understanding of and adherence to necessary medical regimens, (3) integration of illness into family life, especially the reconciliation of family needs with those of the ill child, and (4) adaptation to hospital, school, and peers. In a preventive model, the intervenor functions as a guide and advocate for the child and family through the course of the disease, seeking a reasonable level of adaptation. The success of this expedition depends heavily on the trust that develops between the professional and family. The elusive but powerful concept of trust appears to evolve from the following principles: (1) continuity of relationship, (2) active participation by professional caregivers, (3) mutual participation of child and family, (4) advocacy, (5) a focus on coping and competence, (6) a developmental perspective, and (7) a family-centered focus. These principles will now be elaborated and illustrated in vignettes from our clinical experiences based largely on two model chronic conditions: juvenile diabetes and renal disease. The case examples cover a range of clinical situations encountered in chronic illness.

Continuity of Relationship—The Cornerstone of Preventive Intervention

Our experiences (Ganofsky et al., 1983) and recent research (Haynes, Taylor, & Sackett, 1979) have affirmed the central importance of relationship variables, especially continuity, to successful long-term psychosocial management of a chronic illness and patient satisfaction (Breslau, Haug, Burns, McClelland, Reeb, & Staples, 1975). From the families' vantage point, continuity means that they will not be abandoned at any point in the course of the illness, that they will have a familiar person to turn to in times of crisis and with whom to share moments of triumph over illness-related adversity. From the professional's perspective, continuity provides a critical opportunity for monitoring how a family and child are adjusting to the disease in various life contexts. Continuity of care requires a committed availability in person and by phone, especially at times of crisis. Yet, this commitment does not entail being "on call" at every moment. Rather, the experience of continuity is communicated to children and families in any ways which signal commitment of presence, such as visits during a hospitalization or crisis, remembering a child's birthday, and sharing difficult times. In our experience, a continuous relationship between professional caregivers, the child, and family provides the basis for all subsequent intervention. Continuity of relationship allows the caregiver to build upon prior transactions, provide feedback to the child and family concerning their progress, anticipate future problems, and identify areas that require intervention. In the absence of continuity, chronically ill children and their families do not experience a sense that they are cared for. In this case, the professional caregiver's prospects for providing feedback and anticipating developmental progress are sorely limited.

Active Involvement of Professional Caregivers

Preventive work requires the caregiver to define both the context and focus of intervention rather than rely on the family to identify their problems. The caregiver initiates contact with the chronically ill child and family, facilitates information exchange, and defines the nature of the relationship. Assuming initiative for interchange underscores the message that every family with a chronically ill child is stressed in ways that necessitate intervention. Moreover, structuring opportunities for the child and family to express feelings, and providing direct physical support and information about the disease and its management helps the caregiver build a sense of security in the midst of an anxiety-laden experience. The caregiver's initiation of support, knowledge, and information depends on a thorough knowledge of the disease and its treatment. In addition, the caregiver's understanding of expectable versus deviant psychological reactions can help most families construe their illness-related stress reactions as meaningful and legitimate ways of coping, rather than as deviant behaviors. Finally, the caregiver's anticipation of the emotional impact of developmental and disease-related changes also encourages a sense of mastery. Such anticipatory guidance requires the ability to be informative yet not intrusive, to register concern but not alarm, and to respect families' autonomy and capacity to utilize available information and resources (Drotar & Chwast, Note 2).

Mutual Participation of Child and Family

The active structuring of contacts desirable in preventive work with chronically ill children and their families should not preclude family participation. Quite the contrary, it is critical that the child and family negotiate their relationships with caregivers as active partners rather than as passive recipients of treatment. For this reason, intervenors must structure their contacts with the family to facilitate open and ongoing dialogue concerning perceptions of the illness, its treatment, and changes in life functioning. It is important to create an atmosphere in which the children's and families' perceptions are trusted and believed, and in which families are given clear feedback concerning their responsibilities for treatment regimens and any departures from agreed-upon expectations. Inclusion of families in decisions concerning the illness helps promote a sense of control (Nannis, Susman, Strope, Woodruff, Hersh, Levine, & Pizzo, 1982), which provides an antidote to the inherent constraint associated with the experience of a chronic illness. As families experience their feelings being heard and their wishes being respected, they are more likely to integrate arduous treatment regimens as truly theirs, rather than as alien orders of a feared authority. Shared decision making and responsibility also allows more honest transactions in which professional caregivers are not required to have all the answers and family members are able to admit their anxieties. However, active, autonomous participation in self-care is not easily achieved and usually requires considerable support from the caregiver. The following case is an example.

Diagnosed with diabetes at age three and one-half, Michael was referred to us at age nine and one-half because of problems with his glucose control. Up to this point, he had had little or no involvement in his own care; his mother had always tested his urine, given his insulin, and treated his insulin reactions. At this time, however, his mother asked that he be educated about his disease, hoping that he would assume some responsibility. On the other hand, she described herself as overprotective and willing to assume total responsibility for diabetes-related chores because she viewed Michael's illness as a life and death situation requiring her supervision.

Throughout the next several months, as Michael was trained in urine testing and insulin injections, his mother remained ambivalent about this transition of responsibility, expressing concern that Michael would make many mistakes. Michael himself was unsure about trying new things and was hesitant even in responding to questions about diabetes.

Initially short-term goals were set, for example, one urine test a day or self-injection on the weekend only, with the explanation that Michael was expected to take on these responsibilities gradually. In addition, we supported his new accomplishments with positive reinforcement provided in the form of frequent phone contacts. This helped reduce parental anxiety about the child functioning with less supervision. In addition, our praising Michael about his competence during clinic visits allowed his parents to learn techniques for continuing this support at home, thus increasing Michael's chances of success with his new responsibilities.

Advocacy

Advocacy, defined as the use of professional knowledge of the disease and status to intervene with agencies and institutions on behalf of the family, is another critical ingredient of preventive intervention. This multifaceted intervention can include explanation of the disease and health care setting, help with finances, communication with teachers, or, as in the following case example, the creation of more effective patient-physician interactions.

When 17 year old Jeff was two days post-nephrectomy after a second unsuccessful transplant attempt, the exasperated vascular surgeon bluntly told Jeff he probably would never be transplanted again because he rejected the kidneys too rapidly. (Both were rejected within a week of the transplant.) Jeff was overtly depressed, both from the loss of the second transplant and from the withdrawal of hope. However, Jeff's cadaver kidneys were random HLA antigen-matched grafts and it was thought that with greater effort at subsequent kidney selection, Jeff's chances for a successful transplant could be improved but not guaranteed. Using this knowledge, the social worker approached the pediatric nephrologist, asking him to discuss this information with Jeff and review with him the new experimental anti-rejection drugs. Jeff's depression and sense of hopelessness were also discussed with the physician, who recognized that Jeff could return to his prior level of adequate adjustment only if he reinvested in living. Jeff, his physician, and social worker then met to review all treatment options: hemodialysis (including transfer to a unit closer to his home), home hemodialysis, Continuous Ambulatory Peritoneal Dialysis, and transplant. Jeff fully understood the complications of transplant and wanted only to hear what could be done differently. The decision was made at that meeting to place Jeff's name back on the cadaver transplant list with the proviso of a more stringent match, which would most likely take longer. Jeff's knowledge of the advocate's concern for his best interests and his participation in the process improved his attitude and emotional state considerably.

In a similar vein, physical presence during difficult procedures (for example, in the operating room) can be an effective advocacy intervention. The advocate's direct knowledge of the child's experience facilitates subsequent information exchange and ameliorates feelings of helplessness caused when parents have to separate from their child at a critical juncture. Effective advocacy not only requires a thorough knowledge of the course of a physical disease and the hospital setting, but judgment to determine when to actively intervene on a family's behalf versus facilitating their opportunities for direct negotiation with physicians, teachers, and other professionals.

Emphasis on Coping and Competence

Several special advantages derive from using a competence or coping-based diagnostic perspective to plan preventive intervention. The child's coping strategies can be evaluated in terms of whether they enhance or disrupt life adjustment and compliance with treatment regimens. Coping can also be differentiated in terms of *modes* (for example, information seeking or action) or *functions*, as in altering a stressful situation (Lazarus & Launier, 1978). Coping should be considered as a social transactional *process* (Mechanic, 1974) which involves the chronically ill child and significant peers and adults over time. The emphasis on strengths inherent in the coping perspective communicates a sense of hope and optimism to chronically ill children and their families, who often feel singled out because of the illness. A coping perspective focuses on the stressful, yet manageable, prospect of living with a chronic disease and construes illness as an opportunity for mastery. The caregiver's emphasis on efficacy, for example, what the child and family can actively do to make positive changes in their situation, is a powerful sustaining force that may contribute to self-esteem (Bandura, 1982).

A Developmental Perspective

A developmental perspective is critical to individualize expectations for disease management and to establish a realistic approach in which children gradually assume responsibility for treatment regimens as they relate to their developmental capabilities. Since children's intellectual understanding of their disease (Campbell, 1975; Simeonsson, Buckley, & Monson, 1979), salient emotional concerns (Freud, 1952; Nagera, 1978; Schowalter, 1977) and expectations for management of physical treatment regimens vary considerably with age and level of emotional maturity, the wise clinician structures intervention to emphasize developmental expectations (Cohen & Lazarus, 1979; Mechanic, 1974) and evaluates the child's progress over time to determine subsequent intervention goals. Many chronically ill children who are severely stressed by the onset of a disease, a lengthy hospitalization, or physical deterioration show surprising resilience and regain prior levels of adaptive coping without intensive psychological intervention. On the other hand, a protracted retreat from age-appropriate developmental tasks, particularly in a child with mild physical disease, can signal an ominous disturbance requiring more intensive mental health intervention (Drotar, 1975a, 1978a). Chronic illness-related stress also can be highly intertwined with family developmental issues. For example, the psychological problems of chronically ill children often occur at critical transition points in family development, such as the beginning of school or the onset of adolescence (Drotar, 1978a).

ILLUSTRATION OF THE PRINCIPLES OF PREVENTIVE INTERVENTION

Preventive intervention often involves working with children and adolescents over a protracted period, through times of adversity, periods of calm, and various developmental phases. The following case vignette of a young adult, who endured an array of physical insults throughout the course of her disease, illustrates the following principles of preventive intervention: (1) continuity of relationship, (2) active involvement of professional caregivers, (3) participation of child and family, and (4) advocacy. Angela stands as an impressive tribute to human resilience and to the importance of persistent, available support from professional caregivers.

Angela has end-stage renal disease. She began on dialysis at age 10 and has been cared for by the same network of professionals continuously for seven and one-half years. She is the youngest of eight children in a very closely knit black family. When she began dialysis, Angela was an exceedingly shy, very quiet girl who relied extensively on her mother and father. Six months after she had begun hemodialysis, she was transplanted with a cadaver kidney. The excitement of this transplant was tempered shortly after surgery by numerous medical and surgical complications, hospital admissions, and invasive procedures. The social work staff, physicians, and nursing staff provided considerable support, reassurance, and education to her mother. In turn, the mother became quite effective in helping her daughter with her feelings, utilizing the explanations that the team had given her.

Advocacy was a mainstay of this difficult course of treatment. When confronted with physicians and interchanges about Angela's medical condition, her mother was typically nervous and inarticulate. Although she wanted precise and accurate information about Angela's status, she did not know how to ask for it and did not always understand what the physicians said. To adapt, she asked the physicians to explain it to her social worker. The role of interpreter became a familiar intervention in the subsequent six years of work with the family.

Angela was eventually returned to dialysis as a reliable form of treatment. During this period, an emerging trust developed between the treatment staff and the parents. Angela blossomed into a verbal, open young lady who developed positive relationships with staff and the other children. However, the relief felt by family and staff when Angela was returned to dialysis slowly eroded as her response to dialysis deteriorated over three years. Complicating the seemingly endless dialysis was the parents' unexpected legal separation and eventual divorce, apparently related to previous conflicts rather than Angela's illness. Both parents independently stayed very involved with her, but these problems required considerable supportive counseling time with Angela and her mother.

At age 15, Angela received another transplant with her sister as a donor, but it was again unsuccessful. Angela was hospitalized with complications and the extent of her regression became alarming. However, rather than recommending intervention away from her treatment context, we "accepted" her behavior, explained it to her physicians and nurses, and counseled the family. Angela's family was seen frequently by the social worker and the nephrologist, who apprised them of her medical condition and reassured them that her adjustment would improve. The major psychosocial intervenor again became Angela's mother. Angela slowly recovered from this crisis, and we observed the emergence of a very competent young lady who attends school regularly, has a very active social life, and is well adapted to chronic hemodialysis.

THE FAMILY CONTEXT: A UNIFYING FOCUS OF PREVENTION

Preventive interventions can be structured within a bewildering array of potential modalities, including individual treatment (Drotar & Ganofsky, 1976; Lansky et al., 1975), family therapy (Minuchin et al., 1978), parent guidance (Drotar et al., 1978; McCollum & Gibson, 1970), and groups for parents, ill children or siblings (Cunningham, Betsa, & Gross, Note 3; Heffron, Boomelaere, & Masters, 1973; Mattson & Agle, 1972; Peterson & Brownlee-Duffeck, Chapter 9 of this volume; Schowalter, 1971). However, there are powerful reasons for construing the family context as the primary focus of preventive intervention (Drotar, Crawford, & Bush, 1984; see also Forehand, Walley, & Furey, Chapter 11 of this volume). The family is the chronically ill child's most salient context of socialization, learning, and support (Caplan & Killea, 1976; Power & Dell Orto, 1980; Litman, 1974). Moreover, family influences, such as the quality of intrafamilial coping, openness of disease-related communication, flexibility of problem solving, perceived family cohesion and adjustment, have been shown to be influential mediators of childhood adjustment (Kucia, Drotar, Doershuk, Stern, Boat, & Matthews, 1979; Moise, Note 4; Pless, Roghmann, & Haggerty, 1972; Spinetta & Maloney, 1978). A family-oriented transactional framework (Belsky, 1981) considers the impact of illness-related stress on *all* family members including the affected child, parents, siblings, and the extended family. Finally, a family-centered diagnostic perspective helps identify potentially maladaptive patterns of coping, such as scapegoating of chronically ill children, and facilitates family acceptance of psychological interventions when needed.

Family-centered preventive comprehensive care may be defined as the systematic inclusion of family members and subgroups in the child's physical care in ways that create family contexts for problem solving, decision making, and management of disease-related stress. Our experience indicates that a structural family systems perspective (Minuchin et al., 1978) provides a cogent guiding framework for the family-centered preventive care of chronically ill children. The structural approach focuses on the observable patterns by which family members relate to one another to manage stresses and integrate the child's illness into their lives. An important structural concept is the definition of subsystems (for example, parents, siblings) within the family. Since the quality of the parent relationship is considered especially critical for children's coping, the parent subsystem is often the focal point of the professional's contacts with the family. Successful management of a chronic illness also requires a delicate balance between parental support versus over-involvement in the child's treatment regimen and between concern versus preoccupation with the child's physical and emotional vulnerabilities. A childhood chronic illness can set the stage for maladaptive intrusion of parents into children's activities as well as the detouring of family conflicts onto the chronically ill child. For this reason, natural family-centered preventive interventions include discouraging family members from talking for the chronically ill child, structuring visits to include both parents, involving fathers and siblings in the child's care, and reinforcing the parents' ability to communicate with one another and make decisions as a couple. In the following sections, we consider applications of a preventive, family-centered approach to common illness-related situations.

The Diagnosis of Chronic Illness

The professional's contact with the family of a chronically ill child often begins at diagnosis. The way these initial contacts are structured may have critical import for families' subsequent contacts with caregivers (Ablin, Binger, Stein, Kushner, Roger, & Mikkelsen, 1971). For example, if only the mother is involved, then the family may receive the message that it is more important for her (rather than other family members) to be involved in subsequent contacts with professionals. A mother-centered approach to comprehensive care may also place further responsibilities on an already highly stressed parent and disrupt the parents' capacities to support one another by isolating the father from the child's care. A more adaptive model of family-centered comprehensive care involves salient family members at initial diagnosis, but places primary focus on the parents as shown in the following case.

Dawn is a seven year old child, diagnosed as having diabetes following a mild onset of symptoms. The parents were shocked to be told that Dawn had a chronic illness requiring life-long treatment with insulin.

At the beginning of the hospitalization, Dawn's father asked many questions about the diagnosis and treatment of diabetes in an attempt to confirm in his own mind the reality of his daughter's condition. During the brief four or five day hospitalization, all family members including her siblings learned new information and skills, including insulin injections, urine testing, diet, and recognition and treatment of symptoms. In addition, special emphasis was placed on supporting the parents' relationship with one another.

Inclusion of family members in educational sessions allows them to function as supportive persons to one other, brings out personal strengths that may not otherwise be obvious, and stimulates group feedback. For example, a family member may ask a novel question which exposes the whole family group to new and important information. It is important to recognize that the diagnosis of a chronic illness requires family members to assimilate a great deal of new information and skills very quickly and at a time when they are highly stressed. For this reason, following initial diagnosis, it is particularly helpful to encourage regular phone contact with families to review symptoms and treatment regimens.

Engaging the Absent Father

The adaptive integration of a chronic illness into family life is a slow process often involving setbacks. Since some families appear to resolve the crisis of the chronic illness diagnosis only to break down at subsequent points of stress, caregivers should be sensitized to changes in child or family adaptations that reflect serious psychosocial problems. In such instances, reorientation of the family to their roles and responsibilities in illness management can be a useful preventive tool. However, since maladaptive family patterns are often quite entrenched, concerted efforts may be needed to shift these alignments. The following vignette demonstrates how a shift in the focus of illness-related responsibility from the mother-child dyad to include the father ameliorated the child's behavioral problems. This particular case also illustrates the utility of a home visit, both as a method of family observation and as an intervention technique.

Adopted as an infant, Tricia developed diabetes when she was five and one-half years old. From the beginning, her mother carried the lion's share of responsibility for Tricia's care including giving all of her insulin injections, supervising her diet, and testing her urine. After eight months of diabetes, the mother referred herself to the diabetic clinic because Tricia's diabetic control was erratic. Tricia had had a grand mal seizure which one pediatrician ascribed to low blood sugar and another said was unrelated to the diabetes.

Since the seizure, Tricia's father had become very anxious about her. He no longer wanted to leave the house without her and insisted that the child consume large amounts of food during the evening, hoping to prevent hypoglycemic symptoms. Over the next few years, Tricia developed behavior problems. She fought each insulin injection by becoming hysterical, which only increased the father's anxieties and the mother's frustrations. Although it had been suggested that the father attend clinic appointments and that the family pursue counseling, neither event took place. For this reason and because Tricia was resisting any self-care responsibilities, a home visit was scheduled. The father participated in the discussion and supported his wife's idea that Tricia should at least help with urine testing. Together Tricia and her parents decided that the test before bed would now be her responsibility and, in return, they would stop nagging her so much about urine specimens. The father asked many questions about diabetes, including questions carried over from diagnosis (for instance, how did Tricia get diabetes?) and expressed his fears about her.

After this home visit, Tricia's father began and has continued to bring Tricia for her clinic visits. He always has new questions to ask and generally seems much less anxious about Tricia's condition. Over the subsequent nine months, Tricia gradually took on responsibility for her care, giving all of her own injections and testing all of her own urines.

Preventive Intervention With Siblings

Siblings of chronically ill children are a silent but potentially stressed population (Cairns, Clark, Smith, & Lansky, 1979; Lavigne & Ryan, 1979; Tew & Lawrence, 1973) that should be considered in preventive efforts. Siblings often have a great many worries about what is happening to their chronically ill brother or sister and may feel deprived of parental attention. On the other hand, siblings can be significant sources of support for the chronically ill child over the entire course of the illness, but *only* if they are sufficiently informed and involved so that their experience of their sibling's illness becomes more understandable. An example of productive structuring of sibling involvement during the period of initial diagnosis is seen in the case of a seven year old diabetic child, Abbie, and her eight year old brother, Jamie.

Abbie's parents were always sensitive to Jamie's feelings about his sister's illness and hospitalization. The parents planned for one of them to be home each night with Jamie to maintain some level of usual family activity. Some of this time was spent talking with him about Abbie's diabetes. Thus, Jamie was able to share his concern that he was in some way responsible for Abbie's disease. His parents reassured him that this was not true and described for him how well Abbie was again feeling.

These parents encouraged the children to keep in daily phone contact with each other and when it was suggested that Jamie visit Abbie, they readily agreed. Jamie was included in family educational sessions which provided him an opportunity to observe urine testing and injections and to ask questions. He seemed reassured to know that Abbie could still play sports and eat with him at McDonald's.

After discharge, the family was encouraged to attend clinic visits together which they did often. We continued to involve Jamie in visit activities by weighing and measuring him and giving him a brief physical exam. These activities added little time to the visit and were very important to Jamie, who was just as anxious as Abbie to know how much he had grown. Over the years, Jamie's interest in coming to the clinic lessened as he preferred to stay home with friends. This change was readily accepted by Abbie, who was now quite comfortable coming to visits on her own.

PREVENTIVE INTERVENTION IN THE SCHOOL

School is a significant context in the lives of chronically ill children, who often experience intermittent school absences, limitations requiring special tutoring, or limitations in activity (Pless, 1979). In addition, the necessity of carrying out treatment regimens in school stigmatizes the chronically ill child in relation to physically healthy peers. Transitions between hospital, school, and family contexts also pose even greater dilemmas for chronically ill children and their families than for physically healthy children (Lightfoot, 1978). The parents of chronically ill children are often torn between concerns about informing school personnel of their child's special needs versus not wanting to single out the child as special. It is ordinarily difficult for physicians, family, and school staff to determine and coordinate reasonable expectations for academic functioning, particularly in situations where severe disease-related and emotional factors affect school adjustment. For example, in those instances in which psychologically based somatic symptoms mimic organic disease, potentially remediable adjustment problems such as school avoidance can be very difficult to detect (Drotar, 1978a; Lansky et al., 1975).

The question of special schooling for chronically ill children also has import for preventive intervention. The decision to obtain home tutoring may address the child's short-term physical management, but have negative consequences for long-term socialization. Chronically ill children are educated by teachers who are usually unfamiliar with their disease and its implications for physical activity, socialization, and learning. Our experience indicates that teachers' concern with chronically ill children's vulnerability often contributes to unnecessary restrictions. In recognition of these potential problems, school-related preventive intervention should occur in a number of areas (Crittenden & Gofman, 1976): (1) facilitation of return to school following hospitalization, including normalization of routine, (2) management of the social stresses of illness-related regimens, and (3) preventive educational advocacy with teachers and the school system.

Handling the Social Impact of the Disease in School

Diabetes is one of a number of "invisible" illnesses which contribute to social stigma. For example, the child may require a snack before gym or need to use the bathroom more frequently, things which are noticed by classmates. Fearing ridicule or unwanted attention, some children will at times ignore symptoms or omit snacks, thus placing themselves in jeopardy.

For example, seven year old Lisa repeatedly "forgot" her afternoon snack at school and frequently returned home looking pale and shaky, obviously hypoglycemic. When asked about this, Lisa explained that her friends threatened not to play with her at recess unless she shared her snack. Because she did not have enough food for everyone, she chose not to eat. Lisa was acting in this situation not as a child with diabetes but as a seven year old who did not want to take chances in losing friends.

Kimberly, aged nine, a child with chronic familial pancreatitis requiring partial removal of her pancreas, also had to cope with the considerable social effects of her disease. As a result of the surgery, Kim required daily replacement of insulin by injection and pancreatic enzymes before every meal or snack. After returning to school, Kim frequently had to leave the classroom to take medication or treat low blood sugar symptoms. This singled her out as different and brought many stares and questions from the other children. Kim eventually became so upset by this that she did not want to go to school at all. An intervention was arranged with the school nurse whereby she would hold sessions with each of the fourth grade classes to discuss children who had medical conditions requiring the use of special medication, diet, or equipment. This intervention proved helpful to Kim without making her the specific topic of discussion.

Educational Advocacy with Teachers: The School Visit

At times, school professionals contribute to the chronically ill child's feelings of being different. Most teachers and school nurses have had limited practical experience with chronic illnesses and may base their actions on misinformation.

For example, when Amy, a juvenile diabetic, started nursery school her teachers restricted her physical activities for fear she would become sick. In addition, they asked Amy to carry around a cigar box containing emergency supplies, including instant glucose and a padded tongue blade.

Another example of the barriers faced by chronically ill children was a principal's unwillingness to have a successfully transplanted thirteen year old in school. After considerable prompting, he expressed his concern that the young lady could experience precipitous, irreversible renal rejection in school. When it became clear that he viewed transplant rejection as analogous to a cardiac arrest, it was explained that no tragic medical emergency would occur in the school. With this information, he became less anxious about the girl's return, but still was hesitant. In response to his concerns, it was suggested that the social worker could meet with all relevant staff at the school. When the concepts of renal transplantation and methods for evaluating transplant rejection were explained, the principal and school staff were more than willing to have the adolescent return.

The importance of peer support and academic functioning in the life of a chronically ill child or adolescent cannot be underestimated. To sit alone at home waiting for a tutor, with precious little opportunity for age-appropriate social interactions, inevitably disrupts emotional progress. The stigma associated with chronic illness often contributes to systematic discrimination, which sometimes requires intervention at a programmatic level. For example, local Ohio school officials were initially unwilling to let children with renal failure attend school three days a week (between dialysis) and receive tutoring for the other two. In this instance, the Ohio State Board of Education had to be appealed to in order to provide a flexible, creative program to maintain continuity for the children's school program and social development. Successful intervention involved writing a detailed letter advocating how it was in the child's best interest to modify the school program (Ganofsky, 1981). This case illustrates how some of the most productive interventions may not involve direct psychological treatment, but rather the use of psychological knowledge as the child's advocate in the service of institutional change.

ENHANCEMENT OF SOCIALIZATION

A chronic illness presents many potential hazards to children's socialization in addition to those in the context of the school. Chronically ill children are frequently called upon to transact and compete with physically healthy children, even though hospitalization and physical treatments curtail time and opportunities for socialization. The experience of a chronic illness also requires children to make difficult decisions about how much to tell others about their disease, whether to be identified as a well versus a sick person, and how to cope with others' reactions to their disease. The manner in which these social dilemmas are reconciled may reveal salient aspects of the child's capacity to understand, accept, and negotiate disease-related stress. Given these difficulties, it is not surprising that socialization is an area of special vulnerability for the survivors of chronic illness (Ganofsky et al., 1983; Koocher & O'Malley, 1981; Korsch et al., 1973) and a potential focus for preventive intervention.

Clinical experiences have shown that chronically ill peers can help the child master potentially difficult treatment regimens and feelings of deviance. For example, one of the most beneficial peer-focused interventions for children with chronic renal disease has been the structuring of "old-timers" to orient the newcomers. Children who are being prepared for hemodialysis or kidney transplant are introduced to someone their own age who has been a patient for some time. The more experienced patient describes the treatment, the dietary restrictions, the medication, and shares information on how to get along with the staff. Although some of the specific material offered may be inaccurate, the new patient benefits from seeing that someone else like him or herself has survived the frightening treatments. Our informal policy of introducing newly transplanted patients to other successfully transplanted patients at varying stages posttransplant has helped enhance compliance with steroid medications, which have such upsetting effects on physical appearance, especially for young adults (Korsch et al., 1973). The visual evidence that steroid side effects decrease at lower dosages has helped many newly transplanted patients accept the need for taking the higher doses early in the postsurgery course. In addition, the sense of control children and adolescents achieve by being in a more authoritative role with their peers enhances their self-esteem.

Most children who have chronic illnesses know few, if any, other children with the same condition. Attendance at camp for children with a similar illness provides an opportunity to meet children who also live each day with similar expectations and restrictions. Seeing other ill children participating in a full range of activities helps many children acquire knowledge about their disease and feel more competent (Harkavy, Johnson, Silverstein, Spillar, McCallum, & Rosenbloom, Note 5; Premack & Greifer, 1977). With respect to diabetes, one of the most widely recognized benefits of camp is that many children will begin to take some responsibility for their own self-care, a process with which parents often struggle and have ambivalent feelings. Susan, aged 10, for example, had never given her own insulin injection although her parents had often urged her to do so. After only three days at camp she was drawing up and injecting her insulin twice daily without problems.

For school-aged children, successful camp experiences involve positive role models, support, and an organized program of group reinforcement for peers of the same sex. Living together at camp also provides time for informal discussion of important questions that children do not usually have a chance to discuss. For example, during late night sessions in the cabins, parents are frequently the topic of revealing discussions; some children feel that their parents worry too much about their diabetes, often cautioning them about activities considered quite normal and safe by the children themselves. Finally, parents have also commented on the contact that is established by letter and phone between their children and peers following a camp experience.

SPECIAL CASES OF PREVENTION

Prevention with Reconstituted Families of Chronically Ill Children

Families of chronically ill children who have complex living arrangements caused by divorce, separation, or remarriage pose frustrating problems for preventionists. In reconstituted families, disparate living arrangements and continuing conflicts between the parents can often obscure responsibilities and procedures for decision making concerning illness regimens. In such situations, the professional caregiver can be placed in an untenable, confusing situation by dealing with individual parents who are fighting with one another over the child's care. Successful preventive intervention with such families generally requires a shift in perspective toward the reconstituted family, by emphasizing negotiation with both parents and clarification of their separate illness-related responsibilities. The following vignette illustrates the disruptive effects of a divorce on care for a chronically ill child, and the structuring of preventive intervention designed to ameliorate this stress.

Jason was diagnosed with diabetes at age ten months when he developed severe diabetic ketoacidosis. Jason was the only child of an 18 year old mother and a 30 year old father.

Although both parents were educated in the care of their diabetic infant, the mother assumed the major share of the responsibility from the beginning. The father, on the other hand, remained extremely anxious, expressing fears and concerns about every symptom, dietary requirements, and changes in urinary glucose patterns.

Five months after Jason's diagnosis, the mother left her husband because of his longstanding drinking problem and filed for divorce. At this point, care of Jason's diabetes became very complicated, with his father having visitation rights two days of the week. Many people, including grandparents, aunts, and babysitters became involved in giving Jason insulin, checking his urine, and supervising his diet. On those days when Jason was visiting, the father would frequently call the answering service, saying that Jason was sick because of some mistake made by his mother (for example, she gave him too much insulin, she did not feed him enough, and so on). At the same time, the father seemed uncomfortable and fearful in dealing with any changes in Jason's condition, such as hypoglycemia or acetone in the urine. During this period, Jason's diabetes became more unstable with multiple episodes of hypoglycemia and vomiting with ketonuria.

Faced with this chaotic situation, we structured the intervention to address the parents' conflicts. We asked that both parents attend every clinic visit with Jason. This provided the father an opportunity to ask his questions and hear about Jason's progress from us directly. To simplify decision making, we decided that all changes of insulin would be made through the mother since she was the primary caretaker. Unfortunately, this intervention worked only briefly, as within a few months the father started to withhold child support and money for diabetic supplies, creating even more stress.

We again met with the parents to express concern about their struggles and their negative effect on Jason's psychological development and diabetic care. They were now able to acknowledge their role in Jason's behavioral problems. The mother began to work and used her sister as a consistent babysitter for Jason. She also met a young man with whom she and Jason spent a great deal of time. As these events helped her disengage from the constant struggles with her ex-husband, Jason's diabetes and behavior stabilized.

Primary Postnatal Prevention of Mental Retardation

The birth of a child with a genetic disorder has an enormous, far-reaching impact on the family. Parents often experience guilt about having passed on a defect to their child. Phenylketonuria (PKU) is an example of an inherited metabolic disorder in which the child lacks an enzyme necessary to break down phenylalanine, an essential amino acid. Without treatment, phenylalanine accumulates and has a toxic efect on the central nervous system, producing mental retardation. With careful dietary treatment to restrict the intake of phenylalanine, mental retardation can be prevented. Although the child with PKU now has the potential for normal functioning, the treatment itself may become a serious burden for the family. The diet restricts many foods normally given to children and requires that families use special formula and foods which are often expensive. The burden of this treatment has become an even greater issue in recent years as research has shown that for optimal intellectual development the diet should be continued well into the school-age years (Koch, Azen, Friedman, & Williamson, 1982). The principles of preventive intervention concerning PKU are illustrated in the following case.

Dan was the second child and only son born to a young couple. Within two weeks of his birth, this seemingly normal baby was diagnosed with PKU. Even before hospital admission, the parents were worried that Dan was already retarded because someone had told them that all children with PKU were retarded. From the beginning, both parents expressed concern about Dan's future motor and intellectual development.

Dan's motor development progressed very rapidly. He made the transitions to table foods and self-feeding at the appropriate ages, something which is often difficult and delayed with a restricted diet. On the other hand, Dan was found at 12 months to have a rather short attention span and at 24 months to have deficits in his expressive language. Early identification of these problems enabled the team members to make appropriate suggestions for intervention, much of which was carried out by the parents themselves.

We find it very helpful to introduce new families to other PKU children and their families as soon as possible to reduce parental fears about their child's future and allow them to concentrate on the child's current accomplishments. Regular psychological evaluations can also help reinforce attainment of developmental milestones and to identify areas where special attention is needed. Dan's parents were also involved in a group with other couples who had children with PKU, which served two purposes. First, Dan's parents received support from others who were dealing with the same day-to-day problems and, second, the professionals were able to share information about PKU including the physiology of PKU, the diet plan, and normal development.

Prevention of Life-Threatening Sequelae in Psychosomatic Illness

Psychosomatic illnesses such as diabetes provide one of the most challenging opportunities for preventive intervention. For example, diabetic ketoacidosis, a life-threatening condition often triggered by acute illness, can also reflect psychosocial problems, including poor compliance with the prescribed regimen and a pronounced physiologic response to environmental stress. A small subgroup of juvenile diabetics are repeatedly hospitalized with ketoacidosis in spite of adequate progress during their hospitalization. Health care professionals usually find these patients frustrating, even "hateful" (Groves, 1973), and may threaten them with the potential for long-term complications, such as blindness and amputation, which results in little change in their behavior. On the other hand, systematic attention to family problems which interfere with disease management in the context of comprehensive care can provide an effective tool for dealing with ketoacidosis, as illustrated in the work with Tony, a thirteen year old with diabetes.

Tony had had his illness for three years when he was referred to the Pediatric Diabetes Center because of five hospitalizations for diabetic ketoacidosis in the previous three months. Through frequent clinic visits and phone calls, we identified several problem areas. Tony often ran out of diabetic supplies but did not tell his parents or he would get sick while his parents were out for the evening. Tony also had many questions and concerns about basic diabetes information, such as what caused diabetes, why he could not take pills, and why he got diabetes. Moreover, there were major discrepancies between the parents in their involvement around the diabetes and in their expectations for Tony. The father was intimately involved in every aspect of the care, making all the decisions about insulin dose, controlling Tony's food intake, and nagging Tony about urine testing. He expressed many frustrations about Tony, saying he was not athletic enough, did not apply himself in school, and did not take good care of his diabetes. Each time Tony became sick, this reinforced the father's feelings that Tony could not do it by himself. The mother, on the other hand, had no involvement in the diabetes. She had never given an injection, did not understand the significance of urine test results, and had minimal expectations for Tony. With help, the family, including Tony's four siblings, began to acknowledge how each family member was being affected by Tony's problem. His father was able to pull back and allow Tony more independence while his mother learned more about diabetes and became a new source of support. Tony has now been without diabetic ketoacidosis for more than five years.

OBSTACLES TO IMPLEMENTATION OF PREVENTIVE INTERVENTION

Obstacles to preventive intervention include the pathology-focused training of caregivers, pragmatic difficulties in implementing prevention, and lack of empirical information to guide the planning of preventive, comprehensive care programs. One of the most difficult practical problems is establishing priorities for professional allocation of time to the prevention of psychological problems that accompany chronic illnesses. Lacking systematic evidence to determine priorities, most clinicians divide their time between responding to severe psychological problems and doing minimal prevention on the side. Thus, competing time demands sorely limit the opportunities to sharpen one's skills in preventive work. In addition, medical staff may also pressure caregivers to spend time with more immediate management problems rather than on prevention. Statements such as, "Why are you working with that family when we have sick kids to care for?" and "They don't need it," may be encountered by clinicians who concentrate on prevention of mental health problems in health care settings. Since concepts dealing with prevention of behavioral problems are not emphasized in medical cultures, education of medical staff concerning the necessity and feasibility of preventive intervention is a critical long-range goal.

Difficult logistical problems are also raised by preventive interventions. Most families are not accustomed to working with mental health professionals especially when they do not have severe problems. For this reason, it is useful to structure comprehensive care so that all or most chronically ill children and families have some ongoing contact with psychosocial services, thus enhancing family acceptance of psychological services (Drotar & Ganofsky, 1976) for severe mental health problems should they develop. This context-sensitive model of allocating preventive services also allows psychological problems to be successfully managed in pediatric settings, facilitates professional expertise within a given chronic illness population, and helps humanize patient care by facilitating planning for children's mental health needs.

The logistics of preventive treatment are also complicated by geographical distances between the home communities of chronically ill children and the medical centers where they receive treatment. Although many families prefer to work with mental health professionals in their hospital setting who are therefore more familiar with their child's illness and its treatment, physical distance and strained resources of hospital-based mental health services often prohibit this. When referrals to community mental health services are made, families often require a great deal of support from hospital-based professionals to follow through with recommended treatment. Clinicians in comprehensive care teams in large medical centers have an important task to orient practitioners in community mental health facilities to the special problems experienced by chronically ill children and their families (Brantley, Stabler, & Whitt, 1981). Finally, the families' illness-related experiences can also color their acceptance of preventive mental health intervention. Since chronically ill children and their families are subject to a great many procedures over which they have no control, they may consider mental health intervention as yet another violation of personal autonomy or as a burden. In addition, our wish to help a highly stressed child can sometimes lead to premature mental health treatment at a time when the child's needs for the continued and reliable presence of family and hospital staff are much more compelling (Drotar & Chwast, 1978). At times, the demands of work-related stress can lead a professional staff to label a highly stressed, but emotionally healthy, child as emotionally disturbed and in need of mental health intervention (Meyer & Mendelson, 1961). In such instances, helping medical and nursing staff recognize how their personal reactions may color their appraisals of children and provide more effective emotional support in the setting can be much more productive than direct psychological treatment of the child's "disturbance" (Drotar, 1975b, 1977b; Drotar & Doershuk, 1979; Koocher, Sourkes, & Keane, 1979).

STRUCTURING PREVENTIVELY-FOCUSED COMPREHENSIVE CARE

In principle, the prevention of illness-related behavioral problems is the province of every professional discipline. However, sheer numbers of professional disciplines working with a given chronic illness population do not guarantee that a comprehensive care program will provide effective preventive intervention. In fact, programs in which different disciplines take a "piece" of the child, family, or physical treatment may be counterproductive and confusing to families. Our experience suggests that prevention is much more effective if one nonmedical professional discipline assumes primary responsibility for advocacy or psychosocial intervention and uses the other disciplines as consultants. The individual professional discipline (social work, psychology, nursing) does not appear to matter as much as the personal qualities, experience, and commitment of the individual caregiver.

The design of comprehensive care programs which enhance the chronically ill child's and family's capacities to manage stress is a challenging problem for future service delivery. Unfortunately, medical treatments for chronic illnesses are usually applied well in advance of a thorough understanding of their psychological effects on families. In addition, psychosocial services for chronically ill children usually must be developed after a program of medical care has been established. As consultants to comprehensive care programs for chronically ill children, we have redesigned our services to include preventive interventions such as: (1) greater involvement of fathers and siblings at the time of diagnosis, (2) more frequent family conferences concerning disease-related decisions, and (3) greater contact between professionals and family members at all phases of disease management. Such changes have been accomplished by a persistent, gradual demonstration of their efficacy and a high level of personal commitment to their implementation.

There is also an important need to educate health professionals concerning the strategies of preventive interventions. Experienced clinicians can help medical and nursing staffs develop more adaptive transactions with chronically ill children and families through informal interchange, formal conferences in which patient management issues are discussed, or direct modeling in which the staff has an opportunity to observe interchange with children and families (Drotar & Ganofsky, 1976).

IMPACT ON THE PROFESSIONAL CAREGIVER

Professional caregivers who work with chronically ill children face a number of special problems. The care and treatment of childhood chronic illnesses takes place in a highly charged interpersonal context in which the professional caregiver and family labor under many constraints. Preventive intervention places a special burden on the caregiver to initiate contact and develop meaningful partnerships with children and families who are undergoing considerable physical and emotional pain. The personal involvement of caregiver with family, which in our view is such a critical element of effective preventive intervention, is a double-edged sword. Professionals must live with the knowledge that the human suffering associated with illness cannot be taken away, even by the most skilled and sensitive interventions. Moreover, compelling frustrations are raised by the moral and ethical issues stimulated by the unforeseen stresses of the physical treatment (Illich, 1976; Katz & Capron, 1975), fragmentation of services, and inconsistent planning for the health care of chronically ill children (Mechanic, 1972). For these reasons, caregivers who work closely with chronically ill children and their families cannot help but be stressed by their work (Axelrod, 1979; Cartwright, 1979). The capacity to remain open and available to chronically ill children while somehow not becoming unduly stressed themselves poses a continual dilemma for caregivers. Just as the child and family must perceive hope and meaning in their struggles, professional intervenors must continue to perceive their work as effective and meaningful. To accomplish this, they must acquire a clear understanding of what can and cannot be ameliorated with intervention. The experienced professional learns to set priorities for intervention by devoting greater energies to situations that show a promise of change, while preventing the more intractable family and psychological problems from affecting management of the illness. A respect for the individuality and resiliency of chronically ill children is a critical sustaining force for the professional caregiver. One learns to relish the developmental accomplishments of chronically ill children and their families, especially considering what odds have been overcome. We believe that clinicians derive important benefits from their close involvement, sense of personal participation, and honesty concerning expression of their feelings toward chronically ill children and their families.

Work-related supports are also critical for the professional caregiver (Koocher, 1980). The opportunity to structure one's day in line with specific interests provides a refreshing contrast to the awesome sense of constraint encountered by working with unchangeable illnesses and family situations. Those who work with chronically ill children need ongoing opportunities to ventilate their frustrations, sadnesses, and triumphs, and to realistically appraise their effectiveness. Unfortunately, such supports are often neglected in the design of most hospital work environments. Conferences where difficult, work-related clinical situations are discussed from the standpoint of their emotional impact on their staff are one form of staff support (Drotar & Ganofsky, 1976). The need for reflection to balance the immersion in the difficult day-to-day struggles of children's families can also be achieved through research and writing. Finally, preventive work with chronically ill children can be professionally isolating since it is out of the mainstream of traditional professional activity. Since it is not uncommon for professionals to be the only one in their professional discipline to work with a particular patient population in a given setting, opportunity for interchange with other experienced professionals is of critical importance for professional development.

TRAINING IN PREVENTION CONCERNING CHILDHOOD CHRONIC ILLNESS

Most mental health professionals who utilize preventive intervention strategies with the chronically ill have learned their craft through transactions with children and families, rather than through formal training programs. Although some of the skills acquired in traditional clinical training programs in psychology, psychiatry, social work, and nursing are quite applicable to chronic illness preventive interventions, there is a critical need to develop training models which focus specifically on prevention (Iscoe, 1981). Working with highly experienced teachers who construe their intervention in preventive terms provides the cornerstone of such training (Drotar, 1978b). In addition, the following topic areas are especially relevant to prevention training with respect to childhood chronic illness: (1) family systems concepts which consider how the family group copes with a chronic illness (Power & Dell Orto, 1980), (2) sociological studies of the hospital context and culture, delivery of health care, and its impact on child and family (Friedson, 1970; Mechanic, 1972), (3) symptoms, natural histories, and various chronic illness, and (4) consultation techniques with health care professionals and teachers. Given the complexity of interventions with chronically ill children and their families, no one can realistically expect to acquire suitable skills and experiences in any single training program. For this reason, on the job training and continuing education will assume increasing importance as primary methods of encouraging professional development in preventive work with chronically ill children.

FUTURE DIRECTIONS

The ideas in this chapter represent useful working concepts and promising hypotheses rather than empirically tested methods. We hope that this work will stimulate others to experiment with preventive interventions and help counter the inevitable press for disease centered intervention, which is fueled by modern-day accountability and reimburseability pressures (Iscoe, 1981). With insurance reimbursement tied to services for already identified problems, it is unlikely that preventive services will be expanded without concerted interdisciplinary efforts concerning documentation of their efficacy. In addition, with the rapid expansion of medical technology in the direction of highly stressful physical treatments, such as bone marrow transplantation for severe, life-threatening illnesses like cancer (Patenuade, Szymanski, & Rappaport, 1980), the need for proactive planning to develop prevention-focused services and help counter the impact of such stressful technologies is especially critical. With the exception of controlled studies of the preparation of non-chronically ill children for surgery (Melamed & Siegel, 1975; Peterson, Hartman, & Gelfand, 1980; Peterson & Brownlee-Duffeck, Chapter 9 of this volume), the efficacy of chronic illness preventive interventions has not been systematically evaluated (Johnson, 1979). In fact, descriptions of interventions have generally focused on severe or exceptional disturbances rather than the more common stress-related reactions experienced by the majority of chronically ill children. We believe that empirical documentation of psychosocial interventions, especially of preventive programs, would be an important ingredient of planning for the special intervention, research, and consultation needs of a chronic illness population (Brantley et al., 1981).

What are the priorities for future research and clinical service concerning chronically ill children? One basic priority is descriptive research detailing the relationship of transactions between child, family and intervenors (the frequency, nature, and continuity) with the child's psychosocial, life-functioning outcome. Empirically documented descriptions of the nature of disturbances (both mild and severe) which occur naturally in various chronic illness populations should go hand in hand with the above goal. Our experience indicates that there may be an interesting relationship between the level of contact between family and professionals and the degree to which certain problems are identified. For example, programs which feature regular and continuous involvement of mental health professionals may identify a greater frequency of less severe problems than those programs in which professional contact is less frequent. Psychological disturbances may need to be especially visible to be identified in programs where mental health professionals are not participating.

Long-term outcome studies of special populations such as the survivors of childhood chronic illnesses are needed. In many settings, chronically ill young adults are often cared for by the same caregivers who saw them as children. Although there is no real agreement on the best model for these adults, long-term continuous care provides a unique opportunity to document the quality of survivors' life-functioning and the factors associated with positive adjustment. In this vein, Koocher and O'Malley (1981) noted that the long-term adjustment of young adult survivors of childhood cancer was positively associated with having a type of cancer requiring a relatively short treatment course, a minimum of permanent side effects, a relapse or recurrence-free period, disease onset during early infancy or early childhood, and effective use of denial. Our preliminary observations of young adult survivors of childhood end-stage renal disease treated in a preventively focused comprehensive care program (Ganofsky et al., 1983) indicate far less frequent severe compliance problems with medication than have been reported in similar populations (Korsch et al., 1973).

Prevention-related research might profitably focus on relationship variables that can be objectively defined, such as continuity of care (Breslau et al., 1975) and effectiveness of patient-physician communication (Korsch & Morris, 1968). Since many salient relationship variables occur together in high quality comprehensive care programs, it may be unrealistic to completely separate these factors in order to assess the most critical components. However, the efficacy of alternative preventive treatment models which differ along specific dimensions such as frequency of professional contact, modality (for example, individual versus group) or target focus, can be assessed without depriving children or families of potentially helpful intervention.

The development of objective measures for the efficacy of preventive interventions in chronic illness populations is an important priority. Global measures of psychological disturbance which are unreliable, invalid, and inappropriate for children's problems (Achenbach & Edelbrock, 1978) must give way to specific measures of such variables as adherence to treatment regimens and perceptions of disease (Bibace & Walsh, 1979; Campbell, 1975; Roberts, Beidleman, & Wurtele, 1981) that are relevant to disease management or the assessment of coping (Zeitlin, 1980) and competence (Harter, 1982). Research should be guided by conceptual frameworks which allow assessment of the relative contributions of mediating variables, such as family context and nature of support by professional caregivers, to the outcome.

We are convinced that significant advances in our understanding of prevention in childhood chronic illness will not be forthcoming in individual programs or studies, but will evolve from programmatically applied research in which questions are posed with increasing clarity and measures are slowly refined. Children and families affected with chronic illness have much to teach us about human resilience, courage, and resistance in the face of prolonged stress. Preventively focused intervention research provides a unique vantage point to study factors which enhance or disrupt human resilience under stress. Moreover, the development of preventive interventions which enhance the ability to cope with chronic illness-related stress may suggest principles of intervention that reduce children's vulnerability to other stressful life circumstances (Felner, Norton, Cowen, & Farber, 1981; Felner, Chapter 5 of this volume).

REFERENCES

Ablin, A. R., Binger, C. M., Stein, R. C., Kushner, T. H., Roger, S., & Mikkelsen, C. A. A conference with the family of a leukemic child. *American Journal of Diseases of Children,* 1971, *122,* 362–366.

Achenbach, J., & Edelbrock, C. S. The classification of child psychopathology: A review and analysis of empirical efforts. *Psychological Bulletin,* 1978, *85,* 1275–1301.

Ack, M. The psychological environment of a children's hospital. *Pediatric Psychology,* 1974, *2,* 3–5.

Adams, M. A hospital play program: Helping children with serious illness. *American Journal of Orthopsychiatry,* 1976, *46,* 416–424.

Artiss, K. L., & Levine, A. S. Doctor-patient relation in severe illness. *New England Journal of Medicine,* 1973, *283,* 1210–1214.

Axelrod, B. H. The chronic care specialist "but who supports us." In O. J. Sahler (Ed.), *The child and death*. New York: C. V. Mosby, 1979.

Bandura, A. Self-efficacy mechanisms in human agency. *American Psychologist,* 1982, *37,* 122–147.

Belsky, J. Early human experience: A family perspective. *Developmental Psychology,* 1981, *17*(1), 3–12.

Bergman, A. R., & Stamm, S. J. The morbidity of cardiac nondisease in school children. *New England Journal of Medicine,* 1967, *276,* 1008–1116.

Bergmann, T. *Children in the hospital*. New York: International Universities Press, 1965.

Bibace, R., & Walsh, N. E. Developmental stages in children's conceptions of illness. In G. C. Stone, F. Cohen, & N. E. Adler (Eds.), *Health psychology*. San Francisco: Jossey-Bass, 1979.

Brantley, H. T., Stabler, B., & Whitt, J. K. Program considerations in comprehensive care of chronically ill children. *Journal of Pediatric Psychology,* 1981, *6,* 229–238.

Breslau, N., Haug, M. R., Burns, A. B., McClelland, C. Q., Reeb, K. G., & Staples, W. I. Comprehensive pediatric care: The patient viewpoint. *Medical Care,* 1975, *13,* 562–569.

Cairns, N. V., Clark, G. M., Smith, S. P., & Lansky, S. B. Adaptation of siblings to childhood malignancy. *Journal of Pediatrics,* 1979, *95,* 484–487.

Campbell, J. D. Illness is a point of view: The development of children's concept of illness. *Child Development,* 1975, *46,* 92–100.

Caplan, G., & Killea, M. *Support systems and mutual help: Multidisciplinary explorations*. New York: Grune and Stratton, 1976.

Cartwright, L. K. Sources and effects of stress in health careers. In G. C. Stone, F. Cohen, & N. E. Adler (Eds.), *Health psychology*. San Francisco: Jossey-Bass, 1979.

Cohen, F., & Lazarus, R. Coping with the stress of illness. In G. C. Stone, F. Cohen, & N. E. Adler (Eds.), *Health psychology*. San Francisco: Jossey-Bass, 1979.

Crittenden, M., & Gofman, H. Follow-ups and downs: The medical center, the family, and the school. *Journal of Pediatric Psychology,* 1976, *1,* 66–68.

Dorner, S. Psychological and social problems of families of adolescent spina bifida patients: A preliminary report. *Developmental Medicine and Child Neurology,* 1973, *15,* Supplement 29, 24.

Drotar, D. The treatment of a severe anxiety reaction in the adolescent boy following renal transplantation. *Journal of the American Academy of Child Psychiatry,* 1975, *14,* 451–462. (a)

Drotar, D. Death in the pediatric hospital: Psychological consultation with medical and nursing staff. *Journal of Clinical Child Psychology,* 1975, *4,* 33–35. (b)

Drotar, D. Psychological consultation in the pediatric hospital. *Professional Psychology,* 1976, *8,* 72–80.

Drotar, D. Family-oriented intervention with the dying adolescent. *Journal of Pediatric Psychology,* 1977, *2,* 68–71.

Drotar, D. Adaptational problems of children and adolescents with cystic fibrosis. *Journal of Pediatric Psychology,* 1978, *3,* 45–50. (a)

Drotar, D. Training psychologists to consult with pediatricians: Problems and prospects. *Journal of Clinical Child Psychology,* 1978, *7,* 57–61. (b)

Drotar, D. Psychological perspectives in childhood chronic illness. *Journal of Pediatric Psychology,* 1981, *6,* 211–288.

Drotar, D., Baskiewicz, A., Irvin, N., Kennell, J., & Klaus, M. The adaptation of parents to the birth of an infant with a congenital malformation: A hypothetical model. *Pediatrics,* 1975, *56,* 710–717.

Drotar, D., Benjamin, P., Chwast, R., Litt, C., & Vajner, P. The role of the psychologist in pediatric outpatient and inpatient settings. In J. Tuma (Ed.), *Handbook for the practice of pediatric psychology*. New York: Wiley, 1981.

Drotar, D., Crawford, P., & Bush, M. The family context of childhood chronic illness: Implications for intervention. In M. Eisenberg (Ed.), *The impact of chronic disabling conditions on self and family: A life span perspective*. New York: Springer Press, 1984.

Drotar, D., & Doershuk, C. F. The interdisciplinary case conference: An aid to pediatric intervention with the dying adolescent. *Archives of the Foundation of Thanatology,* 1979, *7,* 79–96.

Drotar, D., Doershuk, C. F., Boat, T. F., Stern, R. C., Matthews, L., & Boyer, W. Psychosocial functioning of children with cystic fibrosis. *Pediatrics,* 1981, *67,* 338–343.

Drotar, D., & Ganofsky, M. A. Mental health intervention with children and adolescents with end-stage renal failure. *International Journal of Psychiatry in Medicine,* 1976, *7,* 181–194.

Drotar, D., Ganofsky, M. A., & Makker, S. P. Comprehensive management of severe emotional reactions of children with end-stage renal failure. *Dialysis and Transplantation,* 1979, *10,* 983–986.

Eissler, R. S., Freud, K., Kris, M., & Solnit, A. *Physical illness and handicap in childhood.* New Haven: Yale University Press, 1977.

Felner, R. D., Norton, P. L., Cowen, E. C., & Farber, S. S. A prevention program for children experiencing life crisis. *Professional Psychology,* 1981, *8,* 444–452.

Ford, A. B., Liske, R. E., & Ort, R. S. Reactions of physicians and medical students to chronic illness. *Journal of Chronic Disease,* 1963, *15,* 785–794.

Fox, R. *Essays in medical sociology*. New York: Wiley, 1975.

Fox, R. C., & Swazey, J. P. *The courage to fail: A social view of organ transplants and dialysis*. Chicago: University of Chicago Press, 1978.

Friedman, S., Chodoff, P., Mason, J., & Hamburg, D. Behavioral observations of parents anticipating the death of a child. *Pediatrics,* 1963, *32,* 610–625.

Friedson, E. *The profession of medicine.* New York: Dodd & Mead Co., 1970.

Freud, A. The role of bodily illness in the mental life of children. *Psychoanalytic Study of the Child,* 1952, *7,* 69–81.

Ganofsky, M. A. Advocacy in the schools. *Council of Nephrology Social Work Newsletter,* 1981, *6,* 3–4.

Ganofsky, M. A., Drotar, D., & Makker, S. P. Growing up with renal failure: Problems and perspectives. *Psychonephrology II.* New York: Plenum Press, 1983.

Geist, R. A. Onset of chronic illness in children and adolescents: Psychotherapeutic and consultative intervention. *American Journal of Orthopsychiatry,* 1979, *49,* 4–22.

Groves, J. E. Taking care of the hateful patient. *New England Journal of Medicine,* 1973, *283,* 883–887.

Haggerty, R., Roghmann, K. J., & Pless, I. B. *Child health and the community.* New York: Wiley, 1975.

Harter, S. The Perceived Competence Scale for Children. *Child Development,* 1982, *53,* 87–97.

Haynes, R., Taylor, D., & Sackett, D. (Eds.). *Compliance in health care.* Baltimore: Johns Hopkins University Press, 1979.

Heffron, W. A., Boomelaere, K., & Masters, R. Group discussion with the parents of leukemic children. *Pediatrics,* 1973, *52,* 831–837.

Heisler, A. B., & Friedman, S. B. Social and psychological considerations in chronic disease: With particular reference to the management of seizure disorders. *Journal of Pediatric Psychology,* 1981, *6,* 239–250.

Hobbs, N. *The futures of children.* San Francisco: Jossey Bass, 1975.

Hofmann, A. D., Becker, R. D., & Gabriel, H. P. *The hospitalized adolescent.* New York: Free Press, 1976.

Holroyd, J., & Guthrie, D. Stress in families with neuromuscular disease. *Journal of Clinical Psychology,* 1979, *35,* 735–739.

Illich, I. *Medical nemesis: The expropriation of health.* New York: Random House, 1976.

Iscoe, I. Conceptual barriers to training for the primary prevention of psychopathology. In J. M. Joffe & G. W. Albee (Eds.), *Prevention through political action and social change.* Hanover, NH: University Press of New England, 1981.

Johnson, M. R. Mental health interventions with medically ill children: A review of the literature 1970–1977. *Journal of Pediatric Psychology,* 1979, *4,* 147–163.

Kagen-Goodheart, L. Reentry: Living with childhood cancer. *American Journal of Orthopsychiatry,* 1977, *47,* 651–658.

Kanthor, H., Pless, I. B., Satterwhite, B., & Myers, G. Areas of responsibility in the health care of multiply handicapped children. *Pediatrics,* 1974, *54,* 779–786.

Katz, J., & Capron, A. M. *Catastrophic diseases: Who decides what?* New York: Russell Sage, 1975.

Koch, R., Azen, C. G., Friedman, B. A., & Williamson, M. L. Preliminary report on the effects of diet discontinuation in PKU. *Journal of Pediatrics,* 1982, *100,* 870–875.

Koocher, G. P. Pediatric cancer: Psychosocial problems and the high costs of helping. *Journal of Clinical Child Psychology,* 1980, *8,* 2–5.

Koocher, G. P., & O'Malley, J. E. *The Damocles Syndrome: Psychological consequences of surviving childhood cancer.* New York: McGraw-Hill, 1981.

Koocher, G. P., Sourkes, B. M., & Keane, W. M. Pediatric oncology consultation: A generalizable model for medical settings. *Professional Psychology,* 1979, *10,* 467–474.

Korsch, B. M., Fine, R. N., Grushkin, C. M., & Negrete, V. F. Experiences with children and families during extended hemodialysis and kidney transplantation. *Pediatric Clinics of North America,* 1971, *118,* 625–637.

Korsch, B. M., & Morris, M. Gaps in doctor-patient communication: Patients' response to medical advice. *New England Journal of Medicine,* 1968, *280,* 535–540.

Korsch, B. M., Negrete, V. F., Gardner, J. E., Weinstock, C. L., Mercer, A. S., Grushkin, C. M., & Fine, R. N. Kidney transplantation in children: Psychosocial follow up study on child and family. *Journal of Pediatrics,* 1973, *83,* 339–408.

Kucia, C., Drotar, D., Doershuk, C., Stern, R. C., Boat, T. F., & Matthews, L. Home observation of family interaction and childhood adjustment to cystic fibrosis. *Journal of Pediatric Psychology,* 1979, *4,* 479–489.

Lansky, S. B., & Gendel, M. Symbiotic regressive behavior patterns in childhood malignancy. *Clinical Pediatrics,* 1975, *17,* 133–138.

Lansky, S. B., Lowman, J. T., Vats, T., & Gyulay, J. E. School phobia in children with malignant neoplasms. *American Journal of Diseases of Children,* 1975, *129,* 42–46.

Lavigne, J. V., & Ryan, M. Psychological adjustment of siblings of children with chronic illness. *Pediatrics,* 1979, *63*(4), 616–627.

Lazarus, R., & Launier, R. Stress-related transactions between person and environment. In L. W. Pervin & M. Lewis (Eds.), *Perspectives in interactional psychology.* New York: Plenum, 1978.

Lightfoot, S. *Worlds apart: Relationships between families and schools.* New York: Basic Books, 1978.

Litman, T. J. The family as a basic unit in health and medical care: A social behavioral overview. *Social Science and Medicine,* 1974, *8,* 495–519.

Mattsson, A. Long-term physical illness in childhood: A challenge to psycho-social adaptation. *Pediatrics,* 1972, *50,* 801–811.

Mattsson, A., & Agle, D. P. Group therapy with parents of hemophiliacs: Therapeutic process and observations of parental adaptation to chronic illness in children. *Journal of the American Academy of Child Psychiatry,* 1972, *11,* 558–571.

McCollum, A. T., & Gibson, L. Family adaptation to the child with cystic fibrosis. *Journal of Pediatrics,* 1970, *77,* 574–578.

Mechanic, D. *Public expectations and health care.* New York: Wiley, 1972.

Mechanic, D. Social structure and personal adaptation: Some neglected dimensions. In G. V. Coelho, D. A. Hamburg, & J. T. Adams (Eds.), *Coping and adaptation.* New York: Basic Books, 1974.

Melamed, B. G., & Siegel, L. J. Reduction of anxiety in children facing hospitalization and surgery. *Journal of Consulting and Clinical Psychology,* 1975, *43,* 511–521.

Meyer, E., & Mendelson, M. Psychiatric consultations with patients on medical and surgical wards: Patterns and processes. *Psychiatry,* 1961, *24,* 197–205.

Minuchin, S., Rosman, B., & Baker, L. *Psychosomatic families.* Cambridge, MA: Harvard University Press, 1978.

Nagera, H. Children's reactions to hospitalization and illness. *Child Psychiatry and Human Development,* 1978, *9,* 3–19.

Nannis, E. D., Susman, E. J., Strope, B. E., Woodruff, P. J., Hersh, S. P., Levine, A. S.,

& Pizzo, P. A. Correlates of control in pediatric cancer patients and their families. *Journal of Pediatric Psychology,* 1982, *7,* 75–84.

Natterson, T. M., & Knudson, A. G. Observations concerning fear of death in fatally ill children and their mothers. *Psychosomatic Medicine,* 1960, *22,* 456–465.

Patenaude, A. F., Szymanski, L., & Rappaport, J. Psychological costs of bone marrow transplantation in children. *American Journal of Orthopsychiatry,* 1979, *49,* 409–422.

Peterson, L., Hartman, D. P., & Gelfand, D. M. Prevention of child behavior disorders: A lifestyle change for child psychologists. In P. O. Davidson & S. R. Davidson (Eds.), *Behavioral medicine: Changing health lifestyles.* New York: Brunner/Mazel, 1980.

Plank, E. M. *Working with children in hospitals.* Cleveland, Ohio: Western Reserve University Press, 1971.

Pless, I. B. Adjustment of the young chronically ill. In R. Simmons (Ed.), *Research in community and mental health.* Greenwich, Conn.: JAI Press, 1979.

Pless, I. B., & Douglas, I. W. B. Chronic illness in childhood: Part I. Epidemiological and clinical characteristics. *Pediatrics,* 1972, *47,* 405–414.

Pless, I. B., & Pinkerton, P. *Chronic childhood disorders: Promoting patterns of adjustment.* Chicago: Year Book Medical Publishers, 1975.

Pless, I. B., & Roghmann, K. J. Chronic illness and its consequences: Observations based on three epidemiologic surveys. *Journal of Pediatrics,* 1971, *79,* 351–359.

Pless, I. B., Roghmann, K., & Haggerty, R. F. Chronic illness, family functioning, and psychological adjustment: A model for the allocation of preventive mental health services. *International Journal of Epidemiology,* 1972, *1,* 271–277.

Power, P. W., & Dell Orto, A. E. (Eds.). *Role of the family in the rehabilitation of the physically disabled.* Baltimore: University Park Press, 1980.

Purcell, K., Brady, K., Chai, H., Muser, J., Mock, L., Gordon, N., & Means, J. The effect on asthma in children of experimental separation from the family. *Psychosomatic Medicine,* 1969, *31,* 144–164.

Purcell, K., Muser, J., Miklich, D., & Dietiker, K. E. A comparison of psychologic findings in variously defined asthmatic subgroups. *Journal of Psychosomatic Research,* 1969, *13,* 67–75.

Primack, W. A., & Greifer, I. Summer camp hemodialysis for children with chronic renal failure. *Pediatrics,* 1977, *60,* 46–50.

Raimbault, G., Cachin, O., Limal, J. M., Elincheff, C., & Rappaport, L. Aspects of communication between patients and doctors: An analysis of the discourse in medical interviews. *Pediatrics,* 1975, *55,* 401–405.

Roberts, M. C., Beidleman, W. B., & Wurtele, S. Children's perceptions of medical and psychological disorders in their peers. *Journal of Clinical Child Psychology,* 1981, *10,* 76–78.

Schowalter, J. E. The utilization of child psychiatry on a pediatric adolescent ward. *Journal of the American Academy of Child Psychiatry,* 1971, *10,* 684–699.

Schowalter, J. E. Psychological reactions to physical illness and hospitalization in adolescence. *Journal of the American Academy of Child Psychiatry,* 1977, *16,* 500–516.

Simeonsson, R., Buckley, L., & Monson, L. Conceptions of illness in hospitalized children. *Journal of Pediatric Psychology,* 1979, *4,* 77–81.

Spencer, R. F. Incidence of social and psychiatric problems in a group of hemophiliac patients. *North Carolina Medical Journal,* 1968, *29,* 332–336.

Spinetta, J. J., & Maloney, L. J. Death anxiety in the outpatient leukemic child. *Pediatrics,* 1975, *56,* 1034–1037.

Spinetta, J. J., & Maloney, L. J. The child with cancer: Patterns of communication and denial. *Journal of Consulting and Clinical Psychology,* 1978, *46,* 540–541.

Spinetta, J. J., Swarner, J. A., & Sheposh, J. P. Effective parental coping following the death of a child from cancer. *Journal of Pediatric Psychology,* 1981, *6,* 251–264.

Steinhauer, P. D., Muskin, D. N., & Rae-Grant, Q. Psychological aspects of chronic illness. *Pediatric Clinics of North America,* 1974, *21,* 825–840.

Sterns, S. Self-destructive behavior in young patients with diabetes mellitus. *Diabetes,* 1959, *8,* 379–385.

Tavormina, J. B., Kastner, L. S., Slater, P. M., & Watt, S. L. Chronically ill children—A psychologically and emotionally deviant population? *Journal of Abnormal Child Psychology,* 1976, *4,* 99–110.

Tefft, B. M., & Simeonsson, R. J. Psychology and the creation of health care settings. *Professional Psychology,* 1979, *10,* 558–570.

Tew, B. J., & Lawrence, K. M. Mothers, brothers and sisters of patients with spina bifida. *Developmental Medicine and Child Neurology,* 1973, *15,* Supp. 29, 69–76.

Turk, J. Impact of cystic fibrosis on family functioning. *Pediatrics,* 1967, *34,* 67–71.

Vance, J. C., Fazan, L. E., Satterwhite, B., & Pless, I. B. Effects of nephrotic syndrome on the family: A controlled study. *Pediatrics,* 1980, *65,* 948–955.

Vernon, D. T. A., Foley, J. M., Sipowicz, R. R., & Schulman, J. L. *Psychological responses of children to hospitalization and illness.* Springfield, IL: Charles C. Thomas, 1965.

Weinberg, S. Suicidal intent in adolescence: A hypothesis about the role of physical illness. *Journal of Pediatrics,* 1970, *77,* 579–586.

Whitt, J. K., Dykstra, W., & Taylor, C. A. Children's conceptions of illness and cognitive development. *Clinical Pediatrics,* 1979, *18,* 327–339.

Zeitlin, S. Assessing coping behavior. *American Journal of Orthopsychiatry,* 1980, *50,* 139–144.

REFERENCE NOTES

1. Mohr, R. *Paradigms in the clinical psychology of chronic illness.* Paper presented at the Annual Meeting of the American Psychological Association, Washington, D.C., September, 1977.
2. Drotar, D., & Chwast, R. *Family-oriented intervention in chronic illness.* Paper presented at the Annual Meeting of Ohio Psychological Association, Cleveland, 1978.
3. Cunningham, C., Betsa, N., & Gross, S. *Sibling groups: Interaction with siblings of oncology patients.* Unpublished manuscript. Case Western University School of Medicine, 1980.
4. Moise, J. *Psychosocial adjustment of children and adolescents with sickle cell anemia.* Unpublished master's thesis. Case Western Reserve University, 1980.
5. Harkavy, J., Johnson, S. B., Silverstein, J., Spillar, R., McCallum, M., & Rosenbloom, A. *Who learns what at diabetes summer camp.* Paper presented at the Annual Meeting of the American Psychological Association, Washington, D.C., August, 1982.

CHAPTER 9

Prevention of Anxiety and Pain

Due to Medical and Dental Procedures

LIZETTE PETERSON AND MARTHA BROWNLEE-DUFFECK

This chapter will deal with preventing children's distress in dental settings, physician's offices, during medical treatment visits and in surgical suites. For the purposes of discussion here, those encounters with individuals seeking to intervene upon children physically (clean their teeth, inoculate them, give them an enema, remove their tonsils) will be referred to as "stressful medical experiences," rather than labeling dental, clinic, hospital, or outpatient surgery settings separately. Commonalities and differences in these varied settings will be discussed as they become relevant.

Because this chapter concerns preventing distress rather than simply studying methods of distress prevention or implementing prevention programs which may or may not actually prevent distress, a dual emphasis is presented here. Individuals interested in the application of preventive techniques require emphasis on reported treatment technology, including a complete description of what was done, what staff, equipment, and temporal demands were, and how effective the treatment was. Individuals with a research perspective require emphasis which additionally details how, when, and where the treatment impact was measured, how treatment effects were separated from uncontrolled variables, and what level of significant effects was achieved. While all of these considerations cannot be completely described for every reported preventive technique, this chapter attempts to present a balanced concern for each perspective.

For many years, the relationship between research and widespread implementation of preventive techniques for children in medical settings was like an open marriage, with each member independently pursuing a separate set of experiences and goals. As will be shown later, this has resulted in an unfortunate bifurcation of interests, needs, and activities and a weakening of the relationship until it sometimes scarcely exists at all. Initially, researchers made contributions to actual program implementation by demonstrating that *any* technique could effectively prevent distress in high risk children scheduled for medical and dental procedures because the idea of prevention per se had not yet been accepted in this area. Similarly, an individual implementing a program could choose from a variety of techniques, since the early studies utilized many techniques which had little independent research support (for example, Prugh, Staub, Sands, Kirschbaum, & Lenihan, 1953). This is no longer the case, however. Current research can now make excellent contributions to actual program implementation by designing low cost, easy to administer, effective programs acceptable to the large number of people making the policy decisions, including hospital and clinic administrators, surgeons, physicians, dentists, nurses, and child life workers. This kind of research emphasis, however, has rarely emerged. Individuals interested in implementing findings could choose from the increasing number of research reports outlining effective preventive procedures. However, recent surveys (Azarnoff & Woody, 1981; Peterson & Ridley-Johnson, 1980) suggest that procedures with strong research support (for instance, film modeling, training coping techniques) are used far less often than methods having equivocal or no support (such as hospital tours, booklets), and the majority of major hospitals employ no preventive programs at all. Indeed, some preventive programs previously offered are now closing (Azarnoff, 1982), partially due to a lack of evaluation support for their effectiveness with children.

These problems do not constitute irreconcilable differences between practitioners and researchers, however. Both groups have much to teach one another concerning what has been learned in the last two decades. Researchers need to relearn how to ask questions which result both in increased academic understanding and increased application of their findings. Individuals interested in implementing preventive programs need to become more familiar with the research literature, both to aid in designing their own programs and evaluating existing programs, and to use when competing for rapidly diminishing social service funds and support staff. This strengthening of the relationship between research and application has already begun.

RESEARCH AND APPLICATION: THE BACKGROUND

In the mid-1930s, there were perhaps two prevention articles a year devoted to the distress experienced by hospitalized children and by the mid-1970s, over 500 articles existed in this area (Azarnoff, 1976). Furthermore, there has been no more rapid growth of the field than that experienced in the last five years. This chapter will draw from those reports of programs which explicitly set out to prevent rather than remediate already existing distress.

The first articles published in this area simply described the problems experienced by hospitalized children (raising concern that long-term harm and transient distress might result from hospitalization) without demonstrating concrete ways to eliminate that distress (for example, Beverly, 1936; Jackson, 1942). However, these descriptive articles were followed by articles which noted that some of the previously experienced distress could be prevented by appropriate in-hospital care (Jensen, 1955) and preparation (Prugh et al., 1953). In the recent past there has been a widespread consensus that preventive preparation for most medical and dental procedures should be a goal for mental health intervention (Ramirez-Johnson,

1979), and an integral component of "A Bill of Rights for Children in Medical Settings" (Seagull, 1978). It has been recommended by the Association for Care of Children in Hospitals and by the American Academy of Pediatrics (Azarnoff & Woody, 1981). An exception to this widespread belief may be based upon studies which suggest that adults who utilize repressive or denying forms of coping may be made more anxious by preparation (see Shipley, Butt, & Horowitz, 1979). Although no definitive data exist for children, some clinicians may have come full circle in believing that at least some children should not be prepared for certain procedures (Melamed, Robbins, & Fernandez, 1982). This is one of several paradoxes which will be addressed.

This chapter will begin by briefly looking at some of the first prevention studies in the area and then follow the literature through its early phases in the late 1950s and 1960s, to the development of some classic techniques in the 1970s, and to the complex and multidimensional research currently being performed. There are three kinds of literature in this field. First, there are a small number of rigorous empirical studies which utilize appropriate experimental design and measurement (for example, appropriate control groups, random assignment to groups, matching experimental groups for relevant subject characteristics and medical procedures, blind observers, reliability data gathered, careful statistical control for inflating alpha). Second, there are a larger number of quasi-experiments which report some useful data in spite of technical flaws, and third, several "I did it and it works great" articles which describe specific technologies without offering any data to support their efficacy. The absence of empirical proof of preventive effectiveness in most of the literature is a problem. An ineffectual procedure could, at worst, sensitize children patients and actually intensify their distress. At best, an ineffectual procedure would have no impact, but even that is costly as hospitals are likely to conclude that prevention procedures used were ineffective, thus limiting the opportunity for future effective endeavors. In a field still trying to prove itself to hospital administrators, physicians, and nursing staffs, the results of a poor program can extend beyond a single hospital. Routine evaluation of programs should become the rule rather than the exception, to ensure the best possible care for children and to aid in program continuation. As funds for social services continue to decrease, programs which can demonstrate their utility have a better chance for survival.

Nevertheless, the few empirical studies, quasi-experiments, and simple descriptions of programs currently make up the "patchwork quilt" data base, which must be utilized to form conclusions and recommendations concerning tomorrow's hospitalized children. The data base received its strongest roots in the early 1950s as concerned professionals in the hospital system attempted preventive interventions.

The Early Studies

Early estimates suggested that the majority of hospitalized children experienced mild distress and many experienced severe emotional reactions (Jessner, Blom, & Waldfogel, 1952). Prugh et al. (1953) reported that 92% of the children they observed experienced moderate or severe behavior problems following surgery. They assessed the impact of a preventive procedure which was remarkably innovative for its time and included multiple components, such as establishing a trusting relationship between nurse and child, creating a play program for the children, daily visitations for parents, and a clearer articulation of the parents' role in caring for the child. Prugh et al. found children in the experimental groups to experience less distress during and following hospitalization than children receiving routine care.

The emphasis on the role of the parents was followed up by Skipper and Leonard, who demonstrated that giving the parents of young surgical patients nursing support and a full explanation of what to expect resulted in diminished distress for both the parents (Skipper, Leonard, & Rhymes, 1968) and the children (Skipper & Leonard, 1968). The emphasis on including parents in the presurgical preparation program has only recently been rediscovered as an important tool in preparing children for medical procedures. Other earlier studies utilized play therapy (Impallaria, 1955), group therapy (Cofer & Nir, 1975), procedural information (Chapman, 1970), and puppet therapy (Cassell, 1965) to provide children with information concerning what to expect and with an emotional release for anxiety feelings about surgical procedures. Other investigators utilized behavioral techniques such as desensitization for dental treatment (Gale & Ayer, 1969) and behavioral rehearsal and imagery for child dental patients (Ayer, 1973). Although there were some methodological shortcomings in this literature which have been discussed elsewhere (for example, Melamed & Siegel, 1975; Siegel, 1976), for the most part these studies also provided convincing evidence for the efficacy of these procedures. By the mid-1970s, there was an air of optimism among prevention researchers working with children. At this point, three fairly different approaches became the focus of attention: (1) film modeling, (2) sensory information, and (3) stress point intervention. The next section reviews the process of replication and refinement used in work on film modeling, and to a lesser degree, on sensory information and stress point intervention.

Film Modeling.

Several studies which demonstrate the utility of film models have been reviewed in more detail elsewhere (Elkins & Roberts, 1983; Melamed, Robbins & Fernandez, 1982; Siegel, 1976), but deserve a brief summary here. Since its early use with childhood phobias (Bandura, 1969), use of a peer model has offered promise for reducing distress in children. Vernon and Bailey (1974), for example, noted that children who viewed a peer model experienced a less distressing anesthesia induction than children without such preparation. Melamed and Siegel (1975), in an often cited investigation, clearly established that viewing a film of a young boy coping with hospitalization and minor surgery resulted in diminished anxiety ratings, less physiological distress prior to surgery and postoperatively, and fewer behavior problems after hospitalization. Melamed, Hawes, Heiby, and Glick (1975) reported similar findings for young dental patients. Children who observed a peer model were slightly more cooperative and less upset than they had been during the pretreatment dental exam, whereas children observing a control film were much more distressed and uncooperative during restoration. Studies like these established film modeling as a technique that was effective, easy to apply, and theoretically integrated with behavior therapy.

Several subsequent studies have added to the knowledge base of preventive film modeling. For example, Melamed, Meyer, Gee, and Soule (1976) assessed the influence of time and length of preparation upon children's anxiety and concluded that older children who viewed the modeling film one week before hospitalization had fewer behavior problems after their hospital experience than older children who viewed a modeling film the day of admission. On the other hand, young children who viewed the film a week before surgery had higher physiological arousal than young children who viewed the film the day of admission. This study also suggested that children benefited more if the race of the child viewing the film was the same as the child model. However, Melamed, Yurcheson, Fleece, Hutcherson, and Hawes (1978) subsequently demonstrated that when dental patients viewed a seven year old black model, white children benefited more from the experience than black children. They also suggested that children with previous dental experience benefited more from a detailed peer modeling preparation. Since some later studies (for instance, Chertok & Bornstein, 1979; Ginther & Roberts, 1982; Klorman, Hilpert, Michael, LaGana, & Sveen, 1980; Melamed & Siegel, 1980) have demonstrated that film modeling is often relatively ineffective with child dental patients and surgery patients who have had previous experience, the issue of previous experience will be considered later in more detail.

Finally, the method used in presenting a model has been analyzed. Past research has utilized puppets, characters in a book, audiotape, videotape, films, and live models. Peterson, Schultheis, Ridley-Johnson, Miller, and Tracy (1984) compared (1) a commercial film previously shown to be successful by Melamed and Siegel (1975), (2) a videotape custom-made for a local hospital, which presented the correct sequence of events and the environment to which the children would be exposed, and (3) a puppet model who outlined its feelings and appraisals of hospital relevant material and who interacted with three-dimensional medical instruments. The comparison demonstrated that all three techniques produced equivalent decreases in anxiety, behavior problems, and parental distress when compared with the hospital routine of preoperative education by the physician, anesthesiologist, and nursing staff prior to young children's surgery. Thus, there have been continuing efforts to assess and refine the use of film models to prevent distress in children.

Sensory Information.

A second successful method of preparation, which has received far less experimental attention with children, is the use of sensory information. This term is most typically associated with Jean Johnson and was described as a method of reducing distress during cast removal by Johnson, Kirchhoff, and Endress (1975). In this study, Johnson and her colleagues advanced the hypothesis that any discrepancy between expected and experienced physical sensations (visual, auditory, taste, smell) during a stressful procedure would result in distress. Children six to 11 years old heard either no information, regular procedural information, or sensory information. Children who heard the sensory information received lower observational distress ratings than children in the other two groups. It is likely that many programs which purport to use simple information or modeling actually employ sensory information by having the narrator or the child model describe and relabel sensations as they occur (for example, "This shot will feel like a stick and will ache for a moment, but will then feel better"). Siegel and Peterson (1980, 1981) recently demonstrated that sensory information is an effective means of decreasing disruptiveness and distress in preschool dental patients. The full usefulness of this technique has not been tested, however. It deserves research consideration in its own right as well as in combination with other procedures like modeling.

Stress Point Preparation.

In a third method of preventing distress, Wolfer and Visintainer (1975) analyzed the effects of stress point preparation, that is, having a famililar nurse present to provide procedural and sensory information, information about appropriate behavior, and supportive care just prior to and during major stress points. Such stress points might include blood tests, introduction to the pediatric ward, preoperative injections, and anesthesia induction. Children receiving such supportive care showed less behavioral upset, more cooperation, and a tendency toward greater ease of fluid intake and postsurgical voiding than children receiving routine nursing care. A later study (Wolfer & Visintainer, 1979) which combined the use of at-home, parent-delivered information preparation with supportive nursing care again supported the premise that both parents and children benefited from stress point nursing care.

In their most recent work, Wolfer and Visintainer (Note 1) further noted that stress point nursing preparation contains information and support which results in diminished distress by simultaneously reducing uncertainty, increasing perceived control, and producing more positive stress appraisal. Their study utilized stress point preparation which, in contrast to preparing children several weeks in advance, was delivered to the children and their parents shortly before the potentially stressful procedures. Children receiving major surgeries (cardiac, renal, and orthopedic) received either stress point preparation, supportive care without stress point preparation, or routine nursing care. The program demonstrated impressive results, with children in the stress point preparation group showing better response to hospitalization and better recovery on 19 of 21 outcome variables ranging from ratings of behavioral distress indices to number of postoperative complications. This type of prevention program can have dramatic effects on hospitalized children's distress, but such a program requires much staff time and cooperation from the nursing service and administration. This may explain why few other researchers have investigated this potentially powerful technique, although some hospitals do utilize such procedures or routinely assign a nurse with no duties other than stress point preparation and support (Robison, 1979). In fact, the extent and difficulty of implementing any one of these three classical treatment techniques has not been reported, and studies assessing the cost-benefit ratio of procedures continue to lag behind research demonstrating treatment efficacy.

This brief review of preventive techniques from the last decade gives a sampling of the research endeavors which have led to the current questions and the research methods used in response. It also gives the reader a perspective on the base upon which the later applied programs have been established. In the following section, some research topics relevant to the current prevention state of the art are described.

AREAS REQUIRING RESEARCH AND APPLIED EMPHASIS

Those studies completed in the mid to late 1970s, which examined preventive techniques in a rigorous, scientific manner, produced some results which are now regarded as classical. They not only demonstrated the utility of techniques such as modeling and sensory information, but also suggested a variety of dimensions which could be considered in future research. These dimensions included the exploration of new preparation techniques and their comparison to classic methods. Other research has considered the expansion of prevention programs to other populations and types of medical procedures, including the extension of preventive preparation beyond at-risk children currently scheduled for medical procedures to population-wide prevention with well children receiving preparation materials. An explicit emphasis on the role and rights of nonpatient family members has served as a new direction for preventive applications and research. A renewed interest in the maintenance of treatment effects also promises to extend the impact of preventive treatment. Finally, a focus on child variables such as age, previous experience, and individual coping style has emerged and expanded the dimensions of prevention. Each of these dimensions has received some recent research consideration and will be examined briefly as they relate to prevention of distress in medical settings.

Preparation Techniques

Expressive Therapy.

There are growing number of studies which advocate expressive therapy both before and after medical procedures to inform the child about what to expect and to prevent later dysfunction. Lewis (1978), for example, described several case histories of children suffering from leukemia, heart disease, and brain tumors who benefited from creative writing exercises. Levinson and Ousterhout (1980) described the use of art therapy and play therapy for child burn victims, advocating that children be introduced to IVs, catheters, and the process of doing skin grafts on dolls prior to actually experiencing the procedures. There are many similar descriptions of the use of art therapy (Crowl, 1980) and play therapy for children experiencing surgery (Chan, 1980) or general hospitalization (Harvey, 1980). Unfortunately, the vast majority of these papers report no data supporting their suggestions for the utility of these procedures. The few studies which have attempted to gather data frequently do not support the utility of these practices and this causes some concern about their apparent increasing application. Williams (1980), in one such study, compared the delivery of information in the form of a story versus the story plus play therapy. She found that grade school children who had received the story alone and children who received both the story and play therapy failed to differ on observed global mood scale ratings. Both treatment groups were, however, rated as less upset than those receiving no treatment.

Writing, art, and play therapy are frequently advocated as preventive techniques which can "enhance a sense of mastery, foster adaptive behavior, and increase cooperation with medical treatment" (Adams, 1976, p. 416). Play therapy has been suggested as the preventive treatment of choice for preschool children (Erickson, 1958; Williams, 1980). There are components of play therapy which past research suggests are beneficial in other theoretical orientations. For example, the simple provision of information is likely to be helpful (Chapman, Loeb, & Gibbons, 1956), and exposure to medical instruments may result in desensitization, a successful method of reducing medical fears (Melamed & Siegel, 1980). Play therapy may even utilize some elements of behavioral rehearsal, a technique which shows much promise for reducing distress in children facing medical procedures (Ayer, 1973; Chertok & Bornstein, 1979). However, being encouraged to experience and express negative emotion in such encounters as "kill the doctor" (Levinson & Ousterhout, 1980) may develop or maintain feelings that are not conducive to quick recovery and low levels of anxiety. Many reports on play therapy programs comment openly on the use of medical equipment like syringes in extremely aggressive play with dolls (Chan, 1980) or even other children (Adams, 1976). Becker (1972) expresses concern that many of the play therapy exercises to alleviate medical fears may actually enhance these fears. It would appear important for future research to rigorously examine the impact of play therapy on children's preparation for medical procedures.

Hypnosis.

Hypnosis is another technology which has been reported to be useful in treating children's medical distress (see reviews by Gardner, 1980, and Olness, 1981), and has been suggested as effective for habit disorders such as nailbiting and enuresis, pain management with migraine headaches and burns, chronic diseases such as asthma and hemophilia, learning disorders, and the elimination of muscular tics and warts (Olness, 1981). Unfortunately, like play therapy, there are many case history and anecdotal reports of the efficacy of hypnosis (Ambrose, 1968; Bernstein, 1965; LaBaw, Holton, Tewell, & Eccles, 1975; Moore, 1981; Olness, 1977), and far fewer well documented studies which empirically demonstrate the use of hypnosis as an effective preventive preparation agent. However, this is an area of advancement, including a rapidly increasing empirical base. For example, two of the first empirically documented programs for the use of hypnosis with leukemic children were recently described (Hodel, O'Grady, & Steffen, Note 2; Katz, Kellerman, & Ellenberg, Note 3). It is anticipated that the next few years will see additional support for the use of hypnosis as an effective preventive technology.

Puppet Therapy.

Puppet therapy also appears to have promise, particularly for younger children. Many recent studies advocate the use of puppet therapy or "participatory puppet therapy'' with no empirical data supporting their programs (Kelfer & Demers, 1980). However, there are some studies which have documented the utility of preparing children in this manner. Cassell (1965) utilized a puppet show in which children interacted with medical equipment prior to the children's receiving cardiac catheterization. Children receiving this treatment were less anxious and more cooperative than a group of nonprepared children. Similarly, Johnson and Stockdale (1975) demonstrated that four to eight year old surgery patients who viewed a hospital-related puppet show had lower palmar sweat readings (the only dependent variable measured) directly following the puppet show and after surgery than those in a control group. However, these authors reported that the puppet show ran nine to 20 minutes, depending upon the number of questions the children asked and the amount of time spent with the medical equipment. Thus, in both of these studies, the children received more than simple information from the puppet. In a previously noted study which limited the puppet preparation to the presentation of information and modeling, Peterson et al. (1984) demonstrated that a puppet working with real medical equipment was as successful at alleviating distress in young children (average age four and one-half years) receiving minor elective surgery as a locally produced or commercially available modeling film. Utilizing the puppet as a model is a flexible, low cost technique which deserves future research consideration. It is likely that successful puppet procedures have several active components worth investigating.

Instructions, Feedback, and Rewards.

The use of simple instructions, feedback, and reinforcers may have similar cost-effective utility in stressful situations which require the child to perform cooperatively for a short period of time. Hedberg and Schlong (1973), for example, reported that simply instructing children who were to receive inoculations that they were to remain on their feet and refrain from any ''arguing or fussing'' until they were out of the clinical area eliminated any negative reactions. A small proportion ($n = 10$ or about 2%) of the control children receiving neutral instructions fainted, and an equal number experienced problems like enuresis, vomiting, and severe crying. Stokes and Kennedy (1980) noted that explaining procedures and suggesting appropriate behavior in combination with trinket reinforcers for cooperative behavior resulted in decreased disruptive responses and increased cooperation in child dental patients. Similarly, Melamed, Bennett, Jerrell, Ross, Bush, Hill, Courts, and Ronk (Note 4) demonstrated that reinforcing feedback (for example, ''Great, you did that really well'') or using reinforcement plus negative feedback (''You are being bad again'') resulted in more cooperative responding in young dental patients compared to a group receiving only negative feedback. Children receiving punishment were even less cooperative than a group receiving no feedback and the punished children also had higher self-reports of fearfulness. In a naturalistic observation study, Weinstein, Getz, Ratener, and Domoto (1982a, 1982b) similarly found that dentists who used negative feedback in the form of coercion or criticism engendered more fearful behavior than dentists using positive or neutral feedback. Thus, feedback and reinforcement procedures seem to be promising techniques for future intervention. However, the use of feedback or reinforcement alone suggests that the treatment agent believes that the child is capable of coping effectively with the stressful encounter and requires only the appropriate instruction and motivation. While this may be a reasonable assumption for some dental restorations and minor medical procedures such as injections, it may not be reasonable for procedures which last for longer periods of time or are more painful or frightening. In such situations, some amplification of the child's natural ability to cope may be needed.

Self-Control or Coping Techniques.

Peterson and Shigetomi (1981) described a set of procedures designed to provide children with additional coping techniques. These techniques were drawn from past research on nonhospitalized individuals and included self-instruction (Meichenbaum & Goodman, 1971), cue controlled relaxation (Russell & Sipich, 1974), and the use of vivid mental imagery (Lazarus & Abramovitz, 1962). These components were selected because they utilized techniques which had appeared in children who coped well with medical procedures. The components also relied on different physical strategies for coping (verbal self-instruction versus muscular relaxation versus visual imagery), thus yielding a greater chance for a match with the child's natural inclination for coping.

For those interested in program implementation, the utility of adding coping skills training to existing technology may not have been clear. Some individuals have suggested that the established technique of film modeling, for example, may have its effect because it (1) delivers information about appropriate patient behavior, (2) desensitizes children to medical equipment and procedures, or (3) demonstrates effective coping techniques (Melamed, Klingman, & Siegel, 1983). If modeling effects were derived from a demonstration of effective coping techniques, it would not be cost-effective to add coping technique training to the well-established modeling technique. Peterson and Shigetomi (1981) therefore examined the extent to which coping technique instruction actually resulted in increased benefit to film modeling.

Children who were to experience elective surgery and their parents thus received one of the following treatment conditions: (1) information from a puppet show, (2) a puppet show plus a successful modeling film (''Ethan Has An Operation,'' the film first demonstrated to be effective by Melamed and Siegel, 1975), (3) a puppet show plus coping skills, and (4) a puppet show, film and coping skills. Parental involvement in the practice and use of the coping skills was urged. When the children returned a few days later for their surgeries, those children receiving the coping skills training were rated as being less anxious and more cooperative than the other groups of children, both before and after surgery. They also showed a nonsignificant trend toward voiding sooner and eating more food following surgery. Their parents likewise rated themselves as feeling less anxious and more competent before and after surgery. These parents also rated the hospital experience more favorably two weeks after hospitalization.

A little more detail not included in the research report by Peterson and Shigetomi (1981) may help to illustrate the flexibility of this kind of coping skills training. As Peterson noted in the original report of this study (1978), careful measures of the amount of practice and use of the techniques were gathered. Parents indicated that they practiced each technique an average of 6.21 times (range 0–21) prior to hospitalization and that they used the self-instruction technique an average of 2.21 times (range 0–10), the relaxation technique an average of 1.73 times (range 0–10), and the imaginal distraction technique an average of 1.50 times (range 0–10). Parents noted that their children could become moderately relaxed using the relaxation technique ($\bar{X}$ = 2.93 on a 1 "not relaxed" to 5 "very relaxed" scale) and that they could imagine the imaginal distraction scene quite clearly ($\bar{X}$ = 3.50 on a 1 "not clear at all" to 5 "very clear" scale). Although only three of the 27 parents who employed the techniques used one technique to the exclusion of the others, the majority of parents still had clear preferences for particular techniques. When asked which technique their child preferred, 11 parents indicated relaxation, 11 indicated imagination and six indicated self-instruction. Thus, the provision of explicit coping skills training appears to add to the benefits of information or information plus a filmed model.

Zastowny, Kirschenbaum, and Meng (Note 5) provided another well-controlled demonstration of the benefits of coping skills training beyond provision of information or simple anxiety reduction. They prepared three groups of elective child surgery patients and their parents using information from a filmed puppet model. The first group of parents was additionally instructed to spend extra time in one-to-one contact with the child the week before surgery, to control for increased contact alone. A second group of parents received both the film and additional anxiety reduction techniques (Melzack, 1973) for use in the hospital setting to enable them to maintain a confident and relaxed stance with their child. This second group was also asked to spend more time than usual with their child. A third group of parents acquired some coping techniques based upon Melzack's (1973) conceptualizations of stress and Meichenbaum's (1975) stress inoculation procedures. Parents were assigned as "coping coaches" to assist their children in deep breathing and relaxation while engaging in four phases of coping from preparing for stress, and confronting and dealing with stress and emotions to self-reinforcement for successful coping. They received a practice booklet to assist in their training. Most families then received about 30 minutes of individualized instruction. While children were present during these treatments, the programs were directed toward the parents.

Parents who both viewed the film and received either anxiety reduction training or coping skills training reported being less stressed prior to and following hospitalization. However, only the children whose parents received coping skills training demonstrated fewer maladaptive responses before, during, and after hospitalization.

The use of coping techniques such as relaxation and self-instruction have similarly been demonstrated to enable preschoolers with no prior experience (Siegel & Peterson, 1980, 1981) and school-age children with prior experience (Nocella & Kaplan, 1982) to cope with dental procedures effectively. These techniques, which can be applied quite flexibly, deserve additional future research.

Summary.

As can be seen from this brief review, the literature of the past few years has suggested a variety of techniques which deserve future attention. Some of the techniques, such as play therapy preparation, are advocated and being used in the absence of empirical data supporting their efficacy. Other techniques such as hypnosis, puppet therapy, and reinforcement-feedback instruction have limited data to demonstrate their utility, but these procedures have not received sufficient experimental attention to document their uses and limitations in applied settings. Finally, techniques such as coping skills training for the parent-child dyad have not only received empirical confirmation of their benefits, but have also been shown to supplement the benefits of already successful techniques. In addition to such classical techniques as the provision of procedural information, film modeling, sensory information, and stress point preparation, the techniques just described may add to the armamentarium of the preventionist seeking to expand the uses of preventive preparation to new populations and new levels of prevention.

Implementation of Research Results

It is unfortunate that so little research has focused upon ways to select an appropriate treatment program for a given setting, but some suggestions can be drawn from past research. The first consideration should be defining what the program is designed to prevent—what level of distress children are currently manifesting, how long it lasts, and what benefits (especially those which the policy makers will attend to) are likely to accrue from prevention. Later, it will be argued in more detail that selecting a particular target system can be very useful, both in terms of conducting methodologically accurate research as well as implementing a program which will be maintained. For example, demonstrating that children who use a given technique respond with more cooperative behavior and fewer complications during anesthesia induction will not only benefit the children, but may also gain the support of the operating room nurse, the anesthesiologist, and the physician. Thus, targeting increased cooperative behavior and decreased crying during anesthesia induction would seem to be a reasonable first step in planning a prevention program to be maintained by hospital staff.

Second, the implementer has to analyze what the system will accept in selecting a program (Peterson, Hartmann, & Gelfand, 1980). Individuals interested in application must be concerned with utilizing available resources far more often than researchers, who may have special funding. Rather than selecting a treatment of convenience, however, the program developer would do better to select a technique which has been demonstrated to produce results, yet which is cost-effective. The treatment of choice may depend upon a variety of factors, including the available resources. For example, if a small hospital wanted to begin a presurgical preparation program and had an enthusiastic staff but no equipment or other niceties, a treatment program utilizing a puppet model could be developed (or even better, utilizing a script requested from a program demonstrated to be successful). If the staff were willing to get some training in coping skills instruction, this component could be inexpensively added to the program. Supportive care might also be applied if the staff's enthusiasm extended to more than a single preparative endeavor.

In contrast, if a hospital preparation program was desired but the staff was over-scheduled and had little desire to participate in a preventive program, a more "canned" approach could be adopted. The use of a modeling film combined with a group tour of the hospital might be a way to utilize minimal staff time and yet present the requisite information. In some cases, an untrained volunteer who would refer questions to appropriate experts might present the program.

A third concern might be the method of evaluating the program's effectiveness. Evaluation may be important to obtain and continue support for the program, as well as to insure that the treatment selected actually impacts the targeted goal. It is not inconceivable that a program might frighten a child or simply have no effect, and in either case changes in the program would be vital. Consumer satisfaction measures are helpful but most policy makers are aware that no matter what is offered, consumers are likely to rate any program positively. Measures of decreased parent and child complaints to the nursing staff, decreased medication requests, and increased fluid consumption may be gathered inexpensively from medical records and may be very useful. Obtaining global ratings from the nursing staff on child distress and behaviors as checked from a prepared list might also be important in such a program. It is not suggested here that rigorous research methods are necessary, but that there must be some way of judging program effectiveness. In the same manner as program selection, the method of informal evaluation will probably be determined based on the targeted program goals and the resources available. It is important that future attention be given to these processes—targeting a prevention goal, selecting a treatment program, and evaluating the program, including the different utilities of different forms of evaluation. In addition, research may focus upon other aspects of prevention which can be useful for future application, including methods of extending prevention to other medical and nonmedical populations.

Populations

The majority of work in preventive preparation has been accomplished either with patients requiring dental examination and restorative treatment (Ginther & Roberts, 1982; Klorman et al., 1980; Machen & Johnson, 1974; Melamed et al., 1975; Melamed, Weinstein, Hawes, & Katin-Borland, 1975; Melamed et al., 1978; Siegel & Peterson, 1980, 1981), or with children requiring minor surgeries such as tonsillectomy, adenoidectomy, myringotomy, oral tumor removal, hernia repair, or genital-urinary tract repair (Burstein & Meichenbaum, 1979; Melamed et al., 1976; Melamed & Siegel, 1975; Peterson & Shigetomi, 1981; Peterson et al., 1984; Wolfer & Visintainer, 1975, 1979). There has also been occasional preparation for patients undergoing cast removal (Johnson et al., 1975) or cardiac catheterization (Cassell, 1965). These populations are among those frequently receiving elective medical procedures and thus have one of the highest baserates for being at risk. Moreover, they are among the most accessible subjects for researchers interested in prevention. However, there are many other populations receiving medical procedures which could benefit from preparation based upon empirical findings.

Any child who is brought to an emergency room can be subject to preventable anxiety and pain, but no interventions with child accident victims have been empirically documented. Nor are there many studies of techniques to prepare children for medical admittance to the hospital where surgery is not required. Children whose diseases may result in disfigurement may be particularly at risk for psychological disturbances (Friedrich, 1977). Yet, while there are reports which discuss methods of preparing children undergoing dermatologic surgery (Gabriel, 1977), or adjusting to severe burns (Knudson-Cooper, 1981), for example, there has been little empirical validation.

Children who are subject to very painful interventions also present an at-risk population. Few of the procedures directed at preparing children for medical procedures have focused upon methods for relieving pain (hypnosis and the coping skills training just described are exceptions), and fewer studies have focused upon a population where pain is a large portion of the stress presented. One example of such a population might include children who have been seriously burned. Such children are in severe pain almost constantly (Savedra, 1977) and yet, because of the necessity of frequent fluid consumption and concerns about pneumonia, sedation must be minimized. Although mortality from burns in children is decreasing, hundreds of children per year are treated for severe burns (Knudson-Cooper, 1981). These children must not only endure the relatively consistent pain from their burns, but must also deal with pain elicited by bathing, changing the burn dressing, and almost daily open treatment in which dead skin and old dressings are scrubbed off with wet gauze. Given the number of burned children who are candidates for both primary and secondary prevention, it is surprising that so little research has been done to aid practitioners in this area.

There are a few studies which provide anecdotal data concerning burn patient treatment. For example, Levinson and Ousterhout (1980), described methods of preparing pediatric patients for medical procedures and surgeries using play therapy and found these interventions were helpful. Similarly, Bernstein (1965) reported several cases in which hypnosis was used to prepare patients for changes in burn dressings, to increase food intake, and to provide analgesia. However, both of these reports rely on a case history approach to demonstrate the efficacy of such procedures. In one of the few empirically based studies in this area, Weinstein (1976) utilized positive self-instruction and meditation to prevent pain during dressing changes in one child burn victim. Similarly, Olson and Elliott (Note 6) in a recently reported study, documented reductions in burned children's distress during invasive procedures when the children were trained in relaxation and distracting imagery. In spite of these movements toward documenting the efficacy of prevention, this area and similar areas in which children must cope with repeated painful interventions, can profit from an expanding of the currently limited data base on preventive procedures for children's pain.

In the same vein, several professionals have also noted the need to intervene with child cancer patients who experience not only pain, but nausea, hair loss, weight loss, and disfigurement in the process of their treatment (Adams, 1976; Azarnoff, 1974). Children with cancer tend to be more anxious and psychologically isolated than other chronically ill children, both in and out of the hospital (Spinetta, 1977). They are subjected to a variety of medical procedures, including surgeries, chemotherapies, and frequent lumbar punctures and bone marrow aspirations (Katz, Kellerman, & Siegel, 1980). Although a technology is emerging for assessing these children's reactions to medical procedures (Katz et al., 1980; Jay, Note 7), few well-documented preventive technologies have yet emerged. Our own experience suggests that brief interventions utilizing modeling and coping techniques, which have been successful with child surgery patients, have little impact on child cancer patients' reactions to repeated invasive procedures. Although there are beginning reports of successful behavioral treatment of distress in child cancer patients (Jay, Note 8) this is another area which may profit from additional examination of preventive preparations.

As additional populations of children who could benefit from preventive treatment become the focus of research, it may prove profitable to explore not only new technologies but new ways of utilizing existing technologies which might lend more impact. Drotar, Crawford, and Ganofsky in Chapter 8 of this volume discuss prevention strategies with chronically ill children and some of these methods are described there in more detail.

There are still other methods of utilizing existing technologies. One such approach may be to expose children to information and coping techniques prior to their need for elective medical intervention. At least for children requiring emergency intervention, this may be the only preventive preparation which is possible. Early prevention might also yield some degree of maintenance which would allow later preparation to occur more effectively. The small number of studies concerned with the preparation of well children who are not currently at risk for hospitalization will be considered next.

Preparation of Well Children

As is the case with other areas of research focused upon preparing children for medical procedures, there are many enthusiastic reports of intuitively appealing programs and a much smaller number of data based studies on the impact of these programs on well children. Pomarico, Marsh, and Doubrava (1979) described the goals for their hospital orientation for well children as including the decrease in children's fears of medical procedures, the dissemination of information, and the increase of pediatric nurses' awareness of children's emotional needs. Their program was announced by radio, newspapers, and flyers and was attended by Girl and Boy Scout troups, Brownies, nursery schools, and early elementary school classes in groups of 15. Children viewed a slide show, had a hospital tour, and were allowed to ask questions. No data are reported on the program's effectiveness.

Similarly, Trouten (1981) described programs which are organized and presented within the schools by a retired pediatric nurse. The programs introduce children to X-rays, casts, stethoscopes, needles, and other items the children might encounter in a medical situation. Stainton (1974) noted a similar program in which children were exposed through play therapy using a hospitalized panda bear. Each child between the ages of three and six became familiar with general hospital equipment and procedures and gave the panda an injection, while many also used a rectal thermometer, bed pan, and other equipment on the bear. Over 1,000 children were prepared in this manner. Linenkugel's (1982) program influenced an even larger number of children by preparing 500 well first grade children using a puppet show, tour, and booklet for parents and then televising their preparation program "Crow Goes to the Hospital" on local stations to gain possible population-wide prevention. While each of these studies utilized components which past research might suggest were beneficial, none of them reported any data on their programs' effects on children.

In one of the few studies to empirically examine the influence of preparation on young well children, Klinzing and Klinzing (1977) used 73 nursery school children between two and five years of age as subjects. Sixteen of the children had been hospitalized in the past. Half of the children viewed a videotape narrated by the television personality Mr. Rogers, which showed both a child and a puppet model undergoing hospitalization from admission to discharge. The other half saw a non-hospital related program featuring Mr. Rogers. The investigators did not utilize common measures of self-reported, observable, or physiological indices of anxiety. Instead, they used four low level questions regarding hospital information (for example, "What does a child's bed look like in the hospital?") and four questions on hospital attitudes (for example, "What is a hospital?"). They did not ask any questions about painful or invasive procedures such as blood tests and injections. Children who viewed the hospital tape demonstrated better knowledge and attitudes than children viewing the control film and there were no age difference factors as the younger children learned as much as the older children. Children who had been in the hospital previously showed higher knowledge and lower attitude scores. These preliminary results suggested that even very young well children without previous experience can benefit from viewing a hospital related modeling film.

Roberts, Wurtele, Boone, Ginther, and Elkins (1981) provided some of the first evidence to suggest that well children's medically related fears could be reduced by modeling and information preparation. Children in second through fifth grade viewed either a slide and audiotape presentation of two coping child models or a slide-audiotape travelogue presentation. Children who viewed the hospital relevant material experienced less self-reported anxiety and reported fewer hospital related fears directly after viewing the program and as well as two weeks later than did children viewing the control film. The hospital program group also demonstrated a slight but significant difference in responding to a measure of medically relevant information acquisition ($\bar{X}$ = 9.94 versus 8.39 out of 11 points).

Although the data are very limited, they suggest that on the average, children benefited from viewing information relevant to hospital procedures. This seems somewhat ironic, since the well child hospital preparation programs started in large numbers in the early 1970s have frequently been cancelled (Azarnoff, 1982). Azarnoff reports that many of the programs have been discontinued because of concern that children's reactions were not being properly monitored, because the procedures took up too much staff time and effort, and because financial support was no longer available. This is another example of the interplay of informal evaluation or formal research and implementation of treatment programs. Programs begun with much enthusiasm failed to be maintained when staff members were unable to see the success of their labors, which even informal evaluation could have shown. Hospital policy making and funding could have been influenced by clear research documentation of the cost-effectiveness of such a procedure, but the research was not yet available. Research evidence for the general effectiveness of similar procedures and evaluation of each individual program's success could have dispelled concerns that children's reactions were not being properly monitored. Because the research base had not kept pace with application, this possibility was lost.

Implementation in Medical and Nonmedical Settings

The communication of needs and possibilities between basic researchers and those implementing prevention programs is vital. Currently, the opportunity exists to intervene with a variety of hospitalized children and research operations must struggle to catch up. On the other hand, research might also suggest other settings for preventive endeavors in which less application has taken place, including preparation for physician visits, routine dental care, and inoculations received at school or at a public health clinic. The chance to prepare groups of well children in a cost-effective manner exists within the schools, religious and community organizations, and community hospital out-patient clinics.

In each of these settings, it will be necessary to communicate with a differing group of individuals in order to implement a program. Even individuals in prevention fields, who have learned to communicate with many disciplines in the hospital community, must relearn skills to influence private practice pediatricians, dentists, public health officials, school boards, and civic leaders. Stolz in Chapter 13 of this volume describes in more detail information dissemination and interpersonal persuasion techniques which may make implementation of prevention more likely. It must be noted that those individuals interested in implementation outside of traditional areas require more than enthusiasm and an effective treatment technology. The implementation of the treatment can require a technology unto itself.

Increasing the Impact of Preventive Programs

In addition to implementing new programs offering preventive preparation to children at risk for distress from medical procedures in any setting, there are other methods to increase the possible impact of the preventive preparation program. One method might involve preparing not only the child but other relevant family members, to maximize the exposure and effect of preparatory techniques.

Focus on the Family.

Separation from one's family has been recognized as a primary source of distress in hospitalized children (Jessner et al., 1952). The Platt Committee on Welfare of Children, formed by the government of Great Britain in 1951, recommended that whenever possible mothers should be allowed to room with their hospitalized children (Roskies, Mongeon, & Gagnon-Lefebvre, 1978). Nine years later, a study completed in England by Brain and Maclay (1968) documented the importance of parental presence for hospitalized children. Half of a group of mothers (all of whom had indicated they would stay with their children if allowed) were randomly assigned to regular hospital treatment while the other half were assigned to accompany their children throughout hospitalization. Children accompanied by their mothers were rated as more satisfactorily adjusted during their hospital stay and emitted fewer maladaptive behaviors at discharge and at a six-month follow-up.

In spite of these findings, not all hospitals allow parents to room with their children (Prugh & Jordan, 1975) and not all parents take full advantage of visiting and rooming privileges when offered (Roskies et al., 1978). In a one year follow-up of their presurgical preparation program, Peterson and Shigetomi (1982) found that the most frequently mentioned stressor for the young children they prepared was spending the night alone in the hospital (injections, vomiting, and postoperative pain were mentioned less often as most stressful aspects of the hospital experience). Interestingly, parents in that study were allowed to remain with their child if they wished.

Parental separation is still frequently mentioned by researchers as the principal cause of anxiety in hospitalized children (Goslin, 1978; Schrader, 1979) and there are many programs discussed in the current literature which provide weekly parent-staff meetings (Chan, 1980) and parental support (Prugh & Jordan, 1975). Johnson (1974), for example, noted that the primary goal of her preparation program was to prepare the parent to care for the child during hospitalization. However, few of these programs have attempted to empirically document the success which their programs have with respect to supporting parents or encouraging their presence in the hospital.

Roskies et al. (1978) provided one of the few attempts to document the success of a parental support program. In an unusually sensitive analysis, these authors pointed out that when the mother is allowed to do the nurturing and routine care and the nursing staff is relegated to medical treatment only, the nursing staff is, in effect, deprived of the most rewarding aspects of their job. Thus, it should not be surprising if nurses do not encourage parents, who are often demanding or critical, to remain with their children. Roskies et al. suggested redefining the nurses' role as a teaching expert who must collaborate with the parent to effect the best medical care possible. Their study utilized weekly meetings with the nursing staff as well as a special orientation program which emphasized parental presence and roles in child care. They found that although mothers under control (regular hospital) conditions came to stay with their children nearly as often as experimental treatment parents (77% versus 82% of possible visits), they remained for shorter periods of time, with both groups remaining a relatively low percentage of the available time (36% versus 55% of possible time). Interestingly, although the program primarily treated mothers, the largest impact was an increase in father visiting. Experimental parents did much of the psychological preparation and routine physical care for their child.

The Roskies et al. study, unlike many in this area, documented that appropriate orientation and support programs can increase parental involvement in child hospitalization. This is important since there is research confirming the important role which the parent has in providing support (Peterson & Shigetomi, 1981; Prugh et al., 1953; Skipper & Leonard, 1968). Since the parent is typically responsible for preparing the child for stressful situations and is aware of the child's unique fears and strengths, it might also be expected that the parent would provide the best preparation for stressful medical procedures. However, this is not necessarily the case. Heffernan and Azarnoff (1971) separately interviewed children who had come to a medical clinic for treatment and the children's mothers. Mothers were asked about their reactions to children's emotions in general and were classified as being suppressive ("It is not okay to cry") or nonsuppressive ("Crying when hurt or upset is okay"). Mothers were also asked to describe what they had told their child about coming to the clinic, how much detail they had used in their description, and who had initiated the preparation. Children received a self-report inventory which assessed their anxiety about the clinic visit.

The results suggest two important findings. First, suppressive mothers tended to have highly anxious children and yet tended to be unaware of their child's anxiety. Second, if the child had initiated the preparation by asking questions, he or she was less anxious while receiving detailed information. However, when the mother initiated the preparation, the child was less anxious when given minimal information (for example, "We are going to the doctor" only) and was most anxious when given detailed information. Heffernan and Azarnoff (1971) noted that there remains a "which came first" dilemma. It is unclear whether (1) children who tend not to seek out information react more fearfully to hospitalization, (2) anxious mothers tend to produce unnecessarily detailed explanations which are anxiety provoking, or (3) anxious children nonverbally alert their mothers to their anxious state and thus provoke more detailed discussions. While future research may need to determine the extent to which parents should offer their children psychological preparation, current evidence appears to support programs which prepare parents to prepare their children.

In one of the earliest attempts to examine this issue, Skipper and Leonard (1968) utilized both regular nursing care for parents, which included moderate amounts of information (what would happen, when, and why), and experimental nursing care in which the nurse spent five minutes longer than regular admission procedures required to discuss the mother's feelings and give information. The nurse also met with the experimental group mothers briefly during other stressful moments of hospitalization (later in the evening after admission, shortly before the child returned from the recovery room, the evening after the operation, and at discharge the following day). The three to nine year old children whose mothers received experimental treatment had lower average blood pressure readings before and after surgery and upon discharge, and showed less physiological distress in measures such as postoperative vomiting and voiding. In addition, more children vomited in the control group than in the experimental group in the week after discharge and children whose mothers were in the experimental group demonstrated quicker recovery time than control group mothers' children. Thus, providing information and support to the mothers had a direct impact on their children. In an important and unusual report, Skipper et al. (1968) also noted that the mothers receiving the experimental treatment were less distressed during their child's surgery and more frequently reported that they would be less distressed in future medical encounters than the control group mothers.

It is interesting that for the most part preventive programs have focused upon the child patient to the exclusion of other interested parties. The parent's distress has often been regarded as important only to the extent that it impacts the child patient. It should be recognized that a parent's anxiety and distress may also require intervention. Smitherman (1979), in an article entitled "Parents of Hospitalized Children Have Needs Too," argued that providing parents with information and a specific role may lower their distress. Peterson and Shigetomi (1981) suggested that parents in their coping conditions responded with feelings of increased competence and diminished anxiety because they were well informed about what to expect and had a defined role with usable technology for combating anxiety and pain. Similarly, Zastowny et al. (Note 5) reported that both parent groups receiving anxiety reduction and coping information were less stressed before and after hospitalization.

Thus, it may prove advantageous to utilize family members, particularly the primary caretaker, as an ally in preventive endeavors. This may magnify the immediate effects of preparation by relieving the anxiety of several interacting individuals. It may also result in longer term anxiety and disturbance reductions as the child who goes home with a prepared parent may be in constant contact with a treatment agent. Such suggestions, however, await further research.

In addition to family member involvement, there are other ways to enhance the carry-over of treatment effects from a single preventive preparation. Some of these strategies will be discussed next.

Maintenance Strategies.

The issue of maintaining treatment effects is not new to clinical psychology studies concerned with remediative treatment effects, where frequent commentary bemoans the inadequate maintenance of treatment gains (Atthowe, 1973; Marholin, Siegel, & Phillips, 1976). When discussing treatment maintenance for preventive endeavors, however, the question becomes even more complicated. Does maintenance of treatment effects refer to the absence of trauma after hospitalization (for example, when the child is home) as well as during hospitalization? There are limited data to suggest that such treatment maintenance is not a problem. Many of the studies which found long-term psychological trauma and behavioral disturbances resulting from hospitalization and surgery (Prugh et al., 1953; Jessner et al., 1952) were completed prior to enlightened surgical, anesthesia, rooming-in, and information preparation endeavors. Two week follow-up of prepared children typically shows minimal upset following minor elective surgery (Melamed & Siegel, 1975; Peterson & Shigetomi, 1981). Similarly, longer term follow-ups of these children do not usually reveal any enduring changes in behavior (Simons, Bradshaw, & Silva, 1980). In a one year follow-up, Peterson and Shigetomi (1982) found that only one of the 40 mothers contacted reported problems such as enuresis, nightmares, or other disturbances. In fact, children tended to recall many more positive than negative aspects of hospitalization. Even major operations such as open heart surgery have reportedly resulted in mild responses which rarely last beyond one month after discharge (Gabriel & Danilowicz, 1978). However, these studies utilized children screened for relatively normal psychological adjustment prior to surgery and even the control subjects received some form of information preparation. Thus, the potential for long-term distress in nonprepared patients or in children with a poor premorbid adjustment remains an issue.

Maintenance of treatment effects might also refer to the extent to which preparing a child for an invasive procedure results in diminished anxiety in future encounters. Few studies have examined the reactions of a previously prepared child to additional procedures. In one such study, Siegel and Peterson (1981) employed an attention placebo control, a sensory information treatment in which the major sensations were positively but accurately redefined, and a coping treatment similar to that used by Peterson and Shigetomi (1981), including relaxation, imaginal distraction, and self-instruction. The preschool subjects in this experiment had no previous dental experience other than one baseline pretreatment session in which their teeth were examined. They were given a single preventive preparation session one hour prior to their first dental restoration. Children who received either of the experimental treatments were less disruptive, more cooperative, and demonstrated less anxiety in the dental session following treatment than did the placebo control group. Furthermore, these differences were maintained several days later when children encountered a separate restorative session. Although there were too few children experiencing three or more restorative sessions to allow definitive statistical analysis, it appeared that experimental subjects continued to show less disruptive and more cooperative responses up to five restorative sessions following treatment. This single study suggests some promise for the maintenance of treatment effects, but a great deal of research will need to be done with children experiencing more stressful procedures at longer temporal intervals before definitive conclusions can be reached regarding maintenance effects for coping and sensory information treatments. Similar research will also need to be conducted on other treatment technologies, as will comparisons between the different treatments.

Finally, maintenance may be viewed as the extent to which preparing a child for one invasive procedure would enable the child to cope well with other similar procedures. Such a view might be more appropriately regarded as addressing the question of generalization rather than maintenance. In any event, there are very few data available to answer this question. In one very limited study, Peterson and Shigetomi (1982) noted that only one third of the parents who received the coping techniques prior to their child's hospitalization utilized the techniques in the year following hospitalization and none utilized the techniques with a child other than the child with which the parent had trained. Considering that parents were taught the procedure only once for about 15 minutes, it may be acceptable that only one-third of them retained the procedure. Future studies will need to devote substantially more attention to this area. Since children may transfer a negative set from one medical experience to another (Melamed, Klingman, & Siegel, 1983), it may also be possible for them to transfer an effective coping technology from a dental to a medical setting or from a hospital to a clinic setting. Preparation with this degree of maintenance/generalization would indeed be cost-effective.

Although little current data exist on the maintenance of treatment effects, there are a few studies which deal with the maintenance of the impact of negative experience–that is, the influence of preexisting experience with dental and medical procedures prior to preventive preparation. This is one of the subject factors which will be discussed in the next section.

Subject Differences.

There are many ways in which children differ; gender, race, and socioeconomic class are all categories commonly assessed by researchers interested in the prevention of child disorders. Becker (1976) noted a variety of factors which place the hospitalized child at risk for trauma, including the child's age, previous hospitalizations or separations from parents, ego integrity, awareness and perception of the world, adequacy of reality appraising abilities, nature of the family, IQ, sensitivity, temperament, and area of adaptive cognitive development. Tsigounis (1978) also noted that the child's anxiety and perception of the parent's anxiety, in addition to the severity of surgery, determined the degree of risk for the child. There are undoubtedly other factors which may impose risk on the hospitalized child. Because it is necessary to limit the focus of the discussion here, only three subject differences, which have been relatively ignored in past research and which current researchers seem to view as important, will be considered. Specifically, the discussion will focus on some of the differences in subjects' preexperience, the very young subject, and on differences in the way children cope with stress.

Preexperience.

Research concerning subject preexperience suggests that, in general, having experienced a stressful situation prior to being appropriately prepared can result in diminished effects for a preparation program received before a second medical procedure. Specifically, Melamed and Siegel (1980) note that children who had previously experienced hospitalization and surgery did not benefit from a modeling film at all, showing no differences from a previously hospitalized control group who did not view the hospital relevant film. Klorman et al. (1980) and Ginther and Roberts (1982) reported similar findings for groups of children having prior dental experience and reporting high dental fears. In the latter study, those children demonstrated no benefit from either a coping or a mastery model film. It is not clear in this case whether the prior experience or the high degree of dental fear contributed to the treatments' impotence, since a similar lack of benefit from the films was observed in a group of children who had no prior dental experience but who reported high levels of dental fears. The extent to which prior experience leads to increased fearfulness may be an important issue to explore. In addition, the search for the preferred preparation techniques to use with children having prior experience should be continued.

Other studies suggest that prior experience may only modify the child's reactions to differing preventive procedures. For example, Melamed et al. (1978) utilized preparations which were either long or short and which demonstrated the dental techniques to be used either in the absence or presence of a peer. They reported that children with previous treatment experience benefited most from viewing the long peer modeling film or the short no-peer film. In fact, the short no-peer film resulted in the least disruptive behavior in the prior experience group and the most disruptive responses in the group with no prior experience. However, these comparisons were made while collapsing across many other differences in the two groups. Overall, younger children (regardless of prior experience) reported fewer fears after seeing either of the longer videotapes and white children reported fewer fears than black children after viewing either of the modeling tapes (interestingly, the model in the film was black). The authors did not report on age, sex, or racial differences between the prior experience and the no prior experience groups, at least age might be strongly related to prior experience. The most accurate general conclusion which might be reached here is that prior experience in combination with other individual variables results in changes in the efficacy of preventive preparation. The use of coping techniques such as relaxation and self-instruction shows promise with children having previous experience (Nocella & Kaplan, 1982). The task of outlining the extent and direction of preexperience influence on filmed modeling and on other treatment approaches falls to future research. It may be necessary, as one treatment agent remarked, to "detoxify" the influence of prior experience before offering preparation for the next experience (Johnston & Salazar, 1979).

Younger Children.

There is a consensus among prevention workers that, in general, the younger the child patient, the greater the risk of psychological disturbance from hospitalization (Mason, 1978; Prugh & Jordan, 1975; Trouten, 1981). Early studies in the field which discovered very severe reactions to hospitalization (Brain & Maclay, 1968; Vernon, Foley, & Schulman, 1967) and those which reported long-term negative reactions to hospitalization (Prugh et al., 1953) noted that these reactions occur primarily in children under the age of four. The recent studies reporting a few severe (Gabriel & Danilowicz, 1978) and long-term (Harvey, 1980) negative reactions to hospitalization mirror the earlier findings, with the greatest distress being experienced by preschool children.

Some practitioners report that the preschool child experiences more anxiety, suffers from greater fear of separation and abandonment, misses household routines more, is more fearful of discomfort, and finds restraint more upsetting than older children (Chan, 1980). Others note that the child's lower level of cognitive development makes it more difficult to understand medical routines (Simeonsson, Buckley, & Monson, 1979) or to ask questions or seek knowledge about what is to happen (Pidgeon, 1981). Preschool children also tend to recall less preparation information (Melamed, Robbins, & Fernandez, 1982). There are many nonempirically documented ideas about the preparation of preschool children discussed in the prevention literature, including notions that children less than age five cannot understand explanations and must be sedated (Karp & Teuscher, 1947), and that it takes much longer and is more difficult to prepare a preschool age child (Gabriel, 1977). The documentation which does exist suggests that regardless of preventive treatment given, younger dental patients (Melamed et al., 1978) and surgery patients (Taylor, 1978) tend to be more distressed by hospitalization than older children. It is important to note, however, that most of these programs were not especially oriented toward the preschool age child. Since children between the ages of four and five tend to be the age group most frequently admitted to U.S. hospitals (Azarnoff & Woody, 1981), the young child seems to be a group which is at once particularly at-risk and yet underserved (Goslin, 1978).

Most rigorously tested prevention programs have incorporated some younger children; reviews of the literature document that a typical lower end range for research on preparation is two to four years and an upper age range is 10–12 years (Goslin, 1978; Melamed, Robbins, & Fernandez, 1982; Siegel, 1976). These different reviews point out a common problem in interpreting research findings on age; most discussions of research (this chapter included) typically note the age *range* of the target subjects without noting the average subject age. As can be seen in Table 9.1, some original research reports indicate either a range or the average age per group—neither method alone allows conclusions about the age of the subjects. When both average age, standard deviation, and range of ages is considered in a sample set of research reports, such as those shown in Table 9.1, it is clear that there are some studies in which preschool children comprise a large portion of the subject

Table 9.1. Age of Children Served

	Range in Years	Average Years*
Examples of Dental Studies		
Ginther & Roberts, 1982	4–12	8.3
Klorman, Hilpert, Michael, LaGana, & Sveen, 1980	Not given	7.80–8.61
Melamed, Bennett, Jerrell, Ross, Bush, Hill, Courts, & Ronk, Note 4	4–12	6.5–8.03
Melamed, Yurcheson, Fleece, Hutcherson, & Hawes, 1978	4–11	Not given
Siegel & Peterson, 1981	3.8–5.9	4.9
Examples of Surgical Studies		
Burstein & Meichenbaum, 1979	4.8–8.6	7.1
Ferguson, 1979	3–7	6.7
Johnson & Stockdale, 1975	5–8	6.7
Knight, Atkins, Eagle, Evans, Finkelstein, Fukushima, Katz, & Weiner, 1979	7–11	Not Given
Melamed, Meyer, Gee, & Soule, 1976	4–12	6.51–8.00
Melamed & Siegel, 1975	4–12	7.24–7.50
Peterson, Schultheis, Ridley-Johnson, Miller, & Tracy, 1984	2.5–11.0	4.77
Peterson & Shigetomi, 1981	2.5–10.5	5.46
Prugh, Staub, Sands, Kirschbaum, & Lenihan, 1953	2–12	Not given
Skipper & Leonard, 1968	3–9	Not given
Visintainer & Wolfer, 1975	3–14	7.1
Williams, 1980	7–13	10.26
Wolfer & Visintainer, 1979	3–12	6.2–7.3
Zastowny, Kirschenbaum, & Meng, Note 5	6–10	7.2

*This is the overall mean age or the mean for each of several experimental groups. The numbers cited are those given in the research report.

population, but more studies in which most of the subjects are school age and older. Since younger children may respond differently to dissimilar preparation techniques, it is particularly important for researchers in the field to examine the use of various prevention techniques with young children and for those implementing research findings to be aware of the age limitations on current findings.

While age is a very important setting variable in children's reaction to medical procedures, it is not the only variable which may mediate children's responses to preparation. The next section explores differences in children's characteristic style of coping with distress and their possible relationship to hospital adjustment.

Coping Styles.

Little definitive information exists concerning the influence of characteristic coping styles on hospitalized adults' and children's distress. The suggestion that such information would be valuable in treating hospitalized children has been advanced only recently (Melamed, Robbins, & Fernandez, 1982; Roberts et al., 1981), and probably stemmed from reports by researchers dealing with adult surgical patients who demonstrated that coping styles influenced the degree of the patients' distress. This is an interesting but difficult area of research to interpret and is probably subject to a larger number of incautious generalizations than most preventive research. Because this is an important area of current research focus, the results of some of the most cited adult studies will be considered here, prior to reviewing the few findings which exist for children.

Part of the difficulty in this research area stems from the multiple methods available for measuring characteristic ways in which children cope with distress, the multiple opportunities for assessing distress and types of measures of distress, and the formation of summary statements based upon some data while ignoring other data. There have been several types of characteristic coping styles in adults in medical settings which have been examined as mediators of their distress, including Internal-External locus of control (Auerbach, Kendall, Cuttler, & Levitt, 1976; Lowery, Jacobsen, & Keane, 1975), high versus low anxiety patients (Auerbach, 1973; Martinez-Urrutia, 1975), and Health Locus of Control (George, Scott, Turner, & Gregg, 1980). However, the most frequently referred to mediators of hospitalized adults' distress may have been a three-dimensional concept which utilizes the following labels, somewhat interchangeably: (1) sensitizer or vigilant, (2) nonspecific defender or neutral, and (3) denier, avoider, or repressor. Vigilants or sensitizers are thought to seek out information, ruminate about it and focus on an upcoming medical procedure, while deniers, avoiders, or repressors tend to avoid information about their condition, fail to think about the procedure, and focus on things other than the upcoming medical intervention (Goldstein, 1973).

There are several frequently cited studies which use these kinds of distinctions and although these studies have some findings in common, it may be premature to accept these commonalities as definitive. In one of two early studies dealing with coping styles and presurgical preparation in adults, Andrew (1970) utilized only two fairly molar dependent variables, time from surgery to discharge and number of medications received. Both variables were obtained from nursing notes in the medical charts. Half of her subjects received audiotaped presurgical information. Andrew noted that neutrals who listened to the tape experienced fewer days to discharge and fewer medications than unprepared neutrals. Prepared avoiders had equal days but more medications than unprepared avoiders, while sensitizers had equal days and equal medications. In a second preparation study, DeLong attempted to replicate Andrew's study (DeLong, 1971; cited in Averill, 1973), and found (in contrast to the previous results) that sensitizers receiving specific information recovered *more* quickly when given specific information about their surgery, while similar information did not influence nonspecific defenders or avoiders.

Two following studies attempted observation of adult patients without manipulating preparation. In one such study, Cohen and Lazarus (1973) interviewed patients to determine their coping type and classified patients as vigilant, avoidant, and neither. The investigators did not prepare the patients; instead, they simply utilized molar measures such as days in hospital and number of pain medications. Vigilant subjects differed from avoidant subjects only by staying more days and having more minor complications. Sime (1976) later suggested that the amount of information requested prior to abdominal surgery did not influence the length of the hospital stay, number of analgesics and sedatives obtained, or the negative affect of adult surgical patients. Thus, these studies suggest that information either has no effect (Andrew, 1970) or a beneficial effect (DeLong, 1971) for sensitizers, who if unprepared, either deal with hospitalization less effectively (Cohen & Lazarus, 1973) or equally as well as (Sime, 1976) other coping styles. Repressors either had a mixed reaction to information (medications but no days increased; Andrew, 1970) or no reaction to information (DeLong, 1971) and recovered either more quickly than (Cohen & Lazarus, 1973) or the same as (Sime, 1976) vigilants. Although it is easier to summarize this research by suggesting that vigilants benefit from information and avoiders do not, the data are not nearly that clear cut.

One of the most recent studies in this area (Hitchcock, 1982) examined 80 patients who were interviewed before their surgeries to determine their level of vigilance and avoidance. Patients were then given (1) minimal procedure information, (2) information plus relaxation training, or (3) sensory information plus cognitive reappraisal. Hitchcock used multiple measures of reaction to hospitalization and reported mixed findings, many of which were discrepant with the earlier studies on preparation. Avoiders (as measured by the amount of information they had about their operation) left their houses sooner after surgery when they had received the cognitive training than when they had received the minimal information, whereas there was no difference between vigilants. Patients low on appraisal of surgery (another method of categorizing avoidants), who had received minimal information, took fewer sleeping pills but the same amount of pain medication as those who had received relaxation or cognitive reappraisal. Patients high on appraisal (vigilants) took the same number of sleeping pills regardless of treatment group, but took fewer pain medications if they had received relaxation training. These were the only variables showing coping disposition interactions with treatment. Overall, vigilants had better recoveries than avoidants. Hitchcock summarizes her interactive findings by noting that ''subjects benefited most from treatments complementary rather than congruent with their preoperative mode of coping'' (p. ix). Again, the conclusions of studies in this area seem far from consistent.

Perhaps a good final example of the difficulty in interpreting this research can be seen in an important paper by Shipley et al. (1979). In their first report (Shipley, Butt, Horwitz, & Farbry, 1978), they noted that adult sensitizers benefited from a film preparation for endoscopy but repressors showed an inverted U-shaped function on two measures (heart rate and tranquilizers obtained) with higher anxiety when they viewed the film once than if they did not view it or viewed it three times. In the second report with patients who had previously experienced an endoscopy procedure, sensitizers showed a decrease in heart rate, amount of gagging, and nurse ratings of anxiety as a function of the number of times they viewed the film. Repressors, however, showed a linear (not curvilinear) increase in heart rate, a *decrease* in the time to insert the endoscope, and no differences in gagging due to number of times they viewed the film. There were also no differences in self-reported anxiety, self-rated discomfort, or number of tranquilizers required. Shipley et al. concluded that these data, in combination with the past findings, suggested that sensitizers benefit from preparation whereas repressors are made more anxious. This is true if only the heart rate data are considered, but it must also be noted that for the majority of the measures, including all the self-report and observable indices of anxiety, the repressors were not substantially influenced by preparation (nor for much of these data were the sensitizers) and the time to endoscope insertion was actually less ($p < .01$) following preparation for repressors. As will be discussed in more detail later, the dependent variable selected as the treatment target will often determine the conclusions to be drawn from a study. Similarly, to suggest that preparation per se is counterproductive rather than noting that modeling and information preparations may not be valuable is inaccurate. In fact, Wilson (1981) cogently argued that preparation is beneficial for patients who use denial as well as those who do not, but in different ways. The search for patterns of characteristic responding which may influence hospitalization is an important one. However, premature and simplistic generalizations about these studies, which differ with respect to subject characteristics, medical procedures, and measurement techniques, may mislead future researchers. It is vital not only to note the threads of similarity but also the number of existing differences.

These data do, however, suggest that in some cases an individual's coping disposition may influence adjustment to hospitalization, recovery time and reaction to some forms of preparation. It seems the zeitgeist currently to inquire if children who are still developing emotionally and cognitively even have characteristic coping styles (Melamed, Klingman, & Siegel, 1983) and if they do, if this may lead them to experience differing reactions to preventive preparation (Melamed, Robbins, & Fernandez, 1982; Peterson, 1981; Roberts et al., 1981; Siegel, Note 9). There are very few studies which have actually examined coping styles which parallel those of adults. The findings of those studies are somewhat limited due to small *n*s and measurement differences. In one preliminary finding of this kind, Knight, Atkins, Eagle, Evans, Finkelstein, Fukushima, Katz, and Weiner (1979) prepared 25 children between ages seven and 11 who were undergoing one of five different kinds of surgery. During the preparation, the investigators made ratings about the children's characteristic defense style. The clinician performing the preparation also gave children the Rorschach, which was rated by a second clinician. A single measure of anxiety—urinary 17-hydroxy-corticosteroids—was collected at three different times: following an outpatient clinic visit, at home (Time 1), at the hospital prior to surgery (Time 2), and the day after surgery (Time 3). Preparation was reported to take place at both Times 1 and 2. There was no relationship between cortisol production rates and any measures of defensiveness during Time 1. During Time 2, there was a relationship between defensive effectiveness and cortisol production rates ($r = -.49$). Children who were rated as utilizing intellectualization, intellectualization with isolation, or a mixed pattern of defenses had lower cortisol production rates than children using denial, denial with isolation, displacement, or projection. In addition, the ratings of children's adjustment to the hospital as measured by ward personnel showed that better adjusted children had lower cortisol production rates. Unfortunately, no definition or further description of the different types of coping dispositions was offered.

In a second study dealing with children's characteristic methods of coping, Burstein and Meichenbaum (1979) utilized two measures of defensive style which were more clearly differentiated. A questionnaire which measured tendency to deny common weaknesses (Wallack & Kogan, 1965) was employed and the opportunity to choose medical (stress-related) toys or nonmedical (nonstress related) toys was made available the week before, during, and the week after hospitalization. Unfortunately, parents prepared the children and no specific information on type or extent of preparation is noted. Also, the authors reported no observational or physiological measures of anxiety. Furthermore, the only measure of self-reported anxiety which they employed, drawn from a doctoral dissertation (Gilmore, 1964), is not described in any detail in their report nor in any of the published reports they cited (for example, Gilmore, 1965). The self-report apparently consisted of several open-ended questions and problems, an adjective checklist, and some sentence completion items. The 20 children, ages 4.8–8.6 (average age 7.1), showed no differences in male and female subjects, anxiety levels, defensiveness scores, or preference for stress related toys within any of the three measurement opportunities. Although there was no relationship between anxiety and play with stress related toys within any time period, there was a significant relationship between tendency to play with stress related toys prior to hospitalization and a low level of anxiety reported after hospitalization. The results indicated that before hospitalization, increased defensiveness was associated with the avoidance of stress relevant toys. A nonrandom selection of four low defensive children was compared with a selected group of four high defensive children seven months after hospitalization. Children responded to a projective test in which they were asked to guess what a peer pictured in eight medical situations was thinking about and were asked what they remembered about the hospital experience. Both groups recalled the same number of events, but the low defensive group remembered more medical and hospital-related procedures and more of the parental preparatory information. Similarly, the low defensive children reported more threats, deprivations, and self-reassurances during the projective test than did the high defensiveness subjects.

In a third study which utilized clear measures of both defensiveness and anxiety, Melamed (1982) reported some preliminary data on 15 subjects ages six to 15 who were seen the night before their scheduled surgery and who viewed a slide-audiotape information presentation. The higher the children's prefilm sweat index, the lower their self-reported anxiety and the greater the amount of information they retained. A lower prefilm sweat index was related to lower amounts of information retained and higher self-reports of fear.

These three studies suggest that preexisting differences in the child's dispositional methods of coping may influence the child's response to information preparation and to surgery. However, the degree to which the types of preparation were similar is unclear, as is the relationship between children with "intellectualizing or mixed defenses," children who play with hospital toys, and children with high prefilm sweating who remember more about the film. Similarly, it is unclear if children who use denial or projection, do not wish to play with hospital related toys, or those with low prefilm sweating who do not receive much film information, are exhibiting the same coping pattern. Even if the somewhat premature generalization is made that all of those studies used some form of information preparation and that children can be dichotomized into patients who seek out information and experience with medical procedures (like adult sensitizers) and those who avoid information (like adult repressors), the suggestion for future preventive endeavors is still not straightforward. Do the data indicate that defensive children should be encouraged in their denial and avoidance, as has been suggested for adults (Shipley et al., 1979) or do they suggest that defensive children require more or different preparation to overcome their characteristic denial, as other adult data would seem to suggest (Hitchcock, 1982)? Melamed's (1982) finding that children who are least aware of hospital relevant information are most frightened might suggest that additional preparation is needed. On the other hand, these children may have more information at their disposal than they admit and may be just utilizing denial when *reporting* their awareness of information pertaining to medical procedures. Perhaps an approach such as the coping techniques mentioned earlier (Peterson & Shigetomi, 1981; Zastowny et al., Note 5) might be useful with defensive children, since techniques such as relaxation and imaginal distraction serve to avoid contact with stressors in the hospital environment. Despite the difficulties involved in this research endeavor, the coping styles of subjects is an area of research interest which promises to yield important information. Additional studies in this area would profit from some standardization in measuring characteristic styles of coping and distress experienced before, during, and after hospitalization. Although multi-modal assessment would continue to be an important endeavor, it may be particularly important to prioritize dependent variables; that is, to form conclusions based upon the effects of treatment on a single target response rather than on any of several possible responses. It may also be vital to guard against premature conclusions regarding when, where, and how treatments should be employed. These last two cautions will be explored further in the next section.

Challenges to Future Research and Implementation

This chapter has attempted to outline the expanse of existing information concerning issues in the area of children's distress prevention in medical settings, and to note repeatedly the areas in which more research is needed. This section will further note some of the methodological, therapeutic, philosophical, and ethical challenges which await researchers as they attempt to answer research questions and treatment agents as they attempt to implement the answers.

Many researchers (for example, Melamed & Siegel, 1975; Peterson & Shigetomi, 1981) have cogently described the necessity for methodological improvements. These include random assignment to conditions; insuring that treatment groups are equivalent in terms of important variables, such as prior experience, surgery type, and age; using blind observers; employing statistical tests to control for the large inflation in alpha level which occurs when multiple comparisons between dependent variables are made; and using multiple measures of distress. With field research conducted with child patients in medical settings, these methodological considerations will continue to be difficult to implement and costly in terms of time, effort, and financial expense. Nevertheless, they are vital if research is to yield interpretable results.

In order to make multiple measures of distress an aid rather than a liability, it may be useful to select a response or small set of responses as a target system and to form conclusions based on changes within this target system alone. Changes in other modalities could be regarded as interesting effects to be investigated by future research, but a procedure which did not impact the selected target system would not automatically be regarded as successful because it impacted any one of the three systems. There are many statistical and pragmatic reasons to describe why this might improve prevention research methodology.

Traditionally, anxiety has been measured in three response systems: physiological, self-report, and overtly observable indices of anxiety (Ax, 1953; Lacey, 1950). The ultimate goal of most prevention programs is to reduce distress in each of these systems. However, since asynchrony of these systems may be more characteristic than parallel changes (Lang, 1978; Lick & Katkin, 1978), changes in all three systems on each of several measurement occasions are likely to be the exception rather than the rule, especially with children. The question thus becomes: In a given evaluation of preventive technology, is there one response system which is a preferred target over the other two response systems? Melamed, Klingman, and Siegel (1983) suggested a complete assessment of the medical procedure to be experienced to determine the behaviors most important to that procedure. If the concern was that the child's vital signs remain stable, then physiological indices of anxiety would be a logical target behavior. If the internal (physiological) and external (observable) manifestations of anxiety were unimportant to a procedure (to take an extreme example, a child is alert but muscles are paralyzed by curare and vital signs are controlled by a machine), then subjectively felt distress would be the logical target response. However, if it were important that the child not show behavioral manifestations of anxiety, then observable distress might be the preferred target. During cardiac catheterization, when it is life-threatening to lose behavioral control (Cassell, 1965), during lumbar punctures or bone marrow aspirations where moving suddenly can cause both pain and tissue damage (Katz et al., 1980), or during anesthesia induction where crying or pulling away leads to increased medical complications (Eckenhoff, 1953), observable manifestations of anxiety may be the most important response system in which to effect a change, even though the other systems are also important indices of distress.

There is a tendency in the literature to refer to a child as "less anxious" if there is a decrease in any one of the response systems. Certainly, each response system is uniquely important to the measurement of hospitalized children's distress and it is not suggested here that measurement of any of the systems be discontinued. However, studies do exist where the conclusions differ based on the specific response system examined. It has already been noted that in the Shipley et al. (1979) adult study, repressors were either unaffected, helped, or hindered depending upon whether self-report, time to insert the endoscope, or heart rate was examined.

Similarly, Melamed et al. (1976) reported that older children benefited most from preparation a week before surgery, whereas younger children benefited most from preparation the day before surgery. However, these authors noted that young children, particularly in the immediate preparation group, showed *more* medical concerns than older children both preoperatively and postoperatively. There was no such difference for children prepared a week before the procedure. Young children in the immediate preparation group also experienced *less* physiological arousal postoperatively as measured by the Palmar Sweat Index than did young children who had received preparation a week in advance. No effects of observable anxiety to differentiate time of preparation for young children were reported. Thus, the data suggest that young children were worse off in terms of self-report, better off in terms of physiological response, and no different in terms of observable anxiety when they had received immediate preparation. Melamed et al. noted that past research (Heller, 1967; Mellish, 1969) had suggested that longer time intervals between preparation and stressor were better for older children, while shorter intervals were better for younger children and suggested that their current findings supported this premise. In part, the results are consistent with the past suggestions. However, some findings within the self-report response system are inconsistent with the past research. The problem arises from the need to summarize research in a journal abstract or review paper. In such a case, one response system is selected for focus, but rather than being the most important system for that procedure, it is often the system which yielded the anticipated results. Thus, the status quo can be maintained even in the face of conflicting evidence.

There was nothing inappropriate in the conclusions drawn by Melamed et al. (1976) in context. However, because the study is so carefully designed and rigorously conducted, it is often cited and only the general conclusions of the study are noted. It is frequently cited to support scheduling preparation times either earlier or later, depending on the child's age, without regard for the different effects on differing response systems. Such studies are extremely difficult and arduous to conduct and, with less interest in replications than in original findings, no one has yet reported a replication of the results. The only similar study which has been conducted since the original study (Visintainer & Wolfer, 1979) found no age by time of treatment interactions. If one response system had been preselected as a target area andconclusions been based only upon the target responses, then the rationale for a defi-nitive conclusion in spite of the mixed results would have been clearer, and individuals using the study to plan programs might recognize what kinds of changes to expect.

Sometimes an investigator has more confidence in the validity of one response system over another and thus might select the system believed to be more valid as a target response. For example, when a child has received numerous drugs postoperatively, physiological signs may be influenced by the drugs and thus may not be a valid indicator of distress. Self-report in very young children may similarly be invalid in some cases. Establishing a single target response would eliminate the need to account for dysynchrony when it occurs. In one such case, Ferguson (1979) found no correlation between child surgery patients' self-report, physiological signs, and behavioral manifestations of anxiety. In order to explain the dysynchrony, she concluded that, "This would suggest that children's outward behavior may not be an accurate assessment of their anxiety level" (p. 663). In the same vein, Hester (1979) noted that her self-report measure of pain was unrelated to the child's facial expressions and motor behaviors and suggested that, "children who respond to painful stimuli with (negative) facial or motor behavior may actually feel less pain." (p. 253). It may be more parsimonious to suspect measurement error, especially with self-report of abstract emotions from young children whose cognitive development makes abstract comprehension difficult, rather than to hypothesize that a crying, complaining child is actually less distressed than a cooperative, smiling child on the basis of other response system measures. Focus on one particular target system may eliminate the need to explain away dysynchrony when it exists. Time will yield further evidence to support or disclaim the utility of this target response suggestion.

Utilization of a single target response system will limit the opportunity for researchers to claim significant treatment effects and for this reason alone it is costly to implement. Another costly suggestion which may produce better, but more difficult to achieve, findings is the use of comparative research design. As this chapter has noted, there are a variety of different treatment technologies which have demonstrated some utility in preventing distress in hospitalized children. Although these technologies typically have a common base of giving information concerning what to expect, they differ in important respects. For example, treatment types vary greatly in the degree to which the stressor is either approached by fully describing the sensations to be experienced or avoided by using mental imagery and relaxation to block experiencing unpleasant sensations. It is likely that, at least for some children experiencing some procedures, one method of preparation will be superior to the others. However, the tradition in the area of children's distress prevention in medical settings has been to identify an effective treatment technology and then to explore various parameters for its use. This is an excellent example of the divergent interests of those who wish to apply research findings by utilizing the most effective technology and those who actually perform the research. Focusing on a single treatment has been typical of therapy research in general in the last two decades. Several clinicians have recently suggested that such an approach is too narrow. Goldfried (1980) argued that far too much effort has been put into the careful analysis of single techniques, which may be less effective than other existing techniques which have remained unexplored. What is the value of knowing everything about a technique which may soon be replaced in application by a more effective technique or used in combination with other techniques which may alter its influence? Similarly, Hersen (1981) noted in the title of his article that "Complex Problems Require Complex Solutions" and suggested that the complex solutions often involve the comparison and combination of differing technologies. One of the most cogent pleas for comparative research was made by Azrin (1977), who argued vigorously against the continued testing of one's own favored technique with no-treatment or attention-placebo controls. It is far more profitable both theoretically and pragmatically to know what works best than to know that multiple techniques are each, one at a time, better than nothing. Those who apply techniques need to know what treatments are available and what the different treatments *do*; it is far less important for them to know all possible parameters of a single type of treatment.

There are many disadvantages of a comparative research approach which have been discussed elsewhere (Peterson, 1981). These include the difficulty in demonstrating statistically significant differences when comparing a very effective and moderately effective technique; the necessity of awaiting the performance component analysis following the attainment of differences in order to determine the active ingredients of any two multi-component techniques; the perceived absence of focus in a research program which utilizes multiple treatment strategies; and the charge that such research is unprogrammatic. In spite of these difficulties, it is likely that the field of preventive preparations for children will advance more rapidly by initially considering and comparing multiple treatment technologies and then following up these comparisons to determine which components are most important to the success of which procedure for each child.

This brings this discussion to its final challenge—that of bearing both the research commitment to design pragmatic, theoretically relevant investigations and the service commitment to design programs which have a high likelihood of being implemented. There can be some legitimate claims of "ivory-towerism" from those individuals actually practicing in the field when they view some of the current directions of research in this area. At a time when funding for psychosocial programs is at a low ebb, preparation programs are closing (Azarnoff, 1982), and only 34% of the general hospitals serving children report any formal preparation (Azarnoff & Woody, 1981), some psychologists are suggesting that the commonly used and cost-effective techniques such as videotaped models, books, and tours are insufficiently individualized and should be replaced by care oriented to each child patient. Such suggestions are directly at odds with the need in the field for a general, easy to administer, low cost program.

There is a similar absence of concern in much preventive research for cost-effective treatment (Klinzing & Klinzing, 1977; Peterson et al., 1980) and for the necessity of examining actual program implementation. Psychologists typically work with the nursing staff when planning preventive programs (probably because the nursing staff is accessible and enthusiastic), yet often the nurses do not have the administrative power to continue the program once the investigator completes the research (Roskies et al., 1978). We do not do research on implementation per se, and we espouse concern for treatment maintenance but not for the maintenance of the treatment program in the actual medical community. We do our research often with a disregard for pragmatics; we remove the parent while the child views a modeling film to control for parent-child interaction, even though the literature consistently shows that parent preparation is important and the parent is typically included in preparation, or we use doctorate level clinicians to train coping skills which must ultimately be applied by individuals who have no behavior therapy training. Is it worthwhile to compare a home visit with in-hospital preparation when most hospitals currently do not bother to prepare a child conveniently located next to the nursing station?

Moreover, the field now shows equivocation about the advisability of routine preparation at all. There are many undocumented suggestions in the literature that "overpreparation" is to be avoided (Levinson & Ousterhout, 1980), that children can assimilate at most one threatening concept at a time (Chan, 1980), and to attempt to explain more is harmful (Becker, 1976). Heffernan and Azarnoff (1971) noted that many physicians and nurses feel describing procedures such as a lumbar puncture or intravenous medication will only agitate the child and that restraining an uninformed child and quickly completing the procedure is less stressful. Such beliefs remain common to many staff members in large hospitals.

It is certainly the case that prevention can be overdone. Similarly, Burstein and Meichenbaum (1979) report that some children actually put their hands over their ears during preparation and we have observed children distracting themselves during our own surgery preparation program. It is probably the case that children differ in terms of how much information is useful and it is undoubtedly the case that individualization of treatment is important. However, the past data would seem to suggest that in most cases for most dependent variables, children and adults are either benefited or unaffected by preparation. To insist that each child be separately screened (in a way yet to be devised) and separately prepared or unprepared in a way which would eliminate any possibility of potential harm from preparation, may in fact result in no children receiving preparation, except in our own research endeavors.

The question becomes whether a program which is beneficial to the large majority of children should fail to receive support or even be discontinued because a minority of children might be sensitized. As scientists, we are trained to answer empirical questions. This question is an ethical and philosophical one which must be answered according to conscience by each researcher and it is unlikely that any individual has the one correct answer.

CONCLUSIONS

After describing the many gaps in our understanding of prevention, and the challenges to future research attempts striving to fill those gaps, it is important to return to the notion that we really do know something about prevention. For most children, merely preparing their parents seems to reduce the children's distress (Skipper & Leonard, 1968) and giving the children information about what to expect is also typically beneficial (Cassell, 1965). We know a great deal about the effectiveness of filmed modeling (Melamed, Klingman, & Siegel, 1983), and techniques such as sensory information (Johnson et al., 1978; Siegel & Peterson, 1980, 1981) and coping skills (Peterson & Shigetomi, 1981; Zastowny et al., Note 5) may offer additional benefits to children. If we combine our desire for increased individualization with a concern for cost-effectiveness, we may yet design programs which can cost-effectively and flexibly draw from the available technologies to yield the best treatment for each child in a large proportion of the hospitals in this country. In the long run, current data suggest that for the most part, children are benefited by rather than traumatized by hospitalization and surgery (Gabriel & Danilowicz, 1978; Peterson & Shigetomi, 1982; Simons et al., 1980). To be able to move in the future from a concept of remediating distress in children in medical settings to a goal of creating an efficacy enhancing experience for each child would be to realize the essence of primary prevention in children.

REFERENCES

Adams, M. A hospital play program: Helping children with serious illness. *American Journal of Orthopsychiatry,* 1976, *46,* 416–424.

Ambrose, G. Hypnosis in the treatment of children. *The American Journal of Clinical Hypnosis,* 1968, *11,* 1–5.

Andrew, J. M. Recovery from surgery, with and without preparatory instruction for three coping styles. *Journal of Personality and Social Psychology,* 1970, *15,* 227–233.

Atthowe, J. M. Behavior innovation and persistence. *American Psychologist,* 1973, *28,* 34–41.

Auerbach, S. M. Trait-state anxiety and adjustment to surgery. *Journal of Consulting and Clinical Psychology,* 1973, *40,* 264–271.

Auerbach, S. M., Kendall, P. C., Cuttler, H. F., & Levitt, N. R. Anxiety, locus of control, type of preparatory information and adjustment to dental surgery. *Journal of Consulting and Clinical Psychology,* 1976, *44,* 809–818.

Averill, J. Personal control over aversive stimuli and its relationship to stress. *Psychological Bulletin,* 1973, *80,* 286–303.

Ax, A. F. The physiological differentiation between fear and anger in humans. *Psychosomatic Medicine,* 1953, *15,* 433–442.

Ayer, W. A. Use of visual imagery in needle phobic children. *Journal of Dentistry for Children,* 1973, *2,* 1–3.

Azarnoff, P. Mediating the trauma of serious illness and hospitalization in childhood. *Children Today,* 1974, *3,* 12–17.

Azarnoff, P. The care of children in hospitals: An overview. *Journal of Pediatric Psychology,* 1976, *1,* 5–6.

Azarnoff, P. Hospital tours for school children ended. *Pediatric Mental Health, 1982, 1*(4), 2.

Azarnoff, P., & Woody, P. D. Preparation of children for hospitalization in acute care hospitals in the United States. *Pediatrics,* 1981, *68,* 361–368.

Azrin, N. H. A strategy for applied research: Learning based but outcome oriented. *American Psychologist,* 1977, *32,* 140–149.

Bandura, A. *Principles of behavior modification.* New York: Holt, Rinehart & Winston, 1969.

Becker, R. D. Therapeutic approaches to psychopathological reactions to hospitalization. *International Journal of Child Psychotherapy,* 1972, *1,* 65–97.

Becker, R. D. Children in the hospital. *Israel Annals of Psychiatry and Related Disciplines,* 1976, *14,* 240–265.

Bernstein, N. R. Observations on the use of hypnosis with burned children on a pediatric ward. *The International Journal of Clinical and Experimental Hypnosis,* 1965, *13,* 1–10.

Beverly, B. I. Effect of illness on emotional development. *Journal of Pediatrics,* 1936, *8,* 533–541.

Brain, D. J., & Maclay, I. Controlled study of mothers and children in hospital. *British Medical Journal,* 1968, *1,* 278–280.

Burstein, S., & Meichenbaum, D. The work of worrying in children undergoing surgery. *Journal of Abnormal Child Psychology,* 1979, *7,* 121–132.

Cassell, S. Effects of brief puppet therapy upon the emotional responses of children undergoing cardiac catheterization. *Journal of Consulting and Clinical Psychology,* 1965, *29,* 1–8.

Chan, J. M. Preparation for procedures and surgery through play. *Paediatrician,* 1980, *9,* 210–219.

Chapman, A. J., Loeb, D. O., & Gibbons, M. J. Psychiatric aspects of hospitalization of children. *Archives of Pediatrics,* 1956, *73,* 77–88.

Chapman, J. S. Effects of different nursing approaches on psychological and physiological responses. *Nursing Research,* 1970, *5,* 1–7.

Chertok, S. L., & Bornstein, P. H. Covert modeling treatment of children's dental fears. *Child Behavior Therapy,* 1979, *1,* 249–255.

Cofer, D. H., & Nir, Y. Theme-focused group therapy on a pediatric ward. *International Journal of Psychiatry in Medicine,* 1975, *6,* 541–550.

Cohen, F., & Lazarus, R. S. Active coping processes, coping dispositions and recovery from surgery. *Psychosomatic Medicine,* 1973, *35,* 375–389.

Crowl, M. Case study: The basic process of art therapy as demonstrated by efforts to allay a child's fear of surgery. *American Journal of Art Therapy,* 1980, *19,* 49–51.

DeLong, D. R. *Individual differences in patterns of anxiety arousal, stress-relevant information and recovery from surgery.* Unpublished doctoral dissertation, University of California, Los Angeles, 1971.

Eckenhoff, J. F. Preanesthetic sedation for children: Analysis of the effects for tonsillectomy and adenoidectomy. *American Medical Association Archives of Otolaryngology,* 1953, *57,* 411–416.

Elkins, P. D., & Roberts, M. C. Psychological preparation for pediatric hospitalization. *Clinical Psychology Review,* 1983, *3,* 275–295.

Erickson, F. H. Play interviews for four-year-old hospitalized children. *Monographs of the Society for Research in Child Development,* 1958, *69,* No. 3.

Ferguson, B. F. Preparing young children for hospitalization: A comparison of two methods, *Pediatrics,* 1979, *64,* 656–664.

Friedrich, W. N. Ameliorating the psychological impact of chronic physical disease on the child and family. *Journal of Pediatric Psychology,* 1977, *2,* 26–31.

Gabriel, H. P. A practical approach to preparing children for dermatologic surgery. *Journal of Dermatological Surgery and Oncology,* 1977, *3,* 523–526.

Gabriel, H. P., & Danilowicz, D. Postoperative responses in "prepared" child after cardiac surgery. *British Heart Journal,* 1978, *40,* 1046–1051.

Gale, E., & Ayer, N. M. Treatment of dental phobias. *Journal of the American Dental Association,* 1969, *73,* 1304–1307.

Gardner, G. G. Hypnosis with children: Selected readings. *The International Journal of Clinical and Experimental Hypnosis,* 1980, *28,* 289–293.

George, J. M., Scott, D. S., Turner, S. P., & Gregg, J. M. The effects of psychological factors and physical trauma on recovery from oral surgery. *Journal of Behavioral Medicine,* 1980, *3,* 291–310.

Gilmore, J. B. *The role of anxiety and cognitive factors in children's play behavior.* Unpublished doctoral dissertation, Yale University, 1964.

Gilmore, J. B. Play: A special behavior. In R. N. Haber (Ed.), *Current research in motivation.* New York: Holt, Rinehart & Winston, 1965.

Ginther, L. J., & Roberts, M. C. A test of mastery versus coping modeling in the reduction of children's dental fears. *Child and Family Behavior Therapy,* 1982, *4,* 41–51.

Goldfried, M. R. Toward the delineation of therapeutic change principles. *American Psychologist,* 1980, *35,* 991–999.

Goldstein, M. J. Individual differences in response to stress. *American Journal of Community Psychology,* 1973, *1,* 113–137.

Goslin, E. R. Hospitalization as a life crisis for the preschool child: A critical review. *Journal of Community Health,* 1978, *3,* 321–346.

Harvey, S. The value of play therapy in hospital. *Paediatrician,* 1980, *9,* 191–198.

Hedberg, A. G., & Schlong, A. Eliminating fainting by school children during mass inoculation clinics. *Nursing Research,* 1973, *22,* 352–353.

Heffernan, M., & Azarnoff, P. Factors in reducing children's anxiety about clinic visits.

Health Services and Mental Health Administration Health Reports, 1971, *86,* 1131–1135.

Heller, J. A. *The hospitalized child and his family.* Baltimore: The Johns Hopkins Press, 1967.

Hersen, M. Complex problems require complex solutions. *Behavior Therapy,* 1981, *12,* 15–29.

Hester, N. K. The preoperational child's reaction to immunization. *Nursing Research,* 1979, *28,* 250–255.

Hitchcock, L. S. *Improving recovery from surgery: The interaction of preoperative interventions, coping processes, and personality variables.* Unpublished Doctoral Dissertation, The University of Texas at Austin, 1982.

Impallaria, C. The contribution of social group work. In R. A. Jensen (Ed.), The hospitalized child: Round table. *American Journal of Orthopsychiatry,* 1955, *25,* 293–318.

Jackson, E. B. Treatment of the young child in the hospital. *American Journal of Orthopsychiatry,* 1942, *12,* 56–67.

Jensen, R. A. The hospitalized child: Round table. *American Journal of Orthopsychiatry,* 1955, *25,* 293–318.

Jessner, L., Blom, G. E., & Waldfogel, S. Emotional implications of tonsillectomy and adenoidectomy in children. In R. S. Eisler (Ed.), *The psychoanalytic study of the child.* New York: International University Press, 1952.

Johnson, B. Before hospitalization. *Children Today,* 1974, *3,* 19.

Johnson, J. E., Kirchhoff, K. T., & Endress, M. P. Altering children's distress behavior during orthopedic cast removal. *Nursing Research,* 1975, *24,* 404–410.

Johnson, J. E., Rice, J. H., Fuller, S. S., & Endress, M. P. Sensory information, instruction in a coping strategy, and recovery from surgery. *Research in Nursing and Health,* 1978, *1,* 4–17.

Johnston, M., & Salazar, M. Preadmission program for rehospitalized children. *American Journal of Nursing,* 1979, *79,* 1420–1422.

Johnson, P. A., & Stockdale, D. F. Effects of puppet therapy on Palmar sweating of hospitalized children. *The Johns Hopkins Medical Journal,* 1975, *137,* 1–5.

Karp, M., & Teuscher, G. W. General anesthesia in difficult pedodontic patients. *Journal of Pediatrics,* 1947, *30,* 317–323.

Katz, E. R., Kellerman, J., & Siegel, S. E. Behavioral distress in children with cancer undergoing medical procedures: Developmental considerations. *Journal of Consulting and Clinical Psychology,* 1980, *48,* 356–365.

Kelfer, L. S., & Demers, P. M. "Floyd and Beasely visit the hospital": A preoperative puppet show. *Nursing Adminstration Quarterly,* 1980, *4,* 27–30.

Klinzing, D. R., & Klinzing, D. G. Communicating with young children about hospitalization. *Communication Education,* 1977, *26,* 307–313.

Klorman, R., Hilpert, P. L., Michael, R., LaGana, C., & Sveen, O. B. Effects of coping and mastery modeling on experienced and inexperienced pedodontic patients' disruptiveness. *Behavior Therapy,* 1980, *11,* 156–168.

Knight, R. B., Atkins, A., Eagle, C., Evans, N., Finkelstein, J. W., Fukushima, D., Katz, J., & Weiner, H. Psychological stress, ego defenses, and cortisol production in children hospitalized for elective surgery. *Psychosomatic Medicine,* 1979, *41,* 40–49.

Knudson-Cooper, M. S. Adjustment to visible stigma: The case of the severely burned. *Social Science and Medicine,* 1981, *158,* 31–44.

LaBaw, W., Holton, C., Tewell, K., & Eccles, D. The use of self-hypnosis by children with cancer. *The American Journal of Clinical Hypnosis,* 1975, *17,* 233–238.

Lacey, J. I. Individual differences in somatic response patterns. *Journal of Comparative and Physiological Psychology,* 1950, *43,* 338–350.

Lang, P. J. The psychophysiology of anxiety. In H. Akiskal (Ed.), *Psychiatric diagnoses: Exploration of biological criteria.* New York: Spectrum, 1978.

Lazarus, A. A., & Abramovitz, A. The use of "emotive imagery" in the treatment of children's phobias. *Journal of Mental Science,* 1962, *108,* 191–195.

Levinson, P., & Ousterhout, D. K. Art and play therapy with pediatric burn patients. *Journal of Burn Care and Rehabilitation,* 1980, *1,* 42–46.

Lewis, N. I probably won't have all the luxuries in the world. *Journal of the Association for the Care of Children in Hospitals,* 1978, *7,* 28–32.

Lick, J. R., & Katkin, E. S. Assessment of anxiety and fear. In M. Hersen & A. S. Bellack (Eds.), *Behavioral assessment: A practical handbook.* New York: Pergamon Press, 1978.

Linenkugel, N. Programs prepare children for hospital procedures. *Hospital Progress,* 1982, *63,* 64.

Lowery, B., Jacobsen, B., & Keane, A. Relationship of locus of control to preoperative anxiety. *Psychological Reports,* 1975, *37,* 1115–1121.

Machen, J., & Johnson, R. Desensitization, model learning, and the dental behavior of children. *Journal of Dental Research,* 1974, *53,* 83–89.

Marholin, D., Siegel, L. J., & Phillips, D. Treatment and transfer: A search for empirical procedures. In M. Hersen, R. M. Eisler, & P. M. Miller (Eds.), *Progress in behavior modification* (Vol. 3). New York: Academic Press, 1976.

Martinez-Urrutia, A. Anxiety and pain in surgical patients. *Journal of Consulting and Clinical Psychology,* 1975, *43,* 437–442.

Mason, E. A. Hospital and family cooperating to reduce psychological trauma. *Community Mental Health Journal,* 1978, *14,* 153–159.

Meichenbaum, D. Self-instructional methods. In F. H. Kanfer & A. P. Goldstein (Eds.), *Helping people change.* New York: Pergamon Press, 1975.

Meichenbaum, D. H., & Goodman, J. Training impulsive children to talk to themselves: A means of developing self-control. *Journal of Abnormal Psychology,* 1971, *77,* 115–126.

Melamed, B. G. Reduction of medical fears: An information processing analysis. In J. Boulougouris (Ed.), *Learning theory approaches to psychiatry.* New York: John Wiley & Sons, 1982.

Melamed, B. G., Hawes, R. R., Heiby, E., & Glick, J. The use of filmed modeling to reduce uncooperative behavior of children during dental treatment. *Journal of Dental Research,* 1975, *54,* 779–801.

Melamed, B. G., Klingman, A., & Siegel, L. J. Childhood stress and anxiety: Individualizing cognitive behavioral strategies in the reduction of medical and dental stress. In A. Meyers & N. E. Craighead, (Eds.), *Cognitive behavior therapy with children.* New York: Plenum, 1983.

Melamed, B. G., Meyer, R., Gee, C., & Soule, L. The influence of time and type of preparation on children's adjustment to hospitalization. *Journal of Pediatric Psychology,* 1976, *1,* 31–37.

Melamed, B. G., Robbins, R. L., & Fernandez, J. Factors to be considered in psychological preparation for surgery. In D. Routh & M. Wolraich (Eds.), *Advances in Developmental and Behavioral Pediatrics.* New York: JAI Press, 1982.

Melamed, B. G., & Siegel, L. J. Reduction of anxiety in children facing hospitalization and surgery by use of filmed modeling. *Journal of Consulting and Clinical Psychology,* 1975, *43,* 511–521.

Melamed, B. G., & Siegel, L. J. *Behavioral medicine: Practical applications in health care.* New York: Springer, 1980.

Melamed, B. G., Weinstein, D., Hawes, R., & Katin-Borland, M. Reduction of fear-related dental management problems with the use of filmed modeling. *Journal of the American Dental Association,* 1975, *90,* 822–826.

Melamed, B. G., Yurcheson, R., Fleece, E. L., Hutcherson, S., & Hawes, R. Effects of film modeling on the reduction of anxiety-related behaviors in individuals varying in level of previous experience in the stress situation. *Journal of Consulting and Clinical Psychology,* 1978, *46,* 1357–1367.

Mellish, R. W. Preparation of a child for hospitalization and surgery. *Pediatric Clinics of North America,* 1969, *16,* 543–553.

Melzack, R. *The puzzle of pain.* New York: Basic Books, 1973.

Moore, C. L. Hypnosis: An adjunct consultation. *American Journal of Clinical Hypnosis,* 1981, *23,* 211–216.

Nocella, J., & Kaplan, R. M. Training children to cope with dental treatment. *Journal of Pediatric Psychology,* 1982, *7,* 175–178.

Olness, K. In-service hypnosis education in a children's hospital. *The American Journal of Clinical Hypnosis,* 1977, *20,* 80–83.

Olness, K. Hypnosis in pediatric practice. *Current Problems in Pediatric Practice,* 1981, *12,* 1–47.

Peterson, L. *The use of a self-control procedure to minimize pain and anxiety in hospitalized children.* Unpublished Doctoral Dissertation, University of Utah, 1978.

Peterson, L. The importance of comparative research in psychological preparation of children. Columbia, Missouri. University of Missouri-Columbia, 1981 (Eric Document Reproduction No. PS012502).

Peterson, L., Hartmann, D. P., & Gelfand, D. M. Prevention of child behavior disorders: A lifestyle change for child psychologists. In P. Davidson & S. Davidson (Eds.), *Behavior medicine: Changing health lifestyles.* New York: Brunner/Mazel, 1980.

Peterson, L., & Ridley-Johnson, R. Pediatric hospital response to survey on prehospital preparation for children. *Journal of Pediatric Psychology,* 1980, *5,* 1–7.

Peterson, L., Schultheis, K., Ridley-Johnson, R., Miller, D. V., & Tracy, K. Comparison of three modeling procedures on the presurgical and postsurgical reactions of children. *Behavior Therapy,* 1984, *15,* 197–203.

Peterson, L., & Shigetomi, C. The use of coping techniques to minimize anxiety in hospitalized children. *Behavior Therapy,* 1981, *12,* 1–14.

Peterson, L., & Shigetomi, C. One year follow-up of behavioral presurgical preparation for children. *Journal of Pediatric Psychology,* 1982, *7,* 43–48.

Pidgeon, V. Function of preschool children's questions in coping with hospitalization. *Research in Nursing and Health,* 1981, *4,* 229–235.

Pomarico, C., Marsh, K., & Doubrava, P. Hospital orientation for children. *AORN Journal,* 1979, *29,* 864–70; 875.

Prugh, D. G., & Jordan, K. Physical illness or injury: The hospital as a source of emotional disturbances in child and family. In I. N. Berlin (Ed.), *Advocacy for child mental health.* New York: Brunner/Mazel, 1975.

Prugh, D. G., Staub, E. M., Sands, H. H., Kirschbaum, R. M., & Lenihan, E. A. A study of the emotional reactions of children and families to hospitalization and illness. *American Journal of Orthopsychiatry,* 1953, *23,* 70–106.

Ramirez-Johnson, M. Mental health interventions with medically ill children: A review of the literature 1970-1977. *Journal of Pediatric Psychology,* 1979, *4,* 147–163.

Roberts, M. C., Wurtele, S. K., Boone, R. R., Ginther, L. J., & Elkins, P. D. Reduction of medical fears by use of modeling: A preventive application in a general population of children. *Journal of Pediatric Psychology,* 1981, *6,* 293–300.

Robison, S. J. A nurse's role in preparing children for surgery. *AORN Journal,* 1979, *30,* 619–623.

Roskies, E., Mongeon, M., & Gagnon-Lefebvre, B. Increasing maternal participation in the hospitalization of young children. *Medical Care,* 1978, *16,* 765–767.

Russell, R. K., & Sipich, J. F. Treatment of test anxiety by cue-controlled relaxation. *Behavior Therapy,* 1974, *5,* 673–676.

Savedra, M. Coping with pain: Strategies of severely burned children. *The Canadian Nurse,* 1977, *16,* 28–29.

Schrader, E. S. Preparation play helps children in hospitals. *AORN Journal,* 1979, *30,* 336, 340–341.

Seagull, E. A. W. The child's rights as medical patient. *Journal of Clinical Child Psychology,* 1978, *7,* 202–205.

Shipley, R. H., Butt, J. H., Horwitz, B., & Farbry, J. E. Preparation for a stressful medical procedure: Effect of amount of stimulus preexposure and coping style. *Journal of Consulting and Clinical Psychology,* 1978, *46,* 499–507.

Shipley, R. H., Butt, J., & Horwitz, E. Preparation to reexperience a stressful medical examination: Effect of repetitious videotape exposure and coping style. *Journal of Consulting and Clinical Psychology,* 1979, *47,* 485–492.

Siegel, L. J. Preparation of children for hospitalization: A selected review of the research literature. *Journal of Pediatric Psychology,* 1976, *1,* 26–30.

Siegel, L. J., & Peterson, L. Stress reduction in young dental patients through coping skills and sensory information. *Journal of Consulting and Clinical Psychology,* 1980, *48,* 785–787.

Siegel, L. J., & Peterson, L. Maintenance effects of coping skills and sensory information on young children's response to repeated dental procedures. *Behavior Therapy,* 1981, *12,* 530–535.

Sime, A. M. Relationship of preoperative fear, type of coping, and information received about surgery to recovery from surgery. *Journal of Personality and Social Psychology,* 1976, *34,* 716–724.

Simeonsson, R. J., Buckley, L., & Monson, L. Conceptions of illness causality in hospitalized children. *Journal of Pediatric Psychology,* 1979, *4,* 77–84.

Simons, B., Bradshaw, J., & Silva, P. A. Hospital admissions during the first five years of life: A report from the Dunedin Multidisciplinary Child Development Study. *New Zealand Medical Journal,* 1980, *91,* 144–147.

Skipper, J., & Leonard, R. C. Children, stress and hospitalization: A field experiment. *Journal of Health and Social Behavior,* 1968, *9,* 275–287.

Skipper, J. K., Leonard, R. C., & Rhymes, J. Child hospitalization and social interaction: An experimental study of mothers' feelings of stress, adaptation and satisfaction. *Medical Care,* 1968, *6,* 496–506.

Smitherman, C. H. Parents of hospitalized children have needs, too. *American Journal of Nursing,* 1979, *79,* 1423–1424.

Spinetta, J. J. Adjustment in children with cancer. *Journal of Pediatric Psychology,* 1977, *2,* 49–51.

Stainton, C. Preschoolers' orientation to hospital. *The Canadian Nurse,* 1974, *70,* 38–40.

Stokes, T. F., & Kennedy, S. H. Reducing child uncooperative behavior during dental treatment through modeling and reinforcement. *Journal of Applied Behavior Analysis,* 1980, *13,* 41–49.

Taylor, F. L. Educational preparation for surgery: An examination of physical and behavioral parameters post-operatively. *Dissertation Abstracts International,* 1978, *38,* 6416.

Trouten, F. Psychological preparation of children for surgery. *Dimensions of Health Service,* 1981, *58,* 9–10; 12–13.

Tsigounis, S. A. The relationship between parent-child perceptions of hospitalization and the child's subsequent psychological response. *Dissertation Abstracts International,* 1978, *38,* 3915.

Vernon, D. T. A., & Bailey, W. C. The use of motion pictures in the psychological preparation of children for induction of anesthesia. *Anesthesiology,* 1974, *40,* 68–74.

Vernon, D. T. A., Foley, J. M., & Schulman, J. L. Effect of mother-child separation and birth order on young children's responses to two potentially stressful experiences. *Journal of Personality and Social Psychology,* 1967, *5,* 162–174.

Visintainer, M., & Wolfer, J. Theater as therapy: How rehearsing your patients can help them cope. *RN,* 1979, *42,* 56–62.

Wallack, M. A., & Kogan, N. *Modes of thinking in young children.* New York: Holt, Rinehart, & Winston, 1965.

Weinstein, D. J. Imagery and relaxation with a burn patient. *Behavior Research and Therapy,* 1976, *14,* 481.

Weinstein, P., Getz, T., Ratener, P., & Domoto, P. The effects of dentist variables on fear-related behaviors of young children. *Journal of the American Dental Association,* 1982, *104,* 32–37. (a)

Weinstein, P., Getz, T., Ratener, P., & Domoto, P. Dentist responses to fear and non-fear related child behaviors in the operatory. *Journal of the American Dental Association,* 1982, *104,* 38–40. (b)

Williams, P. D. Preparation of school-age children for surgery: A program in preventive pediatrics—Philippines. *International Journal of Nursing Studies,* 1980, *17,* 107–109.

Wilson, J. F. Behavioral preparation for surgery: Benefit or harm? *Journal of Behavioral Medicine,* 1981, *4,* 79–101.

Wolfer, J. A., & Visintainer, M. A. Pediatric surgical patients' and parents' stress responses and adjustment. *Nursing Research,* 1975, *24,* 244–255.

Wolfer, J. A., & Visintainer, M. A. Prehospital psychological preparation for tonsillectomy patients: Effects on children's and parents' adjustment. *Pediatrics,* 1979, *64,* 646–655.

REFERENCE NOTES

1. Wolfer, J. & Visintainer, M. *Stress management nursing care for pediatric surgical patients and their parents: Evolution and testing of a practice theory.* Paper presented at the Annual Nursing Research Conference at the Western Council on Higher Education for Nursing. Denver, CO: May 1982.
2. Hodel, T. V., O'Grady, D., & Steffen, J. *Hypnosis for leukemic children for alleviation of anxiety and pain.* Paper presented at the meeting of the American Psychological Association, Washington, D.C., August 1982.
3. Katz, E. R., Kellerman, J., & Ellenberg, L. *Hypnosis in the reduction of acute pain and distress in children with leukemia: Results of a longitudinal controlled study.* Paper presented at the meeting of the Association for Advancement of Behavior Therapy, Los Angeles, November 1982.
4. Melamed, B. G., Bennett, C. G., Jerrell, G., Ross, S. L., Bush, J. P., Hill, C., Courts, F., & Ronk, S. *Dentists' behavior management as it affects compliance and fear in pediatric patients.* Manuscript submitted for publication, 1982.
5. Zastowny, T. R., Kirschenbaum, D. S., & Meng, A. L. *Coping skills training for children: Effects on distress before, during, and after hospitalization for surgery.* Paper presented at the meeting of the Association for Advancement of Behavior Therapy, Toronto, Canada, 1981.
6. Olson, R. A., & Elliott, C. H. *Observations of pain control with children: Burns and invasive procedures.* Paper presented at the meeting of the American Psychological Association, Washington, D.C., August 1982.
7. Jay, S. *Assessment of pain and anxiety in childhood cancer patients.* Paper presented at the meeting of the American Psychological Association, Washington, D.C., August 1982.
8. Jay, S. *Behavioral treatment of procedure-related distress in pediatric cancer patients.* Paper presented at the meeting of the American Psychological Association, Washington, D.C., August 1982.
9. Siegel, L. J. *Naturalistic study of coping strategies in children facing medical procedures.* Paper presented at the meeting of the Southeastern Psychological Association, Atlanta, April 1981.

PART THREE

Population-Wide Prevention

Treatment of Children in Selected Settings

CHAPTER 10

Prevention of Child Problems in the Schools

LEONARD A. JASON, JOSEPH A. DURLAK, AND EVE HOLTON-WALKER

This chapter, along with Chapter 4 by Durlak and Jason, describes preventive interventions for school-aged children and adolescents. Chapter 4 reviewed programs that worked directly with children or adolescents to improve their interpersonal functioning (for example, affective education, school-based secondary prevention). This chapter concerns preventive programming for the same populations; however, the focus here is on an ecological orientation and on the prevention of scholastic/academic problems.

Ecologically oriented programs influence individuals indirectly through environmental manipulation. This can be accomplished by modifying environments or by placing youngsters into more positive environmental situations; the ultimate goal is to identify and then establish environmental settings that are maximally conducive to each child's growth and development. Ecological programs stress the importance of studying environmental-individual transactions, since it is assumed that environments affect individuals differently. Certain children may function best in one type of environment, whereas others may do best in another.

Schools implicitly use ecological principles in their educational programming. For instance, in assigning children to classrooms, they often place children with certain teachers either because of those teachers' interpersonal styles or because of their particular educational practices. In addition, teachers often ask to work with certain types of children. Within classrooms, teachers may place children in different subgroups or vary their instructional methods with different children in the belief that some procedures are more effective with some children than with others. For the most part, this ecological matchmaking is not systematic in the sense that empirical data seldom are the basis for determining different school practices. This chapter discusses research findings from ecologically oriented studies that have preventive implications for school children. The major intent is to illustrate how current theory, research, and practice in ecological psychology can be applied to school settings, either to prevent various educational problems from occurring in the first place (primary prevention) or to engineer prompt interventions for early detected dysfunction (secondary prevention).

An ecological perspective is logically compelling. It is reasonable to believe that pupils react differently to various teaching methods, classroom environments, and school policies; but these ecological interactions are difficult to document precisely. Several fundamental questions might be useful in guiding the progress of ecologically oriented preventive research. Evaluators need to decide which environmental and individual characteristics they must measure before the best person-environmental fits can be determined for different youngsters. Should we study physical design variables (for instance, size of classroom), social climate, and school policies? What student characteristics should be studied: developmental status, intellectual and cognitive assets, past academic performance, current learning styles, personal and motivational variables, or familial educational influences? What teacher characteristics are important: reinforcement patterns, interpersonal warmth, frustration tolerance, technical instructional proficiency, or personal stress and adjustment? Finally, how do all the above variables interact in any given setting for different subject groups? Investigators are just beginning to discover answers to such questions, so the tentative nature of current ecological research must be emphasized. Nevertheless, several sources of information converge to indicate the preventive potential of ecological principles and are highlighted here.

The next section presents a brief review of the relationship between social and academic competence. In developing ecologically sound programs, researchers might need to assess and develop both types of competencies. While Chapter 4 focused more on social competencies, this chapter deals with more academically related abilities. Since teachers represent a critical and dynamic part of school environments, a section is devoted to exploring the relationship between the instructional styles and practices of teachers, and pupil achievement and adjustment. Next, specific approaches for enhancing student achievement (for example, tutoring and individualized instruction) are reviewed briefly. These programs illustrate how resources available in school environments can be mobilized to enhance competencies. Then presented are particular issues in constructing ecologically valid interventions to enhance achievement in youngsters with learning disabilities. Finally, the last sections of the chapter present a schema for conceptualizing the range of organizational and community level interventions which can be employed in preventive school-based programs.

RELATIONSHIPS BETWEEN SOCIAL AND ACADEMIC COMPETENCIES

A central issue in developing school-based ecological programs concerns the relationship between social and academic competence. Investigators wonder whether to focus their attention on enhancing academic skills that might positively affect children's social development, or on developing critical social competencies which might enhance learning and achievement. It is also possible that other variables exist to mediate the progression of both academic and social growth and that the academic and social dimensions are relatively independent.

Unfortunately, answers to the above questions are unclear due to the inconsistent and unreliable ways in which academic and social competence indices have been defined and measured in prior studies. Also, few studies have employed experimental designs that clearly established causal relationships between variables. Despite limitations on the underlying research, there does appear to be some relationship between social and academic competence, with the strongest relationship appearing at the extremes of the distribution. That is, *as a group,* children with emotional, mental or physical disabilities do poorly academically and demonstrate more social and behavioral difficulties compared to children without such handicaps. Likewise, children of superior intellect and cognitive ability as a group are more adept socially than children with fewer intellectual assets. However, there are many exceptions to these findings and the relationship between academic and social skills for the vast majority of school children cannot be accurately predicted.

Relationships between social and academic competencies are illustrated well by Hansford and Hattie's (1982) recent review article. They found an average correlation of only .21 between measures of self-esteem and academic performance or achievement. Across the 128 studies reviewed, however, correlations ranged from − .77 to + .96. Accordingly, Hansford and Hattie (1982) concluded that "Given the volume and diversity of the literature, it is possible to find some support for virtually any viewpoint regarding the relationship between self and performance" (p. 126). Of course, correlations do not imply causality. Many investigators have successfully improved school children's social *or* academic competence but have failed to find corresponding positive changes on the nontargeted competence. Given these findings, it might be best to adopt the conservative position that academic and social competence are relatively independent until research convincingly demonstrates otherwise. Generalization of program effects across social and academic domains may occur, but such findings cannot be expected consistently. Therefore, ecological and preventive investigators who wish to improve academic functioning should focus on such measures for intervention; the same can be said for those interested in improving social competencies. Ways of enhancing social competencies are illustrated by Durlak and Jason in Chapter 4, and approaches for enhancing academic abilities are described in this chapter.

The next section explores the relationships between academic indices and various teacher, curricular, and parent variables. The studies reviewed illustrate the potent effects of several school ecological factors on pupil achievement and performance.

INSTRUCTION, ACHIEVEMENT, AND INTERVENTIONS

School children's achievement in classrooms has been related to the instructional styles of teachers. In Brophy's (1979) comprehensive review article, increases in children's achievement were found to be positively related to the following teaching strategies: (1) monitoring the entire class continuously, (2) conducting more than one activity at a time without breaking the flow of classroom events, (3) moving activities along at a good pace, and (4) providing work at the right level of difficulty and interest to hold the children's attention. These teaching strategies might be thought of as preventive techniques which, to some degree, could obviate the need for using control methods to deal with misconduct. In fact, Brophy (1979) suggests that classroom management skills correlate with student learning gains primarily because teachers who are good managers tend also to be good instructors. These findings are of relevance to school-based mental health professionals, for they suggest that teacher consultation programs might profit from reducing time spent on child management techniques and devoting more energy to developing generic effective teaching strategies.

Teaching strategies for enhancing achievement might need to be individualized to fit the needs of different groups of youngsters (Brophy, 1979). For example, instructors of high socioeconomic status, high ability students are most successful if they teach at a rapid pace, keep the students challenged, and enforce high standards by refusing to accept inferior work. On the other hand, teachers of low socioeconomic status, low ability students are most successful if they are determined to get the most out of their students, but move at a slower pace, allow more time for practice, use considerable warmth, encouragement, and praise, and are supportive in dealing with the concerns of their students. In consulting with teachers, it might be inappropriate to stress universal teaching skills, as teachers in different classrooms might require different strategies for maximum effect.

Another factor influencing students' ability to learn involves teacher anxiety, which might affect up to 200,000 teachers (Coates & Thoresen, 1976). Teacher anxiety may stem from a variety of sources, including inability to maintain discipline, student dislike, lack of knowledge in subject areas, time demands, large class enrollments, and lack of educational resources. When a teacher is anxious, the accompanying classroom climate is not conducive to optimal pupil learning (Keavney & Sinclair, 1978). Mental health professionals can alleviate teacher anxiety by setting up behavioral programs (for example, systematic desensitization, relaxation strategies), providing teachers with more social support and resources, reducing classroom size, or improving teaching techniques.

Curricula which seem to be most effective in facilitating achievement typically focus on structured, task-related activities. Stallings and Kaskowitz (1974), for example, found that time spent on other activities (for instance, arts and crafts) correlated negatively with students' reading and math achievement, and the opportunity to engage in reading and math-related activities contributed to higher test scores in these areas. These findings suggest that an effective way to accelerate achievement or remediate deficiencies in basic subject areas might be to devote relatively large amounts of time to academic-related activities (Centra & Potter, 1980).

One approach that concentrates on intensive academic instruction and skills training is the Direct Instruction Model. Direct Instruction merges Becker's work on classroom-based reinforcement procedures with principles inherent in the successful Bereiter-Englemann preschool program (Becker & Carnine, 1980). The Direct Instruction Model's major elements include step-by-step training in basic skills, systematic reinforcement for correct responses, and effective use of teaching time. This teaching approach emphasizes small group instruction in reading, oral language, and arithmetic, and uses a fast-paced approach with unison group responses and immediate correction of pupil errors. The program is implemented by following a carefully sequenced curriculum that provides teachers with detailed procedural manuals, teaching aides and materials, and methods to monitor student progress.

Direct Instruction was one of 13 teaching strategies evaluated in the nationwide, government sponsored Project Follow Through program. Project Follow Through targets economically disadvantaged children for special instruction from kindergarten through third grade. As a group these children can be considered at high risk for subsequent poor school achievement and thus are good candidates for secondary prevention interventions. Controversy has surrounded the design, results, and interpretation of Project Follow Through (see the *Harvard Educational Review,* 1978). Nevertheless, outcome data are very favorable for the Direct Instruction approach. Of all the programs studied, Direct Instruction produced the greatest gains in academic (particularly language and math skills) and affective areas such as self-esteem (Becker & Carnine, 1980). Moreover, whereas the normative expectation for disadvantaged children without special help is performance at the twentieth percentile, children in the Direct Instruction programs performed close to or above national norms attained by all school children (that is, the fiftieth percentile).

A two year follow-up indicated that, although children in the Direct Instruction programs still significantly outperformed nonparticipating controls, their academic performance reflected some erosion of gains when compared to the national norms (Becker & Gersten, 1982). To overcome this erosion, Becker and Gersten suggest the development of direct instructional programs for older children using the same principles found effective with younger children (for example, high levels of feedback and incremental steps to develop independent reading, writing, and critical thinking skills).

Research data suggest that children's school achievement is more strongly related to such familial variables as parental encouragement and stimulation of learning than to demographic variables such as socioeconomic status (White, 1982). This implies that another strategy to increase children's academic performance would be to involve parents directly in educational programs. Basically, this strategy can be accomplished in three ways: (1) use of parents as classroom-based teacher aides either on a volunteer or paid paraprofessional basis (Cohen, 1976), (2) training parents to administer tutoring programs, and (3) home-based reinforcement systems. Each of these strategies has met with some success, but only the last is discussed here.

In home-based reinforcement systems, teachers communicate with parents regarding the child's school behavior. Then parents reinforce appropriate behaviors contingently at home, in accord with teacher reports (Atkeson & Forehand, 1979; see also Forehand, Walley, & Furey, Chapter 11 of this volume). Recent studies conducted by Blechman and her colleagues represent successful examples of such an approach. Blechman, Kotanchik, and Taylor (1981) selected children for their intervention who were inconsistent in their daily classwork (such children tend to perform more poorly on social, emotional, and academic indices than youngsters who do not manifest inconsistent performance). Parents of the target children were provided a one hour session in a clinic where they were taught how to implement contingency contracts. When children brought their parents notes from the teacher indicating more consistent classroom performance, parents were to reward the children. Teachers also called parents weekly, to monitor and assess how the contracting system was operating. At program end, the target children's classroom work had improved. In a later program, Blechman, Taylor, and Schrader (1981) found that the accuracy of the target children's classroom work improved significantly, even on probe days when children were not reinforced, suggesting that the effects had begun to be generalized. Developing programs that link family cooperation with teacher efforts might be particularly useful, from a preventive perspective, at critical transition points such as when children initially enter school or during the first weeks of class with a first-time teacher (Douglas & Jason, 1979).

INTERVENTIONS TO INCREASE ACHIEVEMENT AND MOTIVATION

Tutoring

There are many ways to enhance achievement in school children. One method for maximally using resources within schools and helping resolve mental health manpower shortages involves using school youngsters to tutor other children. Cross-age and peer tutoring projects represent constructive approaches for harnessing underutilized student resources and directly changing the learning environment by creating behavior settings where children directly participate in teaching other youngsters. Cross-age tutoring projects involve older children tutoring younger children. For example, college students have tutored seventh graders (Schwartz, 1977), high school youngsters have worked with fourth and fifth graders (Cloward, 1967), and fifth and sixth graders have tutored kindergarten youngsters (Johnson & Bailey, 1974). Peer tutoring projects have featured children in the same grade level tutoring one another. Youngsters from first grade (Jason, Ferone, & Soucy, 1979) to the college level (Coyne, 1978) have been used effectively in peer tutoring projects. Both cross-age and peer tutoring projects represent innovative approaches for allowing children to assume more responsibility in helping one another enhance learning competencies.

Cohen, Kulik, and Kulik (1982) have recently conducted a meta-analysis of tutoring studies. Starting with about 500 articles, they selected only those projects which (1) occurred in elementary or secondary schools, (2) reported quantitative data on experimental and control groups, and (3) were free from crippling methodological flaws. Findings of this meta-analysis revealed that tutored youngsters outperformed their control peers on achievement tests. In addition, the facilitating effects of tutoring were stronger in more structured programs, in projects of shorter duration, when lower level skills were taught, and when math rather than reading was the subject of tutoring. In addition, children expressed more positive attitudes toward the tutored subjects. Tutors also developed more positive attitudes toward the subject areas and evidenced significant gains in achievement. Finally, neither tutees nor tutors changed in self-esteem as a result of the projects.

While these favorable results (particularly the enhanced achievement scores) are encouraging, tutoring projects reviewed thus far have primarily been restricted to aiding youngsters with academic and social difficulties. In other words, few attempts have been made to employ these tutoring programs with normally functioning youngsters. As an example of this approach, Harris and Sherman (1973) arranged an entire class of fourth graders in groups of two and three to help one another solve math problems. The percentage of correct math problems and problems worked on were highest when the math period was preceded by peer tutoring. In another example, Jason, Frasure, and Ferone (1981) had a class of eighth graders supervise an entire class of first graders. The first graders were placed in groups of three for two 15-minute tutoring sessions each week. In each group, three first graders were assigned the roles of tutor, tutee and scorekeeper. Roles were switched every five minutes so that each first grader had the opportunity to play all three roles. The eighth graders systematically established three critical tutoring behaviors (correcting incorrect answers, re-presenting the questions following wrong answers, and using contingent praise) in all the program youngsters. At the end of the project, the first grade children registered significant improvements on standardized achievement tests as well as in teacher perceptions of their abilities (grades). In addition, the tutored first graders as compared to a control classroom had fewer overall adjustment problems. This program suggests that tutoring projects can foster academic and interpersonal skills in all children, not only in those identified as having academic or social skill deficits. Mental health professionals might be particularly interested in establishing behavior settings where all children can help one another learn, assume positions of responsibility, and adopt a more active stance in the learning process.

Besides extending tutoring programs to more youngsters, school-based professionals might also explore ways of developing more comprehensive tutoring programs in which significant individuals actively influence children's development. For example, children transferring into a new school, who might be academically behind peers, could immediately be provided tutoring projects to ensure that academic or behavioral difficulties do not occur. In addition, home notes could be delivered to parents, so they could reinforce and build upon progress occurring in the school. In other words, multifaceted preventive programs featuring, for example, tutoring and parent involvement, could be implemented to avert problems and prevent early maladjustment.

From another perspective, providing a tutor changes the child's ecological sphere. By placing a child in a situation involving direct individual assistance, educators can almost completely eliminate the tutee's off-task behavior (Jason, Christensen, & Carl, 1982). Behavior changes can occur when children are placed into settings which encourage the display or development of specific behavior patterns. This idea will be explored more thoroughly in the sections dealing with organizational interventions, such as the influence of environmental dimensions on achievement and adjustment.

Individualized Programming

In the 1950s, programmed instruction was introduced into school systems in the form of teaching machines. At that time, this educational innovation promised to free teachers from routine instructional tasks and enable pupils to move at their own pace through carefully sequenced material, with continuous reinforcement for accurate responses (Connolly, 1972). The movement toward this instructional form peaked in the mid-1970s, and today many teachers and administrators resist implementing this form of instruction because they feel individualized programming is too demanding, costly, and difficult (Rothrock, 1982). As a consequence, instruction in schools today is still predominantly teacher administered and group-oriented; however, school principles relevant to individualized forms of instruction currently influence school systems (Lahey, 1979). For example, more teachers now place value on developing specific behavioral objectives, encouraging active pupil responses in the educational process, and providing positive reinforcement for step-by-step learning progress.

Over the past two decades, many studies have compared the achievement of students who were taught in either a programmed or a more conventional method. Kulik, Schwalb, and Kulik (1982) recently did a meta-analysis of 48 relatively well designed comparison studies. Their general findings were that programmed instruction did not improve the effectiveness of secondary school learning. In comparison to conventional instruction, programmed instruction did not raise student achievement on final examinations and did not make students feel more positive about the subject matter. The authors did note that in the more recent studies, programmed instruction boosted student achievement more than in the earlier applications, suggesting that the more recent investigations used better developed and more refined programs.

Computers and their applications in educational settings have replaced much of the enthusiasm once directed toward programmed learning. Computers are now used in nearly every school system in the U.S. Currently, they are used more frequently for completing assignments for computer courses or in playing educationally related games with canned programs. Finkel (1982) has criticized some of the assumptions upon which the computer revolution is based. Many qualities in effective teaching, he claims, involve processes foreign to computers (for example, enthusiasm, hope, energy, and the intuitive ability to find the right words to communicate with a given child). Evans (1982), foreseeing a future trend, counters these arguments with the upcoming portable, personal teaching computers. Students will be given the impression that these teaching computers are interested in teaching, since communications will be structured so that pupil needs are being met continually. One day, Evans claims, powerful interactive systems will be developed, allowing teaching computers to teach and have "intellectual chats" and "conversations" with their students. Rather than identifying dull and tedious programs as the limiting factor in computer system growth, we might see future dangers in a further division of learners who embrace technology thoroughly and reap the benefits of an increasingly computer-sophisticated society, and others who fail to learn new computer technologies and consequently are ill-fit to function effectively in society. Once again, the ecological challenge is to match student learning styles and instructional techniques effectively, so that all students benefit.

In order to ensure that all children learn appropriate core academic material as well as technological advances, educational settings might increasingly tap into multimedia sources and mastery learning. Media sources, including television and computers, could be used to create conditions conducive to learning and to prevent problems. Bruffee (1982), for example, suggests that television could be used in a collaborative mode, whereby people learned from one another. Youngsters in different educational settings could be linked together through computer systems to ensure mastery learning (each child mastering a predetermined set of objectives through instruction which can include large group, small group, one-to-one teaching, combinations of computer assisted instruction, programmed instruction, games and worksheets). These technologies have important preventive implications. For example, a child who was required to stay home for a period of time due to illness could continue interacting with classmates by viewing parts of the classroom through a home video terminal. The pupil could be tutored by an older child or participate in a group discussion, though not physically present in the classroom. In addition to preventing academic deficits, these strategies could do much to reduce the isolation and loneliness which homebound youngsters experience, particularly when they are unable to attend school for extended periods of time.

Preventive mental health professionals might participate in developing and evaluating these technological systems which might have far-reaching effects on our educational systems. If school mental health professionals can design educational systems which ensure that all children master critical academic and interpersonal competencies, it is highly probable that many youngsters' later mental health problems will be averted.

Reservations about the introduction of technologically-aided instruction should be heeded. By early 1982, reports were beginning to appear in the popular literature concerning youth who were becoming "mesmerized" or "addicted" to computers, television, or video games and whose academic and social development was suffering. Whether or not these cases are representative is unknown; however, attempts to bring technological innovations into the classroom must be attuned to possible deleterious effects. Nonetheless, in the coming decades, there will be exciting possibilities for preventive mental health professionals with interests in developing and integrating technological innovations into school systems.

PREVENTION OF SERIOUS LEARNING DIFFICULTIES: LEARNING DISABILITIES AND MENTAL RETARDATION

While previous sections have dealt with the prevention of poor achievement in schools, this section discusses learning disabilities and mental retardation. Successful prevention of either of these conditions would have far-reaching positive effects. Depending on one's criteria, approximately 3% of the population functions in the mentally retarded range (Coleman, Butcher, & Carson, 1980) and approximately 2–16% are considered to be learning disabled (Clarizio & McCoy, 1976). Each condition can have long-term negative consequences. Learning disabilities have been linked with juvenile delinquency, school dropout rates, and antisocial behavior. Many mentally retarded children who do not receive the necessary academic, vocational, and social skills training during their school careers, demonstrate marginal social and vocational adjustment as adults. Furthermore, both learning disabled and mentally retarded children often are actively rejected and ostracized by their nonhandicapped peers (Gresham, 1981). It is not hard to see how learning problems compounded by frequent negative peer interactions can take their toll on learning disabled and mentally retarded children's levels of aspiration, goal-directed behavior, and feelings of self-worth.

The above discussion is not meant to imply that negative outcomes inevitably follow mental retardation or learning disabilities, but indicates that learning disabled and retarded children are at risk for a variety of adjustment difficulties. Successful preventive programming for these populations could have a substantial impact on the functioning of a significant minority of school children. Since preventive interventions for the learning disabled and mentally retarded involve different issues, each condition is discussed separately. We also note that the presentation of these two developmental problems together does not imply a relationship in etiology, characteristics, needed interventions, or outcomes. These are two particular types of learning problems or handicaps confronting prevention programmers in the school. Although our discussion centers on learning disabilities and mental retardation, as examples of neurological and intellectual problems respectively, other preventive efforts can be fruitfully applied to handicaps resulting from muscular difficulties such as cerebral palsy and sensory problems such as deafness and blindness.

Learning Disabilities

Comments regarding the prevention of learning disabilities must be offered cautiously, since there is no agreement on the exact definition or parameters of learning disabilities. Conceptual confusion surrounding the description of learning disabled children compromises efforts at measurement and prediction of this problem. For example, Sabatino and Miller (1980) noted that there are at least 60 definitions of learning disabilities and school districts do not apply uniform criteria in labeling children as learning disabled. Furthermore, many of the instruments used to identify the presence of learning disabilities have been constructed for other purposes; consequently, use of such measures may provide an incomplete or a highly inaccurate assessment of the phenomenon in question.

Learning disabilities can be prevented by designing interventions that promote academic achievement for all children, or by identifying at-risk children and providing them special attention. Since programs illustrating the former approach have been discussed in earlier sections, only efforts exemplifying at-risk identification are discussed here.

Before at-risk children can be helped, they must be reliably identified. Several investigations have attempted to predict the occurrence of learning disabilities, but these studies vary in terms of which variables are used as predictors and criteria and when data are collected. Many studies collect initial data immediately prior to, or at the point of, school entry in an attempt to predict children's learning status after one or two years in school. Most commonly, one or more measures of aptitude or school readiness are used as predictors. Teacher ratings and academic achievement in one or more subject areas usually serve as criteria in assessing children's school performance. Occasionally, data on physical health and development and information about the family are used.

When predicting who will develop learning problems, it is important to know how accurately individual children are classified. True positives are those children who are predicted to have learning problems and actually experience such difficulties; false positives are those expected to have difficulties but do not. False negatives are those children who have learning problems that were not predicted, and true negatives consist of those who were correctly predicted as being free of serious learning difficulties. Most investigators try to maximize the percentage of true positives that are correctly classified in the belief that the failure to identify children with learning problems is a serious error. However, efforts to increase the percentage of true positives usually increase the percentage of false positives. The identification of false positives increases the risk of a negative self-fulfilling prophecy for the child, family, and teacher.

Six recent investigations illustrate efforts to predict learning problems (Dunleavy, Hansen, Szasz, & Baade, 1981; Friedman, Fuerth, & Forsythe, 1980; Gallerani, O'Regan, & Reinherz, 1982; Ireton, Shing-lun, & Kampen, 1981; Margolis, Sheridan, & Lemanowicz, 1981; Lewis, 1980). Using the best predictions from each study, the percentage of correctly classified children ranged from 36 to 74 for true positives, 26 to 64 for false positives, 74 to 97 for true negatives, and 3 to 26 for false negatives. These data indicate the variability and error involved in current efforts to predict which children will or will not eventually display learning difficulties. It is unlikely that substantial improvement in predictive validity will occur until greater precision is attained in the specification and measurement of learning dysfunctions.

Notwithstanding the problems inherent in identifying learning disabilities, it is possible to discuss a variety of interventions for children with learning problems. Once a child is diagnosed as having a learning disability, there are several ways to intervene. Learning disabled children can be provided tutoring in the classroom (Jason et al., 1982), or they can be provided remedial work in a resource room on the subject area of greatest difficulty (Wender & Wender, 1978). A preventive strategy might entail identifying basic academic competencies each child needs to master. If a basic task were not mastered, the child would immediately be provided extra instruction (for example, tutoring). In addition, since children learn at different rates, different levels of instruction might be needed within each class. Children with advanced academic skills could serve as teacher aides, helping youngsters who learn material at slower paces. A child with difficulties in academic areas might be particularly adept in a nonacademic field and could share these competencies with other youngsters to promote a sharing of resources and develop each child's sense of worth.

When preventive programs such as the one outlined above cannot be implemented, there is a need to develop programs for youngsters with deficits so severe that they cannot be kept in regular classrooms. These children have frequently been placed in alternative psychoeducational programs. Hobbs (1966) has called for an ecological perspective in conceptualizing and developing these types of alternative educational settings. Within such a system, when a child's behavior departs from environmental expectations, the problem is perceived as an indication of a malfunctioning system. In other words, whereas a traditional posture has been to ask "What is wrong with the learning disabled child?", the question now becomes, "Why is the typical educational process often ineffective with learning disabled children?" After understanding why the system no longer is working, interventions are developed with members of the child's ecosystem, which includes the child, the family, agencies, and institutions in the child's environment. Neuhaus, Mowrey and Glenwick (1982) recently described this type of psychoeducational program as a comprehensive intervention utilizing psychological and educational consultants to help identify and utilize community resources which will help youngsters with significant behavior problems and learning disabilities. In a special school, children in groups of six to eight were provided instruction using a token economy system and help from a diverse group of professionals. A supervisor in Learning Disabilities/Behavior Disorders was available to the two teachers in each classroom for curriculum assistance and individualized educational planning. Two part-time clinical child psychologists provided therapy for the program children when needed, and parent counseling and liaison work with relevant community agencies. Comprehensive health, occupational therapy, and language evaluations were provided by a local pediatric hospital, and a county welfare department helped place youngsters into foster homes or residential facilities, or re-integrate them back into their homes. In terms of outcome, 61% of junior and senior high students eventually graduated from the program and made successful transitions to their home schools or work settings. Successful return to home schools for primary and intermediate age students was 86%. These statistics point to the advantages of early detection and treatment before problems have become entrenched and difficult to remedy.

Behavioral investigators claim that reading, writing, and arithmetic difficulties can be corrected by reinforcing academic behaviors. Stromer (1977), for example, worked with five third grade children who showed reversal problems (b for d, p for g). In the tutoring program of 30 minute sessions four to five times weekly, the children wrote down letters which were dictated to them. The reversal letters were placed on flash cards. Youngsters first matched the letters dictated by the teacher on a choice card and praise was used as a reward throughout the sessions. At posttesting and a two month follow-up, reversals had been eliminated. Since children with learning disabilities frequently manifest conduct problems (noncompliance, aggression, disruption), behavioral investigators have shown that these problems can be brought under control by reinforcing terminal academic behaviors which appear also to control classroom misbehavior (Lahey, Hobbs, Kupfer, & Delamater, 1979). One problem with these behavioral techniques is that teachers sometimes are not willing to use them on an independent basis (Lahey, Busemeyer, O'Hara, & Beggs, 1977). Perhaps preventive approaches would be more favorably accepted if teacher input was more actively solicited prior to program implementation in order to assess children's academic progress and correct early signs of underachievement.

Interventions for learning disabled children should not be limited to academic problems. Many learning disabled children have poor social skills; in particular, they engage in less positive and more negative behaviors during their peer interactions (LaGreca, 1981). Cooke and Apolloni's (1976) study is a good example of an attempt to improve learning disabled children's social-emotional behavior with peers. These investigators reported success in training children to increase their rates of smiling, sharing, positive physical contact, and verbal complimenting of peers. Moreover, data were obtained to support the generalization and durability of training effects.

Current problems in the reliable identification and measurement of learning disabilities preclude reaching any definitive conclusions regarding preventive programming. Nevertheless, it appears that intervention agents should be prepared to promote learning disabled children's social development and academic performance.

Mental Retardation

By the time a child reaches elementary school, the critical period for the primary prevention of mental retardation has passed. Approximately 25–35% of mental retardation has some organic basis and the remainder is believed to result from inadequate cultural and social enrichment and stimulation (Coleman et al., 1980). Effective prenatal and postnatal medical care including genetic counseling can reduce the incidence of organic cases (Kornberg & Caplan 1980; see Magrab, Sostek, and Powell, Chapter 2 of this volume), and family-oriented interventions during infancy and the preschool years have potential for reducing cases in the latter category. (See Chapter 3 in this volume by Rickel, Dyhdalo, & Smith.) Therefore, the elementary school years are the time for secondary prevention efforts aimed at reducing the severity of problems that subsequently may be associated with mental retardation.

The mentally retarded require multiple services if they are to achieve their educational and social potential. They need intensive instruction in basic academic skills and training in vocational and community living skills. Community living skills include general social skills (see Chapter 4 by Durlak & Jason) as well as adaptive behaviors in such areas as personal safety and hygiene, shopping, budgeting, homemaking, and leisure activities. There are examples of successful programs in each of these areas. By and large, highly structured programs that emphasize systematic reinforcement, step-by-step learning, and continued repetition of tasks until mastery is achieved have produced some promising results in the educational domain. Sheltered workshops and specialized job training programs that develop students' skills to fit job requirements have achieved success in the vocational area. Finally, several behaviorally oriented investigators have improved community living skills in retarded populations. Matson and McCartney's (1981) text contains chapters evaluating research and practice in each of the above areas.

Although success has been achieved in promoting the academic, vocational, and social development of the retarded, the authors hesitate to draw conclusions about the preventive impact of these efforts. Unless coordinated, comprehensive services are offered to the retarded, the impact of any one program is diminished. For example, interventions may improve community living skills, but unless the retarded also receive the necessary prevocational and vocational training, they will not be able to secure gainful employment. Alternately, the retarded may obtain jobs successfully but lack the necessary interpersonal skills to function effectively in social settings. Therefore, preventive programs for the retarded should involve comprehensive interventions that respond to the multiple needs of this population.

A Word of Caution

In developing preventive, school-based programs, investigators need to exercise care in deciding which children are in need of corrective intervention. This is particularly true of minority youngsters, who represent a disproportionate number of high-risk youngsters in schools and are more frequently labelled as learning disabled or mentally retarded than nonminority children (Tucker, 1980). More than likely, some of these youngsters are misdiagnosed because standardized intelligence and achievement tests often do not measure the culturally different skills and abilities of minorities (Bernstein, 1970), and they are more easily labelled as deficient due to their different dialects (Williams, Whitehead, & Miller, 1971). In response to this controversy, some culture fair tests have been developed. Mercer's System of Multicultural Pluralistic Assessment, which uses standardized tests but interprets them according to the norms of the child's sociocultural group, is an example (Mercer, 1979).

Many bicultural children come from backgrounds different from the middle-class white background the schools represent. Because of this, their families' and schools' educational roles tend to be different, often in conflict. Since academic success is more likely to occur when the families' and schools' educational roles are complementary, a preventive, ecological approach could involve bringing the community culture into the schools. Interventions to alleviate bicultural underachievement might then incorporate teacher educational and in-service programs, community and parental involvement workshops and activities, and various student instructional strategies. Many teachers do not have the specific training necessary for optimum interaction with bicultural children and in-service programs addressing the special needs of these youngsters are frequently not available. Therefore, preventive interventions involving teachers might focus on providing consulting services to school boards and institutions of higher education that offer programs designed to transmit knowledge about bicultural youths. Components of these programs might cover such topics as the "Pygmalion Effect," value transmission, and dialect differences that are especially pertinent to bicultural youths. Parents could be periodically invited to the schools to individually obtain a firsthand impression of their children's educational experiences and to aid in school programs such as tutoring. Community activities (such as holding a "Culture Day") also could be planned to promote cooperation and learning among diverse ethnic groups. With this kind of ecological approach, greater harmony and interests are likely to develop between bicultural communities and their school administrators.

ORGANIZATIONAL LEVEL INTERVENTIONS

The preceding sections have discussed how preventive ecological programs might be developed. Student achievement can be markedly affected by changing teacher instructional style, altering curricula, and developing tutoring programs, to name just a few possible approaches. There is a need, however, to place ecological-type interventions into a larger and more delineated conceptual framework, which will be addressed in the following two sections.

When school-based mental health professionals select organizational type interventions, they might bring about changes in the following four areas: (1) the inanimate environment (that is, physical design, resources, ambient conditions), (2) characteristics of individuals inhabiting the setting, (3) policies and contingencies, and (4) the setting's social climate (Jason & Glenwick, 1980).

Inanimate Environment

Physical Design.

One component of the inanimate environment involves a school's physical design including architecture, physical layout of rooms, furniture arrangements, seating positions, and size. A school's size has been the subject of several rather classic investigations by Barker (1976). In examining differences between small and large high schools, he found that students in small schools participated in more than six times more responsible positions (for example, officers of organizations, members of athletic teams) than those in large schools. In addition, students in the smaller schools were more motivated and challenged, and engaged in more experiences relating to competency development. Finally, Barker found that academically marginal students were provided five times more attention and assistance in the smaller schools. School-oriented mental health professionals might use these robust findings to consider methods of redesigning larger school systems to include either smaller units or to facilitate aspects of smaller schools. Placement of children into these types of health and competence promoting settings might serve as a potent preventive strategy for enhancing adjustment, particularly among marginally capable students.

Glass and Smith (1978) reported additional evidence supporting smaller sized units in their meta-analysis, which found dramatic gains in achievement when class size was reduced to 15 or less. Even within classrooms, mental health professionals might explore ways to restructure space to capitalize on positive features of smaller behavior settings. As an example of this concept, Jason and Nelson (Note 1) investigated the influence of different teacher-supervised class units with identified problem and nonproblem first graders. Nonproblem children manifested low levels of disruptive behavior in the small group and in the larger classroom; however, the problem children's acting-out behavior averaged 15% in the small group and 30% in the larger classroom. In addition, problem youngsters were reinforced by the teacher for appropriate behavior 9% of the time in the smaller group, but only 5% in the larger ecological unit. These findings suggest that smaller behavior settings, at least in this case, enabled children with acting-out tendencies to capture more teacher attention for on-task behavior, and consequently the youngsters manifested an unusually high degree of self-control. Once again, the implications are clear that placement of children in ecological units which have a constructive influence on social behavior might represent an alternative strategy for promoting healthy functioning.

A considerable amount of research has been focused on comparing traditional with more open-space schools, which are characterized by lack of interior walls and the existence of instructional areas ranging in size from two ordinary classrooms to more than ten. In a review article, Weinstein (1979) reported that teachers in these open-space settings had greater feelings of autonomy, satisfaction, and ambition, and the children had greater feelings of autonomy, were more willing to take risks, and could persist longer at tasks. Gump (1980), however, cites data indicating that certain children, particularly those from inner cities and students with lower IQs, do not perform well in open classrooms. These results emphasize the need to take into account characteristics and abilities of children when examining the influence of environmental variables (Solomon & Kendall, 1976; Thomas & Berk, 1981).

Resources.

Another aspect of the inanimate environment involves the materials and resources used in play and instruction. In a previous section of this chapter, the shaping influences of different curricula on students' activities were discussed. Besides examining the effect of curricula on achievement, school mental health professionals could develop curricula which mitigate the harmful effects of prevalent stereotypes. As an example, Guttentag (1977) devised and evaluated a curriculum to modify children's sex role stereotypes. Following the intervention, kindergarteners were better able to understand how the same job could be held by either a man or a woman. The belief among fifth grade girls that they could have varied and successful careers was strengthened, but attitudes among ninth graders became more stereotyped. More than likely, by the ninth grade, biases had become more entrenched and were therefore more difficult to modify. These findings suggest a need to develop several preventive curricula at primary grade levels, focusing on such diverse topics as age, sexism, racism, and moral development (Lockwood, 1978), before youngsters develop rigid stereotypic attitudes and beliefs.

Ambient Conditions.

A third category in the inanimate scheme involves ambient conditions within the schools, including noise, lighting, temperature, odors, and vibrations. As an example, a number of studies have found that temperature has a prominent effect on children's learning and adjustment (Horner, 1974). Russell and Bernal (1977) found more deviant child behaviors (for example, name calling, destructiveness) on cold days. Christie and Glickman (1980) report that classroom noise affects the task performance of girls more adversely than boys. Hyperactive children also demonstrate negative shifts in their task attention and levels of inappropriate behavior as a result of ambient noise levels in a classroom setting; at the same time, hyperactive children create more noise levels in the environment due to their verbalizations and motor behavior (Whalen, Henker, Collins, Finck, & Dotemoto, 1979). The above findings suggest that mental health professionals consulting in school systems need to adopt a comprehensive perspective to fully recognize and analyze ambient conditions which exert strong influences on children's behavior. Creating settings which have regulated temperatures, appropriate lighting levels, and nonaversive noise levels might prevent or at least moderate some conduct and learning problems among school children.

Inhabitants of School Settings

While the previous organizational component referred to the inanimate environment, the inhabitant category includes qualities or characteristics of the people inhabiting settings (for example, the number of people, density, stability). A study by Kelly (1969) illustrates the strong effects of member stability. He investigated two high schools, one characterized as fluid (more than 42% of the students left in a year) and the other as stable (less than 10% of its students departed). Students in the stable school were generally unresponsive to outsiders and tended to ostracize nonconforming members. In contrast, students in the fluid school helped newcomers adjust to their setting through an informal welcoming committee and nonconforming behavior was accepted.

Frequently, problems in social programs and institutions are caused by placing children into settings populated by youngsters who demonstrate delinquent, antisocial behaviors (for example, juvenile detention centers, prisons). Mental health professionals could utilize inhabitant characteristics to strengthen and build competencies in school children. As an example, Jason, Robson, and Lipshutz (1980) identified groups of children in a classroom evidencing high rates of sharing. When isolated low sharers were placed in groups of high sharers, the low sharers evidenced significant increases in sharing behaviors. Strategic placement of high-risk children with early identified problems into settings populated by socially competent children (Hartup, 1979) or adults (Skeels, 1966; Winick, Meyer, & Harris, 1975) represents a relatively unexplored ''behavioral matchmaker'' role for preventive psychologists.

Policies and Contingencies

Within all school settings, teachers, administrators, and school children are affected by the overall policies of the organization. Some of these policies include the degree to which autonomy is given to staff members (Tizard, Cooperman, Joseph, &

Tizard, 1972), roles are specified for various staff positions, activities are subject to standard procedures, rules are written, and the locus of control is confined to higher levels of the organization (Landy & Trumbo, 1976; McDonald, 1976). Another policy concerns the degree to which students participate in classroom decision making. Richter and Tjosvold (1980) investigated the effects of allowing students to help select topics and learning materials. Compared to members of more traditional teacher-planned classrooms, youngsters with input into decision making showed greater gains on achievement tests, more favorable attitudes toward school, more positive interactions toward peers, and more unsupervised work.

Some policies can be conceptualized as contingencies, either strictly or loosely controlled. For example, a teacher might be responsible for maintaining a certain amount of discipline in the classroom. Consistent failure to do so might result in the principal either not enforcing the rule violation, reprimanding the teacher, or not renewing the teacher's contract for the subsequent year. Policies and contingencies can be conducive toward personal satisfactory growth and development or inefficiency and pathology. Behaviorally oriented preventive psychologists could identify schoolwide consequences which enhance certain behaviors and reduce the probability of others. Identifying and altering contingencies established by school personnel might represent one effective preventive measure for establishing transactions more conducive toward teachers' and children's adjustment and development. As an example of this approach, Barber and Kagey (1977) increased classroom attendance among children in an entire elementary school when the amount of time children could spend in monthly school parties was made contingent upon classroom attendance.

Social Climate

Social climate, the last organizational dimension, focuses on the perceptions and feelings of individuals concerning their environments. A setting's social climate has strong influences on mood, behavior, health, sense of well-being and social, personal, and intellectual development (Moos, 1975). Several questionnaires have been developed by Moos (1975) to assess social climate. Three general dimensions have emerged in a variety of social milieus, including relationship (personal involvement in the setting, support, and free and open expression), personal development (personal growth and development), and system maintenance (an environment's orderliness, clarity of expectations, maintenance of control, and responsiveness to change). In school settings, students are more satisfied when there are personal student-teacher relationships, innovative teacher methods, and student involvement (Trickett & Moos, 1974). Mental health professionals might assess these social climate variables (Prawat & Solomon, 1981) and mount interventions which systematically alter the social climate within school systems, particularly in settings which have unclear expectations, lack group spirit, and discourage independence and leadership. In studying the perceived school environment, there is also a need to adopt an interactional model which recognizes that youngsters with varying abilities or characteristics might react differently to alternative social climates (Marjoribanks, 1980).

COMMUNITY LEVEL INTERVENTIONS

The sections above focused on programs occurring within organizations. In contrast, community level interventions investigate relationships between school systems and their communities. Communities can be categorized into four components: the natural environment, the built environment, overall characteristics of the community's inhabitants, and systems which interconnect throughout the community. In the following sections, the relationships between these dimensions and possible school-based preventive programs will be reviewed. (See Chapter 12 by Masterpasqua & Swift for other community-wide prevention interventions.)

Natural Environment

The first component of a community includes the land and climate where schools are located, as well as available natural resources and park lands. Climate and geographic features can exert subtle effects on the culture and activities of a community in which school systems are located (Moos, 1975). Mental health professionals might work with ecologically oriented school-based groups to preserve the natural environment. As an illustration of this approach, Bogat (1982) evaluated an intervention whereby school affiliated Boy Scout troops throughout a city "adopted" small, one acre parks. The project provided school youngsters in the community an opportunity to take active responsibility for public areas and also led to improvements in the aesthetic condition of many parks.

Built Environment

All manufactured structures, superimposed upon the natural environment, comprise the built environment. Mental health professionals might collaborate with citizen groups in designing school systems which are functional, attractive, and safe from crime. Activities which occur in built environments frequently generate a host of pollutants, including noise, litter, heat, and chemicals. Mental health professionals could help identify dangerous by-products of the built environment which pose health risks to school children. As an example, Cohen, Evans, Krantz, and Stokols (1980) found that children who were in schools built under an airport air corridor manifested elevated blood pressure and were more likely not to persist in test items. Programs could be devised to insulate buildings against aversive noise levels; the source of the harmful noise levels could be shifted (for example, plane routes could be changed so that their flight patterns were not directly over schools); or from the start, schools could be built in areas which do not have pernicious noise levels. Most mental health practitioners probably have not been involved directly in programs focusing on natural and built environmental variables; however, these types of preventive environmental activities and collaborative efforts represent untapped and challenging directions for school-based professionals.

Aggregate Inhabitant Characteristics

While the previous two categories focused on inanimate qualities of the natural and built environment, the inhabitant dimension refers to characteristics of the people who live in communities surrounding schools. Aggregate inhabitant characteristics include objective dimensions such as socioeconomic status, ethnicity, and density. As an example of how conditions in the community might affect school performance, Saegert (1980) found that increases in the number of people in students' living quarters were associated with increases in emotional and behavioral disturbances in school settings. Such findings suggest that, at least with some youngsters, if enduring changes are to occur, family and community members might need to participate actively in preventive programs.

Aggregate inhabitant characteristics also include more subjective indices, such as inhabitant perceptions of their environments (for instance, community satisfaction, neighborhood cohesion) and the extent to which youngsters fit into their communities. The relevance of this latter category was explained by Moritsugu and Sue (1983), who reviewed studies indicating that problems arise when groups live in social environments where they constitute minorities on one or more dimensions. If the majority of children in a school are members of a gang, considerable pressure will be exerted on nonmembers to join, and if youngsters refuse, it is more than likely they will be ostracized from the main group. Preventive-oriented psychologists in this situation might work toward developing alternative social support groups, which enable school children to be validated and reinforced for more prosocial and antidelinquent behaviors.

Social networks are another part of the aggregate inhabitant dimension. Networks include friends and family, neighborhood (for example, parent-teacher associations), self-help (teacher support groups), and social action groups (for instance, National Organization for Women). Social networks exist throughout schools and communities and provide individuals the opportunity for socialization and emotional support (Hirsch, 1980), moderate various types of life stress (Cobb, 1976), and enable relatively unimpeded access to information (Mitchell & Trickett, 1980). In working with these groups, community psychologists might evaluate outcomes of participating in them, organize new social networks, encourage professionals to make referrals to these networks, and strengthen already existing support groups. For example, Jung and Jason (Note 2) consulted with school affiliated 4-H Clubs in a metropolitan area. They were able to identify effective techniques for increasing membership in child-oriented 4-H support groups. These clubs provide youngsters important socialization experiences and increasing membership in such groups represents a viable preventive strategy for community-oriented mental health professionals.

Systems

Schools within a community represent one system embedded within a complicated web of other community-wide macrosystems. Systems which directly and indirectly influence the functioning and vitality of educational settings include the political process, economic conditions, the media, social service agencies, transportation systems, medical care agencies, juvenile correctional facilities, religious institutions, and recreational facilities.

Political Processes.

Decisions and policies at the executive, legislative, and judicial levels can exert strong influences on communities and school systems. Educational psychologists with particular interest in political affairs might engage in any of the following activities: (1) alert public officials to the community residents' attitudes toward upcoming school policy decisions, (2) collaborate with citizen groups in lobbying efforts to enact or alter legislation, and (3) present expert testimony at key court cases to induce change through the judicial process (Knitzer, 1980). As an example, the Education for All Handicapped Children Act (PL 94-142) is legislation which passed Congress and was designed to assure that all handicapped children receive education appropriate to their needs. While this legislation has expanded the educational opportunities for handicapped children, Durlak (1983) notes that advocacy groups, with which mental health professionals might work, will have to ensure that local school districts establish proper criteria under PL 94-142 to diagnose and place children, and that adequate resources are available to successfully implement the program.

During the well-known court case of Brown versus the Board of Education, psychologists testified concerning the effects of school segregation on prejudice, self-esteem, and achievement. Although the social scientists were incorrect in their expectation that desegregation would reduce the prejudice of whites toward blacks (Stephan, 1978), their testimony was instrumental in this landmark judicial decision banning segregation in school systems. Mental health professionals can play a critical role in helping to reform deleterious system-wide policies and practices which deprive children and adults of their basic human rights.

Economic Conditions.

The health of a school system is at least in part determined by the community's economic base; that is, the types of business and industry, the available employment, the opportunities for advancement, and the percent of unemployed and underemployed. Community-minded psychologists have evaluated social programs which directly affect income levels among community members (Catalano & Dooley, 1980). As an example, Maynard and Murnane (1980) found that in those families which received a negative income tax (that is, a guaranteed level of support below which a participant's income cannot fall), significant increases were found in school children's reading achievement scores. Finding appropriate jobs, training programs, or economic resources for unemployed parents might represent a potent preventive strategy for stabilizing family life and ultimately enhancing children's adjustment in both the family context and school settings. Pointing out to various public and private organizations the mental health consequences for children of various economic policies at the local, state, and federal levels is another role for mental health professionals.

Media.

Another system interconnecting a community is its network of media sources (television, radio, newspapers, and magazines). The media, which reaches nearly all members of the community, transmits information and images which influence the promotion of both healthy and unhealthy life patterns. By the age of 16, children have spent more time watching television than attending school. This is particularly troubling because television programming features violence in most cartoons, shows more than half of all prime time characters committing violence, and rarely shows the accompanying pain and suffering (Baker & Ball, 1969). Moreover, the majority of scientific studies have indicated that children and adults tend to become more aggressive after exposure to aggressive stimuli (Berkowitz & LePage, 1967). School psychologists might work with community groups to decrease negative media images which predispose adolescents to violence and unhealthy lifestyles. Mental health professionals might also work with youngsters to aid them in better utilizing the media. As an example, Rooney-Rebeck (Note 3) developed a school-based program in which school children and parents were given behavioral contracts to decrease excessive television viewing. In this successful project, children earned points for engaging in prosocial activities and the points were then exchanged for time to watch television.

Implementation of Preventive Programs

Many of the interventions discussed in this chapter require care and sensitivity in their implementation since they often invoke substantial changes in customary educational practices. For example, teachers are asked to use new classroom management techniques, to instruct children differently, to individualize instruction, and to create new groupings or subgroupings of students. Parents and volunteers may become involved in the educational process and their roles and responsibility vis-a-vis school staff must be clarified and negotiated. Finally, in some cases substantial organizational changes are required in classroom procedures and school policies to accommodate innovative services. Therefore, it is important to discuss how new programs can be implemented most easily and effectively.

Implementation refers to the way in which a proposed program is put into practice. The actual day-to-day functioning of a program may differ considerably from what is expected, given the intervention's theoretical and conceptual orientation. Indeed, many proposed programs are never begun or completed; many that are initiated are not adapted as planned; and other seemingly successful interventions are prematurely discontinued or fail to gain widespread adoption. As a result, several writers believe that program implementation is a critical factor affecting the generality and effectiveness of an intervention (Berman & McLaughlin, 1976; Fullan & Pomfret, 1977; Mannarino & Durlak, 1980; Stolz, 1981).

It is not possible in this chapter to conduct a comprehensive theoretical discussion of the implementation process. The factors that affect program implementation are rarely studied and published reports seldom contain enough administrative and practical details to permit an adequate analysis of the program implementation variables. Nevertheless, several sources of information converge to suggest the importance of certain factors (Sarason, 1972; Reppucci & Saunders, 1974; House, 1975). At the risk of simplifying a complex topic, researchers might identify at least four critical elements: (1) the program's problem-solving potential, (2) program costs, (3) meaningful program input from school personnel, and (4) effective interpersonal skills by the change agent.

Problem-solving potential refers to whether or not a proposed program is a potential solution to locally identified needs and problems. It should be noted that positive research findings seldom are sufficient to ensure adoption of a new program; rather, school personnel must believe that a proposed program has value and is needed. One cannot assume that the school staff will initially evaluate preventive programs favorably. For example, in a study described later in detail, only 31% of 221 principals surveyed perceived preventive mental health services as helpful (Senft & Snider, 1980). Therefore, it is important that change agents offer effective arguments regarding the practical payoffs and values of proposed innovations. Unless such arguments are convincing, school staff members are unlikely to commit to new programs.

Program costs involve not only money but also the time, energy, and changes in roles and behaviors required of participants. The more costly a program, the less the likelihood of effective implementation unless adequate steps are taken to meet or reduce program costs. Teachers may need additional training if new behaviors and teaching techniques are required, and they will need additional training and consultation once they begin to apply these new behaviors. Administrators may have to oblige by discharging teachers from some of their regular responsibilities so they can participate in new programs; extra pedagogical resources must also be procured if needed.

The implementation process usually is enhanced when school personnel are given meaningful input into the program's planning, execution, and evaluation. Hence, a change agent must be flexible, responsive, and sensitive to suggested program changes. The ultimate goal is to maintain the basic integrity of a program model while matching the innovation of the unique features of the setting and the preferences and reactions of relevant staff. Change agents must learn to negotiate and compromise during the delicate interpersonal exchanges that occur while a program is being implemented.

Change agents also must possess other social skills, including: (1) good communication, (2) the ability to solve problems effectively despite unexpected obstacles and dilemmas, and (3) the ability to develop and project genuine understanding and respect for the needs, values, and traditions of the school. Ultimately, the change agent's interpersonal skills and personal influence may be the most important factors determining whether schools adopt and maintain innovative preventive services.

The above discussion is intended to alert the reader to the interpersonal and administrative complexities of conducting innovative school-based programs. Any of a number of issues may work against an otherwise effective program. The benefits of proposed interventions may remain obscure to school staff; teachers may feel uncomfortable in learning new behaviors and dispensing with customary classroom practices; a proposed program may be impractical in a particular setting unless it is modified substantially in scope or design; and finally, school personnel may be suspicious of a change agent's personal motivation and commitment to the schools. Those who attempt to introduce preventive-oriented services into schools should examine possible problems involved in program implementation and ways these problems may be overcome.

DISCUSSION

Whether intervening with academic difficulties, promoting prosocial behaviors, or mounting organization or community level interventions, mental health professionals operating within a preventive ideology maintain the primary objective of developing children's competencies. Preventive-oriented professionals have a unique role in developing competencies within school systems through the following activities: (1) focusing on the mental health implications of social system policies and practices for school children, (2) mounting efforts geared toward analysis and modification of children's behaviors and attitudes, (3) helping design and evaluate community initiated preventive school interventions, and (4) serving as the catalyst for mobilizing interdisciplinary investigation teams to work with communities in comprehensively analyzing and ameliorating school needs.

The preventive, organizational, and community interventions presented herein represent a commitment toward bringing relevance, creativity, and innovation into school settings. These qualities were essential characteristics of the Dewey school (Sarason, 1972), whose educational philosophy considered school a crucial part of life instead of a preparation for life. Along these lines, schools might consider being rooted in real world experiences, so that students might perceive participation outcomes and consequences as more useful and practical. For example, curricula for caring could be as important a core area as reading and arithmetic. These curricula would offer students opportunities to learn skills and competencies while providing substitute care for working mothers, or visiting elderly citizens, or assisting families in emergencies (Bronfenbrenner, 1977). School-based professionals and community members need to explore ways to integrate the activities and functions of schools into the mainstream of community life.

With massive cutbacks in federal and state funds for social service programs, the consequences are that fewer mental health personnel and financial resources will be allocated to preventive and nontraditional service modalities. In other words, many school systems increasingly will expect school counselors and psychologists to assume traditional roles of assessment and one-to-one therapy. As demand and need for services overwhelm service providers, restrictive conventional treatment approaches will be embraced as the major solution to children's social and behavioral adjustment problems. As a consequence, the traditional roles and functions of school professionals will be preserved at the expense of more preventive-oriented services.

Survey data support this contention. Senft and Snider (1980) found that 99% of a nationwide, random sample of school principals believed that psychological testing conducted by school psychologists was helpful, but only 31% perceived preventive mental health services as helpful. Twenty-two percent of the principals had no experience with preventive programs and the remaining respondents either believed preventive programs were not helpful (29%) or were uncertain of their worth (17%). Furthermore, only 17% of those principals who indicated preventive services were not available in their schools expressed a desire for such services.

There are several antidotes for this rather discouraging tendency. First, even within traditional roles, opportunities for more preventive projects can arise. For example, after treating several youngsters for emotional problems stemming from parent death or divorce, schools could set up support groups for others who have been less severely affected, or for youngsters not presently manifesting outward signs of maladjustment. Second, some mental health professionals might be able to persuade policy officials that indirect services (training paraprofessionals, consultation) might be more cost-effective and might reach more troubled youngsters. These approaches might allow traditional practitioners to involve at least some resources in more preventive and community-based interventions.

Even if the roles of mental health professionals become somewhat more rigid and traditional, preventive programs increasingly will be mounted by nonmental health groups. For example, industrial firms in Chicago have begun adopting schools and implementing a host of competency building projects. Grass roots organizations are continuing to request more input into local school decisions and policies. Both students and parents increasingly are challenging somewhat authoritarian school administrations in order to introduce more democratic practices, ones which might better prepare youngsters to actively participate in responsible positions in our society. As schools are influenced to be more sensitive to student and parent input and to develop closer ties with community and industrial environments, substantial structural changes will occur in educational settings. It is hoped that mental health professionals will participate actively in these changes which will ultimately transform schools into more humane settings for the encouragement of learning and competency development.

REFERENCES

Atkeson, B. M., & Forehand, R. Home-based reinforcement programs designed to modify classroom behavior: A review and methodological evaluation. *Psychological Bulletin,* 1979, *86,* 1298–1308.

Baker, R. K., & Ball, S. J. *Mass media and violence*. (Vol. 9). Washington D.C.: U.S. Government Printing Office, 1969.

Barber, R. M., & Kagey, J. R. Modification of school attendance for an elementary population. *Journal of Applied Behavior Analysis*, 1977, *10*, 41–48.

Barker, R. G. On the nature of environment. In H. M. Proshansky, W. H. Ittelson, & L. G. Rivlin (Eds.), *Environmental psychology*. New York: Holt, Rinehart & Winston, 1976.

Becker, W. C., & Carnine, D. W. Direct instruction: An effective approach to educational intervention with the disadvantaged and low performers. In B. B. Lahey & A. E. Kazdin (Eds.), *Advances in clinical child psychology* (Vol. 3). New York: Plenum, 1980.

Becker, W. C., & Gersten, R. A follow-up of follow through: The later effects of the direct instruction model on children in fifth and sixth grades. *American Educational Research Journal*, 1982, *19*, 75–92.

Berkowitz, L., & LePage, A. Weapons as aggression-eliciting stimuli. *Journal of Personality and Social Psychology*, 1967, *7*, 202–207.

Berman, P., & McLaughlin, M. W. Implementation of educational innovation. *Educational Forum*, 1976, *40*, 345–370.

Bernstein, B. A. A sociolinguistic approach to socialization: With some references to educability. In F. Williams (Ed.), *Language and poverty*. Chicago: Markham, 1970.

Blechman, E. A., Kotanchik, N. L., & Taylor, C. J. Families and schools together: Early behavioral intervention with high risk children. *Behavior Therapy*, 1981, *12*, 308–319.

Blechman, E. A., Taylor, C. J., & Schrader, S. M. Family problem solving versus home notes as early intervention with high-risk children. *Journal of Consulting and Clinical Psychology*, 1981, *49*, 919–926.

Bogat, G. A. *An investigation of Boy Scouts adopting parks in a metropolitan area*. Unpublished doctoral dissertation, DePaul University, 1982.

Bronfenbrenner, U. Toward an experimental ecology of human development. *American Psychologist*, 1977, *32*, 513–531.

Brophy, J. E. Teacher behavior and its effects. *Journal of Educational Psychology*, 1979, *71*, 733–750.

Bruffee, K. A. CLTV: Collaborative learning television. *Educational Communication and Technology*, 1982, *30*, 26–40.

Catalano, R., & Dooley, D. Economic change in primary prevention. In R. H. Price, R. F. Ketterer, B. C. Bader, & J. Monahan (Eds.), *Prevention in mental health: Research, policy, and practice*. Beverly Hills, Sage, 1980.

Centra, J. A., & Potter, D. A. School and teacher effects: An interrelational model. *Review of Educational Research*, 1980, *50*, 273–291.

Christie, D. J., & Glickman, C. D. The effects of classroom noise on children: Evidence for sex differences. *Psychology in the Schools*, 1980, *17*, 405–408.

Clarizio, H. F., & McCoy, G. F. *Behavior disorders in children* (2nd ed). New York: Thomas Y. Crowell, 1976.

Cloward, R. D. Studies in tutoring. *Journal of Experimental Education*, 1967, *36*, 14–25.

Coates, T. J., & Thoresen, C. E. Teacher anxiety: A review with recommendations. *Review of Educational Research*, 1976, *46*, 159–184.

Cobb, S. Social supports as a moderator of life stress. *Psychosomatic Medicine*, 1976, *38*, 300–314.

Cohen, P. A., Kulik, J. A., & Kulik, C. C. Educational outcomes of tutoring: A meta-analysis of findings. *American Educational Research Journal,* 1982, *19,* 237–248.

Cohen, R. "New Careers" Grows Older: A perspective on the paraprofessional experience, 1965–1975. Baltimore: Johns Hopkins Press, 1976.

Cohen, S., Evans, G. W., Krantz, D. S., & Stokols, D. Physiological, motivational, and cognitive effects of aircraft noise on children. *American Psychologist,* 1980, *35,* 231–243.

Coleman, J. C., Butcher, J. N., & Carson, R. C. *Abnormal psychology and modern life* (6th ed.). Glenview, Il: Scott, Foresman, 1980.

Connolly, J. A. Basic education—A mastery approach. *Phi Beta Kappa,* 1972, *54,* 211–212.

Cooke, T. P., & Apolloni, T. Developing positive social-emotional behaviors: A study of training and generalization effects. *Journal of Applied Behavior Analysis,* 1976, *9,* 65–78.

Coyne, P. D. The effects of peer tutoring with group contingencies on the academic performance of college students. *Journal of Applied Behavior Analysis,* 1978, *11,* 305–307.

Douglas, J. A., & Jason, L. A. Transitions: Utilizing behavioral technology to facilitate entry into a school and an occupation. *Crisis Intervention,* 1979, *10,* 68–79.

Dunleavy, R. A., Hansen, J. L., Szasz, C. W., & Baade, L. E. Early kindergarten identification of academically not-ready children by use of human drawing developmental score. *Psychology in the Schools,* 1981, *18,* 35–38.

Durlak, J. A. Providing mental health services to elementary school children. In C. E. Walker & M. C. Roberts (Eds.), *Handbook of clinical child psychology.* New York: Wiley, 1983.

Evans, C. An invitation to the (near) future. *Today's Education,* 1982, *71,* 12–15.

Finkel, E. The computer: Myths and promises. *Curriculum Review,* 1982, *21,* 11–15.

Friedman, R., Fuerth, J. H., & Forsythe, A. B. A brief screening battery for predicting school achievement at ages seven and nine years. *Psychology in the Schools,* 1980, *17,* 340–346.

Fullan, M., & Pomfret, A. Research on curriculum and instruction implementation. *Review of Educational Research,* 1977, *47,* 335–397.

Gallerani, D., O'Regan, M., & Reinherz, H. Prekindergarten screening: How well does it predict readiness for first grade. *Psychology in the Schools,* 1982, *19,* 175–182.

Glass, G. V., & Smith, M. L. *Meta-analysis of research as the relationship of class size and achievement.* Boulder, Colorado: Laboratory of Educational Research, University of Colorado, 1978.

Gresham, F. M. Social skills training with handicapped children: A review. *Review of Educational Research,* 1981, *51,* 139–176.

Gump, P. V. The school as a social situation. *Annual Review of Psychology,* 1980, *31,* 553–582.

Guttentag, M. The prevention of sexism. In G. W. Albee & J. M. Joffe (Eds.), *Primary prevention of psychopathology: The issues* (Vol. 1). Hanover, NH: University Press of New England, 1977.

Hansford, B. C., & Hattie, J. A. The relationship between self and achievement/performance measures. *Review of Educational Research,* 1982, *52,* 123–142.

Harris, V. W., & Sherman, J. A. Effects of peer tutoring and consequences on the math performance of elementary classroom students. *Journal of Applied Behavior Analysis,* 1973, *6,* 587–597.

Hartup, W. W. Peer relations and the growth of social competence. In M. W. Kent & J. E. Rolf (Eds.), *Primary prevention of psychopathology: Volume III. Social competence in children.* Hanover, NH: University Press of New England, 1979.

Harvard Educational Review, 1978, *48*(2).

Hirsch, B. J. Natural support systems and coping with major life changes. *American Journal of Community Psychology,* 1980, *8,* 159–172.

Hobbs, N. Helping disturbed children: Psychological and ecological strategies. *American Psychologist,* 1966, *21,* 1105–1115.

Horner, D. P. A review of research concerning the thermal environment and its effects on learning. *Dissertation Abstracts International,* 1974, *34,* 4620.

House, E. *The politics of educational innovation.* Berkeley, CA: McCutchan, 1975.

Ireton, H., Shing-lun, K., & Kampen, M. Minnesota Preschool Inventory identification of children at risk for kindergarten failure. *Psychology in the Schools,* 1981, *18,* 394–401.

Jason, L. A., Christensen, H., & Carl, K. Programmed versus naturalistic approaches in enhancing study-related behavior. *Journal of Clinical Child Psychology,* 1982, *11,* 249–254.

Jason, L. A., Ferone, L., & Soucy, G. Teaching peer-tutoring behaviors in first- and third-grade classrooms. *Psychology in the Schools,* 1979, *16,* 261–269.

Jason, L. A., Frasure, S., & Ferone, L. Establishing supervising behaviors in eighth graders and peer-tutoring behaviors in first graders. *Child Study Journal,* 1981, *11,* 201–219.

Jason, L. A., & Glenwick, D. S. Future directions: A critical look at the behavioral community approach. In D. S. Glenwick & L. A. Jason (Eds.), *Behavioral community psychology: Progress and prospects.* New York: Praeger, 1980.

Jason, L. A., Robson, S. D., & Lipshutz, S. A. Enhancing sharing behaviors through the use of naturalistic contingencies. *Journal of Community Psychology,* 1980, *8,* 237–244.

Johnson, M., & Bailey, J. S. Cross-age tutoring: Fifth graders as arithmetic tutors for kindergarten children. *Journal of Applied Behavior Analysis,* 1974, *7,* 223–232.

Keavney, G., & Sinclair, K. E. Teacher concerns and teacher anxiety: A neglected topic of classroom research. *Review of Educational Research,* 1978, *48,* 273–290.

Kelly, J. G. Naturalistic observations in contrasting social environments. In E. P. Willems & H. L. Rausch (Eds.), *Naturalistic viewpoints in psychological research.* New York: Holt, Rinehart and Winston, 1969.

Knitzer, J. Advocacy and community psychology. In M. S. Gibbs, J. R. Lachenmeyer, & J. Sigal (Eds.), *Community psychology: Theoretical and empirical approaches.* New York: Gardner, 1980.

Kornberg, M. S., & Caplan, G. Risk factors and preventive intervention in child psychotherapy: A review. *Journal of Prevention,* 1980. *1,* 71–133.

Kulik, C. C., Schwalb, B. J., & Kulik, J. A. Programmed instruction in secondary education: A meta-analysis of evaluation findings. *The Journal of Educational Research,* 1982, *75,* 133–138.

LaGreca, A. M. Social behavior and social perception in learning-disabled children: A review with implications for social skills training. *Journal of Pediatric Psychology,* 1981, *6,* 395–416.

Lahey, B. B. (Ed.). *Behavior therapy with hyperactive and learning disabled children.* New York: Oxford University Press, 1979.

Lahey, B. B., Busemeyer, M. K., O'Hara, C., & Beggs, V. E. Treatment of severe perceptual-motor disorders in children diagnosed as learning disabled. *Behavior Modification,* 1977, *1,* 123–140.

Lahey, B. B., Hobbs, S. A., Kupfer, D. L., & Delamater, A. Current perspectives on hyperactivity and learning disabilities. In B. B. Lahey (Ed.), *Behavior therapy with hyperactive and learning disabled children.* New York: Oxford University Press, 1979.

Landy, F. J. & Trumbo, D. A. (Eds.). *Psychology of work behavior.* Homewood, IL: Dorsey, 1976.

Lewis, A., The early identification of children with learning difficulties. *Journal of Learning Disabilities,* 1980, *13,* 102–108.

Lockwood, A. L. The effects of values clarification and moral development curricula on school-age subjects: A critical review of recent research. *Review of Educational Research,* 1978, *48,* 325–364.

Matson, J. L., & McCartney, J. R., *Handbook of behavior modification with the mentally retarded.* New York: Plenum, 1981.

McDonald, F. J. *Summary report: Beginning teacher evaluation study, Phase II* (PR-76-17). Princeton, NJ: Educational Testing Service, 1976.

Mannarino, A. P., & Durlak, J. A. Implementation and evaluation of service programs in community settings. *Professional Psychology,* 1980, *11,* 220–227.

Margolis, H., Sheridan, R., & Lemanowicz, J. The efficiency of Mykelbust's Pupil Rating Scale for detecting reading and arithmetic difficulties. *Journal of Learning Disabilities,* 1981, *14,* 267–268; 302.

Marjoribanks, K. Person-school environment correlates of children's affective characteristics. *Journal of Educational Psychology,* 1980, *72,* 583–591.

Maynard, R. A., & Murnane, R. J. The effects of a negative income tax on school performance. In E. W. Stromsdorfer & G. Farkas (Eds.), *Evaluation Studies Review Annual (Vol. 5).* Beverly Hills: Sage, 1980.

Mercer, J. R. *System of multicultural pluralistic assessment.* New York: The City Psychological Corporation, 1979.

Mitchell, R. E., & Trickett, E. J. Task force report: Social networks as mediators of social support. An analysis of the effects and determinants of social networks. *Community Mental Health Journal,* 1980, *16,* 27–44.

Moos, R. H. *Evaluating correctional and community settings.* New York: Wiley, 1975.

Moritsugu, J., & Sue, S. Racial and ethnic factors in mental health. In R. D. Felner, L. A. Jason, J. Moritsugu, & S. S. Farber (Eds.), *Preventive psychology: Theory, research and practice.* New York: Pergamon, 1983.

Neuhaus, S. M., Mowrey, J. D., & Glenwick, D. S. The cooperative learning program: Implementing an ecological approach to the development of alternative psychoeducational programs. *Journal of Clinical Child Psychology,* 1982, *11,* 151–156.

Prawat, R. S., & Solomon, D. J. Validation of a classroom climate inventory for use at the early elementary level. *Educational and Psychological Measurement,* 1981, *41,* 567–573.

Reppucci, N. D., & Saunders, J. T. Social psychology of behavior modification: Problems of implementation in natural settings. *American Psychologist,* 1974, *29,* 649–660.

Richter, F. D., & Tjosvold, D. Effects of student participation in classroom decision making on attitudes, peer interaction, motivation and learning. *Journal of Applied Psychology,* 1980, *65,* 74–80.

Rothrock, D. The rise and decline of individualized instruction. *Educational Leadership,* 1982, *39,* 528–530.

Russell, M. B., & Bernal, M. E. Temporal and climatic variables in naturalistic observations. *Journal of Applied Behavior Analysis,* 1977, *10,* 399–405.

Sabatino, D. A., & Miller, T. L. The dilemma of diagnosis in learning disabilities: Problems and potential directions. *Psychology in the Schools,* 1980, *17,* 76–86.

Saegert, S. Crowding and cognitive limits. In J. Harvey (Ed.), *Cognition, social behavior and the environment.* Hillsdale, NJ: Erlbaum, 1980.

Sarason, S. B. *The culture of the school and the problem of change.* Boston: Allyn & Bacon, 1972.

Schwartz, G. J. College students as contingency managers for adolescents in a program to develop reading skills. *Journal of Applied Behavior Analysis,* 1977, *10,* 645–655.

Senft, L. B., & Snider, B. Elementary school principals assess services of school psychologists nationwide. *Journal of School Psychology,* 1980, *18,* 276–282.

Skeels, H. M. Adult status of children with contrasting early life experiences: A follow-up study. *Monographs of the Society for Research in Child Development,* 1966, *31,* No. 3.

Solomon, D., & Kendall, A. J. Individual characteristics and children's performance in "open" and "traditional" classroom settings. *Journal of Educational Psychology,* 1976, *68,* 613–625.

Stallings, J. A., & Kaskowitz, D. *Follow through classroom observation evaluation 1972–1973.* Menlo Park, CA: Stanford Research Institute, 1974.

Stephan, W. G. School desegregation: An evaluation of predictions made in Brown vs. Board of Education. *Psychological Bulletin,* 1978, *85,* 217–238.

Stolz, S. B. Adoption of innovation from applied behavioral research: "Does anybody care?" *Journal of Applied Behavior Analysis,* 1981, *14,* 491–505.

Stromer, R. Remediating academic deficiencies in learning disabled children. *Exceptional Children,* 1977, *43,* 432–440.

Thomas, N. G., & Berk, L. E. Effects of school environments on the development of young children's creativity. *Child Development,* 1981, *52,* 1153–1162.

Tizard, B., Cooperman, D., Joseph, A., & Tizard, J. Environmental effects on language development: A study of young children in long stay residential nurseries. *Child Development,* 1972, *43,* 337–359.

Trickett, E., & Moos, R. Personal correlates of contrasting environments: Student satisfaction in high school classrooms. *American Journal of Community Psychology,* 1974, *2,* 1–12.

Tucker, J. Ethnic proportions in classes for the learning disabled: Issues in nonbiased assessment. *Journal of Special Education,* 1980, *14,* 93–105.

Weinstein, C. S. The physical environment of the school: A review of the research. *Review of Educational Research,* 1979, *49,* 577–610.

Wender, P. H., & Wender, E. H. *The hyperactive child and the learning disabled child.* New York: Crown Publishers, 1978.

Whalen, C. K., Henker, B., Collins, B. E., Finck, D., & Dotemoto, S. A social ecology of hyperactive boys: Medication effects in structured classroom environments. *Journal of Applied Behavior Analysis,* 1979, *12,* 65–81.

Williams, F., Whitehead, J., & Miller, L. *Attitudinal correlates of children's speech charac-*

teristics. Final Report, No. 00336, Grant No. OEGO-70-7868 (508). Washington, D.C.: U.S. Government Printing Office, 1971.

Winick, M., Meyer, K. K., & Harris, R. C. Malnutrition and environmental enrichment by early adopting. *Science,* 1975, *190,* 1173–1175.

REFERENCE NOTES

1. Jason, L. A., & Nelson, T. *Engineering reductions in problem behaviors through environmental design*. Paper presented at the meeting of the Midwestern Association of Behavior Analysis, Chicago, May 1978.
2. Jung, R., & Jason, L. A. *Enhancing preventive social support systems for children*. Paper presented at the meeting of the Association for Behavior Analysis, Milwaukee, 1981.
3. Rooney-Rebeck, P. *A behavioral program for reducing heavy television viewing*. Unpublished manuscript, DePaul University, 1982.

CHAPTER 11

Prevention in the Home

Parent and Family

REX L. FOREHAND, PAGE B. WALLEY, AND WILLIAM M. FUREY

> Preparing for effective parenthood is an extremely complex task. There seems to be an amazing lack of information among young parents today of the social, emotional, education, and health needs of children and of the role of parents in fostering a child's development. Parents seem ill prepared to meet the problems encountered in rearing children. [Huntington, 1979, p. 846]

> At times many a parent of an adolescent is convinced that the teen-age years represent a form of mental illness. [Decker, 1982, p. 25]

> We have a society that claims love and concern for its young, and yet it leaves parents to raise their children virtually unprepared and alone. [Weissbourd, 1981, p. 160]

Being a parent is not only difficult but is one occupation for which there is typically no training prior to taking on the job. Furthermore, once the job is assumed, few resources are available to offer answers and provide guidance. For example, Roberts and Wright (1982) reviewed studies indicating that pediatricians, who are often the first professionals contacted with parental questions, are not adequately trained to address questions about child behavior and additionally spend only a minimum of time (an average of 13 minutes) with each child patient and his or her parent. These circumstances are particularly unfortunate as a variety of problems are faced daily by parents. For example, Macfarlane, Allen, and Honzik (1954) followed a group of normal children from 24 months to 14 years of age and found that over one third of the parents reported some specific problems at each age. In a survey of mothers of normal children, Heinstein (1969) reported that stubbornness and temper tantrums were reported by about 60% of the mothers of children under two years of age. Achenbach and Edelbrock (1978), reviewing the frequency of problems reported by parents of children six to 11 years old, indicate that 64% and 58% of boys and girls argue frequently, 40% and 37% are disobedient at home, and 45% and 37% are sullen, stubborn, and irritable. Mesibov, Schroeder, and Wesson (1977) collected data on parental concerns about their children which were expressed in a pediatrician's office or by phone to a child development specialist. The results indicated that almost 15% of the concerns focused on negative child behaviors. Clearly, problems exist for children of all ages. Furthermore, parents are concerned about such problems and are constantly seeking effective child-rearing techniques as is evident by the sale of childcare books (Clarke-Stewart, 1978).

A knowledge of good parenting skills alone is not sufficient, as a certain amount of problem behavior is normal. That is, although the behavior may be aversive to the parent, it may be typical for a child of that age or a given situation. In order to cope as a parent, effective childrearing techniques and a knowledge of developmental norms are necessary. Without the latter, a parent can be over or under concerned with a behavior or have unrealistic expectations, leading him or her to respond inappropriately to the child's behavior and intensify the normal difficulties to a problematic level. For example, unrealistic expectations may lead a parent to make extreme demands upon an infant or child (for example, to be toilet trained by 12 months) or to fail to make sufficient demands (for instance, continuing to dress a six year old rather than having the child dress him- or herself).

Several formulations have been offered to explain how unrealistic expectations and use of inappropriate parenting procedures may cause, intensify, and maintain problem behavior. These have been reviewed by Wells and Forehand (1981) and will be reiterated briefly here. Patterson (1976) has developed a ''coercion hypothesis'' to account for the development and maintenance of childhood problem behaviors. According to this hypothesis, rudimentary aversive behaviors such as crying may be instinctual in the newborn infant. Such behaviors could be considered highly adaptive in the evolutionary sense as they quickly help the mother develop skills necessary for the infant's survival (such as feeding and temperature control). Presumably, as infants grow older, they substitute more appropriate verbal and social skills for the rudimentary coercive behaviors. However, according to Patterson (1976), a number of conditions might ensure that some children continue to employ aversive control strategies. Of most importance here, parents may continue to respond inappropriately to the child because of poor parenting skills or unrealistic expectations. Based on a negative reinforcement paradigm, coercive behavior by the child (for example, a tantrum) is reinforced when it results in the *removal* of an aversive event being applied by a parent (such as a command to clean a room). Subsequently, parental coercive behavior toward the child may be reinforced in a similar manner (the child terminates the tantrum when the parent screams at him or her, for instance). Significant increases in rate and intensity of these coercive behaviors occur as both family members are reinforced for higher amplitudes of negative behavior.

Although the ''negative reinforcement trap'' delineated above is probably the most powerful process contributing to deviant child behavior, Wahler (1976) has also emphasized the role of positive reinforcement in shaping these behaviors. In this model, the parent applies positive reinforcers, such as verbal or physical attention, to the child's deviant behaviors (for example, the child is given a cookie in an attempt to terminate a tantrum), thus increasing the frequency or intensity of such behavior. Reinforcement of deviant behaviors may occur because the parent does not have realistic expectations (such as not realizing that a tantrum is inappropriate for a seven year old) or lacks appropriate parenting skills.

Thus, unrealistic or inappropriate expectations and utilization of poor child-rearing skills can lead to early problems, which are good predictors of later problems. Olweus (1979) reviewed studies dealing with aggressive boys and concluded that this is a stable behavior across time. In the Isle of Wight Study (Rutter, Graham, Chadwick, & Yule, 1976), a relationship was found between early child and adolescent problems. Robins (1966) has reported a relationship between certain childhood problems and later adult problems as have Jenkins, Bax, and Hart (1980). These examples suggest a need for prevention efforts in home problems.

Prevention of home problems can be approached from two levels. First, there is primary prevention which intervenes before problems occur. This consists of steps taken at the formative period in the child's development when patterns of interaction are being set and before difficulties or coercive cycles emerge. A second level of prevention is the treatment of early problems to prevent later, more severe problems. The work reviewed in the preceding paragraph suggests that such secondary prevention is important. In this chapter we will selectively review both types of prevention where data are available to provide the reader with an overview of the *data based* studies pertaining to prevention efforts at home.

AREAS OF PREVENTION

There are three important areas in the prevention of home problems. First, unrealistic parental expectations about child behavior and insufficient knowledge of developmental norms should be addressed. Second, the actual childrearing skills utilized by parents may need to be modified to prevent problems. Third, parental distress, such as depression or marital discord, may be associated with either unrealistic expectations or poor parenting skills and should be modified as part of a prevention effort.

Expectations and Norms

If a parent's expectations of his or her child are not met, it has been hypothesized that the parent will be less satisfied as a result of perceiving the child as difficult, noncompliant, or oppositional (Cahill, 1978; Kempe & Kempe, 1978). This may result in the parent placing more pressure on the child to perform. Unfortunately, if the parent's expectations are too high, the child's behavior may become more problematic. A parent may react further with guilt about causing the child's problems, frustration by their inability to deal with the child, or anger at the child for the trouble or embarrassment he or she causes. These parental reactions can lead to the parent and child becoming enmeshed in a vicious cycle of conflict similar to Patterson's coercion model. Such an established pattern of conflict may persist into subsequent periods of development or escalate the intensity or frequency of other normal behaviors to a problematic level.

Although data are not available concerning the long-term effects of unrealistic expectations, there is some evidence to suggest that such expectations may be quite common. For example, Heinstein (1969) reports that the second most common problem reported by mothers of children under the age of two is toilet training. This problem has been reported by over 50% of the mothers of boys and girls between the ages of 18 months and 23 months. Literature concerning the normal acquisition of this developmental task shows that the majority of children are not toilet trained until after two years of age, and many not until three years of age (White, 1975). A year or more of negative interactions between parent and child regarding toileting may be sufficient to establish a general pattern of conflict.

In a study of mother's perceptions of independent and responsible behaviors in their preschool children, Hildebrand (1975) found 14 instances where the percentage of mothers saying "I expect this" exceeded the "should be old enough" responses. The most extreme contradiction was that only 60% of the four year old boys' mothers indicated their children "should be old enough" to wash their hands and yet 98% indicated they expected the child to do the task. Thirty-eight percent of these children were expected to do a task but were not developmentally ready, thereby establishing a pattern of negativism.

Perhaps the best example of a relationship between potentially preventable unrealistic expectations and their effects upon the parent-child interaction pattern comes from child abuse literature. In a comparison of abusive, neglectful, and normal parents, Spinetta (1978) reported that abusive parents had the highest expectations of their children. Similar conclusions have been reported elsewhere (Gladstone, 1965; Melnick & Hurley, 1969; Steele & Pollock, 1968). This suggests that unrealistic high expectations may lead to parental frustration and, subsequently, to child abuse.

Parental expectations and perceptions are mediated, at least in part, by a knowledge of normal development and of established child reactions to certain events. Both of these norms should be considered in primary and secondary prevention. When considering developmental norms, child development specialists White (1975), Caplan and Caplan (1977), and Brazelton (1971) noted that different types of positive behaviors appear at varying stages of development. These include motor, cognitive, verbal, social, and self-sufficiency skills. Similarly, some problem behaviors (for example, separation anxiety, imagined fears, tantrums, "terrible two's," and adolescent rebellion) have been identified as age-related.

To illustrate the relationship between knowledge of normal development and parental expectations, one might consider a child's cognitive level. Not only does it set limits on the types of thinking the child can employ and the strategies used in coping with stress, but the child's cognitive level also influences the parents' coping strategies. For example, the three to four year old lacks a firm grasp on logic, thus preventing the parent from rationally discussing real and imagined dangers. The parent who does not have a knowledge of the child's logic skills would be unable to understand why the child is afraid of fantasy monsters and unwilling to go into the house alone but, on the other hand, does not stop and look before crossing the street. Attempting to teach a child of this age how and when to cross the street may be unrealistic.

A second example of the relationship between developmental norms and parental expectations is adolescent rebellion. Parents abound with questions and expectations: Do all adolescents go through this stage? Should rebellion be expected and tolerated or should the adolescent be strictly disciplined? Should parents worry if their adolescent is rebelling or, conversely, should a parent worry if their adolescent is *not* rebelling? A casual conversation with the parent of any adolescent will confirm these questions and expectations plus other similar ones. Parental behavior, based on their expectations, can do much to foster or prevent adolescent problems in the home.

Unfortunately, the psychological literature does little to help parents of adolescents develop realistic expectations, as there are two contradicting theories concerning adolescent rebellion. Some view adolescence as a period of disruption and see maladaptive behavior as inevitable (Freud, 1958; Buntman & Saris, 1981). Others have proposed that modern civilized society makes adolescence a time of rebellion (Bandura, 1964; Bettelheim, 1969; Bronfenbrenner, 1974; Elder, 1980; Keniston, 1965). The expectations about an adolescent will clearly differ depending on the theory adopted.

In addition to developmental norms, another norm should be considered: childhood behavior which is associated with specific events not necesssarily tied to developmental stages. Examples include the arrival of a sibling (Dunn & Kendrick, 1980), the death of a parent, sibling, friend, or relative (Koocher, 1974; Kessler, 1966), and the separation or divorce of parents (Atkeson, Forehand, & Rickard, 1982). To illustrate, separation or divorce will be examined here in detail. (For a further discussion of prevention of problems associated with life transitions, see comments by Felner, Chapter 5 of this volume).

It is conservatively estimated that by 1990 approximately one third of all children will experience a parent's divorce before they reach the age of 18 (Glick, 1979). Systematic research concerning the impact of divorce on children is just beginning. Most studies (for example, Kalter, 1977; McDermott, 1970; Rutter, 1971) have found that children of divorce have more difficulties with aggressive, antisocial, predelinquent, or delinquent behaviors than children of intact families. Further, divorce has been related to greater detrimental effects on children than the absence of a parent due to death, desertion, or separation (Crescimbeni, 1965; Ferri, 1976; Santrock, 1972). Developmental differences have also been noted in reactions toward divorce. For example, Wallerstein and Kelly (1976) found that children in three age ranges (6–8, 9–10, and adolescence) differed in their reactions to divorce. The first group displayed more of a sense of loss, the second group displayed more anger, and the third group withdrew more. Thus, specific events such as divorce may be associated with different reactions at different ages.

The research currently available suggests that there are a number of mediating factors in determining the effects of divorce on children (Hetherington, Cox, & Cox, 1978; Kelly & Wallerstein, 1977; Wallerstein & Kelly, 1974). These factors include the quality of a child's relationship with both parents, the parents' personal adjustment, the relationship between parents, and extrafamilial support systems (Atkeson et al., 1982). Such mediating factors are at the heart of preventing or at least minimizing behavior problems in the home when a divorce occurs.

In summary, unrealistic expectations may be quite common among parents and may pose an excellent target for preventive programming. Such expectations are not confined to a particular age group of children, but can exist in infancy through adolescence. Lack of knowledge about developmental norms and children's reactions to specific events can lead to unrealistic expectations and, as a consequence, use of poor parenting skills.

Child Rearing Skills

Although some behavior problems of children are age appropriate and therefore expected, there are others which should not occur at any age. Both situations can be changed if parents possess the appropriate skills. This section will focus on the identification of parenting skills which prevent or foster behavior problems in the home.

Several studies have compared the behavior of parents who have conduct problem children and those whose children are viewed as normal. Patterson (1976) noted that parents of conduct problem boys fail to appropriately consequate deviant behavior more often than parents of nonproblem children. In a review of the literature, Rogers, Forehand, and Griest (1981) concluded that mothers of behavior problem children give significantly more commands, display more negative behavior, and criticize more than parents of nonproblem children. These types of coercive parental behaviors serve to increase negative child behavior when viewed in light of Patterson's coercion hypothesis (1976).

Beyond consequating deviant behavior and reducing their coercive behavior, what parental actions promote positive reactions in children? Gordon (1970, 1976), the developer of Parent Effectiveness Training (PET), assumes that a better relationship between parents and children will occur if parents acquire and use skills employed by professional psychotherapists. The most important of these include "active listening," "I-messages," and the "no-lost" method of conflict resolution. Unfortunately, there has been no research on the effectiveness of the various program components. In addition, the overall effectiveness of PET as a prevention or intervention strategy has not been supported (Rinn & Markle, 1977).

Moore and Arthur (1982) have identified three critical ingredients for promoting positive child behavior and development: (1) the quality of the parent-child affiliative relationship, (2) the style and consistency of parental supervision, and (3) the quality of parental socialization of the child. A relationship was shown between love-oriented parents who demonstrated consistent disciplinary techniques and positive development in children. The ability to show affection and concern for the child was particularly important, as was the ability to use consistent, contingent social approval and disapproval. Finally, children whose parents modeled appropriate lifestyles had more favorable outcomes in terms of adjustment than children whose parents did not. Substantial research supports the importance of these three parenting skills. For example, data indicate that parental social reinforcement for the child's appropriate behavior (Bernhart & Forehand, 1975), clearly stated parental commands (Roberts, McMahon, Forehand, & Humphreys, 1978), and the use of a consistent disciplinary procedure such as timeout (removing the child from positive reinforcement contingent upon inappropriate behavior; Hobbs, Forehand, & Murray, 1978; Scarboro & Forehand, 1975) increases desirable child behavior.

In summary, there is evidence that coercive parental behavior and inconsistency with consequences are associated with an increase in child behavior problems. A positive loving relationship, consistency in interactions with the child, and modeling appropriate behavior produce positive child behavior.

Parental Distress

> There is ample evidence to assume that the mental health of children is closely related to that of the parents and, specifically, that the parents' sense of confidence, competence, and self-worth has a direct impact on the nature of the parent-child interaction and therefore on the child's self-image. . . . If we are concerned with children's welfare, we must look at the parents' state of being [Weissbourd, 1981, p. 1975]

The literature suggests that a relationship exists between the psychological adjustment of parents and the behavior of their children. Parental depression, anxiety, marital discord, and isolation from friends each have been related to child behavior problems (Forehand, Furey, & McMahon, 1982; O'Leary & Emery, 1982). In fact, these characteristics have been found to be highly interrelated, with correlations ranging from .54 to .83 (Forehand et al., 1982). This led Forehand et al. to suggest that the different measures of parental adjustment may be tapping a common construct which can be labeled as parental distress.

Before reviewing the data, it should be noted that the bulk of the research has been completed with clinic samples. While the relationship between adjustment measures of parents and the behavior of children is particularly strong in clinical samples, generalizations must be limited because differences in clinic and nonclinic samples are important. For example, O'Leary and Emery (1982) concluded that while a relationship exists between marital discord and child behavior problems in nonclinic samples, the relationship is substantially weaker than in clinic samples.

Several studies have noted relationships between the personal distress of parents and the behavior problems of their clinic-referred children. Johnson and Lobitz (1974) reported a relationship between fathers' elevated MMPI scores and deviant child behavior. A study by Griest, Forehand, Wells, and McMahon (1980) focused upon maternal adjustment. In a comparison of clinic and nonclinic children, the investigators documented that, in addition to clinic-referred children being less compliant, their mothers rated themselves as significantly more depressed and anxious. This suggests a relationship between child behavior problems (for example, noncompliance) and parental adjustment problems. Furthermore, maternal depression is frequently related to parental perceptions of child adjustment in clinic samples (Griest et al., 1980; Griest, Wells, & Forehand, 1979) and to parental satisfaction with their children in a nonclinic sample (Furey, Note 1).

Several studies have assessed the relationship of marital status to child behavior problems. Most (for example, Johnson & Lobitz, 1974; Oltmanns, Broderick, & O'Leary, 1977) have provided evidence suggesting that children with higher levels of deviant behavior are more likely to have parents with marital problems than are children with lower levels of deviant behavior. Emery (1982) found in the general population that the probability of having a discordant marriage given a child with psychological problems is less than the probability of having a child with psychological problems given a discordant marriage. This study suggests that marital problems lead to problem behaviors in the child more often than vice versa.

Attention has also been focused on the relationship of parental divorce to child behavior problems. Hetherington, Cox, and Cox (1979) reported that children, particularly males, whose parents are divorced demonstrated more behavior problems than children from intact families for at least two years subsequent to the divorce. Furthermore, level of parental conflict and the married-divorce status of the parents appeared to interact, at least for males. Hetherington (Note 2) reported that boys from divorced families in which parents continue to engage in a high level of conflict manifested more problems than boys from divorced-low conflict, intact-high conflict, and intact-low conflict families. Thus, evidence supports the existence of a relationship between child behavior problems and parent-to-parent problems, divorce, and the interaction of both.

There are some data which link parents' interpersonal relationships outside the family to the occurrence of child behavior problems. Wahler and Afton (1980) identified two groups of parents: those with infrequent and negative interactions outside the home and those with frequent and positive interactions outside the home. The former was termed *insular* and the latter *noninsular*. Observations of these two groups in the home indicated that mothers and children from insular families displayed more oppositional behavior than those from noninsular families, suggesting that factors outside the home which affect the parents are related to parenting style and child behavior problems.

In summary, the data show that parental distress is related to child behavior. The distress may be in the parents' personal, marital, or extrafamilial adjustment. Furthermore, the intercorrelations of these different measures of parental adjustment suggest that parental distress in any area may signal the possibility of maladjustment in the other areas which also influence the child's behavior.

PREVENTION

To this point, we have presented an argument for the need for prevention of childhood problems in the home. We now turn to primary and secondary prevention of childhood problems in the home setting. The work reviewed here centers around the three areas described previously: expectations and norms, child rearing, and parental distress.

Expectations and Norms

> An introduction to growth and development, primarily through norms, acquaints new parents with behaviors of the infant and toddler but perhaps even more importantly,

begins to shape the parents into observers of child behavior. [Christophersen, Barrish, Barrish, & Christophersen, 1982, p. 5]

This comment reflects the importance they place on introducing parents to child behaviors associated with various stages of development, so that parents may develop accurate, age-appropriate expectations. Unfortunately, Christophersen et al. provide no data as to whether instructing parents in developmental norms/expectations leads to a change in parental understanding/expectations of their child's development and, subsequently, to changes in the child's behavior. For the most part, this lack of data-based research is characteristic of the literature focusing on modification of parental expectations and norms related to their children's home behavior.

Primary Prevention

In a recent study, Myers (1982) reported a successful attempt to increase parental knowledge of typical infant behavior in which 42 middle class, married couples with a firstborn infant participated. Families were assigned to one of three groups: mother treatment, father treatment, or no treatment. Treatment, consisting of one training session, was based on an experimenter teaching the parent to administer items of the Neonatal Behavior Assessment Scale (Brazelton, 1973) to his or her infant. The session included "eliciting reflexes . . . habituation . . ., and visual and auditory following and noting unique patterns in ability to be soothed, temperature adaptation, and state change." (p. 464). The results indicated that, relative to the no treatment group, mothers and fathers who participated in training demonstrated more knowledge of infant behavior. This effect was maintained at a four week follow-up.

In a large study involving 35 physicians and over 450 mothers and their young infants, Chamberlin, Szumowski, and Zastowny (1979) evaluated the effects of pediatricians' efforts to educate mothers of firstborn children about child development and behavior. Physicians were divided into low, medium, and high groups based on the degree of their efforts. The results indicated that mothers gained more in knowledge about child development as the physician effort level increased. Mothers with more child development knowledge reported more positive physical contact with their child, suggesting a relationship between knowledge and positive parenting skills.

In a similar research project with parents of six to nine year olds, Biferno (1978) compared the effects of a Cognitive Development Parent Education Group and an Adlerian Parent Education Group on parental expectations, acceptance, and parental acceptance as perceived by children. He found that accurate parental expectations of children's behavior did *not* result from participation in either parent education program. Both parent education programs did produce an increase in parental acceptance of child behavior, but failed to produce an increase in the child's perception of parental acceptance.

Although expectations per se have not been measured, Gordon (1975) has introduced Parent Effectiveness Training (PET) to modify parent attitudes and acceptance of their children. These procedures were developed initially for parents and children who had relationship problems. However, according to Gordon (1975), PET evolved into a means of teaching parents skills which *prevent* problems between their children and themselves. In 1975, Gordon reported that there were a quarter of a million parents who had gone through PET and 7,000 persons who had been professionally trained to teach PET courses, with 1,500 more being trained every year.

Rinn and Markle (1977) have summarized and critically evaluated the research literature (14 studies) regarding the effects of PET on parents and their children. Of particular note is that only one of the 14 studies had appeared in a professional publication. Criticizing the studies as being inadequate in design and limited in scope and dependent measures, Rinn and Markle conclude that there are currently no experimentally rigorous data available to support the assumption that PET is effective.

Secondary prevention.

Data are equally scarce in secondary prevention of parental expectations. The only available research related to the modification of parental expectations focuses on identification of infants who are at risk. Beller (1979) reviewed a number of programs for such infants, including the New Orleans Model which focused on teaching parents child development norms and methods of facilitating child development. No direct measures of change in parental knowledge of norms or parental expectations were reported; however, a number of positive changes in the parents' behavior toward their children occurred, including more sensitivity, cooperation, and acceptance. From these results, one could infer that changes occurred in parental expectations and understanding of their children's needs. A second program, the Birmingham Model, attempted to increase the parenting skills of the participants and their planning of daily activities and social interactions. One outcome measure indicated that mothers became more flexible and tolerant of their children's socialization and maturation processes. This *suggests* a change in maternal expectations.

The Upsilanti Infant Education Project was the only program to directly measure parental perceptions of general child development and parental expectations of their own child. Parents in the treatment group observed a home visitor who worked with their infant using a curriculum associated with Piaget's sensorimotor period. Mothers then were encouraged to take responsibility as the infant's teacher. Two types of control groups were utilized. One was labeled a contrast group and involved home visitors introducing informal intuitive play activities. The other control group was exposed to a test-retest only condition. Although more positive changes did occur on some measures for the experimental mothers than for those in the two remaining groups, the three groups did not differ on measures of "perceptions of and expectations for child development" (p. 865).

Conclusions.

Minimum data are available to support the effectiveness of primary or secondary prevention efforts which modify parental expectations and knowledge of child development norms. As Rickard (Note 3) has noted, the paucity of studies may result from the absence of instruments to measure parental expectations. Rickard recently developed the PEABS (Parents' Expectations, Attitudes, and Beliefs Scale) to measure this concept. Obviously, such instruments should be developed and utilized to assess the impact of prevention programs aimed at modifying parental expectations.

Childrearing

More research efforts have been directed toward modifying childrearing skills than toward changing expectations in the areas of both primary and secondary prevention.

Primary Prevention.

Substantial research has been focused on the area of primary prevention of preschool home behavior problems. A common form of intervention in this area appears to be the use of self-help programs which are totally self-administered and require a minimal amount of professional time (McMahon & Forehand, 1980). These take the form of "how to parent" books, manuals, and leaflets, which parents may obtain from professionals or bookstores.

One such book used widely by parents in primary (as well as secondary) prevention of childhood problems is *Toilet Training in Less Than a Day* (Azrin & Foxx, 1974). Azrin and Foxx (1973) used an intensive learning procedure in which experienced trainers successfully toilet trained 34 children, ranging in age from 20 to 36 months, in an average of four hours. Accidents remained near zero over four months of follow-up, leading the authors to suggest that virtually all healthy children of at least 20 months of age could be toilet trained in a matter of hours. This technique was then developed into book form for consumption by the general public.

Butler (1976) and Matson and Ollendick (1977) subsequently replicated the toileting program and obtained positive results when using the book plus supervision in implementing the toileting procedures. However, Matson and Ollendick found the book alone was not effective. The results of the evaluations of the Azrin and Foxx book (1974) indicate that the procedures described are effective in teaching toileting skills to preschool children when there is some amount of outside supervision by a professional.

Moving to more traditional training programs, Toepfer, Feuter, and Maurer (1972) demonstrated that attempts at primary prevention can change the obedience of normal preschool children. Mothers were taught contingent social reinforcement to increase their nonclinic children's obedient behavior. Based on the positive results, the authors concluded that increasing preschool children's obedience to maternal commands in an analogue setting was attainable through a program requiring less than five hours of parent training. Using substantially less time, Forgatch and Toobert (1979) found that the whining of preschool children could be decreased significantly by a 40-minute training program consisting of time-out and positive reinforcement. In a second experiment reported in the same study, child noncompliance was decreased by a similar 30-minute parenting program. As noted earlier, data from the University of Georgia Research Program have supported the importance of using clearly stated commands (Roberts et al., 1978) and a time-out procedure (Hobbs & Forehand, 1977) with preschool normal children.

Primary preventive research efforts have also been undertaken with school-age and adolescent populations. Self-help programs (McMahon & Forehand, 1980) have been developed for instructing parents or caregivers to teach their normal children adaptive family shopping trip behaviors (Clark, Greene, Macrae, McNees, Davis, & Risley , 1977), and assumption of morning time responsibilities (McManmon, Davis, & Clark, Note 4). In the McManmon et al. study, an advice program known as MAK-IT was devised, which defined each morning household responsibility, assigned responsibilities to each child, scheduled the order in which the responsibilities should be completed, prompted the parent to monitor the children's progress throughout, and provided the children with a motivational system for assuming these responsibilities. Two women from the community were paired with elementary school-age children who were residents at a group home for dependent-neglected children. During the program, mothers received and read a package of instructional materials, asked questions during the first two days of implementation, received verbal feedback from the experimenter, and were cued by the experimenter when they explained the program to the children. Thus, this program combined self-instruction with therapist supervision similar to the Matson and Ollendick (1977) and Butler (1976) studies on toilet training. Results of the study revealed that children in both "families" increased the amount of time spent on their assigned chores and completed more during the program than during baseline. This had the additional effect of reducing the time the "analogue" mothers themselves spent on chores.

Secondary Prevention.

A number of studies have also addressed the issue of secondary prevention or treatment of relatively minor problems in order to prevent subsequent major problems. These prevention procedures have been implemented with infants, preschoolers, and school age children, including adolescents.

As noted earlier, Beller (1979) reviewed a number of programs for at risk infants, many of which taught parents skills to prevent the infants from developing subsequent serious problems. In the Milwaukee Project, Heber and Garber intervened to prevent cultural familial retardation in cases where all mothers had IQ scores under 80 and newborn infants. Mothers attended adult education classes where job training, child rearing, and homemaking skills were taught. Infants participated in programs which emphasized the development of cognitive, language, and social skills. The results indicated that, relative to a control group, the children in the treatment group communicated better and demonstrated more problem solving skills, advanced language development, and higher IQ scores. Beller concluded that while dramatic changes occurred for the treatment group, the intensive training received by the mothers cannot be considered responsible for the improvements as few measures collected on maternal functioning changed. This suggests that teaching more than parent skills may be necessary in low IQ, high-risk families. For example, occupational skills training and how to cope with life stresses may be a necessary part of a program for this population.

Self-help programs have been used with preschoolers in secondary prevention as well as in primary prevention. For example, McMahon and Forehand (1978) selected three mothers who were having mealtime problems with their preschool children and examined the effectiveness of a brochure teaching these mothers to modify their children's inappropriate mealtime behaviors. The brochure described the procedures of differential attention and time-out as they might be applied to mealtime. No feedback or information other than the brochure was employed. The results were assessed in the home by a multiple-baseline across-subjects design. Inappropriate mealtime behavior decreased substantially for each child, with reductions ranging from 50% to 80%. Maternal use of rewards and consequation of inappropriate mealtime behavior also changed in the desired directions. Changes were maintained at a six-week follow-up and were comparable to results obtained in more intensive parent training programs.

A number of prevention programs have been developed for preschoolers which involve direct contact between a professional and parent. One such program was implemented at the University of Georgia to increase child compliance. The problem of noncompliance was identified as an important behavior because it is the most frequently reported problem by parents who refer their children for treatment *and* by parents of nonclinic children who are not seeking treatment (Forehand, 1977). Therefore, the behavior appears to be a ubiquitous one that causes parents considerable concern. Robins' (1966) data suggest that children who demonstrate various types of noncompliance (for example, refusing to work, running away, fighting) may well experience poor adjustment as adults (for instance, arrests, poor marriages, alcoholism), which indicates the need for prevention strategies at an early age. Furthermore, Conger (1982) has identified noncompliance as an important elicitor of child abuse; therefore, modification of this behavior may prevent more serious behavior problems and potential harm to the child.

To date, over 100 mother-child pairs, for whom extensive data have been collected, have participated in the University of Georgia ongoing project. The children have ranged in age from three to eight and have manifested difficulties with noncompliance and other behavior problems. The majority of the families have been of a lower middle-class status.

The parent training program employs a controlled learning environment in which parents are taught to change their interactions with their child. Sessions are conducted in a clinic setting with individual families rather than in groups. Treatment occurs in clinic playrooms equipped with one way mirrors for observation, sound systems, and a bug-in-the-ear (Farrell Instruments) device by which therapists can unobtrusively communicate with parents. A number of discrete parenting skills are taught in a systematic manner by way of didactic instruction, modeling, and role playing. The parent also practices the skills in the clinic with the child while receiving prompting and feedback from the therapist through the earpiece. Finally, the parent employs these newly acquired skills in the home setting.

The treatment program consists of two phases. During the differential attention treatment phase (Phase I), the parent learns to be a more effective reinforcing agent by increasing the frequency and range of her or his social rewards and reducing competing verbal behavior. First, the parent is taught to attend to and describe the child's appropriate behavior. All commands, questions, and criticisms directed to the child are eliminated during the therapy session. The second segment of Phase I consists of training the parent to use verbal and physical rewards contingent upon compliance and other appropriate behaviors. The parent is taught to reward the child's ongoing appropriate behavior and ignore minor inappropriate behavior.

Phase 2 of the treatment program consists of training the parent to use appropriate commands and a time-out procedure to decrease noncompliant behavior exhibited by the child. The parent is taught to give direct, concise commands one at a time and to allow the child sufficient time to comply. If compliance is initiated, the parent is taught to reward or attend to the child within five seconds of the compliance initiation. If compliance is not initiated, the parent learns to implement a time-out procedure that involves placing the child in a chair for three minutes (Forehand & McMahon, 1981). Following time-out, the command that originally elicited noncompliance is repeated and compliance is then followed by social reinforcement from the parent.

Our outcome measures have included the collection of behavioral data in the home setting during 40-minute observations by trained observers. Four observations each are collected at pretreatment, posttreatment, and follow-up with naive undergraduate and graduate students as observers. The coding system used in the home setting is presented in detail by Forehand and McMahon (1981). The following classes of parent behaviors are recorded: rewards, attends, contingent attention, questions, commands, warnings, and time-out. Child behaviors which are recorded include appropriate, inappropriate (deviant), compliance, and noncompliance. A second outcome measure is three of the scales from the Parent Attitude Test (Cowen, Huser, Beach, & Rappaport, 1970). These have been employed to assess parental perceptions of child behavior.

Our research has progressed through three stages. Initially, our efforts were directed at demonstrating the short-term effects of the program (Forehand & King, 1974, 1977). In the second stage, we turned our attention to evaluating the generality of the program (Baum & Forehand, 1981; Forehand, Sturgis, McMahon, Aguar, Green, Wells, & Breiner, 1979; Humphreys, Forehand, McMahon, & Roberts, 1978; Peed, Roberts, & Forehand, 1977; Wells, Forehand, & Griest, 1980). And in the third stage, we examined ways to enhance generality of treatment effects (McMahon, Forehand, & Griest, 1981; Wells, Griest, & Forehand, 1980). In general, research results indicate the following: use of the parent training program leads to changes in parent and child behavior; the changes generalize over time, settings, behaviors, and siblings; and the addition of two procedures (teaching parents self-control techniques and teaching them a thorough knowledge of social learning principles) to the basic parent training program enhances generality beyond that obtained with the program alone (Forehand & McMahon, 1981; McMahon & Forehand, 1982).

A major focus on our research is now directed toward dissemination of our procedures. Forehand and McMahon (1981) published a book describing the parenting program, the exact procedures utilized, and the outcome data. Even more directly related to prevention, Dr. Robert McCall visited the program, interviewed participating parents, and wrote an article for *Parent's Magazine* based on our procedures. Articles such as this should extend our technology from scientific journals to magazines typically read by parents. Only then will large numbers of parents have access to the techniques that hopefully can prevent problems in children.

Other investigators have also designed programs for parents of preschoolers which are primarily preventive in nature. Of particular interest are those which, in contrast to the University of Georgia program, have utilized group training procedures. Prevention procedures ideally should be designed to reach a large number of parents and require minimum professional involvement. Thus, group procedures to teach preventive child rearing skills would appear important.

Most of the programs developed for groups of parents are based on behavioral principles similar to those used in the University of Georgia program. That is, parents are taught to reinforce appropriate behavior and to ignore or use a time-out procedure for inappropriate behavior. In an interesting prevention study, Rinn, Markle, and Wise (1981) trained foster parents in behavioral principles since corporal punishment was no longer permitted by the state's child welfare agency. All data were collected by the foster parents and indicated that participation in the group training was associated with more child improvement than that demonstrated by children of foster parents who dropped out of the program. In a second study utilizing foster parents, Hampson and Tavormina (1980) compared behavioral group training to a reflective group training procedure. The latter procedure was more effective in changing parental attitudes toward the children, whereas the former group procedure was more effective in decreasing problem behaviors, improving parent-child interactions, and satisfying parents (that is, overall ratings of improvement and treatment effectiveness). Thus, different types of group procedures may be associated with different outcomes.

Several studies have not only been concerned with parent group training but also with the most effective way to teach the parenting skills. Each of these studies has involved teaching parents to use a time-out procedure for disruptive behavior in the young normal child. The various procedures used to teach time-out have included distribution of a written manual, a didactic presentation, an audiotaped presentation, a videotaped modeling presentation, a live modeling presentation, and an opportunity to role-play the procedure. In general, a procedure that involved modeling alone or in combination with another procedure (such as role-playing, brief individual checkout in using the skill) has been found to be most effective (Flannagon, Adams, & Forehand, 1979; Nay, 1975; O'Dell, Mahoney, Horton, & Turner, 1979). Drawing from these studies, Webster-Stratton (1981) exposed groups of parents to a videotape modeling program designed to change general maternal parenting behaviors (positive affect, nonacceptance, dominance, leadtaking, and watching the child play) and parent attitudes toward the child. The results indicated changes in the expected direction for four of the five parent behaviors, but not for parent attitudes. In addition, all parents reported being "very positive" about the program.

In general, the results of the various studies suggest that minor problems of preschool children can be effectively reduced and parents are satisfied with the implemented programs. The programs can be effectively utilized in either an individual or group format. When the latter method is used, modeling appears to be an important ingredient. The primary question at this time is whether these strategies are as effective as preventive ones. That is, are the gains maintained over an extended time period and do the parents remain satisfied with the results or seek subsequent help with childhood problems? The only data available beyond a rather brief posttreatment interval (one year or less) are those recently reported by Baum and Forehand (1981) on the University of Georgia program. At periods ranging from one and one-half to four and one-half years after termination of treatment, children maintained their behavior change and parents maintained their perceptions of child adjustment, reported satisfaction with treatment, and had sought additional treatment for only six of 34 children. Clearly, more data using longer follow-up periods are needed before the effectiveness of programs for young children (which are designed to alleviate minor problems in order to prevent subsequent major ones) can be determined.

Substantial research efforts have also been directed toward school age children. Some of these projects are similar to the ones described with preschool populations (for example, Patterson & Fleischman, 1979), whereas others deal with different types of early problem behaviors or are designed to prevent major problems like delinquency. To avoid redundancy, projects similar to those with preschool children will not be described here.

Stuart and his colleagues have utilized contingency contracting (a written agreement between parent and child specifying responsibilities, privileges for fulfilling the responsibilities, and sanctions for failure to meet responsibilities) with predelinquent adolescents in order to prevent delinquency. In one report, Stuart, Tripodi, Jayaratne, and Camburn (1976) compared 57 clinic-referred families of predelinquents treated with contingency contracting to 45 waiting list control families. Results indicated that, relative to the controls, the adolescents treated with contingency contracting displayed small but significant improvement on five measures of school and home behavior, including parental ratings of the adolescent behavior in the home.

A model that has received substantial attention with parents and adolescents is a problem solving, communication skills training program. The rationale behind this model is that some parents and adolescents do not have the skills to resolve conflicts or solve problems. From a preventive viewpoint this difficulty could lead to further problems and possible delinquency. Therefore, parent-child dyads are taught to define the problem, list the solutions, evaluate each option by reviewing positive and negative consequences of each, and plan the implementation of the chosen solution.

A study by Robin, Kent, O'Leary, Foster, and Prinz (1977) indicated significant improvement for a treatment group on several measures collected in the clinic; however, ratings on a communication checklist failed to yield substantial evidence of improvement at home. The authors concluded that this lack of improvement in the home should prompt a search for procedures to enhance generalization, such as use of homework assignments and incorporation of other relevant family members into treatment.

In a subsequent study, Robin (1981) incorporated procedures designed to enhance generalization in the problem solving model. This treatment was compared to a waiting list control group and an alternative family therapy model consisting of a mixture of family systems, dynamic, and eclectic family therapy. Both treatment conditions, but not the control condition, resulted in significant reductions from pre- to postassessment in self-reported disputes and conflicting communication at home; however, only problem solving communication training resulted in significant improvements in behavior coded during family discussions. Most of the significant treatment effects were maintained at a 10 week follow-up.

A child/adolescent behavior problem which is particularly noteworthy is stealing. Data by Moore, Chamberlain, and Mukai (1979) and Mitchell and Rosa (1981) indicate that young children who are identified as stealers are at high risk for later delinquency. Of the stealers referred for treatment, Moore et al. found that two to nine years later 77% of them had court-referred records, whereas Mitchell and Rosa found that stealing in children was the best predictor of a criminal record 15 years later. Therefore, in terms of secondary prevention, it is important to identify these children early, develop programs for their stealing behavior, and evaluate the effectiveness of the programs.

Reid, Hinojoa-Rivera, and Lorber (Note 5) have developed a program which involves four major components. First, emphasis is removed from stealing per se and placed on possession of objects for which the child cannot account. Second, the parent is the sole judge of whether or not stealing occurred. The parent does not attempt to elicit a confession from the child, but simply decides if the child has or has not stolen an object. Third, if the parent decides that stealing has occurred, a mild consequence (for example, one hour of work for stolen objects valued under $1.00 and two hours of work for stolen objects valued over $1.00) is imposed. Fourth, a system is implemented which requires the child to check-in with parents on a regular basis. This is implemented for children who previously have been allowed to wander outside the home for long periods of time.

Using this program with children ranging from five to fourteen years of age, Reid et al. (Note 5) evaluated treatment outcomes based on parental reports of stealing events. Analyses of the data for the 28 families who completed at least five weeks of treatment demonstrated significant declines in stealing events and other referral problems from baseline to posttreatment. In addition, the six month follow-up measures on 10 available families indicated that changes were maintained.

The studies with adolescents address a variety of problems. In general, the programs have reduced minor problems; however, the effects do not appear to be as dramatic as those obtained with younger children. From a preventive perspective, this is not surprising as behaviors are more ingrained by the adolescent years. Unfortunately data are not available to indicate the long-term effects of treatment projects with adolescents (such as whether later serious problems are prevented).

Conclusions.

Substantial research has been directed toward prevention in the area of parenting skills. The data suggest that both primary and secondary preventive efforts have been successful with infants, preschool children, and adolescents. The earlier in the life of the child that preventive programs are implemented, the more successful they appear to be. A major need at this time is to conduct long-term evaluations of the preventive programs currently being utilized.

Parental Distress

In addition to prevention programs for child problems in the home, which focus on changing parental expectations of children and parental child rearing skills, a third approach is to reduce parental distress (depression, marital problems). Because previous data indicated a relationship between parental distress and child behavior problems, this approach would appear to be a logical and important one when considering preventive strategies of children's problems.

Green, Forehand, and McMahon (1979) conducted an investigation in which mothers of clinic-referred children and mothers of nonclinic children were asked to make their children ''look compliant'' in one condition and ''look noncompliant'' in a second condition. Both were effective in making their children look compliant and nondeviant in the ''look compliant'' condition, and look noncompliant and deviant in the ''look noncompliant'' condition. Furthermore, parents in both groups utilized the same types of behaviors (for example, increases and decreases in certain types of commands and increases in positive statements) to accomplish the requested child behavior. These results led us to suggest that parents of clinic-referred children may have the behaviors necessary for child management in their repertoire but may not be utilizing them. Although parental distress was not measured in the Green et al. study, it would appear plausible that this factor may be one reason for the absence of child management skills. Therefore, secondary prevention efforts may be successful by reducing parental distress and allowing the appearance of appropriate parenting skills to prevent or reduce child problems.

Although some data suggest that reducing child oppositional behavior is associated with reductions in parental depression (Forehand, Wells, & Griest, 1980), parental anxiety (Patterson & Fleischman, 1979), and parental marital problems (Forehand, Griest, Wells, & McMahon, 1982), we found no empirical investigations treating parental distress and examining the effects on the prevention or treatment of child problems. Clearly, this area is worth investigating.

Griest, Forehand, Breiner, Rogers, Furey, and Williams (1982) partially address the question in a study to determine if treatment of mothers' personal adjustment, marital adjustment, and extra-familial relations would enhance treatment outcome and generalization beyond the positive effects typically obtained in the University of Georgia program. Seventeen mothers and their clinic-referred, noncompliant children were assigned to either a parent training only group or a parent training plus enhancement therapy group. Fifteen mothers and their nonclinic children served as a quasi-control group. All clinic-referred mother-child dyads were treated individually by way of the parent training program. In addition, mothers in the parent training plus parent enhancement therapy received ''distress'' treatment in the following areas: parent's perception of their child's behavior (presentation of developmental norms in order to change unrealistic expectations), marital adjustment (spouse communication and problem solving skills), parent's personal adjustment (modification of depression and anxiety by cognitive restructuring), and parent's extrafamilial relationships (increasing positive and decreasing negative community interactions). Components of the enhancement treatment were presented intermittently with the standard parent training program.

The primary outcome data in this project consisted of independent home observations prior to treatment, after treatment, and at a two month follow-up. The results indicated that the parent training plus parent enhancement therapy was more effective than parent training alone in changing child deviant behavior at posttreatment and maintaining improvements in compliance, child deviant behavior, parental rewards, and parent contingent attention two months later. The control group did not change over the three assessment periods, suggesting that the behaviors measured were generally stable.

This study suggests that focusing not only on child behavior but also on parental distress may facilitate the effectiveness of preventive programs. What effects preventive efforts aimed just at parental distresss would have on child behavior is uncertain, but warrants investigation. One model for such a program was proposed by McGuire and Gottlieb (1979). In an attempt to reduce distress of new parents, social support groups of six couples were formed. Although few significant differences between treatment and control groups were found, the idea of utilizing other parents to prevent distress caused by the birth of child (for example, isolation, changes in the marital relationship, fears concerning child rearing) deserves further investigation.

Conclusions.

Substantial research is needed to identify the best procedures for preventing childhood problems in families that are experiencing other distresses. For example, focus could be placed on reducing the parental distress and examining the effects on childhood problems. Alternately, if needed, emphasis could be placed on teaching parenting skills and realistic expectations and on monitoring the family to determine if childhood problems are prevented *and* distress dissipates. Perhaps most logically, some combination of the two preceding approaches may be utilized. Data are needed to determine how to approach prevention and intervention efforts with distressed families.

FINAL COMMENTS

The literature reviewed indicates that unrealistic expectations, inadequate parenting skills, and parental distress affect the well-being of children. Unfortunately, our attempts to develop preventive programs in these three areas lag substantially behind our identification of the effects they have on the child. In particular, little research exists to guide our efforts to effectively modify unrealistic parental expectations and parental distress (and the effects on children). In the area of parenting skills, initial research efforts appear promising. However, more work is needed, especially long-term evaluations of existing programs.

Once research in these areas has been completed, the focus will be on dissemination of the procedures. Magazine articles and books designed for the lay person are two obvious ways to disseminate information. Pamphlets could be distributed through schools, preschools, and physicians' offices as well as brief messages over radio and television. Preventive hotlines could be set up where parents call-in to professionals during specified hours to ask questions about their child's behavior. This procedure is part of an excellent, comprehensive program that Schroeder (1979) established for psychologists working within the context of a private pediatric practice. However, it is important to emphasize, as shown elsewhere (McMahon & Forehand, 1980), that the preventive procedures *must* be developed and demonstrated to be effective when used by the public *before* dissemination occurs.

When the prevention of children's problems in the home is considered, we do not view our goal as one of simply making children less trouble for their parents. As has been noted in another context (Forehand & Baumeister, 1976), if this were the goal, a hammer would probably be a useful tool. In contrast, our goal is to facilitate *positive* parent-child interactions. Therefore, in our opinion, prevention of childhood problems in the home can be best achieved by promoting a positive environment for the family. Unfortunately, increasing concern is being expressed about the state of the American family (Bazar, 1982), and its ability to provide a nurturing environment. Divorce, economic factors, lack of support systems (for example, extended families), and inadequate childcare outside the home are examples of the many pressures being exerted on the American family.

Home environments can be designed to prevent childhood problems and foster positive parent-child relationships. However, professionals need to look beyond their traditional therapeutic procedures in search of preventive strategies. Not only will parental expectations, parenting skills, and distresses need to be addressed, but an ecological approach will have to be implemented. As Bronfenbrenner (1974, p. 55) has asserted, it will be necessary "to provide those conditions which are necessary for life and for the family to function as a child rearing system. These include adequate health care, housing, employment, and opportunity and status for parenthood." Such an approach would begin well before the birth of a child and would be an ongoing part of our society. As Weissbourd (1981) has noted, initiation of programs based on this philosophy will have to involve a *community commitment* to "supporting parents as people and parents as parents" (p. 178). We readily support such a philosophy and such programs—for the sake of our children and their children.

REFERENCES

Achenbach, T. M., & Edelbrock, C. S. The classification of child psychopathology: A review and analysis of empirical efforts. *Psychological Bulletin,* 1978, *85,* 1275–1301.

Atkeson, B. M., Forehand, R., & Rickard, K. M. The effects of divorce on children. In B. B. Lahey & A. E. Kazdin (Eds.), *Advances in clinical child psychology* (Vol. 5). New York: Plenum, 1982.

Azrin, N., & Foxx, R. *Toilet training in less than a day*. New York: Simon & Schuster, 1974.

Bandura, A. The stormy decade: Fact or fiction? *Psychology in the Schools,* 1964, *1,* 224–231.

Baum, C. G., & Forehand, R. Long term follow-up asessment of parent training by use of multiple outcome measures. *Behavior Therapy,* 1981, *12,* 643–652.

Bazar, J. Families in need. *APA Monitor,* 1982, 13–14.

Beller, E. K. Early intervention programs. In J. Osofsky (Ed.), *Handbook of infant development*. New York: Wiley, 1979.

Bernhart, A. J., & Forehand, R. The effects of labeled and unlabeled praise upon lower and middle class children. *Journal of Experimental Child Psychology,* 1975, *19,* 536–543.

Bettelheim, B. Obsolete youth. *Encounter,* 1969, *23,* 29–42.

Biferno, K. A comparison of the effects of cognitive, developmental, and Adlerian parent education groups on parental expectations, parental acceptance, and parental acceptance as perceived by children. (Doctoral dissertation, California School of Professional Psychology, Los Angeles, 1977). *Dissertation Abstracts International,* 1978, *38,* 4999B–5000B.

Brazelton, T. B. *Infants and mother: Differences in development*. New York: Delacorte Press, 1971.

Brazelton, T. B. *Neonatal Behavioral Assessment Scale*. Philadelphia: Lippincott, 1973.

Bronfenbrenner, U. *Is early intervention effective? Report of longitudinal evaluations of preschool programs* (Vol. 2). Washington, D.C.: U.S. Department of Health, Education, and Welfare, 1974. Cited in Weissbourd, B. Supporting parents as people. In B. Weissbourd & J. Musick (Eds.), *Infants: Their social environments*. Washington, D.C: National Association for the Education of Young Children, 1981.

Buntman, P. E., & Saris, E. M. *How to live with your teenager: A survivor's handbook for parents*. Pasadena, CA: Birch Tree Press, 1981.

Butler, J. The toilet training success of parents after reading *Toilet Training in Less Than a Day*. *Behavior Therapy,* 1976, *7,* 185–191.

Cahill, M. F. A search for the meaning of the "difficult" child. *Dissertation Abstracts International,* 1978, *39,* (1-B), 154.

Caplan, F., & Caplan, T. *The second twelve months of life*. New York: Grosset & Dunlap, 1977.

Chamberlin, R. W., Szumowski, E. K., & Zastowny, T. R. An evaluation of efforts to educate mothers about child development in pediatric office practices. *American Journal of Public Health,* 1979, *69,* 875–886.

Christophersen, E., Barrish, H., Barrish, E., & Christophersen, M. Continuing education for parents of infants and toddlers. In R. F. Dangel & R. A. Polster (Eds.), *Behavioral parent training: Issues in research and practice*. New York: Guilford, 1982.

Clark, H., Greene, B., Macrae, J., McNees, M., Davis, J., & Risley, T. A parent advice package for family shopping trips: Development and evaluation. *Journal of Applied Behavior Analysis,* 1977, *10,* 605–624.

Clarke-Stewart, K. A. Popular primers for parents. *American Psychologist,* 1978, *33,* 359–369.

Conger, R. D. Behavioral intervention for child abuse. *The Behavior Therapist,* 1982, *5,* 49–53.

Cowen, E. L., Huser, J., Beach, D. R., & Rappaport, J. Parental perceptions of young children and their relation to indexes of adjustment. *Journal of Consulting and Clinical Psychology,* 1970, *34,* 97–103.

Crescimbeni, J. Broken homes do affect academic achievement. *Child and Family,* 1965, *4,* 24–28.

Decker, M. L. Parent teen relationships. *The Christian Home,* 1982, June-August, 25–26.

Dunn, J., & Kendrick, C. The arrival of a sibling: Changes in patterns of interaction between mother and first-born child. *Journal of Child Psychology and Psychiatry,* 1980, *21,* 119–132.

Elder, G. H. Adolescence in historical perspective. In J. Adelsen (Ed.), *Handbook of adolescent psychology,* New York: Wiley, 1980.

Emery, R. E. Interparental conflict and the children of discord and divorce. *Psychological Bulletin,* 1982, *92,* 310–330.

Ferri, E. *Growing up in a one-parent family: A long-term study of child development.* London: National Foundation for Educational Research, 1976.

Flannagon, S., Adams, H. E., & Forehand, R. A comparison of four instructional techniques for teaching parents the use of time-out. *Behavior Therapy,* 1979, *10,* 94–102.

Forehand, R. Child noncompliance to parental commands: Behavioral analysis and treatment. In M. Hersen, R. M. Eisler, & P. M. Miller (Eds.), *Progress in behavior modification* (Vol. 5). New York: Academic Press, 1977.

Forehand, R., & Baumeister, A. A. Deceleration of aberrant behavior among retarded individuals. In M. Hersen, R. M. Eisler, & P. M. Miller (Eds.), *Progress in behavior modification* (Vol. 2). New York: Academic, 1976.

Forehand, R., Furey, W. M., & McMahon, R. J. A review of the role of maternal distress in a parent training program to modify one aspect of aggression: Noncompliance. *Analysis and Intervention in Developmental Disabilities,* 1982 *20,* 429–436.

Forehand, R., Griest, D. L., Wells, K. C., & McMahon, R. J. Side effects of parent counseling on marital satisfaction. *Journal of Counseling Psychology,* 1982, *29,* 104–107.

Forehand, R., & King, H. E. Pre-school children's non-compliance: Effects of short-term behavior therapy. *Journal of Community Psychology,* 1974, *2,* 42–44.

Forehand, R., & King, H. E. Noncompliant children: Effects of parent training on behavior and attitude change. *Behavior Modification,* 1977, *1,* 93–108.

Forehand, R., & McMahon, R. J. *Helping the noncompliant child: A clinician's guide to effective parent training.* New York: Guilford, 1981.

Forehand, R., Sturgis, E. T., McMahon, R. J., Aguar, D., Green, K., Wells, K. C., & Breiner, J. Parent behavioral training to modify child noncompliance: Treatment generalization across time and from home to school. *Behavior Modification,* 1979, *3,* 3–25.

Forehand, R., Wells, K. C., & Griest, D. L. An examination of the social validity of a parent training program. *Behavior Therapy,* 1980, *11,* 488–502.

Forgatch, M. S., & Toobert, D. J. A cost-effective parent training program for use with normal preschool children. *Journal of Pediatric Psychology,* 1979, *4,* 129–145.

Foxx, R., & Azrin, N. Dry pants: A rapid method of toilet training children. *Behaviour Research and Therapy,* 1973, *11,* 435–442.

Freud, A. Adolescence. In R. S. Eissler et al. (Eds.), *The psychoanalytic study of the child* (Vol. 13). New York: International Universities Press, 1958.

Gladstone, R. Observations on children who have been physically abused and their parents. *American Journal of Psychiatry,* 1965, *122,* 440–443.

Glick, P. C. Children of divorced parents in demographic perspective *Journal of Social Issues,* 1979, *35,* 170–182.

Gordon, T. *Parent effectiveness training*. New York: Wyden Books, 1970.

Gordon, T. *P.E.T.: Parent effectiveness training*. New York: New American Library, 1975.

Gordon, T. *P.E.T. in action*. New York: Wyden Books, 1976.

Green, K. G., Forehand, R., & McMahon, R. J. Parental manipulation of compliance and noncompliance in normal and deviant children. *Behavior Modification,* 1979, *3,* 245–266.

Griest, D. L., Forehand, R., Breiner, J., Rogers, T., Furey, W., & Williams, C. A. Effects of parent enhancement therapy on the treatment outcome and generalization of a parent training program. *Behaviour Research and Therapy,* 1982, *20,* 429–436.

Griest, D. L., Forehand, R., Wells, K. C., & McMahon, R. J. An examination of the differences between nonclinic and behavior problem clinic-referred children and their mothers. *Journal of Abnormal Psychology,* 1980, *89,* 497–500.

Griest, D., Wells, K. C., & Forehand, R. An examination of predictors of maternal perceptions of maladjustment in clinic-referred children. *Journal of Abnormal Psychology,* 1979, *88,* 277–281.

Hampson, R. B., & Tavormina, J. B. Relative effectiveness of behavioral and reflective group training with foster mothers. *Journal of Consulting and Clinical Psychology,* 1980, *48,* 294–295.

Heinstein, M. *Behavior problems of young children in California*. Berkeley: State of California Department of Public Health, 1969.

Hetherington, E. M., Cox, M., & Cox, R. The aftermath of divorce. In J. H. Stevens, Jr., & M. Matthews (Eds.), *Mother-child, father-child relations*. Washington, D.C.: National Association for the Education of Young Children, 1978.

Hetherington, E. M., Cox, M., & Cox, R. Play and social interaction in children following divorce. *Journal of Social Issues,* 1979, *5,* 26–49.

Hildebrand, V. Mothers' perceptions of independent and responsible behaviors of their preschool children. *Psychological Reports,* 1975, *37,* 631–641.

Hobbs, S., & Forehand, R. Important parameters in the use of timeout with children: A reexamination. *Journal of Behavior Therapy and Experimental Psychiatry,* 1977, *8,* 365–370.

Hobbs, S. A., Forehand, R., & Murray, R. G. Effects of various durations of time-out on the noncompliant behavior of children. *Behavior Therapy,* 1978, *9,* 652–656.

Humphreys, L., Forehand, R., McMahon, R. J., & Roberts, M. Parental behavioral training to modify child noncompliance: Effects on untreated siblings. *Journal of Behavior Therapy and Experimental Psychiatry,* 1978, *9,* 253–258.

Huntington, D. S. Supportive programs for infants and parents. In J. Osofsky (Ed.), *Handbook of infant development*. New York: Wiley, 1979.

Jenkins, S., Bax, M., & Hart, H. Behavior problems in preschool children. *Journal of Child Psychology and Psychiatry,* 1980, *21,* 15–17.

Johnson, S. M., & Lobitz, C. K. The personal and marital adjustment of parents as related to observed child deviance and parenting behavior. *Journal of Abnormal Child Psychology,* 1974, *2,* 193–207.

Kalter, N. Children of divorce in an outpatient psychiatric population. *American Journal of Orthopsychiatry,* 1977, *47,* 40–51.

Kelly, J. B., & Wallerstein, S. Brief interventions with children in divorcing families. *American Journal of Orthopsychiatry,* 1977, *47,* 23–39.

Kempe, R. S., & Kempe, C. H. *Child abuse.* Cambridge: Harvard University Press, 1978.

Keniston, K. Social change and youth in America. In E. H. Erikson (Ed.), *The challenge of youth.* New York: Doubleday & Company, Inc., 1965.

Kessler, J. W. *Psychopathology of childhood.* Englewood Cliffs, NJ: Prentice-Hall, 1966.

Koocher, G. P. Talking with children about death. *American Journal of Orthopsychiatry,* 1974, *44,* 404–411.

Macfarlane, J. W., Allen, L., & Honzik, M. P. *A developmental study of the behavior problems of normal children between twenty-one months and fourteen years.* Berkeley and Los Angeles: University of California Press, 1954.

Matson, J., & Ollendick, T. Issues in toilet training normal children. *Behavior Therapy,* 1977, *8,* 549–553.

McDermott, J. F. Divorce and its psychiatric sequelae in children. *Archives of General Psychiatry,* 1970, *23,* 421–428.

McGuire, J. C., & Gottlieb, B. H. Social support groups among new parents: An experimental study in primary prevention. *Journal of Clinical Child Psychology,* 1979, *8,* 111–116.

McMahon, R. J., & Forehand, R. Nonprescription behavior therapy: Effectiveness of a brochure in teaching mothers to correct their children's inappropriate mealtime behavior. *Behavior Therapy,* 1978, *9,* 814–820.

McMahon, R. J., & Forehand, R. Self-help behavior therapies in parent training. In B. B. Lahey & A. E. Kazdin (Eds.), *Advances in clinical child psychology* (Vol. 3), New York: Plenum, 1980.

McMahon, R. J., & Forehand, R. Suggestions for evaluating self-administered materials in parent training. *Child Behavior Therapy,* 1982, *3,* 65–68.

McMahon, R. J., Forehand, R., & Griest, D. L. Effects of knowledge of social learning principles on enhancing treatment outcome and generalization in a parent training program. *Journal of Consulting and Clinical Psychology,* 1981, *49,* 526–532.

Melnick, B., & Hurley, J. Distinctive personality attributes of child-abusing mothers. *Journal of Consulting and Clinical Psychology,* 1969, *33,* 746–749.

Mesibov, G. B., Schroeder, C. S., & Wesson, L. Parental concerns about their children. *Journal of Pediatric Psychology,* 1977, *2,* 13–17.

Mitchell, S., & Rosa, P. Boyhood behaviour problems as precursors of criminality: A fifteen-year follow-up study. *Journal of Child Psychology and Psychiatry and Allied Disciplines,* 1981, *22,* 19–33.

Moore, D. R., & Arthur, J. L. Juvenile delinquency. In T. Ollendick & M. Hersen (Eds.), *Handbook of child psychopathology.* New York: Plenum, 1982.

Moore, D. R., Chamberlain, P., & Mukai, L. H. Children at risk for delinquency: A follow-up comparison of aggressive children and children who steal. *Journal of Abnormal Child Psychology,* 1979, *7,* 345–355.

Myers, B. J. Early intervention using Brazelton Training with middle-class mothers and fathers of newborns. *Child Development,* 1982, *53,* 462–471.

Nay, W. R. A systematic comparison of instructional techniques for parents. *Behavior Therapy,* 1975, *6,* 14–21.

O'Dell, S. L., Mahoney, N. D., Horton, W. G., & Turner, D. E. Media assisted parent training: Alternative models. *Behavior Therapy,* 1979, *10,* 103–110

O'Leary, K. D., & Emery, R. E. Marital discord and child behavior problems. In M. D. Levine & P. Satz (Eds.), *Developmental variation and dysfunction.* New York: Academic Press, 1982.

Oltmanns, T. F., Broderick, J. E., & O'Leary, K. D. Marital adjustment and the efficacy of behavior therapy with children. *Journal of Consulting and Clinical Psychology,* 1977, *45,* 724–729.

Olweus, D. Stability of aggressive reaction patterns in males: A review. *Psychological Bulletin,* 1979, *86,* 852–875.

Patterson, G. R. The aggressive child: Victim and architect of a coercive system. In E. J. Mash, L. A. Hamerlynck, & L. C. Handy (Eds.), *Behavior modification and families.* New York: Brunner/Mazel, 1976.

Patterson, G. R., & Fleischman, M. J. Maintenance of treatment effects: Some considerations concerning family systems and follow-up data. *Behavior Therapy,* 1979, *10,* 168–185.

Peed, S., Roberts, M., & Forehand, R. Evaluation of the effectiveness of standardized parent training program in altering the interaction of mothers and their noncompliant children. *Behavior Modification,* 1977, *1,* 323–350.

Rinn, R. C., & Markle, A. Parent effectiveness training: A review. *Psychological Reports,* 1977, *41,* 95–109.

Rinn, R. C., Markle, A., & Wise, M. J. Positive parent training for foster parents: A one-year follow-up. *Behavior Counseling Quarterly,* 1981, *1,* 213–220

Roberts, M. C., & Wright, L. The role of the pediatric psychologist as consultant to pediatricians. In J. M. Tuma (Ed.), *Handbook for the practice of pediatric psychology.* New York: Wiley-Interscience, 1982.

Roberts, M. W., McMahon, R. J., Forehand, R., & Humphreys, L. The effect of parental instruction-giving on child compliance. *Behavior Therapy,* 1978, *9,* 793–798.

Robin, A. L. A controlled evaluation of problem-solving communication training with parent-adolescent conflict. *Behavior Therapy,* 1981, *12,* 593–609.

Robin, A. L., Kent, R., O'Leary, K. D., Foster, S., & Prinz, R. An approach to teaching parents and adolescents problem-solving-communication skills. *Behavior Therapy,* 1977, *8,* 639–643.

Robins, L. N. *Deviant children grown up.* Baltimore: Williams & Wilkins, 1966.

Rogers, T., Forehand, R., & Griest, D. L. The conduct disordered child: An analysis of family problem. *Clinical Psychology Review,* 1981, *1,* 139–147.

Rutter, M. Parent-child separation: Psychological effects on the children. *Journal of Child Psychology and Psychiatry,* 1971, *12,* 233–260.

Rutter, M., Graham, P., Chadwick, O. F. D., & Yule, W. Adolescent turmoil: Fact or fiction? *Journal of Child Psychology and Psychiatry,* 1976, *17,* 35–56.

Santrock, J. W. Relation of type and onset of father absence to cognitive development. *Child Development,* 1972, *43,* 455–469.

Scarboro, M. E., & Forehand, R. Effects of response-contingent isolation and ignoring on compliance and oppositional behavior of children. *Journal of Experimental Child Psychology*, 1975, *19*, 252–264.

Schroeder, C. S. Psychologists in a private pediatric practice. *Journal of Pediatric Psychology*, 1979, *4*, 5–18.

Spinetta, J. J. Parental personality factors in child abuse. *Journal of Clinical and Consulting Psychology*, 1978, *46*, 1409–1414.

Steele, B. B., & Pollock, C. B. A psychiatric study of parents who abuse infants and small children. In R. E. Helfer & C. H. Kempe (Eds.), *The battered child*. Chicago: University of Chicago Press, 1968.

Stuart, B., Tripodi, T., Jayaratne, S., & Camburn, D. An experiment in social engineering in serving the families of pre-delinquents. *Journal of Abnormal Child Psychology*, 1976, *4*, 243–261.

Toepfer, C., Reuter, J., & Maurer, C. Design and evaluation of an obedience training program for mothers of preschool children. *Journal of Consulting and Clinical Psychology*, 1972, *39*, 194–198.

Wahler, R. G. Deviant child behavior within the family: Developmental speculations and behavior change strategies. In H. Leitenberg (Ed.), *Handbook of behavior modification and behavior therapy*. Englewood Cliffs, NJ: Prentice-Hall, 1976.

Wahler, R. G., & Afton, A. D. Attentional processes in insular and noninsular mothers: Some differences in their summary reports about child problem behaviors. *Child Behavior Therapy*, 1980, *2*, 25–41.

Wallerstein, J. S., & Kelly, J. B. The effects of parental divorce: The adolescent experience. In E. J. Anthony & C. Kouperik (Eds.), *The child in his family: Children at psychiatric risk*. New York: Wiley, 1974.

Wallerstein, J. S., & Kelly, J. B. The effects of parental divorce: Experiences of the child in later latency. *American Journal of Orthopsychiatry*, 1976, *46*, 256–269.

Webster-Stratton, C. Modification of mothers' behaviors and attitudes through a video-tape modeling group discussion program. *Behavior Therapy*, 1981, *12*, 634–642.

Weissbourd, B. Supporting parents as people. In B. Weissbourd & J. Musick (Eds.), *Infants: Their social environments*. Washington, D.C.: National Association for the Education of Young Children, 1981.

Wells, K. C., & Forehand, R. Childhood behavior problems in the home. In S. M. Turner & H. E. Adams (Eds.), *Handbook of behavior therapy*. New York: Wiley, 1981.

Wells, K. C., Forehand, R., & Griest, D. L. Generality of treatment effects from treated to untreated behaviors resulting from a parent training program. *Journal of Clinical Child Psychology*, 1980, *8*, 217–219.

Wells, K. C., Griest, D. L., & Forehand, R. The use of a self-control package to enhance temporal generality of a parent training program. *Behaviour Research and Therapy*, 1980, *18*, 347–353.

White, B. L. *The first three years of life*. New York: Avon, 1975.

REFERENCE NOTES

1. Furey, W. *An examination of predictors of maternal perceptions of satisfaction with their nonclinic children*. Unpublished master's thesis, University of Georgia, 1982.

2. Hetherington, E. M. Colloquium presented at the University of Georgia, Athens, Georgia, October 31, 1980.
3. Rickard, K. M. *A measure of parent conceptions of children's behaviors: The parent expectations, attitudes and beliefs scale (PEABS)*. Unpublished manuscript, 1981.
4. McManmon, M., Davis, J., & Clark, H. *An analysis of a parental advice procedure for distributing morning responsibilities among family members*. Paper presented at the Meeting of the Fourth Annual Western Regional Conference: Humanistic Approaches in Behavior Modification, Las Vegas, March, 1978.
5. Reid, J. B., Hinojoa-Rivera, G., & Lorber, R. *A social training approach to the outpatient treatment of children who steal*. Unpublished manuscript, 1978.

CHAPTER 12

Prevention of Problems in Childhood on a Community-Wide Basis

FRANK MASTERPASQUA AND MARSHALL SWIFT

Prevention of mental health problems across entire communities is an inherently amorphous goal, but no more so than the task of encapsulating within one chapter the variety of prevention programs emanating from community mental health/ mental retardation centers. We have not attempted to compile a compendium here of early preventive services in community mental health/retardation centers (CMHC's). Such a listing, while of value, would not necessarily enhance the ultimate goal of providing a firm base for prevention services in CMHC's. Rather, the purpose of this chapter is threefold: first, to outline a model based on years of experience in prevention programming and planning (which has been and can be used as a framework for providing and evaluating prevention programming); second, to describe exemplary prevention/promotion projects which fall within this framework and have proven to be applicable and effective across the entire range of community settings; and third, to increase awareness that the implementation of preventive services for children is as much a political as a scientific challenge.

PROBLEMS ASSOCIATED WITH PREVENTION PROGRAMMING IN COMMUNITY MENTAL HEALTH/MENTAL RETARDATION CENTERS

The Unfulfilled Mandate

In their important history of the community mental health center movement, Snow and Newton (1976) noted that political and financial support for ''indirect'' (preventive) services has not been commensurate with the mandate for services as stated in the original Community Mental Health/Mental Retardation Act. CMHC's were designed to be more than conduits for the provision of clinical services to previously underserved populations. Centers were also designed to promote the mental health of catchment areas, particularly through consultation and education. Unfortunately, a number of obstacles continue to interfere with the development of preventive services in CMHC's. Before discussing specific prevention services, it is important to discuss the nature of these constraints.

Political Impediments.

There can be little question that a major hindrance in preventive services development has been the dominance of the traditional clinical waiting mode in mental health services. Characteristics of the waiting mode include (1) services offered by an expert who is highly educated in a mental health profession, (2) services rendered in the expert's office, hospital, or a CMHC, (3) the expert passively waiting for clients to reach him or her, with no attempt at initiating mental health contacts (Heller & Monahan, 1977). Decision making regarding programming within CMHC's continues to be biased toward the provision of clinical services. Preventionists have always had to confront the inertia of the passive traditional medical model.

Conceptual Impediments.

Unlike clinicians, preventionists have lacked working models upon which to base interventions. As a result, projects frequently lack explicated designs and objectives. This unstructured approach to prevention has contributed to the ability of traditionalists to assimilate and transform preventive services into clinical services.

Financial Impediments.

Unlike clinical services, there have been few, if any, reimbursable early prevention efforts. Thus, preventionists have had to seek grants and contracts from increasingly limited private and public sources, and have been the first to be eliminated under conditions of austerity.

Absence of Forum for the Exchange of Information Regarding Prevention Services.

Unlike their academic colleagues, preventionists in CMHC's have only recently begun to exchange knowledge about programming. As a result, preventionists frequently found themselves working in isolation, limiting the development of effective prevention efforts. Fortunately, this void is now being filled by journals devoted to applications in preventive mental health (such as the *Journal of Primary Prevention,* and *Prevention in Human Services*).

This chapter addresses the means of overcoming these obstacles to prevention of childhood problems. We begin by outlining a framework for the delivery of such services across entire communities.

A CONCEPTUAL FRAMEWORK FOR PREVENTION SERVICES FOR CMHC'S

We have already noted how the intrinsically vague task of preventing childhood disorders on a community-wide basis is made more difficult by the lack of an applicable model. Only recently have trends within the field of developmental and child psychology lent themselves to the crystallization of a framework usable in CMHC's. The traditional model has been based upon reductionistic (Gibbs, 1979), laboratory-based research (Bronfenbrenner, 1974) with an overriding objective being the enhancement of intellectual performance. Such an approach, in conjunction with the deficit model in mental health, is not easily translated into CMHC services designed to promote the full range of development (emotional, social, physical, and cognitive) of children in their real-life settings.

On the other hand, the more recent emphasis in developmental and child psychology on the ecology of childhood (Bronfenbrenner, 1979), on enhanced social competence as a criterion of success (Zigler & Trickett, 1979), and on personal social networks (Gottlieb, 1981; Cochran & Brassard, 1980) lends itself to prevention services (see Masterpasqua, 1981). Drawing upon these recent trends, we have developed a framework for the projects described in this chapter. The model (Swift, Notes 1 and 2) is based upon Snow and Newton's (1976) "sociopsychological" approach to mental health in that it includes "a conception of individual psychology together with a social structural understanding of the collective contexts in which personality and psychopathology develop throughout the life cycle" (p. 592).

Using Research as a Basis for Prevention.

The trend in academic psychology to ask ecologically valid, yet experimental, questions like, "Is it important for mother-newborn to be together during the postpartum period?" or "What are the effects of day-care?" has led to a bridging of the schism between research and application in CMHC's. Thus, Klaus and Kennell's (1982) research indicating that early development is promoted by hospital maternity wards which allow mother-newborn contact has led to increased interventions during this sensitive period. Similarly, Shure and Spivack's (1980) research, demonstrating that real life interpersonal competence can be enhanced in children, has led preventionists working in CMHC's to provide decision-making training to children through schools and caregivers. Therefore, preventionists should now base their interventions on ecologically valid research in child development.

Where Do Preventionists in CMHC's Work?

In which settings should these research-based early preventive interventions take place to be most effective? Traditional approaches indicate that the individual should be the focus, yet a hallmark of early prevention services is interventions with populations, not individuals. In the current model we identify five ecological levels within the community which must be addressed: individuals (through direct promotion of individual competence); caregivers; social networks; organizations and agencies; and policy makers. These eco-levels can be viewed as elaborations of Bronfenbrenner's (1979) description of the contexts of human development, in which there is a

> progressive, mutual accommodation between an active growing human being and the changing properties of the immediate settings in which the developing person lives, as

> this process is affected by relations between settings, and by the larger contexts in which the settings are embedded. [p. 21]

This view of human development has profound implications for the creation of community-wide prevention programs. It suggests that to be effective across entire communities, early preventionists must address each of these levels as well as their complex interrelationships (Bronfenbrenner's mesosystem). We will describe here the research-based programs which address each of these levels, from the individual child to policies and policy makers.

It must be emphasized that division of the community into five ecological levels is an arbitrary convention. One of the facts of life for preventionists is that one can seldom design a program for one level (the individual) for example, which does not have impact at other levels (such as the caregiver). In describing these efforts we have attempted to choose those programs which were well researched and resulted in positive outcomes. In other instances, programs are described which hold considerable promise but whose results may not yet be conclusive.

Promotion of Individual Competence

Emphasis at this level is on individual development and competence enhancement (Bloom, 1979; Sundberg, Snowden, & Reynolds, 1978). One approach to fostering individual development is the interpersonal cognitive problem solving (ICPS) approach of Shure and Spivack and their colleagues (Shure & Spivack, 1980; see also Rickel, Dyhdalo, & Smith, Chapter 3 and Durlak & Jason, Chapter 4 of this volume). Their direct work with children from a wide age range has shown that certain cognitive skills play an important role in social-behavioral adjustment. More importantly, they have demonstrated that enhancing these thinking skills contributes to "healthy social adjustment and interpersonal competence at an early age" (Shure & Spivack, 1980, p. 29). The skill which best distinguishes various adaptation degrees among young children is the ability to generate different solutions to interpersonal problems. Other skills include the ability to conceptualize consequences of an act and a tendency to think spontaneously about cause and effect in social situations. Shure and Spivack report further that in all of their studies IQ scores did not mediate between these cognitive skills and social competence/behavioral adaptation.

In a two year study emanating out of our CMHC, 113 inner-city children attending day-care centers were the subjects of the intervention group while 106 served as controls (average age for both groups was 4.3 years). The goal of the intervention was to determine whether the behavior of ICPS deficient children could be improved by teaching them *how* to think, rather than *what* to think. Results showed that "increased ability to conceptualize alternative solutions to interpersonal problems significantly related to improved social adjustment" (Shure & Spivack, 1980, p. 29).

In another project based upon individuals' social competence research, Sarason and Sarason (1981) reported on a program designed to reduce the drop out and delinquency rate of high school students. Using 127 ninth graders (mean age 14.8 years), the program utilized modeling and role playing of social cognitive skills.

There were two experimental groups and one control group, all comparable demographically. The interventions, given as part of regular classroom studies, emphasized (1) the consequences of actions, (2) the alternatives available in a situation, and (3) an increased emphasis on "the other's" perspectives and communications skills, particularly with nonpeers. Results showed that:

> subjects who received special training were able to (a) think of more adaptive ways of approaching problematic situations and (b) perform more effectively in a self-presentation situation (job interview). In addition, in a 1-year follow-up, they tended to show lower rates of tardiness and fewer absences and behavioral referrals. [p. 908]

The work of Shure and Spivack, Sarason and Sarason, and others (for example, Gesten, Flores, De Apodoca, Rains, Weissberg, & Cowen, 1979) highlights the inherent interrelatedness of eco-levels described above. These successful individually oriented programs have had a direct impact on educational offerings in day-care centers and schools. Indeed, based on this applied social competence research, a number of schools have begun to integrate decision making training as a routine part of the curriculum (for example, Healey, Jackson, & Ellis, Note 3). There is now ample empirical evidence that interpersonal problem-solving techniques are effective in enhancing behavioral adaptation. Preventionists in CMHC's should actively seek opportunities to offer such services to children in various settings, such as schools, clinics, and churches.

Direct Work with the High-Risk Newborn.

It has been estimated that approximately 10 percent of the U.S. population has handicaps or defects at birth or soon after (Niswander & Gordon, 1972). Sameroff and Chandler (1975), in their review of research on the sequelae of reproductive risk, concluded that

> the environment appears to have the potential for minimizing or maximizing such early developmental difficulties. High socio-economic status dissipates the effects of such perinatal complications as anoxia or low-birth weight. Poor social environmental conditions tend to amplify the effects of such early complications. [p. 236]

Moreover, there is now a substantial body of research indicating that direct environmental intervention strategies for high-risk infants can ameliorate the effects of reproductive risk (Field, Sostek, Goldberg, & Shuman, 1979; Magrab, Sostek, & Powell, Chapter 2 of this volume). For instance, Powell (1974) reported on work in which low birthweight and low SES newborns were handled daily by nursery personnel or by their mothers. Infants who received stimulation, compared to non-handled controls, regained their birthweight faster, had higher Bayley Mental and Motor scores at four months, and performed better on the Bayley Behavior Record at six months. Masi (1979) concluded in her review of such supplemental stimulation strategies that

> the physical growth and responsiveness of the premature infant can be facilitated by supplemental stimulation during the early weeks and months of life. The effects of

> tactile-kinesthetic, auditory and visual stimulation have been demonstrated on several dependent measures. [p. 380]

One can only speculate on the benefits, both with regard to the quality of life and the economy of the nation, if the preventionists' goal in CMHC's were the delivery of these early stimulation techniques to all high-risk infants in hospitals.

Summary.

Direct interventions with individuals are consistent with the more traditional mental health approaches. The distinction is the emphasis on beginning early in child development, preventing disorders, and promoting competence. As we have seen, there is now ample empirical evidence that efforts, such as infant stimulation/enrichment and interpersonal problem solving training, are effective in enhancing early child development.

Prevention of Childhood Problems Through Caregiver Interventions

A second ecological level of preventive intervention consists of caregivers (for example, parents, teachers, physicians). In his important review of early intervention programs, Bronfenbrenner (1974) reported that a critical determinant of the long-term impact of early preventive interventions was whether or not parental involvement was maintained. Consonant with Bronfenbrenner's findings, a large number of early prevention programs in CMHC's have focused on parenting interventions, designed to enhance the behavior and attitudes of parents as well as the development of their children.

Johnson, Leler, Rios, Brandt, Kahn, Marzeika, Frede, and Bissett (1974) reported on a two year project for Mexican-American children and their parents. The program began when the children were a year old and continued for two years. Intervention included weekly home visits during the first year by bilingual educators who assisted mothers in learning about developmentally appropriate activities. The first year of the program also included four weekend family workshops which focused on strengthening communications skills, decision making, and other aspects of family functioning. During the second year, mother and child participated in a center-based program which began with four mornings per week and was gradually reduced to two mornings. This second year effort emphasized home management and child development skills. The results indicated an enhancement of treatment mothers' interaction with their young children and improvement in Bayley mental and psychomotor subscale scores compared with the control group. The Johnson et al. project is typical of hundreds of efforts nationwide which, though perhaps equally beneficial (for example, Silver, 1979), have not been presented in a research or published format.

In another program designed to assist caregivers, Masterpasqua (1982) reported on a CMHC project designed to enhance maternal perceptions of newborns in a low income population of young Black and Hispanic mothers. The advantage of the program was that it emanated from a neighborhood health clinic accessible to virtually all families living in this high-risk neighborhood. The treatment group consisted of 30 pregnant women who attended a childbirth education course in the clinic. One control group consisted of 30 pregnant women who had attended the clinic during the previous year, before childbirth classes were available. A second control group consisted of 30 pregnant women who attended the clinic at the same time as the treatment group, but chose not to attend childbirth classes. All groups were demographically comparable and received routine prenatal care. The treatment group attended five consecutive weekly sessions of childbirth education and anticipatory guidance in infant development. When mothers were subsequently administered the Neonatal Perception Inventory (NPI) (Broussard & Hartner, 1970) during a postpartum feeding session, the percentage of mothers who believed they would have more problems with their own newborns than normal (and were thus designated as at-risk) was significantly smaller in the treatment group compared with the two controls. These data are significant since Broussard and Hartner reported that subsequent follow-up psychiatric interviews with children at four and one-half years found more psychiatric problems among at-risk newborns.

A final example of CMHC caregiver interventions comes from the work of Shure and Spivack (1980). Shure and Spivack trained both teachers and parents to teach Interpersonal Cognitive Problem Solving (ICPS) to their students and children. It was found that teachers could improve classroom behavior with ICPS training. Similarly, during a three month period mothers were trained to initiate 20 minute ICPS games and dialogues with their children each day, resulting in reduced impulsive and inhibited behaviors of inner-city four year olds.

> One important result is that children exposed to ICPS training in one environment (the home) improved in their behavior as observed in a different one (the school). The finding is particularly important because behaviors were judged by teachers unaware of the training procedures and goals. [Shure & Spivack, 1979, p. 215]

Summary.

The three projects described represent only a small portion of the preventive interventions which demonstrate that caregivers with structured guidance in child rearing can promote the mental health of their children. Unfortunately, primarily because they have not been reimbursable services, such efficacious caregiver interventions have not been accessible to large populations served by CMHC's. Again, we can only speculate on the mental health (as well as long-term economic) benefits which would accrue if these direct, preventive services were made available to all parents.

Recently, we began a project which may be a step toward economic self-sufficiency in prevention services. After many years of providing consultation services to adoption and foster care agencies and programs for adolescent parents, access to large populations of high-risk infants in the community has been established. The purpose of the project is to assess the developmental status of at-risk infants in each of the programs and to design and implement (when necessary) a program of parent/caseworker intervention where parents and caseworkers become partners in direct preventive interventions emanating from our CMHC. The advantage of these kinds of direct services is that while they are preventive, they are also frequently reimbursable through third party or direct payments.

Personal Social Network Intervention

The third level of intervention consists of work to enhance the natural supports to individuals under various stressful life conditions (Caplan, 1981; Cassel, 1974). For example, Polansky, Chalmers, Buttenweiser, and Williams (1979) reported that neglectful parents tend to have a history of social isolation. A recent text (Gottlieb, 1981) outlines the various methods of assessing and enhancing the impact of social support and social networks.

More specifically, Cochran and Brassard (1979) suggested three ways in which social support influences parents and their children. First, support provides access to emotional and material assistance. "By providing a loving and relatively consistent social environment that allays the doubts and frustrations of parents, the social network may enable them to be more sensitive to the needs of their children" (p. 603). Second, social networks provide sanctions and controls over child-rearing techniques used by parents (such as extreme techniques used by abusive, neglectful parents). Third, social networks provide parents with alternative role models from which to learn new child-rearing behaviors.

Empirical support for the importance of social support interventions comes from Crockenburg (1981), who reported that the best predictor of infant-mother attachment was the support mothers received in their parenting capacity. Moreover, the impact of such support was especially beneficial for mothers with irritable babies (that is, infants whose temperaments might otherwise lead to a parent-child conflict).

Further direct evidence of supportive network influence on child rearing is derived from Garbarino (1980). In that study, a neighborhood's "risk score" for child maltreatment (the difference between actual and predicted rates of child maltreatment) "was associated with important aspects of stress and supports as perceived and reported by mothers in the interview study" (p. 74). Thus, in addition to projects designed to directly enhance early development or to promote caregiver competence, there is now reason to believe that preventionists in CMHC's should serve as catalysts in the creation of supportive milieus in their neighborhoods and communities. There are already excellent examples of such efforts.

For instance, Masterpasqua (1982) reported findings from a CMHC project noted earlier in which it was suggested that the psychological benefits of an intervention during pregnancy were due to developmental guidance and the support created among these young mothers. Pregnancy and the birth of a child are potentially stressful life events for all parents; for young, low income, inner-city participants these experiences can be especially troublesome. Childbirth classes may not only provide anticipatory guidance, but may also create peer and professional support systems that will continue to be helpful during subsequent sensitive periods in parent-child relations.

In another study, Minde, Shosenberg, Morton, Thompson, Ripley, and Burns

(1980), created a support group for parents of premature infants. Parents in the intervention group met weekly for seven to 12 weeks. They were encouraged to express their feelings about their new children and were provided with anticipatory guidance about what to expect medically and psychologically about their premature newborns. Compared to a control group, the supportive group showed greater understanding of their infants' conditions, visited their infants more frequently in the hospital, and showed enhanced child-rearing behaviors.

Finally, McGuire and Gottlieb (1979) reported a study involving two family physicians who created support groups for parents of firstborns. One-half of the new parents received literature in the mail on a wide range of infant developmental issues. A second group received these materials, but also met for seven weekly support group sessions moderated by the physicians and their spouses during which parents were encouraged to share their concerns. Results indicated a trend toward support group parents expanding their own social supports (apart from the study's support group) and increasing the frequency with which they discussed child-rearing matters with members of their expanded social network.

These and other research projects have direct implications for prevention programming. In addition to providing direct interventions or changing the settings in which children develop, preventionists in CMHC's need to seek out opportunities to create social support groups for parents and other caregivers.

Organizational Interventions

Masterpasqua (1982) has argued that important loci for preventive interventions in childhood are the various organizational settings (for example, hospitals, schools, day-care centers) through which children pass during their development. Inherent within the notion of "developmental rights" is the idea that preventionists must combine two knowledge bases in their interventions: the ecology of child development and strategies for organizational change. First, they must have a "social structural" understanding of negative and positive influences on individual child development. Second, they must be willing and able to foster changes within organizations and agencies which will best accommodate the developmental needs of individual children. When working at the organization and agency level, there should be two evaluative criteria. First, to what extent has the preventive intervention been integrated ("routinized") into the everyday activities of the organization? Second, (the more traditional criterion) what impact is the innovation having on the individuals served? In this section we outline specific programs which have fulfilled either or both of these criteria.

Masterpasqua, Shuman, O'Shea, and Gonzalez (1980), working out of a CMHC, recently described prevention efforts designed to integrate early preventive services into an inner-city, neighborhood clinic. The project began with prevention staff providing assistance to the physicians and nurses. Preventive innovations included classes in childbirth education, providing anticipatory guidance to new mothers during the postpartum period, and home-and center-based infant enrichment classes. Because of the transience of the population served, the long-term impact of the project on each mother-infant pair has been difficult to evaluate. There are, however, data indicating that mothers enrolled in the project acquired enhanced perceptions of their newborns, (that is, they believed they would have fewer problems with their own infants relative to the average baby, Masterpasqua, 1981). Furthermore, there is a trend toward fewer perinatal complications among infants whose mothers were recruited into the project during pregnancy (Hermalin, Note 4). Based on the evaluative criterion of ''routinizing'' the prevention services into a setting already serving children, the project has been a success. The innovation has been assimilated into the health clinic and despite time and fund shortages, the clinic health staff has taken on the responsibility of conducting classes in anticipatory guidance and childbirth education.

Based on a scientific understanding of hospital conditions which are likely to promote or impede development of infant-parent attachment, Garbarino (Note 5) reported on a survey of hospital policies and practices in metropolitan Omaha. The following are examples of questions asked of hospital health staff to determine how well they met the needs of parents and infants during the prenatal and labor/delivery periods and during the first five days postpartum.

Prenatally

1. Does the hospital sponsor prenatal classes?
2. Does the hospital systematically assess whether or not expectant parents are at risk for child maltreatment as a basis for providing services?

Delivery and the First Twelve Hours

1. Does the hospital support the presence of prepared fathers in the delivery room through cooperative hospital staff action?
2. What is the typical duration of contact between infants and parents immediately after delivery, particularly with the firstborn?

First Five Days

1. What provisions are made for rooming-in?
   How is rooming-in defined? What support and assistance is given?
2. What are the visitation policies for fathers and children?
   For others?

From this survey, Garbarino concluded that ''progress has been made in establishing hospital policies and practices that enhance parent-child bonding'' (p. 7). However, six recommendations were made for changes in hospital practices. First, further progress is needed in identifying the at-risk status of all families, not only those who show obvious signs of maladaptation. Second, hospitals should allow and encourage bonding (Klaus & Kennell, 1982) during the sensitive early period of development. Third, more attention should be paid to the development of adaptive or maladaptive patterns in the infant-parent bond. Fourth, further active participation by fathers should be encouraged by hospitals. Fifth, efforts should be made to minimize separations between medically at-risk infants and their parents. Sixth, health care deliverers (physicians and nurses) should receive more training in the mechanisms underlying parent-infant attachment.

In this section we have focused on changes needed in health care settings (see also Magrab, Sostek, & Powell, Chapter 2 of this volume). We have intentionally emphasized this setting because (1) there has been a void in mental health preventive services for children in health facilities (that is, despite the fact that virtually all infants and parents pass through the nation's health care facilities, only recently have practices and policies been created to accommodate the developmental needs of children), and (2) there is already substantial literature describing changes in other institutions such as schools (Jason, 1980), and courts (Vandenbos & Miller, 1980).

Policy Intervention

The fifth level of intervention concerns governmental policy issues relating to prevention services. Such policy influences are perhaps most significant for preventive interventions since most prevention services require funding through government supported contracts and grants. In the late 1970s the President's Commission on Mental Health recommended several actions, including the establishment of a Center for Prevention within NIMH, the prioritization of primary prevention within this center, and the allocation of $10 million dollars for NIMH prevention efforts with a 10 year goal of 10% of the NIMH budget being allocated for prevention (President's Commission on Mental Health, 1978). In 1982, NIMH began implementing these recommendations. Similarly, the Surgeon General's Report on Health Promotion and Disease Prevention (1979) concluded:

> There are three overwhelming reasons why a new, strong emphasis on prevention—at all levels of government and by all our citizens—is essential. First, prevention saves lives. Second, prevention improves the quality of life. Finally, it can save dollars in the long run. In an era of runaway health costs, preventive action for health is cost-effective.[p. 9]

As frequently seen in American politics, the pendulum of governmental support for prevention swung abruptly to conservative policies with the election of Ronald Reagan in 1980. Prevention once again became the stepchild of mental health and the distant cousin of "hard science." Yet, prevention is no less a valid endeavor of intervention now than it was in 1979. It is clear that politics, not scientific evidence, decides which areas of research will reach the public. Peters (1980) concluded in discussing the Head Start movement that first, programs such as Head Start and other early intervention efforts result from economic, social, and political forces and not directly from social science research; second, research determines the particular context and direction of a program, not the demand for such efforts; and third, as scientists and practitioners we ourselves are products of the sociocultural climate. That is:

> Research does not, and perhaps cannot, provide solutions to broad social problems. Decision making of the sort that initiates and maintains social programs is accomplished within a value context that permits "scientific data" to be used in multiple ways. Decisions on which alternatives are to be selected and implemented, however, require value judgements and the "selling" of the selected alternative constitutes advocacy. The social scientist who fails to recognize the distinction courts frustration and disillusionment, and risks his "scientific credibility." [p. 25]

A further point to be analyzed is that prevention will become a respected applied science/intervention (as are medicine and, to a lesser degree, clinical psychology), not based exclusively on its empirical support, but if and when it becomes politically acceptable. Thus, Lamb and Zusman (1979) criticized prevention as being amorphous and without conclusive results. Yet, Plaut (1980) noted that the White House Office on Science and Technology reported only 15% of generally accepted medical interventions (for example, surgery, pharmacological treatments) have been fully evaluated and found to be effective. Our message is that until prevention becomes as widely accepted as other intervention modes, preventionists must wear two hats: that of scientist and that of political advocate willing to sell prevention to formulate public policy. There are a number of political avenues in which preventionists must be willing to sell their trade.

Levels of Political Advocacy

Advocacy Through Citizens in the Catchment Area.

It is perhaps ironic that at the local level the strongest political support for prevention has frequently come from community members. It has been enlightening to note that early intervention programs, which many professional colleagues have considered abstract and without substance, have been accepted by community members as valid enterprises. *We cannot stress enough the importance of forging alliances with members of the community who are instrumental in making decisions within the CMHC*. Among the most significant of these are members of the community mental health center's community board, key neighborhood "gate keepers," and local clergy.

Advocacy at Governmental Levels.

At all levels of government (city, state, federal) there are mental health professionals committed to the prevention of childhood problems. It is essential that preventionists in CMHC's create and nurture contacts with such individuals. The purpose of these contacts is twofold. First, acquaintance with policy makers at these levels ensures that preventionists will keep abreast of future decisions which will affect the course of prevention programming (such as the recent federal emphasis on aftercare and high-risk children) as well as future funding. Second, it is indeed possible for local preventionists to have an impact at all levels of policy making. There have been a number of instances in which a few individuals have altered the course of large-scale decisions impacting programs for children.

With initiation of block grant funding, local policy makers have become especially influential in deciding priority areas for mental health funding. Preventionists must ensure that their voices be heard at these local governmental levels as it has been our experience that such advocacy can be effective. For instance, despite an extremely austere local budget, Philadelphia has decided to allocate grant money for projects designed to promote the development of young children at risk.

Advocacy Groups/Lobbying.

Recognition that prevention of childhood problems is as much a political as a scientific process implies the need to form self-help groups of prevention advocates. For instance, the National Council of Community Mental Health Centers has organized a council on prevention and many states have organized lobbying groups of preventionists. Similarly, strong preventive organizations have arisen to advocate for particularly vulnerable age groups and populations (for example, Councils on Aging and the International Infant Mental Health Association).

ISSUES IN EVALUATION OF PREVENTION IN CMHC'S

Probably no other field within mental health has been scrutinized as much as prevention. Preventionists are continually asked to justify their work, whereas therapeutic efforts frequently come under less scrutiny but receive more funding. Clearly, there is a double standard applied to prevention and there is a tendency for most preventionists in community settings to therefore react with ambivalence. On one hand, they feel as though they are being asked to constantly prove efficacy compared to those providing remediation or therapy. On the other hand, the consumer orientation of preventive services demands accountability in the delivery of such services. Resolving the ambivalence will occur somewhere between rigorous research methods applicable only in laboratory settings and the carefree application of unproven methods. In this section we highlight salient issues in evaluation of prevention programs for children in CMHC's.

The Need to Distinguish Research from Evaluation

The distinction between laboratory and community evaluation research was recently clarified by Cowen (1978) when he wrote:

"Although community program evaluation studies can surely be improved, it is unlikely that the purity of antiseptic laboratory research will ever be attained" (p. 792). Later in the same paper, he noted "The vulnerability of findings from any single community evaluation study points to the importance both of replication and of tolerance for a slow accretive process in which small pieces in a puzzle gradually cumulate toward weight-of-evidence conclusions about major new programming approaches'' (p. 804).

Preventionists need to walk a fine line between empirical research and program implementation without abdicating responsibility for proof of efficacy. ''The importance of replication and of tolerance for a slow accretive process'' implies the need for communication between preventionists who are working on similar projects. Unfortunately, despite the recent appearance of journals devoted to prevention (for example, *Prevention in Human Services*), the lack of forums for the exchange of program evaluations has further impeded the accretive process. Indeed, it is likely that CMHC prevention projects for children are being replicated throughout the nation, with each program implementor unaware of similar efforts. We strongly urge organization to further develop national and international forums to exchange information on prevention program evaluations.

When Does Research Become Preventive Intervention?

Because of the double standard applied to prevention services, much of prevention programming has been framed within a quasi-experimental framework. As a result, an inordinate amount of the time of preventionists working in CMHC's is devoted to evaluation and applied research. There is little question that such effort is essential for *unproven* or untested procedures. But repeated research on successsful interventions is not an efficient use of preventionists' time nor that of the population they serve.

Such redundancy of efforts seldom occurs in medicine or clinical psychology. When the efficacy of procedures within these fields is empirically determined, practitioners are expected to employ the intervention, not research its effectiveness. The blurred distinction in prevention between research and practice limits the progress of the field in two ways: First, it conveys the impression that nothing is known about how to prevent problems or promote mental health, and that the field has little to offer in the way of effective interventions; second, it continuously raises ethical questions since preventionists must always create nontreatment control groups despite the fact that there are control participants who may be of equal need and who are just as likely to benefit as treatment participants.

For example, Lazar and Darlington (1982) recently synthesized results from 12 early education programs for low income children which began in the 1960s. A collaborative follow-up was conducted in 1976 when subjects in all studies ranged in age from nine to 19. Secondary analysis of these data revealed ''that early education programs for children from low-income families had long-lasting effects in four areas: school competence, developmental abilities, children's attitudes and values and impact in the family'' (p. vi). Clearly, this kind of strong longitudinal empirical support for early intervention does not mean that any program will be effective nor that preventionists can abdicate the responsibility of determining particular program effectiveness. On the other hand, after obtaining such data on large populations of children who received a variety of early interventions, it would be absurd to create another experimental study to determine whether early intervention is effective.

Likewise, Broman, Nichols, and Kennedy (1975) reported on a study of more than 26,000 children nationwide, stating that "within race, sex, and socioeconomic subgroups, mean IQs were significantly higher among children of mothers who had more prenatal visits, whose pregnancy was less advanced at the time of registration for prenatal care, and who were not anemic during pregnancy" (p. 245). Based on this research, we have developed a community outreach program designed to increase the numbers of low income pregnant women receiving prenatal care. Given the overwhelming evidence of the importance of prenatal care, what purpose is served by establishing a control group of mothers who, while equally desirous and in need of prenatal care, would be placed in a nontreatment control?

The Need to Expand Criteria for Evaluation

Evaluation problems are further exacerbated by the use of one dimensional criteria or criteria not directly relevant to program goals. Zigler and Trickett (1979) recently criticized the use of IQ as the sole criterion of early intervention, instead suggesting that "social competence" be the goal of early intervention projects. Social competence should include measures of (1) physical health, (2) cognitive development, (3) social-emotional development, and (4) school achievement. It has been our experience that including these measures more adequately defines "healthy" development and is also more likely to convince skeptics about the true impact of preventive interventions.

Summary.

In this discussion of program evaluation in CMHC's, we focused on points which should serve to enhance the efficacy and viability of such services. First, it is essential to recognize that there are indeed "proven" preventive interventions; that is, interventions that are at least as efficacious as remediative interventions. Second, while we are obligated to evaluate each program, such evaluation (particularly of efforts already proven to be effective) must not be confused with research. Third, in establishing criteria for evaluation we must expand our objectives to include measures of social competence and physical health as well as the traditional IQ.

INNOVATIONS AND FUTURE DIRECTIONS

The effects of governmental budget cutbacks on CMHC's have always been most salient for consultation/education and prevention services. For the most part, prevention services for children have been dependent on federal funding for their survival. Unlike the proverbial barefoot doctors of China who are paid only as long as they keep their patients healthy, in America no one pays to prevent or promote. Nevertheless, during all periods of fiscal austerity in the coming years, preventionists in CMHC's will need to devise innovative means for funding their services.

As preventionists, we have developed services which have become increasingly independent of governmental grants, such as an infant mental health project. The roots of this service were established over the past 10 years through close ties with a wide range of hospitals, clinics, and agencies serving at-risk infants and their parents. These have included hospital pediatrics departments, adoption and foster care agencies, and programs for infants born to high school age parents. In the past, evaluation, intervention, and consultation services were provided to these agencies without reimbursement. More recently, several steps have been taken to ensure continuation of services despite federal cutbacks. First, we have requested funds from each of the agencies which will allow services to continue. While the amount of money from any one agency is small, the total sum is substantial. Second, these prevention services have been integrated into outpatient child clinical services in the CMHC. In this way, client centered services such as evaluations and interventions for infants from the various agencies can be reimbursed through direct or third party payments. Again, while the number of reimbursable services may be limited, they complement other funding sources. Finally, funds in some instances have been obtained from local philanthropic and corporate sources.

It is clear that, in order to survive, preventionists in CMHC's must be willing to compromise. A major compromise is the realization that prevention services cannot always be free and indirect. There is a large group of children at risk for psychopathology (for example, low birthweight, in foster care, reared by disturbed or retarded parents) for whom direct and reimbursable services are appropriate.

A second recent and innovative thrust has been the integration of decision-making and interpersonal problem-solving courses into school curricula. We have already discussed research demonstrating the effectiveness of ICPS training with a variety of populations. Our personal experience with ICPS skills training from preschool to high school levels indicates a willingness by school authorities to fund such training. Indeed, one of our current goals is to make decision-making/ICPS training an integral part of public school training.

SUMMARY AND CONCLUSIONS

In this chapter we have outlined (1) problems associated with the provision of preventive services across entire communities and through CMHC's, (2) a model designed to provide a focus for such services, (3) exemplary prevention projects targeted at the various ecological levels within a community, (4) guidelines for evaluating prevention projects for children, and (5) innovative techniques designed to ensure the viability of prevention/promotion in CMHC's during these austere times.

A few conclusions can be drawn from this overview. First, it is no longer necessary to be defensive about the efficacy of prevention/promotion in mental health. Extensive research literature now indicates that, depending on the target population served, prevention/promotion is as efficacious as other modes of intervention. There will always be a need for prevention research and evaluation to serve as the source for service delivery. On the other hand, a sufficient amount is known about the efficacy of procedures, such as early intervention for at-risk infants or problem-solving and decision-making techniques, to make these and other services available.

CMHC's remain the most likely conduit for the provision of preventive/promotive mental health. But preventive interventions will reach large segments of communities only when preventionists (1) refuse to capitulate to the double standard applied to prevention, (2) realize that prevention remains a stepchild of mainstream mental health for political rather than scientific reasons, and (3) accept the dual roles of applied social scientists and political advocates. Preventionists can become passive in the face of a return to traditional values and techniques in mental health, or can *actively* use the substantial body of empirical support as the basis for political advocacy for prevention services for children.

REFERENCES

Bloom, B. L. Prevention of mental health disorders: Recent advances in theory and practice. *Community Mental Health Journal,* 1979, *15,* 179–191.

Broman, S., Nichols, P. L., & Kennedy, W. A. *Preschool IQ: Prenatal and early developmental correlates.* Hillsdale, N.J.: Lawrence Erlbaum, 1975.

Bronfenbrenner, U. Developmental research, public policy and the ecology of childhood. *Child Development,* 1974, *45,* 1–5.

Bronfenbrenner, U. *The ecology of human development.* Cambridge, MA: Harvard University Press, 1979.

Broussard, E. R., & Hartner, M. S. S. Maternal perception of the neonate as related to development. *Child Psychiatry and Human Development,* 1970, *1,* 16–25.

Caplan, G. Mastery of stress: Psychosocial aspects. *American Journal of Psychiatry,* 1981, *138,* 413–420.

Cassel, J. Psychosocial processes and "stress." Theoretical formulations. *International Journal of Health Services,* 1974, *4,* 471–482.

Cochran, M. M., & Brassard, J. A. Child development and personal social networks. *Child Development,* 1979, *50,* 601–616.

Cowen, E. L. Some problems in community program evaluation research. *Journal of Consulting and Clinical Psychology,* 1978, *46,* 792–805.

Crockenburg, S. Infant irritability, mother responsiveness, and social support influences on the security of infant-mother attachment. *Child Development,* 1981, *52,* 857–865.

Field, T. M., Sostek, A., Goldberg, S., & Shuman, H. H. (Eds.), *Infants born at risk: Behavior and development.* New York: SP Medical and Scientific Books, 1979.

Garbarino, J. Preventing child maltreatment. In R. C. Price, R. F. Ketterer, B. C. Bader, & J. Monahan (Eds.), *Prevention in mental health: Research, policy, and practice.* Beverly Hills, CA: Sage, 1980.

Gesten, E. L., De Apodoca, R. F., Rains, M., Weissberg, R. P., & Cowen, E. L. Promoting peer-related social competence in schools. In M. W. Kent & J. E. Rolf (Eds.), *Primary prevention of psychopathology. Volume 3: Social competence in children.* Hanover, NH: University Press of New England, 1979.

Gibbs, J. C. The meaning of ecologically oriented inquiry in contemporary psychology. *American Psychologist,* 1979, *34,* 127–140.

Gottlieb, B. H. (Ed.), *Social networks and social support.* Beverly Hills, CA: Sage Publications, 1981.

Heller, K., & Monahan, J. *Psychology and community change.* Homewood, IL: Dorsey Press, 1977.

Jason, L. A. Prevention in the schools: Behavioral approaches. In R. C. Price, R. F. Ketterer, B. C. Bader, & J. Monahan (Eds.), *Prevention in mental health: Research, policy and practice.* Beverly Hills, CA: Sage Publications, 1980.

Johnson, D. L., Leler, H., Rios, L., Brandt, L., Kahn, A. J., Marzeika, E., Frede, M., & Bissett, B. The Houston parent-child development center: A parent education program for Mexican-American families. *American Journal of Orthopsychiatry,* 1974, *44,* 121–128.

Klaus, M., & Kennell, J. *Parent-infant bonding* (2nd ed.) St. Louis: C. V. Mosby, 1982.

Lamb, H. R., & Zusman, J. Primary prevention in perspective. *American Journal of Psychiatry,* 1979, *136,* 12–16.

Lazar, I., & Darlington, R. Lasting effects of early education: A report from the consortium for longitudinal studies. *Monographs of the Society for Research in Child Development,* 1982, *47* (2–3, Serial No. 195).

Masi, W. Supplemental stimulation of the premature infant. In T. M. Field, A. M. Sostek, S. Goldberg, & H. Shuman (Eds.), *Infants born at risk: Behavior and development.* New York: SP Medical and Scientific Books, 1979.

Masterpasqua, F. Toward a synergism of developmental and community psychology. *American Psychologist,* 1981, *36,* 782–786.

Masterpasqua, F. The effectiveness of childbirth education as an early intervention technique. *Hospital and Community Psychiatry,* 1982, *33,* 56–58.

Masterpasqua, F., Shuman, B. J., O'Shea, L., & Gonzalez, R. Integrating early intervention into neighborhood health clinics: An ecological intervention. *Infant Mental Health,* 1980, *1,* 108–115.

McGuire, J. C., & Gottlieb, B. H. Social support groups among new parents: An experimental study in primary prevention. *Journal of Clinical Child Psychology,* 1979, *8,* 111–116.

Minde, K., Shosenberg, N., Morton, P., Thompson, J., Ripley, J., & Burns, S. Self-help groups in the premature nursery: A controlled evaluation. *Journal of Pediatrics,* 1980, *96,* 933–940.

Niswander, K. R., & Gordon, M. (Eds.), *The collaborative perinatal study of the National Institute of Neurological Diseases and Stroke: The women and their pregnancies.* Philadelphia: Saunders, 1972.

Peters, D. L. Social science and social policy and care of young children: Head Start and after. *Journal of Applied Developmental Psychology,* 1980, *1,* 7–27.

Plaut, T. F. A. Prevention policy: The federal perspective. In R. H. Price, R. F. Ketterer, B. C. Bader, & J. Monahan (Eds.), *Prevention in mental health: Research, policy and practice.* Beverly Hills, CA: Sage Publications, 1980.

Polansky, N., Chalmers, M., Buttenweiser, W., & Williams, D. The isolation of the neglectful family. *American Journal of Orthopsychiatry,* 1979, *49,* 149–152.

Powell, L. F. The effect of extra stimulation and maternal involvement on the development of low birth weight infants and on maternal behavior. *Child Development,* 1974, *45,* 106–113.

President's Commission on Mental Health. *Report to the President. Volume I.* Washington, D.C.: U.S. Government Printing Office, 1978.

Sameroff, A. J., & Chandler, M. J. Reproductive risk and the continuum of caretaking casualty. In F. D. Horowitz, M. Hetherington, S. Scarr-Salapatek, & G. Siegel (Eds.), *Review of child development research (Vol. 4).* Chicago: University of Chicago Press, 1975.

Sarason, I. G., & Sarason, B. R. Teaching cognitive and social skills to high school students. *Journal of Consulting and Clinical Psychology,* 1981, *49,* 908–918.

Shure, M. B., & Spivack, G. Interpersonal problem solving thinking and adjustment in the mother-child dyad. In M. W. Kent & J. E. Rolf (Eds.), *Primary prevention of psychopathology* (Vol. 3), *Social competence in children.* Hanover, NH: University Press of New England, 1979.

Shure, M. B., & Spivack, G. Interpersonal problem solving as a mediator or behavioral adjustment in preschool and kindergarten children. *Journal of Applied Developmental Psychology,* 1980, *1,* 29–44.

Silver, B. J. Overview of clinical infant programs. In *Clinical infant intervention research programs: Selected overview and discussion.* Washington, D.C.: National Institute of Mental Health, 1979.

Snow, D. L., & Newton, P. M. Task, social structure and social process in the community mental health center movement. *American Psychologist,* 1976, *31,* 583–594.

Sundberg, N. A., Snowden, L. R., & Reynolds, W. M. Toward assessment of personal competence and incompetence in life situations. *Annual Review of Psychology,* 1978, *29,* 179–221.

Surgeon General's Report on Health Promotion and Disease Prevention. *Healthy People.* DHEW (PHS) Publication No. 79-55071. Washington, D. C.: U. S. Government Printing Office, 1979.

Vandenbos, G. R., & Miller, M. O. Delinquency prevention programs: Mental health and the law. In R. H. Price, R. F. Ketterer, B. C. Bader, & J. Monahan (Eds.), *Prevention in mental health: Research, policy and practice.* Beverly Hills, CA: Sage Publications, 1980.

Zigler, E., & Trickett, P. K. The role of national policy in promoting social competence in children. In M. W. Whalen & J. E. Rolf (Eds.), *Primary prevention of psychopathology (Vol. III), Social competence in children.* Hanover, NH: University Press of New England, 1979.

REFERENCE NOTES

1. Swift, M. *A working model for prevention.* Paper presented at the Annual Convention of the National Council of Community Mental Health Centers, Kansas City, March 1977.
2. Swift, M. *Prevention goals and program development: A working model for service providers in mental health.* Paper presented at the Annual Convention of the American Orthopsychiatric Association, Boston, March 1983.

3. Healey, K. H., Jackson, D. J., & Ellis, B. *Problem-solving for seventh graders*. Unpublished manuscript, 1982. (Available from JFK CMH/MR Center, 112 N. Broad St., Philadelphia, Pa. 19102.)
4. Hermalin, J. *Prenatal education and reproductive outcome*. Unpublished manuscript, 1981 (Available from JFK CMH/MR Center, 112 N. Broad St., Philadelphia, Pa. 19102.)
5. Garbarino, J. *Becoming a family: A review of metropolitan Omaha hospital policies and practices affecting parent-child relationships*. Unpublished manuscript, 1982 (Available from J. Garbarino, Division of Individual and Family Studies, College of Human Development, Penn State University, University Park, Pa. 16802.)

PART FOUR

Conclusions

CHAPTER 13

Preventive Models

Implications for a Technology of Practice

STEPHANIE B. STOLZ

Our culture proclaims the efficacy of preventive practices at least to the extent of a truism: An ounce of prevention is worth a pound of cure. Yet society does not back this proclamation with behavior. To use another well-known phrase, it does not put its money where its mouth is. Much greater resources are expended to study, develop, and provide cures than are spent for comparable activities in primary prevention.

In contrast to our culture's practice of ignoring prevention, this book reports a wide range of models for preventing problems in childhood. Some of these models were studied as part of research programs, some originated in clinical settings; many were implemented for a time in real world settings, even though their main intent was often research rather than service. The authors have provided anecdotes and data regarding the effectiveness of these preventive efforts.

EFFECTIVE PREVENTIVE MODELS: IDEAL CHARACTERISTICS

What is a good preventive model? The essential characteristic is that it be effective, but additionally, a good model for preventing childhood problems should encompass a range of preventive activities, be well specified, allow for both active and passive prevention, and include an implementation program. The first three characteristics will be addressed briefly before turning to implementation, the chapter's main focus.

Range of Activities

A good prevention model must provide for the range of preventive activities found in practice. Some preventive procedures are required only a few times in a person's

---

This chapter was written when Dr. Stolz was Director of the Division of Alcoholism, Drug Abuse, and Mental Health Programs in the Kansas City Regional Office of the U.S. Public Health Service.

life (vaccination), some daily (flossing), some several times a day (nutrition), and some occur only in particular settings (seat belt use).

Specification

A preventive model should be sufficiently specific that one can measure when the prevention technology is being used as originally devised, being used in a changed form, or not being used. A case in point is one of the best known prevention programs for children, the Primary Mental Health Project developed by Cowen and his colleagues (Cowen, Dorr, Izzo, Madonia, & Trost, 1971; Cowen, Gesten, & Wilson, 1979). This intervention has four essential characteristics: a focus on primary-grade children, systematic screening for early identification of children with school adjustment problems, use of nonprofessional aides to serve identified children, and alteration of traditional professional roles by using these professionals only for consultation and for selection, training, and supervision of aides (Cowen, Spinell, Wright, & Weissberg, 1983).

Cowen and his associates report widespread use of the Primary Mental Health Project (PMHP) model (Cowen, Davidson, & Gesten, 1980; Cowen et al., 1983). However, because the key characteristics of this model are so general, the researchers themselves are unsure as to whether schools reporting use of the model are actually using it. "One cannot know for sure, from the present data, the extent to which the new implementations preserve PMHP essences. Most likely, some essences are lost" (Cowen et al., 1983, p. 125). The "essences" of a preventive model should be measurable, so research can show what these essences are or at least what an effective package of interventions is.

Active and Passive Prevention

Preventive procedures can be active or passive (see also Roberts & Peterson in Chapter 1 of this volume), and a good preventive model includes both. In an active program, children engage in some specific behavior to prevent some childhod problem, or their parents engage in behavior to protect their children. Passive programs involve changing a part of the children's environment to provide prevention. Examples of environmental arrangements that protect children include fluoride in the drinking water, childproof medicine containers, and air bags in automobiles. In each case, neither the child nor the parent has to engage in any special behavior for the prevention program to be effective.

This distinction does not mean that passive programs are passive from their initiation:

> It is very obvious that any passive strategy must be an active strategy at one time or another. For instance, the failure of the United States Congress to pass a mandatory air bag law, of various local governmental bodies to pass mandatory motorcycle helmet legislation, of hospital administrators to require or insist on legislatively mandated cervical screening for all female patients, "active" processes for these legislative

bodies, makes impossible a "passive" activity for recipients of these procedures. [Kegeles, Lund, & Weisenberg, 1978, p. 200]

Before an environmental change can occur, such as introducing fluoride into drinking water, social change must precede it, including at least some government action and often some pressure by citizens' groups.

Implementation Plan

In order for prevention practices to have an impact on children, someone must use a preventive model. The user may be individual children, parents, professional practitioners, or government bodies. Children can select nutritious foods and floss their teeth. Parents can put their infants in child restraining car seats, preventing serious injury in the event of an accident. Practitioners can paint fluoride on children's teeth; and, as noted previously, governing bodies can legislate preventive activities as public policy.

A preventive model, designed to be implemented at one of these levels, should include this crucial step: how to get the model used. In the literature in the field—and in most chapters of this book—the description tends to cover research and clinical activities that took place after someone began to use the preventive model, such as the authors themselves (Drotar, Crawford, & Ganofsky, Chapter 8), school teachers (Durlak & Jason, Chapter 4), or parents (Forehand, Walley, & Furey, Chapter 11). A few chapters (Albino, Chapter 7; Jason, Durlak, & Holton-Walker, Chapter 10; Masterpasqua & Swift, Chapter 12), however, do deal with the process by which the preventive model was implemented.

OVERVIEW OF THIS CHAPTER

The focus of this chapter is on the implementation of preventive models. Once research has demonstrated the effectiveness of a preventive model, what is required for its implementation? That few of the chapters in this book deal with the issue is not unusual. Characteristically, psychological research findings are not implemented by service providers, either in therapy (Stolz, 1981) or in primary prevention (Lund & Kegeles, 1982).

This chapter will first review what is being done to implement preventive models, describe the available theories that attempt to explain how implementation occurs, and finally, propose some practical methods for implementing prevention programs.

IMPLEMENTATION IN PRACTICE

How do researchers and other developers of preventive models disseminate information about their procedures so that they are used by individuals, professionals, and agencies? The literature on prevention, as exemplified by the work reported in this book, offers little evidence that knowledge gained from research on models preventing the problems of childhood is disseminated systematically.

Information Lacking

Unfortunately, the literature often reports only that preventive programs were used successfully, without giving any information on how people came to use them. Researchers rarely study what affected their program's implementation, and thus rarely publish details that would enable subsequent analysis of the variables affecting program implementation (for example, Jason et al., Chapter 10). Instead, researchers almost always measure the impact of the preventive intervention, rather than evaluate the process by which the intervention comes to be used (for example, Peterson & Brownlee-Duffeck, Chapter 9; Masterpasqua & Swift, Chapter 12). As a result, although a body of knowledge is developing about what kinds of preventive models can be successful, this literature does not increase related knowledge on how to get these successful models used.

Usually, the topic of implementation is ignored. To take some examples from the chapters in this book as reflective of the literature as a whole, Rickel, Dyhdalo, and Smith (Chapter 3) describe a prevention-oriented preschool screening program. But how did Wayne State University and the Detroit Public Schools come to set up such a project in the Title I preschool programs in Region 7 of the school system? Forehand et al. (Chapter 11) describe a parent training program, but give no information on how participants were motivated to stay in the course, learn the materials, and use the procedures learned. The programs described by Peterson and Brownlee-Duffeck (Chapter 9) were announced on radio and in the newspapers and were attended by Scouts and school classes. Again, why did the media carry these announcements, and what variables led to group participation by Scouts and schools?

Sometimes when ideal preventive programs are described, the authors fail to deal with the practical issues involved in putting those programs into use. Discussing perinatal prevention, Magrab, Sostek, and Powell (Chapter 2) call for physicians to give new types of tests or advice, and for public policy changes so that government at some level pays for home assessments, especially for high-risk mothers. What must be done to achieve those goals? Durlak and Jason (Chapter 4) would like school systems to provide competency building preventive programs for school age children and adolescents. How could events be arranged to encourage the schools to participate?

Even when the practical issues of getting prevention programs are discussed, the literature commonly deals with them only on a general level. For example, Rolf, Bevins, Hasazi, Crowther, and Johnson (1982) emphasized "the extraordinary degree of social-political skills which the [prevention] project's spokesperson must possess and the endless hours of staff time which must be invested in order to generate and maintain community support" (pp. 114–115). However, no details were provided concerning what actions were taken so that the Vermont Vulnerable Child Development Project continued in the community for an extended period of time. Can the behaviors necessary to obtain community cooperation be specified?

As a consequence of the common failure to get preventive models used by individuals or adopted by legislatures or communities, authors in the prevention area often call for psychologists and other researchers to use the political process to change the system and achieve these goals (for example, Roberts, Elkins, & Royal, Chapter 6; Jason et al., Chapter 10; Masterpasqua & Swift, Chapter 12; Liberman, 1980; Peterson, 1981; Skinner, 1981). The same question remains: How are these changes to be brought about (McAlister & O'Shea, 1981)?

Implementation Is Not Studied

In part, we do not know the answers to these questions. Typically, after researchers have demonstrated the effectiveness of a new preventive model, they move on to another research question. Very little research has developed methods for implementing preventive models so that they are continued in use once the research project is over (compare Peterson & Brownlee-Duffeck, Chapter 9). A possible technology for disseminating information about new preventive procedures will be discussed in detail later.

Publish and Hope

Once researchers have developed a new preventive model, they typically publish it in the scientific literature and hope it will have some impact, such as being followed up by others or used in applications (Stolz, 1981). This book itself is an example of publishing information about preventive programs, with the hope that the mere availability of this information will lead more people to become interested in studying prevention or applying preventive techniques. Some of the individual chapters have their own dissemination agendas. For example, Felner (Chapter 5) hopes by this publication to convince other scientists to change their view of the relationship of life changes and stress, adopting a new view that "may lead to more effective preventive efforts being developed for children."

Hoping that publication will result in increased use of preventive methods is mentioned in several chapters here, most explicitly by Forehand et al. (Chapter 11). After describing the empirical support for a parent training program devised by McMahon and Forehand (1978), Forehand et al. note that "a major focus of our research is now directed toward dissemination of our procedures." According to the chapter, this dissemination thrust involves publishing a nontechnical book on the training program, plus publishing in popular magazines such as *Parents' Magazine*. The authors believe that when large numbers of parents read these publications, they will use the procedures described. Forehand et al. (Chapter 11) are also planning other dissemination methods, including pamphlets.

Several chapters recommend presentations in the media as one way to get preventive measures implemented (for example, Jason et al., Chapter 10). Forehand et al. (Chapter 11) are planning announcements on radio and television to supplement dissemination through print. In a sense, film modeling shown on television is the ultimate in dissemination, because the preventive technique itself is what is disseminated, rather than simply information about the availability of preventive technology. Peterson and Brownlee-Duffeck (Chapter 9) cite a number of research examples in which favorable behavior change was obtained through the observation of film models.

A variant of Publish and Hope is Nag and Hope: explaining to parents how they encourage behavior incompatible with good performance by their children in school and hoping that, as a result, the parents will use different child rearing methods (Rickel et al., Chapter 3).

Do these techniques work? Do people act on what they read? According to Shore (1972), "only 9% of the innovations in mental health services are believed to be stimulated by use of printed research findings" (p. 383).

I know of little empirical research evaluating the effectiveness of using publication alone to get preventive models used. Although McMahon and Forehand (1978) reported a study in which they measured the effectiveness of a brief brochure (containing instructions on how to use behavioral technology to decrease children's inappropriate mealtime behavior), their study included too many additional factors to allow an evaluation of publication per se as a dissemination method. For example, study participants responded to advertisements in the newspaper, and only three mothers were included in the study, thus involving some uncontrolled selection variables. Further, all data were collected by the experimenters' observers in the home, presumably adding demand characteristics to the impact of the experimental brochures.

A careful study by Iwata and Becksfort (1981) examined the effects of education on the later use of preventive dental hygiene methods. This method might be called "educate and hope." Iwata and Becksfort (1981) showed that a group getting only instruction, compared to those receiving instruction plus a monetary incentive, evidenced short-term behavior change; the initial improvement in dental hygiene no longer remained at the six-month follow-up. In contrast, the group receiving the additional monetary incentive showed significant change and clinical improvement both after training and at a six-month follow-up.

Although much is published about preventive models, people are generally agreed that preventive techniques are used little. This suggests that some additional or alternative methods of dissemination are required (compare Albino, Chapter 7).

Reinforce Use

Psychologists and other researchers have developed a technology of behavior change based chiefly on stimulus control and the principle of reinforcement. This technology can produce meaningful behavior change (Baer, Wolf, & Risley, 1968) that may be maintained over time (Stokes & Baer, 1977). Presumably, one way to get people to use preventive models is to change their behavior by means of this established technology. The reinforcers used to effect behavior change might be extrinsic (that is, separate from and different from the preventive model), or intrinsic (integral to the preventive technique).

The technique of Publish and Hope (or Educate and Hope) assumes that the information transmitted provides intrinsic motivation, that something about knowing the disseminated information will result in behavior change. However, the literature suggests that this effect will not be a powerful one, because people generally fail to use procedures they read or are taught.

Some preventive techniques, if used, do provide intrinsic reinforcers. For example, people commonly report that aerobic exercise and running makes them feel better, which is apparently enough reinforcement to keep many people exercising and running, despite the aversive consequences also intrinsic to those behaviors. Iwata and Becksfort's (1981) subjects reported that they "were surprised by the amount of debris that accumulated between the teeth in spite of daily flossing, and that this feedback served to maintain regular and thorough dental self-care" (p. 118). The discovery of debris between the teeth is an automatic—and evidently reinforcing—consequence of flossing, and apparently functioned as an intrinsic reinforcer for those subjects.

One way to motivate physicians and other health caregivers to provide preventive models for their patients would be to alter the insurance reimbursement system to allow insurance policies to pay for such services (Roberts et al., Chapter 6). This change is likely to have the desired result, as suggested by the impact other changes in reimbursement rules have had on physicians' choices of procedures. When physicians are reimbursed for using new procedures, those are adopted (Bunker, Fowles, & Schaffarzick, 1982). Thus, payments to health caregivers could be designed as extrinsic reinforcers, increasing the use of preventive models.

The Northeast Guidance Center, a community mental health center in Detroit, provides presumably reinforcing consequences for attendance at a new-mothers community event where prevention is the main topic. The prevention functions of the Annual Community Baby Shower are to identify the stressors associated with pregnancy and parenting, increase the coping skills of expectant mothers, increase social supports and networks, and provide anticipatory guidance for the processes of birth and parenting (Keeler & Swift, 1982). The attendees are mainly young, low income, first-time mothers, who receive a gift package of miscellaneous baby items, a free lunch, and a chance at winning a door prize, in addition to hearing talks on preventive topics. Although no systematic evaluation has been done, the gifts, door prizes, and lunches are considered to be important in encouraging participation.

Only a few studies report experimentally programming reinforcers to increase the use of preventive models. In one such study (Reiss, Piotrowski, & Bailey, 1976), the researchers attempted to get low income parents to take their children for at least one dental screening plus some follow-up visits. Techniques used were either (1) a note to the parents, (2) a combination of the note, a telephone call, and a home visit by a hygienist, or (3) the note plus a payment of five dollars for visiting the dentist. In the latter two groups, nearly three times as many families went to the dentist for screening as those in the group receiving only the note (23%, 60%, and 67%, respectively).

Reanalysis of the data reported by Reiss et al. (1976) shows that of those families who went to the dentist at least once, subsequent visits (in the next 17 weeks) were made about as often by the group getting the calls and home visits and by the payment group (approximately two visits per participating family). This was more than ten times the number of visits made by participating families in the note-only group (0.16 visits per participating family). Of the two successful interventions, the cheaper was the payment group (five dollars per family). This relatively inexpensive intervention produced a great increase in dental care, presumbly saving future costs. Although few families were involved in this study, the intergroup differences reported were large. Perhaps these results can be applied to other programs.

Kegeles and his associates (Kegeles et al., 1978; Lund & Kegeles, 1982; Lund, Kegeles, & Weisenberg, 1977) investigated the effects of extrinsic reinforcers on seventh graders' preventive dental behavior in a series of studies involving 100 or more students in each experimental condition. In the earlier studies (Kegeles et al., 1978; Lund et al., 1977), all of the children were given information (a slide show and demonstration), after which some received either two discussions with groups of their peers or small reinforcers for preventive behavior. These carefully designed studies demonstrate the irrelevance of the particular school the children attended or their particular teachers. Two types of preventive behavior were studied: fluoride applied to the children's teeth at three appointments spread over a year (Lund et al., 1977), and a topical fluoride mouth rinse self-administered by the children daily for twenty weeks (Kegeles et al., 1978).

A high level of compliance was obtained with reinforcement; less with information only; and much less with the peer group discussions. Kegeles and Lund (1982) suggest "greater use in school health programs of techniques developed within applied behavior analysis such as self-management, external contingent rewards, social contracts, and specific instructions" (p. 110).

These techniques increase preventive behavior by making small payments to individuals for performing that behavior. The public health issue (raised also by Lund et al., 1977) is whether preventive behavior established by extrinsic reinforcers will generalize; that is, whether people will continue the behavior over time in the absence of reinforcers.

One possible answer to this question is that society should not terminate the extrinsic reinforcers, but rather ensure generalization over time by continuing the consequences that maintain the preventive behavior. Where the cost of reinforcers and program administration is modest, as in the studies cited, and where, at the same time, the cost is high of dealing with any disease resulting from an absence of preventive behavior, society may well choose to continue payments, although such a decision is by no means automatic. Where considerable cost occurs in maintaining preventive behavior, or where the disease resulting from the lack of preventive care has little long-term social or health cost, society is unlikely to provide extrinsic reinforcers for prevention. In these instances, technology more subtle than the application of contingent money will have to be developed in order to get preventive models used.

IMPLEMENTATION IN THEORY

How do researchers and theorists dealing with preventive models describe the processes of dissemination and implementation? More generally, what explanations are available of the dissemination process and the use of new knowledge?

The Health Belief Model

In the field of prevention, a classic theory treats the issue in terms of beliefs. The Health Belief Model (Rosenstock, 1966) postulates why people engage in preventive health behavior in the absence of illness. People will take such actions, in response to appropriate internal or external cues, if they believe that:

they are susceptible to a disease,

contracting the disease would be serious,

preventive behavior would enable them to avoid the disease or minimize its effects, and

the preventive behavior would not be worse than getting the disease (Becker, 1974; Rosenstock, 1966, 1974).

According to this model, if people are not engaging in preventive health behavior, the way to develop the desired behavior is to provide relevant information. The model assumes that this will change their beliefs about health to those listed above; then, when suitably cued, the preventive behavior will occur. That is, preventive behavior occurs when persons holding a particular set of attitudes are exposed to the relevant cues.

Such an approach is implicit in some chapters of this book. For example, Albino (Chapter 7) suggests that people would be more consistent in their primary prevention of dental diseases if they took dental problems more seriously ("contracting the disease would be serious"). Several authors mention the importance of people perceiving prevention as a possible solution to a problem (Jason et al., Chapter 10), and seeing a clear relationship between the preventive behavior and health (believing that the preventive behavior results in avoidance or minimization of the disease). Albino further notes that the progress of dental disease is too slow to make obvious the relationship between flossing and dental health (compare Iwata & Becksfort, 1981). Drotar et al. (Chapter 8) credit their success in medical staff adopting their preventive procedures to a demonstration of the procedures' efficacy.

Unfortunately, the Health Belief Model has not held up well under rigorous empirical test. Although retrospective reports from respondents obtained in surveys support the model, those data are correlational, with causal relationships indeterminable. In contrast, prospective research typically finds weaker or nonsignificant relationships between beliefs and preventive behavior, and sometimes finds results in the opposite direction from those predicted by the model (Kegeles & Lund, 1982; Weisenberg, Kegeles, & Lund, 1980).

A special issue for this book is that most of the research supporting the Health Belief Model was done with adults. The prospective empirical research done by Kegeles and his associates with children (Kegeles & Lund, 1982; Weisenberg et al., 1980) consistently failed to support the Health Belief Model. Although their program caused seventh-grade children to use preventive techniques over a relatively long period of time, the children did not change their beliefs about their susceptibility to illness, the seriousness of dental illness, or the effectiveness of the preventive interventions they were using, contrary to the expectations of the Health Belief Model.

Overall, research has not shown that information leads to changes in attitudes and, as a consequence, changes in behavior (Kegeles & Grady, 1982). The research cited (Kegeles & Lund, 1982; Weisenberg et al., 1980) suggests that in children, there was no relationship between these beliefs and the relevant behavior. Weisenberg et al. (1980) summarize their findings as follows:

> Efforts to achieve children's acceptance of preventive health procedures by emphasizing the changing of health beliefs seem unlikely to succeed, both because children's beliefs seem unrelated or negatively related to behavior and because such efforts are unlikely to change these target beliefs. . . . These data, combined with other studies of health beliefs with both children and adults, suggest the possible absence of a causal relationship between health beliefs and health behavior. [p. 72]

Contrary to this suggestion, much prevention is based—sometimes only implicitly—on a model of information input as the central factor in preventive behavior. Considerable resources are devoted to media campaigns and health education classes, for example. The failure of research to provide consistent support for the Health Belief Model should stimulate a search for other variables.

Good Data Are Not Enough

One of the factors considered important in getting preventive models used is having data on the models' effectiveness. Is clear evidence of effectiveness, perhaps cleverly presented, all that is needed? For example, discussing the adoption of new programs for preventing children's academic problems in school, Jason et al. (Chapter 10) note that effectively presented information on the "practical payoffs and value" of the proposed programs is crucial for getting school staff members to use the new programs.

Some social scientists typically operate on the premise that "once knowledge and truth are assembled, . . . transfer of knowledge . . . will take care of itself" (Cowen et al., 1980, p. 36). Although Albino (Chapter 7) discusses many different aspects of the problem of getting preventive programs used, she also notes that it is "important to develop the data base that will substantiate, and therefore sell" such programs. Peterson and Brownlee-Duffeck (Chapter 9) likewise suggest that a helpful method for getting medical personnel to use new preventive methods is to provide clinical data in support of the new methods.

However, as Cowen et al. (1980) despairingly conclude, "life is neither so simple nor so just" (p. 36); rather, there is a "serious gap" (p. 37) between data and their use (compare Peterson & Brownlee-Duffeck, Chapter 9; Jason et al., Chapter 10). Preventive interventions are used not because of the elegance of the supporting data, but because of economic, social, and political forces (Peters, 1980). Noting this relationship, some authors urge political advocacy (Masterpasqua & Swift, Chapter 12), that is, working through the political system to sell prevention as an essential component of public policy (compare Liberman, 1980; Peterson, 1981; Skinner, 1981).

The empirical results are not consistent concerning whether good research data are important in initiating the use of preventive models and other innovations. Some studies show that research quality is an important determinant of later use (Baer, Johnson, & Merrow, 1977; Weiss & Bucuvalas, 1977), others that quality is irrelevant (Patton, Grimes, Guthrie, Brennan, French, & Blyth, 1977; Useem & DiMaggio, 1978). At best, however, clear data demonstrating the effectiveness of a preventive model are not a sufficient explanation for the use of that model (Sherman, 1981). Indeed, because some good data lead to preventive models being used and some do not, and because some models poorly supported by evaluation results or having no evaluation at all are used even so (Durlak & Jason, Chapter 4; Masterpasqua & Swift, Chapter 12), good data must be neither necessary nor sufficient for implementing preventive models.

Getting New Programs Used

If reinforcers could be discovered for each person and someone were there to deliver those reinforcers, individuals could be reinforced directly for using preventive models. This is obviously an expensive and cumbersome technique. How else could people learn to use preventive models?

The field that deals with this question is a subfield of political science; in the technical language of that field, the process of informing people about new models is called *knowledge diffusion,* and the process of using that information, *knowledge utilization.* The literature on the diffusion and utilization of scientific knowledge in general is extensive, including thousands of published articles and technical reports.

However, despite the immensity of the published literature, few empirical studies have been done on the diffusion or utilization of scientific knowledge, and little theory has developed from the available evidence. In terms of theory, what is available is acknowledged to be a preliminary sketch (Nelson & Winter, 1977) or framework (Pelz & Munson, 1982), rather than a fully developed theory.

The published literature on the diffusion and utilization of knowledge also lacks an effective technology, a set of interventions that would result, for example, in preventive models being used. It also does not even contain evidence for powerful variables on which such a technology might be built (Stolz, 1981; Yin & Gwaltney, 1981). Rather, it consists of numerous anecdotal and correlational reviews that produce lists of possibly effective variables, each of which appears weak (Roessner, 1980; Stolz, 1981), and most of which are not manipulable. Researchers' and theorists' lists are so numerous, in fact, that some publications contain lists of the lists (Human Interaction Research Institute, 1976). "One might gain the impression," Salasin and Davis (1977) commented, "that there is something a bit short of consensus" (p 430).

It might be useful to analyze the variables considered most important—perhaps those which appear on the largest number of lists—to discover whether an underlying behavioral principle exists. For example, my review of this literature and case study analysis (Stolz, 1981) suggest that the strongest single variable in the lists is the personal interaction between the person deciding to use the innovation and a colleague or friend who promotes its use. Several other studies agree (DiMaggio & Useem, 1979; Glaser, 1973; Rich, 1981; Yin & Gwaltney, 1981; Jason et al., Chapter 10). Social reinforcement may be the behavioral mechanism underlying the personal factor, but that hypothesis requires repeated empirical testing.

IMPLEMENTATION TECHNOLOGY

The gap between the discovery and publication of new knowledge and practical use of that knowledge has created increasing interest in the study of dissemination itself (Cowen et al., 1980; Fairweather, Sanders, & Tornatzky, 1974; Jason et al., Chapter 10). Thus far, this interest has generated lists, but no organized technology (Stolz, 1981).

How could we develop a technology for getting preventive models used? The standard method is to cite various techniques that might be effective and test them empirically, one by one. This approach seems unlikely to work quickly, or to produce any unifying theoretical thread. An alternative is to draw out a set of feasible techniques, explicit and implicit, from the literature. This would be analogous to Stokes and Baer's (1977) development of what they called an implicit technology of generalization: a list of generalization-promoting techniques reported to be sometimes effective. I have found it fruitful to look at the possibility of direct analogies to Stokes and Baer's techniques.

What follows is a preliminary step toward a technology for getting preventive models used. The techniques involve empirical manipulation of measurable variables and thus could be implemented for use with realistic problems. Because the technology is developed by analogy with the problem of generalization, extensive empirical testing is needed to establish the actual value of these techniques for the problem of implementation.

Publish and Hope

This previously discussed technique is analogous to Stokes and Baer's (1977) first "nonmethod" of generalization, Train and Hope. Publish and Hope (or Educate and Hope) is a common method of attempting to get preventive models used by children and their parents. Children are given lectures and shown models in school and at home; parents are given pamphlets, films, and talks by teachers and other professionals; continuing education courses are provided for school nurses, pediatricians, and other professions working with parents and children, to teach them what to teach the parents and children. Rowland's "Pierre the Pelican" series, 28 family bulletins on child care, are mailed to all new parents in several states during their child's first six years. Those bulletins give parents information on child development and management, and attempt to prevent problems in childhood. Sometimes these methods are effective. However, simply communicating the availability of a preventive model, and then hoping that people will use it, is not consistently effective, much as Train and Hope is only somewhat effective in obtaining generalization of learned behavior (Stokes & Baer, 1977).

Sequential Implementation

Sequential Modification, Stokes and Baer's (1977) second technique for obtaining generalization of learned behavior, accomplishes generalization by systematic sequential modification in every condition in which generalization is desired (rather than simply hoping for generalization and failing to schedule necessary consequences in every relevant condition). Sequential Implementation, the analogy in the technology of getting preventive models used, involves establishing a program exemplifying use of a preventive model and then determining where future uses should occur. Model preventive programs are eventually repeated sequentially in every desired setting where such control is possible and use does not otherwise occur.

The technique of Sequential Implementation calls for extraordinary expense, pluck, and commitment, because it may require that the program eventually be implemented in every possible setting. This seems to be what is happening with state laws requiring that children in cars either have a safety belt fastened or be placed in a special restraining seat, depending on the child's age (Fawcett, Seekins, Cohen, Elder, Jason, Schnelle, & Winett, Note 1). A national organization concerned with the issue is attempting to get laws passed in every state, using the results in the first few states. Note that the innovating agency in this example—the agency deciding to adopt the preventive model—is the state legislature, rather than an individual, caregiver, or service agency (Roberts et al., Chapter 6).

Albino (Chapter 7) makes a recommendation for gaining widespread use of health-enhancing habits, which sounds like an instance of Sequential Implementation. Albino calls for changes in "schools, community organizations, health care and social services, and other institutions serving children." Were these changes to be introduced initially in a few agencies, and later in those agencies not adopting the changes despite seeing initial models, the process would exemplify Sequential Implementation.

Introduce to Natural Maintaining Contingencies

Using this technique would involve identifying naturally occurring reinforcers for potential users, so as to entrap them with these reinforcers into using the new preventive model.

One example of this technique is the personal factor (Patton, 1978), which would exemplify Introduce to Natural Maintaining Contingencies if the key variable that makes the personal factor significant is the reinforcement provided to the potential user by a colleague (Stolz, 1984). For example, suppose a goal were to get the local PTA to include mental health education on its agenda and to provide health promotion workshops for parents as one of its activities. A strategy for doing this might be to identify the decision makers in the PTA, befriend them, and use the opportunity of interaction to describe the value of such programs for, perhaps, the prestige of the organization or other natural reinforcers for the group.

The anecdotal literature on the adoption of new technologies strongly supports the importance of this technique. For example, Shore (1972) claims that most innovations in service delivery come as a consequence of informal personal contacts. Masterpasqua and Swift (Chapter 12) stress that persons interested in disseminating preventive models should nurture contacts with key government administrators to have an opportunity to affect policy making. In the opinion of Jason et al. (Chapter 10), "the change agent's interpersonal skills and personal influence may be the most important factors determining whether schools adopt and maintain innovative preventive services."

Theories of knowledge utilization include a personal factor as an important variable. For example, Pelz and Munson (1982) emphasize the role they call the Innovation Advocate, the person who champions the innovation within the organization. Empirical research, too, has shown the importance of this variable (Patton et al., 1977). For example, research has shown that youths start smoking in response to pressure from a favorite peer (Albino, Chapter 7). They continue because of their addiction, another form of Natural Maintaining Contingency.

The technique of Introduce to Natural Maintaining Contingencies involves entrapping the potential user with naturally occurring reinforcers. A variant of this involves explicitly programming reinforcers that occur in the natural environment but might not otherwise be contingent on behavior associated with using preventive models. For example, the associates of a pediatrician or school nurse might ordinarily provide social reinforcers for interesting or creative work; using the logic of Introduction to Natural Maintaining Contingencies, these associates would make a special effort to deliver reinforcers when preventive models are being tried with child patients or with their parents.

Drotar et al. (Chapter 8) discuss the problems of working with chronically ill children, including maintaining the behavior of staff who must assist the children in mastering illness-related anxieties, adhering to medical regimens, and so on. They suggest designing the environment to provide opportunities for reinforcement when appropriate staff behavior occurs. For example, conferences and other opportunities for contact with professionals could be arranged, and time out from caregiving for research and writing could be provided after a period of caregiving. The conferences, research, and writing opportunities are already presumably available; the suggested rearrangement of the environmental contingencies takes advantage of naturally occurring reinforcers and provides them contingent on behavior otherwise only minimally reinforced.

Influencing individual behavior by social reinforcement and personal interaction or by environmental redesign is certainly feasible, but it is difficult to implement on a large scale and may also be difficult within a single organization, even if a suitable key individual is located. Introduction to Natural Maintaining Contingencies suggests another way would be to design the information received by the decision maker so that the information itself is reinforcing. The literature indicates that the new information should be congruent with the decision maker's previously held beliefs. Most of us are reinforced by being told something with which we agree. In one extensive series of case studies (DiMaggio & Useem, 1979), the single most important reason given by a number of organizations for the use of new research findings was that the findings fit their preconceptions. This is a type of personal factor and has the advantage of being intrinsic to the information, rather than requiring the engineering of interpersonal interaction.

Implement Sufficient Exemplars

This technique, the analogy to Stokes and Baer's (1977) Train Sufficient Exemplars, involves promoting the use of preventive models by establishing some model programs. This technique is similar to Sequential Implementation, but involves implementation in fewer settings, using the shrewdest possible choice of exemplars that best represents the dimensions of the problem (Baer, 1981). Unlike Sequential Implementation, Implementing Sufficient Exemplars rests on the possibility that use by others will occur if only the right few examples are provided.

To put this technique into practice, researchers need to modify their usual research style. Typically, researchers try an applied technology, such as a new preventive model, to see what variables produce a significant effect. Once they have their results, the innovative preventive program is discontinued as the researcher moves on to something else, while publishing the results from the first study and hoping that someone else will implement them. The innovative preventive program, although feasible as part of a short-term research study, may not be feasible as part of an on-going service program. In contrast, in the course of implementing a few exemplars, if practical problems can be worked out and feasibility demonstrated, the new preventive model may be continued even after the researchers depart.

A common recommendation for promoting the use of new programs is to have potential users view a few well chosen model programs (Stolz, 1981) that is an example of Implementing Sufficient Exemplars. Drotar et al. (Chapter 8) comment that they believe one of the keys to the success of their program is that medical staff have the opportunity to observe Drotar et al.'s on-going, effective preventive program. Similarly, to get a community to establish workshops or support groups for families involved in divorce, model programs could be set up in a few communities and key staff of agencies in other communities invited to visit and learn about the procedures and their impact on the mental health of the children in the participant families.

Implement Loosely

In obtaining the generalization of learned behavior, the technique of Train Loosely (Stokes & Baer, 1977) means to teach with relatively little control over the stimuli presented and the correct responses allowed, to maximize sampling of possibly relevant dimensions for transfer to other situations and other behavior. Implement Loosely, the analogous technique for dissemination, refers to changing the intervention to suit local circumstances, so that each new use is somewhat different from the others as well as from the initial model.

This process is widely recognized in the dissemination literature. It is sometimes called adaptation (Emshoff Note 2; Roitman & Mayer, Note 3) or reinvention (Fawcett, Mathews, & Fletcher, 1980; Rice & Rogers, 1980). To the extent that empirical evidence is available, the data neither provide strong support for the value of this technique, nor suggest that it should not be used (Stolz, 1984). Anecdotally, it appears that the procedures actually implemented often differ in some respects from their model. What is unclear is whether that is a virtue, making it more likely that the new technology is used, or a problem, attenuating the effectiveness of the model.

One of the factors Jason et al. (Chapter 10) include as important for getting a preventive program used is that the program should be robust enough that adaptation to the unique features of the site does not change the original system or decrease its effectiveness: this recommendation is similar to Implement Loosely.

Cowen and his associates (Cowen et al., 1980; Cowen et al., 1983) have been working since 1972 to get their Primary Mental Health Project used nationwide. This research group viewed adaptation of their model for early detection and prevention of school adjustment problems as ''both inevitable and desirable'' (Cowen et al., 1983, p. 125), reflecting their opinion that one of the factors in their successfully getting the Project used in many school systems was their willingness to have school personnel change the model to fit the local setting.

Use Indiscriminable Implementation

Use Indiscriminable Contingencies (Stokes & Baer, 1977) refers to designing the environment in such a way that the subject cannot discriminate in which settings the response will or will not be reinforced, so that the learned behavior is generalized to all settings. A loose analogy, Use Indiscriminable Implementation, emphasizes how the new preventive model differs little from that currently in use, and then gradually alters current practice in the direction of the new model. One aspect of such a program might be to avoid giving the new preventive model a distinctive name.

As laws requiring seat belts and car restraints for children and infants are being introduced around the country, a consistent pattern has appeared: the initial law carries little or no penalty, with penalties increased by later legislatures (Fawcett et al., Note 1). Gradually strengthening penalties in this fashion is an example of Using Indiscriminable Implementation.

A problem with using this technique is that for many preventive models, it is difficult to make the intervention indiscriminable from current practices. Using a new preventive model generally involves changes in individuals' behavior or staff routines, plus other costs in money, time, or energy (Jason et al., Chapter 10). Still, it is worth asking empirically whether those changes can be accomplished gradually and if doing so would facilitate use of new preventive models.

Program Common Stimuli

Program Common Stimuli, the seventh of Stokes and Baer's (1977) techniques, would, in the area of preventive models, have elements in common between some preliminary form of the preventive model and the ultimate use. An example of a common element might be the training materials used to inform potential users about a program. Potential users visiting a model preventive program would receive a training course to help them understand the program; the same training materials would be available to those who decide to set up their own program following the model.

Giving teachers training prior to their use of a program for preventing children's academic problems, and subsequently giving them more training once the program is in use (as recommended by Jason et al., Chapter 10), is another example of this technique. The training program, occurring both before and during use of the new preventive model, might facilitate the continued use of the model.

Teaching children at school to use preventive dental techniques has little value unless the children practice the techniques at home. Bringing the children's parents into the school during teaching sessions guarantees common elements between the initial training and later use. The children's continued use of the preventive dental techniques represents use of a preventive model on the individual level. Although many programs taught to children could make use of Programming Common Stimuli by involving family members in the children's training, the practical problems of doing so preclude this in most school systems.

Mediate Dissemination

To Mediate Generalization (Stokes & Baer, 1977), a response likely to be used in other problems is established as part of the newly learned behavior so as to result in generalization. Mediating Dissemination involves ensuring that those who ultimately decide on the use of a preventive model are among those who ask for a preliminary test of the new method. School principals who volunteer their pupils for experimental or demonstration preventive programs would be more likely to decide later to use the programs as a regular part of their schools' routine. A community that volunteers to participate in a demonstration of a new method to increase the use of seat belts and car restraints is likely to institutionalize that method as an ordinance when the demonstration study is over.

Rickel et al. (Chapter 3) recommend that teachers and administrators be more involved in the use of early intervention programs in preschools, so that such procedures would become an accepted part of the preschools' programs. In general, an effective technique for promoting the use of new technology is to involve those who will later have the opportunity to use the innovation in planning and designing preliminary research evaluating the innovation (DiMaggio & Useem, 1979; Stolz, 1981). These are all examples of the technique of Mediating Dissemination.

Train "To Implement"

This technique involves establishing training programs focused on teaching people to acquire knowledge that has been disseminated and to use innovations, as well as how to influence others to use innovations, such as through selective reinforcement and resistance to counter-control (Knapp, 1982). One could look at the curriculum of schools of public health, education, and other fields that teach students who will later become school nurses, principals, hospital administrators, and service-agency personnel, to see whether their curriculum includes explicit training in the use of innovative preventive models. Currently, this training emphasizes research and provision of service, rather than preventive models (Broskowski & Baker, 1974). However, training in the use and evaluation of preventive models could be provided by schools of public health and the health professions. Even more broadly, society could do a more systematic job to prepare its citizens to take advantage of new preventive techniques, for themselves and for their children.

Rather than teaching the use of new models to individuals, another way to Train "To Implement" is to design the environment to promote the use of new preventive models, either through designing organizations so that their structure results in preventive models being used (Kilmann, 1981), or through designing environmental contingencies so that use of preventive models is reinforced. The staff of Michigan's prevention unit, for example, has suggested (Tableman, 1980) that one way to persuade community mental health agencies to use preventive models is to design the state's funding rules so that community agencies meeting the requirements for their basic program receive extra funding which can only be used for preventive services (Tableman, 1980).

Reinforcement for implementing innovative preventive models might be accomplished on a broad scale through legislation that provides either positive incentives for complying, or threats of punishment for failure to comply. This would be feasible only for those preventive activities that can be monitored publicly, such as wearing seat belts or being immunized, and unsuitable for private preventive activities, like flossing teeth.

The power to tax is currently being used to discourage behavior considered to cause poor health. One intent of increasing taxes on alcohol and cigarettes is to reduce use. Governments also use tax laws to encourage citizens to engage in particular behavior, by giving individuals or companies tax credits for cooperation. An industry could be taxed less, for example, if it provided courses in parenting for its employees. Schools could be given extra operating funds if their staffs were given training in the latest preventive models. Private industry can also offer individuals incentives for using preventive models. Some insurance companies currently charge lower rates for customers who practice healthful preventive behavior (such as not drinking or not smoking), and no-smoking motels charge less than those that allow smoking.

CONCLUSIONS

This chapter has addressed a relevant problem: Preventive models exist and yet are not being widely used. To solve that problem, a new technology needs to be developed that would prescribe procedures for getting models used.

The techniques described here comprise what might be an implicit technology for getting preventive models used. I developed this list theoretically, by analogy with known techniques for the generalization of learned behavior. Much empirical work remains before an explicit (rather than implicit) technology is available (McAlister & O'Shea, 1981). Kegeles et al. (1978) concur with the process described here: Do experimental research on techniques shown in nonhealth contexts to be effective in changing behavior, determine their effectiveness as techniques for getting preventive models used, and assess the generality of any effective techniques. Once empirically based techniques are available, they can be employed to get preventive models, like the ones described in this book, used.

One question that research should address is whether the variables that result in the use of preventive models are the same or different, depending on the target user. The target user can be a person who actually is engaging in preventive behavior (for example, flossing teeth), engaging in preventive behavior on behalf of others (such as a parent buckling a child's seat belt), supervising another's preventive behavior (for instance, parents using contingency contracting at home to support the schools' educational goals), an organization devising a policy on preventive models (for example, training all third graders in the school system to floss their teeth), or a legislature adopting laws to require prevention (such as seat belt laws).

The contingencies of the world make it especially challenging to get primary preventive programs adopted. The world is already full of disease victims who have specific and urgent needs for secondary and tertiary prevention (that is, acute and long-term treatment). Primary prevention, when successful, reduces incidence (Bloom, 1979), but does not change prevalence, because those with diseases continue to need treatment. Those not working with primary prevention may see the ultimate users of primary preventive models as an intangible, "abstract, collective set of potential victims and persons at risk" (Vosburgh, 1982, p. 78), and of lower priority than disease victims. The challenge is to raise the priority of primary prevention.

This book recognizes the need to achieve several important goals. There is a need for systematic and effective diffusion of knowledge about preventive programs for children, for promotion of effective programs so that children, hospitals, schools, parents, and other agencies will use them, and for legislation to promote preventive models, such as environmental changes (child-proof medicine bottle caps), and to introduce penalties for unsafe behavior (not using child restraints in cars). The development of an empirically tested, effective technology for getting preventive models used will give us the opportunity to reach these goals.

ACKNOWLEDGMENT

I thank D. M. Baer for his helpful comments on an earlier version of this manuscript. The opinions expressed in this chapter are mine and do not necessarily reflect the views of the Department of Health and Human Services. This chapter is in the public domain, and is not copyrighted.

REFERENCES

Baer, D. M. The nature of intervention research. In R. L. Schiefelbusch & D. D. Bricker (Eds.), *Early language: Acquisition and intervention*. Baltimore MD: University Park Press, 1981.

Baer, D. M., Wolf, M. M., & Risley, T. R. Some current dimensions of applied behavior analysis. *Journal of Applied Behavior Analysis,* 1968, *1,* 91–97.

Baer, W. S., Johnson, L. L., & Merrow, E. W. Government-sponsored demonstrations of new technologies. *Science,* 1977, *196,* 950–957.

Becker, M. H. (Ed.). The health belief model and personal health behavior. *Health Education Monographs,* 1974, *2,* 326–473.

Bloom, B. L. Prevention of mental disorders: Recent advances in theory and practice. *Community Mental Health Journal,* 1979, *15,* 179–191.

Broskowski, A., & Baker, F. Professional, organizational, and social barriers to primary prevention. *American Journal of Orthopsychiatry,* 1974, *44,* 707–719.

Bunker, J. P., Fowles, J., & Schaffarzick, R. Evaluation of medical-technology strategies. *New England Journal of Medicine,* 1982, *306,* 620–624; 687–692.

Cowen, E. L., Davidson, E. R., & Gesten, E. L. Program dissemination and the modification of delivery practices in school mental health. *Professional Psychology,* 1980, *11,* 36–47.

Cowen, E. L., Dorr, D., Izzo, L. D., Madonia, A., & Trost, M. A. The Primary Mental Health Project: A new way of conceptualizing and delivering school mental health services. *Psychology in the Schools,* 1971, *8,* 216–225.

Cowen, E. L., Gesten, E. L., & Wilson, A. B. The Primary Mental Health Project (PMHP): Evaluation of current program effectiveness. *American Journal of Community Psychology,* 1979, *7,* 293–303.

Cowen, E. L., Spinell, A., Wright, S., & Weissberg, R. P. Continuing dissemination of a school-based mental health program. *Professional Psychology,* 1983, *14,* 118–127.

DiMaggio, P., & Useem, M. Decentralized applied research: Factors affecting the use of audience research by arts organizations. *Journal of Applied Behavioral Science,* 1979, *15,* 79–94.

Fairweather, G. W., Sanders, D. H., & Tornatzky, L. G. *Creating change in mental health organizations.* New York: Pergamon, 1974.

Fawcett, S. B., Mathews, R. M., & Fletcher, R. K. Some promising dimensions for behavioral community technology. *Journal of Applied Behavior Analysis,* 1980, *13,* 505–518.

Glaser, E. M. Knowledge transfer and institutional change. *Professional Psychology,* 1973, *4,* 434–444.

Human Interaction Research Institute. *Putting knowledge to use: A distillation of the literature regarding knowledge transfer and change.* Rockville, MD: National Institute of Mental Health, 1976.

Iwata, B. A., & Becksfort, C. M. Behavioral research in preventive dentistry: Educational and contingency management approaches to the problem of patient compliance. *Journal of Applied Behavior Analysis,* 1981, *14,* 111–120.

Keeler, K., & Swift, C. The Community Baby Shower: Detroit packages prevention messages to teenage parents. *Journal of Primary Prevention,* 1982, *3,* 48–51.

Kegeles, S. S., & Grady, K. E. Behavioral dimensions. In D. Schottenfeld & J. F. Fraumeni (Eds.), *Cancer epidemiology and prevention*. Philadelphia: Saunders, 1982.

Kegeles, S. S., & Lund, A. K. Adolescents' health beliefs and acceptance of a novel preventive dental activity: Replication and extension. *Health Education Quarterly*, 1982, *9*, 96–112.

Kegeles, S. S., Lund, A. K., & Weisenberg, M. Acceptance by children of a daily home mouthrinse program. *Social Science and Medicine*, 1978, *12*, 199–210.

Kilmann, R. H. Organization design for knowledge utilization. *Knowledge: Creation, Diffusion, Utilization*, 1981, *3*, 211–231.

Knapp, C. W. The acquisition and maintenance of behavioral skills: A response to Michael. *The Behavior Analyst*, 1982, *5*, 77–93.

Liberman, R. P. A review of Paul and Lentz's *Psychological treatment for chronic mental patients: Milieu versus social-learning programs*. *Journal of Applied Behavior Analysis*, 1980, *13*, 367–371.

Lund, A. K., & Kegeles, S. S. Increasing adolescents' acceptance of long-term personal health behavior. *Health Psychology*, 1982, *1*, 27–43.

Lund, A. K., Kegeles, S. S., & Weisenberg, M. Motivational techniques for increasing acceptance of preventive health measures. *Medical Care*, 1977, *15*, 678–692.

McAlister, A. L., & O'Shea, R. Community oral health promotion. *Journal of Behavioral Medicine*, 1981, *4*, 337–347.

McMahon, R. J., & Forehand, R. Nonprescription behavior therapy: Effectiveness of a brochure in teaching mothers to correct their children's inappropriate mealtime behaviors. *Behavior Therapy*, 1978, *9*, 814–820.

Nelson, R. R., & Winter, S. G. In search of useful theory of innovations. *Research Policy*, 1977, *6*, 37–76.

Patton, M. W. *Utilization-focused evaluation*. Beverly Hills: Sage, 1978.

Patton, M. W., Grimes, P. S., Guthrie, K. M., Brennan, N. J., French, B. D., & Blyth, D. A. In search of impact: An analysis of the utilization of federal health evaluation research. In C. H. Weiss (Ed.), *Using social research in public policy making*. Lexington: Heath, 1977.

Pelz, D. C., & Munson, F. C. Originality level and the innovating process in organizations. *Human Systems Management*, 1982, *3*, 173–187.

Peters, D. L. Social science and social policy and care of young children: Head Start and after. *Journal of Applied Developmental Psychology*, 1980, *1*, 7–27.

Peterson, D. R. Overall synthesis of the Spring Hill Symposium on the Future of Psychology in the Schools. *School Psychology Review*, 1981, *10*, 307–314.

Reiss, M. L., Piotrowski, W. D., & Bailey, J. S. Behavioral community psychology: Encouraging low-income parents to seek dental care for their children. *Journal of Applied Behavior Analysis*, 1976, *9*, 387–397.

Rice, R. E., & Rogers, E. M. Reinvention in the innovation process. *Knowledge: Creation, Diffusion, Utilization*, 1980, *1*, 499–514.

Rich, R. F. *Social science information and public policy making*. San Francisco: Jossey-Bass, 1981.

Roessner, J. D. Technological diffusion research and national policy. *Knowledge: Creation, Diffusion, Utilization*, 1980, *2*, 179–201.

Rolf, J. E., Bevins, S., Hasazi, J. E., Crowther, J., & Johnson, J. Prospective research with vulnerable children and the risky art of preventive intervention. *Prevention in Human Services,* 1982, *1*(4), 107–122.

Rosenstock, I. M. Why people use health services. *Milbank Memorial Fund Quarterly,* 1966, *44,* 94–127.

Rosenstock, I. M. The health belief model and preventive health behavior. *Health Education Monographs,* 1974, *2,* 354–386.

Salasin, S. E., & Davis, H. R. Facilitating the utilization of evaluation . . . A rocky road. In I. Davidoff, M. Guttentag, & J. Offutt (Eds.), *Evaluating community mental health services: Principles and practices* (DHEW Publication No. (ADM)77-465). Rockville, MD: U.S. Department of Health, Education, and Welfare, 1977.

Sherman, J. G. Do the data count? In S. W. Bijou & R. Ruiz (Eds.), *Behavior modification: Contributions to education.* Hillsdale, NJ: Erlbaum, 1981.

Shore, M. F. The federal scene. *Professional Psychology,* 1972, *4,* 383–384.

Skinner, B. F. Innovation in science teaching. *Science,* 1981, *212,* 283.

Stokes, T. F., & Baer, D. M. An implicit technology of generalization. *Journal of Applied Behavior Analysis,* 1977, *10,* 349–367.

Stolz, S. B. Adoption of innovations from applied behavioral research: "Does anybody care?" *Journal of Applied Behavior Analysis,* 1981, *14,* 491–505.

Stolz, S. B. Dissemination of standardized human service models: A behavior analyst's perspective. In S. C. Paine, G. T. Bellamy, & B. Wilcox (Eds.), *Human services that work: From innovation to standard practice.* Baltimore, MD: Paul H. Brookes, 1984.

Tableman, B. Prevention activities at the state level. In R. H. Price, R. F. Ketterer, B. C. Bader, & J. Monahan (Eds.), *Prevention in mental health: Research, policy, and practice.* Beverly Hills, CA: Sage, 1980.

Useem, M., & DiMaggio, P. An example of evaluation research as a cottage industry: The technical quality and impact of arts audience studies. *Sociological Methods and Research,* 1978, *7,* 55–84.

Vosburgh, W. W. Primary prevention, priorities, and implementation: The case of the New Zealand Accident Compensation Act. In F. D. Perlmutter (Ed.), *New directions for mental health services: Mental health promotion and primary prevention* (No. 13). San Francisco: Jossey-Bass, 1982.

Weisenberg, M., Kegeles, S. S., & Lund, A. K. Children's health beliefs and acceptance of a dental preventive activity. *Journal of Health and Social Behavior,* 1980, *21,* 59–74.

Weiss, C. H., & Bucuvalas, M. J. The challenge of social research to decision making. In C. H. Weiss (Ed.), *Using social research in public policy making.* Lexington, MA: Heath, 1977.

Yin, R. K., & Gwaltney, M. K. Knowledge utilization as a networking process. *Knowledge: Creation, Diffusion, Utilization,* 1981, *2,* 555–580.

REFERENCE NOTES

1. Fawcett, S. B., Seekins, T., Cohen, S. H., Elder, J. P., Jason, L. A., Schnelle, J. F., & Winett, R. A. Experimental analysis of child passenger safety legislation in seven states. In S. W. Fawcett (Chair), *Interstate research collaboration: The case of child*

passenger safety legislation. Symposium presented at the meeting of the American Psychological Association, Washington, D.C., August 1982.

2. Emshoff, J. G. Innovational processes: The issues and the research. In C. H. Blakely (Chair), *Adoption, implementation, and routinization of organizational innovations*. Symposium presented at the meeting of the American Psychological Association, Washington, D. C., August 1982.
3. Roitman, D. B., & Mayer, J. P. Fidelity and reinvention in the implementation of innovations. In C. H. Blakely (Chair), *Adoption, implementation, and routinization of organizational innovations*. Symposium presented at the meeting of the American Psychological Association, Washington, D.C., August, 1982.

Author Index

Subject Index